A Treasure Hunting Text

In 1623, a fleet from Havana was struck by a storm at the mouth of the Bahama Channel somewhere near the coast of Florida. "The treasure-laden galleon *Espiritu Santo el Mayor*, 480 tons, Captain Antonio de Soto, opened up and sank so quickly that only 50 of the 300 persons aboard her could be saved by other ships, and all her treasure, *amounting to one million pesos*, was totally lost." Such catastrophes at sea (among the many described in this book) have long fueled dreams of finding sunken ships awash in gold doubloons and fabulous jewels, and have tantalized archaeologists with the prospect of recovering valuable historic artifacts.

This Book tells exactly how to go about locating a sunken vessel and what to do after it is found, and also offers a comprehensive catalog of more than 4,000 authenticated wrecks and their locations. The book is divided into two parts:

Part I offers a wealth of expert information on the history of salvage; locating shipwrecks; surveying, mapping and excavating a site; identification and dating of shipwrecks and their cargoes; preservation of artifacts, and much more.

Part II comprises a carefully researched guide to every major shipwreck in the western hemisphere, from the time of Christopher Columbus to 1825. Descriptive captions on each wreck include year, captain, ports of origin and destination, probable location, cargo, lives lost, and prior salvage, if any. These captions amount to a treasure hunter's guided tour of ships waiting to be discovered in the waters of Canada, the United States (including an entire chapter on Florida, a major location of shipwrecks), Mexico, the Lesser Antilles, Bermuda, the Bahamas, Cuba, Hispaniola, Jamaica and the Cayman Islands, Puerto Rico and the Virgin Islands, Central America and off-lying areas, and South America.

Ram Publications
Hal Dawson, Editor

Sunken Treasure: How to Find It
One of the world's foremost underwater salvors shares a lifetime's experience in locating and recovering treasure from deep beneath the sea.

Treasure Recovery from Sand and Sea
Step-by-step instructions for reaching the "blanket of wealth" beneath sands nearby and under the world's waters, totally rewritten for the 90's.

Modern Metal Detectors
Comprehensive guide to all types of metal detectors; designed to increase understanding and expertise about all aspects of these electronic marvels.

Let's Talk Treasure Hunting
The ultimate "how-to" book of treasure hunting — with or without a metal detector; describes all kinds of treasures and tells how to find them.

Buried Treasure You Can Find
Complete field guide for finding treasure in the United States; includes state-by-state listing of thousands of sites where treasure is believed to exist.

Gold Panning is Easy
Excellent new field guide shows the beginner exactly how to find and pan gold; follow these instructions and perform as well as any professional.

The New Successful Coin Hunting
The world's most authoritative guide to finding valuable coins, totally rewritten to include instructions for 21st Century detectors.

Modern Electronic Prospecting
Explains in layman's terms how to use a modern detector to find gold nuggets and veins; includes instructions for panning and dredging.

Weekend Prospecting
Offers simple "how-to" instructions for enjoying holidays and vacations profitably by prospecting with metal detectors and gold pans.

Treasure Hunting Pays Off
A basic introduction to all facets of treasure hunting...the equipment, targets and terminology; totally revised for 21st Century detectors.

Treasure from British Waters
One of Great Britain's best known detector hobbyists tells how and where to find treasure in the waters of England and the Balearic Islands.

*True Treasure Tales - **Gar Starrett Adventures***

The Secret of John Murrell's Vault
The Missing Nez Perce Gold

New World Shipwrecks
1492–1825

RAM
BOOKS

A Comprehensive Guide

By Robert & Jenifer Marx

ISBN 0-915920-84-0
Library of Congress Catalog Card No. 94-65593
New World Shipwrecks 1492-1825
First Edition.
© Copyright 1994
Robert and Jenifer Marx

First Edition Printing, March 1994.

Book and cover design by Mel Climer

iv

This book is dedicated to

the Divers

who pursue their dream

Contents

About the Authors ix
Preface to the 1993 Edition 1
Introduction 9

Part One

1 The Ships.. 19
2 Early Salvors, THers and Marine Archaeology 55
3 Locating Shipwrecks.................................... 71
4 Surveying, Mapping, and Excavating a Site 95
5 Identification and Dating Shipwrecks and Cargoes..... 119
6 Preservation of Artifacts 155

Part Two — The Shipwrecks

1 Canada.. 165
2 The United States 179
3 Florida 217
4 Mexico 255
5 The Lesser Antilles 273
6 Bermuda 303
7 The Bahamas.. 315
8 Cuba 341
9 Hispaniola 359
10 Jamaica and the Cayman Islands 369
11 Puerto Rico and the Virgin Islands 387
12 Central America and Off-lying Areas 397
13 South America... 409
    Select Bibliography 425

By Robert Marx

The Underwater Dig
The Lure of Sunken Treasure
Port Royal Rediscovered
Sea Fever: Famous Underwater Explorers
Shipwrecks in Mexican Waters
Shipwrecks in Florida Waters
Shipwrecks of the Western Hemisphere: 1492-1825
Always Another Adventure
Pirate Port: The story of the Sunken City of Port Royal
They Dared the Deep: A History of Diving
The Battle of Lepanto: 1571
The Battle of the Spanish Armada: 1588
The Treasure Fleets of the Spanish Main
Following Columbus: The Voyage of the Niña II
The Voyage of the Nina II
The Capture of the Treasure Fleet
Buried Treasure of the U.S.
Spanish Treasure in Florida Waters
Quest for Treasure: the Maravilla
Sunken Treasure: How to Find It
Buried Treasures You Can Find

Robert and Jenifer Marx

About the Authors

obert F. Marx is one of the most successful and well-known specialists in the field of marine archaeology and has an equally strong reputation for his work in naval and maritime history. His particular area of interest is Spanish naval activity in the Caribbean during the Colonial Period. He and his wife, historian Jenifer Marx, have together written 41 books and published more than 700 scientific and popular articles and reports.

Robert Marx is perhaps best known to the general public for such feats as his voyage from Spain to San Salvador in the Niña II, a replica of Columbus's ship, on which he served as co-organizer and navigator. For this voyage he was made a Knight Commander in the Order of Isabella the Catholic by the Spanish government, the highest honorific order given to any foreigner.

Jenifer Grant Marx is a writer interested in history and an associate of her husband in underwater archaeology projects. A graduate of Mount Holyoke College, she also studied history at the University of Florence in Italy. She was a member of the first U.S. Peace Corps contingent, serving in the Philippines from 1961 to 1963 where she worked on the islands of Negros and Mindanao. She subsequently lived in Europe, Africa, the West Indies and Asia.

The Marxs, who have three daughters, met in Jamaica where Jenifer assisted Robert who spent four years excavating the sunken city of Port Royal. They live in Indialantic on Florida's east-central coast.

Their latest book is *In Search Of Sunken Treasure*, an illustrated volume published by Key Porter, Toronto.

New World Shipwrecks 1492-1825

Preface

Searching for sunken treasure is nothing new. People have been doing it, as a profession or avocation, for some four thousand years. In our day when the average person punches a time clock and runs double-time to keep up with the rat race, the lure of sunken treasure offers a fascinating and romantic change of pace. As professionals in the business will tell you, the search for shipwrecks is inevitably challenging. They'll also tell you it can be very frustrating and incredibly expensive if you don't go about it properly. Still, it is one of the few endeavors that can make a man a millionaire with just one lucky strike — as a number of my friends have discovered. Even if you don't turn up a gleaming chest of treasure, you'll have fun searching for and exploring wrecks...and, if fortune shines, finding something you will cherish for a lifetime.

To anyone who has donned a scuba tank and set off to explore the watery depths the fantasy is common: to find a piece of treasure, an historical artifact, or even the mother lode itself — a sunken ship beckoning like a siren from the ocean's floor. A diver's dream of shipwrecks laden with treasure generally conjures up images of Spanish galleons, their holds crammed with gleaming riches. And, not without reason, for in the years between 1492 and 1820 more than two thousand Spanish treasure ships were lost in the waters of the New World, and the vast majority of them still lie undiscovered with the fabulous treasures they went down with.

Most of these shipwrecks lay untouched for centuries until scuba equipment was introduced in the early 1950s. Interest in skin diving has increased each year and now millions of people are hooked on exploring the seductive underwater world. Most divers are content with exploring the beautiful reefs and photographing those wonders around them, but each year more and more divers find that the search for shipwrecks pumps adrenaline into their system. This book is written for them.

1

When I started in this business over 40 years ago, most people regarded anyone questing after sunken treasure as a romantic crackpot who was no more likely to succeed than someone chasing the pot of gold at the end of the rainbow. Not anymore! Major underwater treasure finds have been made every single year since I got started. Today treasure hunting is "big business," utilizing the latest developments in scientific knowledge and high-tech equipment. There are a number of companies that think nothing of spending as much as $50,000 a day in the quest for undersea riches.

Ironically, however, most of the major discoveries in the past four decades have been made by amateur divers. That's right. It has been the little guy, driven by bubble-bright visions of gleaming doubloons and chests crammed with jewels, who has made dreams come true. Every summer during the past 25 years an average of 40 small salvage vessels have worked on a group of wrecks known as "the 1715 Fleet" and other shipwrecks scattered along the east central coast of Florida between Stuart and Melbourne. Some of these operations are so small that they don't even use excavation equipment. It's just two or three guys using underwater metal detectors. As I write this in the late summer of 1993, there are currently 52 salvage boats working this coast with varying degrees of success.

The wreck of the flagship of the 1715 Fleet lies in a lease area which I own with Mel Fisher by virtue of an Admiralty Arrest Permit. Just yesterday I got a call from a local group, Historical Research and Development, Inc., which is working the site on a sub-lease from us. They invited me to go out with them. My inclination was to say no since I was still suffering from jet lag, having returned only two days earlier from a two-month expedition in the South China Sea working on a 10th-century Song dynasty Chinese junk loaded with beautiful porcelain. But when I heard what the divers had found the day before, I jumped at the chance to go. Searching less than 100 yards offshore in eight feet of water they had found two long gold chains, two large ornate gold rosaries, five sets of gold cuff-links, two large gold buckles, two exquisite manicure sets, two ornate gold tooth picks, a gold holy medallion, nine gold rings and one silver ring.

Although I have been finding shipwrecks and treasure all my life, my pulse still quickens at the prospect of finding *more*. When I went out with the HRD divers, they were working in a new spot because they thought they had found all there was to find in the "treasure hole." I thought I'd check out the treasure cache area with my Garrett Sea Hunter underwater detector anyway. To everyone's amazement and my great delight, within minutes I located a set of intricately-wrought gold filigree cuff-links. The HRD team is out again today and I'm having a tough time convincing myself that writing this book is more important than exploring that wreck.

Another Fantastic Find

Less than a month ago another fantastic find was made on this same wreck by another small group. For years Bob Weller, a kitchen cabinet builder from Palm Beach, has spent a couple of summer months working off the east coast. A veteran of the Korean War in which he led an underwater demolition team, he works from his small boat *Pandion* with his wife Margaret and partner Christopher James. His recent find was made when he decided to rework an area close to shore which had been gone over hundreds of times by others through the years.

After opening a hole in less than 10 feet of dirty water, Weller went down with a metal detector. He turned up only an old beer can and was ready to head for the surface when his detector went wild. Digging down a few inches into the sand he pulled out an elaborate gold brooch about the size of a man's hand set with 171 diamonds. After deepening the hole a bit more with the boat's prop-wash, all three divers were in the water with detectors. They soon found another brooch about the same size with 161 diamonds, followed by two matching gold earrings each containing 53 diamonds, two gold tooth picks and a gold manicure set. The following day in the same area they found a silver candelabrum, two silver belt buckles and a handful of silver coins. His years of persistent searching finally paid off!

Inevitably, when word of the thrilling find leaked out, more than 20 salvage boats converged on the scene. For over a week it was pure mayhem with boats running over divers and everyone fighting for the best spots to dig. As soon as news is out about Historical Research and Development's discoveries, this scene will be repeated — but for the moment they're keeping their secret in hopes of finding more gold in the same area.

Between the two above-mentioned finds Mel Fisher's son, Kane, made another...five miles to the south off Wabasso Beach. Like the 1715 flagship the galleon *San Martin*, lost in 1618 while sailing between Honduras and Spain, has been extensively excavated by dozens of groups over the years. But, as we know in the business, no matter how much a wreck is dug and how much is found, there always seems to be more to find at a later date. This time Kane, using a detector, found a bronze navigational astrolabe, valued at somewhere between $250,000 and $300,000. Fewer than 60 astrolabes dating from the Colonial Period exist.

Less than 100 miles to the east in the Bahamas, several valuable discoveries have been made this summer. John Brandon was working on the site known as the "Lucaya Wreck," where one of the Spanish galleons captured by the Dutch privateer Piet Heyn in Matanzas Bay, Cuba, in 1628 was lost while being taken back to Holland. The veteran treasure diver found a bronze astrolabe, as well as several hundred thousand dollars worth of other treasures. This wreck lays on a shallow reef off Freeport, Grand Bahama. The wreck has been worked over for decades and local dive shops take hundreds of divers each day to see the wreck's cannon; yet it goes to show that without a good underwater detector you can swim over a fortune of treasure and never know it.

On the other side of Grand Bahama island, to the north on the Little Bahama Bank, four other treasure hunting groups are hard at it as well. Marex International of Memphis is still working on the 1656 *Maravillas* galleon and rarely a day goes by without recovery of gold or at least quantities of silver specie and bullion. They have three boats following a scatter trail hoping to find the elusive solid gold life-size Madonna and Child which was aboard the *Maravillas* when she went down. By the time this year's salvage season ends more than $20 million in treasure and artifacts will have been brought up by the various salvage companies working in Florida, the Bahamas and the Caribbean. This figure pertains to the salvage groups working shipwrecks with permits. Probably an equal amount will be found by divers working clandestinely — most of whom would prefer being legitimate, but are forced to be "pirates" because for one reason or another they couldn't obtain official government permission. With each year it becomes more difficult to obtain permits to locate and salvage shipwrecks.

This is true throughout the world. All but 21 nations now have specific laws governing shipwrecks. Until 1981 27 states of the U.S. had laws, differing widely from state to state, that laid claim to sunken historical sites. In 1981, these laws were challenged in the Supreme Court by Mel Fisher. After a lengthy fight the states lost the rights to shipwrecks. Federal laws give the government

4

control over natural resources out to the 200-mile (320-km) limit, although the states retain ownership of resources within the three-mile (4.8-km) coastal area. However, these laws do not cover shipwrecks or other man-made objects.

By contrast, the right of states to manage archaeological sites buried on land is explicitly stated in U.S. law. Until recently, in the absence of a law recognizing the special nature of ancient ship-wrecks, these sites were covered by the "finders-keepers" principle that applies to modern wrecked and abandoned commercial vessels. It meant that federal admiralty law took precedence over state law. For seven years, Congress labored over the passage of a new law granting states the right to jurisdiction over all shipwrecks a hundred years old or older which are within three miles of the coast.

Sport divers, treasure hunters and archaeologists contributed their points of view on the management of shipwrecks at congressional hearings held by the House Merchant Marine and Fisheries Subcommittee. In April 1987, the Reagan administration endorsed the Abandoned Shipwreck Act of 1987. The bill was approved by the House of Representatives on December 19, 1987, by a vote of 340 to 64 and on April 14, 1988, by an overwhelming majority of the Senate . On April 28, 1988, the president signed the bill, which is now known as Public Law 100-298.

The new law covers 5 to 10 percent of the estimated 50,000 shipwrecks inside the three-mile limit. Other shipwrecks both within and outside this limit continue to be covered by federal admiralty law. The shipwrecks affected by the new law are:

(a) Those defined as historic abandoned shipwrecks that are "substantially" buried in submerged state lands;

(b) Those embedded in coral formations; and

(c) Wrecks listed in the National Register of Historic Places (fewer than 100 are currently so designated).

Each state has the right to determine how recovered artifacts and treasures are to be divided and to establish guidelines for the search and excavation of shipwrecks. Most states employ archaeologists to oversee their shipwreck programs. Unfortunately, most of them would rather see shipwrecks in their waters destroyed by dredging or landfill operations than let sport divers or treasure hunters explore them. Countless times I have heard state archaeologists express the opinion that "The wrecks have been down there for hundreds of years so what's the rush to excavate them now?"

The rush is that they are deteriorating in the hostile undersea environment, and in many places face obliteration by dredging and other threats. Why not find them today and bring up their treasures for everyone to enjoy? Coastal states and divers would mutually benefit if they could work together in a spirit of cooperation to excavate shipwrecks.

Bob Marx and Demostines Molinar admire 1715 flagship treasures they found in 10 feet of water 100 yards offshore Florida during the summer of 1993.

From Bob Marx

Introduction

Many years ago, when I first became interested in old shipwrecks, I was inspired by several books on the subject that were extremely exciting to read. They described sunken galleons, lying intact with chests of gleaming treasure in their holds and skeletons at the wheel. These thrilling volumes also included "Authentic Treasure Charts" that pinpointed the locations of many wrecks "containing millions in treasure." I had to learn the hard way that all that glitters on an "authentic" treasure map is definitely not gold. I spent three exciting years exploring Mexican waters and — without help from the books — located and excavated several Spanish wrecks which yielded a vast number of important artifacts and some treasure.

Encouraged by that experience, I determined to find other Caribbean wrecks. I reasoned: Why spend weeks and months snorkeling over coral reefs and the sea floor searching for wrecks when I had all the information I had accumulated from books and treasure charts? I selected 100 wrecks from these sources. They were scattered all over the Caribbean, and I set off to track them down. Fifteen months later, after exploring from the Gulf of Honduras to the San Blas islands off Panama and from Trinidad to the Bahamas, diving on almost every island, reef and rock in between, I had located only two of the hundred wrecks, and neither had anything of interest on them.

This was not surprising, as I was to learn during years of research of primary sources in European archives. Out of the 100 "authen-

Golden treasures recovered by Bob Marx from the wreck of the famed *Maravillas*, a Spanish galleon lost in 1656 in the Bahamas.

tic" wrecks, 74 existed only in the fertile imaginations of the authors of the books I had used as sources. Of those that did exist 18 had in fact sunk with treasure on board, but on the high seas (where there was little chance of recovery) and not in the shallow waters close to land, where these authors had conveniently placed them. Four others had indeed sunk in shallow waters, but hundreds of miles from the locations given. The remaining four also existed. I found two of them but their cargoes were ordinary trade goods and not dazzling treasure. Because professional wreck-hunters have long since realized that most of the information in such books is fictional, they label the wrecks "Ghost Wrecks" and have a good laugh whenever they hear of newly organized expeditions setting out after them.

I know of several groups of "professionals," however, which have spent at least $100,000 searching for a Spanish wreck that sank in the 17th century with a vast amount of treasure on board. A book considered the most reliable on the subject placed the wreck in the Florida Keys. My research in the Spanish archives has since proved that the ship wrecked in the Bahamas. Even the assistance of so-called experts on maritime history cannot always be relied upon. A good example is the late Kip Wagner, one of the most successful treasure-hunters in the world. In his early days, before he realized that the only place to get authentic information was in the Spanish archives, he sought assistance from an expert at the Smithsonian Institution and was told that the 1715 treasure fleet was lost in the Florida Keys. If Wagner had followed this expert's advice, he would never have discovered the fantastic treasure he eventually recovered more than 200 miles from the Keys.

Some people erroneously believe that with today's fantastic underwater electronic location equipment, it isn't necessary to do extensive research as long as the general area of a wreck is known. A well-known mineral company decided to enter the field of treasure-hunting. Equipped with a deep submersible vehicle and the latest in electronic detection gear, it proudly announced that it was about to make the biggest treasure recovery in history. I contacted the director of the operation and offered to supply authentic original documentation. The shipwreck in question was lost off the coast of Colombia during a naval engagement between the Spaniards and the English. This ship, flagship of a Spanish treasure fleet, carried over 22 million pesos in treasure and was blown up in about 600 feet of water.

10

They refused my assistance, confident that with the general location they could easily locate the wreck site. Three months later, having spent a quarter-million dollars, they begged for my research, but I had decided to go after that wreck myself one day and didn't help them. Their submarine has since been put to use in searching for marine deposits, the original purpose for which it was designed.

Quite a few significant underwater treasure recoveries have made by lucky souls who never did a bit of research. Teddy Tucker of Bermuda, one of the world's most successful treasure hunters and prototype for the protagonist of the movie *The Deep*, started off by searching the reefs surrounding Bermuda, using a glass-bottom bucket. When he sighted something that did not appear to be made by nature, he would dive and check it out. Over the years, this led to many discoveries. But for the few who have been successful, there have been hundreds who have failed miserably. Most professionals agree that it is best to have the odds in your favor, which means doing proper research before you set out after a wreck.

There are two schools of thought on the business of wreck research. One is to first find a wreck in the manner that Tucker did and then do research to determine its identity, what it carried, etc. The other school holds that the first thing to do is to decide on an area to work in; then, research those wrecks that are the most promising, or conduct research to determine the areas with the most promising wrecks. The latter method has proven the most successful for me and many others in the business. This book is written in order to assist the treasure-hunter to identify a wreck which has already located, as well as to indicate areas of potential with other promising wrecks.

From my research I have amassed a file comprising data on more than 37,000 shipwrecks around the world, dating from the time of the Greeks to the modern era. For this book I have selected the most significant shipwrecks lost in the Western Hemisphere from the time of Columbus until about 1825. In a future book I plan to tackle the important wrecks postdating 1825. Actually, when a diver locates a wreck postdating 1825, it is fairly simple to establish its identity and other pertinent data because newspapers of the period contained notices of ship disasters. Once the treasure-hunter pinpoints the period of disaster by dating artifacts from the wreck within 10 or 20 years, he can consult old newspapers of the place in which he located the wreck. He may also learn its identity by reading history books on the area or from a local historian or museum curator.

It is even simpler to obtain information on ships that were lost off the coast of the United States after 1825, since records of these losses can be obtained from various governmental agencies. The best source is in the Treasury section of the National Archives in Washington, D.C.. Other good sources include the archives of the United States Coast Guard, the United States Naval Hydrographic Office, and United States Maritime Commission, all located in Washington, D.C. Over the years the Public Information Division of the United States Coast Guard has published lists of ship losses, which can be obtained free of charge. Two currently in print are: "Principal Marine Disasters 1831-1932," which lists over 600 shipwrecks; and "United States Merchant Ship Losses, December 7, 1941-August 14, 1945."

Of the many books currently available containing information on shipwrecks postdating 1825, I recommend only the following as completely reliable: *A Guide to Sunken Ships in American Waters*, by Lieutenant Commander Adrian L. Lonsdale and H. R. Kaplan, which contains information on over 1,100 shipwrecks off the coast of the United States and in the Great Lakes and major rivers; a 42-volume work entitled *Records of the Navies of the Civil War*, published by the U.S. Government Printing Office, which contains data on almost every military and merchant ship lost during the Civil War; and *Graveyard of the Atlantic*, by David Stick, which lists over 800 shipwrecks off the coast of North Carolina.

If I were to write a multi-volume work listing every shipwreck on which I have collected information, it would still be far from a complete list of all the ships lost in the Western Hemisphere over the centuries. Hundreds of ships have been lost without a trace all over the world, many of them no doubt in waters of the Western Hemisphere. To cite but one example, a Portuguese fleet consisting of 21 ships carrying 23,740 ounces of gold in different forms and 439,980 crusadoes of silver bound for Lisbon sailed from Pernambuco, Brazil, in 1746. About a week out of port it was struck by a storm and had to run before it toward the Caribbean. The fleet was still intact when it passed within sight of Barbados, but shortly afterward the storm developed into a full hurricane and the ships were widely dispersed. Thirteen disappeared without a trace. Documents carrying news concerning various shipwrecks back to Europe or elsewhere were in many cases lost because the ships themselves were lost.

European depositories contain masses of documents concerning shipwrecks, but until they are cataloged they are not fully accessible to researchers. The major reason information on many shipwrecks will never be discovered, however, is that thousands upon thousands of historical documents have been destroyed by man and nature. All of the documents predating 1671 that were kept in Old Panama City went up in flames when Henry Morgan and his men burned the city to the ground. Additionally, documents postdating 1671 have been destroyed by the humid climate of the Panama area. Complete archives in Cartagena and Bogota, Colombia, were destroyed during the War of Independence; similarly, a great number of documents were destroyed in Veracruz and Mexico City during the Mexican War of Independence.

The Cuban Archives

When Cuba revolted against Spain near the end of the last century, the colonial archives were fortunate to survive. After the war the Cubans turned over the whole archives to the Spaniards, who took them back to Seville. Seventy years later these thousands of bundles of historical documents still remain stacked and unopened as they were when they arrived, collecting dust and being chewed up by rats in an old building in Seville. The main archive in Lima, Peru, was destroyed twice by earthquakes in the 18th century. Even in Spain, vast numbers of documents have been destroyed — in 1551, for example, when the House of Trade building burned to the ground, and as recently as 1962, when thousands of documents were destroyed during a flood.

Spanish colonial history is not alone in suffering the destruction of documents. Those of most of the other major European nations have shared similar fates. Portugal experienced by far the worst loss in 1755 when its main depository of historical documents the *Casa da India* sank into a Lisbon river during a terrible earthquake. During World War II there were great losses of historical documents from fires caused by bombing in London, Paris, Rotterdam and Amsterdam.

The greatest collection of Spanish colonial records is stored in the Archives of the Indies in Seville, which was the original House of Trade building. The original state archive of Spain was the Simancas Archive, located near Valladolid. It became so overcrowded with documents that in 1784 the King ordered all documents dealing with the New World shipped to Seville, thus creating the Archives of the

Indies. However, in recent years it has been discovered that about six to seven hundred bundles (called *legajos*) of documents dealing exclusively with the New World still remain in Simancas.

I have discovered that vast numbers of documents on the flotas and shipwrecks are in erroneously titled legajos in Simancas. While researching 16th-century Portuguese voyages to India, I found four thick legajos entitled *Papers of Portugal Sixteenth Century*, but to my amazement I found that they had nothing to do with Portugal or those voyages. Instead, there were thousands of pages dealing with the day-by-day salvage operations on the 1715 shipwrecks on the coast of Florida. There is also documentation on Spanish maritime history in other depositories in Spain, such as the Museo Naval, Museo Nacional, Biblioteca Nacional, Archivo Historico Nacional and Academia Real de la Historia, all in Madrid. But they pale in comparison to with the Archives of the Indies in Seville. If a team of 100 researchers spent their whole lives searching through the more than 250,000 legajos in the Archives of the Indies, I doubt they could locate all the important documents concerning Spanish maritime history in the New World. The majority of the legajos are not cataloged, and about 20 percent of those shipped from Simancas in 1784 have never been opened.

Very few documents concerning Dutch maritime history in the New World have survived the ravages of man and nature, and there is virtually nothing known on Dutch shipwrecks in the New World other than what can be found in Spanish or British depositories. Many documents on French maritime history in the New World have been lost, but when the French archives are better cataloged, we will be able to learn more about their ship losses in the New World. England is the easiest place to work in research. The depositories are generally well-cataloged and the staffs very helpful.

The main depositories for research on shipwrecks in the waters of the New World are The British Museum, Public Records Office, Admiralty Archives, the National Maritime Museum and the archives of Lloyd's of London, all of which are in or very near London. In making the best use of information in this book concerning shipwrecks, the following factors should be taken into consideration. All of the information on Spanish shipwrecks was obtained from original documents. In some cases a wreck or wrecks were mentioned in only a few words while for others there were thousands of pages concerning the loss of a fleet, or even an individual wreck. Where vital information is lacking on a wreck, it is because it could not be found in the original documents.

Concerning those instances when I have stated the amount of treasure reported to have been carried on a ship, there are two factors to take into account. Because a wreck might have been salvaged over the years, there is no record to indicate how much treasure was recovered. In addition, so much treasure was smuggled back to Spain to avoid taxes that a vessel sometimes carried as much as four or five times the amount registered on its manifest. A good example of this occurred in 1743, when some English warships captured a Spanish galleon named *San Antonio*. Her manifest indicated she was carrying slightly over 800,000 pesos, but the English discovered treasure on her worth more than four million pesos.

Modern Place-Names

In some cases I have given the modern place-name where a shipwreck occurred, but only when I was positive that the place-name in the documents corresponded to place-names today. In many cases I have used the original place-name as given in the document, because the place cannot be identified today, or because the place-name was used at different places at different periods. Cayo de Viboras is an example: in some 16th-century documents all of the Florida Keys are called Cayos de los Vivoras; on some 17th-century charts it is shown near Plantation Key; and on 18th-century charts it is shown between Vaca and Matacumbe Keys.

There are various reasons for the lack of precise shipwreck locations in primary documents. In the early days there were very few place names on charts of the coast of Florida that were used by Spanish navigators. On most 16th-century charts only two places are named: Martires (spelled many different ways), which was the Florida Keys; and Cabo del Canaveral, or Cape Canaveral. By the middle of the 17th century a few more place-names had been added: Las Tortugas (the Dry Tortugas), Vivoras, Matacumbe, Rio de Ais and La Florida, which was the name for St. Augustine. By the beginning of the 18th century, many other places were named, rendering charts more accurate.

Another important reason Spanish documents are vague on shipwreck locations is because when writing to Spain about a disaster, it mattered little to the officials in Seville exactly where the shipwreck had occurred. What mattered mainly was what was lost and what could be or had been recovered.

15

Some of the information in this book concerning the wrecks of English, French, Dutch and American ships is brief and the location of the wreck is vague. This isn't because charts had too few landmarks for reference, since most of these wrecks occurred after good charts were available. It is chiefly because those who wrote about the occurrence didn't consider it important to mention the precise location of a wreck. If a shipwreck could be reached, it was usually salvaged long before news of the disaster ever reached Europe or America. Thus, it wasn't essential that the precise location of a disaster be made known to either the admiralty, in the case of naval vessels, or to the public or insurance firms, in the case of merchant vessels.

The best source for British warships is in the Admiralty Section of the Public Records Office. Because of the Great Fire of London in 1666, there are virtually no extant documents on British shipwrecks in the New World prior to this date; but then again, there was not much British shipping to the New World prior to 1666. Between 1666 and 1740, there is a limited amount of original documentation on British shipwrecks in New World waters, but I found very little concerning shipwrecks in the Western Hemisphere. The best sources of information on British shipwrecks since 1740 have been *Lloyd's List* and *Gentleman's Magazine*, both of which were first published in that year. *Lloyd's List* was basically a newspaper giving the movements of British shipping around the world, as well as brief accounts of ship losses and the movements of other foreign shipping, including the Spanish flotas and French fleets returning from the Caribbean. In many cases the names of foreign ships, persons, and place-names were misspelled, and I have corrected only those about whose spelling I am positive.

Although *Lloyd's List* has been in continuous existence to the present day, the volumes for various years are missing and no copies are known to exist. The years of the missing volumes are 1742, 1743, 1745, 1746, 1754, 1756, 1759, 1776 and 1778. The Lists from October 15, 1770, through the end of that year are also missing. While carrying out research in the Archives of Lloyd's of London (I preferred it over various libraries because on many of the printed Lists notes had been added by contemporary members of the staff), I found that there is never any mention of merchantmen or other ships carrying cannon, although we know that most of them did indeed carry cannon. It should be noted that when the List mentions "a cargo being saved," this doesn't necessarily mean it was saved before the ship sank or broke up, because the word "saved" was also used to mean "salvaged."

All of the ships built and used by the American colonies until the War of Independence were under British registry, and most of the documentation on these ships' losses I found in British Archives. After the United States became independent and our ships were of American registry, the vast majority were still insured by Lloyd's of London, and the List published notices of the majority of American ship losses. I found a limited number listed in early American newspapers in the Library of Congress.

I have taken the liberty of converting the dates of ships' losses and other events mentioned in this book to our modern calendar. In 1582, Pope Gregory XIII ordered that 10 days of that year be omitted in an effort to bring the calendar and sun into correspondence again. This created the Gregorian calendar, which we use today. All of the Protestant nations stuck to the old calendar for many years; England, until 1752. Before England made this change, her new year began on March 25; thus, a date of February 11, 1733, to the English was February 21, 1734.

Finding no reliable means to convert the value of the monetary units used in the old days to our present-day monetary system, I have used the values of treasures and cargoes in the terms in which they are described in the old documents.

Chapter One

The Ships

Between 1492 and 1830 the Spaniards mined a total of 4,035,156,000 pesos of gold and silver in the New World, which was registered in the Royal Mints. Of this amount, 493 million pesos, or slightly over one-tenth, consisted of gold and the remainder of silver. About 40 percent of the above total was mined in Mexico, while almost all of the remainder came from Peru, with a small amount also from Colombia and Chile. During this period, in an average year, about 17,500,000 pesos of gold and silver were shipped to Spain, while small amounts remained in the Spanish colonies for local use. There is no way to determine the amount of unregistered gold and silver mined during this period, but it is estimated that it amounted to between one and two billion pesos. Some of this unregistered treasure was smuggled back to Spain, but the majority was used in purchasing contraband goods from other European nations. Until Columbus' discovery of the New World, economies of the European nations were stagnant because of a severe lack of precious metals which were so critical for expanding mercantile trade.

It was the search for gold, in fact, that led to the discovery of the New World. Columbus had read of Marco Polo's travels in which he mentioned a land called Zipango (Japan) so filled with gold that even the roof tiles were made of it. Columbus was convinced that by sailing westward from Europe or Africa, he could reach Zipango, the source of more than enough gold and silver to satisfy Europe's needs. As it turned out, treasure was obtained not from Zipango but from the mines of Peru and Mexico.

The importance to Spain of treasure from the New World can readily be understood from the following dispatch sent from the Venetian ambassador in Spain to the Doge in September 1567: "At the time of writing my last dispatch to you, I informed you that there was great anxiety all over Spain, over the delay of the arrival of the treasure fleet from the Indies and, when the Genoese bankers informed the King that unless the fleet reached port shortly, they would be unable to negotiate any further loans for him, Philip II fell into such a state of shock that he had to be confined to bed by his physicians. The King then ordered some 10,000 Ducats, which was about all the treasure left in his royal coffers, to be sent all over his realm and distributed to various churches and monasteries for the saying of masses for the safe arrival of the treasure fleet. I am happy to inform you that news has just arrived from Seville that the fleet has made port safely and there is now great rejoicing not only here in the Royal Court, but throughout the land."

From the thousands of documents that have survived in various European archives, I discovered that the above account was by no means exceptional; in fact, it was almost a yearly occurrence over a period of three centuries. The importance of the Indies treasure was such that any delay in its arrival damaged Spanish credit disastrously and caused great concern in all the major financial centers of Europe. Although generally between a quarter and a third of the returning Indies treasure was consigned to the Crown, it never seemed to be enough and the Crown was constantly in debt to international bankers. Sometimes the Crown's share of the Indies treasure was pledged to these bankers for as much as four or five years in advance.

Treasure from the New World was of critical importance to the other European nations as well, since it furnished nearly 95 percent of the precious metals on which their monetary systems were based. There is a popular misconception that only Spain benefited, when in fact she benefited less than England, France, Holland and Italy. The reason is that throughout the 16th, 17th and 18th centuries, when heavily laden and usually cranky ships carried immense amounts of treasure, there was virtually no industry of any kind in Spain. Spain was totally dependent on other nations for manufactured goods, both for export to the New World and for domestic consumption. Therefore, nearly all her treasure was used to pay for these goods.

From the beginning of the Age of Discovery the city of Seville held a monopoly on New World trade until superseded by the seaport of Cadíz early in the 18th century. During the first five decades following the discovery of the New World, Seville, which was Spain's main commercial and financial port was the best choice for the main terminus for ships sailing to and from the New

20

World. Although Seville is 60 miles up the Guadalquivir River, it offered no handicap, because ships in those days were quite small. Around the middle of the 16th century, however, when the first organized fleet came into existence and ships began to double in size, Seville could no longer accommodate large numbers of ships and it became extremely hazardous for the bigger ships to navigate the river.

As a result of the larger ships, even though control of the Indies trade remained in the hands of merchants and royal officials in Seville, the seaports of Sanlucar and Cadíz replaced Seville as the chief ports. Yet both of these ports also had their drawbacks. Sanlucar, which is situated at the mouth of the Guadalquivir River, had a very dangerous sandbar over which ships had to pass when leaving port. During the three-century period when treasure ships were plying the seas between Spain and the New World, more than 200 ships were lost on this sandbar. Cadíz, although much larger than Sanlucar, was vulnerable to attacks by enemy fleets and was afflicted at times by a dangerous wind called a levanter. As a result of these obstacles, more than 500 ships engaged in the Indies navigation were lost during that period.

In 1503, when Columbus was in the New World on his fourth voyage of discovery, Queen Joanna put the Indies trade on an organized basis with the founding of the House of Trade in Seville. Its purpose was to promote and regulate trade and navigation with the New World, to make certain that all royal orders were carried out, to collect taxes and duties on both outward-bound and returning cargoes and to supervise the preparations and dispatching of all ships sailing for the New World. At first the officials of the House of Trade made their headquarters in the Cathedral of Seville, much to the great discontent of the local populace. But in 1572, construction was begun on a new building; and when it was completed a few years later it served as the home for the House of Trade officials until the Indies trade monopoly was transferred to Cadíz. Today this building is the Archives of the Indies, which houses millions of pages of priceless documents dealing with the ships in the Indies navigation and other aspects of New World history.

In 1519, the year that Cortez sailed from Cuba to begin his infamous conquest of Mexico, Charles I determined that the business of administering the affairs of the New World was taking up too much of his time and created a new administrative body, the Council of the Indies. The Council was part of his royal court, and its main function was to keep the King advised on matters concerning his New World possessions, to appoint both royal officials to govern in the New World and commanders of the treasure fleets, to organize the conquest of new lands in the New World and to act as a middleman between the House of Trade and the King.

Still another administrative body was created in 1543 to aid in trade and navigation. It was called the Merchant Guild, and its officials were selected from among the richest and most influential merchants engaged in commerce with the New World. Its three main functions were to supervise marine insurance, which was necessary to equalize losses from shipwrecks and ships captured by enemies or pirates, to serve as a clearing house for all manufactured goods arriving from European nations for transshipment to the New World and to maintain civil jurisdiction for its members, all of whom were merchants and businessmen engaged in trade with the New World.

One of the earliest laws concerning the Indies navigation was that ships must be of Spanish construction and ownership. Over the entire period of the Indies navigation, about half of the ships that sailed for the New World were of foreign construction, for rarely was there a sufficient quantity of Spanish-built ships available. The *ownership* aspect of the law, however, was more strictly enforced. During the first half of the 16th century ships were astonishingly small, most of them less than 100 tons and many as small as 30 to 40 tons, which was the size of the Niña, the smallest vessel used by Columbus on his first voyage of discovery. To get a better idea of the diminutive size of these early ships, one has only to look at their tonnage: a ship of fifty tons was 35 to 40 feet long and from 12 to 15 feet in the beam; while a ship of 100 tons was 50 to 55 feet in length and 16 to 18 feet in the beam. These ships were in a class called caravels but were often referred to in documents as *naos*, which merely means a ship. Caravels were first built early in the 15th century by the Portuguese for voyages of exploration.

By making slight modifications in the sails and rigging, the Spaniards found the caravels well-adapted for transatlantic voyages. Although they were quite fast and much more seaworthy than any of the later classes of ships used by the Spaniards for Indies navigation, their relatively small size was a handicap, as it restricted the amount of cargo that could be carried and afforded very limited quarters for crew and passengers.

In the early 1540s, when the New World's demand for imports from Europe increased greatly, along with the export demands of Spain, it was necessary to replace the caravel with a much larger vessel. At that time the standard vessel in Europe for carrying bulky cargoes was the *carrack*, which ranged in size from 100 to 800 tons. It was a large, round and bulky tub. Although it was capable of carrying large cargoes, its shape made it so slow that after several years of trial and error on transatlantic voyages, this type of vessel was found impractical and never used again.

The Spaniards next tried galleys, which were larger and faster than caravels, but they too were impractical because they accommodated less cargo since so much space in the hold was taken up with water and victuals for the large number of slaves needed to propel them. The galleys rode very low in the water and were extremely hazardous in any kind of storm.

By the early 1550s, when large quantities of treasure began reaching Spain from the New World, the Spaniards were hard-pressed to find a suitable vessel. The ship not only had to be larger in size but also more defensible — since hostilities had broken out between France and Spain many of the smaller caravels were falling prey to French privateers. The solution was found by Don Alvaro de Bazan, Spain's foremost 16th-century naval leader. By combining the bulkiness of the carracks with the swift-sailing lines of the galleys and the sail patterns and rigging used on caravels, he invented the galleon, which became the standard class of ship used throughout the remainder of the Indies navigation. Its average size was from 300 to 600 tons, but late in the 16th century many were as large as 1,200 tons. They were constructed with two or three spacious decks, large fore-and-stern castles, and carried from three to four masts. Though slower than caravels or galleys, they could average about four knots on a transatlantic crossing, if not overloaded and with their bottoms properly cleaned — more than twice as fast as the carracks. Their disadvantage was the massive size of the fore-and-stern castles, which made the ships top-heavy and placed them in great peril of capsizing in storms. Not until early in the 18th century was this danger properly understood and these castles reduced in size.

Although the galleon became the standard vessel used in the Indies navigation, this vessel was called a galleon only when it carried a large number of cannon. When used as a merchant ship carrying fewer cannon, it was called à nao. Thus, on one voyage to the New World, a ship might be called a nao and on the next a galleon.

Other classes of smaller vessels, ranging in size from 40 to 100 tons, were also used in the Indies navigation. Caravels, pinks, flyboats, sloops and pinnaces varied widely in construction and rigging but the Spaniards referred to them all as *pataches*. They served various purposes, such as reconnaissance vessels in convoys, advice boats between Spain and the New World, and transporting small cargoes to outposts like St. Augustine, Florida, which, as a settlement of minor importance, did not warrant sending a larger ship.

Although the main terminus for Indies navigation was centered in southern Spain, very little suitable timber was available in this area. Thus, most of the Spanish-built ships were constructed in the provinces of northern Spain. After the turn of the 17th century a large number were also built in Cuba and other New World ports. Most of the masts, spars and other heavy rigging came from as far away as Russia and Poland; cordage and sails were imported from Scandinavia and Holland; and until the end of the 16th century, when factories producing a good grade of iron were founded in Biscay Province in northern Spain, most of the metal fittings, anchors and iron cannon were imported from various countries of northern Europe.

From the beginning, even the small caravels were obliged to carry several pieces of artillery, the number depending on the ship's size and the purpose it served. For example, a galleon of 400 tons used as a merchant nao was required to carry only 10 or 12 guns, but the same vessel serving as a flagship of a convoy and entrusted with bringing back a large amount of treasure would be required to carry as many as 50 cannon of various calibers. Unless they were new, iron cannon were used only to fire salutes or as a signal between ships, because the iron cannons heated too quickly after firing and would crack or burst apart, often rendering more damage to those firing than those fired upon.

When the galleons superseded the earlier class of Indies vessels, it became standard practice for them to carry only brass cannon, if such cannons were available. The largest brass cannon used on the

Diver displays coin and three 80-pound silver bars, part of the treasure recovered over the years from the 1656 wreck of the *Maravillas* in the Bahamas.

galleon in the 16th and 17th centuries was called a demiculverin, which weighed about two tons and fired an iron ball weighing from seven to twelve pounds at a maximum distance of 1,000 paces at point blank range and more than twice that distance when fired in a trajectory. In those early days, ships usually sailed in small convoys, not only for the sake of mutual protection against corsairs and foul weather but to pool navigational knowledge, for there was a great scarcity of navigators.

During the first three decades of the 16th century, before sizable conquests had been made in Mexico and Peru, virtually all the shipping between Spain and the New World was focused on Hispañiola. The number of ships sailing each year depended on the availability of ships, the number of corsairs hovering off the Azores in wait for returning ships, and the amount of exports and number of settlers going to the New World in that particular year. For example: In 1508, 66 ships sailed to the New World; in 1520 the number reached 108; in 1529, when a great number of French privateers were off the Azores, only 60 sailed, and of the 42 that attempted to return to Spain, 11 were captured by French privateers.

Columbus was the first to have dealings with corsairs and privateers which were a menace from the very beginning. On his very voyage of discovery in 1492, when approaching the Canaries, he sighted two French corsair vessels, but because his ships were better armed the corsairs gave him a wide berth. Returning from his third voyage, only foul weather saved his flagship from falling prey to a fleet of French corsairs off Cape St. Vincent at the southern tip of Portugal. Although corsairs were lucky enough to capture a few returning Indies ships each year from 1505 onward, they never seized any of major importance until 1521, when two caravels loaded with treasure for the King were captured.

This resulted in the formation of a special fleet, which was maintained by a special tax, the *averia*, placed on all cargoes to and from the New World. The purpose of this new fleet, which was named the Armada of the Ocean Sea, was to escort convoys of ships from Spain as far as the Canary Islands and then take up station off

Manila galleons brought vast quantities of such price-less Oriental objects as this jewel-studded Kris handle that were then lost while being shipped to Spain.

the Azores, where it would search out and destroy corsair vessels as well as meet homeward bound convoys and escort them to Spain. This fleet of warships became of such major importance to Spain that it became the Royal Fleet of Spain and existed throughout the duration of the Indies navigation.

The first "treasure fleet" sailed to the Indies in 1537, when war with France broke out once again. Consisting of six warships and 20 merchant ships, it sailed directly to Nombre de Dios on the Isthmus of Panama to collect the treasures sent up from Peru, then to Cartagena to receive gold and emeralds sent down from the interior and pearls sent from the Island of Margarita, off the coast of Venezuela. Then it sailed to Havana, where it met with ships arriving from Veracruz with treasures and products from Mexico. After taking on water and provisions at Havana, it sailed up through the Bahama Channel and headed for the Azores, where it united with the Armada of the Ocean Sea to sail jointly for Spain. This system of treasure fleets remained in effect until about 1552, when galleons came into use and a new convoy system was established.

New Convoy System

This new convoy system consisted of sending two separate convoys of ships each year to the New World. Although other European nations referred to these convoys as treasure fleets, the Spaniards called them *flotas*, which means just plain fleet. Each of these flotas consisted of four heavily armed galleons of at least 300 tons and two 80-ton pataches, in addition to 10 to 90 merchant naos. One flota generally sailed in March and the other in September. After passing the Canaries they would generally make first landfall at either Guadeloupe or Martinique in the Caribbean. There the ships would split up: those sailing for Mexico would sail along with the vessels bound for Puerto Rico, Hispañiola, Cuba, Jamaica and Honduras; and the four galleons and two pataches would sail with those remaining ships for Venezuela, Colombia (which was then called the Nuevo Reiño de Granada) and the Isthmus of Panama.

The galleons would make their usual stops at Nombre de Dios and Cartagena before sailing to Havana to await arrival of the ships from all the other Spanish settlements in the New World that were returning to Spain. In theory, only the four galleons were permitted to carry treasure on the voyage to Spain, but this regulation was often ignored by merchants, who preferred to carry their treasure with them on other ships.

28

The organization of this flota system had one big drawback. After the ships separated after making their Caribbean landfall, many of those ships bound for Mexico were left without the protection of the four galleons and two pataches and fell prey to pirates and privateers. As a result of this deficiency, a much better flota system was put into effect in 1564 and retained for nearly a century. There were still two flotas sailing to the New World each year, one called the *Tierra Firme Flota* and the other the *New Spain Flota*. Each consisted of two heavily armed galleons and two pataches, plus the merchant naos sailing under their protection. The larger galleon, which was the flagship, was called the *Capitaña* and the smaller the *Almiranta*. The New Spain Flota generally sailed from Spain in April; however, the incurable dilatoriness of the Spaniards made it difficult for either of the flotas to be dispatched on time.

The voyage from Spain to Veracruz generally took from two to three months, depending on the weather and condition of the ships. The ships sailing for the Greater Antilles islands and Honduras would sail with this flota. By this time it had become the practice for the flotas to winter in Veracruz because such a large number of ships had been lost in the Gulf of Mexico after sailing from Veracruz between October and February, the time of the year when dangerous "northers" blow in the Gulf. They now would not sail until February or March of the following year, either to wait in Havana and sail jointly with the Tierra Firme Flota or to continue on alone for Spain.

The Tierra Firme Flota usually sailed in August, taking under its protection all the ships destined for ports along the Spanish Main. After it received the treasure from Peru in Nombre de Dios, it proceeded to Cartagena and wintered there, like the New Spain Flota did at Veracruz. Then in January it sailed for Havana and either met with the New Spain Flota or continued back to Spain alone. Political conditions in Europe during this period sometimes made it necessary to increase the number of galleons in the Tierra Firme Flota to six or eight, in which case it was called the Armada of Tierra Firme, or simply the Galleons. During such times the New Spain Flota either sailed back to Spain with the Galleons or left the Mexican treasure in Havana to be picked up by the Galleons.

In 1591, the threat of English capture of homeward-bound treasure galleons led to yet another reorganization of the Indies navigation which continued until about 1650. Under the new system three fleets were dispatched each year to the Indies. The Tierra Firme Flota and the New Spain Flota were still maintained, except for the fact that the former sailed earlier in the year and instead of wintering at Cartagena returned to Spain the same year, usually in convoy with the new fleet, which was called the Armada of Tierra Firme, the Silver Fleet, or simply the Galleons. This new fleet consisted of eight to 12 galleons and two or more pataches, and, like the Capitaña and Almiranta in the flotas, it was not permitted to carry cargo to or from the New World, except for treasure. The average size of these galleons was about 600 tons, but the Capitañas and Almirantas were sometimes as large as 1,000 tons. Besides being heavily armed with brass cannon, they each carried a company of two hundred marines.

With the reorganization of the Indies navigation, the Tierra Firme Flota usually sailed first in March and the Galleons either sailed at the same time or a month or so later. The New Spain Flota would now sail in May or June, attempting to reach Veracruz before the northers started blowing in October. After the Galleons picked up the treasure in Nombre de Dios, or later Portobelo, it went to Cartagena and then sailed alone or with the Tierra Firme Flota to Havana, where it would either meet with the previous year's New Spain Flota or pick up the treasure this flota had left in Havana. Then it would sail for Spain. Only on a few occasions between 1591 and 1650, when the treasure was urgently needed in Spain to avoid royal bankruptcy, did the New Spain Flota carry treasure back to Spain unescorted by the Galleons.

Throughout three centuries of the Indies navigation single ships, called *sueltos,* were also permitted to sail to the New World, in addition to the ships sailing in convoys. Depending on the political climate in Europe, the number sailing each year varied from a few to as many as 50. Most of the sueltos were small ships and their destinations were out-of-the-way places that larger merchant naos didn't visit. Although they were easy prey to enemy or pirate ships, the Crown benefited from their sailing, because they served as a year-round communication system with the New World colonies. To protect these sueltos, as well as the smaller and relatively unprotected settlements, Spain maintained a squadron of from four to eight galleons, called the Windward Armada, in the Caribbean.

After the conquest of Peru in the early 1540s, a squadron of from two to four ships, the Armada of the South Seas, was created for the purpose of carrying treasure from Peru to Panama City, where it was transferred to either Nombre de Dios or Portobelo, and for transporting European products and passengers brought from

Spain who went down to Peru. The home port of this armada was Callao, a seaport located six miles from Lima.

The most dangerous navigation undertaken by the Spaniards during these three centuries was the voyage between Manila in the Philippines and Acapulco, Mexico. From 1565 onward and nearly annually until 1815, ships called *Manila Galleons* made the perilous voyage between Manila and Acapulco. Three or four sailed annually until 1593, when a law was passed limiting the number of these sailings to two a year in each direction. The largest ships used by the Spaniards in the 16th century, they averaged about 700 tons; in the 17th century the average was 1,500 tons; and in the 18th they were between 1,700 and 2,000 tons.

The voyage from Acapulco to Manila was usually pleasant, with only an occasional storm to unsettle the routine sailing of from eight to 10 weeks. On the other hand, the voyage from Manila to Acapulco was known as the most difficult navigation in the world and dozens of ships were lost over the years. Because winds in the latitude of the Philippines are from the east, the Manila Galleons had to beat their way as far north as Japan before reaching the belt of westerly winds, which would carry them across the Pacific until they made a landfall on the coast of California and worked their way down to Acapulco. This voyage took from four to eight months, depending on luck. Counting the crews, from 300 to 600 persons sailed on each galleon. On average from 100 to 150 of them perished on each voyage from epidemics, scurvy, thirst, starvation or cold. On one of two Manila Galleons sailing jointly in 1657, all 450 persons died from a smallpox epidemic and about half of the 400 on the other.

Notwithstanding the great risks this navigation posed to ships, property and life, the financial gain made by those involved in this trade and by the Crown made it seem worth the hardships. The cargoes carried from Acapulco to Manila were basically the same as those carried on the flotas between Spain and the Indies ports, but these galleons also carried silver specie and bullion from the mines of Peru and Mexico to pay for the cargoes sent from Manila. The Crown restricted the amount to be sent to Manila at 500,000 pesos a year, but like most other laws, this one was disregarded and an average of 3 to 5 million pesos was sent to Manila each year. In 1597 the fantastic amount of 12 million pesos reached Manila.

The cargoes from Manila to Acapulco were of a more interesting and diversified nature. The main item was Chinese and Japanese silks of various styles and descriptions. There were also crepes, velvets, taffeta, damasks in cloth materials; fans, rugs, combs, exquisite jewelry (rings, bracelets, pendants, earrings, etc.); devotional pieces, such as crucifixes, reliquaries and rosaries; jewel-studded sword hilts, ornaments made of pearls, objects made of ivory and sandalwood, copper cuspidors, gold bells, beautiful porcelain ware and a variety of drugs and spices.

When the Manila Galleons reached Acapulco, merchants converged from as far away as Peru and a fair was held in which the bulk of the goods was sold. Peruvian merchants carried their goods to Panama City and sailed later in the year on the ships of the Armada of the South Seas. Mexican merchants had their goods carried over the mountains by mules. The agents who represented the Seville merchants also used mules and traveled all the way to Veracruz to return to Spain aboard the New Spain Flota.

All officers and royal officials serving on ships in the Indies navigation were Spanish citizens by birth, with the exception of navigators who were often either Portuguese or Italian. On the other hand, the crews on these ships were made up of men and boys from every European country. This was the case throughout the history of the Indies navigation; Spaniards sometimes making up less than 20 percent of the crew, even though contrary to royal regulations. Due to the chronic shortage of seafaring Spaniards, however, officials of the House of Trade turned a blind eye. At times as many as 12 European nations were represented by members of the crew on a single merchant nao, Since these men did not share a common language the result oftentimes was confusion and conflict between the seamen.

The maximum number of passengers permitted on each ship was computed to be 30 for each 100 tons of shipping. The ship's owner or captain was responsible for providing each passenger with a pound and a half of biscuit, two pints of drinking water, and one pint of water for bathing purposes. Passengers provided all other victuals and liquids.

The seamen and marines on both the galleons and merchant naos shared a diet which varied very little throughout three centuries. Daily rations consisted of two pounds of biscuit, one quart of wine and one quart of water each day. Four days a week they received eight ounces of dried fish and two ounces of peas or beans; on the other three days they received eight ounces of salt pork and one and a half ounces of rice. Once a week they were given a small amount of olive oil, vinegar and cheese. They supplemented this monotonous diet by catching fresh fish during the voyage. Officers and royal officials had to supply their own victuals. Lists of their personal victuals include every known species of live domestic beast and fowl, smoked hams, bacon, sausages, salted cow's tongue, various types of pickled or dried fish, olives, olive oil, biscuit, bread, chocolates, noodles, rice, beans, spices, starch, lentils and as many as 20 different varieties of wines and stronger liquors.

Preparing for dispatching a flota was a long, drawn-out, frustrating affair lasting from three to five months, depending on the availability of supplies, ships, men and money to purchase what was needed. The merchant naos were the responsibility of their owners, but the House of Trade officials were in charge of preparing the Capitañas, Almirantas and pataches of the flotas, as well as all the ships in the Galleons. These officials prepared the galleons and pataches for sailing. They also inspected the merchant naos to ensure they were capable of making the voyage and that they carried sufficient armaments and munitions. These officials also made certain that all cargo had been properly registered with all taxes and duties paid and that only licensed passengers were aboard the ships. The officials were sometimes aided in these inspections by officers and officials of the flotas, who knew that if a merchant nao was overloaded or unfit to make the voyage, it would slow down the progress of the convoy which sailed at the speed of the slowest ship.

Early colonists in the New World were forced to depend on Spain for almost every essential item needed for subsistence. Thus. ships' cargoes consisted basically of foodstuffs, tools, agricultural and mining implements, domestic animals, seeds, weapons, cloth and sundries. Even the ballast of the early ships consisted of bricks or dressed stones, which were used for building in the new settlements. After the discovery of the rich New World mines and the foundation of the flota system in mid-16th century, the nature of the cargo began to change. By this time the colonists were able to supply themselves with their own foodstuffs, and because of the wealth they were obtaining from the mines they demanded vast quantities of manufactured goods, not just hardware, weapons, and household items, but luxury items — books, paper, musical instruments, religious objects, leather goods, etc.

The departure of a fleet from Spain was a ceremonious occasion and brought crowds of spectators from far and wide to witness the event. The sailing date was always preceded by several days of fiestas and religious ceremonies. Once at sea, after the excitement of the departure had died down, the normal routine of each ship was set and maintained throughout the voyage. The men were placed on different watches, assigned sleeping areas and messmates, and assembled to hear a reading of rules governing the voyage.

Spaniards were never noted for cleanliness, especially on ships, and most of the epidemics that broke out aboard their ships resulted from poor sanitation. An Englishman writing in the early 17th century said, "Their ships are kept foul and beastly, like hog-sties and sheep-cots in comparison of ours; and no marvel, for there is no course taken to correct that abuse by appointing men purposely for that office as we do in our ships."

In contrast to the voyage from Manila to Acapulco, the transatlantic crossing was child's play. Even so it was still a long and trying experience. Quarters were painfully restricted for all but the senior officers and rich passengers, and the quantity and quality of the victuals left much to be desired. To break the monotony of the voyage they improvised mimic bullfights, held cockfights, celebrated as many religious holidays as possible, and did a great deal of fishing. But the main pastime for most of the crew and passengers was gambling, which, although forbidden by royal decree, met with little opposition from ships' officers and officials. Predicting the weather was a continuous source of interest. Old salts could fairly accurately forecast the weather by various means. A heavily clouded sky at night, for example, meant rain would soon fall; when extra-large rays accompanied a rising or setting sun, bad weather was usually at hand; the brighter the moon at night, the better the weather the following day; deep red clouds on the horizon at dawn or dusk meant the approach of a tempest; a halo around the moon foreshadowed rain, etc.

Older seamen predicted bad weather when their rheumatism flared up just as people still do because the high humidity that precedes most storms at sea inflames arthritic joints. What men dreaded most was an exceptionally calm sea lasting for several days accompanied by unusually clear water and many more fish than usual seen near or on the surface, followed by huge swells when there was no wind about. This meant the approach of a hurricane.

From beginning to end, the voyage to and from the New World was a hazardous undertaking. Shipwrecks were the greatest danger. During the three centuries slightly more than five percent of the ships in the Indies navigation wrecked, mostly due to bad weather but also to incompetent navigators. A small percentage capsized because of overloading or perished from fires on board. There were also relatively small losses due to ships being destroyed or captured by enemy or pirate ships.

Throughout the Indies navigation, once the Americas-bound ships sailing for the New World passed over the dangerous sandbar at Sanlucar, very few were lost until after they reached the Caribbean. The winds were nearly all in their favor, there was little danger of bad storms in the latitudes these ships sailed in, and, of course, there was little danger of running up on a reef in the deep ocean waters.

Dangerous Return Voyage

The return voyage was far more dangerous, in addition to sometimes being twice as long. The hulls of the Spain-bound ships were riddled with worms and slowed by heavy growths of barnacles and moss. Passage homeward encountered many dangerous areas, including the hostile reefs and shoals on both sides of the Bahama Channel. Another problem was that crews were smaller because of deaths and desertion in the New World.

Among the most interesting aspects of these voyages were the methods, or lack of methods, used in navigation. Many, including Spaniards themselves, have written scornfully of Spanish navigational practices. Shortly after the foundation of the House of Trade in Seville, a school of navigation was founded there for the express purpose of training navigators.

The science of navigation came into being during the early 15th century under the auspices of such Portuguese as Prince Henry the Navigator. By the time Columbus sailed for the New World, navigation appeared to have reached its zenith and very few improvements were made until the 19th century. Basically, the navigator depended on dead-reckoning navigation because there was no way to establish longitude until the 19th century. The compass was used to maintain a course. Such instruments as astrolabes and quadrants were used to reckon latitude at midday. Various methods were used to estimate a ship's speed, and navigators employed a fair amount of guesswork in deciding such things as a ship's drift in ocean currents or the magnetic variation of the compass. Charts were generally so inaccurate that many navigators preferred to rely on their own knowledge and experience.

Rarely did two navigators in the same convoy agree on the position of the ships or even the proper compass headings to take, which led many ships to be wrecked. In a New Spain Flota sailing in 1582, the captain-general summoned all the navigators to his ship to determine their position after five weeks at sea. The estimates ranged from being two weeks away from Guadeloupe to one day. The majority placed the convoy ten days from the island while one man predicted they would reach the island within 24 hours. He was laughed at, but that very night the three leading ships ran upon reefs on the eastern side of Guadeloupe.

The flota system followed the New World routes with little variation except during time of war, when they were altered to avoid capture or destruction. Upon leaving Spain, all fleets passed within sight of the Canary Islands and then made landfall at either Guadeloupe or Martinique, where they spent a day or two refreshing themselves. The New Spain Flota then set a course for St. Croix, Virgin Islands, and passed within sight of the southern coast of the island. While dropping off various ships along its way, the fleet continued along the south side of Hispañiola and Cuba and, after sighting Cape San Antonio on the western tip of Cuba, headed for Cape Catoche on the Yucatan peninsula staying in sight of land until it finally reached Veracruz.

Between Veracruz and Havana

The voyage from Veracruz to Havana generally took from four to five weeks, since the flotas sailed an indirect route because of contrary winds. After leaving Veracruz they headed north until sighting land in the vicinity of Pensacola, where they turned and followed the length of Florida's west coast, where winds were usually favorable. Not until reaching the vicinity of the Dry Tortugas in the Florida Keys could they steer a direct course for Havana.

Both the Tierra Firme Flota and the Galleons followed the same routes. After leaving Guadeloupe or Martinique, they steered for a point on the Spanish Main called Cabo de la Vela, or Cape of the Sail, so called because from a distance it resembled a large sail. Once in sight of the cape, they stayed within sight of the coast until reaching Cartagena. To sail from Cartagena to Nombre de Dios, or Portobelo (which superseded Nombre de Dios near the end of the 16th century) the fleets sailed in a direct line because of prevailing winds, but they would first have to sail northwest for several days before changing course to southwest. The voyage back to Cartagena was more direct and generally made within sight of land all the way.

36

In sailing between Cartagena and Havana, the Spaniards used an unorthodox method, also employed between Havana and Spain. Instead of attempting to steer a course to pass between the dangerous reefs of Serrana and Serranilla on the west and Pedro Shoals on the east, they steered directly for either one of these reefs. They believed it was better to know they had reached a dangerous area by sighting it rather than trying to sail between reefs on both sides, not knowing their position or that of the dangerous reefs. Not surprisingly, these reefs occasionally ripped the bottoms out of vessels that reached them on dark nights. After sighting whichever of these perilous reefs they had been steering for, the fleet then changed course, heading for Grand Cayman Island. Upon sighting it they would again alter course at a point on the southwestern coast of Cuba. Once in sight of the Cuban coast, they would hug it until reaching Havana.

After departing from Havana on the voyage for Spain, they once again executed the unorthodox practice of heading directly for the Florida Keys, an area that has claimed more Spanish shipwrecks than any other in the New World. With the Bahama Channel being no narrower than 50 miles at any point, it seems incomprehensible that they would not try to steer up its middle rather than so close to such a dangerous area. In that day and age, however, navigation practice dictated sighting as many known points of land as possible to establish a ship's true position. Not even the loss of a great number of ships on the Florida Keys was enough to change this practice. Once the Keys were sighted, a more northerly course was taken. Generally the ships stayed within sight of the Florida coast until sighting Cape Canaveral, when they changed course, heading for Bermuda. While reefs around Bermuda also claimed many Spanish ships, navigators felt it was absolutely necessary to sight Bermuda in order to know their true position before turning on an easterly and heading toward the Azores.

The route used on the return voyages to Spain remained constant throughout the Indies navigation. By about 1650, however, when most of the islands of the Lesser Antilles began to be settled by the English and colonists from other European nations, both fleets sailing to Mexico and the Spanish Main had to change their routes. The New Spain Flota would make its first Caribbean landfall in the vicinity of the Virgin Islands and then pass along the northern coast of Puerto Rico before sailing south down the channel separating Puerto Rico from Hispañiola. Once in sight of the southern coast of Hispañiola, the rest of the route was the same as before.

The fleets sailing for the Spanish Main would make their first landfall at Trinidad and Tobago and pass between both these islands on the body of water that retains the name of Galleon Passage. They would then head directly for Cabo de la Vela and proceed along the routes used previously. The main ports visited were Nombre de Dios, Portobelo, Cartagena, Havana and Veracruz. At first the Caribbean terminus for receiving the Peruvian treasures was at Nombre de Dios, the narrowest point on the Isthmus. Because of the unhealthy nature of this port which was surrounded by malarial swamps, however, the Crown in 1584 ordered the town moved to Portobelo, a few miles to the southeast and a much safer port for shipping. The actual move was delayed for some time because a new jungle trail had to be cut to connect Portobelo to Venta Cruz, the midway point along the trail between Portobelo and Panama City. The move was greatly hastened after Drake destroyed Nombre de Dios in 1596, when Portobelo finally superseded it. Portobelo was never a settlement of significant size. Except at the time of the visit of the fleets, it was more or less a ghost town containing a small garrison of Spanish soldiers who manned the forts plus several hundred Negroes and mulattos.

The main Peruvian port was Callao, six miles from Lima. Cconsisting of a natural harbor defended by a strong fort, it was home base for the Armada of the South Seas. This armada, formed after the rich ore discoveries at Potosi, usually consisted of from two to four galleons responsible to carry the Peruvian treasures up to Panama City and return with cargoes brought from Spain. The Potosi mines were high in the mountains and llama trains took about two weeks to carry the treasure to Arica, the nearest port. From Arica to Callao the treasure was carried on small pataches, taking an average of eight days. The voyage of the Armada of the South Seas from Callao to Panama City averaged about three weeks, but the return voyage was twice and sometimes three times as long, with ships bucking contrary currents and winds.

Usually, a few weeks before the Galleons were to leave Spain, an advice boat was sent to Nombre de Dios (or Portobelo) with news of the approach of the Galleons. By sea and land, this news was rushed south to Lima, and measures were taken to assure that the Peruvian treasures would be in Panama City about the time the Galleons arrived at the Isthmus. Once the Galleons reached the Isthmus, word sped overland to Panama City ordering transportation of the treasure to Nombre de Dios or Portobelo.

This was executed in one of two ways: either the treasure was transported entirely overland on mules, or partly by mules and partly on water. A short distance south of Portobelo is the mouth of the Chagres River, which has its head at Venta Cruz, the halfway point across the Isthmus. When water was high enough on the river, treasure would be taken off the mules at Venta Cruz and placed aboard flat-bottomed barges and carried down the river. At the mouth of the river, where there was a strong fort, the treasure would then be transferred to either galleys or other small vessels and taken to Portobelo. Bars of silver were stacked like heaps of stones in the streets or the main square of Portobelo without causing any fear or suspicion of loss, since the owner of each bar had his marks stamped on it. The gold, all coinage and the Kings treasure were kept in the large Customs Warehouse.

Each year a fair was held in Nombre de Dios or Portobelo and the town accommodated an enormous crowd of traders, soldiers, sailors, etc. who found shelter and food obtainable only at outrageous prices. Merchants paid as much as a thousand pesos for a building in which to house their goods. Yet Portobelo wasn't much healthier than Nombre de Dios, and each year large numbers perished from dysentery and malaria. The fair generally lasted a month, but occasionally epidemics or the urgent need for the treasure in Spain would cut its duration as short as a week. Once the fair ended and the ships sailed for Cartagena, the port would once again become a ghost town.

Cartagena served as the port for Santa Fe de Bogota, which was the capital of New Granada (today called Colombia). Here pearls from the various fisheries along the Spanish Main were placed aboard the galleons, as well as gold and emeralds sent from Bogota. Before the fleets left for Havana, they obtained fresh victuals and water and made repairs to the ships.

Veracruz was the most dangerous port visited by the flotas, exposed as it was to hurricanes in the summer and violent northers during most of the fall and winter months. It was an open roadstead, and entry to the port was made hazardous by sandbars and reefs at its mouth. Large ships anchored at or were tied up in the lee of a small island named San Juan de Ulza, located 15 miles down the coast from Veracruz, and the goods destined for Mexico City and elsewhere had to be transported to Vera Cruz on small boats.

The town of Veracruz was completely moved in 1600, down the coast directly opposite San Juan de Ulza. This town, like all others visited by the fleets, was never of major importance, being nothing more than a shanty town that served as a base for the flotas that wintered there. The only buildings of note were the forts, a customs house and several churches. A fair was held there, as in Portobelo, and when it was over, goods were carried overland on mules to Mexico City and other places, including faraway Guatemala City.

Havana was the only Indies port at which nearly every ship returning to Spain from the New World stopped. The town itself was the most impressive of any visited by the fleets, and it was here that the fleets would unite for the homeward voyage. The surrounding countryside provided plenty of provisions for the homeward-bound ships as well as wood for necessary ships' repairs.

Without the discovery of the rich mines of precious metals in the New World, there would not have been any treasure fleets and the whole course of American history would have taken a different turn. The first treasure to reach Spain was brought by Columbus. It was followed by much larger amounts from Hispañiola during the next two decades, amounts obtained by the use of Indian slave labor. When this labor source was quickly exhausted, others emerged with the conquests of Peru and Mexico. By 1530 some enterprising Spaniards and a large number of Germans sent by the Emperor began serious mining by digging out deposits of ore, mainly silver, from rich surface deposits, and each year larger and larger amounts were shipped back to Spain.

The breakthrough came in the year 1545 in Peru with the discovery of the prodigious silver mountain of Potosi (today located in Bolivia), which contained the greatest concentration of silver found anywhere in the world. This mine was discovered by an Inca Indian named Hualpa. While stalking a deer up the steep slopes of this mountain, he grabbed a shrub to pull himself up. The shrub gave way and its cavity he discovered a mass of pure silver. The Spaniards began working this mine on a large scale, and three years later rich silver mines were discovered in Mexico at Zacatecas and Guanajuato, precipitating a mad silver rush to the areas.

With the exception of Peru's Huancavelica mercury mine, the Spanish Crown never exploited the mines on their own account but gained revenue from the collection of the King's Royal Fifth on all precious metals mined. Although some Spaniards, and even Indians, worked small claims by hand, the typical silver miner was a capitalist. He supplied the money that it took to mine, refine and transport the gold and silver to the seaports.

Another boost in the amount of precious metals reaching Spain came in 1555 with the discovery by an unknown German alchemist of refining precious metals with the use of mercury or quicksilver. Within a year this mercury amalgamation process was employed in the New World with good results. The Crown, realizing that supplying miners with mercury would be a lucrative source of income, shrewdly placed a Crown monopoly on mercury. The mercury mine of Huancavelica, which had been discovered prior to 1555, was seized by the Crown and its owners were miserably compensated. This mine was in steady use to provide all the mercury for South American mines until the 19th century, except during rare periods when production was halted by cave-ins or flooding.

No mercury mines were ever discovered in Mexico, and all the mercury used there had to be shipped from Peru and Spain. The mercury brought from Spain came from two sources. A mine named Almadin in southern Spain, first used by the Romans, was exploited, but when it couldn't produce sufficient quantities to meet the demands of the Mexican mines, large quantities were imported from Hungary, the nearest source of mercury. Mercury was so important that any interruption in its delivery resulted in great financial problems to the Crown, since it meant a decrease in the amount of precious metals refined and subsequently lesser amounts of revenue paid to the Crown.

Before the discovery and exploitation of the silver mines, gold was the chief source of mineral wealth. This gold was obtained from conquest of new lands as well as by panning rivers and streams in the areas that had already been settled. Deposits of gold ore were frequently discovered, but were generally too expensive to mine when compared with silver mining, which proved more profitable. Between 1550 and 1700 so little gold was mined that it accounted for less than one percent of the total value of precious metals, with most of this a by-product of silver production.

Silver production expanded continuously throughout the second half of the 16th century, reaching a peak in the 1590s. Production declined slowly between 1600 and 1630; after 1630 the decline was precipitous. The main reason was the exhaustion of deposits near the surface. Miners were forced to dig deeper and deeper which greatly increased production costs. Also at these deeper levels they found poorer grades of ore. For example, at the Potosi mine in 1560 a pound of silver ore yielded two ounces of pure silver, but by 1630 it took over one ton of ore to yield the same amount.

Besides necessitating much more labor to mine, the inferior grades of ore required such greater amounts of mercury for refining that there was never enough to meet demands. By the middle of the 17th century over half the mines that had been in operation in 1600 were closed, either because labor conditions kept them from making a profit, or because of such technical difficulties as not being able to drain deep shafts, prevent cave-ins or supply adequate ventilation to miners.

Around the end of the 17th century production of both gold and silver took a turn for the better, chiefly because of technical advances in mining techniques, such as the abilities to drain and provide ventilation down the deep shafts. By 1700 and during every year of the 18th century more precious metals were mined in America than during even the peak years during the last decade of the 16th century. Many of the gold mines that had been discovered as much as two centuries earlier but never mined were put into production, and throughout the 18th century the value of mined gold was about ten percent of the total value of precious metals.

The refining of both gold and silver was left in the hands of individual miners, but the Crown provided assayers to test all the precious metals for their fineness and also collected the Kings Royal Fifth and other smaller taxes. There were royal mints in most of the major cities of the New World, including Lima, Mexico City, Guatemala City, Bogota and even at Potosi. Most of the Kings Royal Fifth was kept in bars or smaller wedges of silver. Some of it was used in the Indies to pay the salaries of royal officials and

Above

These three pistols and lead musket balls were among the many artifacts recovered by the author from the sunken Jamaican city of Port Royal.

Below

Manila galleons brought from the Orient as many as 400,000 pieces of porcelain, such as these excellent examples from the Ming Dynasty.

BANCOS SAN JOSE- BAY OF PANAMA
SITE TWO- 18TH (MID) CENT CANNON WRECK

T = TIMBER
OJ = OLIVE J.
P = POTTERY
CB = CANNON B
B = BALLAST

BALLAST PILE

N

BOTTOM-M

DEPTHS-
24-30 me

0   10   20   30   40   50   60   70
METERS

soldiers. After private individuals had paid their Royal Fifth, they were free to keep the gold or silver in bars or wedges, or have it minted into coins.

Most of the coins minted in the Indies remained in circulation there, but large amounts changed hands at the fairs in Portobelo or Veracruz and were carried back on ships by Spanish merchants who had sold merchandise at the fairs. Gold coins were called escudos, or, from about 1700, doubloons. Silver coins were called reals, and both gold and silver were minted in denominations of eight, four, two, one and halves. The value of gold coins compared with silver in the 16th and 17th centuries was 16 to one; but during the 18th century, when gold production was greatly increased, this value dropped to eight to one. There were all sorts of frauds committed by the men entrusted with the refining, assaying and minting gold and silver. On many occasions silver bars were found to have centers of lead or copper and occasionally other base metals. During minting, base metal, including platinum which was considered of no value then, was sometimes added. Coins were also minted weighing less than they should have.

Before any treasure was embarked on the galleons, manifests, or registers, were made in triplicate listing every bar, wedge or chest of coins. The bars and wedges had various marks on them that indicated where they were mined and assayed, whether the Royal Fifth had been paid, the owner's mark, the mark of the assayer, the fineness of the metal, the weight, and the value of each piece. The average weight of a silver bar was 70 pounds, a wedge was between 10 and 20 pounds, and gold bullion weighed from several ounces up to 30 pounds.

Above

This illustration depicts a large late-16th-century Spanish galleon under full sail. Finding the wreck of such a treasure-laden vessel is a diver's dream.

Below

Site plan of the San Jose, lost in the Pacific off Panama in 1631, shows that this wreck in relatively deep water is not scattered like those in most shallower sites.

Smuggling of unregistered cargoes, both to and from the Indies, was the most frustrating problem confronting the Spanish Crown throughout the period of the Indies navigation. In 1510 an ordinance was issued ordering that any unregistered treasure brought back from the Indies was subject to confiscation with the smuggler forced to pay a fine of four times its value. None of these elaborate precautions exercised by officials of the Crown were ever totally effective. Before a fleet entered Sanlucar, all other ships in the port were forced to move to Cadíz to prevent any treasure from the returning Indies ships being sneaked aboard them. Patrol boats were stationed up and down the coasts between Cape St. Vincent and Gibraltar to make certain that no boats approached or left the returning Indies ships. The beaches were patrolled with savage dogs. From 1576 onward, informers were paid one-third of the value of any unregistered treasure recovered. Every ship returning from the Indies was also closely inspected by royal officials of the House of Trade. Notwithstanding these precautions, an estimated 20 percent of the gold and silver mined in the New World was smuggled into Spain or other European nations in return for payment of contraband goods that had been sold in the Indies by foreigners.

Gold, ounce for ounce far more valuable than silver, was the first choice of smugglers, but great amounts of silver, both in specie and bullion, also were smuggled, and the smugglers never seemed to tire of devising new methods to avoid detection. On one occasion a royal official scratching the surface of a suspiciously painted anchor found it was made of solid gold. The most common method used, however, was smuggling the gold and silver in bales, boxes or chests of unimportant commodities like sugar, molasses, tobacco, etc., since it was almost impossible for the royal officials to open every single container on board a ship.

In some cases the amounts of unregistered treasure on board ships was greater than that registered. A good example was in 1555, when a ship returning from New Spain wrecked on the southern coast of Spain between Cadíz and Gibraltar. Divers sent to salvage the wreck recovered over 500,000 pesos in treasure, of which less than 150,000 pesos was registered. All the ship's officers were sentenced to 10 years as galley slaves.

A gradual decline in the flota system began around 1600, and by 1650 the flota system had almost ceased to exist. There were multiple reasons for this but the most important were the decrease in silver production, a great increase in contraband goods in the Spanish Indies sold by interlopers; insufficient vessels and crews for the Indies navigation; poor leadership by inept rulers; bankruptcy of the Crown on several occasions; and the depredations executed on the shipping and American colonies by Spain's enemies and pirates.

Ever-increasing amounts of contraband were brought over by interlopers and sold at far more attractive prices which caused Spanish America's demand for merchandise from Spain to fall steadily. Consequently, the number of ships in the flotas kept decreasing. So great was the amount of contraband goods reaching Portobelo that 1648 was the last year that a Tierra Firme Flota ever sailed to the Indies. Thereafter, the small amount of goods carried there was embarked aboard the Galleons. A few years later, with so little merchandise to carry, and the mining industry in such a poor state, the Crown seriously considered the cessation of the whole flota system.

From 1650 onward the New Spain Flota and the Galleons, which previously had sailed yearly, sailed only at irregular intervals of every four or five years, and the number of ships in these fleets was negligible. Between 1570 and 1599 an average of 110 ships sailed yearly to the Indies; between 1600 and 1610 the number dropped to 55; between 1640 and 1650 to 25; and between 1670 and 1690 to 17.

In 1661 the situation was so dire that Spaniards had to use a Dutch fleet of 20 ships under the command of Admiral Ruiter to protect their returning treasure ships from English attack. The Dutch were willing, since most of the returning treasure was consigned to Dutch merchants in payment for goods they had shipped over earlier in the year. Even after 1700, when the production of gold and silver in the American mines greatly increased, the overall flota system showed very little improvement, chiefly because Spanish-American colonists preferred buying European merchandise more cheaply from the English, Dutch and French, all of whom had established settlements throughout the West Indies. During the War of Spanish Succession, which lasted from 1700 to 1713, the French took over virtual control of the flota system, and most of the ships used were French with predominantly French crews.

Between 1715 and 1736, small flotas continued to sail to Veracruz every two or three years, but during this same period of 21 years only five convoys of treasure galleons sailed to Portobelo and Cartagena. In 1736, the threat of war with England caused the Spanish Crown to suspend sailing of the New Spain Flota and the Galleons. In 1740 the Crown went a step further and ended the sailings of the Galleons permanently. Thereafter, a new system had to be devised to bring back the Peruvian treasures. Large, solitary galleons, or occasionally two, would sail directly from Cadíz to Callao and back. Great improvements in the design and rigging of the galleons now made the perilous voyage around Cape Horn much safer. Some foreign ships, mainly French, had been making this long nad perilous voyage from 1700 onward.

The long war with England disrupted sailings of the New Spain Flota until 1754, and during this period when no flotas sailed to Veracruz, single registered sueltos made the voyage yearly. Between 1754 and 1778, the year when the last New Spain Flota returned to Spain, only six flotas sailed to Veracruz, and all of them had to be escorted by large squadrons of warships, which made it too costly to continue future sailings.

In 1778, when the Spanish Crown finally declared free trade for her American colonies, the flota system came to an end. Spanish ships still sailed to the New World with European products and returned with treasure, but no longer in convoys. Two or three ships generally sailed jointly but sometimes only one made the voyage.

Throughout the 16th century the waters of the New World were more or less a "Spanish Lake" and almost all the ships sailing in these waters were Spanish-built, had Spanish crews and carried cargoes and treasures between Spain and the Spanish-American colonies. Ships of other European nations made occasional voyages to the New World, however, generally to the detriment of the Spaniards. The Portuguese were the one exception. Soon after the founding of the early Spanish settlements, the Portuguese were granted exclusive permission by the Spanish Crown to carry limited numbers of Africans to be sold in the New World ports as slaves. They were in especially great demand in areas where the indigenous population had been decimated, either by wholesale Spanish massacres or by diseases the conquistadors introduced from the Old World. During the period 1525 to 1550 an average of six to eight Portuguese slave ships a year visited various ports in the New World, sometimes making additional profits by selling contraband European products to the Spanish colonists at much cheaper prices than they could obtain from the Seville monopolists. With the great increase in mining after the mid-16th century, the number of Portuguese slave ships increased to as many as 40 to 50 annually. This continued until 1640, when Portugal revolted against the Spanish Crown and eventually won total independence. Dutch, and later English, took over the lucrative trade of supplying the Spanish colonies with a steady supply of African slaves.

The first interlopers in the waters of the New World were the French pirates and privateers, who appeared during the third decade of the 16th century. Throughout this century the French made sporadic voyages to the New World, generally for the sake of attacking Spanish settlements and shipping. They also made several abortive attempts to establish settlements on the coast of Florida. On the other hand, the English, like John Hawkins, began activity in this area with the intent of peacefully trading with the Spanish colonists, but the Spaniards had such complete mastery over their colonies that these voyages were rarely profitable. It took the English many years to realize that the only way to make any profit in the New World was to take what they wanted by force. During the last three decades, Francis Drake and a host of other famous English privateers infested the West Indies and settlements on the coast of Central America (the Spanish Main) to wage war on the Spaniards and accumulate great amounts of plunder. Spain considered these privateers and all who trespassed on their rich preserve to be pirates. But many of these forays were profitless, because the Spaniards were not always easy to overcome.

The Dutch showed no interest in the New World until the last two decades of the 16th century, and this came about not because of greed or plunder or to make a profit out of contraband trade with the Spaniards but because of their great need for salt. Fishing was the main industry of 16th century Netherlands and processing the catch required immense amounts of salt. Until 1580, when Portugal was annexed to Spain, the necessary salt was obtained from great salt pans on Portugal's southern coast. This ended, however, when Spain took over the government of Portugal, and further trade with the Dutch (with whom Spain had been at war for over 20 years) was discouraged.

The Dutch economy faced collapse until the discovery of vast deposits of salt in the New World, in several of the Bahama Islands, St. Martin, and at Junta de Araya on the coast of Venezuela. As early as 1582 there were as many as 150 Dutch ships making annual voyages to the Caribbean for salt. By 1600 this number increased to over 200 ships (actually more ships than were sailing from Spain to the New World at this time), and in the year 1616 a total of 279 Dutch ships made the round trip, most of them loading salt at Punta de

Araya, where they had constructed permanent warehouses to store any surplus that might accumulate. They continued extracting huge amounts of salt from the Caribbean until near the close of the 17th century, when large salt mines were discovered in Germany and elsewhere in Europe.

Early in the 17th century, Sir Walter Raleigh founded several small English settlements near the Orinoco River on the northeastern section of the South American coast. The Dutch and the French soon followed, establishing settlements in the same general area, but none of them amounted to much until later in the century, when the settlements were put on a firmer footing (some are still held today). Most of the ships returning from these settlements sailed directly to Europe and didn't come up through the Bahama Channel except when a captain decided to chance meeting some small Spanish ship he might capture.

New Era Dawns

A new era in the maritime history of the New World dawned with the second quarter of the 17th century as the Caribbean ceased to be a "Spanish Lake." The English, French and Dutch, no longer content to be thought of by the Spaniards as interlopers and pirates, established themselves as permanent settlers.

The English settled the Island of St. Christopher (St. Kitts) in 1624, and the following year a large group of French settlers joined them. To avoid friction between the colonists, the island was divided in two. In 1627 the English colonists reached Barbados, and in 1628 English colonists settled on Nevis and on Providencia (called Santa Catalina by the Spaniards), which is located in the western Caribbean off the coast of Nicaragua.

The Spaniards were livid about this encroachment . On September 7, 1629, a Spanish fleet of more than 30 large ships under the command of Admiral Fadrique de Toledo dropped anchor at Nevis and captured and destroyed several English ships anchored there. Then Spanish soldiers were sent ashore to ravage the few buildings the settlers had just built. The fleet then moved to St. Kitts, only a few miles to the north, and although the English and French put up some resistance the Spaniards quickly captured it.

Admiral Toledo provided several ships and ordered the settlers to return to their respective countries (for which he was severely criticized by the King of Spain). Although most of the French colonists returned to France, the English soon returned to St. Kitts and began all over again. Some of the English ships sailing between England and Virginia or New England preferred taking the southern route in crossing the Atlantic, and on many of these voyages additional colonists were brought to St. Kitts and other newly founded English settlements.

The Dutch, not wanting to be outdone by their French and English neighbors, were quick to grab the islands they wanted and to found their own settlements. In 1628 they settled on Tobago Island, but it was a bad choice, as Trinidad, the next island to the south, was settled by the Spaniards. The Spaniards, making use of the cannibalistic Carib Indians, soon forced the Dutch to flee from Tobago in 1630. The directors of the Dutch West Indies Company, who were entrusted with the founding of these settlements, sent another group of colonists to Tobago in 1633, but in 1637 the Spaniards mounted a surprise attack and put every one of the settlers to the sword. The Dutch had better luck on other Caribbean islands. By the time of the Treaty of Westphalia in 1648, when the war between the Dutch and Spanish came to an end after almost a hundred years of bloody conflict, the Dutch had permanent settlements on Aruba, Bonaire, Curaçao, Saba, St. Martin and St. Eustatius; and the Spaniards were forced to recognize the existence of these Dutch colonies in the New World.

In 1635 the French formed the Compagnie des Iles d'Amerique to compete with the Dutch and English. By 1648 they had settlements on Martinique, Guadeloupe, St. Bartholomew, St. Croix, St. Lucia and Grenada. By this time the English had gobbled up most of the remaining islands in the Lesser Antilles and later were to win, through the spoils of war, some of those in French hands; yet they were still unsatisfied. No foreign nation had attempted to take an inhabited Spanish possession by force until 1655 when Cromwell sent a massive military force to the Caribbean. After failing to capture either Puerto Rico or Santo Domingo, he finally took the Island of Jamaica, more or less as a consolation prize. Spain was too weak to recapture the island, and in 1670 she ceded Jamaica to England as part of a peace treaty.

Jamaica soon became England's most profitable overseas possession. Piracy and privateering was conducted from here, as well as illegal commerce with the Spanish colonies. Eventually, however, agriculture, made Jamaica valuable to England, mainly because of the cultivation of sugar and its by-products. The French followed the English by attacking the western half of Hispañiola, which was

51

finally ceded to them by Spain in 1697. Thus, throughout the 17th century, especially during the second half, there were great numbers of European ships in Caribbean waters and returning through the Bahama Channel. The majority of these ships sailed singly or in small groups and carried back cotton, tobacco, indigo, spices, lumber and rum, as well as gold, silver and whatever else obtained from the Spaniards through plunder or illegal trade.

Toward the end of the century the English organized merchant fleets, generally convoyed by warships. The usual practice was for the convoy to split up when reaching the Caribbean while the merchant ships sailed to various islands to unload cargoes and load homeward-bound cargoes. Then all of the ships would sail to Kingston, Jamaica, and then back to England in a large convoy, passing through the Bahama Channel. As early as 1697 one of these fleets numbered 116 merchantmen and six warships. In 1758, a fleet leaving Jamaica numbered 150 ships, and this was only one of two fleets that sailed from there that year. As early as 1723 there were three fleets sailing from England to the Caribbean: one to Barbados and two to Jamaica, totaling over 425 ships for that year. Not all of them sailed to England; many went to various ports in the American colonies.

These American colonies were also sending substantial numbers of merchant ships to the Caribbean, supplying the English islands with items they could not get from the Mother Country or those they could supply at cheaper prices, such as a wide variety of foodstuffs and various types of lumber. As years passed and the population grew, maritime traffic also increased. By 1750, in Kingston alone, more than 800 ships from other Caribbean islands, Europe, Africa, North America and the Spanish colonies entered the port. The Dutch colonies were small by comparison and they did not use convoys.

Although their colonies were not as large as those of the English, the French also inaugurated a convoy system. The majority of their homeward-bound traffic, however, did not pass through the Bahama Channel. French ships from the Lesser Antilles would unite in one of their several Hispaniola ports and sail through what was known as the "Windward Passage," which took them to the Atlantic Ocean, passing to the east of Great and Little Inagua and Mayaguana islands and to the west of Caicos Island. The largest French merchant fleet to leave Hispaniola sailed in 1782 and totaled 190 ships.

Not all the shipping of these nations was of a mercantile nature. Warships were used to escort merchant fleets and to wage war on each other, which seemed to be a chronic situation throughout both the 17th and 18th centuries. The warships also attempted to capture returning Spanish flotas when their nations were at war with Spain. Although at least 50 attempts were made by the English, French and Dutch between 1550 and 1750 to capture an entire flota, it was only accomplished once. In 1628 a Dutch West Indies Company fleet under the command of Peit Heyn, captured all 24 ships of the New Spain Flota commanded by Captain-General Juan de Benevides y Bazan and won a booty of over 14 million pesos.

Smaller vessels also sailed the waters of the Caribbean and passed through the Bahama Channel. There were packet boats that brought news from and took news back to the Mother Country; and there were fishing vessels of various kinds; coastal, or inter-island, traders, salvage boats and numerous pirate and privateering vessels (about which so much has been written). As the New World colonies of the European nations grew rapidly in population, shipping between Europe and the Western Hemisphere expanded correspondingly. In 1785 a total of 1,347 European ships sailed to the Western Hemisphere and to Europe. And, inevitably, with a greater number of ships plying the seas, the number of ship losses increased.

Chapter Two

Marine Archaeology
Early Salvors and Treasure Hunters

Man has gone down to the depths of the sea since earliest times. From archaeological evidence we know that free divers were used in Mesopotamia as early as 450 B.C. to recover murex shells, from which a precious purple dye was obtained. Divers were also used by the Egyptians about 3200 B.C. to recover mother-of pearl shells; and Greek divers were bringing up sponges as early as 2500 B.C.

The earliest account of divers recovering sunken treasure is in the writings of Herodotus, a Greek historian around the middle of the 5th century B.C. About 50 years earlier a Greek diver named Scyllias and his daughter Cyane had been employed by Xerxes, the King of Persia, to recover an immense treasure from several Persian galleys that had been sunk during a battle with a Greek fleet. They managed to recover the treasure, but Xerxes cheated them out of the reward he had promised them. There are hundreds of other accounts of divers recovering treasures from sunken ships all over the seas of the Old World. Diving was certainly an established profession long before the discovery of the New World.

We know that diving was done by the Indians of Peru as early as the 3d century A.D. Long before Europeans reached the Western Hemisphere many aboriginal people dived for food in the sea and in lakes and rivers. North American Indians used diving as a basic hunting technique. By swimming under water and breathing through reeds they were able to approach unwary fowl and game and capture them with nets, spears or their bare hands. Diving for pearls didn't become a major industry until the coming of the Spaniards, but it was done on a small scale in the Caribbean by the Lucayan, Carib and Arawak tribes. In 1498, during Columbus's third voyage of exploration, his small fleet anchored off the Venezuelan coast at the Island of Cubagua for fresh water and fruit. While some of his men were ashore they noticed a Carib Indian woman wearing a pearl necklace. They made inquiries, then informed Columbus that the natives possessed great quantities of exquisite and valuable pearls that were to be found in the waters all around the island. Columbus sent Indian divers in search of the pearl oysters, and the results confirmed the story of his men. Returning to Spain, Columbus reported the good news to the King, who ordered a pearl fishery established on Cubagua.

Other large pearl beds were discovered during the next few years in the same area, including the area around Margarita Island, which eventually became the center of the pearl industry, a position it has maintained. The Caribbean pearl fisheries furnished Spain with a source of wealth surpassed only by the gold and silver from the mines of Peru and Mexico.

Soon after the opening of the pearl fisheries around Cubagua and Margarita, the local supply of divers was exhausted. Many died from diseases carried by the Spaniards, others from overwork at the hands of their greedy employers, who often forced them to dive as many as 16 hours a day. The next source of divers tapped by the Spaniards was the Lucayan Indians of the Bahamas, the first people Columbus and his men had encountered on their epic voyage of discovery. These Indians were then considered the best divers in the New World. The Spanish historian Oviedo, writing in 1535, gave an account of his visit to the pearl fishery at Margarita in which he marveled at the fantastic abilities of the Lucayan divers and stated that they were able to descend to depths of 100 feet and remain submerged as long as 15 minutes (no doubt an exaggeration). He added that, unlike the Carib Indians, who had less stamina, they could dive from sunrise to sunset, seven days a week, without appearing to tire.

As the divers of the Old World had done for thousands of years, they descended by grasping stone weights in their arms and jumping overboard, completely naked except for a net bag around their neck for the oysters. So great was the demand for the Lucayans that within a few years all of them were enslaved and the Bahamas were bereft of the native inhabitants who had greeted Columbus just a few years before.

Like the Carib Indians before them, the Lucayans were soon wiped out. Thus, by the middle of the 16th century the Spaniards were again hard-pressed for divers. They solved the problem by importing slaves from Africa, most of whom had never dived and in many cases had never seen the sea until their enforced voyage. Amazingly, they adapted at once and became good divers. Women slaves were preferred to men, probably because the extra layers of body fat in their tissues prevented chilling and enabled them to spend longer hours in the water.

Divers Become Salvors

The Spaniards knew that they were on to a good thing with these slaves and soon found another use for their talents just as important as pearl-diving, and even more profitable — salvage work on shipwrecks. In major colonial ports like Havana, Veracruz, Cartagena, and Panama, teams of African divers were kept aboard salvage vessels that were ready to depart on short notice to attempt recovery of sunken treasure and other valuable cargoes. During the 16th century, and on to the end of the 18th, more than 100 million pesos in treasure alone was recovered by these African divers. Ironically, when the other European nations began colonizing the New World, these same divers were instrumental in depleting the Spanish exchequer. Their new employers used them to salvage Spanish wrecks, but this time the profits went into English, French, and Dutch treasuries.

Soon after they settled in Bermuda at the beginning of the 17th century the English were next to enter the salvage field, which they called "wracking." They worked their wracking vessels all over the Caribbean, and during the second half of the century Port Royal, Jamaica, became the center of the wrackers. It was there that the American William Phips went to recruit divers to help salvage a Spanish galleon, laden with an immense treasure, that had sunk in 1641 on Silver Shoals, off the northern coast of Hispañiola. Using African divers, he recovered the greatest amount of treasure from any single wreck until the 20th century.

The Spaniards learned early that the Indians of Florida were also excellent divers but considered them too dangerous to work with. There are documents dated as early as 1544 stating that Indians on the coast of Florida were diving for and recovering vast amounts of treasure from shipwrecks. Although no known pearl deposits exist today in Florida waters, there are several 16th-century accounts stating that Indians dived for pearl oysters along the east coast of Florida. The famous Dutch historian John Huigehen Van Linschoten wrote in 1598, "Gold and silver wherewith the Indians trafficke, they had it out of ships which fall on ground (wreck) upon the Cape of Florida, because most of the ships lost here are lost on this said cape...."

Although the diving bell was first invented early in the 16th century, neither the Indian nor the African divers made much use of it, preferring to stay below for as long as they could hold their breath. On some occasions Europeans did the diving on wrecks, and they almost always used diving bells.

Since something like 97 percent of the ships that have been lost over the centuries in the New World went down in shallow waters, generally wrecking on shallow reefs or shoals, almost all of these wrecks were at depths that early salvors could reach. Thus, it would seem that little treasure or other items of historical value would remain on shipwrecks today, but this is not the case. When ships broke up on reefs or on a coastline, especially during hurricanes, their cargoes were often scattered over wide areas and covered by shifting sands. A good example was the loss of the 1715 fleet on the eastern coast of Florida. Although the Spaniards carried out extensive salvage operations on these wrecks, they were only able to recover about half the treasure. An exception occurred with the loss of the 1733 fleet in the Florida Keys when more treasure was recovered than had been registered.

In many cases when ships were lost there were no survivors; either everyone drowned or was killed by Indians. Obviously, the Spaniards couldn't salvage wrecks the locations of which were unknown and some of these virgin wreck sites have been discovered by 19th and 20th-century salvors and fishermen.

Key West, which was founded as a base for salvors at the beginning of the 19th century, was actually a latecomer in the game. Nassau, settled a century earlier, had replaced Port Royal as the main base of Caribbean wreck salvors. With salvage vessels working out of both ports from the early years of the 19th century onward, there were very few shipwrecks that were not salvaged even before they broke up and their cargoes scattered or hidden beneath shifting sands or coral growth.

During the first half of the 20th century few attempts were made to recover sunken treasures or salvage old shipwrecks, although a gullible public, fascinated with tales of sunken treasure, gobbled up fictional articles and books telling of brave divers finding intact Spanish galleons with skeletons still at the wheel and holds crammed with chests of gold and gems. Almost always in these yarns a giant octopus or schools of voracious sharks prevented the actual recovery of the treasure.

In fact, it was one of these romantic and totally bogus stories that got me interested in old shipwrecks at an early age. The author spun a good yarn about having gone to Jamaica in the 1930s and dived on the sunken city of Port Royal. He wrote of water 10 times deeper than it actually is and told of walking the streets of this sunken city in helmet diving gear and going past a standing cathedral full of golden church relics that were guarded by a twelve-foot crab and finding taverns in which skeletons sat at tables with tankards in their bony hands. He assured me along with other pop-eyed readers that chests of gold and precious stones were strewn about ready for the taking. What a surprise I was in for when I eventually dived on this sunken city!

The only major recovery of sunken treasure in the early 20th century was not in the sea but in fresh water. For centuries a legend persisted about the Mayans sacrificing virgin maidens covered with ornaments of gold and jade in a sacred well, called a cenote, at the ruins of Chichin Itza in Yucatan, Mexico. In 1904 a young American, Edward Thompson, who was the American consul to Merida, capital of Yucatan, decided to see if there was any truth to this legend. The murky waters of the cenote were between 60 and 70 feet deep and the bottom was thick mud. Thompson first learned to dive with a helmet, then enlisted the services of a professional Greek diver to assist him. Initially they had no luck, but Thompson was persistent. Eventually they found gold jewelry and ornaments, as well as many archaeological treasures. Realizing that the bulk of the artifacts were beneath the mud on the bottom of the cenote, Thompson rigged a drag-bucket at the top of the cenote and was aboe to recover a great deal more. His primitive equipment, however, did not permit him to salvage all of the treasure. Recently, several well-equipped expeditions have recovered a great amount of priceless artifacts and treasure there.

In 1906 a fisherman from Grand Cayman Island was working in the area of Pedro Shoals, about 130 miles south of Kingston, Jamaica. While rowing over a shallow reef he saw something gleam. Without any diving equipment at all, he dove and brought up a Spanish gold bar. On subsequent dives he brought up six other gold bars and several handfuls of gold Spanish coins. Not realizing the value of his find, he sold all of the treasure for its gold value. When news of his find spread, several expeditions explored the area but could find nothing more. They didn't realize that the rest of the treasure and cargo of the shipwreck was probably buried under coral growth or sand. In recent years over a dozen expeditions have set out to find this particular wreck, but the exact location where the fisherman found his treasure has been lost and none of the expeditions have been successful.

I have been unable to verify any of the tales about Greek helmet divers from Tarpon Springs, Florida, who supposedly found various sunken treasures while harvesting sponges in Florida and Bahamian waters.

During the summers of 1934 and 1935, the Mariner's Museum of Newport News, Virginia, conducted salvage operations on two British warships that were sunk in the York River during the Siege of Yorktown in 1781. The locations of both wrecks were found by oystermen who accidentally snagged their nets on them. Helmet divers used water-jets to remove the mud over the wrecks, which were in 40 feet of water. A great number of interesting artifacts were recovered: cannon, cannonballs, swords, axes, tools of various types, many pieces of rigging, a brass ship's bell, sounding leads, glass bottles of many descriptions and other personal items belonging to the crews of these ships. Fortunately, great efforts were undertaken to preserve these artifacts and most of them can today be seen in the Mariner's Museum.

In December 1938, several black fishermen sighted a large number of coral-encrusted cannons on a reef off Key Largo. They reported this to Charles Brookfield, who had long dreamed of locating sunken treasure. Brookfield hired a young diver and the

This contemporary drawing illustrates how an 18th-century diving bell would have been used to recover treasure from a shipwreck.

For J. Hinton at the King's Arms in Newgate Street.

cannons were relocated. In addition to cannons they brought up many cannonballs, lead musket balls, bits of rope, anchors, a silver porringer and several silver and brass coins. Their most interesting recovery was small fragments of pages from a prayer book that was found beneath a cannon. Through the British Admiralty, which they contacted after identifying the cannon as British from the markings, they learned the wreck was *H.M.S. Winchester*, of 933 tons and 60 guns, which was lost on September 24, 1695.

During World War II, when there was a great demand for scrap iron, salvage boats scoured the East Coast of the United States and the Caribbean stripping thousands of cannons and anchors from old shipwrecks and selling them for scrap-iron value. The salvors were no doubt unaware of how greatly they had diminished chances that future marine archaeologists and wreck-divers could ever locate many of these shipwrecks, since cannon and anchors are the main indications of a wreck site.

In the chapters of this book that list shipwrecks of the Western Hemisphere, we have covered the most significant recoveries since the introduction of scuba-diving equipment as well as other pertinent information that will help the wreck-diver.

The first people to show an interest in marine archaeology were a group of English archaeologists and antiquarians in 1775 who sponsored an expedition to recover historical artifacts from the Tiber River, near Rome. Greek divers, using a diving bell, worked for three years with very little success, for they had no means of removing the accumulation of river mud that covered the Greek and Roman artifacts they were hoping to recover. After that there was very little

Above

The flagship of the 1715 fleet off Florda produced these treasures in eight feet of water in 1993, three decades after recoveries were first made from it.

Below

The late Art McKee, considered the father of modern day treasure divers, displays a large silver bar he recovered from a galleon wreck in 1948.

interest in recovering relics until early in the 20th century, when objects brought up from the Mediterranean by Greek and Turkish sponge divers aroused the interest of archaeologists working on land sites nearby. The archaeologists hired divers to recover more artifacts, which turned out to have a historical importance as great as anything dug up on land sites.

Today, almost all marine archaeological work is confined to the Mediterranean. In the late 1930s, even before scuba equipment was available, the underwater explorer Dimitri Rebikoff began surveying and excavating dozens of ancient shipwrecks and sunken cities off the coast of France, Italy and Greece. He was followed by Jacques Cousteau and his team of divers, who worked several ancient shipwrecks off France and Tunisia.

In the last 30 years or so significant marine archaeology projects have been undertaken in Greek and Turkish waters, largely because of the enthusiasm of an American, Peter Throckmorton, who in 1959 discovered 35 ancient shipwrecks. His most important find was a shipwreck dating from 1200 B.C. called the "Bronze Age Wreck," which lies in 120 feet of water off Cape Gelidonya, Turkey. Soon after the discovery, Throckmorton became associated with the Department of Archaeology of the University of Pennsylvania, and under the direction of Dr. George Bass, major excavations were carried out for six seasons. During the past summer no less than 20 major marine archaeological expeditions took place all over the Mediterranean: in Spain, France, Italy, Greece, Yugoslavia, Turkey, Israel, Tunisia, Malta and Crete. The sad fact is that most of the Americans who are qualified to conduct a proper marine archaeological excavation prefer working on the more ancient sites in the Mediterranean, resulting in a scarcity of archaeologists to aid the many amateurs who work at sites in the Western Hemisphere.

The most difficult, expensive and time-consuming marine archaeological project ever undertaken in Europe was the raising of the Swedish 64-gun warship *Vasa*, which sank in Stockholm Harbor in 1628 shortly after being launched. Early salvage efforts failed, as the deepest parts of the wreck lay in a hundred feet of water, a depth too great for the diving bells then in use. However, a few cannon were recovered from higher parts of the wreck within reach of the diving bells. The wreck lay at the bottom of the harbor for more than 300 years, and because there are no sea teredo, or shipworms, in the harbor, the ship remained totally intact.

In 1956 a Swedish petroleum engineer, Anders Franzen, became interested in the *Vasa* and located the wreck using a core sampler. Swedish naval divers sent down to investigate the wreck reported that it was intact and, plans were made to raise it. With the aid of the Swedish government and funds from private sources, a team of helmet divers went to work under Franzen's supervision. It was a challenging task. The *Vasa* was huge, having a displacement of 1,400 tons and it was deeply buried in mud. First, the divers had to remove all of the loose objects aboard. Next, with the use of a water-jet, they had to blast tunnels under the wreck (a perilous job, for the ship could easily have slipped farther into the mud and crushed them) so that steel lifting cables could be inserted under the wreck. The construction of the tunnels alone took three years.

While all of this was going on, other divers were busy removing the masts, spars, and rigging. Two more years were spent sealing off the gun ports and other openings in the ship, as well as tying down all the cannons to prevent them from moving and possibly damaging the hull. Finally, cables were strung through the tunnels and attached to pontoons on the surface. On April 24, 1961, five years after the work began, the *Vasa* broke the surface. It was placed in a specially constructed dry-dock, where it is still undergoing preservation. To date, over 30 million dollars has been spent in the salvaging and preservation of this ship

The first marine archaeological excavation in the Western Hemisphere was undertaken by Edward Thompson at Chichin Itza (mentioned earlier in this chapter). Under the dynamic leadership of Pablo Bush Romero, the founder and president of CEDAM (the Marine Archaeological Society of Mexico), two other excavations took place in the Sacred Well in 1960-61 and 1967-68.

A 1980's Recovery

A more recent major underwater archaeology recovery was that of King Henry VIII's *Mary Rose*, which sank in 1545 off Portsmouth, England, while setting sail to repel a French invasion. Before any shots were fired this top-heavy 91-gun vessel suddenly capsized and went to the bottom in only a matter of minutes with more than 700 men aboard. In 1836 it was partly salvaged by the Deane brothers who invented the first practical diving helmet. In 1968 the wreck was located by Dr. Harold Edgerton using sub-bottom profiling sonar. During the next decade a few surveys of the site took place.

Then in 1979 Dr. Margaret Rule, a land archaeologist turned diver, began a full-scale excavation of this famous wreck. Over the next four summers she recovered over 17,000 priceless artifacts with the assistance of hundreds of volunteer divers. The climax of the project occurred on October 11, 1982, when a large portion of the ship's lower hull was brought to the surface. Despite the use of volunteers the project still cost upwards of $8 million, and another $5 million was spent later for conservation of the wooden hull and the myriad objects and artifacts found on the site.

The most extensive marine archaeological excavation undertaken in the Western Hemisphere was my own work on the sunken city of Port Royal, which was conducted over a period of three years during which more artifacts were recovered than had been gathered from all the old shipwrecks salvaged in the Western Hemisphere in the last 20 years. Later in this chapter as well as in the chapter dealing with Jamaica I will go into more detail on the Port Royal project.

Marine archaeology, a science still in its infancy, poses problems that do not arise in the excavation of a land site. Ideally, archaeological excavation should be taken stratigraphically, or layer by layer, with the exact depth of each find recorded. Stratigraphic digging on land often leads to very precise determination of the age of the object uncovered and reconstruction of the society it belonged to. On most marine sites, because the sea floor is constantly subjected to the disturbances of currents, storms and the like — to say nothing of the disturbances caused by man — such results are the exception rather than the rule.

One case in which land archaeological methods were applied under water with outstanding results occurred a few years ago, when George Bass undertook the excavation of the three-thousand-year-old "Bronze Age Wreck" discovered by Peter Throckmorton. Bass had every advantage. The wreck lay in crystal-clear water at a depth of 150 feet, too deep for salvors of the past. No storm had broken it to pieces over the centuries, nor had currents disturbed the artifacts aboard. Besides having sufficient funds with which to finance his work, Bass had a full archaeological team of divers, draftsmen, artists, a photographer, a historian, a classicist and several preservation experts. With their help he was able to map the site on a grid chart, dig stratigraphically and record the position and depth of the timbers remaining on the ship as well as every artifact recovered. Later, he was able to reconstruct the wreck completely, ascertaining how the ship was built, what it carried and how each item was stowed aboard. His work on this site was an archaeologist's dream, the equivalent of the Roman city of Pompeii, which was covered over by volcanic ash in A.D. 79 and remained a fantastic time capsule until archaeologists began excavating it over 200 years ago.

In 1984, a Bass-led expedition from the Institute of Nautical Archaeology (INA) of Texas A & M University discovered another Bronze Age wreck: a 3,400-year old shipwreck near the seaport of Kas off the southern coast of Turkey. This wreck of a trading ship from biblical Canaan was two centuries older than the previous Bronze Age ship. Dating from the time when Tutankhamen sat on the throne of Egypt and Troy was in its heyday, it has furnished us with an unequaled look at seaborne trade in antiquity. The ship, about 65 feet (20 meters) in length, was laden with a cargo of raw materials that included 150 intact amphorae containing over a ton of resin, six tons of copper and tin ingots, cobalt-blue glass ingots, elephant tusks, dozens of logs of uncorked ebony wood, jars of olives, tortoise shells and even pomegranates and hollow ostrich eggs. The wreck lies on a ledge in depths of between 150 and 170 feet (46 and 52 m), depths that restrict the time divers can work on the site each day. INA has spent six summers on the excavation, and it may be another five seasons before it is completed.

In 1990, while INA divers were working at Kas, a Greek sponge diver chanced upon what is believed to be the oldest known ship-wreck in the world: a Bronze Age ship dating from 2250 B.C. The wreck, only 65 feet deep, lies off the northern coast of the tiny Greek island of Dokos. A team of 20 divers, led by archaeologist George Papathanasopoulos, spent two summers on this early Hellenic period site mapping and photographing. They recovered hundreds of ceramic objects and several stone anchors. Work on this extraordinary wreck will continue for many more years.

The chances of obtaining such sensational results are rare in the Western Hemisphere, where almost every marine archaeological site is located in shallow waters and has been subjected to countless disturbances from nature and man. The exception would be the discovery of an shipwreck at a depth of 100 feet or more. Unfortunately, only a small number of old wrecks are known to have sunk in such depths, and unless the ship was known to be carrying treasure there is little likelihood that anyone would attempt to excavate it, because of the great expense involved in working a deep wreck.

The sunken city of Port Royal is the only site in the Western Hemisphere in which any attempt has been made to thoroughly and completely excavate under the archaeological standards of the "old school" archaeologists. It was excavated using methods similar to those used by land archaeologists and Bass, which meant gridding the site off, making a thorough survey, recording the position and stratigraphy of all the artifacts and buildings uncovered, making drawings and photographing everything recovered, carrying out proper preservation work, and, most important, publishing the scientific results of the overall excavation. As in Bass's case, however, I had many advantages that archaeologists and divers will not have on other sites in this hemisphere. The city sank quickly and was soon covered over by harbor sediment which more or less kept the artifacts and buildings in situ. Because the site is in a protected harbor, it has not been greatly disturbed by storms or currents — unlike most shipwreck sites, which lie exposed in shallow-water areas. A certain amount of disturbance was caused over the centuries, however, by ships' dragging their anchors through the site, and this resulted in artifacts being moved from their original positions. Also, the site was contaminated by items from later shipwrecks and by trash thrown into the area over the years.

Since most sites in this hemisphere do not fit into the category of these Mediterranean sites or Port Royal, just how much archaeological information can they yield to science? Archaeologists and historians would like to learn the following about most old shipwrecks: How and out of what material were the ships constructed? What type of rigging, anchors and armament did they carry? What were their cargoes, and where were they stored aboard the ships? Some of these questions can be answered from the average shallow-water wreck, but others, such as where the cargoes were stored, can only be answered from deep-water shipwrecks.

More than 98 percent of all ship losses in the Western Hemisphere occurred when a ship wrecked in shallow water. Either immediately upon wrecking, or soon after (even when ships wrecked in good weather), the ship broke up. The superstructure was the first to go. Being buoyant, it generally washed up on a beach or into a more shallow area, spilling cannon and other items along the way after it broke away from the main hull. What remained of the main hull was generally lost. On reefs the wood was either eaten by teredos or broken up and carried away by wave action or currents, so that items stored in the hull were widely scattered over the reef or caught in sand pockets.

When a ship wrecked on a sandy or muddy bottom, generally the lower section of the hull — keel, keelson, and lower ribs — was buried, while protruding sections were either eaten by worms or washed away, and again the items carried would be widely scattered. Consequently, it is impossible to determine accurately the original position of cannon, anchors, equipment or cargo. Nor can very much be learned about type and methods of construction of the actual ships, except for the lowest sections, which might be buried beneath sand or mud.

The marine archaeological data that can be collected are what these ships carried, even it isn't possible to determine where and how cargo and other items were stowed. When a ship is properly identified and dated, the items recovered from it are of immense value to science because they can be used to corroborate dates of items found on land archaeological sites. Yet this is not always foolproof, because a wreck can be contaminated in several ways. Salvors may throw objects on a shipwreck many years after it was wrecked, items from a later shipwreck might be carried into the area, or someone on a passing vessel might toss a bottle or something else overboard.

My advice to anyone working a shipwreck or other marine archaeological site is to gather all the archaeological data possible. This will include a description and drawings of the site, photographs of everything uncovered (both in situ underwater and when brought to the surface) and any other pertinent information. Then, turn it all over to a university or institution which can put the information to scientific use.

The big problem with regard to marine archaeology, as already mentioned, is that there are too few qualified people working in the field and the average wreck-diver has no one to go to for assistance in recording archaeological data he has obtained from a site.

Chapter Three

Locating
Shipwrecks

Approximately 98 percent of the ships lost in the Western Hemisphere prior to 1825 lie in water no deeper than 30 feet, which makes them much easier to locate and salvage than deep wrecks. In the Mediterranean, however, the reverse is true; at least 95 percent of the shipwrecks lie in depths of over 100 feet. The major causes of shallow water ship losses were storms which drove them onto reefs, shoals or coastlines; and faulty navigation, which is easy to understand given the primitive navigational equipment and inaccurate charts available The two percent of Western Hemisphere wrecks in deep water broke up or capsized in storms, were destroyed by fire, were sunk in battle or scuttled, either to prevent capture or by their captors after being stripped of most valuables.

About 95 percent of shallow water shipwrecks are on sandy bottoms; the others are almost equally divided between those covered by mud and silt in harbors such as Havana and Veracruz, those at river mouths and those covered by coral growth on reefs.

Consider what happened to ships that wrecked in shallow water. When a ship struck on shallow reefs, it was sometimes so badly broken up that no trace of its wooden hull remains. The wood either floated away or was completely devoured by teredo worms. Teddy Tucker worked several such sites in Bermuda; and the *Matanceros* site, which I worked on the coast of Yucatan, is another good example, as we found only a few pieces of ship timbers buried under sand. Other ships wrecked on shallow reefs sometimes had all or part of their hulls carried to sandy bottoms or small sand pockets by wave action or currents, so that their timbers were covered over by sand before the worms could totally destroy them.

Coral growth varies a great deal in different areas of tropical and subtropical waters, depending on temperature and salinity of the water and wave action. In areas where coral growth is slow, most of the items on a wrecked ship are carried away to areas at varying distances, depending on the weight and shape. Very little, in some cases nothing at all, can be found on the reef where the ship was lost. Along the Caribbean coastline of Yucatan, for instance, where coral growth is rapid, the major portion of a ship's cargo would be buried under coral growth before it could be washed ashore or off the area of the wreck site. Another good example of rapid coral growth is on Silver Shoals on the eastern edge of the Bahama archipelago. When Sir William Phips's divers located the *Concepcion*, a richly laden treasure galleon in 1682, only 41 years after it had been wrecked, they found it completely buried in coral. In some places the coral was five feet thick, preventing them from entirely salvaging the wreck.

Many followed in Phip's wake in search of the *Concepcion*, among them Mel Fisher and Jacques Cousteau. In 1978, Burt Webber, a part-time bookseller, mason and welder, succeeded where so many had failed. Webber, fascinated with sunken treasures since childhood, had spent time treasure hunting in the Florida Keys before he went after the *Concepcion*, but he had found very little. With $2.5 million in funding and a team of 30 men he hit the jackpot when he located the fabled galleon and brought up over $10 million of treasures. Webber proved that Phips had left plenty of treasure behind and, convinced there is still more left on the *Concepcion*, is planning a future expedition to the wreck.

Ships lost in mud or silt are generally the best-preserved because the weight of the ship forces the lower hull of the vessel down into the sediment very quickly, preventing attacks on the wood by the teredo. In the harbor of Cartagena, Colombia, I dived on two large warships that had been scuttled by the Spaniards in 1740 to prevent capture by the English. Several months before I arrived, both wrecks had been uncovered during dredging operations to deepen the harbor. I was thrilled to see how remarkably well preserved the hulls were, having been protected by a shroud of soft mud and silt. Other examples are the two ships run aground in 1504 by Columbus in St. Anne's Bay, on the northern coast of Jamaica. Because bad leaks on both ships had filled them with water, a great portion of their lower hulls was pushed down into the soft silt of the bay, preserving them to this day. The main disadvantage of excavating a wreck lying on a mud or silt bottom is that during the actual excavation, underwater visibility is generally reduced to nil because of stirred up sediment.

The preservation of ships wrecked on sandy bottoms varies depending on two major factors — how quickly the weight of the wreck pushes the hull into the sand, and how quickly ocean or tide currents cause sand to build up over the wreck. In some areas where there are only a few inches of sand covering a limestone or coquina bottom very little of a ship's hull will be preserved. Sometimes wrecks were covered over so quickly that even contemporary salvors, who knew the precise location, were prevented from salvaging them. The *Atocha*, which was lost in 1622 in the Florida Keys, is a prime example. It sank on the edge of the Gulf Stream, where the currents run between one and three knots, and the sand built up so rapidly over the wreck that within two months Spanish divers reported that only the masts remained above the sea floor and there was an average of two fathoms of sand over the main deck of the wreck. A great deal of documentary evidence exists showing that this happened on many other wrecks.

Cargoes Often Scattered

When ships are wrecked during hurricanes, generally their hulls and cargoes are scattered over wide areas, sometimes several square miles, but there are exceptions. During the disaster of the 1715 treasure fleet 10 of the ships were completely broken up. Very little of the hulls exists today and cargoes are scattered over large areas. Yet the eleventh ship of this fleet wrecked close to shore and its hull remained intact for a long period, thus enabling the Spaniards to salvage her complete cargo.

During the hurricane of 1733 in which 21 Spanish ships were wrecked off the Florida Keys, the majority of the ships remained almost totally intact until the Spaniards salvaged them. Then they burned those parts of the wrecks that remained above the waterline.

I once spent several months excavating the *San Jose*, a galleon of the 1733 fleet. From our excavation I discovered the following facts. The ship apparently struck on an offshore reef with an average depth of 10 feet, or it may have been thrown completely over the reef by the high seas during the hurricane. About a quarter of a mile closer to shore from the reef the ship struck on a sandy bottom approximately 20 feet deep, losing its rudder, five cannons (which were possibly carried on the stern) and a substantial amount of cargo that spilled out of the ship in this general area.

The galleon's main hull was carried about 250 feet farther, sinking in 30 feet of water, probably because she lost her stern section which permitted her to fill rapidly with water. Most of the cannon she carried were discovered either right on top of the ballast on the lower deck or relatively close to the main section of the lower hull. Most of the starboard section of the hull was lying between 10 and 20 feet from the lower section of the wreck, which consisted of the lower deck over the ship's keel. We discovered about 200 tons of ballast rock covering the lower deck, with a trail of ballast rock leading to the area where the ship had lost its rudder and part of its stern.

From these discoveries we can conclude that the *San Jose* was one of the ships that remained intact after wrecking, otherwise we wouldn't have discovered most, or all, of her cannon so close to the main section of the wreck. This would also indicate that most of her cargo would have remained inside the hull of the wreck, or fairly close to it.

In cases such as the ships of the 1715 fleet we know, both from contemporary documents and actual salvaging of the wrecks, that when they broke up during the hurricane the lower sections of the hulls, containing the ballast and most of the bulky cargoes, sank farther offshore than the upper decks and superstructures. This is verified by the fact that most of the cannon, carried on the upper decks of the ships, were discovered closer to shore than the main ballast piles; and by the fact that most of the gold jewelry was discovered close to shore. The most valuable items, such as gold and silver, were always carried in the captain's, or some other ranking officer's, cabin in the superstructure of the old ships, generally in the stern castle. This was so that the chests of treasure could be kept under close surveillance. When a vast amount of silver, either in specie or bullion, was carried, it was always stored in the main hold over the ballast.

There are also instances in which ships wrecked during good weather and their cargoes were still scattered over large areas. Sometimes when a ship struck on a reef, sustaining holes in the hull, the captain would keep the sails up and try to run the ship as close to shore as possible to lessen the loss of life and facilitate salvage operations. Typically, when this happened, a great deal of ballast and cargo spilled out of the vessel between the area where she had hit and where she eventually sank. Off the coast of Nicaragua near Providencia I worked on a site which illustrates this type of disaster. In 1641 a Portuguese ship, chased by several Spanish warships, struck on a shallow reef fairly close to shore. To elude the pursuers the captain kept the ship sailing, staying right over the dangerous reef, either hoping that the pursuers would also wreck on it or that they would cease their pursuit to avoid the danger. The ship traveled over two miles before finally sinking. In searching for the wreck, by snorkeling I discovered the area where the ship first struck the reef. I followed the trail of ballast stones until I reached the main section of the wreck. Mixed in with the trail of ballast rock were a large number of artifacts that had fallen out through the hole in the ship's hull.

Cannons, Anchors and Ballast

The three principal signposts of old shipwrecks are the cannon, anchors and ballast; finding any of the three, however, does not always indicate that you have found a shipwreck. On many occasions some or all of the cannon were thrown overboard when a ship was in danger of capsizing during a storm. When a ship ran aground on a reef or shallow area, cannon were thrown overboard to lighten the ship and sometimes the ships were refloated. At times even large amounts of ballast and cargoes of the least value were thrown overboard to lighten and refloat a stranded ship. I have dived off areas close to old waterfront forts around the world and discovered large numbers of cannon that were not from shipwrecks but from the forts. During hurricanes and earthquakes they might have fallen into the sea when sections of the forts collapsed; or they may have been thrown in because they were too old and dangerous to use, or to prevent their capture by an enemy, or they might have been thrown in by the enemy after the capture of a fort.

Old cannon were sometimes used as ships' ballast and occasionally jettisoned. Diving off the eastern end of the Bon Aire some years ago, for example, I located more than 200 cannon in a relatively small area; but what amazed me the most was the fact that they ranged in age over a period of 250 years. The mystery was cleared up by a local historian who explained that this area was where ships coming from Holland had anchored to load cargoes of salt from the island. The cannon had been used as ballast on various ships and jettisoned when they took on heavy cargoes of salt.

Generally, finding anchors that are not near cannon or a ballast pile simply signifies that a ship lost an anchor — but not always. When a storm drove a ship toward a dangerous reef or coastline, anchors were naturally thrown out to prevent the ship from wrecking. In these situations one or more anchors would have been lost seaward from the shipwreck and can provide a clue to the wreck's location. Since most — in some cases, all — of a ship's anchors were carried high on the bow and stern of the ship, and we know that in many cases these sections of a shipwreck were carried closer toward shore than the main section of a shipwreck. Anchors can also be found shoreward from a wreck site, providing a clue in locating the main wreck site. In either event, whether the anchor is seaward or shoreward from a wreck, knowing the wind and sea direction as well as the current directions prevalent in the area helps determine the approximate position of the wreck site.

As noted earlier, finding a ballast pile does not always indicate a shipwreck, especially when discovered near or in ports or harbors. Sailing ships occasionally sailed without cargoes, which necessitated carrying large amounts of ballast to stabilize them. Before or after entering a port where a heavy cargo was to be loaded, most and sometimes all of the ballast was thrown overboard. If the ship remained in the same position when this operation was underway, the ballast pile would resemble one similar to that of a shipwreck site. If the ship was swinging on its anchor, then the ballast would be scattered as it is on a site where a wreck was badly broken up and the ballast strewn over a large area.

Ancient mariners were not overly cautious about sanitation, particularly the Spaniards, who were known to have the dirtiest ships afloat. Since many seamen, as well as the poorer passengers, lived below deck a great amount of fish, animal, and fowl bones, broken pieces of ceramic, glassware, etc. were thrown into the hold with the ballast. This sometimes fools salvors into thinking they have found a shipwreck when in fact the artifacts are mixed in with ballast rock.

Most old ships carried round ballast rocks ranging in size from several ounces to 200 pounds. The larger rocks were usually placed over the lowest deck, then smaller rocks filled in the spaces. On some of the early French and English ships, a substantial amount of ballast rock was cemented together with mortar for use as permanent ballast. I have not discovered whether ships of other nationalities followed this practice.

Since most ships took on their ballast in ports or harbors, and most of them had rivers or streams emptying into them, the round "pebble" or "river rock" ballast was the most commonly used. In many instances however, when this type of rock wasn't available, mariners were forced to use other types. Their preference was naturally round rocks which wouldn't pierce wooden hulls in rough weather.

A late-16th-century wreck, either of Spanish or French origin, salvaged by Teddy Tucker in Bermuda contained flint rock for ballast. Documents dated 1570 tell of a Spanish merchantman sailing from Cuba to Spain with copper ore for ballast; of a Spanish ship sailing in 1638 from Venezuela to Spain with saltpeter for ballast; and still another sailing in 1760 from Cadíz to Venezuela with gypsum rock for ballast.

As early as 1614 there is mention of Spanish ships carrying bars of iron from Spain to America as ballast, but this happened only when iron was being carried for sale or use in the New World colonies. From 1700 onward, English warships used pigs (ingots) of iron as ballast, a practice that took hold with French warships from 1707.

There are several reasons why a wreck site may not have any ballast on it at all. When ships carried enormous cargoes they didn't take on ballast to avoid being dangerously overweight. Sometimes, when ballast rocks were scarce, sand was used. Also, on small vessels the limited space below decks necessitated an alternate means of carrying ballast. Therefore, as casks and barrels containing water, beer, wine, vinegar, etc., were consumed they were filled with sea water. This method had the advantage of lightening a ship quickly during a storm. The casks and barrels could either be emptied into the bilges and the salt water pumped overboard, or they could be jettisoned quickly, which ships carrying ballast in the form of rocks or pig iron couldn't do.

Before going into the methods of locating shipwrecks, several physical facts should be considered. Over the centuries, shorelines have receded in some places and have extended farther into the sea in others. Those that have built out mainly affect the modern-day salvors, since many shipwrecks have been covered over by land. The Jamaican city of Port Royal sank into the sea in an earthquake and tidal wave in 1692. Approximately 60 percent of the sunken pirate port city is covered by land today. On the other side of the harbor from Port Royal, the shoreline has been built out by sediment brought down by rivers and recently three 18th-century shipwrecks have been found buried on land there. This is known to have occurred in many other areas as well.

Many small islands or cays that once existed have disappeared, others have built up...some are actually manmade. On modern charts there is an area west of Grand Cayman Island called Mysterious Bank, which is as shallow as four fathoms on some parts. Throughout the 16th century various navigators mentioned passing a small island in this area, but sometime around 1600 it disappeared beneath the sea. North of Memory Rock on the Little Bahama Bank many old charts show several small islands or cays which no longer exist.

The mouths of rivers and streams have in some cases changed their courses considerably over time. Several inlets on Florida's east coast have been closed and others opened, some by nature and others by man.

Special caution should be exercised when dealing with old charts. Many are grossly inaccurate. Whenever I use old charts to locate a shipwreck, I try to consult as many charts as possible that were published around the time of the disaster, because place-names changed considerably over the centuries. Memory Rock, for example, had six different names on Spanish charts over a 300-year period and was given still other names on charts of different nations. We can assume that navigators used the most up-to-date charts, so the names on them would be the ones they used to describe the location of a shipwreck.

Positions of latitude taken on a rocking ship were not always accurate, but it was generally the practice to establish the latitude of a shipwreck by taking the position from the nearest piece of firm ground. I have found that on the whole these positions are accurate to within a few miles, even from the earliest days of navigation in the New World.

Diver displays coins that were discovered with a metal detector, one of the methods used for locating and inspecting possible shipwrecks.

The distance, or measurement, of a mile and league was not universal in the old days. From the end of the 15th until well into the 19th century, the Spanish and Portuguese divided a degree of latitude into 70 miles of 5,000 feet each, or into 17 1/2 leagues of four miles each. The English and French divided it as we know it today — 60 nautical miles, or 20 leagues of three miles each. The Dutch divided it into 60 nautical miles, and 15 leagues of four miles each.

All nations used the fathom as the unit to describe depths of water, but its true depth, or length, was not uniform. Especially during the 16th and 17th centuries it depended on the size of the seaman who made the measurement which was figured by measuring the distance between the fingertips of a man's outstretched arms A sounding lead on a line was lowered and the depth established by the pulling in the line. If a man had short arms the fathom could be as little as 5 1/2 feet; if he had long arms it could be as long as 6 1/2 feet.

In areas where there is considerable difference in tide levels, care must be exercised in using depths given in old documents, since there is never any mention of what state the tide was in when depth was measured. I have also found that when a document states that "a ship was lost in so-many fathoms," it does not always indicate the true water depth in the area but the depth from the surface to the main deck of a shipwreck.

Methods thAT A modern-day salvor can use depend on circumstances, such as how accurate a position one might have of a ship location, its size, the depth and area in which it was lost, the cause of the disaster, and other factors. I shall try to cover them all in this chapter.

Assuming that a salvor decides to locate one or more particular shipwrecks in a given area, the prerequisite is to obtain permission from the government in whose water the wreck is located. It is good practice next to establish contact with local historians or archae-

Spanish fascination with pre-Colombian artifacts resulted in vast numbers of objects such as this Mayan jade that can be found on wrecks of Spanish galleons.

ologists in the area because they can be helpful to you in many ways, e.g. providing pertinent historical data on the wreck you are trying to locate.

Depending on the nationality of the wreck, write to the major archives, libraries and naval museums of the country and request any historical information they can provide. In the case of, say, a Spanish shipwreck, it would be advisable to write to the Naval Museum in Madrid and the Archives of the Indies in Seville. Do this well in advance, for it sometimes takes many months for them to locate the material you request. Further information can often be obtained by writing to the nearest port captain or harbor master in the area you plan to explore, since fishermen who might drag up some artifacts from a shipwreck usually report these facts to the port authorities.

You should read every history book dealing with the area, especially those written shortly after the period in which your wreck was lost. Such books are not easy to find, but major American libraries may have them; they can also be obtained through the interlibrary system. Before heading for any new area to search for a shipwreck, I usually spend a few days or a week at the Library of Congress in Washington, D.C., and read any books that may be helpful. The Library of Congress also has the most complete collection of old charts and maps of the Western Hemisphere, and I get photocopies of those which might be helpful.

Several times I have discovered old wrecks simply by following old charts, and on a few occasions even modern charts led me to old wrecks when they contained place-names that aroused my suspicion. I located the *Matanceros* wreck off the coast of Yucatan by becoming curious why modern charts called it "Punta Matanceros, Slaughter Point." This, I assumed, could have been a place where many persons were slaughtered by Indians after staggering ashore from a shipwreck.

Modern charts are useful in other ways. By studying them before actually going to the area of the shipwreck, one can determine the most promising areas to search from taking into account water depths, positions of reefs and other shallow areas, as well as the direction of prevailing currents and winds. Sailing directions and coastal pilot books also provide essential information for a successful search.

Weather is a major factor in the failure of many expeditions. Obtain as much meteorological data as possible about the area you plan to explore. Then select the best time of year for the venture. Throughout the Western Hemisphere the summer months are generally the most favorable, but there are exceptions. Off Padre Island, Texas, the winter months are best, when the seas are calm and the water visibility clear. Remember that since seasons south of the equator are opposite of those north of the equator, the best months there are our winter months.

The science of weather forecasting is still in its infancy as far as I am concerned, for I have more than once encountered the opposite weather pattern from the one predicted by the experts whom I consulted before setting off on an expedition. In 1963 I mounted a major expedition down on Serranilla Bank during the month of June, supposedly the best of the year. The result was that during the 30 days we were in the area the wind never dropped below 20 knots and we could not even attempt to search for the wrecks we were after. The following year I decided to spend August and September on Serrana Bank, actually living on a small cay and working out of a small skiff. Meteorological experts assured me that no hurricane had ever visited that area during those months. But one struck anyway, and if a passing vessel had not stopped by to pick me up and get me to safety, I would have perished because the hurricane washed most of the cay away.

Hurricanes can be helpful or harmful to salvors. Some of them may completely uncover a shipwreck, making locating and salvaging it much easier. On the other hand, hurricanes have also deposited as much as 15 feet of sand over known wreck sites. The huge seas associated with hurricanes generally help establish shipwreck locations in two ways. Artifacts that may be buried offshore on a wreck are often thrown up on adjacent beaches; also, when beaches become badly eroded by the wave action, artifacts, treasure and sometimes even parts of the ship may be revealed.

Upon arriving in a new area it is always advisable to inquire about items the local inhabitants might have found on the beach. Remember that the main reason the 1715 fleet shipwrecks were discovered is that Kip Wagner found coins and other items from these galleons washed up on the beaches between Sebastian and Fort Pierce inlets on Florida's east central coast.

After arriving in the area where you plan to work, make contact with the authorities who have granted you permission to work in their territorial waters. This applies not only when one is in a foreign country, but in one's own as well. A few days spent in the local archives and libraries will also prove useful. If the wreck you are after occurred after the area was first settled, chances are more than likely that some local newspaper was in existence at the time and carried news about it. The local archives might also have documents concerning the loss of the ship, provided documents have survived over the years.

In my experience fishermen have been the best sources of information on shipwreck locations. On my first night ashore I usually visit bars frequented by fishermen. While they may not be very talkative to a stranger during the working day, they generally loosen up when you are buying them drinks. If you just ask if they know the locations of any wrecks, they'll probably lead you to a modern-day shipwreck. It is much better to ask if they've ever seen "old guns" or a pile of "river stones." They usually know the surrounding areas as well as the palm of their hand. In many of the Caribbean islands they dive on known ballast piles to recover the rocks to use as ballast on their own fishing boats.

Local divers are also good contacts. Throughout the Caribbean and Bahamas there are thousands of divers who spear fish, grab lobsters or dive for conch. If your wreck is in a harbor or port there are commercial divers who know the surrounding bottom and can lead you to different wrecks — one of which may be the one you are seeking. I also consult the captains or operators of dredging barges, since they can tell me where they may have dredged up items from shipwrecks.

Check out all the locations supplied by your contacts. Then, if the water visibility is clear, you should make an aerial survey of the suspected area. The preferred tool for an aerial survey is a balloon, which proved very successful for Teddy Tucker in Bermuda. Also useful are either a seaplane, a Bensen gyrocopter or helicopter, or a light single-engine plane. The balloon and the Bensen gyrocopter can be made compact enough to enable the explorer to ship it to the area he plans to search. Remember however, that since helium is virtually impossible to obtain outside the United States, a hot-air balloon may be a better bet.

The reason I prefer the balloon is that it has to be towed by a surface vessel, and it is always easier to obtain a good position with electronic equipment from a surface vessel than from an aircraft. Furthermore, as soon as something is sighted from a balloon it can be hauled in and divers sent to investigate the suspected area. If a balloon is not available, then I suggest using either a seaplane, a gyrocopter or a helicopter with floats, which enables the salvor to land right over the suspected area and inspect it, provided sea conditions are good. Prior to obtaining his balloon, Teddy Tucker located more than 50 wrecks around Bermuda using a small, light seaplane. Dimitri Rebikoff used a Sea-B seaplane, and aboard it he not only carried sufficient diving equipment but a small portable air-compressor for refilling his scuba tanks.

When an aircraft cannot land in promising areas, I suggest that a surface vessel be used in conjunction with the search. By radio communications the surface vessel can be directed to suspect areas and divers sent down to investigate, or a vessel can assist in placing buoys over the area for future investigation. Without the aid of a surface vessel it is often difficult to establish the precise position of a shipwreck sighted from the air, particularly if the location isn't close to a noteworthy landmark.

Loran and GPS

If you are operating alone in the air, however, there are several methods that can be used. A loran or global positioning system (GPS) are your best tools. Flying several timed compass headings from the wreck site to known positions is another method; still another is the use of a radio directional finder, but it is not as accurate as the other methods. From the gyrocopter or helicopter, buoys can be dropped on top of the wreck, but it is more difficult to do this from a circling plane. Several small sonar transmitters are available. Dropped over a wreck site, some produce a continuous sonar signal for as long as 2,000 hours, and with the use of a boat and sonar-receiving equipment the position can be located.

To obtain the best results from an aerial survey the sea should be flat calm and your altitude between 100 and 500 feet. Polaroid glasses are a must, as is a good chart of the area on which to mark approximate positions of anything you sight. Not only can items such as ballast piles, cannon and anchors be detected, but I have also located wrecks that were completely buried under sand. On wreck sites that have a mass of metal, such as large cannon, iron oxide from metal masses generally darkens the sand over the site. Another good indication is a small, solitary coral reef or several small patches of coral reefs in areas where there are no others. In most instances these small reefs started building up when some part of a shipwreck was exposed above the sand and continued to grow after the wreck was buried.

Photography can also be very helpful in locating shipwrecks. Using infrared film in a 35mm still camera, I located three shipwrecks on a reef along the northern coast of Jamaica that I hadn't spotted from a light plane. Regular color film with the use of a Polaroid filter occasionally produces good results. The main difficulty with aerial photography lies in establishing the precise area of the photographed wreck.

Provided a wreck is not buried under sand, sediment or coral growth, there are simple methods that can be used to search for it. I shall begin with the simplest and cheapest methods and progress up to those which are more elaborate and costly. Although I suggest that every vessel carry a good fathometer to keep track of the depth, this instrument is practically useless in locating shipwrecks in both shallow and deep water. To get a reading on the fathometer, a considerable part of the wreck has to be protruding above the sea floor and the search vessel has to pass directly over it.

If the water is reasonably clear, if you have good eyes, and if you have had considerable experience, you can use the "Teddy Tucker Method." This requires standing either on the bow or a higher spot on a boat and searching for large objects like ballast piles, cannon, etc. But, the sea must be flat calm, as it is in Bermuda for months at a time. Once, using this method under ideal (and rare) conditions, I located 14 old wrecks on the Little Bahama Bank in less than three hours. Polaroid glasses are very useful when using this method.

When I first started, I preferred searching for wrecks either by snorkeling on the surface or by being dragged behind a small boat holding on to a line. I still use this method whenever it is feasible. With this simple "shark line" I have found hundreds of old wrecks. Its disadvantages are that it's more time-consuming than most other methods, such as using a magnetometer, and it is dangerous in areas with heavy concentrations of sharks. Whenever sharks have forced me to abandon these two methods I have usually resorted to a glass-bottom boat.

Other divers prefer using sea sleds or towing vanes, but I prefer snorkeling or the towline behind a boat which offer greater freedom of movement.

Various types of sea scooters and the Rebikoff Pegasus can also be used. Their big disadvantage is that the maximum length of time they can operate is two hours, after which they usually require from eight to 24 hours for recharging. To overcome this major problem,

Rebikoff Underwater Products developed another type of Pegasus, which I have found much more adaptable to searching in shallow water. It is powered by a surface engine that is floated on a small pontoon and connected by an umbilical power line to the underwater vehicle, which drags it behind on the surface. In recent tests we mounted a magnetometer on this new type Pegasus and it worked quite well.

Wet submarines offer no advantage over any of the above methods other than giving the diver some protection in the event of a shark or barracuda attack. And while I highly recommend dry submarines for locating deep shipwrecks, I have found them practically useless on shallow-water searches. Not only are they quite expensive to operate and maintain, but they require constant maintenance; also, their weight generally requires large surface support vessels, and they are difficult to launch or retrieve in rough seas.

In 1963 I rented the original Perry Cubmarine for a month, and from the start it was a headache. Before sailing for our wreck location in the Caribbean we decided to test it at Fort Lauderdale. During the test dive it ventured too close to the salt-water-intake system of the city's electric-power plant and was sucked against the huge pipe's protective screen. The two men inside were trapped for eight hours before we finally located it and had the plant intake pump stopped for a few minutes. On the few occasions we were able to use it, we constantly suffered from electric shocks due to minor water leaks reaching the batteries, which were located under both seats. When navigating it in shallow water, we repeatedly collided with coral reefs.

Locating shipwrecks that are completely buried or lying in areas with poor underwater visibility requires other, more sophisticated methods. Sometimes these methods should also be used in clear water because they can considerably reduce the time involved in locating a wreck. Also, some of the methods will locate a shipwreck whether it is visible or buried.

In areas of poor visibility, especially in bays and harbors, the old method of locating a shipwreck — provided that some part of it protruded above the sea floor — was to drag a cable between two vessels or to drag a line with grappling hooks from a single vessel. The big disadvantage of this method was that it could be used with a degree of success only when the sea floor was flat and reefs and rocks were not prevalent. Otherwise the drag line was constantly snagging on various underwater obstructions.

Sidescan sonar, developed during World War II to detect submerged submarines, is useful in locating wrecks — but, once again, only if some part of the wreck protrudes above the surface of the sea floor. Yet in deep water this is the primary search tool. In 1967 it proved useful in locating a Roman wreck in 300 feet of water off Yasse Ada, Turkey. Since that time more than 300 ancient shipwrecks have been located with sidescan sonar. The late Dr. Harold Edgerton was responsible for improving the old World War II sonar devices for use in finding very small objects on the sea floor. In 1973 he used one of his own sidescan sonar units on a National Geographic Society-financed expedition to locate the fabled Civil War-era *Monitor*, the Federal ironclad which sank off Cape Hatteras, North Carolina in 1862. Prior to his death several years ago Dr. Edgerton participated in shipwreck-hunting expeditions all over the globe and located hundreds of old wrecks with his sonar.

Dr. Edgerton, who was with Massachusetts Institute of Technology, also invented another type of sub-bottom sonar, called the "pinger" and "boomer," which locates and records the shape and position of objects buried beneath the sea floor. Both units have been used with great success on marine archaeological sites all over the globe. During January and February of 1968, I was fortunate to have Edgerton run his sub-bottom sonar surveys at both Port Royal and St. Anne's Bay, the site of the two Columbus shipwrecks which he located in short order.

Most of his efforts were devoted to mapping the sunken city of Port Royal. A series of shore points, each about 10 meters apart, were located, numbered, then plotted on an existing map of the area. Offshore buoys had to be placed, also 10 meters apart; then the survey ship, with its sonar equipment, made runs between the shore markers and the buoys at a constant speed. Since the site extends almost a mile in length, the sonar survey took about three weeks; however, the results were excellent.

From hundreds of feet of sonar recording paper several draftsmen helped us produce four large charts that covered the whole site, showing the precise position of a tremendous number of walls of the old buildings, as well as of several shipwrecks. Another important feature of this survey was that it defined the total extent of the whole site.

Magnetometers were developed during World War II to detect submerged submarines. Basically, a magnetometer detects gradients in the earth's magnetic field produced by local concentrations of ferro-magnetic materials such as cannon, anchors or any other ferrous metal objects from a shipwreck. The larger the object and the longer it has remained in the same position, the better the chances are of locating a wreck it represents.

There are four types of magnetometers, each working on a different principle: the rubidium, proton, caesium, and differential fluxgate. The usual method of operating a magnetometer is to tow it behind a boat at speeds of from two to 10 knots, depending on the sensitivity of the particular instrument and the size of the object being sought. On several occasions shipwrecks have been located using a magnetometer from a helicopter, with the sensing probe dragged through the air on a long cable. During the 50s a few attempts were made to utilize magnetometers to locate shipwrecks, but none seemed to meet with much success. Fay Fields with Treasure Salvors Company designed a mag which he says has proved very effective. According to Fields, his magnetometers have located more than a hundred ancient shipwrecks just off the coast of Florida.

Until a few years ago a good magnetometer cost well over $15,000, with some as high as $30,000. Recently a magnetometer came out on the market that is as sensitive, if not more so, than the $30,000 models and sells for $3,500. It is a Differential Flux Gate magnetometer and has several important features that many of the other magnetometers lack. It operates at full efficiency regardless of geographic location; it eliminates problems resulting from orientation in the earth's magnetic field, and it is unaffected by ignition interference and atmospheric conditions.

The control unit is watertight and tested to a depth of 200 feet. It has negative buoyancy and, with an optional sensing probe, can be operated by a diver in an underwater environment. Indications of magnetic anomalies are provided both visually and aurally. The visual indication is a 4-inch meter, calibrated in field strength (Gamma), with an 0 to 10 scale, subdivided into two-tenths divisions. Eight field-strength scales are provided, 0 to 3 Gamma, the most sensitive, and decreasing by a factor of our per-switch position, i.e., scale 8 is 0 to 3 Gamma, scale 7 is 0 to 12 Gamma, etc. Aural indication is provided by earphones. Power is provided by the power case and consists of rechargeable nickel cadmium cells. Total drain is approximately 4.5 watts. The power case will provide 20-hour operation between charges. A charger operating from 115 v. A.C., with overcharge protection and undervoltage protection, is part of the power case.

This magnetometer senses gradients in the earth's magnetic field produced by local concentrations of ferro-magnetic material. It employs two sensors, elements that are mounted in a rigid submersible container, and measures the difference between the two sensor outputs. These sensors are balanced, so that orientation in the earth's magnetic field is not critical. The instrument is also insensitive to ignition interference and atmospherics. This device can detect magnetic-field strength at the two sensors less than o.s Gamma, independent of the external-field strength as long as this field does not exceed three times the maximum value of the earth's field. This makes the unit's operation independent of geographic location.

The instrument consists of three basic units, sensing probe, control unit and power case. The sensing probe is designed to be towed and a 100-foot cable is supplied. The towable sensing probe is extremely stable and can be adjusted to run at predetermined depths to 200 feet. A given underwater altitude can be maintained over a range of several hundred engine RPM's. Buoyancy is slightly negative. Altitude is maintained during turns.

Prior to the introduction of precision navigation equipment we were forced to lay out a series of lines of buoys in order to survey an area carefully with either sonar or magnetometers. Today, we use inexpensive LORAN and Global Position Positioning (GPS) systems which makes it much easier. Evenly spaced, accurate survey runs can be made with these instruments. The position readings are so accurate, usually within 15 feet, that they eliminate the need to use buoys to mark targets located. You can find something and get a position with a GPS unit, no matter where you are in the world, and go back 10 years later and find it in minutes. Locating and salvaging shipwrecks in deep water is attracting more and more interest for many different reasons. Since exploring shipwrecks caught on in the early 50s, we've known that wooden wrecks in deep water are much better preserved than those in shallower sites because they lie beyond the reach of the ship worm and other marine borers.

Quite a few old deep wrecks were discovered during searches for other things. In 1952 a closed-circuit television search for the wreckage of a commercial airline in the Mediterranean, off the island of Elba, resulted in discovery of a Roman amphora wreck a half mile down. In 1966 during the search for the hydrogen bomb lost off Palomares, Spain, the crew of the submersible *Aluminaut* reported a remarkable sighting. Sitting on the ocean floor in 2,000 feet of water were two intact wooden ships, their masts still standing and cannon projecting from the gun ports, just like a Hollywood fantasy wreck.

Big companies soon realized the potential in deep water after the recovery of gold bars valued at $91 million from the *HMS Edinburgh*, a British cruiser sunk by a German U-boat off Murmansk in the Barents Sea during World War II. Divers using mixed-gas deep diving techniques worked at a depth of 820 feet to bring up the 431 gold bars after cutting their way into the large hulk. Then, in 1985 the discovery in the North Atlantic of the world's best known shipwreck, the *Titanic*, located in two and a half miles of water and the subsequent recovery of many of her treasures two years later by a French expedition proved that depth was no longer a deterrent to recovering deep water treasures. To most treasure hunters the recovery of over a half billion dollars in gold from the *Central America* is even more fascinating, since it occurred closer to home. This ship sank during a storm in 1857 about 160 miles off Charleston, South Carolina, in 8,000 feet of water. The Columbus-America Discovery Group located her with sidescan sonar and then used a remote-operated-vehicle (ROV) named *Nemo*, to recover the tons of gold specie and bullion.

In 1965, not far off the Dry Tortugas west of Key West, the shrimp boat *Trade Winds* was dragging her nets in 1,500 feet of water and snagged into a major obstruction. When the nets were pulled up they contained a substantial amount of early 17th-century material from a Spanish shipwreck. In 1972 I teamed with a group of oceanographers to go after the wreck. We chartered the sophisticated oceanographic research vessel *Alcoa Seaprobe* for the search. Deepwater technology at the time was in its infancy, and we failed to locate the wreck. Several months later I resorted to a low-tech method used by salvors for thousands of years. By dragging a steel cable between two boats we snagged into the wreck and were able to bring up a huge anchor. ROVs were not available at the time and the fast current in the area prevented the use of a submersible for diving the site.

By 1988 when I teamed with Tampa-based Seahawk Deep Water Technology Inc., deep water exploration had made giant strides. The wreck was easily located with my LORAN bearings, despite its location 40 miles from the nearest land. A small ROV went down to the wreck and as it glided gracefully over the sea bed, a video camera transmitted a clear look at the ghostly remains of the Spanish ship, which later proved to be a sister ship of the *Atocha* and *Margarita* of the ill-fated 1622 fleet. An extensive mound of ballast, ships timbers, heaps of Spanish olive jars and countless other artifacts were seen on the video screen.

Later this same ROV with its manipulator arms recovered the ship's bronze bell. This artifact was used to obtain an Admiralty Arrest claim giving Seahawk ownership of the wreck which lies in international waters. A larger ROV dubbed *Merlin* was then specially constructed for use in excavating this wreck. Built at a cost of $2 million, *Merlin* is a technological marvel. It has three video cameras capable of providing 180-degree underwater vision, and three 70mm still cameras for taking pictures of artifacts in situ to be digitized into a computer for later mapping of the site. The *Merlin* is also equipped with two manipulator arms, suction pumps and water jets to remove bottom sediment as well as a number of other revolutionary devices. It is amazing how technology has exploded since I first dove over 40 years ago, going down in a hard-hat suit to find my first gold coin!

Over a period of three seasons the Seahawk group brought up a fantastic array of treasure and artifacts including dozens of gold ingots, three bronze astrolabes and even small objects such as over 8,000 small pearls. My favorite was a rat's tooth.

In 1965, the same year that the shrimper found the 1622 wreck off the Dry Tortugas, another shrimper snagged into a Spanish wreck about 60 miles east of St. Augustine in 1,200 feet of water. Six large cooking kettles, three cannon balls and some ballast rock came up in his nets. Again teaming with Seahawk I used a submersible to explore this wreck which proved to be one of the 1715 fleet. We signed a research agreement with Harbor Branch Oceanographic Foundation in Fort Pierce and got underway in October 1990. Working at this great depth aboard the submersible *Sea-Link* was one of the most exciting thrills of my life. At first everyone was skeptical that a wreck could be excavated from a small submersible but I knew it could be done. Each day we made two dives of three to four hours duration and I spent over 150 hours working this wreck.

I first made a comprehensive survey, after using the manipulator arm to lay out a series of buoys. Using both still and videos cameras I made a complete mosaic of the entire site which had 13 cannon and two anchors lying on top of the ballast and ship's timbers with artifacts scattered all over them. We were able to recover a large variety of artifacts including two small cannon, a brass telescope, a stone grinding wheel, rum bottles, copper kettles, hundreds of cannon balls, lead musket balls and ceramic objects.

In April 1991 I returned with a thruster mounted on the bow of the submersible which worked in the same manner as a prop-wash. I also took along my Garrett XL500 Sea Hunter underwater detector to indicate an object hidden beneath the sediment. With these two new tools we were able to recover hundreds of objects such as wooden pulley blocks, more cannon and cannon balls, pewterware, brass buttons and buckles, tools, small weapons, animal bones and six silver coins.

At present more than two dozen companies around the world are engaged in deep water shipwreck work and I'm sure that in the next few years the number will double. Although deep water work is costly in comparison with shallow water exploration, the wrecks are easier to find since they lie on the sea floor and make excellent targets for the sidescan sonar. The shipwrecks are virgin and have never been salvaged. In addition, they are usually contained in a very small area in contrast to most shallow water wreck sites which are spread over several square miles or more. Best of all, in most cases no permission is required from any government because they lie in international waters and the finders get to be keepers.

Chapter Four

The Site
Surveying, Mapping and Excavating

SURVEYING

One of the major mistakes modern-day salvors make is failing to make a accurate survey of a wreck site once it has been located and before beginning excavation. Many expeditions have failed with a tremendous loss of money, time and labor because a proper survey wasn't done. For example, a group from Miami, armed with historical documents giving the location of a rich galleon wreck in the Bahamas, first searched with a magnetometer dragged from a helicopter. In less than a week they located a shipwreck in the general area given in the documents.

Instead of first making a survey of the site to determine if the wreck was the one they were after, they outfitted a large vessel for salvaging the site, only to discover — many thousands of dollars later — that this wreck was a late-19th- century vessel with nothing of value on it. Amazingly, the group didn't learn their lesson and actually repeated the scenario. After returning to Miami with their salvage vessel, 'they resumed their magnetometer search from a helicopter and located what they were sure was the wreck of "their" galleon.

Once again, however, they failed to make a survey of the suspected area and brought their large (and expensive) salvage vessel back to the Bahamas. This time they uncovered a modern missile cone instead of a galleon. In both cases they could have saved time and money by renting a small boat along with a minimum of diving and excavating equipment.

There are other reasons why a wreck site should be surveyed before bringing in a salvage vessel. Establishing the overall extent of the site is important because it will give an idea of how long the excavation will take and whether it is economically feasible to salvage the wreck. A wreck contained in a small area, say about the size of a football field, is certainly more economical to excavate than one spread over several square miles. Another reason for surveying is to determine the type of excavation equipment best suited to the site. An expedition in the Bahamas failed because of imiproper equipment. Salvors who located a wreck site by searching with an airplane, sighted a large number of cannon on a sandy bottom. Believing that a wreck was buried in the sand, they outfitted their salvage vessel with airlifts and a prop-wash. When they arrived at the wreck site, they quickly discovered that the sand was only several inches deep and that the wreck was buried in thick coral growth which they couldn't penetrate without the proper equipment, such as pneumatic hammers or powerful water-jets.

In areas such as Florida, where salvors must obtain a pinpoint lease on a wreck site, it is imperative to know the total extent of the site, or else a salvor may apply for a lease which does not cover the total area. When this occurs, and it has on several occasions, other salvors are able to obtain leases adjacent to that of the original discoverers of a shipwreck.

The initial step of any survey is to locate all visual traces of the wreck by diving and placing buoys over objects found. I make it a practice to have someone follow me in a small skiff. After I place a buoy over each object, I surface and identify the object to the person in the skiff who records and plots it on a chart. Mapping and identifying objects as they are located eliminates the danger of not being able to find them again should the buoys be lost.

The next step is to locate all concentrations of metal, which is absolutely necessary when no trace of a wreck is visible above the sea floor. A good magnetometer locates ferrous metallic objects and, from the size of the anomalies recorded, an experienced magnetometer operator can determine the size of the metallic concentration. This information should also be plotted on a chart.

This drawing illustrates the method by which intact shipwrecks in water depths to 2,000 feet can be salvaged today using saturation diving techniqes

Sub-bottom-penetrating sonar can be used to locate large metallic objects as well as ballast piles and wood. Hand-held magnetometers and metal detectors should be used for locating smaller metal objects on a site. If the wreck is scattered over a large area this can be very time-consuming. When time and capital permit, however, I recommend it.

A diver proved the value of a metal detector on a wreck during the summer of 1968. Wanting to test a new detector he had recently invented, he decided to use it on the wreck of the *H.M.S. Looe*, which had been worked over by hundreds of divers. Everyone assured him there was nothing left on the wreck. Although all of the sandy areas had been excavated with airlifts, many artifacts were buried in coral growth, which he easily located with his detector. On the first day he discovered a silver plate, a silver spigot, a pewter plate, two pewter spoons, a pewter tankard, a brass scale weight, four copper coins, lead musket balls, many iron cannonballs, and several other items made of iron.

Deciding what the next step is in surveying a wreck site depends on the nature of the sea floor. Objects buried in coral growth are the most difficult to survey, since test holes must be made all over the area until the overall extent of the site is determined, which can be a lengthy undertaking. If the coral growth is soft, either a strong water-jet or coring device can be used.

In hard coral growth, such as we experienced on the *Matanceros* wreck off Yucatan, small pneumatic hammers are best, but you can always small sledge hammers and chisels. On reefs where wrecks are located, there are generally many small sand pockets not more than a few inches deep. I have found that a scuba tank with several feet of hose attached can be used as an air-jet and is quite effective for blowing away the sand. Of course, you can fan the sand away by hand, but it is more time-consuming.

Other methods can be used to survey a site in mud or silt after magnetometer and sub-bottom sonar surveys have been completed (or when such sophisticated instruments are not available). The fastest, but not always the most effective, method is to make test

Airlifts are now used widely in underwater excavation activities such as this diver recovering a Portugese anchor from a ship lost in the Bahamas in 1551.

holes on the site using an airlift, hydrolift or small prop-wash. In some areas these excavation tools can be used when there is only a few feet of sediment over the site; small test holes can be made quickly.

If the sediment is hard and compact, small test holes can be made with these tools to reach quite deep in the sediment. When the sediment is soft and silty, however, it continually caves in so much that larger test holes have to be made. At Port Royal I found areas where the sediment was so soft that in order to make a test hole with an airlift to a depth of 20 feet, the diameter of the hole had to be over 60 feet.

To overcome the problem I used five sections of concrete water pipe, which were four feet in diameter and five feet long. After driving the first section as far down into the sediment as possible, I began excavating with a small airlift, and as I went deeper the pipe also sank. When it sank below the level of the sea floor I attached the next length of pipe and continued this method until I reached the desired depth. This method had one big disadvantage. It was almost impossible to retrieve the concrete water pipes without excavating a large hole around them, which in my case did not really matter, since I had access to unlimited pipes.

I later learned a simpler way to obtain the same results from Art McKee, who developed it, by making test holes on wreck sites located in deep sand. Instead of using water pipes, he used a long metal tube and an airlift. The diameter of the tube should be a few inches wider than the airlift-tube diameter. His method is quicker than mine and safer because the diameter of the test hole is smaller. The metal tube is easier to handle than the larger water pipes. The diver operating the airlift in the water pipe remains on the sea floor operating the airlift as it and the metal tube sink deeper into the sediment. Best of all, he doesn't risk having the water pipe collapse, trapping him under tons of sediment.

To determine the stratigraphic depth beneath the sea floor at which items are located by the airlift, the diver simply measures the length of the metal tube remaining above the sea floor and subtracts it from the total length of the tube. Recovering the metal tube from the sediment can be accomplished with the aid of lifting bags or lifting equipment from a boat, such as an anchor winch.

At Port Royal I used an iron rod, a quarter-inch-thick and 12 feet long, with a wooden handle, to locate large objects that were buried under up to 10 feet of mud After we located the two Columbus ships with Dr. Edgerton's sonar equipment, I attempted to determine the overall extent of both wrecks by using the metal-rod-probe method. The sonar indicated that the wrecks were beneath sediment from 10 to 12 feet in depth. In some areas on both wrecks I was able to reach these stratigraphic levels and discovered the presence of wood and ballast rock. In other places, however, concentrations of very hard mud kept my probe from penetrating more than a few feet. Instead, I then used another tool, which I have dubbed the Judd air probe.

Dr. George Bass helped me obtain a coring device from Columbia University for bringing up test samples of the wreck to prove their identity. Columbia also sent an experienced operator, Bob Judd, to help me. When Judd saw the problems I was having with my metal-rod probe, he invented his air probe right on the spot. It consisted of a 20-foot section of galvanized iron water pipe of one-inch diameter. The air hose of an Aquanaut diving unit attached to the top of the pipe, sent down a continuous stream of compressed air that cut through the concentrations of hard mud. It not only penetrated the sediment quickly but was easy to pull out because of the compressed air blowing out the pipe's bottom.

Coring tubes are useful not only in mud or silt but on sandy bottoms and even in soft coral growth. Those generally used by marine geologists are driven into the sea floor by explosives or equipment operated from a surface vessel. Those used by divers can be very low-tech, like the one I used on the Columbus shipwrecks which consisted of four-foot sections of four-inch- diameter iron tubing. One diver held the tube vertically while another drove it into the sediment by hitting the top of the tube with a heavy sledge hammer. As each section sank into the sediment another was attached, and the operation continued until we reached a depth of 20 feet beneath the sea floor. Before the coring tube was pulled up by means of a lifting bag, a rubber plug was inserted into the top of it to maintain suction in the tube, otherwise the sediment and artifact sample would fall out as the tube was pulled up.

Either aboard a vessel or ashore, the sample in the tube was recovered by simply removing the plug and holding the tube almost horizontally and shaking it lightly. We recovered sufficient amounts of material, including wood, glass, flint, iron nails and tacks, small ballast rock, animal bones, ceramic shards and beans, to determine their exact stratigraphic depth as well. This method also eliminated the danger of disturbing the historic site.

A coring tube used in coral growth requires a sharp edge for cutting through the coral and will have to be sharpened often. The length of each section of the tube should not exceed four feet, a length which enables the diver who is pounding the tube into the sediment to stand on the sea floor, giving him more power in swinging the hammer than if he had to swing it while swimming underwater.

Surveying a wreck site on a sandy bottom is relatively easy. Test holes can be made with small airlifts, hydrolifts or the prop- wash of a small boat. I have operated both small airlifts and hydrolifts without the use of even a small boat when the sites were located relatively close to shore. The air compressor for an airlift and the water pump for the hydrolifts were mounted on a platform floated on a truck inner tube. A small prop-wash, which would be effective on a site no deeper than 10 or 12 feet, can even be mounted over the propeller of an outboard engine. The advantage of the airlift and hydrolift in making test holes is that they can be used in any reasonable depth; however, an airlift will not work in less than 10 feet of water.

Test holes can also be made in areas of shallow sand over a wreck by using an air-jet or water-jet, both of which can be operated from a small float or boat. In shallow water the air-hose from an Aquanaut diving unit can be used effectively. The unit has two hoses: one can provide the diver with air to breathe and the other used to make test holes. I don't recommend the use of the air- or water-jets in muddy areas because they quickly reduce underwater visibility to nothing.

A good system for surveying a wreck site uses a prop-wash mounted on a large vessel. Long test-trenches are dug by continually excavating with the prop-wash and "walking" the vessel on a straight course over a large area. This is done by first determining the length of time needed to excavate to the desired depth in the sand and by playing out the stern anchor lines and taking in on the two bow anchors respectively. While the vessel is "walking" and excavating the trench, divers follow behind the vessel at a safe distance and search in the trench. This system has the advantage of covering a larger area much faster than by making test holes with any of the other equipment I have mentioned. The disadvantage of making test-trenches is that they require a large vessel, which increases the cost of the survey.

MAPPING

A common mistake made by modern-day salvors is their failure to map a wreck site. They generally consider it too time-consuming and may believe that the information obtained is useful only to archaeologists. But this isn't so. By mapping and recording all the information gathered during the surveying of a wreck site, the salvor not only determines the overall extent of the site but collects a great deal of useful information. By studying the pattern of the sunken ship's remains the salvor can often determine what caused the wreck. This is useful in figuring out whether it was salvaged by contemporary salvors. For example, a wreck that has remained intact for a long period is more likely to have been salvaged than one that is scattered over a large area. A wreck lying on the surface of the sea floor or not buried very deep was most likely salvaged soon after being lost and again over the centuries by other salvors, whereas a wreck buried deep was most probably covered over before anyone could have salvaged it.

Another reason to map a wreck is to determine its size, which is useful in identifying it. This is made easier if its size, tonnage or the number of cannon it carried is known. Size can be determined by measuring the length of the keel of a wreck (if it exists), estimating the amount of ballast the ship carried or discovering the number and size of cannon.

Mapping or plotting the locations of major artifacts discovered during the actual excavation aids the salvor in many ways. From the nature of the different items recovered, he or she can usually determine the bow and stern of a wreck. Since the largest anchors were generally carried on the bow of the ship, anchors found on one end of a ballast pile or section of a ship that was wrecked more or less intact generally indicate the bow of the ship. Unfortunately, this by itself is not always a safe assumption because anchors were also carried on the stern, and sometimes several were stored in the hold as spares. If seamen, in danger of wrecking, threw several overboard off the bow she might wreck with some on her stern, which can confuse the issue.

Most salvors make an attempt to distinguish the bow and stern of a wreck as quickly as possible. Knowing that most of the significant treasure on old ships was carried in the stern they naturally want to salvage that area of the wreck first.

In many cases the most likely areas for finding treasure on a wreck which was not widely scattered can also be determined through mapping the position of artifacts recovered. Since the most valuable treasure was kept in the stern castle where officers and rich passengers lived, this is the most likely area in which good silver or pewterware, fine chinaware or similar items are likely to be discovered. A number of factors must be considered, however, before such general assumptions can be made. If items show no sign of use, such as knife-scratch marks on a pewter or silver plate, then these items could have been carried as cargo elsewhere on the ship.

Because there are various methods to map a wreck site, the method the salvor selects will depend on such factors as visibility, distance from shore, bottom topography and wind, waves and currents. The grid system, used by land archaeologists, can also be used underwater when visibility is good, the sea floor more or less level, the wreck contained in a relatively small area, and a prop-wash not used. (The prop-wash will blow the grid lines away.)

Grid lines can be laid out in a predetermined pattern, generally running on a north-south and east-west axis and spaced from 10 to 20 feet apart, making squares of equal size. Each square is marked with a number under water and plotted on a chart. As each square is excavated, the locations of artifacts are plotted on the chart as well as locations of such things as ballast piles, ship's timbers and other items that cannot be raised (like a heavy cannon).

In most cases, the grid system is neither practical nor economically feasible. It works best in deeper, calm water on compact sites. On wrecks that are scattered over large areas, with parts lying in the shore breakers, the system can't be used.

Mendel Peterson developed a method of mapping wrecks contained in a relatively small area that is less time-consuming and less expensive than the grid system. It consists of an azimuth circle marked with the degrees of the compass, which is mounted on a brass rod and driven into the bottom near the center of the wreck site to become the datum point. Using an underwater compass, the azimuth circle is lined up with magnetic north. A chain is connected to the center of the circle and distances are marked on the whole length of the chain. When the chain is stretched to a cannon, or whatever artifact is to be mapped, the diver notes the compass bearing on the azimuth circle to the object and the distance from the datum point and plots the information on a chart. This system has an advantage over the grid when the bottom is not uniformly level. The device is compact and can be built inexpensively.

If the wreck site is close to shore, the best mapping method is to erect shore markers and plot their positions on a chart. Compass bearings taken on these shore markers will indicate the position of the items that must be plotted on the chart. Taking compass bearings from a rocking boat is not easy, nor is it accurate. After first surveying the wreck site, buoys should be placed on all important items. Their locations can be obtained by taking compass bearings from the shore. During the salvage operation itself someone ashore should take compass bearings, communicating with the salvage vessel by walkie-talkie.

At Port Royal I used shore markers erected by the Jamaican Survey Department and plotted on special grid charters. When major finds were made, one of my team on shore established the precise position of the find by taking compass bearings from three or more shore markers to the top of the airlift tube, which protruded vertically above the water right over the position of the recovery. Since stratigraphic information was important on this particular site, the depth of the recovered item was simultaneously established by determining the length of the airlift tube remaining above the surface of the water. Taking the water depth and state of the tide into consideration, we were able to determine the exact stratigraphic depth.

Mapping a wreck site that is scattered over a large area and not close to shore can be more challenging. First, using good electronic equipment and a sextant, a datum point must be established. A buoy placed on the datum point provides one compass-bearing source, but at least two others are required, preferably forming a triangle, and the other buoys must be placed in precisely known locations, possibly established by measuring the distance and bearing from the datum point

I used this method on the excavation of the *San Jose*, (wrecked in 1733 in the Florida Keys). Since we were fortunately in sight of land, we could determine the precise position of the actual hull of the shipwreck and its ballast pile. A datum point was established on the seaward end of the wreck and buoys were positioned over other areas of the overall wreck site. The State of Florida official aboard the salvage boat used these buoys to take compass bearings and map our excavation. On several occasions when buoys disappeared during bad weather, it was easy to replace them because we could locate their original position by establishing their compass bearing and distance from the datum point.

The most accurate way to map a wreck site is with a new system called SHARPS (Sonic High Accuracy Ranging and Positioning System) which is manufactured and sold by Marine Telepresence Inc. of Pocasset, MA. This system provides fast and accurate three-dimensional acoustical mapping of a wreck site. Four receivers are used; three are positioned in a triangular arrangement, while the fourth is held by a diver. The three stationary transceivers, which track the one in the diver's hand, are connected to the surface by a coaxial cable, feeding the data into the SHARPS control unit and into a computer. Each time a diver wants to plot the position of another object, he activates a transmitting button which relays the information to the surface through the other three transceivers and the precise position of the object is recorded with X, Y and Z coordinates. During this operation a map is traced on a computer screen and stored for later use or printed out on recorder paper.

Where visibility is good and the site contained in a small area, underwater photography is helpful in mapping a wreck site. Generally, the wreck is first marked with the grid system, a grid frame is used to hold the camera, and photographs are taken of each square grid. The photographs are then made into a large mosaic showing the entire area of the wreck. Marine archaeologists take photographs of each square at different stratigraphic levels and, provided the wreck sank relatively intact in deep water and has been relatively undisturbed by man or nature over the years, obtain a great deal of information concerning facts about the ship's construction, how and where the cargo was carried and other information. On shallow-water wreck sites, however, such data cannot be obtained.

I recommend making a photographic mosaic of wreck sites when large sections of the actual ship may exist, because it will assist in establishing the type, size and sometimes the nationality and identity of the ship. This must be done after the wreck has been uncovered and all of the ballast stones removed from it. The best way to make a good mosaic of a wreck site, and one that is not too expensive, is to use the Pegasus or a similar underwater vehicle with a pulse camera mounted on it. The focal width of the camera lens and the clarity of the water will determine the elevation above the wreck from which the photographs will be taken and the total number of photographs required to make a complete mosaic. In making a complete mosaic of the *San Jose* site which encompassed a 200x100-foot area only 14 individual photographs were required. Good underwater visibility in the area, the depth of the wreck, which averaged 30 feet, and a wide-angle corrected Rebikoff lens on the camera from a height of 25 feet over the wreck enabled us to make a mosaic with such a relatively few photographs.

Hand-held cameras can also be used to make a photographic mosaic of a wreck site, but the diver must remain at a constant elevation over the wreck and swim on a straight course. Otherwise, the mosaic will not be accurate and it will be difficult to match the photographs when assembling the mosaic. The Pegasus eliminates this problem because it has a complete navigational system and can be flown at a constant depth on a straight course. Video cameras are very useful in mapping a wreck site.

EXCAVATING

Before discussing the tools and methods for excavating a shallow wreck site, I want to address diving equipment. Most divers prefer using a surface-supplied source of air, which eliminates having to surface and change scuba tanks every hour or so. Back in the 1930s, when Art McKee started exploring shipwrecks, the standard diving rig was the bulky shallow-water diving helmet, which required the diver to keep his head upright so that large amounts of water would not enter. After World War II this rig was superseded by the Desco diving mask, which consisted of a full- face mask connected to the surface air compressor by means of a rubber hose, like the shallow-water helmets. The Hookah diving rigs came into use around 1955, consisting of the breathing air reaching the diver through a regular scuba regulator connected by an air hose to the surface air compressor.

In 1965 the Outboard Marine Corporation introduced a new SAS (Surface Air Supply) diving rig that I found far superior to those I had used in the past. The exact same unit *except for different exterior colors* is distributed by Johnson Motors as the Air Buoy and by Evinrude Motors as the Aquanaut. The unit, which weighs only 40 pounds, consists of an engine-pump assembly that is encircled and floated on the surface by an inflatable tube. The 2-HP, 2-cycle engine delivers 2.5 CFM of clean air to each diver at a depth of 25 feet, which is the length of the two hoses provided with each unit. This is actually twice the amount of air normally required at this depth. I found that by attaching additional lengths of hose I could safely and comfortably use my Aquanaut as deep as 50 feet. Depending on the carburetor adjustment, the unit will run from 45 to 60 minutes on each filling, taking a quart of regular gasoline with an oil mixture of 24:1. It is cheaper to use than compressed-air refills for scuba.

This system has several unique features that I particularly like. The air delivered by the unit is the cleanest I have ever breathed under water, the hoses do not kink or sink to the bottom and get tangled on obstructions and the full-face mask fits all faces, child or adult. Another great advantage of the unit is the relatively small amount of maintenance it requires — and I'm speaking from long experience because my divers and I logged over 13,000 hours with these units during the three-year excavation of Port Royal. About every 30 or 40 hours the spark plugs had to be cleaned, and about every 100 hours we would have to take off the exhaust and scrape out the carbon deposits. Other than a few times when some idiot failed to put gas in the fuel tank, the unit did not stop and cut off our air supply.

The system's only disadvantage is the small capacity of its fuel tank. Rather than come topside every hour to refuel, however, we ran each unit continuously for eight to 10 hours daily, and about every 40 minutes someone topside would refuel the units without stopping them. The only problem here came when someone goofed and spilled gas on the unit, which resulted in gas fumes being pumped to the divers which caused some discomfort for a few minutes. The compact size and light weight of this unit is another of its great advantages over the other sources of breathing air for a wreck-diver. It is especially useful when going to a remote area to search or undertake a survey on a wreck site and can even eliminate the need of a boat if the wreck is located close to shore.

None of the surface-air-supply diving rigs should be used when excavating with a prop-wash. The air hose might be caught in the vessel's turning propeller and be cut or, even worse, might wrap around the propeller pulling the diver into it. Instead, scuba-diving equipment should be used. Scuba gear should also be used for deep-water shipwrecks.

Even in the warm waters of the Caribbean, wet suits are needed, because most divers will be chilled after several hours in the water. They also offer protection from coral cuts and scratches, burns from fire coral, stings from jellyfish, and bites from small fish.

During the actual excavation of a wreck, large amounts of sea worms and other marine life are uncovered. This provides a feast for small fish, and during their eating sprees it is not uncommon for them to take occasional bites out of a diver. I have several scars from the bites of trigger fish which are especially aggressive. Because most bites are to the fingers (probably because they most resemble sea worms), gloves are essential on most excavations. Of course, the danger of attacks by sharks or barracudas is always a possibility, but I have found that the noise created by a salvage operation tends to scare them away. For obvious reasons you should never spear fish around a wreck site or throw any garbage in the water. In 1981 while I was working on a wreck in the Bahamas, I suffered an unprovoked attack by a mako shark and had to have 268 stitches in my upper right arm.

Everyone participating in excavating a wreck should be instructed about the nature of the site and the physical appearance of items and artifacts likely to be uncovered. A silver coin, for example, after long years under the sea has so changed in appearance that it might be mistaken for a dark sea shell. Most iron objects that become heavily encrusted with coral growth are very difficult to distinguish from ordinary pieces of coral. Divers should also be instructed in how to handle fragile artifacts. Small, fragile items should be placed in a jar or plastic bag and brought to the surface; bigger items can be placed in plastic buckets or larger containers.

The usual method of sending up non-fragile items is in metal buckets or baskets made of wire mesh. Heavy objects can be raised by pulling them aboard the salvage vessel by lines or lifting bags. Some salvage vessels are rigged with lifting equipment to raise cannon, anchors and similar heavy items. There are also lifting bags on the market with a lifting capacity as great as a ton.

Large or heavy objects can also be brought to the surface using 55-gallon fuel drums. The drums are sunk and attached by steel cables or lines to the object, then filled with compressed air to raise them to the surface. Using this method, I have seen salvors recover large cannon and anchors while operating from a small boat. After the drums and attached objects are lifted to the surface, the salvors tow them to shore, where they can be removed from the water by different methods.

Every diver should carry a "goodie bag," a small cloth or plastic bag for storing small items (coins, musket balls, etc.) until he surfaces. Many valuable items have been lost when divers try to hold them inside their gloves or rubber suits. Use of the goodie bag may also prevent a diver from "accidentally" forgetting about a gold coin he may have found and placed inside his rubber suit for safekeeping.

Surveying the wreck site carefully will assist the salvor in deciding on the best method of operation and excavation tools required. Other factors, such as surface and tidal currents, should also be considered when excavating areas where sand, mud or silt is being removed from a wreck. Selecting the proper area to begin your excavation is very important. The currents should be used to carry the sediments away from the wreck site, or at least into areas that have already been excavated. A common mistake of salvors is to begin their excavation in the middle of the site. This usually results in the excavated sediment being deposited in areas not yet excavated, which can result in having to move the same sediment many times.

The most difficult wreck site to excavate is one embedded in coral growth, like the *Matanceros* in Yucatan. On this wreck our main excavation tools were sledge hammers and chisels to chop into the coral and extract artifacts. We usually attempted to chop or cut out pieces of coral about the size of a basketball, or larger. These pieces were raised aboard the salvage vessel and later broken apart to extract the artifacts they contained. In many instances we had no idea of the contents of a chunk until it was broken apart. From one clump of coral weighing about 20 pounds, we extracted over 200 individual artifacts. Because parts of artifacts could usually be seen embedded in the surface growth, we dug into these areas, sometimes as deep as five feet, until there were no more artifacts to be recovered. In areas where no artifacts were seen in the surface of the coral, we dug as deep as three feet before locating any artifacts.

Large artifacts (pewter plates, wine bottles, etc.) were carefully extracted from the coral on the bottom, because it was too difficult to dig out a large enough section of the coral growth in which they were embedded.

During the third year of excavation on this wreck, I obtained three pneumatic hammers, which were quite effective in chopping through the coral. The largest was used only in excavating cannons and anchors. The medium, only 12 inches in length with a cutting chisel six inches long and two inches wide, was used to excavate the basketball-size chunks of coral containing the smallest artifacts. For excavating fragile items like wine bottles or small items such as a brass medallion or crucifix, we used the smallest pneumatic hammer, whose chisel was only four inches long and three-fourths of an inch wide.

The overall area of the *Matanceros* wreck site is smaller than a football field, and although over the years thousands of man-hours have been spent by hundreds of divers chopping into the coral growth on this wreck, it is far from being completely excavated. This wreck was the most difficult shallow water site to excavate that I have ever seen or heard about. Other wrecks located in coral growth have proved easier to excavate because, in most cases, a large portion of the wreck was actually buried in sand pockets on a reef. In addition, because most of the parts usually buried under coral can be found in softer growth than that at the *Matanceros* site, high-pressure water-jets can be used to blast the coral apart.

When excavating on muddy or silty bottoms, the only recommended excavation tool is an airlift. It consists of a metal tube into which a continuous stream of compressed air is ejected through one or more holes, depending on the size or diameter of the tube, which will also determine the pressure and volume of air that is required. A three-inch-diameter airlift requires between 20 and 50 cubic feet of air per minute at a pressure of about 50 PSI. One of six-inch diameter requires 50 to 200 cubic feet of air per minute and about 100 PSI of pressure. The effective working depth of an airlift depends on the air pressure being provided, which must be greater than the surrounding water pressure. For example, the maximum effective depth for an airlift using only 50 PSI of air pressure is 40 feet, whereas one using 100 PSI of air pressure can work in depths up to 100 feet.

The principle of the airlift is that when air is forced into its bottom it rises rapidly, creating suction and sucking up bottom sediment and small objects. There should be a control valve on all airlift tubes enabling a diver to control the amount of air entering the tube. When removing overburden, the airlift is run at full power to remove sediment as rapidly as possible, but when areas containing artifacts are reached, the speed of the suction should be reduced to permit a diver to grab artifacts before they are sucked up by the tube or damaged by striking against the bottom of the tube. When small objects, e.g. coins, buttons, or musket balls, are sucked up by the tube, the spill from the top of the tube should be directed onto a floating screen or onto a boat or barge containing a screen.

Never use an airlift with a diameter larger than six inches, because these are difficult for divers to control and many artifacts will be destroyed or lost. This occurred in 1959 during a six-week excavation of the sunken city of Port Royal when a 12-inch-diameter airlift was used.

During my excavation of Port Royal I used a four-inch-diameter airlift with good results. On the bottom of the tube I attached two wires, crossing the tube in opposite directions, which permitted only the smallest artifacts to go up the metal tube where they landed on a screen placed on a barge. Two men stood guard to recover them the moment they landed on the screen. Using only 50 PSI of air pressure meant that sediment was removed at a slower rate than if I had used a higher pressure, but it prevented artifacts from being sucked with great force against the bottom of the tube and being damaged.

The advantage of using the airlift on muddy or silty bottoms is that spill from the top of the airlift can be directed and carried away by the current, preventing underwater visibility from becoming too bad. Since there was rarely any underwater visibility at Port Royal — and then for only a few inches — the only advantage in using the currents to carry away the sediment pump-up was to prevent it from sinking back down on unexcavated areas. Until the development of the prop-wash, the airlift was also the main excavation tool used on wrecks in sandy areas, and it is still used on many wrecks today, especially on those in waters below the effective working depths of the prop-wash.

The prop-wash, also called a "blaster" or "mailbox," was invented early in the century to blow away sediment covering Chesapeake Bay oyster beds. In 1962 salvors working on the 1715 wrecks off the coast of Florida accidentally discovered its effectiveness as an excavation tool. Confronted with very murky waters, they devised a type of prop-wash for the purpose of pushing clear water from the surface down to the bottom, which is always dirtier and darker. To their great surprise they discovered the prop-wash to be a much better excavation tool than airlifts and hydrolifts they had been using.

The prop-wash is simple and inexpensive to construct and easy to operate. It consists of an elbow-shaped metal tube several inches larger in diameter than the vessel's propeller diameter and is attached to the transom of the salvage vessel so that the wash of the propeller is forced into the tube and deflected downward to the sea bottom. Generally, the upper end of the tube is attached from one to three feet behind the propeller with a wire-mesh cage covering the propeller area to prevent divers from being cut.

On twin-screw vessels, two prop-washes can be used side-by-side. The length of the prop-wash will depend on the diameter of the tube. On a small prop-wash, such as those used on outboard engines, they are generally about three feet in length. On larger vessels, such as those having propellers as large as four feet in diameter, the length of the tube is usually six to eight feet long, and half of this length is used in the section of the tube running out horizontally from the propeller to the elbow part of the tube.

Four anchors must be put out to hold the salvage vessel in place when the prop-wash is being used. The vessel's engine is then started and the propeller turned at varying speeds, depending on the depth of water and amount of sediment that must be blasted away. The wash of the prop deflected downward creates a whirlpool action that forces water to the bottom at a terrific velocity, blasting away sediment at a rapid rate. It is so powerful that it also cuts through coquina, a type of limestone coral growth, almost as fast as through sand.

Effective depth of a prop-wash depends on two factors, the size of its tube and the highest velocity at which the vessel's propeller can be run. A small prop-wash on an outboard engine is effective only up to 15 feet. Those on a vessel with a propeller of two to three feet in diameter can be used up to 35 feet, and on one with a four-foot-diameter propeller it can be used up to 50 feet. In 20 feet of water a prop-wash of two to three feet in diameter can excavate a hole 20 feet in diameter to a depth of 15 feet into sediment in only a few minutes. A larger prop-wash can excavate a hole in 50 feet of water to a diameter of 50 feet and 20 feet deep in the same period of time.

The secret in using a prop-wash is being able to control its speed. This means running it at high speeds to remove overburden on a wreck yet knowing to slow it down when the level of the wreck or artifacts is reached to prevent the artifacts from being blown away. I have learned that in order to remove 12 feet of sand over a wreck, I must run the engine so that the propeller makes 1,200 revolutions per minute for a period of exactly three minutes. Then I reduce the speed to 400 RPM and send divers down to operate under this slow speed picking up artifacts as they are uncovered. At this speed the prop-wash will remove approximately an inch of sand per minute, which is slow enough to enable the divers to catch all the artifacts before they are blown away. If the prop-wash is not properly controlled, many artifacts will be destroyed or blasted away into other areas. With a prop-wash running at full speed I have seen a six-pound cannonball blasted over 50 feet from its original position. Some prop-washes are so powerful that they can be used to remove ballast stones off a wreck, but I do not recommend this since there generally are many valuable artifacts mixed in with ballast piles and these will also be blasted away.

When a good area, e.g. one where jewelry or gold coins, or porcelain chinaware, is uncovered by the propeller, stop the prop-wash and continue the excavation either by fanning by hand or using a small airlift or hydrolift so you have more control. I have had experiences where a prop-wash uncovered a layer containing a large number of coins or other items and, even while it was running at its slowest speed, I was unable to grab all the items before they were blasted away.

The one disadvantage of the prop-wash is that as it excavates a hole, sediment is thrown or blasted over unexcavated areas, and this overburden must always be removed from the virgin areas. Yet the speed at which the prop-wash can excavate makes this really a minor problem.

The hydrolift, also known as a transfer tube and gold dredge, is mainly used in surveying a wreck or when excavating in a hot area, like that mentioned above. It works on the same principle as the airlift, except that water pressure is used instead of air pressure to create the suction in the tube. The tube used is rarely more than six feet long and discharges its spill behind the diver instead of discharging on the surface. The spill should be directed to fall on a screen so that small artifacts can be found or a diver should be stationed at the exhaust end of the tube to search for artifacts as they come out of the tube.

Shipwrecks are not all at the bottom of the sea, yet archaeologists in Spain are using destructive methods here to salvage the remains of an old shipwreck.

Water-jets, which consist of nothing more than a hose pushing water out at a high pressure, and air-jets, which operate on the same principle, are mainly useful as tools to blow away sediment under a ship's timbers or in ballast piles, where an airlift or prop-wash might not be used as effectively.

The depth into sediment or coral growth that one must excavate can be determined only by trial and error. I have worked on some wrecks in which everything found was under the first two feet of sediment, and on others in which 25 feet of overburden had to be removed before everything was discovered in the next five feet.

The ballast piles of every wreck should be thoroughly investigated, because valuable artifacts will be found mixed in with the ballast rock. Moving ballast rock is the most time-consuming and hardest part of any wreck excavation. The best way is to excavate all the areas adjacent to a ballast pile and then move the ballast rock into these areas. Sending the ballast rock to the surface vessel in baskets can require months of time and is not really necessary, provided the same ballast rock can be moved on the bottom to an area already excavated. A friend of mine is working on a system that will move ballast rock on a wreck site to other areas by means of a conveyer belt.

Nothing is more frustrating than to excavate a hole and then discover a beer can one of your crew has flung overboard. This can be avoided by keeping proper records. Systematically excavating a wreck and recording data is the only way to thoroughly and accurately salvage a shipwreck. Many modern-day salvors, however, still prefer to rely on intuition and ESP in deciding where to excavate. They jump from one spot to another and in many cases miss the best finds. When a wreck is worked systematically, salvors can easily keep track of the areas excavated each day.

The "blaster" technique, utilizing propwash from a ship's propellors, is used by a diver to remove sand overburden at a shipwreck site.

At the end of each day, all the artifacts retrieved that day should be laid out on the deck of the salvage vessel and photographed with a record made of where they were found. It definitely pays to work in an organized and orderly way, even if it sometimes seems tedious.

Chapter Five

Wrecks/Cargoes
Identification and Dating

The identification and dating of shipwrecks, equipment and cargoes can be difficult and time-consuming, especially for the salvor with little background in history or research. Fortunately, there are many experts who generously share their expertise to assist in bringing a shipwreck to life by "filling in its blanks." Even with a library of thousands of books and scientific reports relating to my work, I still find myself puzzled from time to time. I have been helped enormously over the years by scholars and scientists in many fields ranging from authorities on Chinese coastal trade to geologists and biologists.

Very often my books and reports enable me to establish a positive identification and date of an item, particularly when a great deal has been published on such an item. Still, to avoid possibility of error and for verification I consult experts specializing in various articles. On items on which little or nothing has been published, I rely solely on the assistance of experts. Some items can't be precisely identified, either because there are no experts who have focused on that object or because nothing has been written, e.g. ship's pumps, fastenings, lead shipping seals or sewing thimbles.

There are many challenges associated with identifying and dating a shipwreck and its items. The more articles the salvor has to work with, the better his chances are of establishing a positive identification and date. Artifact contamination post-dating a shipwreck is always possible. This would include items from other wrecks lost in the same area that might get mixed in with an earlier shipwreck; articles thrown off a passing ship or a ship salvaging a shipwreck which may also contaminate a nearby site.

During a salvage operation in the Florida Keys the first item recovered was an anchor dating from the second half of the 19th century. If the salvors had relied on dating the shipwreck from this one item alone, they would been mistaken. The century-old anchor had apparently been lost after snagging on a 17th-century wreck, thus contaminating the shipwreck site.

On the other hand, many shipwrecks will have items predating the period of the shipwreck. From reading old documents I have found many instances where items carried on ships were much older than the ships and men sailing them. A Spanish sea captain wrote to the King in 1728 that he would defend his ship against any enemy attacks with the same sword that one of his ancestors had used during the famous Battle of Lepanto in 1571. Another captain reported in 1682 that since he was unable to obtain the required number of cannon for his ship making a voyage to Mexico, he had hired divers to recover several from a shipwreck in Cadíz Bay dating from the middle of the 16th century. He knew they could not be fired and admitted that he carried them to make his ship appear heavily armed to enemy ships he might encounter. In 1794 an English ship was lost without a trace in the Caribbean during a hurricane; its principal cargo consisted of treasure recovered from a Spanish galleon that had sunk on the coast of Panama around 1560.

I have had firsthand experience with this problem. While I was living in Seville the director of the local archaeological museum asked me to make a survey on a shipwreck recently located by fishermen near Malaga. He told me that the fishermen had sighted a large marble statue on the shipwreck. The statue was of Roman origin, but the rest of the ship's cargo as well as the ship itself dated from the latter part of the 19th century. Through research we discovered that the ship had been sailing from Sicily to Spain with a general cargo. Either the statue was being brought to Spain to be sold or was being used as ballast.

Establishing the nationality of a shipwreck from items discovered on it is not as easy as it would seem. As I mentioned in an earlier chapter, the majority of the cargoes brought from Spain to the New World were manufactured in many different countries. This also applies to ships of other nationalities. Even during times of war, when rulers prohibited trade between their subjects and the enemy, trade continued as usual, sometimes involving merchants of neutral nationals as middlemen. The *Matanceros* is an illustration of this. Although Spain and England were at war at this time, over half of the cargo carried on the ship was of British origin. To further complicate identification of this wreck, the major portion of the remainder of the ship's cargo came from countries other than Spain, including France, Germany, England, Holland and Brazil.

At the close of our first season of excavation on the *Matanceros* we sought the assistance of an expert from the Smithsonian Institution in identifying and dating the wreck. He assured us the wreck was definitely an English merchantman. Nevertheless, my partners and I disagreed, mainly because we found a vast number of Catholic religious articles, which we felt certain no English ship would carry. Consequently, we kept researching and were finally able to identify the shipwreck positively as a Spanish merchantman. After obtaining copies of the original cargo manifest from the Archives of the Indies in Seville, we were able to match the majority of the items that we had recovered from this wreck with those listed on the cargo manifest.

There are many cases in which ships of European nations also carried cargoes manufactured in various other countries. In 1620 a Dutch merchantman was captured after entering a small port in Cuba while attempting to carry on illegal trade with the local residents. The bulk of its cargo consisted of merchandise from England, France and Italy. Many European ships sailing to the New World made it a practice to stop at one of the Canary Islands to take on fresh water and victuals before making the long ocean crossing. Because they often also purchased Spanish wine and other spirits, it is not unusual to find a number of Spanish olive jars in which these liquids were carried on non-Spanish ships. Other items manufactured in Spain, such as swords made in Toledo and held in great esteem by men of different nationalities, might also have been obtained in the Canaries.

Ships of all nations sailing back to Europe from the Western Hemisphere also carried goods manufactured in various countries. Items such as navigational equipment might have been carried throughout the life of the ship, whereas trade items might have been obtained in the ports they visited or they could be items from the Old World that a ship failed to sell. These items could also have been captured them from ships of other nations.

Discovering Spanish specie or bullion on a shipwreck is definitely not evidence that the ship is Spanish because Spanish coinage circulated in European nations with settlements in the New World.

121

It remained legal tender in the United States until the beginning of the 19th century. The vast amount of silver and gold mined and minted by the Spaniards and the scarcity of these precious metals in the other European nations made this necessary. Through legal trade, contraband trade and as the result of plundering by privateers, most of the precious metals mined in Spanish America eventually reached other European countries. Many of these nations used the Spanish coinage on a large scale, rather than melt down the precious metals to make new coins. On various occasions the English Crown had huge amounts of Spanish coinage melted and recoined into English coinage, but very few of these coins ever reached the New World. To encourage the English subjects to purchase only merchandise manufactured in Mother England, merchant ships sailing to the New World were forbidden to carry English currency. Thus, the thousands of English merchantmen that came to obtain New World products could only offer English-manufactured merchandise in exchange.

Spanish coinage was used throughout the world. Each year huge sums were shipped from Mexico to the Philippines to purchase goods to be shipped to Acapulco from the Orient. Large amounts of this specie eventually reached other nations. A Dutch ship, the *Golden Dragon*, wrecked in 1656 on the west side of Australia, was salvaged in the 1970s. Among the items recovered were 7,500 silver coins dated 1654-55 from the Mexico City and Potosí) mints.

The nationality and date of some shipwrecks can be established by the size of the vessel and the objects found on them, but again, caution must be exercised, as there are many exceptions. During the period covered in this book, the smallest vessels were those used by early explorers like Columbus — advice or mail boats, reconnaissance boats, salvage vessels and coastal, or inter-island, trading vessels.

The small caravels and pinnaces used by early explorers should be fairly easy to identify by the artillery they carried, which differed greatly in size and construction from that of later-period ships. Because of the risk involved in sailing in uncharted waters, the officers and crew avoided bringing such valuable items as silverware or glassware. Instead they ate and drank from wooden or ceramic objects. An exception occurred when one of these ships carried colonists or government officials to a newly settled area, in which case they would bring all their earthly possessions with them. Such a ship might carry agricultural, mining, masonry and carpentry tools which should enable the salvor to differentiate between a vessel on an exploratory or colonizing voyage. Any treasure found on such a Europe-bound shipwreck will most likely be gold or silver of an unrefined and unminted nature, or items manufactured by the Indians.

Advice and mail boats, and even reconnaissance boats for that matter, appear very similar in appearance under water. Unlike the early exploratory or colonizing vessels, these carried more armament and can be dated by their guns. They were not armed to fight large vessels but only to repel ships their own size and smaller ones that might overtake them. Their lightness and construction enabled them to outrun the larger vessels. Since these vessels had to be light to maintain fast speeds, they rarely carried any cargo at all. On occasion, advice boats returning to Spain carried small amounts of treasure to drop off at places along the way to pay officials or garrisons; and sometimes they carried it to the hard-pressed Spanish kings to tide them over until the treasure fleets reached Spain at later dates.

Small pirate and privateering vessels also fit into this description and would be difficult to distinguish from the other ships.

Salvage vessels also carried a substantial amount of armament to protect the items they might recover. Finding diving bells, or any of the many instruments used in early salvage operations, might aid the modern-day salvor in identifying the type of ship he has located. If the early salvors were successful, then a diversified cargo of treasure and artifacts might also be found on the wreck.

Shortage of Artillery

Throughout the centuries covered in this book, there was a chronic shortage of artillery throughout the Western Hemisphere. Very few small vessels carried any. If they did, the pieces were rarely larger than swivel guns, capable of repelling boarders but of little use in combat with other vessels. Since lack of armament and slow speeds, caused by the weight of cargoes, made trading ships vulnerable to attack, they sailed only when it was safe. And, even when they sailed, they usually carried cargoes of little value because of the risk of capture.

Small Spanish vessels were forbidden by the Crown from carrying any treasure. This rule like so many others, however, was not strictly enforced. Documents tell of many ships lost with treasure aboard. Occasionally these small trading vessels were used to carry large amounts of treasure, but then they were guarded by armed galleys or other warships. The gold and emeralds that were sent annually from Bogota to Cartagena for transshipment to Spain were brought down the Magdalena River in these small vessels which then sailed along the coast to Cartagena. When the Chagres River was used to transport the treasure by rafts from the Pacific to the Caribbean side of the Isthmus, the small trading ships carried the treasure from the mouth of the river to Nombre de Dios or Portobelo. Virtually all non-precious cargoes such as lumber and agricultural products carried on these small traders would have disappeared long ago on a shipwreck and few traces of the wreck would remain today, especially if the ship carried no armament or ballast.

The sites of larger merchant ships may also be unmarked since they generally carried such perishable cargoes to Europe as tobacco, cocoa, sugar, rum, cotton, drugs, indigo, cochineal and lumber. Finding a shipwreck that fits this description could falsely lead a salvor to conclude that the ship was empty when it was lost, since only shipboard items, cannon, anchors, weapons and cooking and eating utensils would be found.

Their cargoes make merchantmen arriving from Europe by far the easiest to identify. In most cases these cargoes consisted of objects of various metals, glass and ceramicware (things that would not disappear from a shipwreck over the years). Remember that many of the items carried on these merchantmen to be sold in the New World were also used on all types of ships. Thus a large number of different individual articles must be recovered before a salvor can determine that he has found a merchantman. It would be normal to find several dozen, or even several hundred, shoe buckles on a number of different types of shipwrecks, but finding thousands of them, as we did on the *Matanceros* wreck, enabled us to recognize that she was a merchantman.

A Spanish treasure ship is easily identifiable by the large amounts of treasure it carried, as well as the number and size of its cannon, greater in quantity and size than those of the average merchantman. The size of the ship furnishes another clue because only the largest ships were generally used to carry treasures back to Spain. During the second half of the 16th century the average size of a Spanish merchantman was about 450 tons and a galleon around 800 tons. During the 17th century the merchantmen averaged 600 tons and the galleons between 800 and 1,000 tons. During the 18th century the merchantmen barely increased in size, but most of the treasure-carrying galleons were between 1,500 and 2,000 tons. Galleons were required to carry anywhere from 100 to 250 marines; consequently, finding a large number of weapons in association with great amounts of treasure will help identify a shipwreck as a galleon.

All treasure-laden ships were not necessarily Spanish galleons, because ships of other nations also carried Spanish treasure to Europe from the New World. In 1755 because Spain and England were at war, no Spanish ships were available to carry treasure to Spain, and French vessels were used. A French ship, the *Notre Dame de Deliverance* disappeared without a trace somewhere between Havana and Cadíz. Her cargo consisted of 1,170 pounds of gold bullion carried in 17 chests, 15,399 gold doubloons, 153 gold snuff boxes weighing six ounces each, a gold-hilted sword, a gold watch, 1,072,000 pieces of eight, 764 ounces of virgin silver, 31 pounds of silver ore, a large number of items made of silver, six pairs of diamond earrings, a diamond ring and several chests of precious stones, plus general cargo consisting of Chinese fans, cocoa, drugs and indigo and, of course, an unknown amount of smuggled treasure.

A large ship with many cannon and weapons but little or no treasure will most likely prove to be a warship. Generally, warships of all nations were forbidden to carry cargo of any description, and the scarcity of the kinds of artifacts normally found on merchantmen helps identify a warship. In most cases it is impossible to distinguish between a Spanish treasure galleon sailing from Europe to a New World port and a warship. Neither would be carrying cargo, and both would carry large numbers of cannon and hand weapons. Because mercury was occasionally shipped from Spain to the New World on the treasure galleons, discovery of mercury on a wreck site would indicate it was a treasure galleon arriving from Spain.

British warships are easily identifiable because of the broad-arrow mark on many objects found in association with them. I have seen the broad arrow on cannon, weapons, copper sheathing, cutlery, bottles and a variety of other articles. The origin of the mark is obscure, but it was in regular use by the second half of the 16th century to denote all Crown property and continued until the end of the 19th century. Finding a few items with the broad arrow on a shipwreck indicates that the items once belonged to the British admiralty, but does not necessarily prove that the shipwreck itself is British. Items marked with the broad arrow have been found on several of the 1715 Spanish shipwrecks as well as on other wrecks that proved to be non-British.

Slave ships sailing to or from the New World are usually identifiable by the equipment found on them. One located recently near Panama contained hundreds of leg and arm bracelets attached to chains which were used on the wretched human cargoes these ships carried. Because almost every inch of a slave ship was used to carry the slaves and water and victuals to sustain them, most ships of this type carried only a few cannon. Other than the slaves, the only cargo these ships carried was ivory and gold dust, also obtained on the African coast. After selling their cargoes on this side of the Atlantic, slavers returned to Europe with gold or silver specie or bullion received as payment.

Before discussing identification and dating of items discovered on shipwrecks by their physical appearance, I shall mention various scientific methods that can aid in establishing the origin or date, or both, of various materials. Radiocarbon 14, or C-14, can be used to date old organic items such as wood, bone, charcoal, peat, shell or plant material. This method was conceived by the noted nuclear physicist W. F. Libby, who discovered that all organic material absorbs carbon-14 from the earth's atmosphere until it dies, and that this absorption ceases and disintegrates at a known rate over a period of time. By measuring the amount of C-14 remaining in organic material, scientists can determine the length of time that has elapsed since the object died; e.g. approximately how long ago a tree was cut down. Only small samples of the materials are required for this method of dating an object, but objects recovered from the sea must be kept wet until tested. Many universities have facilities for C-14 dating, and there are of commercial laboratories that do it as well. The procedure takes about two to six weeks.

A serious drawback of this method for dating shipwrecks in the Western Hemisphere concerns the uncertainty of the date an item itself was obtained. I once submitted a wood sample from a shipwreck and received a date of 420 years, plus or minus 150 years. This meant that the wood sample could date from 1400 to 1700, which was no help at all. When C-14 dating is used on items that are many thousands of years old, the plus or minus factor is of little significance; but on items only several hundreds of years old, it is important. Furthermore, in many cases the date obtained by this method will have no relationship to the date of the shipwreck. The ship may have been many decades old (some were used for as long as fifty years) when it sank yet the ambiguous date obtained by this method would relate to the date when trees was cut to build it. There are many instances when a ship was constructed from timbers of older ships, which in turn could have been constructed from the timbers of an even older ship. Other articles such as bone or charcoal found on a shipwreck are preferable to submit to testing, since they date within a few years of the loss of the ship.

Dendrologists can determine the place of origin of wood. Frequently they can identify not only the country of origin but even narrow it down to a small section of the country. This information is extremely useful in establishing the country in which the ship was constructed. This was one of the factors that contributed to the positive identification of the two shipwrecks of Columbus in St. Anne's Bay, Jamaica.

Botanical testing is also helpful. During our preliminary survey of the St. Anne's site we found several black beans that botanists identified as a species grown only in Spain. On another occasion a botanist identified several tobacco leaves I had found on a shipwreck as coming from Venezuela, thus aiding me in identifying the shipwreck. Most plants or seeds discovered on shipwrecks can be identified as to their species and place of origin.

Zoologists Sometimes Required

Zoologists are helpful in identifying bones of animals, birds and fish. Identifying large numbers of human bones on a shipwreck would indicate either that many of the persons were killed during a sea battle or as a result of a hurricane that caused the ship's loss. Investigating a shipwreck site near Jamaica, I noticed that there were a great many fish bones mixed in with the ballast. I assumed that they were either from native fish that had died over the years on the wreck or were the remains of meals eaten by the ship's crew. The latter assumption proved correct when a marine zoologist identified the bones as belonging to a fish never found in the warm Caribbean. They were herring bones from the North Sea. This information, combined with my discovery of many Dutch items on the wreck, identified it as a Dutch merchantman.

Geologists can usually establish the place of origin of most ballast rock found on a shipwreck, information which can be used to identify the ship's nationality. There are certainly exceptions to the rule, but generally a ship carried ballast rock from its home port or other ports belonging to the same country either in the Old or New World.

Scientists specializing in metallography can determine the origin of minerals and metal alloys used in different metal items. This will not necessarily identify the particular nationality of a wreck, but will give the precise origin of the metallic objects carried on it. This is especially useful in instrances where metal fastenings were used in construction of a ship's hull. Because fittings were probably manufactured near the source of those minerals of which they are composed, this would identify the locality where the ship was constructed.

The Corning Glass Museum in Corning, New York, has conducted extensive research in methods of identifying and dating glassware. Throughout history, different methods and minerals have been used in making glassware, and through scientific analysis experts are able to identify the place of manufacture of most glassware. Several years ago, the museum's Dr. Robert Brill developed a method of precisely dating glass recovered from the sea. By counting the number of layers of the weathering crust on the glass fragment, he establishes the length of time it has been under the sea. I have submitted many samples of glassware from shipwrecks, and his findings are always accurate to within a year or two of the known date of the wreck.

Ceramics and other objects made of clay, such as building bricks, can be rather accurately dated by a process called thermoluminescence, which was developed at the Oxford Research Laboratory in England. This process is based on the fact that radioactivity from certain isotopes in clay remains trapped there until a ceramic object is fired in a kiln. The firing releases the electrons in a "thermoluminescent glow." When the object cools, electrons are again trapped but continue to increase with the process of decay, and the number of electrons released increases with the length of time. Measuring the number remaining in the object, can establish its date with from 50 to 100 percent accuracy.

It is very difficult to establish a ship's nationality when it was lost merely from a visual inspection of the shipwreck. Captured ships were used by all European nations in their navies and merchant fleets; others were bought or hired from different nations. Scarcity of Spanish shipping in 1593 led the King to order seizure of all foreign ships in Spanish ports to assemble a fleet to sail to the New World. Of the 62 ships in this fleet, only 14 were Spanish-built. The others came from 12 European nations, including Greece and Sweden.

Too little usually remains on shipwrecks in shallow waters to determine the location where the ship was constructed. Yet, even if this site could be established, this fact would not necessarily indicate the nationality of the ship at the time it was lost. One of the 1715 ships was originally built in England and served as a warship for many years until captured by the French and converted into a merchantman; she was eventually sold to the Spaniards and converted to a treasure galleon.

Spikes, nails, tacks and other metal fastenings are no help in identifying a ship's nationality or the date of its construction because their shapes and sizes changed so little over the centuries. Brass tacks discovered on a Roman shipwreck dating from the 3d century A.D. are identical to those found on an 18th-century French warship. Treenails (wooden pegs) used to fasten the planking to the frame of a ship, are no help either since they remained the same over the centuries. If they were turned on a lathe rather than shaped by hand, it indicates only that the wreck is dated after 1825. Nor will the types of wood used in a ship's construction provide the salvor with any valuable clues, because the types of wood used by the various nations generally depended on what was most readily available. The earliest mention of a ship built in Europe using teakwood was in 1821. A ship built with mahogany planking might indicate that it was built near Honduras, which was the major source of mahogany in the old days.

From consulting thousands of documents concerning the size and tonnage of ships of different types and nationalities, I have devised the table on the following page to assist the salvor in establishing the size and draft of old ships. If documentary sources indicate that his ship was of 500 tons or so, the keel should be about 92 feet long. This information can be used in reverse. Locating a shipwreck, the salvor might discover that the keel length was 120 feet which would indicate that his ship was 1,400-1,500 tons, which would aid him greatly in identifying a wreck as the one he is seeking.

Tonnage	Length of Keel	Width of Beam (all others in feet)	Draft
100 tons	52 feet	19 feet	7 1/2
200	66	24	9 1/2
300	'76	27 1/3	15 1/2
400	84	30	12
500	92	33	13
600	98	35	14
700	102	36 3/4	14 5/8
800	104	37 1/2	15
900	107 1/2	38 1/2	15 1/4
1,000	109	39 1/5	15 1/3
1,400-1,500	120	44	16
1,600	132	48	16
2,000	152	60	18

Preventing the borings of the teredo and accumulation of marine mollusks on the hulls was a constant problem, especially in the warm waters of the New World. One method used by most of European maritime nations was to careen their ships and singe the ships' bottoms before applying various tar and pitch-based protective compounds. The Spaniards generally used a mixture of tar and lime. Some Spanish ships in the 18th century used a layer of wooden sheathing and placed a compound of tar and animal hair between the sheathing and hull. The English used too many different compounds on their ships' bottoms to describe here. In 1745, for example, it was a mixture of 100 parts of pitch, 30 parts of brimstone and 35 parts of brick or marble dust.

The earliest mention of Spanish ships sheathed with lead occurs in 1508. This practice continued until 1567 when the King ordered it to cease, claiming that the added weight caused his ships to sail too slowly. Lead sheathing was again applied to Spanish ships sailing to the New World in 1605, but only to those going to Mexico. The sheathing protected their hulls from the teredo during the long months that these ships wintered in Veracruz. The only other nation that employed lead sheathing was England, which used it on a small scale, mainly as an experiment on warships in the Caribbean at different periods.

There was a brief mention in 1735 that 20 English warships were sheathed, but the type of material used was not mentioned. Several English warships were sheathed with copper in 1766, and by 1780 this condition existed on all their ships, both naval and merchantmen. The first French ships to use copper sheathing sailed in 1775, but this practice did not catch on with the Spaniards or Portuguese until the first decade of the 19th century.

The majority of masts, yards, spars and rigging used on ships of all nations came from the Baltic region; their shapes differed so little over the years that they are not helpful in identifying the nationality or construction date of a ship. Size of such items, however, could be used to establish the size of the ship.

Anchors are very difficult to date because their shapes changed so little over the centuries, nor can their place of origin be established by the shape of the anchor. From the time of the Vikings until about 1825, all anchors were hand-forged from several pieces of iron. After this period many were cast in one piece. The stocks were made of wood until the middle of the 19th century, when they were replaced by iron bars. First mention of chains used on an anchor was in 1817 and referred to those on an English warship.

The number and size of anchors a ship carried depended on its size and type. Because anchors were frequently lost, many extra ones were carried. Until 1579 there was no regulation concerning how many anchors a Spanish ship had to carry, but that year the King issued an order that ships over 100 tons going to Tierra Firme must carry five anchors and those going to Mexico must carry seven. The first mention of their sizes dates to 1620, when a galleon of 500 tons carried seven anchors on a voyage to Veracruz, including one of a ton weight, two of 1,800 pounds, two of 1,600 pounds, one of 450 pounds, and one of 350 pounds. In 1709 an order was issued that the total weight of anchors on all Spanish warships must be equal to five percent of the total weight of the ship.

After 1634 French merchantmen were required to carry a minimum of four large anchors and warships at least six. One large French warship lost in the Caribbean near the end of the 17th century was carrying 10 anchors, while another that was lost during the same hurricane, had only two available. When the cables of both these anchors parted, she wrecked on a reef.

English warships in 1688 were required to carry the following number of anchors: a ship of 2,000 tons, known as a first-rater, nine anchors weighing a total of 17 tons; a second-rater of 1,500 tons, nine weighing a total of 12 1/2 tons; a third-rater of 1,000 tons, six weighing a total of 8 1/2 tons; a fourth-rater of 700 tons, six weighing a total of 5 1/2 tons; and a fifth-rater of 500 tons, five weighing a total of 4 1/2 tons.

131

Cannon are very beneficial in determining the size, type and approximate date of a ship, but not necessarily the nationality, because cannon manufactured in several countries can be found on a single ship. During the second half of the 16th century the majority of cannon on Spanish ships were made in England and Holland and during the 17th and 18th centuries a large percentage were also of foreign manufacture. A Spanish merchant ship sailing to Veracruz in 1616 had three English guns, one Italian, three Dutch, two Portuguese, five French, and three Spanish cannon as her armament! In 1623 a critical shortage of cannon kept the flotas and treasure galleons from sailing for the New World because none of the ships that had gone to the New World the previous year had returned to Spain. To arm the ships 30 cannon were bought from Portugal, 200 from Denmark and 300 from England. Many other European ships carried cannon of foreign manufacture, most of which had been taken from captured ships.

Most bronze and iron cannon were struck with dates at the time they were founded and many also bore the coat of arms of the monarch of the country of manufacture. The majority of English cannon were struck with a crowned rose and the initials GR for "George Rex" or "King George." On bronze cannon these marks always survive, but on the iron cannon oxidation of the exterior of the pieces has caused the markings to disappear. When cannons bear no visible mark of their founding date, they can still be dated by shape and other distinctive characteristics.

All European nations have artillery museums, and their experts can generally date pieces to within 50 years. In the United States the Smithsonian Institution and the National Park Service have experts who can aid a salvor in identifying and dating cannon. Various books have been published on cannon of different nations.

During his voyages Columbus's ships were armed with two types of cannon — lombards and versos, also called swivel guns. The lombards were made of forged-iron strakes running the length of the barrel and held together by iron bands spaced every four to six inches. The piece was open at both ends and a breech block

An intact English musket which the author recovered from a shipwreck off Jamaica helped date the wreck to the end of the 17th century.

loaded with powder was wedged against the back end after a ball was inserted. The cannon were mounted on wooden cradles and carried on the main deck of the ship. These pieces varied from six to 12 feet in length, weighed from 500 to 2,000 pounds, and fired a ball of stone between four and 10 inches in diameter. The weight of the ball depended on the type of rock. A distinctive feature of this type of cannon was the absence of trunnions on the cannon, unlike cannon used at later dates.

Versos were either cast in bronze or made of iron in the same manner as the lombards. Around the end of the 16th century they began casting them in iron as well. They were mounted on a pivoting frame and attached to the bulwarks of ships. They varied in length from four to 10 feet, weighed between 150 and 1,800 pounds, and fired a stone or iron ball between 1 1/2 and three inches in diameter. These small-caliber guns were mainly used to attack personnel on the decks and castles of an enemy ship rather than a ship's hull, which was capable of resisting the shock of the projectiles. This type of cannon was carried on ships of all types and nations as late as the end of the 18th century. It was also used as a signal gun and by officers at times of mutiny.

As early as 1504 some of the larger Spanish ships sailing to the New World were carrying bigger cannon, mounted on two wheeled wooden gun carriages. A merchant nao sailing to Santo Domingo that year carried one bronze demiculverin, 11 feet in length, weighing two tons and firing a 12-pound ball; four iron cannon serpentines, eight feet in length, weighing 2 1/2 tons and firing a 40-pound ball; one bronze saker, seven feet in length, weighing 1,200 pounds and firing a six-pound ball; and three versos of unknown size and weight which fired a four-pound ball.

In 1552 a royal order commanded all Spanish ships sailing to the New World to carry the following amounts of armament. Merchant ships between 100 and 170 tons were each required to carry one bronze saker, one bronze falconet, six iron lombards and 12 iron versos. A ship of 170 to 220 tons had to carry one bronze demicul-

This Roman bronze statue represents a mystery of the deep because it was snagged in the nets of a fishing boat off the coast of Argentina. How did it get there?

verin, one bronze saker, one bronze falconet, eight iron lombards and 18 iron versos. Ships of 220 to 320 tons carried one iron demiculverin, two bronze sakers, one bronze falconet, 10 iron lombards and 24 iron versos. Treasure galleons of between 400 and 600 tons were required to carry all bronze cannon, which consisted of 30 to 50 culverin cannon, four to six demiculverins, two to four sakers, four falconets and an unknown number of versos.

The demiculverins fired balls weighing from seven to 12 pounds, were 25 to 40 times their bore diameter in length and weighed between 3,000 and 4,000 pounds. The sakers fired balls weighing from five to 10 pounds, were from five to eight feet in length, and weighed between 1,700 and 2,400 pounds. The falconets fired a three- or four-pound ball, were 30 to 36 times their bore diameter in length and weighed between 1,500 and 2,500 pounds. Lombards were then made with trunnions and were about the same size and weight as earlier types, as were versos. Culverin cannon were the main armament for fighting against enemy ships. They were made in many different sizes and fired balls weighing between 20 and 40 pounds. Their lengths were 30 to 32 times their bore diameter and their weight from two to three tons.

When a scarcity of copper prevented the manufacture of bronze culverins and other types of cannon for Spanish ships around 1570, many began carrying more iron cannon. The largest was called just plain cannon. It fired a 40-pound ball, was 17 times its bore diameter in length and weighed 6,200 pounds. There were also demi-cannons, which fired balls weighing between 12 and 20 pounds, were between 12 and 20 times their bore diameters in length, and weighed between 2,300 and 3,600 pounds.

Small vessels frequently used several other types of cannon, including the pasavolante, which fired a ball weighing between two and 15 pounds; the moyana, which fired a ball weighing from six to 10 pounds; and the esmeril, about which very little is known. During the 16th and 17th centuries a type of cannon named pedrero was occasionally carried on Spanish ships, but very little is known about it. Some documents mention them being small in size and weight and firing balls of only a few pounds; others mention them weighing as much as two tons and firing 40-pound stone balls.

With the exception of the lombards, which went out of use near the end of the 16th century, all the other cannon described above remained in use until the beginning of the 19th century, when carronades replaced most of the larger cannon on Spanish ships.

In 1599 the Spaniards apparently had a sufficient supply of bronze, since all cannons aboard the 12 galleons in that year's Tierra Firme Armada were made of bronze as were those of the Capitañas and Almirantas of both flotas. A royal order in 1605 stated that all treasure galleons and the Capitañas and Almirantas of the flotas must carry only bronze cannon and that all merchantmen must carry at least two bronze pieces. By 1644, however, only the two main flagships of the Tierra Firme Armada carried bronze cannon exclusively, while the other galleons carried but a few. All of the merchantmen sailing that year carried only iron cannon. In a fleet of 11 ships sailing to the New World in 1680, only 15 of the 467 cannon carried were bronze. In 1715 all the cannon on the 12 ships returning to Spain were iron and in 1733 on the 21 returning vessels, the cannon were iron with the exception of several small-caliber pieces.

Of English-made cannon, the robinet, falconet, falcon, minion, saker, demiculverin and culverin were generally made of bronze. Different types and sizes of cannon were generally made of iron.

A new type of cannon, the carronade, was introduced on English ships in 1779. The carronade is easily distinguished from earlier guns because of its large bore and short length of from three to six feet. They fired balls weighing nine, 12, 24, 32, 42 and 68 pounds. Those manufactured up to 1800 had low trunnions; after 1800 the trunnions were centered. After 1825, however, many of them had no trunnions but were mounted with lugs on the gun carriages. From 1800 onward the carronade replaced most of the large-caliber cannon on ships of all nations.

The principal cannon carried on 16th-century English ships are given below with their average weights and measurements:

Name	Weight in pounds	Length in feet	Caliber in inches	Shot Weight in pounds
Robinet	200	5	1 1/4	1
Falconet	500	4	2	2
Falcon	800	6	2 1/2	2 1/2
Minion	1,100	6 1/2	3 1/2	4 1/2
Saker	1,500	7	3 1/2	5
Demiculverin	3,000	10	4 1/2	9
Bastard Culverin	3,000	8 1/2	4 1/2	11
Culverin	4,000	11	5 1/2	18
Demi-Cannon	5,000	9	6 1/2	30
Cannon	7,000	12	8	60

Because cannon were also scarce in England, the number and types carried on English merchantmen depended on the size of the ship and their availability. This also applied to English warships until about the middle of the 17th century, when the admiralty issued an order specifying the number and types of cannon that must be carried on their ships.

In 1762 a first-rater of 100 cannon carried 30 42-pounders, 28 24-pounders, 30 12-pounders, 10 eight-pounders, and two six-pounders. A second-rater of 90 cannon carried 26 32-pounders, 26 18-pounders, 26 12-pounders, 10 eight-pounders, and two six-pounders. A third-rater of 74 cannon carried 28 32-pounders, 30 24-pounders, 14 nine-pounders, and two six-pounders. A fourth-rater of 50 cannon carried 22 24-pounders, 22 12-pounders, and six six-pounders. A fifth-rater of 36 cannon carried 26 12-pounders and 10 six-pounders. A sixth-rater of 28 cannon carried 24 nine-pounders and four six-pounders.

French cannon were very similar in size, shape and weight to the English cannon, but were generally lavishly marked with decorations, especially those cast in bronze. The number and types of cannon carried on French merchantmen and warships varied greatly until 1643, when the King issued an order concerning armament on all the country's ships. Merchantmen sailing to the New World were required to carry the following number and sizes: a ship between 200 and 300 tons, six demiculverins of 2,400-pounds, 12 sakers of 1,600-pound weight, two minions of 1,000-pound weight, one falconet of 300-pound weight and one robinet of 200-pound weight.

The principal cannon carried on 17th-century English ships are given below with their average weights and measurements:

Name	Weight in pounds	Length in feet	Caliber in inches	Shot Weight in pounds
Robinet	120	3	1 1/4	3/4
Falconet	210	4	2	1 3/4
Falcon	700	6	2 1/2	2 1/4
Minion	1,500	8	3	4
Saker	2,500	9 1/2	3 1/2	5 1/4
Demiculverin	3,600	10	4 1/2	9
Culverin	4,000	11	5	5
Demi-cannon	6,000	12	6	27
Cannon	7,000	10	7	47
Cannon Royal	8,000	8	8	63

The principal cannon carried on English ships during the 18th century, until the introduction of the carronades, are given below with their average weights and measurements:

Name	Weight in pounds	Length in feet	Caliber in inches	Shot Weight in pounds
Robinet	150	3 1/2	1 3/4	1/2
Falconet	700	4 1/2	3	3
Falcon	800	6	3 1/4	4
Minion	2,000	7 1/2	3 3/4	6
Demiculverin	2,600	8	4 1/2	9
Culverin	3,200	9	4 3/4	12
18-Pound Cannon	3,900	9	5 1/3	18
24-Pound Cannon	4,600	9	5 4/5	24
32-Pound Cannon	5,500	9 1/2	6 1/2	32
42-Pound Cannon	6,500	10	7	42

French ships of larger sizes had to carry the smaller number and sizes of cannon, with the exception of the number and weight of the demiculverins, which increased with the size of the ship. A 300-ton vessel carried nine demiculverins of 3,000-pound weight, a 500-ton ship carried 16 demiculverins of 3,200-pound weight, and a 700-ton ship carried 22 demiculverins of the same weight.

All first- and second-raters were required to carry only bronze cannon, with the smaller French warships required to carry one-quarter of their cannons made of bronze and the remainder of iron.

Dutch cannon were very similar to the English and French guns. They used bronze cannon almost exclusively on all their ships, including the majority of their large merchantmen. Portuguese cannon differed vastly in shape from any of the others manufactured in Europe, and many of those carried on Portuguese ships were actually manufactured in India or in other Portuguese possessions in the Far East.

The basic cannon projectile was the round shot, generally made of iron, but sometimes of stone or lead. The size of the shot used for each cannon was one-quarter inch smaller in diameter than the caliber of the piece. Because there was no difference in the appearance of the round shot made by all the countries, the only information that can be obtained from them establishes the caliber of the cannon carried on the shipwreck in the event that the cannon are found to have been previously salvaged.

Bar shot and chain shot were primarily used during sea battles to destroy the sails and rigging of enemy vessels. The first mention of bar shot was by the Dutch in 1619. Some were made by attaching an iron bar measuring six to 12 inches in length between two round shot; others were made with two halves of a round shot, and some with round disks. Chain shot was introduced by the Dutch in 1666, with chain replacing the iron bar of the bar shot.

Two types of antipersonnel shot were also used: grape shot and canister shot, sometimes called case shot. The earliest mention of grape shot was in 1556 aboard English ships. It consisted of 20 to 50 small cast-iron balls of one to two inches in diameter held in place between two or more wood or metal disks connected to a central rod. The balls were lashed to the frame with cords or leather, and the cylindrical projectile was covered with canvas and coated with wax, paint or pitch. The diameter of the projectile depended on cannon's caliber; its height was between six and 12 inches. Canister shot, introduced by the French in 1745, consisted of a thin cylindrical metal can containing various-shaped objects, such as glass fragments, nails, tacks, musket balls and small pebbles.

Carcass shot was an incendiary projectile, consisting of a hollow cast-iron ball filled with combustible materials. When fired, flames streamed out through small holes in the side of the ball. The period when this projectile first came into use is unknown, except that it was during the second half of the 17th century.

The table below gives the average weight of iron round shot in relation to its size.

Diameter in inches	Weight in lbs and ozs	Diameter in inches	Weight in lbs and ozs
2	1.2	5 1/4	20.1
2 1/4	1.9	5 1/2	23.2
2 1/2	2.2	5 3/4	26.6
2 3/4	2.14	6	30
3 1/4	3.12	6 1/4	34
3 1/2	4.12	6 1/2	38
3 3/4	6. 1	6 3/4	42
3	7. 5	7	48
4	8.15	7 1/4	53
4 1/4	10.10	7 1/2	58
4 1/2	12. 10	7 3/4	64
4 3/4	14.14	8	71
5	17. 5	8 1/4	78

Carronade shot also consisted of a hollow cast-iron ball but did not contain any combustible material or have holes in it.

Weapons of many different types were carried on the ships, and it is relatively simple to identify them and establish their date and place of manufacture since many books are available on this subject. On ships of all nationalities, even passengers were required to carry at least one hand-held weapon. Crossbows were used until the end of the 16th century, but generally only small numbers of these were carried aboard ships because arquebuses and muskets were considered better weapons.

Matchlock arquebuses, which were introduced in the 14th century, were generally five or six feet long, weighed as much as 60 pounds and fired an iron or lead ball ranging from half an inch to an inch in diameter. The firing mechanism consisted of an S- shaped lever pivoted to the stock near its center and forked at its upper end to hold the match. By pressing the lower end of the lever the match was forced down into the flashpan and ignited the primer. The disadvantage of this weapon was the necessity of keeping the match lit or having the means to light it when needed.

The Wheel Lock and Flintlock

In 1517 a German invented the wheel lock, which replaced the matchlock, consisting of two main parts. A steel-tooth wheel was wound up by a key to tighten a spring; by pulling the trigger, the wheel, which contained a lump of pyrite or a flint, struck the firing pan and ignited the primer. Around the end of the 16th century another improvement was introduced on the firing mechanism when the flintlock superseded the wheel lock. In the flintlock, a piece of flint held in the jaws of the cock was released by pulling the trigger, which struck a piece of steel, sending a shower of sparks into the priming powder pan. The flintlock remained in continuous use on all firearms until about 1820, when it was replaced by the percussion lock. Although it was invented near the end of the 16th century, it wasn't widely used for many years. In France, for example, the flintlock was not used on a large scale until 1670.

Muskets, introduced in 1521, were the largest guns fired by a single man. Some were as long as 10 feet and weighed over 100 pounds and, because of their size and heavy recoil, had to be supported by a rest. The average size of the ball was about an inch in diameter. These weapons gradually decreased in size and by 1690 the average musket was about five feet long. From about 1700 onward the name *musket* was used to identify any type of firearm shot from the shoulder.

The English introduced the carbine during the second half of the 16th century. Similar in appearance to a musket, it was much smaller and fired a lead ball less than an ounce in weight.

Pistols were first used in England in 1521 and in most other European countries soon afterward. They were actually a smaller version of the arquebus — lighter and easier to handle, primarily invented for use by men on horseback who could handle a weapon with only one hand. By the middle of the 16th century pistols were standard equipment for all officers aboard ships.

The firing mechanisms on the muskets, carbines and pistols changed at the same time as those of the arquebuses.

Although full suits of armor were not used aboard ships during the period covered in this book, armored breast plates and helmets were used until the end of the 16th century. Other primitive weapons still in use were boarding axes, pikes, lances and shields.

Many of the swords, daggers, rapiers and poniards worn by all officers and wealthy passengers on ships have been discovered on shipwrecks. Cutlasses were used by the seamen and marines during battles from about the middle of the 16th century onward.

Bayonets were introduced by the Spaniards in 1580, but not adopted by the French until 1647 and the English until 1690.

Hand grenades were used on ships as early as 1467 and remained in use until the middle of the 19th century. They took many forms, but were usually round, made of various metals, glass or ceramic and filled with gunpowder. A small hole held a fuse which was lit before the grenade was thrown.

The average underwater explorer will probably need to consult an expert to establish the place and date of manufacture of most navigation instruments because few reference books are available. The navigation instruments used at the time of Columbus consisted of astrolabes and quadrants to establish the ship's latitude; nocturnals to establish the approximate time of night; the compass and dividers to mark off distances on charts. About the middle of the 16th century the cross-staff, or Jacob-staff, came into general use. The sextant was invented simultaneously in 1732 by John Hadley in England and Thomas Godfrey in Philadelphia, but it did not come into general use until about 1750.

Several bronze astrolabes and a large number of dividers have been recovered from shipwrecks, but none of the other navigation instruments mentioned above have been discovered on shipwrecks, with the exception of several sextants dating in the 19th century.

Quadrants and the cross-staves were made of wood and probably have not been found either because they floated away or were devoured by worms. Since nocturnals were made of brass, it is strange that none have been discovered. The same applies to compasses, because compass housings were usually made of lead or other non-magnetic metals.

Glass bottles are very good for establishing the date of a shipwreck, as their shapes changed quite often and they can be dated to within 10 years of their date of manufacture.

Glass was first discovered by the Phoenicians and the Egyptians, who made many beautiful glass objects. At the time of Columbus' discovery of America, Venice was the only place in Europe where glassware was being made, specializing in drinking glasses and decanters. Glass factories were founded in Antwerp in 1550 and in London in 1557. Another was founded in Jamestown, Virginia, in 1608, but it went out of business in 1624. A factory was started in Salem, Massachusetts, in 1632, making bottles to transport rum and cider to the West Indies and England. The next glassworks to open was in Brussels in 1662, and soon after others were founded in Spain, France, Holland and Germany.

Glass bottles that contained any type of liquor are generally called "wine bottles." The first ones manufactured were those in Salem, in 1632. The exact date when they were being manufactured elsewhere is not known, but it is believed that they were being made in England around 1650. Other European nations were not manufacturing wine bottles until well after 1700. At least 95 percent of all wine bottles discovered on 17th- and 18th-century shipwrecks will be of English manufacture because the English produced them on a large scale and exported them all over Europe. Wine bottles manufactured in Holland are very similar in appearance to those of the English, but those made in other European countries have their own distinct characteristics.

Some bottles bear the dates of manufacture and others have seals identifying the person for whom they were made, such as a tavern owner. Bottles were sealed with plain cork stoppers until near the end of the 17th century, when brass wire was used to hold the corks in place. Late in the 18th century copper wire came into general use to hold them in place. All bottles were blown by hand until the second decade of the 19th century, when molds were introduced. Thus, any bottle discovered with mold marks or with the maker's or owner's name molded on it must date later than 1810.

There are various books available to identify and date drinking glasses, but I suggest sending photographs and measurements of any glasses discovered on a shipwreck to the Corning Glass Museum. Glass plate for windows and mirrors was first made in England in 1673

White clay smoking pipes are also valuable for establishing the date, but not the nationality of a shipwreck since almost all pipes were manufactured in England and Holland. Most clay pipes can be dated to within 10 years of their date of manufacture, with the exception of a few manufactured in Virginia and Jamaica. Unlike many other items discovered on shipwrecks, the life span of a clay pipe was short, so those located on a wreck will date very close to the time when the ship was lost. Life span of a pipe was short because they were fragile and broke easily. Pipes were inexpensive to purchase and almost as expendable as cigarettes are today.

The use of tobacco was unknown in Europe until after the discovery of the New World. Columbus and his men saw Indians on various Caribbean islands smoking cigars, and later explorers in North America saw Indians smoking tobacco from clay pipes. Although the Spaniards started cultivating tobacco and exporting it from the New World colonies about the end of the 16th century, the use of tobacco in Spain was prohibited by the Church until the beginning of the 19th century. Most of the tobacco imported into Spain was sold to England and Holland.

On his voyage to the West Indies in 1565, John Hawkins gathered a large amount of tobacco and introduced it to England upon his return. The first mention of the manufacture of clay pipes in England occurred in 1573, and by the end of the 16th century the use of tobacco and clay pipes was widespread both in England and Holland. By 1619 there were so many manufacturers of clay pipes in England that they incorporated into a guild. Dutch pipe makers formed a guild in 1660. Clay pipes were first made in Denmark in 1655 and in Switzerland in 1697, but very little is known concerning the dates when they were first manufactured in the other European nations. It is believed — but not certain — that small numbers were being manufactured in Virginia and Jamaica in the late 17th century, but it wasn't until about the beginning of the 19th century that the United States first manufactured clay pipes on a massive scale.

There are many distinctive features about clay pipes that aid in dating them. When smoking first came into vogue in England and

144

Holland the cost of tobacco was very expensive because all of the tobacco used had to be purchased from the Spaniards; consequently, pipe bowls was small. After the English began cultivating tobacco in the New World and exporting it to England, the cost became progressively less and the size of the pipe bowls increased progressively. And, ass the bowls increased in size their shapes changed. Thus, pipe bowls can be dated to within 10 or 20 years by their shapes.

Dating Theory Disproved

Prior to my excavation of the sunken city of Port Royal it was believed that clay pipes could be dated by the diameters of the bore of their stem. The theory was based on the assumption that as the pipe bowls grew larger the diameter of the bore became smaller. At Port Royal I discovered a total of 7,133 pipes with intact bowls and over 5,000 with semi-intact bowls. From a very thorough examination of these clay pipes, ranging in dates from 1650 to 1850, I found that this theory was baseless and should never be used in trying to establish a date on a pipe.

Most of the pipes manufactured in England were marked with either the initials or full name of the manufacturer. Records exist in England listing 3,400 pipe-makers from 1600 onward. Several good reference books on the subject are available to help identify the maker, place of manufacture and date range of any particular pipe. These marks can be found on the bowls, heels, spurs or stems of the pipes.

Decorated pipes were made as early as 1600; the earliest have a fleur-de-lis or rosettes etched on them. Among the many designs on later pipes are oak leaves, a bowl or bunch of grapes, flowers and anchors. From the end of the 18th century to the middle of the 19th century, pipe decoration became much more elaborate, with some adorned with busts of the British monarchs or intricate coats-of-arms. Little is known about markings on pipes from other European nations until well into the 19th century. The same applies to the red clay pipes believed to have been made either in Virginia or in Jamaica.

The discovery of large numbers of pipes on a shipwreck usually identifies it as being English or Dutch, but small numbers have been discovered on a few Spanish shipwrecks. Since the use of snuff became general around 1700, the discovery of snuffboxes on a wreck would date it after 1700. Tobacco stoppers, generally made of brass or pewter, are first mentioned as being used in 1640, and many contain distinctive markings that can be used to establish a date or place of manufacture.

Gold, Silver and Pewter

There has been a great deal published about gold, silver and pewter items that enable a salvor to establish a precise date and place of manufacture. The majority contain identifiable hallmarks and touch marks, and those that do not can be identified by their shape or form.

Such items are generally easy to identify and date. At Port Royal, for example, I found tankards, spoons, knives, etc., and with only a few exceptions I was able to identify not only the place and date of manufacture but in many cases the names of the actual owners of the items. The majority were stamped with only the owner's initials, but some items contained the owner's full name. From historical records in the Jamaican archives I matched initials with the names of their owners, enabling me to identify the owners of the buildings I was excavating. I have also done this with items recovered from various shipwrecks by matching the names or initials on items recovered with passenger or crew lists of the ship.

The English had a virtual monopoly on the manufacture of gold, silver and pewter items, and more than 95 percent of those found on shipwrecks are of English manufacture, with the exception of jewelry. A small quantity of silver items — mainly spoons, forks, plates and cups of Spanish and French manufacture — have been found on various shipwrecks, and all contained sufficient markings to identify and date them. Even on most Spanish wrecks, however, the vast majority of items of this type were English made. Of the more than 100 pewter and silver articles found on the *Matanceros*, all were English save one fork of Spanish make.

All items made of gold, silver or pewter which might be found in association with a shipwreck of the period dealt with in this book were in use throughout the period, with the exception of snuffboxes and forks. Large serving forks were in use as early as 1300, but the use of small forks to transfer food from the plate to the mouth is not mentioned until the latter part of the 16th century, when they came into general use for the upper class. Their use did not catch on with the lower class until the end of the 17th century. The cutlery used by the lower classes until late in the 18th century was usually made of iron or brass.

Since only the very rich could afford articles of gold or silver, relatively small quantities of such items will be found on shipwrecks. Items made of pewter were used by the vast majority of the upper and middle classes. Pewter ware was first used by the Romans and has remained in continual use until the present time.

Pewterware is easy to identify. All pieces bear a variety of markings. The touch mark, for example, identifies the manufacturer. After being admitted to the Pewterers' Guild, each pewter-maker was given permission to strike an identifying mark of his choice — from one to two inches in height — on all pieces he made. The touch marks of over 6,000 English pewter makers are recorded and have been published in various reference books. The majority consist of some type of design, flower, animal, crown, etc., with the maker's name or initials around it. The crowned Tudor rose mark signifies that the item was manufactured in London; the letter X with a crown above it denotes items made of extraordinary quality. In addition, many items were also stamped with their place and date of manufacture.

Hallmarks similar to those used on gold or silverware can be found on many articles of pewterware. These marks were not authorized for use by the Pewterers Guild, however, and were illegally struck by the pewter-makers. Struck in the shapes of shields or cartouches, they average about three-eighths of an inch in height, and are aligned in a straight row, unlike the marks mentioned above. The first hallmark denoted the place of manufacture. The crowned leopard's head was the mark of the London manufacturers, the anchor for those in Birmingham and a plain crown for those in Sheffield. The second mark consisted of a letter of the alphabet and denoted the year of manufacture. Every 27 years the makers started again from the beginning of the alphabet. The third hallmark denotes that the piece was of good quality. In England the lion was used; elsewhere in the British Isles other devices, such as the thistle in Edinburgh. The fourth hallmark denoted the identity of the maker and usually consisted of his initials.

Gold and silverware feature the same kinds of hallmarks described above in addition to other distinctive marks that can be easily identified. American-made silverware of the 17th and 18th centuries bore only the maker's mark; thus these pieces can only be dated as being made sometime during the life span of a known craftsman.

Silver plating on copper items was first done in 1743, but not on a large scale until 1833, when electroplating was invented.

Enormous amounts of porcelain have been found on shipwrecks and most pieces can be identified and dated fairly accurately. The distinguishing feature of porcelain is that it is translucent, as opposed to pottery, which is opaque. All porcelain found on a 16th-century shipwreck and the majority found on shipwrecks of the 17th century is of Chinese or Japanese manufacture. All these pieces bear marks of the province in which they were made in addition to the name of the reigning ruler of the country at that time.

The first exact date or place of manufacture of porcelain in Europe is not known, but it is believed to have been in Florence around the close of the 16th century with production on a small scale and no items exported. The English began producing small amounts of porcelain about 1745; the Dutch, a few years later. Most of these pieces bear makers' marks, making it possible to establish the date and place of manufacture. Porcelain was not produced in most the other European countries or the United States until the 19th century. Identification of unmarked porcelain should be left to experts, but amateurs can discover approximate dates and places of manufacture by consulting various references.

The most common type of pottery discovered on shipwrecks is utilityware which consists of a coarse hard paste, usually red but sometimes gray or brown. Only small amounts of utilityware were glazed, generally green. This pottery used by the lower classes was rarely decorated and lacks distinctive features that would facilitate identification of place or date of manufacture. Approximate dates can be fixed by the shapes of various vessels of this type, however, if the vessel is found intact or enough pieces are found to establish its original shape.

On all Spanish ships — and on those of many of other nations — a type of vessel resembling the amphorae used by the Greeks and Romans was used to carry liquids and a wide variety of solids such as olives and grain. These vessels, known as Spanish *olive jars*, were manufactured in Seville and the surrounding countryside and exported all over Europe and the New World. An approximate date can be obtained from the shape of the vessel and by a maker's mark on some. They were made of utilityware, usually of a gray exterior, and ranged in size from two to six gallons in capacity.

Another type of large vessel that can be dated fairly accurately is the bellarmine jug. These were manufactured in Germany of a type of ceramic called stoneware. The clay had flint in its composition, was fired at much greater temperatures than utilityware, and

148

was coated with a salt-glaze that gave it a distinctive whitish-gray interior and textured brownish exterior. Most of the necks of the bellarmines were decorated with a human face and some have armorial medallions on the bodies. These jugs range in size from one-pint to five-gallon capacity.

Another commonly used type of pottery was known as delftware to the English, Dutch and other northern Europeans. In France and Italy, however, it was called faience and in Spain and its New World possessions majolica. Widely manufactured in every country and used mainly by the upper and middle classes, it was generally made of the same clay as utilityware but was coated with a glaze of tin oxide, which appeared white in color after firing. The surface of the glaze was then decorated in a wide range of colors and designs.

Most of the pieces manufactured in Europe and some of the later pieces made in the New World have distinctive makers' marks on them, which can be used to establish date and place of origin. Experts should be consulted to date unmarked pieces.

Dating by Coins

Coins can generally be used to date a shipwreck within a few years of its loss, especially when large numbers of coins bearing the same dates or dates that span a short period of time are discovered. Coins have been found, however, that were more than a hundred years older than the shipwreck itself. Remember that a shipwreck must date from the same year, or earlier, than the latest dated coin found on it. Since probably 99 percent of all coins dated prior to 1825 found on a Western Hemisphere shipwreck will be of Spanish-American colonial mintage, I describe below only these coins and the means by which they can be dated.

Very little is known about the earliest coins minted in the New World. Several documents mention that private persons minted their own issues of gold and silver coins in Mexico City as early as 1528, but nothing is known of them. In 1535 a mint was established in Santo Domingo, where copper maravedi coins were first minted. Practically nothing is known about this coin, except that it was also minted at Mexico City and Panama City, among other places, and was used until the beginning of the 19th century. Very few 'were stamped with distinctive markings such as dates, mint marks or assayers' initials. Some, dating from the second half of the 16th century and minted in Santo Domingo, had an anchor on one side and a fort on the other. Others, minted there in 1636, had a fort on one side and two ships on the other. Occasionally, maravedi coins minted in Spain and bearing dates and other marks have been discovered on shipwrecks. The known denominations of these coins were eight, four, and two maravedis, but they may have been minted in other denominations as well. Their actual buying value was small and they were basically used as small change in the New World. A silver one-real coin was worth 34 maravedis and an eight-real coin, or piece of eight, was worth 272 maravedis.

Silver coins were first officially minted at Mexico City in 1536, at Lima in 1568, at Potosí) in 1572, at Bogota in 1622, at Guatemala City in 1733 and at Santiago (Chile) in 1751. It is believed that they were also minted at Cartagena and Panama City for short periods at various times during the 17th century. The basic silver coin was the eight-real piece, which weighed an ounce. The other real denominations were the four, two, one, 1/2 and 1/4 coins, which were smaller in size and weight.

Gold coins were first officially minted at Cartagena in 1615; Bogota, 1635; Mexico City, 1679; and at Lima and Potosí) about 1697. They were also minted for a six-month period during the year 1698 and again after 1750 at Cuzco, Peru. The gold coins are of the same size and weight as the silver and are in denominations of eight, four, two, one and 1/2 escudos.

The screw press was used to mint round milled coins in England as early as 1610, but it was not used in Spanish America until 1732, when the first round milled coins were made at the Mexico City mint. The Lima mint did not produce round milled coins until 1752, and the other mints at even later dates.

Prior to 1732 almost all gold and silver coins minted in the New World were not round in shape but of many irregular patterns. There were some exceptions. The silver coins minted in Mexico City during the first 20 or 30 years of operation were almost perfectly round, and over the years all of the mints made small

Markings on this cannon were helpful in dating a shipwreck since it bears the Portugese royal crest and the date 1704.

numbers of perfectly round gold and silver coins. The round gold coins are known as royals and are quite rare. It is believed that each mint made several royals each year and sent them to the King to show that they were capable of producing good coinage.

The irregular-shaped gold and silver coins were called cobs, a name probably derived from cabo de barra, which means *end of a bar.* To make these coins molten metal was poured on a flat surface in long, thin strips. When it cooled, pieces of the approximate size and weight of the desired coin were cut from the strip and trimmed to their proper weight. The planchet was then placed between two dies and struck with a heavy hammer. Since one or both sides of the coin were not perfectly flat, the dies only marked the highest surfaces of these sides. This resulted in the majority of cob coinage not having full die marks. Also, because such large quantities of coins were minted each year, care was not always exercised in marking them. Many, therefore, bear die marks only on various sections of their surfaces. The coins made at the Mexico City mint during the 17th and 18th centuries are poor in quality, show faulty die marks and are the most difficult to date. Of the coins recovered from the 1715 shipwrecks, 95 percent of which were from the Mexico City mint, only 15 percent of the gold coins and less than one percent of the silver bear dates. Other mints appeared to have exercised better workmanship, with larger amounts of both their gold and silver coins having fuller die marks in addition to bearing dates. At Port Royal I recovered about 2,500 silver coins from the Potosí) and Lima mints dated from 1658 to 1690, and 98 percent of these coins had dates on them.

There are many books that can be used to date Spanish-American colonial coins, and in most large cities have numismatists who can be consulted. When dates are not visible on coins, there are other ways to date them. With the majority of coins having the shield or coat-of-arms of the monarch on the obverse side the coin can be dated

This late-17th-century piece represents the most ornate of all Colonial Period bronze cannon which were generally manufactured by the French.

to the period in which that king reigned. From 1772 to 1825, the end of Spanish rule in America, both gold and silver coins carried the portrait of the Spanish king. All coins were also
marked with the initials of the assayer and cover the period in which a particular assayer was in charge of a mint. On small numbers of coins the reigning monarch's name or initials were also marked.

The place in which a coin was minted can be determined from the mint marks on each coin. The letter L for Lima, P for Potosí), M for Mexico City, C for Cartagena, G for Guatemala, S for Santiago, and NR for Bogota. When mint marks are not visible on the coin, the place where it was minted can be identified by its die markings. Almost all the Mexico City coins had a Jerusalem cross, a square cross with balls on all four ends, on the reverse side, as did some of the Bogota and Cartagena-minted coins. The Lima and Potosí-minted coins had a plain cross with the arms of Castile and Leon on their reverse sides. Even if only a small amount of the die is visible, the place in which it was minted can generally be established.

Platinum was probably discovered at an early date in the New World, but the first mention of its use in coinage was in 1651, when it was illegally used in both gold and silver coins in Lima. When this fact was discovered the assayer of the mint was beheaded and its further use strictly forbidden, but it might have been used both before and after this date. It was not considered a precious metal until late in the 19th century.

Chapter Six

Preserving Artifacts

S ome items, notably gold and porcelain, that are found on shipwrecks are unaffected by long underwater immersion and are recovered in a perfect state of preservation. On the other hand, most items deteriorate in varying degrees. The purpose of this chapter is to acquaint the salvor with appropriate methods for protecting and restoring artifacts. Such protection can begin when the artifact is discovered, even before it is brought to the surface, where the task must continue. Then, comes the challenge of restoring items to their original state, when possible, and preserving them for posterity.

Most organic items, like wood, come under immediate attack from the teredo, fungi and bacteria. The more these items are exposed to salt water, the more they suffer and the quicker some of them disappear. When buried deep under sediment, many of the same objects will suffer less, or not at all, and on occasion will be discovered in an excellent state of preservation.

Of the various types of metals lost on a shipwreck, iron and silver suffer the most, because of the effects of electrolysis under water. Different types of metal and salt water act as a gigantic galvanic battery. With salt water as the electrolyte, metals of two or more different molecular weights become opposite poles and a current of electrons is created between them. The galvanic current flowing between dissimilar metals will attack them with the highest electrode potential and convert them to one of its compounds. Silver converts to silver sulfide and iron to iron oxide. The metals with the lowest electrode potential are preserved by cathodic protection. Electrolysis occurs when metals are buried under sediment or are exposed to sea water on the surface of the sea floor.

Items recovered from the sea can be divided into three distinct classes:

1. Those recovered in their original condition (like gold) that require no treatment at all or only a brief immersion in fresh water to remove the salts on their exterior surfaces;

2. Those that have suffered marked physical and chemical changes and can be preserved by various methods;

3. Those that have suffered to such a degree that they cannot be restored to their original state. In this case, what remains of the original object can be saved by completely embedding it in plastic. In some cases nothing will remain of the original object other than a hollow form inside a coral-encrusted conglomerate, which can be recorded through X-ray photography or by making a replica of it by using the hollow form as a mold.

No shipwreck-recovered item that requires preservation should be exposed to the air for any length of time, and it must be kept wet, preferably in salt water. Water's heavy weight makes it impractical sometimes to transport it. An item can be wrapped in plastic wrap or placed in an airtight plastic bag or container. Large items are best transported from the salvage vessel to a preservation laboratory in wooden barrels or boxes containing moist sawdust.

Glass, Jewels and Related Materials

Hard gem stones (sapphires, rubies, emeralds, and agate) do not suffer from immersion in sea water and are recovered in their natural state. Softer gem stones such as beryl are sometimes found scratched by the abrasive action of sand and other materials moving against them under water, and these scratches should be removed by lapidary treatment.

Glass is affected in varying degrees, depending on its composition. Optical glass generally survives in a good state of preservation but is occasionally found pitted on its exterior. White-lead glass objects, such as plate glass, wine glasses, tumblers and pharmaceutical vials or medicine bottles are generally found free of calcareous deposits — though most will be covered with a thin coating of lead oxide and sometimes iron oxide when discovered in close association with iron objects.

To clean and preserve these items place the item in a 10-percent solution of nitric acid for the time required to remove the lead oxide. If iron oxide is present, after using a 5-percent solution of sulfuric acid to remove the oxide, follow through with several thorough washings in distilled water. When dry, if the item shows signs of flaking on its exterior, it should be coated with several layers of clear plastic spray, such as Krylon.

As a rule, most bottles postdating 1750 are found well preserved and require very little treatment. Sediment inside the bottle can be removed with careful use of a high-pressure hose or with something like a wire or an ice pick. Remove exterior calcareous growth by tapping gently on the bottle with a rubber mallet or immerse it in a bath consisting of 0.2-percent solution of sulfuric acid for from several hours to as long as a week, depending on the amount of growth on it. It must then be thoroughly washed in several baths of fresh or distilled water until it is free of alkalis. Test with litmus paper to determine if the glass is free of alkalis. Upon drying, the surface of some bottles may tend to look dull or develop a very thin layer of pearly iridescence in spots. No further treatment is necessary, although the iridescence, if it is especially fragile, may tend to flake off.

It is very difficult to preserve badly decomposed glass, which is the state of most bottles predating 1750. If the glass is not impregnated in some way, it is very likely that the exterior weathering crust will crumble away when it dries out. This may be a matter of minutes or of some months, depending on the item itself. This was one of the major preservation problems encountered during the Port Royal excavation. In consultation with Dr. Robert Brill of the Corning Glass Museum, I attempted to discover why the wine bottles were recovered in a worse state of preservation than others of the same manufacture and period that were found elsewhere. The weathering crust on those at Port Royal was thicker than on other bottles of the same period, and this made them more difficult to preserve. He theorized that the heavy concentration of bauxite in the harbor sediment may have created electrolysis with the lead components in the glass, thus causing accelerated deterioration.

Most bottles predating 1750 can be cleaned and preserved in the following manner: 0.2-percent solution of sulfuric acid will remove the calcareous growth and stains. Depending on the fragility of the bottle, a high-pressure hose or probe can be used to remove the sediment inside the bottle. While the bottle is still west after being thoroughly rinsed in distilled water until free of all alkalis, bathe it in wood, denatured ethyl or rubbing alcohol. This helps remove remaining water without causing the decomposition crust to crumble away. Then, after air-drying the bottle for a short period, impregnate it with several coatings of clear lacquer spray.

Through experimentation I discovered that the above method failed to preserve the more badly decomposed bottles, such as those recovered at Port Royal. After several months the glass began flaking under the lacquer coatings, and in many cases the bottles completely disintegrated. To prevent this, we follow the same procedure described above, except that instead of coating the bottles with lacquer we immersed them for a week or two in a solution consisting of 50 percent distilled water and 50 percent vinyl acetate, which is the same material used in making the glue used in bookbinding. (It is marketed as padding cement.) After removing the bottle, we wiped off the excess solution with a slightly damp cloth before air-drying it in a cool area. After the bottle was completely dry, we coated it with several layers of lacquer.

For mending or piecing together broken glass or bottles, any number of convenient epoxy cements can be used (a small amount works best). The most important step in cementing glass is cleaning the surfaces to be joined. Caution must be exercised in cementing the glass correctly the first time, because once the cement sets, the bonds are permanent and cannot be loosened.

Different types of ceramics are affected in varying degrees by immersion in salt water. Porcelain survives the best, although its painted exterior may have eroded. Because of its nonporous surface porcelain is rarely found with any adhering calcareous marine growth. When such growth is found, however, it can be removed by tapping the object lightly with a rubber tool or by bathing it in a 10-percent solution of nitric acid. Iron or lead-oxide stains can be removed by a bath in a 5-percent solution of sulfuric acid. The sulfuric-acid bath removes both calcareous deposits and oxide stains from porcelain. Thorough washing in fresh water will remove all traces of alkalis and acids from the object.

Glazed pottery, covered as it is with a waterproof vitreous layer, survives much better than unglazed pottery. If, however, the glazed layer is incomplete or imperfect, soluble salts can get into the body of the ware and crystallize, forming efflorescence, which causes the glaze to flake off. If the glazed layer on a piece is intact, use the methods for removing calcareous deposits and oxide stains from porcelain. If the glaze is not intact, or is flaking (which occurs on a great deal of the delftware items recovered) no acid of any kind should be used to remove deposits or stains. The pieces should be immersed in fresh water to remove the sea salts, then air-dried and coated with several layers of clear plastic or lacquer spray.

No acid of any type should be used on unglazed porous pottery, such as utilityware or olive-jar pottery. Removal of calcareous deposits must be done with small tools, then the pieces should be immersed for a number of days in several baths of fresh water to remove the sea salts. To assure that these pieces are free of water they must be dehydrated in several baths of alcohol and then coated with plastic spray. This treatment should be used only on ceramic objects that show signs of crumbling. Approximately 95 percent of ceramic pieces will require no treatment other than the freshwater baths to remove sea salts.

Nature handles the removal of calcareous deposits on clay smoking pipes. After their recovery they should be air-dried. When this is completed, the pipe actually decreases slightly in size which causes the calcareous deposits to fall off. The removal of various stains on pipes is best accomplished by washing with a mild detergent and soft brush.

Repairing or piecing together all types of ceramics is relatively simple. The joints must be first cleaned of any foreign bodies and then cemented together with a cement like Durofix or Elmer's Glue. While the glue is drying the pieces should be held in place by tape or placed in a sandbox.

Organic Materials

All organic material recovered from salt water must be bathed in fresh water from two to four weeks, depending on their size, to remove all sea salts before any preservation treatment can begin. Ideally, the bath consists of running fresh water, which carries away the sea salts as they are leached from the items. Large items, like wooden ship's timbers, can be placed in a freshwater stream or river, provided the water is not contaminated by industrial waste. If a running-water bath cannot be provided, the bath water should be changed at least daily.

Such organic materials as sisal or hemp fibers, beans and pods, tortoise shell, hair, textiles, leather, horn, bone or paper will generally disintegrate totally upon drying if not treated appropriately. Sometimes organic materials such as wood or bone have been preserved underwater because they were saturated by iron oxide while lying close to iron objects and consequently became mineralized and hard in texture.

Organic animal material must first be thoroughly dehydrated in successive baths of alcohol to remove all water. The first bath should consist of 40 percent alcohol and 60 percent water, the second of 60 percent alcohol and 40 percent water, and the third of 100 percent alcohol. The length of each bath depends on the size of the object — say, an hour for a small fragment of leather and several hours for a bone object weighing several pounds. The object must next be placed in two successive baths of xylene, the first for a week and the second for four weeks In the second bath paraffin chips should be added until a saturated solution of paraffin is obtained. After the object is removed from the second bath and allowed to solidify by air-drying, a small amount of paraffin crystals may remain on the exterior of the object. They can be removed by heating the object in an oven until the excess crystals melt off or by brushing the object with a fine-bristled brush.

Very fragile organic animal materials such as small objects of ivory or horn which might suffer from preserving them with the above method, can best be preserved by being embedded in clear plastic blocks after they have been dehydrated.

Organic vegetable materials such as wood, sisal and hemp fibers, textiles, paper, and beans and pods can also be preserved by the method described above for organic animal materials, but there are several other methods that can be used. The following alum and glycerin process has been used with good results, especially on wood, because the alum crystallizes and replaces the water in the wood, preventing it from shrinking or losing its original shape. After all foreign matter has been removed, the object is immersed in a boiling solution containing equal parts, by weight, of alum, glycerin, and water. As soon as the object is placed in the solution, this bath is taken away from the heat source and allowed to cool slowly. The object should remain in the bath from one to two days, depending on its size. After the object has hardened and air-dried, it should be coated with a solution of 50 percent turpentine and 50 percent linseed oil.

The following polyethylene glycol process has also proven to be quite successful. The great advantage in using PEG is the elimination of dehydrating the object before it is immersed in its chemical bath. Polyethylene glycol is a polymer formed by the condensation of ethylene glycol into a wax-like water-soluble preservative. It is sold commercially under the trade names of Polywax and Carbowax. The length of time that the object remains in the chemical bath varies from four hours to several weeks, depending on the type of PEG used and the size of the object.

Inorganic Materials

Iron accounts for approximately 95 percent of the metal objects that will be discovered on a shipwreck. Unfortunately, iron's highly corrosive nature makes it extremely difficult to preserve. In many cases cast-iron objects corrode into a crystalline form and are so totally destroyed that only powdered oxide remains. Wrought-iron objects are not as corrosive, probably because they contain a greater nickel content. The same applies to steel, which has a high nickel content. The amount of metal remaining in an iron object can best be determined by its weight or by application of a magnet. If the object has no magnetic attraction, it is evident that it is completely oxidized. When laboratory facilities are available, this can also be determined by the use of X-ray photography or a fluoroscope.

The first step in treating ferrous metals (iron or steel) is to remove any exterior calcareous encrustations, which can be attempted only when a substantial amount of the original metal remains in the object. These deposits can best be removed from cannon and similar large objects by tapping them gently with a hammer or other hand tool. Small, delicate objects can be cleaned in ultrasonic electrical baths or chemically. Ultrasonic baths range in price from $100 dollars upward and are easy to operate. The chemical process consists of a bath in a solution of 10 percent nitric acid and 90 percent water, with several washes in fresh water to remove the alkalis.

The object must then be treated by electrochemical reduction. It is placed in a bath consisting of 10 percent sodium hydroxide and 90 percent water and soaked for a period of four to eight weeks. The object is then removed and a new bath of the same solution is made, following which the entire object is covered with zinc chips or surrounded by zinc plates. Soon after the zinc is added to the bath the solution will begin to bubble, continuing to bubble throughout the two to four weeks the object is kept in the bath. Upon removal, the object will be covered with a white coating, which can be removed by placing it in another bath consisting of 5 percent sulfuric acid and 95 percent fresh water.

The next step is placing the object in a running-water bath for at least a week, then in a bath of distilled water for another week. The bath should be tested to make sure that it is free of both alkalis and chlorides. If it is not free of these elements, then more baths in distilled water are required until there are no traces. The object is then dried, preferably in an oven at a high temperature. After drying it can be coated by melted paraffin wax or a clear synthetic plastic or lacquer to seal the exterior and prevent further corrosion.

When little or none of the original ferrous metal remains, objects can be treated by one of the following methods. The object can be embedded in a plastic resin, such as Selectron 5,000. First, the object must be thoroughly dehydrated, either by heat or the alcohol process; otherwise it will continue to disintegrate inside the plastic blocks. This can be a lengthy process if the object is large, because only very thin layers of the plastic can be placed in the mold containing the object.

When an object is found in encrusted conglomerate, an exact replica can be made in plaster of paris or other materials. By X-raying the object, its size and location in the conglomerate can be determined, then the conglomerate must be cut in half by a diamond saw. The two halves will be hollow inside where the original object was and will serve as the mold into which the plaster of paris is placed to make the replica. Another method is to drill a hole into the conglomerate and force the plaster-of paris compound into the cavity. After hardening, the exterior encrustation can be removed by grinding or hand tools.

Nonferrous metals are always recovered in a far better state of preservation than the ferrous and are usually easier to clean and preserve. Some of the metals are recovered in such condition that they require no treatment other than cleaning with fine steel wool and water.

A gold object is almost always recovered as richly gleaming as the day it was made and requires no preservation treatment. Occasionally gold will be tarnished by close underwater association with other metals. In this case soak the piece in a bath of 10 percent nitric acid and 90 percent water. The same bath also removes calcareous deposits on gold.

Silver is affected in varying degrees under water, depending on conditions. A silver coin lying on the sea floor and not protected by electrolysis from other metals — even other silver coins — may be converted to silver sulfide, and nothing can be done to preserve it, other than casting it in plastic. When this occurs, a silver coin or other small object will weigh as little as one-fifth of its original weight and may be two or three times its original thickness. Caution must be exercised in handling silver in this fragile condition, as it will easily disintegrate into powder.

When silver has been protected by electrolysis, it will survive intact, sometimes with only a superficial amount of corrosion which can be removed by the electrochemical bath described above for preserving ferrous metals.

Another method is the electrolytic reduction process. The corroded silver object is made the negative electrode (cathode) and is placed between two plates of sheet iron (acting as the positive electrode, or anode) in a glass or plastic container filled with water and a 5-percent amount of caustic soda, which acts as the electrolyte. Electrical current, generally from a six- or 12-volt battery, is also required. The object is connected by copper wire to the negative pole of the battery, and the iron anodes are connected to the positive pole through an ammeter and adjustable resistance unit. When current passes into the bath, hydrogen evolves at the cathode, with the result that the corrosion is gradually reduced. As the reduction progresses, chlorides are transferred from the cathode to the iron anode. The length of the process depends on the amount of corrosion on the object. The object should be removed and inspected periodically until all corrosion has been removed. When this has been completed, there will be a thinner layer of insoluble oxides and metallic powder on the object which can be removed by brushing under running water. Then the silver object should be rubbed with a paste of water and baking soda.

On some occasions, e.g. when large amounts of silver coins or items are found together, the majority will be in a very good state of preservation and only require a cleaning with the paste method to remove the black silver-sulfide patina on them.

Pewter is generally found in a good state of preservation. Of the pewter recovered from the sunken city of Port Royal, about 20 percent required very little treatment. Rubbing it with a soft cloth in water and a mild detergent removed a thin black film from its surface, and its luster was restored by the paste treatment. The remaining 80 percent was recovered with only a small amount of external corrosion and occasionally with small amounts of calcareous deposits. Both were removed by immersion in a bath consisting of a solution of 20 percent hydrochloric acid and 80 percent fresh water followed by thorough washings in running fresh water, generally for a period of several hours. After the surface was rubbed gently with fine steel wool to remove the black patina, the object was again placed in a bath of running water for several hours. The same paste treatment is used to restore its original luster.

On some sites, pewter is occasionally found badly corroded, and in some cases the only means of preservation is to embed it in plastic. Badly corroded pewter can be cleaned and preserved as follows: A lye bath is prepared by dissolving a pint of lye in two gallons of fresh boiling water. When the object is placed in the solution, this bath is taken off its heat source and allowed to cool. Generally, a period of 10 to 30 minutes is required to remove the corrosion. Caution must be observed to prevent the lye solution from contact with skin or eyes. Then the same procedure is carried out as on pewter objects cleaned by the hydrochloric-acid process. If the object is bent out of its original shape, the best time to restore it, normally with a rubber mallet, is when it is just removed from the lye bath and is warm and malleable.

Lead changes very little in the sea other than acquiring a thin coating of lead oxide on its surface, which is easily removed by immersion in a bath of 10 percent acetic acid and 90 percent fresh water, followed by a running-water bath of several hours. Because lead is naturally soft, many pieces are bent and lose their original shape on shipwrecks.

Copper, brass and bronze objects also usually suffer few ill affects from salt-water immersion. Calcareous deposits on large objects can be removed by tapping with a rubber mallet and on smaller objects by immersion in a bath consisting of 10 percent nitric acid and 90 percent fresh water followed by a washing for a short time in running water. The acid bath is used to remove the green patina found on these objects, which can also be removed with judicious use of steel wool.

Since objects made entirely of magnesium, tin, aluminum, zinc or nickel will not be discovered on a shipwreck predating 1825, their preservation is not discussed here.

Chapter One

Canada

Bad weather, rough seas, and ice-cold water throughout most of the year make Canada one of the least attractive areas in the Western Hemisphere for underwater explorations and salvage work. As a consequence, there has been very little exploration of old shipwrecks in Canada's waters. In fact, most Canadian divers who are interested in shipwrecks head south to Bermuda or the Bahamas for their diving.

There are exceptions. During the summer months amateur divers under the supervision of archaeologists from the Toronto Museum and the National Historical Park Service have been employed for the past six years to locate and salvage several small vessels that were sunk in lakes and rivers during the French and Indian Wars.

The only major salvage operation in Canadian waters occurred during the summers of 1965 and 1966, when three amateur divers located the 18th-century French warship *Le Chameau* off Cape Breton Island, Nova Scotia. They found the site by dragging a grappling hook where the ship was known to have been lost, and when it snagged on something a diver went down to inspect the object. The shipwreck was first located in 1914, when a helmet diver surveying a modern shipwreck spotted gold and silver coins on the sea floor. He planned to recover the treasure as soon as his modern shipwreck job was finished, but he drowned a few days later and the secret of its location died with him and remained unknown for half a century

The three divers who worked the site in the 1960s, Alex Storm, David MacEachern and Harvey MacLeod, were faced with hostile conditions. The water temperature was never higher than 45 degrees F. and high tides meant there were always currents of several knots around the site. During the two summers, however, they discovered over 2,000 gold French Louis d'or coins and 11,000 silver French livres coins, as well as a silver pocket watch, silver and pewter cutlery, weapons of different types, a vast number of cannonballs, cannon, ceramics and many other artifacts.

When they began work on the *Chameau*, there were no laws concerning the recovery of sunken treasure, but soon after they brought up their first finds the Canadian government ordered them to turn everything over to officials while the matter was investigated. This prevented them from selling anything to raise more capital to carry on their work. A court battle over legal ownership of the treasure and artifacts dragged on into 1968 when the courts decided that the government should retain only 10 percent of the find and return the rest to the salvors. The cargo manifest of the ship stated that she was carrying over 300,000 livres, so the trio still has a great deal of work left to complete the job. The government has since passed a law stating that no work on old shipwrecks can be undertaken without permission from the National Historical Park Service. The law also requires that a competent archaeologist supervise all such salvage operations.

In 1978 a team of underwater archaeologists from Parks Canada, the Canadian government agency responsible for national parks, discovered a Basque whaling ship in the harbor of Red Bay, Labrador. They had been led to the site by historian Selma Huxley Barkham whose sleuthing in the Spanish archives turned up information regarding the loss in 1565 of a whaling vessel called the *San Juan*. The archaeologists found the *San Juan*, which is Canada's oldest shipwreck, on their first exploratory dive. The whole lower hull was intact. The frigid water had protected it from sea worms, which would have devoured a wooden ship in such shallow, exposed conditions.

The sleepy fishing port of Red Bay was invaded by a team of 50 underwater archaeologists and support staff the following summer, and excavation of the wreck began. Directed by Dr. James Tuck and Robert Grenier, the excavation continued for seven more summers. To survive in the icy waters, divers had hot water from the surface continuously circulated through their rubber suits. Though frigid, the sea was crystal clear, which greatly facilitated the collection of archaeological data.

When they removed the mud and marl covering the site, the Canadian archaeologists found one of the best preserved lower hulls in the western hemisphere. Instead of bringing material to the surface, they made latex molds of all the wooden remains in situ. Later these molds were used to reconstruct a model of the ship. When the excavation was completed, the entire site was reburied and left intact for future study.

The *San Juan* was a particularly significant find because it furnished modern scholars with tens of thousands of fascinating 16th-century maritime artifacts, many of them very rare, including half of a brass navigator's astrolabe, the ship's compass, intact wooden barrels for storing whale oil, and even the ship's whaleboat, the only one of its kind in existence. The extremely low water temperature had preserved the wreck's oak timbers so well that they still shone with a honeyed hue. Generally, next to ballast stones, iron objects account for the greatest quantity of things found on old shipwrecks. The only iron objects on the *San Juan* site, however, were an anchor and a small swivel gun. No one is sure why this is so.

Recent excavations in the pioneer field of deep-water archaeology, where the water is very cold and deeper than compressed air diving capabilities, have also yielded surprisingly little iron. Two other Basque whaling ships of the same vintage were discovered in Red Bay in 1983 and 1984 by Parks Canada divers. Preliminary investigation indicates they are in an excellent state of preservation, and the government plans to excavate them when and if funds become available.

One of the greatest concentrations of shipwrecks in Canadian waters is around Sable Island, located 150 miles off the coast of Nova Scotia. At its strategic location far from the mainland where several different ocean currents flow toward the island, at least 500 ships have wrecked on Sable. Although more than 90 percent of these wrecks are dated after 1825, many of them carried various amounts of treasure as well as interesting cargoes. Working conditions in these waters, however, are extremely difficult and shifting sands have tended to cover most of the ships very soon after they wrecked.

Shipwrecks in Canadian Waters

Year Sometime before 1583. English warship *Delight* in the fleet of Admiral Sir Humphrey Gilbert sank on a shoal near Sable Island, off Nova Scotia.

Year 1710. In late August, a fleet of New Englanders set out to capture Port Royal, a port in eastern Canada, but one of the troop-transport ships from Rhode Island, the sloop *Caesar*, Captain Jeremiah Tay (or Taye), ran ashore on Digby Cut in the Bay of Fundy and 26 men were lost.

Year 1725. The French frigate of war *Le Chameau* sailed from Louisburg, a French stronghold on the eastern tip of Cape Breton Island, Nova Scotia, heading for Quebec carrying a valuable treasure of gold and silver as well as a large number of passengers. As the ship was rounding Cape Lorenbec, Nova Scotia, a squall struck and the ship capsized and sank with almost a complete loss of crew and passengers. Many of the bodies washed ashore, but nothing of the wreck was ever found until recent times.

Year 1748. During a freak violent wind on February 26, nearly every French merchant and warship in the harbor of Louisburg, Cape Breton Island, Nova Scotia, was sunk.

Year 1752. During a hurricane that struck Louisburg Harbor on October 1, over 50 merchant and warships were driven ashore or sunk.

Year 1752. English merchantman *Elizabeth*, Captain Carter, coming from Poole, England, was lost in the harbor of Fogo, in Newfoundland.

Year 1753. During a very bad storm on October 7, over 40 large ships were wrecked at Cape Breton Island, Nova Scotia.

Year 1755. English warship *H.M.S. Mars*, 64 guns, Captain John Amherst, was wrecked at Halifax, Nova Scotia, in June.

Year 1755. English merchantman *Jersey*, Captain Giffred, coming from Jersey Island, off the coast of France, was wrecked on the coast of Newfoundland.

Year 1757. During a hurricane on September 24, two English warships were sunk in Louisburg Harbor: *H.M.S. Tilbury*, 60 guns, Captain Henry Barnsley, and *H.M.S. Ferret*, 10 guns, Captain Arthur Upton.

Year 1757. English merchantman *Buchanan*, Captain Lawrence, sailing from Gibraltar to Maryland, was captured by a French privateer and on her passage to Louisburg was wrecked on Sable Island, Nova Scotia, on April 22.

Canadian weather can require unusual recovery techniques such as the ROV that recovered these gold bars in 1,500 feet of water from a 1622 wreck off Dry Tortugas.

Year 1758. The following ships were scuttled by the French in Louisburg Harbor on June 28 because they did not have enough men to defend against an impending attack by the English: *Apollon*, 50 guns; *Fidile*, 26 guns; *Chirre and Biche*, each of 16 guns. While still awaiting the English attack, three of the major French warships were burned by accident in the same harbor: *Entreprenant*, 74 guns, *Capricieux* and *Cilibre*, each of 64 guns. During the English attack, which took place a few weeks later, an English frigate, *H.M.S. Tilbury*, the payship for Admiral Edward Boscawen's fleet, was wrecked on a reef near Louisburg.

Year 1759. Four ships were wrecked in the St. Lawrence River: the English warship *H.M.S. Terrible*, 74 guns; and three French warships: *Le Smecterre* and *Le Soleil Royal*, each of 24 guns, and *Duc de Fronfac*, 20 guns.

Year 1760. English merchantman *Cupid*, Captain Trimett, sailing from Newfoundland to the Leeward Islands, was lost in bad weather returning to St. John's Harbor, Newfoundland.

Year 1760. Two English warships were wrecked in the St. Lawrence River: *H.M.S. Lowestoft*, 28 guns, Captain Joseph Deane, on May 17; and *H.M.S. Eurus*, 20 guns, Captain John Elphinstone.

Year 1760. During an attack by an English fleet commanded by Captain Byron, 25 French ships were sunk in Chaleur Bay, in the Gulf of St. Lawrence, on July 8. Twenty-two of the ships were small vessels carrying provisions and stores; the other three were warships: *Marchault*, 32 guns, *Bienfaisant*, 22 guns, and *Marquis Marlozee*, 18 guns.

Year 1761. Four ships were lost on the St. Lawrence River: the English ship *Success*, Captain Friend, wrecked on the river approaching Quebec, coming from London; English merchantman *General Gage*, Captain Power, wrecked in the river after leaving Quebec for London; English ship *Isaac and William*, Captain Gregory, lost on the Orleans Shoals in the river after leaving Quebec for London, but her cargo was saved; and the French warship *Leopard*, 60 guns, arrived at Quebec with the plague on board and was burned.

Year 1762. English merchantman *Charming Nancy*, Captain Hume, coming from London, sank at Quebec but most of her cargo was recovered.

Year 1762. English ship *Charming Nancy*, Captain Haynes, sailing from London to Halifax, Nova Scotia, was lost entering this port and nothing was salvaged from her.

Markings on this bronze Dutch cannon identify it as belonging to the Dutch East Indian Company, with the "A" indicating ownership by its Amsterdam chapter.

Year 1763. Two English merchantmen were wrecked in the St. Lawrence River: *Providence*, Captain Pinkham, sailing from Quebec to Ireland and London, the crew and some of her cargo were saved; and the *Good Intent*, Captain Wood, sailing from London to Quebec, most of her cargo was saved.

Year 1763. English ship *Bonetta*, Captain Frampton, sailing to Poole, England, was lost near St. Mary's in Newfoundland with a total loss of crew and cargo.

Year 1764. Three English merchantmen were lost in the Gulf of St. Lawrence: *Lord Elbank*, Captain Warrell, sailing from New York to Quebec, was lost near Gaspe, New Brunswick, but part of her cargo was saved; *Margaret & Harriot*, Captain Cordova, sailing from Plymouth, England, to Quebec, was lost on rocks near the island of Anticosti, one member of the crew drowned and the rest were forced to spend six months in great misery on that deserted island; and the *Greyhound*, Captain Shaw, sailing from Liverpool to Quebec, was lost out of sight of land but her crew was saved.

Year 1765. English troop-transport *Loyal Pitt*, Captain Davis, sailing from London to Quebec, was lost in strong gale of wind on the St. Lawrence River between the islands of Caudre and Travers on August 6.

Year 1765. A small American schooner, acting as a tender for the frigate *H.M.S. Maidstone*, foundered on the south shoal of George's Bank, off Nova Scotia; all 12 of her crew perished.

Year 1766. American or English ship *Minehead*, Captain Gwyn, sailing from Bristol, England, to Boston, was a total wreck on Sable Island, off Nova Scotia, 15 of the crew drowned.

Year 1768. English ship *Mary & Susannah*, Captain Muire, sailing from London to Quebec, was a total loss in the St. Lawrence River.

Year 1771. Ship of unknown registry, *Rose*, Captain King, sailing from Quebec to Cork, Ireland, was lost on the St. Lawrence River.

Year 1771. Three English merchantmen were lost at Nova Scotia: *Nassau*, Captain Smith, sailing from London to Boston, was a total wreck near Canso but her crew was saved; *Swansey*, Captain David, sailing from Rhode Island to Newfoundland, was lost on Sable Island; and the sloop *Grandy* (or Granby), Captain Hay, was wrecked off the Lighthouse Rocks in Halifax Harbor and all 16 men aboard her were lost. She carried military stores and 3,000 pounds sterling in coins for the Halifax Navy Yards.

Year 1773. English merchantman *Sophia*, Captain Hastington, sailing from Philadelphia to Quebec, was lost on Sable Island, Nova Scotia.

Year 1773. English ship *Matilda*, Captain Blyth, sailing from Philadelphia to Quebec, was lost on October 18 in the St. Lawrence River after being on the rocks for five days.

Year 1775. English merchantman *Sally*, Captain Brame, sailing from London to Quebec, was lost off Newfoundland.

Year 1775. English warship, *H.M.S. Savage*, 8 guns, Captain Hugh Bromelye, was lost near Louisburg, Cape Breton Island, Nova Scotia.

Year 1776. Two English ships were lost near Halifax, Nova Scotia: *Dolphin*, Captain Thomas, sailing from Newfoundland to Halifax, was lost near that port; *Euphrates*, Captain Gordon, a transport coming from London, was lost entering the port of Halifax.

Year 1776. An English transport ship, *Favorite*, Captain Bishipprick, was lost in the Gulf of St. Lawrence.

Year 1776. Two English ships were lost on the St. Lawrence River: *Bosphorus*, a victualer; and *St. George*, Captain Gill, was wrecked on Red Island in the river but the crew was saved.

Year 1777. Three ships were lost off Nova Scotia: English ship *Mary & Frances*, Captain Sutton, sailing from Cork, Ireland, to Quebec, was lost in the Bay of Canso; the English ship *Aurora* was lost on Sable Island; when survivors got ashore from this wreck they found seven Negro women who had been wrecked there 16 years earlier on a French ship.

Year 1777. English merchantman *Lock*, Captain Gowland, coming from London, sank in the St. Lawrence River.

Year 1777. Two English warships foundered off Newfoundland: *H.M.S. Pegasus*, 16 guns, Captain J. Hamilton Gore; and *H.M.S. Vestal*, 20 guns, Captain James Shirley.

Year 1778. English warship *H.M.S. Dispatch*, 14 guns, Captain J. Botham, capsized in the Gulf of St. Lawrence.

Year 1778. Three English warships were lost off Newfoundland: the armed transport *Grampus*, 32 guns, Captain John Frodsham, foundered; *H.M.S. Cupid*, 16 guns, Captain William Carlyon, foundered; and *H.M.S. Spy*, 12 guns, Captain Thomas Lenox Frederick, was wrecked near the island.

Year 1779. English armed-transport *Tortoise*, 32 guns, Captain Jahleel Brenton, foundered off Newfoundland.

Year 1779. Two ships were lost near Nova Scotia: a ship of unknown registry, *Fame Murphy*, was wrecked on Sable Island; and the English armed-transport *North*, 20 guns, Captain George Selby, was wrecked near the coast of Nova Scotia.

Year 1780. English ship *Margaretta Christina* foundered on a voyage between Halifax, Nova Scotia, and Newfoundland but the crew was saved.

Year 1780. English merchantman *Jane*, Captain Wilson, sailing from London to Halifax, was lost on Sable Island, Nova Scotia, but the crew was saved.

Year 1780. Three English ships were lost at Quebec: the *Sharp*, the *Valiant*, and the *Lizard*.

Year 1780. English warship *H.M.S. Viper*, 16 guns, Captain John Augusta, was wrecked in the Gulf of St. Lawrence on October 11.

Year 1780. Three English merchantmen were lost at Newfoundland: *William*, Captain Washman, coming from Lisbon, was wrecked on the coast and all of its crew perished; *Peggy*, also known by the alias *Wolf*, coming from Liverpool, was wrecked on St. Peter's Island; and the *Adventure*, sailing from St. Eustatius Island to Newfoundland was forced onshore by an American privateer near the Port of St. John's, vessel and cargo a total loss.

Year 1781. English ship *Ann*, Captain M'Clue, sailing from Quebec to Barbados, was wrecked on the Isle of Orleans, in the Gulf of St. Lawrence.

Year 1781. English ship, *Captain Mitchell*, sailing from London to Quebec, was captured by an American privateer and later wrecked on Sable Island, Nova Scotia.

Year 1781. Three English ships sank in the St. Lawrence River: *General Haldemand*, Captain Love, one man drowned; *Harvey*, Captain Harvey [sic], her crew was saved; and the *London*, Captain M'Cullough, her crew was saved.

Year 1781. Two English ships wrecked at Newfoundland: warship *H.M.S. Dutchess of Cumberland*, 16 guns, Captain Edward March; and merchantman *Venus*, Captain Millet, sailing from Jamaica to Quebec, wrecked at Cape Ray, with a total loss of men and cargo.

Year 1782. Two English ships were lost going up the St. Lawrence River. One was not identified, except as a transport, and the other was the *Christie*, Captain Bodfield.

Year 1782. Two English warships were lost at Newfoundland: *H.M.S. Placentia*, 14 guns, Captain Charles Anderson, wrecked near the island; and *H.M.S. Hector*, 74 guns, Captain John Bourchier, sank on the Grand Banks of Newfoundland.

Year 1782. Two English merchantmen were lost at Nova Scotia: *Endeavour*, Captain Simpson, coming from Exeter, England, to Quebec, was wrecked 25 leagues eastward of Halifax, in December, and part of its cargo was saved; *Tom*, Captain Smart, sailing from Antigua to Halifax, was lost at the entrance of the port but all of its cargo was saved.

Year 1783. Three English merchantmen were lost on the St. Lawrence River: *Hope*, Captain Cameron, sailing from Tortola to Quebec, was lost two leagues below Tadefase but part of its cargo was saved; *Betsey*, Captain Anderson, sailing from Quebec to Barbados, was totally wrecked by a violent gust of wind on Hare Island on October 24 and one of the crew drowned; and the *Noble*, Captain Taylor, sailing from Halifax to Quebec, was lost near Quebec but all of its cargo was saved.

Year 1783. Three English ships lost at Nova Scotia: *Peter*, Captain Bruce, sailing from St. Lucia Island to Halifax, was lost near that port; a transport ship, *Lion*, Captain Davis, was lost near Cape Sable; and a merchantman, *Sampson*, Captain Wood Whitehove, sailing to Quebec, was totally wrecked on Cape Breton Island and three of the crew drowned.

Year 1785. English merchantman *Coleman*, Captain Pickmore, was wrecked on Newfoundland but the crew was saved.

Year 1785. English packet boat *Hermoine*, sailing from Halifax to Port Roseway, was wrecked on Cape Sable, Nova Scotia.

Year 1785. English merchantman, *Warrior*, Captain M'Donough, sailing from St. John's Island to Cadíz, was wrecked at Merrygomish in the Gulf of St. Lawrence on December 28, her total cargo was lost but the crew was saved.

Year 1786. Ship of unknown registry, *Telemachus*, Captain Sargeant, sailing from Georgia to Amsterdam, was lost with most of her cargo on Sable Island, Nova Scotia.

Year 1786. English ship *Renuse*, Captain Bully, was lost at Newfoundland.

Year 1788. English merchantman *Favorite*, Captain Robertson, sailing from London to Quebec, was lost on the lower part of the St. Lawrence River.

Year 1788. English merchantman *Elizabeth and Mary*, Captain Lethbrige, was lost at Newfoundland.

Year 1788. Three English merchantmen lost at Nova Scotia: *White*, Captain Gill, sailing from Cowes, England, to Quebec was lost at Seaton off the Cape Breton Island; *William*, Captain Losh, sailing from London to Quebec, was lost near Cape Breton on April 28; and *Betsey*, Captain Young, sailing from Scotland to Halifax, was lost on the coast but the crew was saved.

Year 1790. Ship of unknown registry, *St. Joseph*, Captain Barnveth, was lost onshore at Newfoundland shortly after sailing from there.

Year 1790. English ship *Lynx*, Captain Murphy, sailing from Newfoundland to Cape Breton, was lost on July 9 near the Laun Islands, in the Gulf of St. Lawrence.

Year 1791. English merchantman *Fanny*, Captain Bugs, arriving from Grenada Island, was burned at St. Andrews, New Brunswick.

Year 1791. Four English merchantmen lost around Newfoundland: *Hope*, Captain Anderson, coming from London, wrecked on the coast; *Monkey*, Captain Palmer, was a total loss on the Banks of Newfoundland but the crew was saved; unidentified ship sailing from Liverpool to Quebec was lost off Cape Ray; and *Fame*, Captain Meggetson, sailing from London to Quebec, was wrecked on St. Pierre Island, near Newfoundland, but the crew and part of her cargo were saved.

Year 1792. Two ships of unknown registry were lost on Sable Island, Nova Scotia: one was not identified; the other was the *Rambler*, Captain Kaquet, sailing from Philadelphia to Boston.

Year 1793. Three English merchantmen were wrecked on the coast of Newfoundland: *Diana*, Captain Greaves, coming from Dartmouth, England, but the crew was saved; *Hornet*, Captain Priddes, coming from St. Ubes, England; and Manacles, Captain Jones.

Year 1794. Two English merchantmen were lost on the coast of Labrador: *Charlotte*, Captain Godfrey, coming from Dartmouth, England; and *Polly*, Captain Graves.

Year 1794. English warship, *H.M.S. Placentia*, Captain Alexander Shippard, was lost near Newfoundland.

Year 1794. Two English ships were lost on the St. Lawrence River: *Augusta*, Captain Cole, sailing from Quebec to the West Indies, was burned by accident on October 24; and the schooner *Charlotte*, sailing from Quebec to Halifax.

Year 1795. Two English merchantmen lost at Nova Scotia: *York*, Captain Norton, sailing from Liverpool to Boston, was wrecked at Cape Negro; and *Orb*, Captain Brigs, sailing from Liverpool to Halifax, was wrecked on Sable Island on January 6.

Year 1795. Two unidentified English merchantmen were lost on the Grand Banks of Newfoundland but both crews were saved.

Year 1796. English warship *H.M.S. Active*, 32 guns, Captain Edward Leverson Gower, was wrecked in the St. Lawrence River on July 5.

Year 1797. Two English ships were lost at Nova Scotia: merchantman *Stag*, leaving Halifax Harbor for Jamaica, overset when leaving the harbor and was lost; warship H.M.S. Tribunee, 32 guns, Captain Scory Barker, was wrecked near Halifax on November 16.

Year 1798. English warship *H.M.S. Rover*, 16 guns, Captain George Irwin, was wrecked on June 23 in the Gulf of St. Lawrence.

Year 1798. English merchantman *Susannah*, Captain Doucett, sailing from Quebec to Halifax, was lost in the St. Lawrence River.

Year 1798. English merchantman *Britannia*, Captain Adney, was lost at New Brunswick but the crew was saved.

Year 1798. During a gale in Halifax Harbor on September 25, many ships were sunk. Among them were two American ships: the *Libertye* and *Penelope*; a Danish ship; the English warship *H.M.S. Lynx*; and the brig *Betsey*, of unknown registry. Total loss of shipping was over 100,000 pounds sterling.

Year 1799. English merchantman *Lucy*, sailing from Quebec to Greenock, England, was lost on September 11 on the coast of Labrador but part of her cargo was saved.

Year 1800. English merchantman *Enterprize*, Captain Cummings, sailing from London to Quebec, was lost in November on Anticosti Island in the Gulf of St. Lawrence.

Year 1800. English ship *Francis*, sailing from London to Halifax, was totally lost on Sable Island, Nova Scotia, and all of the crew perished.

Year 1800. English merchantman *Turk*, Captain Thomas, sailing from Bristol, England, to Newfoundland, was lost on the Banks of Newfoundland.

Year 1801. English merchantman *Sovereign*, Captain Ramshaw, sailing from London to Quebec, was lost in May at Cape Breton, Nova Scotia.

Year 1801. Two English merchantmen were lost in the St. Lawrence River: *Industry*, Captain Young, sailing from Quebec to Leith, Scotland; and *Dalrymple*, Captain Marsh, sailing from Barbados to Quebec, but part of its cargo was saved.

Year 1802. Two English warships foundered off Newfoundland: *H.M.S. Scout*, 18 guns, Captain Henry Duncan, and *H.M.S. Fly*, 14 guns, Captain Thomas Duvall, both with a total loss of crews.

Year 1802. Three English merchantmen were lost at Nova Scotia: *Union*, Captain Hooper, sailing from Spain for Boston, wrecked on July 10 on Sable Island, but the crew was saved; *Mars*, Captain Clemente, sailing to India, and *Eagle*, sailing to the West Indies, were lost at Cape Sable but their crews were saved.

Year 1802. Ship of unknown registry, *Terpsichore*, Captain Burge, sailing from Quebec to Bristol, England, was lost on Flatt Island in the Gulf of St. Lawrence but its crew was saved.

Year 1802. During the winter months 10 ships were lost on the St. Lawrence River but only one was identified: *Mary*, Captain Montburne, sailing from Newfoundland to Quebec.

Year 1803. Twelve unidentified vessels lost on the St. Lawrence River.

Year 1805. English merchantman *Atlanta*, Captain Gammell, sailing from Grenada Island to Halifax, was wrecked at Torbay, Newfoundland, on January 29 but part of its cargo was saved.

Year 1806. Two ships of unknown registry were lost in the St. Lawrence River: the brig *Mineroa*, heading to Quebec, on March 19; and the *Liberty*, Captain Clark, sailing from Quebec to Plymouth, England.

Year 1807. English storeship *H.M.S. William*, 12 guns, Captain John Foxton, was wrecked in the Gut of Canso, Nova Scotia, on November 11.

Year 1807. English schooner *Doncet*, coming from Halifax, was totally lost in the St. Lawrence River but the crew was saved.

Year 1808. Three English ships were lost on the St. Lawrence River: warship *H.M.S. Banterer*, 22 guns, Captain Alexander Shippard, on December 4; merchantman *Speeddwell*, Captain Lawson, sailing from Madeira Island to Quebec, but most of its cargo was saved; and the merchantman *Hamilton*, Captain Gilchrist, sailing from Clyde, Scotland, to Quebec, but most of the cargo was saved.

Year 1810. English warship *H.M.S. Plumper*, 12 guns, Captain W. Frissel, foundered in the St. Lawrence River in November.

Year 1812. English warship *H.M.S. Avenger*, 16 guns, Captain Urry Johnson, was wrecked off St. John's, Newfoundland, on October 8.

Year 1812. Three English warships were lost at Nova Scotia: *H.M.S. Chubb*, 4 guns, Captain Samuel Nisbett, capsized off Halifax on August 14 with all hands lost; *H.M.S. Emulous*, 18 guns, Captain Williams Howe Mulcaster, and *H.M.S. Barbadoes*, 28 guns, Captain Thomas Huskisson, were wrecked on Sable Island on August 3 and September 28, the latter ship was carrying over $500,000 in gold and silver specie and bullion.

Year 1813. English warship *H.M.S. Atalante*, 18 guns, Captain Frederick Hickey, was wrecked off Halifax, Nova Scotia, on November 10.

Year 1813. English warship *H.M.S. Bold*, 12 guns, Captain John Skekel, was wrecked on Prince Edward Island, in the Gulf of St. Lawrence, on September 27.

Year 1813. English warship *H.M.S. Tweed*, 18 guns, Captain William Mather, was wrecked in Shoal Bay, Newfoundland, on November 5.

Year 1814. Three English warships were lost near Halifax, Nova Scotia: *H.M.S. Fantome*, 18 guns, Captain Thomas Sykes, wrecked on November 24; *H.M.S. Cuttle*, 4 guns, foundered: and *H.M.S. Herring*, 4 guns, Captain John Murray, foundered; date of losses of last two ships not known.

Year 1814. English troopship, *H.M.S. Leopard*, 50 guns, Captain Edward Lowther Crofton, was wrecked on Anticosti Island, in the Gulf of St. Lawrence, on June 28.

Year 1815. English troopship, *H.M.S. Penelopee*, 36 guns, Captain James Galloway, was wrecked off Newfoundland on May 1.

Year 1822. English warship, *H.M.S. Drake*, 10 guns, Captain Charles Adolphus Baker, was wrecked with the loss of many lives off Newfoundland on June 20.

Year 1822. French ship *L'Americaine*, carrying over a million dollars in gold and silver bullion and specie, was lost in 72 feet of water off Wallace Lake, on Sable Island, Nova Scotia.

Chapter Two

The United States

Since the Abandoned Shipwreck Act of 1987 was passed, every state bordering the sea and the Great Lakes has enacted laws relevant to shipwrecks and other underwater cultural resources. Before attempting to carry out salvage work in any body of water in the United States, it is essential to know both local and federal regulations. In many states unlawful recovery of artifacts from a shipwreck can result in seizure of the vessel used, large fines and even incarceration.

Due to changing underwater-visibility conditions, the best time of the year to search for and salvage a shipwreck varies throughout the states. It is advisable for prospective salvors to make their own investigations. Some areas have rather unusual seasons in which diving conditions are the best. Off the Gulf Coast of Texas, for example, the water is the clearest in winter.

I have excluded from the following list a total of 1,167 shipwrecks about which I found references in documents because their locations were too vague. For example, over 300 shipwrecks were listed only as being lost on "the New England Coast;" others were lost on "the Carolinas," on "the American Coast," or on "the North American Continent."

I have listed only a few shipwrecks on the Pacific coast, because there was virtually no shipping at all in this area prior to 1825. There are books listing numerous treasure-laden Manila galleons lost off the coast of California on Santa Catalina Island, Cortez Bank and elsewhere. Many divers have searched in vain for these shipwrecks. According to my research they never existed. There are two known galleons off the California coast, however: at Drake's Bay off Cape Mendocino and another off the coast of Oregon.

I have made a separate chapter to cover Florida waters because of the extraordinary number of shipwrecks there.

Shipwrecks in U.S. Waters

East Coast

Maine

Year 1743. English warship *H.M.S. Astrea*, Captain Robert Swanton, was accidentally burned at the mouth of the Piscataqua River and several of the crew perished.

Year 1758. English merchantman *Phoenix*, Captain Barter, sailing from England to Boston, wrecked in Casco Bay but some of her cargo was saved.

Year 1779. Four American warships were burned on August 14 at Portland to prevent their capture by the British: *Warren*, 32 guns, Captain Dudley Saltonstall; *Diligent*, 14 guns, Captain Brown; *Hazard*, 16 guns, Captain John Foster Williams; and the *Tyrannicide*, 14 guns, Captain Cathcart. Some of the cannon were recovered several years later.

Year 1807. American merchant schooner *Charles*, Captain Adams, was wrecked on a reef of rocks to the westward of the Portland Lighthouse and only six of her crew of twenty-two were saved.

New Hampshire

Year 1760. English merchantman *Friends Adventure*, Captain Hamilton, sailing for Jamaica, was lost when leaving Portsmouth Harbor.

Year 1774. American merchantman *Scripio*, Captain Moore, sailing for the West Indies, was wrecked on a rock at Fernands Point in Piscataqua Harbor.

Year 1780. Three unidentified American merchantmen returning from Jamaica with rum and sugar products were totally lost on Appledore Island, on the Isle of Shoals, and many persons from the crews were lost.

Year 1817. American merchantman *Commerce*, Captain Roberts, sailing from Jamaica to New York, was totally lost on May 14 on Portsmouth Beach but the crew and some of her cargo of rum were saved.

Massachusetts

Year 1614. The earliest known shipwreck in this state was an unidentified French trading vessel which went aground off Peddock's Island near Boston. The Indians killed all of the men aboard and burned the vessel, probably in retaliation for some injustice.

Year 1624. Small English vessel, *Sparrow Hawk*, carrying settlers and supplies to the newly founded Virginia Colony, was wrecked on the beach near the site of the present town of Orleans on Cape Cod. She was recently excavated and many recovered items were placed in a museum.

Year 1635. During a gale the 400-ton British merchant ship *Great Hope*, arriving from Ipswich, England with a very valuable cargo, was totally lost at Hoffe's Point near Charleston (Boston).

Year 1636. British bark *Warwich*, 10 cannon, sank near the mouth of the Neponset River but nothing else known about this disaster.

Year 1640. British merchant ship *Mary Rose* of 200 tons, 32 guns, was anchored off Charleston (Boston) on July 27 carrying a large amount of silver specie and a cargo of powder. She caught afire, exploded and went down. There was only one survivor.

Year 1678. An unidentified French merchantman coming from Canada with a cargo of hides was totally lost on Nantucket Shoals.

Year 1682. An unidentified brig of about 100 tons arriving from the West Indies attempted to enter Boston Harbor during a blinding snow storm and wrecked on a reef between Faur Bar and Deer Island. Only 10 of her crew were saved.

Year 1697. American brig *Providence*, Captain Michael Gill, returning from Barbados with a cargo of rum, wrecked on Harding's Ledge near Boston in a storm on September 28 and was a total loss. In recent years divers recovered three of her iron guns.

Year 1709. English warship *H.M.S. Solebay*, 32 guns, was totally lost on December 25 at Boston Neck and all of her crew perished.

Year 1714. English sloop of war *H.M.S. Hazard*, bringing munitions from England, wrecked in Green Bay, 30 miles from Boston, all of her crew perished.

Year 1717. Pirate ship *Whidah* (or *Whydah*), Captain "Black Sam" Bellamy, wrecked on a shoal near Wellfleet on Cape Cod, only one of her crew of 102 survived. She was reported to be carrying a considerable treasure at this time, but this probably isn't so. In 1984 Barry Clifford located the wreck and recovered more than 1,000 silver and gold coins, several small gold ingots, dozens of pieces of gold jewelry and hundreds of artifacts.

Year 1731. Two English merchantmen lost: the *John & Mary*, Captain Quirk, near Boston; and the *Anne*, Captain Goodridge, coming from Barbados, on Martha's Vineyard.

Year 1744. English warship *H.M.S. Astrea*, 20 guns, Captain John Barker, was accidentally burned in Boston Harbor but no lives were lost.

Year 1749. During a hurricane on October 8, seven unidentified ships were wrecked on Martha's Vineyard and many lives were lost.

Year 1757. American merchantman *Clinton*, Captain Hughes, coming from Jamaica and South Carolina, was wrecked on August 12 on No-man's Land, a small island near Martha's Vineyard, but some of her cargo was saved.

Year 1760. English merchantman *Claremont*, Captain Newton, sailing to Jamaica, was wrecked on Cape Cod, several of her crew perished.

Year 1762. English merchantman *Mary*, Captain Nain, sailing from Halifax to Gibraltar with a cargo of hides and furs, was lost near Boston.

Year 1766. English merchantman *Pembroke*, Captain Taylor, arriving from England with a valuable cargo was wrecked on Lynn Beach, near Boston, but some of her cargo was saved.

Year 1767. Scottish merchantman *Betsey*, Captain MacFarlan, sailing for London, was wrecked after leaving Boston near Race Point on Cape Cod, but most of her cargo was saved.

Year 1768. American merchantman *Hawke*, Captain Norton, carrying a cargo of salt from the Bahamas, was wrecked on Shagg Rock near Boston, but all of her crew was saved.

Year 1768. Unidentified brig, Captain Morton, arriving from the West Indies with a cargo of rum, sugar, molasses and a large chest of gold and silver specie, wrecked in a gale on December 4 on Shag Rocks near Boston. The treasure was never recovered.

Year 1773. English troop-transport *Britannia*, Captain Walker, after arriving from London, was accidentally burned in Boston Harbor but there was no loss of life.

Year 1774. During a gale in December, two unidentified merchantmen arriving from the Leeward Islands and a schooner from Virginia were totally lost in Buzzards Bay.

Year 1775. British naval schooner *Diana* was burned and destroyed by American patriots on May 27 at Noddle Island near Boston.

Year 1778. English frigate of war *H.M.S. Somerset*, 70 guns, Captain George Curry, carrying a large cargo of war materials, was wrecked near Provincetown, on Cape Cod.

Year 1782. French warship *Magnifique*, 74 guns, was wrecked August 15 on Lowell's Island which is near the entrance to Boston Harbor. Of her crew of 750 men only seven were lost. Most of her cannon were salvaged after the disaster.

Year 1782. English warship *H.M.S. Blonde*, 32 guns, Captain Edward Thornborough, was wrecked on a rock on Nantucket Shoals and several of her crew perished.

Year 1783. During a gale on October 9, three unidentified ships sank in Boston Harbor.

Year 1784. Three ships were lost: Spanish merchantman *Julius Caesar*, coming from Cadíz, on Cape Cod; American merchantman *Peace & Plenty*, Captain Calahan, on Cape Cod; and a ship of unknown registry, *Fanciculetta*, arriving from Tobago Island, on Nantucket Shoals.

Year 1785. American packet boat *Ross*, sailing from Newfoundland to New York, sank after entering Boston Bay.

Year 1786. Unidentified French brig sailing from the Caribbean to France, was lost on July 31 on Nantucket Shoals, but all of her crew was saved.

Year 1786. Brig *Lucretia* arriving from St. Croix with a cargo of coffee was wrecked in a snow storm on December 4 off Deer Island, near Point Shirley and only five of her crew were saved.

Year 1786. Six days later during another snow storm an unidentified large brig was totally lost on Ram Head, a bar extending off the northern part of Lowell's Island. She was carrying four chests of silver coins.

Year 1789. English merchantman *Mary & Ann*, Captain Evers, arriving from London, wrecked on Plumb Island, four persons of her crew were lost.

Year 1791. English merchantman *Hopewell*, Captain Harrison, arriving from London, was wrecked near Boston.

Year 1792. Three merchantmen were lost: English ship *Rodney*, Captain Wytock, sailing from Boston to the Caribbean, on Cape Cod; American ship *Marretta*, Captain Barnes, on Cape Cod; and American ship *Columbia*, Captain Chauncey, arriving from Liverpool, off Plymouth, only two of her crew survived.

Year 1793. Danish merchantman *Gertrude Maria*, Captain Klein, arriving from Copenhagen, was lost near Boston, some of her cargo was saved.

Year 1794. American merchantman *Fanny*, Captain Stevens, arriving from Virginia, was totally lost on Martha's Vineyard.

182

Year 1795. Three merchantmen were lost: English ship *Clarissa*, Captain Scott, arriving from London, on Nantucket Isle, crew and cargo were saved; ship of unknown registry, *Margaret*, Captain Mackay, arriving from Amsterdam, near Cape Ann; and American ship *Industry*, Captain Barnes, sailing from Portsmouth to Boston, totally lost near Cape Ann, with total loss of lives.

Year 1796. English ship *Julianna*, Captain Ingraham, arriving from South Carolina, was lost at Nantucket Isle.

Year 1797. English merchantman *Three Sisters*, Captain Delano, arriving from Liverpool, was wrecked on Cape Cod, but all of her crew was saved.

Year 1798. Three merchantmen were lost: American ship *Charming Betsey*, Captain Foffey, arriving from Martinique, wrecked on Martha's Vineyard; English ship *Delight*, Captain Wilson, sailing from Virginia to London, lost on Cape Cod; and English ship *Commerce*, sailing from Havana to Bristol, lost on Nantucket Shoals.

Unidentified year prior to 1799. A Spanish chart of New England published 1799, mentions that two Spanish warships, the *Magnifico* and *Cibila* were sunk in Boston Harbor at a previous date.

Year 1800. English merchantman *Delight*, Captain Williams, arriving from Gibraltar, was wrecked on a shoal off Martha's Vineyard.

Year 1802. Four merchantmen were lost on Cape Cod: American ship *Astrea*, sailing from Boston to the West Indies; English ship *Minerva*, Captain Phelim, arriving from Madeira Island, on January 11; two ships of unknown registry, *Brutus*, Captain Brown, and *Ulysses*, Captain Cock, both sailing from Salem to Europe.

Year 1802. American brigantine *Elizabeth*, arriving from St. Vincent Island in the Caribbean, lost on December 15 in a gale on a bar off Point Allerton near Boston.

Year 1804. Three merchantmen were lost: American ship *Semiramis*, Captain Smith, arriving from South Carolina, on Nantucket Shoals, only a small part of her cargo was saved; Spanish ship *Protecto*, sailing from Boston to Lima, Peru, on Cape Cod; and French ship *Alert*, arriving from France, near Boston on December 24.

Year 1811. Five merchantmen were lost: American ship *Four Brothers*, arriving from Russia, all of her cargo was saved; English ship *Neutrality*, Captain Forster, arriving from Liverpool; ship of unknown registry, *Florenza*, Captain King, arriving from London, crew and some of her cargo saved; French ship *Abeona*, Captain Blunt, sailing from Boston to Portsmouth, her crew saved; and Irish ship *Alknomack*, carrying immigrants from Ireland to New York, her crew and all passengers were saved. The first four were lost on Cape Cod and the fifth on Martha's Vineyard.

Year 1812. American merchantman *Alfred*, sailing from Russia to Boston, was lost on January 3 near Cape Ann, her crew was saved.

Year 1813. American ship *Princess*, sailing from London to New York, was totally lost on April 27 on Cape Cod, salvors failed to recover several chests of silver specie from this wreck.

Year 1814. Swedish merchantman *Nordkoping*, Captain Nordstrom, sailing from Cuba to Boston, was lost on Nantucket Shoals in July.

Year 1815. English merchantman *Matchless*, after arriving from London, sank at anchor in Boston Harbor during a gale on September 23.

Year 1817. Three vessels were lost: American packet boat *Dispatch*, Captain Lovett, arriving from the Virgin Islands, wrecked near Boston; American merchantman *Fox*, Captain Williams, arriving from Guadeloupe Island, wrecked January 18 on Martha's Vineyard; and the English merchantman *Robert Todd*, Captain Campbell, arriving from Liverpool and the Bahamas, totally lost on Nantucket Shoals on October 21.

Year 1817. The *Canton* packet of 350 tons, engaged in the West Indies trade was ready to sail on May 30 with a very valuable cargo valued at $400,000, including a large amount of silver specie, when she blew up with a total loss of life and cargo.

Year 1818. Two American merchantmen were lost on Cape Cod: *Mary Ann*, Captain Robinson, arriving from Baltimore, part of her cargo saved; and the *Warren*, Captain Knowles, arriving from Brazil, during the month of November.

Year 1820. Spanish brig *Midas*, Captain Varina, arriving from Santo Domingo with a general cargo and a chest containing over 10,000 silver coins, wrecked in five fathoms of water near George's Island near Boston. One of her crew and all of her treasure were lost.

Year 1821. American merchantman *Paragon*, Captain Hardon, arriving from Havana, totally lost on February 16 near Cape Ann.

Year 1822. American merchantman *Favorite*, Captain Webster, sailing from Honduras to Boston, wrecked on May 7 near Edgartown but her crew was saved.

Year 1824. American merchantman *Federal George*, Captain Davis, sailing from Philadelphia to Boston, was totally lost on January 20 near the Scituate Lighthouse off Boston Harbor; all of her crew and part of her cargo was saved.

Rhode Island

Year 1765. Irish merchantman *Golden Grove*, Captain Chitty, sailing from Cork to Halifax with a cargo of dried meats and butter, was wrecked on Block Island, crew and some of her cargo saved.

Year 1772. Two English ships were lost near Newport Harbor: warship *H.M.S. Gaspee*, on June 10; and merchantman *London*, Captain Folger, sailing for London.

Year 1777. Two English warships wrecked near Point Judith: *H.M.S. Triton*, Captain Woolcomb; and *H.M.S. Syren*, 20 guns, Captain Tobias Furneaux, on November 10.

Year 1778. Seven English warships were burned and sunk in Narragansett Bay during the War of Independence: *H.M.S. Kingfisher*, 16 guns; *H.M.S. Juno*, 32 guns, Captain Hugh Dalrymple; *H.M.S. Lark*, 32 guns, Captain Richard Smith; *H.M.S. Orpheus*, 32 guns, Captain Charles Hudson; *H.M.S. Flora*, 32 guns, Captain John Brisbane; *H.M.S. Cerberus*, 28 guns, Captain John Symons; and *H.M.S. Falcon*, 16 guns, Captain Harry Harmood.

Year 1779. American ship *Minerva*, Captain Cranston, sailing to New York, was wrecked near Westerly.

Year 1805. Ship of unknown registry, *Anna and Hope*, coming from France, was totally lost on Block Island.

Year 1806. English schooner of war *H.M.S. Redbridge*, 12 guns, Captain Edward Burt, wrecked on November 4 near Providence.

Year 1807. English ship *Brutus*, Captain Tobey, arriving from Liverpool, was wrecked on Block Island.

Year 1813. American merchantman *Ann*, Captain McDonald, wrecked near Barrington, her crew and cargo were saved.

Year 1815. During a hurricane on September 23 at Providence, four large ships, nine brigs, seven schooners and 15 sloops were wrecked or sunk.

Year 1818. American ship *Governor Hopkins*, arriving from Savannah, Georgia, wrecked during a storm in December on Brenton's Reef but most of her cargo was saved.

Year 1819. Two American merchantmen were lost: the *Montgomery*, arriving from Honduras, near Sakonnet Point; and the American, *Captain Lincoln*, sailing from the West Indies to Boston, on May 25 off Block Island.

Connecticut

Year 1770. During a hurricane on October 19, two unidentified large merchantmen were wrecked at New London.

Year 1812. American merchantman *Osprey*, Captain Cook, sailing from Pernambuco to New York, wrecked during a gale in February near New London.

Year 1816. Spanish merchantman *Anion*, sailing from Italy to New York, sank during October near New London because of a bad leak.

Year 1817. Two American merchantmen were lost: the *George*, Captain Speeding, sailing to Grenada, October 16, near New London, her crew and cargo saved; and the *Mary*, Captain Hanly, sailing for Liverpool, March 25, while crossing the bar at Darien.

New York

Year 1657. Dutch ship *Prins Maurits*, carrying immigrants to Nieuw Amsterdam (New York City), was lost on Fire Island, but Indians rescued all of the crew and passengers.

Year 1710. German ship *Herbert*, bringing immigrants from the Palatinate, wrecked on July 7 on the east end of Long Island; no lives were lost but only a small part of her cargo was saved.

Year 1719. Spanish privateer of 12 guns and 133 men was blown up during a battle with a New York privateer off the east end of Long Island, 91 of the Spaniards perished.

Year 1738. German ship *Princess Augusta*, Captain Brook, carrying 350 German immigrants from Amsterdam to New York, was wrecked on the northern tip of Sandy Point, Block Island. Before the disaster 250 of the passengers and some of the crew had died from contaminated water. In addition to a considerable amount of personal valuables belonging to the immigrants, the ship carried more than two million pounds sterling in gold and silver specie for a New York bank. None was ever recovered.

Year 1760. Scottish merchantman *Adventure*, Captain Auld, sailing from New York for Dublin, was lost in lower New York Bay.

Year 1761. American ship *City of Werry*, Captain Patterson, arriving from Boston, was sunk in the Narrows of New York Bay but her crew was saved.

Year 1763. American coastal schooner *Marey*, Captain Samuel Vetch, wrecked at Montauk Point, Long Island, carrying a cargo of contraband goods from French Canada.

Year 1769. Scottish merchantman *Elizabeth,* Captain Consy, arriving from Dublin, was totally lost on the south side of Long Island.

Year 1773. Scottish merchantman *Hope,* Captain Stewart, sailing from New York City to Dublin, was wrecked on Staten Island but her crew was saved.

Year 1776. American troop-transport *Generous Friends,* sank near Coney Island, but no lives were lost.

Year 1777. Four ships were lost: English warship *H.M.S. Liverpool,* 28 guns, Captain Henry Bellow, wrecked on the south side of Long Island; Irish merchantman *Diamond,* Captain Lanning, arriving from Cork, struck on some rocks at the entrance to the East River and sank near a wharf close to Manhattan; American warship *Congress, 28 guns, burned on the Hudson River to prevent her capture by the British; American warship Montgomery,* 24 guns, captured and blown up on the Hudson River by the British.

Year 1778. Three ships were lost: English warship *H.M.S. Mercury,* 24 guns, Captain James Montagu, wrecked near New York City; American naval vessel *Rose,* Captain Anderson, wrecked during a gale in December on Staten Island; and American merchantman *Jenny,* sailing for London, wrecked during a gale on Staten Island.

Year 1779. Three ships were lost: American merchantman *Colpoys,* arriving from St. Kitts, totally lost on Long Island, but only one man drowned; English troop-transport *James & William,* arriving from Rhode Island, totally lost at Hell Gate on the East River of New York City but all of her crew was saved; and the English warship *H.M.S. Hussar,* 28 guns, Captain Charles Maurice Pole, sank at Hell Gate, quite close to the *James & William.* Although there have been several articles in recent years stating that the *Hussar* was carrying a large amount of treasure, I have not discovered any documentary evidence to support this claim.

Year 1780. Four ships were lost: English troop-transport *Betsey,* Captain Obrien, was wrecked on some rocks in lower New York Bay and many lives were lost; English ship *Mercury,* Captain Monkhouse, sailing to Portugal, lost on March 2 during a gale on Long Island; American ship *Watt,* Captain Coulthard, sailing to Jamaica, was totally lost on Long Island and 26 men perished; and American privateer *Patience,* Captain Chase, wrecked on Long Island.

Handsome gold chain and locket which were recovered from the Almiranta of the 1715 Spanish fleet off Vero Beach, Florida.

Year 1781. Two English warships were wrecked on Long Island: *H.M.S. Swallow*, 16 guns, Captain Thomas Wells; and *H.M.S. Culloden*, 74 guns, Captain George Balfour, on January 23.

Year 1783. Three ships were lost: English troop-transport *St. James*, wrecked on Staten Island; English supply ship *Elizabeth*, Captain Griffith, wrecked on Long Island; and American merchantman *Huzzar*, Captain Wilson, arriving from Jamaica, wrecked on Long Island, but part of her cargo was saved.

Year 1784. Unidentified French packet boat was wrecked on Long Island on January 15 and several of her crew perished.

Year 1785. Two ships were lost: Spanish merchantman *Nuestra Señora del Rosario*, Captain Moratus, arriving from the Canaries, was wrecked near New York City but part of her cargo was saved; and the Swedish ship *Alstromer* was wrecked on Governor's Island during a gale on September 29.

Year 1786. Ship of unknown registry, *Mary Ann*, Captain Stewart, coming from the Far East, wrecked on Long Island in August.

Year 1788. English merchantman *Betsey & Amy*, Captain Watts, arriving from Liverpool, wrecked on Long Island.

Year 1789. American merchantman *Sally*, Captain Matthews, arriving from Grenada, wrecked on Coney Island.

Year 1792. Two ships of unknown registry were wrecked on Long Island: the *Eliza*, Captain Hughes, arriving from Jamaica, and *George*, Captain Gregorio, arriving from Madeira Island.

Year 1795. American merchantman *Neptune*, Captain Wallace, arriving from Dominica Island, wrecked on the south side of Long Island but some of her cargo was saved.

Year 1796. During a gale at New York City on January 11, eight unidentified ships sank at anchor or at the wharves, one of them was an English packet boat.

Year 1797. Spanish merchantman *Enrique*, Captain Cuzana, arriving from Cadíz, wrecked on Long Island but crew and some of her cargo saved.

Year 1798. American merchantman *Jenny*, Captain Dickson, sailing to Jamaica, wrecked in lower New York Bay.

Many other valuable items can be recovered from shipwrecks in addition to precious metals and jewels, such as this 1670 English rum bottle.

189

Year 1800. Two ships were lost: German ship *Ocean*, sailing from Bremen to Philadelphia, wrecked on the south side of Long Island; only the captain perished; and the American merchantman *Experiment*, arriving from Havana, sank shortly before reaching Manhattan.

Year 1801. Three ships were lost: English merchantman *Thomas*, sailing for Londonderry, totally lost on the East River; American ship *Traveller*, Captain Russell, sailing from the West Indies to Boston, wrecked on Long Island; and a ship of unknown registry, *Ann*, sailing from New York City to Liverpool, wrecked on Long Island, near Brookhaven.

Year 1802. Two ships were lost: Dutch ship *Mary*, Captain Seimen, arriving from Amsterdam, lost in lower New York Bay; and a ship of unknown registry, *Catherine Ray*, Captain Benthall, arriving from Lisbon, wrecked on February 21 on Long Island, crew and part of her cargo saved.

Year 1804. Ship of unknown registry, *Nelly*, Captain Nueller, arriving from Newfoundland, wrecked on Long Island.

Year 1805. American merchantman *Cato*, Captain Updell, arriving from New York, wrecked on January 16 on Long Island.

Year 1806. Scottish merchantman *Edward*, Captain Babcock, arriving from Dublin, was totally lost on Long Island but all of her crew was saved.

Year 1807. Three merchantmen of unknown registry were lost: the *Nereus*, Captain Stowe, arriving from St. Vincent's, wrecked on Long Island; the *Selby*, Captain Pratt, arriving from Jamaica, wrecked on March 25 near Manhattan; and the *Mississippi*, Captain Stedmore, arriving from London, wrecked in lower New York Bay, crew and some of her cargo saved.

Year 1808. Two American merchantmen were lost: the *Flora*, Captain Adams, arriving from New Orleans with a cargo of cotton, burned on the East River; and the *Little George*, arriving from Newfoundland, wrecked on January 29 near Long Island.

Year 1809. American merchantman *True American*, Captain Newson, arriving from Haiti, wrecked on February 20 near The Narrows in upper New York Bay.

Year 1810. American merchantman *Cincinnati*, bound for Lisbon, wrecked on Governor's Island during a gale on November 10.

Year 1811. During a violent storm on December 23 and 24, between 50 and 60 large unidentified ships were wrecked on the south side of Long Island. Two other ships were lost on Long Island earlier in the year: the English merchantman *Olive Branch*, Captain Newman, arriving from Liverpool, crew and passengers were saved; and the English warship *H.M.S. Thistle*, 10 guns, Captain George McPherson, on March 6; six of her crew of 50 perished.

Year 1812. American ship *Lucy & Elizabeth*, Captain Bray, arriving from Lisbon, lost in lower New York Bay, but all of her crew was saved.

Year 1815. Four English ships were lost: warship *H.M.S. Sylph*, 18 guns, Captain George Dickens, wrecked on Southampton Bar, Long Island, 115 of her crew of 121 perished; and three merchantmen: *Nelson*, Captain Scoffin, arriving from London, sank in lower New York Bay; *Vidette*, Captain Hammond, arriving from Guadeloupe, wrecked October 28 on Long Island, three persons drowned; and the *Friendship*, sailing from Halifax to Jamaica, wrecked during a gale on September 23 on Staten Island, but most of her cargo was saved.

Year 1818. English merchantman *Albion*, Captain Cox, wrecked on Coney Island in February; her crew and cargo saved.

190

Year 1821. During a hurricane on September 4, New York City suffered severe damages. A large ferryboat sank at Whitehall Dock, a sloop sank at Coenties Slip, 10 large ships sank at the Quarantine, 12 other large ships sank at Public Store Dock #12, four ships wrecked at Fountain Ferry, five ships wrecked at the Kiln, and a large number were wrecked along the south side of Long Island. Earlier in the year, two American merchantmen were wrecked on Long Island: the *Savannah*, Captain Holdridge, arriving from Savannah, but most of her cargo was saved; and the *Albert*, Captain Salter, sailing from Portsmouth, New Hampshire, to Philadelphia.

Year 1822. Four American merchantmen wrecked on Long Island: the *Savannah*, Captain Cole, arriving from Liverpool, during October, with a total loss of lives; the *Elizabeth*, Captain Williams, arriving from Amsterdam, on May 22; all of her crew and part of her cargo saved; the *Ruth*, Captain Hughson, sailing from South America to Canada, near Mount Desert on April 2; and the *Augusta*, Captain Peterson, during a gale on October 27, at Shrewsbury Beach.

Year 1823. Spanish schooner *Ligera*, Captain Rock, arriving from Havana, wrecked at Montauk Point, Long Island, and only a small part of the specie she carried was recovered.

Year 1824. Three merchantmen wrecked on Long Island: the American ship *Pocahontas*, Captain Grover, arriving from Jamaica, on April 11, one person drowned; English ship *Edward Douglas*, Captain Carlew, sailing to Haiti, on September 14, no lives lost; and the English ship *Nestor*, Captain Pease, arriving from Liverpool, on November 28.

Year 1825. During a hurricane on June 3 or 4, the Colombian warship *Venezuela* wrecked in New York Harbor and the American schooner *Hornet* foundered off Long Island.

New Jersey

Year 1704. A privateer vessel, *Castle del Rey*, 18 guns, 130 tons, Captain Otto Van Tyle, was struck by a gale after sailing from Manhattan and wrecked on a shoal near Sandy Hook. Of her crew of 145 only 13 survived, as the ship quickly went to pieces.

Year 1768. English merchantman *Sally*, Captain Rankin, sailing from England to Philadelphia, wrecked off Little Egg Harbor.

Year 1777. Irish merchantman *Norbury*, Captain Wood, sailing from Cork to New York, wrecked at Sandy Hook, crew and most of her cargo saved.

Year 1778. English warship *H.M.S. Zebra*, 16 guns, Captain Henry Collins, wrecked during October at Egg Island Harbor.

Year 1779. Three American merchantmen were lost: *Mary*, Captain Peppard, arriving from St. Kitts, sank near Sandy Hook during a gale; an unidentified ship, arriving from Antigua with a cargo of rum, was also lost at the same time near the above- mentioned ship; and the *Betsey*, Captain Parke, sailing from Providence, Rhode Island, to New York was wrecked at Great Egg Harbor.

Year 1783. Nine merchantmen were lost: *Jupiter*, Captain Rumage, sailing from Jamaica to New York, totally lost off Cape May, two men perished. During a gale on September 19, four others were lost at Cape May: *New York*, Captain Fortey, sailing from Glasgow to New York, but her crew was saved; *Two*

Friends, Captain Bevan, sailing to Philadelphia; *Betsey*, Captain Brown, sailing to Philadelphia; and the *Mercury*, Captain Herpin, sailing from Dunkirk to Philadelphia. During another gale, on October 8, two unidentified ships sank at Cape May and two others near Great Egg Harbor.

Year 1784. American merchantman *Charming Nancy*, Captain Penkham, sailing from Philadelphia to the West Indies, wrecked during a gale at Cape May Roads but some of her cargo was saved.

Year 1789. American merchantman *Nymph*, Captain Palmer, sailing from Oporto to New York, wrecked during November near Barnegat.

Year 1791. Two ships were lost: English merchantman *Betsey, Captain Douglas*, sailing from London to New York, wrecked at Barnegat; and a ship of unknown registry, *Boston & Liverpool*, Captain Laud, sailing from Liverpool to Philadelphia, wrecked near Barnegat.

Year 1792. Two merchantmen of unknown registry were lost: *Fanny*, Captain Johnson, sailing from the Virgin Islands to Philadelphia, wrecked at Cape May; and the *Wilhelmina*, Captain Steele, sailing from New London to Dublin, wrecked north of Cape May but her crew was saved.

Year 1793. Three merchantmen were lost: English ship *Manchester*, Captain Clay, sailing from Liverpool to Philadelphia, wrecked on Egg Island Shoals; American ship *Swallow*, Captain Wright, sailing from Antigua to New York, wrecked near Sandy Hook; and the American ship *Edward*, Captain Goodrich, arriving from Turk's Island, Bahamas, lost on Barnegat Shoals.

Year 1794. Italian ship St. *Francesco de Paola Costellina*, Captain Genovese, sailing from France to New York, lost on Little Egg Harbor Bar.

Year 1802. Spanish warship *Juno*, 34 guns, sailing from Mexico to Spain, was driven off course by strong winds and due to many leaks sank on October 29 near Cape May, carrying all of her 425 persons and over 300,000 pesos in silver to the bottom.

Year 1803. American ship *Virginia*, Captain Darby, sailing from London to New York, lost south of Sandy Hook, several of her crew and passengers perished.

Year 1804. Two American merchantmen were lost: *William*, Captain Ashton, arriving from the Canary Islands, sank near Sandy Hook; a gale caused an unidentified ship to wreck on Absecon Beach (present-day Atlantic City) on October 9.

Year 1805. English brig *Recovery*, sailing from England to New York, wrecked at Sandy Hook.

Year 1806. Two American merchantmen were lost: the *Columbia*, Captain Lewis, sailing from Lisbon to New York, totally lost near Little Egg Harbor on January 4; during a hurricane on August 24, the *Rose in Bloom* sank off the central New Jersey coast.

Year 1807. Ship of unknown registry, *Wakers*, Captain Homer, sailing from Amsterdam to New York, wrecked on January 16, near Sandy Hook but all of her crew was saved.

Year 1808. Three merchantmen were lost: English ship *Ida*, sailing from Lisbon to Philadelphia, lost near Cape May on February 16; Italian ship *Thetis*, Captain Granbury, wrecked on Cape May on February 16; and American ship *Cato*, Captain Darrell, arriving from the Bahamas, lost November 11 at Sandy Hook.

Year 1809. American merchantman *Harnett*, Captain Gardner, arriving from Jamaica, lost on February 20 near Sandy Hook.

Year 1810. Ship of unknown registry, *Sally*, Captain Moffet, sailing from England to New York, totally lost on September 22 near Barnegat.

Year 1811. Three merchantmen were lost: American ship *Success*, Captain Forbes, sailing from the Virgin Islands to New York, wrecked on January 16 near Sandy Hook; English ship *Arnelia*, sailing from England to New York, wrecked February 16 at Sandy Hook; and a ship of unknown registry, *Belle Air*, Captain Allen, sailing from Norway and Cork to Philadelphia, wrecked near Egg Harbor, but her crew was saved.

Year 1815. American ship *Clarendon*, Captain Gainess, sailing from Bermuda to New York, wrecked at Sandy Hook on April 7, crew and passengers saved.

Year 1816. English merchantman *Robert Walne*, sailing from London to New York, wrecked on Sandy Hook on August 22; a small part of her cargo was saved.

Year 1817. Ship of unknown registry, *Hannah*, Captain Askwith, sailing to New York, wrecked on April 19 off Tom's River, crew and cargo saved.

Year 1819. English merchantman *Andrew*, Captain Hathaway, sailing from Liverpool to Philadelphia, wrecked at Barnegat, her crew was saved.

Year 1820. English merchantman *Caledonia*, Captain Struthers, sailing from Liverpool to New York, wrecked on December 28 about 10 miles south of Sandy Hook; three persons were drowned.

Year 1821. English ship *Syren*, sailing from the Caribbean to Boston, wrecked around February at Great Egg Harbor. During a hurricane on September 3, a large number of unidentified ships sank in the vicinity of Cape May.

Year 1822. Three merchantmen were lost: English ship *Enterprize*, sailing from Maine to Philadelphia, lost in May near Little Egg Harbor, her crew was saved; Scottish ship *Hind*, sailing from Dundee to New York, wrecked at Sandy Hook on January 28; and a ship of unknown registry, *Citizen*, Captain Loring, sailing from Manila to New York, wrecked on April 9 on Brigantine Shoals, near Egg Harbor, but then drifted off and sank in five fathoms of water, her crew was saved.

Year 1823. American ship *Union*, Captain Cotter, sailing from Londonderry and Bermuda to New York, wrecked at Sandy Hook, but her crew was saved.

Year 1824. Two merchantmen of unknown registry were lost: the *Rebecca*, Captain Stairs, sailing from the West Indies to Halifax, wrecked on December 2 at Sandy Point; and the *Hunter*, sailing from France to Philadelphia, wrecked at Cape May, crew and cargo saved.

Year 1825. American merchantman *Trumbell*, Captain Hitchcock, sailing from Trinidad to New York, wrecked at Sandy Hook.

Delaware Coast, Bay and River

Year 1751. English merchantman *Mercury*, Captain Hogg, sailing from Philadelphia to London, lost near the Delaware River.

Year 1757. Three English merchantmen lost: *Sally*, Captain Saze, sailing from Philadelphia to Antigua, lost at Brandy Wine on the Delaware River; *Pusey*, Captain Good, arriving from Jamaica, wrecked on Reedy Island in the Delaware River; and the *Cornelia*, Captain Smith, sailing from Philadelphia to Gibraltar, sank between capes Henlopen and May, three of her crew perished.

Year 1760. Scottish merchantman *Molly*, Captain Stewart, sank in the Delaware River.

Year 1763. Two English merchantmen lost: the *Vaughan*, Captain Foster, sailing from Bristol to Philadelphia, wrecked in Delaware Bay; and the *Pitt Packet*, Captain Montgomery, sailing from Belfast to Philadelphia with a large number of passengers, foundered in Delaware Bay with total loss of life.

Year 1766. American merchantman *Charlestown*, Captain Simpson, sailing from Hamburg to Philadelphia, wrecked on January 25 on the Branclawine Bank in Delaware Bay.

Year 1768. Ship of unknown registry, *Kildare*, Captain Nicholson, sailing from Barbados to Philadelphia, lost at the mouth of the Delaware River.

Year 1771. English merchantman *Commerce*, Captain Addis, sailing from England to New York, wrecked at Cape Henlopen; very little of her cargo was saved.

Year 1774. English merchantman *Severn*, Captain Hathorn, sailing from Bristol to Philadelphia, wrecked in Delaware Bay, but all of her crew was saved.

Year 1775. English merchantman *Endeavor*, Captain Caldwell, sailing from Philadelphia to Londonderry, caught fire and sank off Reedy Island in the Delaware River, but most of her cargo was saved.

Year 1777. Seven American warships were lost during a battle with the British in Delaware Bay: *Washington*, 32 guns; *Effingham*, 28 guns; *Sachem*, 10 guns; *Independence*, 10 guns; *Dolphin*, 10 guns; *Wasp*, eight guns; and the *Mosquito*, four guns. Another American warship, the *Andrea Doria*, 14 guns, was burned to prevent her capture, also in Delaware Bay.

Year 1783. During a severe gale in the fall, nine large unidentified ships were wrecked at Cape Henlopen and many lives were lost.

Year 1784. Ship of unknown registry, *Peace*, Captain Star, sailing from London to Virginia, wrecked on Hog Island in Delaware Bay; some of her cargo was saved.

Year 1785. Scottish immigrant ship *Faithful Stewart*, Captain M'Causland, sailing from Londonderry to Philadelphia, sank near Cape Henlopen; over 200 persons perished.

Year 1788. Spanish merchantman *Santa Rosalea*, Captain Pardenus, sailing from Baltimore to Havana, wrecked near Cape Henlopen but some of her cargo was saved.

Year 1789. English ship *Pomona*, Captain Hopkins, coming from Quebec; sank in Delaware Bay on October 30.

Year 1790. English merchantman *John*, Captain Staples, arriving from England, wrecked December 5 on the Delaware River, near Philadelphia but some of her cargo was saved.

Year 1793. American merchantman *Industry*, Captain Carson, sailing from France to Philadelphia, sank in Delaware Bay, near Cape May.

Year 1794. Two merchantmen were lost in Delaware Bay: a Spanish ship, *San Josiph*, sailing from Philadelphia to Cuba, lost due to ice crushing her hull; the American ship *Peggy*, sailing from Philadelphia to Savannah.

Year 1795. Ship of unknown registry, *Lively*, Captain Lawrence, sailing from Amsterdam to New York, sank near Lewes, only her crew was saved.

Year 1796. Three American merchantmen were lost: *Henry & Charles*, sailing from Philadelphia to Hamburg, wrecked near Cape Henlopen; the *Favorite*, sailing from Cadíz to Philadelphia, sank in Delaware Bay; and the *Minerva*, sailing from Lisbon to Philadelphia, wrecked near the mouth of the Delaware River, seven of her crew perished.

Year 1797. American ship *John*, Captain Folger, sailing from Hamburg to Philadelphia with over 300 immigrants, wrecked near Cape Henlopen.

Year 1798. English warship *H.M.S. De Braak*, 16 guns, Captain James Drew, capsized and sank near Lewes, 35 of her crew perished. She was carrying 70 tons of copper ingots and a large amount of gold and silver bullion and specie. Over the years there have been many attempts to locate this shipwreck. In 1983 it was finally located and salvaged. In attempting to raise part of the ship's lower wooden hull, many artifacts and pieces of treasure were lost.

Year 1799. American merchantman *New Jersey*, Captain Clay, sailing from Puerto Rico to Philadelphia, wrecked on the west side of Delaware Bay.

Year 1800. Three merchantmen were lost: English ship *George*, preparing to sail for England, sank at Philadelphia; American ship *Susannah*, Captain Medlin, sailing from Hamburg to Philadelphia, wrecked in Delaware Bay; and an unidentified ship sank near the mouth of the Delaware River.

Year 1801. Two American merchantmen sank in Delaware Bay: *Adriana*, sailing from Philadelphia to Dublin, due to heavy ice, and the *Constellation*, sailing for New York.

Year 1804. During a hurricane on October 9, a large newly arrived unidentified ship sank at Philadelphia.

Year 1805. Two merchantmen of unknown registry sank in Delaware Bay: *China*, Captain M'Pherson, sailing from Batavia to Philadelphia; part of her cargo was saved; and the *Fanny*, Captain Wing, sailing from France to Philadelphia.

Year 1811. American ship *Matilda*, sailing from the Canary Islands to Baltimore, wrecked on the north side of Delaware Bay, crew and part of cargo saved.

Year 1824. American merchantman *Adeline*, Captain Israel, sailing from North Carolina to Philadelphia, wrecked December 9 at Cape Henlopen.

Maryland

Year 1753. English merchantman Swan, *Captain Clarkson*, sailing from Baltimore to London with 300 hogsheads of tobacco, burned shortly after leaving Baltimore.

Year 1758. Merchantman *Unity*, Captain Joseph Richardson, caught fire on May 5 while anchored in the northwest branch of the Patalsco River and was a total loss. Some of her cannon were recovered at the time.

Year 1759. American merchantman *Sophia*, Captain George Kimpber, was anchored with a cargo of tobacco off Charleston on the Chester River when she caught fire and was a total loss.

Year 1766. English merchantman *Hawke*, Captain Price, sailing for Cadíz, sank in the upper reaches of Chesapeake Bay, but all members of her crew was saved.

Year 1768. Merchantman *Nisbit*, Captain Hugh Wylie, 10 cannon, loaded with a cargo of tobacco, was waiting to sail for Scotland when an explosion aboard totally destroyed the ship near Annapolis. Some of her were saved.

Year 1769. Scottish merchantman *Earl of Chatham*, Captain Wolsey, sailing from Dublin to Maryland, was lost near Cambridge but some of her cargo was salvaged.

Year 1770. English merchantman *Boyne*, Captain Howard, arriving from St. Kitts, wrecked in Chesapeake Bay near Baltimore.

Year 1775. English ship *Totness*, Captain Wafing, was set afire by Indians and totally destroyed near St. Mary's City, but no lives were lost.

Year 1779. Scottish merchantman *Earl of Chatham*, 90 tons, Captain George Woolsey, just arrived from Ireland was anchored on the Choptank River near Cambridge, She blew up and was a total loss.

Year 1781. Early in the year a storm severely damaged the British fleet, and the *H.M.S. Culloden*, 74 guns, was lost, except for her masts, which were later salvaged. Later in the year the British scuttled three of their warships in the northern part of Chesapeake Bay: *H.M.S. Guadeloupe*, 28 guns, Captain Hugh Robinson; *H.M.S. Charon*, 44 guns, Captain Thomas Symonds; and the fire ship, *H.M.S. Vulcan*, eight guns, Captain George Palmer.

Year 1806. English merchantman *Ruthy*, after arriving from Liverpool, wrecked at the mouth of the Baltimore River, crew and some cargo saved.

Year 1808. Ship of unknown registry, *Mary*, Captain Hunt, was lost during a gale on September 12 at Baltimore.

Year 1817. Canadian brig *Hannah*, arriving from St. Johns, New Brunswick, wrecked at the mouth of the Potomac River at the end of May.

Virginia

Year 1689. English warship *H.M.S. Deptford*, 10 guns, Captain Thomas Berry, wrecked on August 26 near Cedar Island, but no lives were lost.

Year 1706. During a hurricane, a fleet of 14 unidentified merchantmen was lost on the northern coast of Cape Charles after setting sail for England.

Year 1724. During a hurricane on August 12, several ships were wrecked on the James River, but most of their cargoes were saved.

Year 1738. British merchantman *Richmond*, Captain Smith, richly laden and coming from Bristol, England, was totally lost on April 4 on a shoal in the center of the Chesapeake Bay.

Year 1738. American ship *Needham*, Captain Harwood, carrying a cargo of tobacco was anchored at the mouth of the York River when she caught fire and sank on February 21.

Year 1739. In January an unidentified ship carrying over 300 immigrants from Germany to the James River wrecked off Cape Henry, there were only 10 survivors.

Year 1741. English merchantman *Sea Nymph*, Captain Ecles, sailing for England, was lost on Hog Island; many of her crew perished.

Year 1746. Two Scottish merchantmen, *Prince George*, Captain Coulter, and the *Glasgow*, Captain Montgomery, were captured near Cape Charles by a French warship. After the crews and cargoes were transferred to the French ship, both merchantmen were burned.

Year 1747. American brig *Raleigh*, Captain Samuel Allyn, was ready to sail for Madeira with a cargo of wheat and four chests of silver specie, when she wrecked at Norfolk on March 21. The ship was a total loss. Her coinage was never recovered.

Year 1747. Unidentified ship bringing hundreds of Irish indentured servants sank during a hurricane on September 3 on the Rappahannock River just south of Urbana in five fathoms of water. Over 50 souls drowned.

Year 1749. The worst hurricane in memory occurred on October 7 and over 50 ships were lost along the Virginia coast. One of them was the *Glasgow*, Captain Hunter, arriving from England with a large amount of silver specie. This ship was totally lost at Cape Henry.

Year 1749. English merchantman *Tamphough*, Captain Brag, arriving from England, wrecked on Cobb Island, but her crew was saved.

Year 1750. A hurricane on August 18 struck the New Spain Flota of Captain-General Juan Manuel de Bonilla off Cape Hatteras, North Carolina, and four ships were lost in this vicinity. Three other Spanish ships were lost on the coast of Virginia: *Nuestra Señora de los Godos*, near Cape Charles, *La Galga*, 15 leagues north of Cape Charles, and an unidentified brigantine, six leagues north of this cape. The Capitana *Nuestra Señora de Guadalupe* and the galleon *Zumaca* reached Norfolk; however, both of these ships and 12 unidentified English merchantmen were lost during another hurricane several weeks later.

Year 1751. English merchantman *King's Fisher*, Captain Bibby, sailing from New England to South Carolina with a cargo of prisoners, was captured by these prisoners who murdered the captain and crew then wrecked the ship at Wallop's Island.

Year 1752. Large merchantman *Peggy and Nancy*, Captain Isaac Johns, loaded with a cargo of tobacco, lost in a gale at Willoughby Point; crew saved but all else lost.

Year 1753. Two merchantmen were lost: Irish ship *Flower of Cork*, Captain Chip, arriving from Cork, was wrecked on the coast five leagues south of Cape Henry but the crew was saved; American ship *Lucy*, sailing from Maryland to Lisbon with a cargo of wheat, wrecked on the Middle Ground, between capes Henry and Charles.

Year 1754. English ship *Pearl* caught fire and blew up in the vicinity of Cape Charles.

Year 1757. Five English merchantmen were lost: *Duke*, Captain Maitland, sailing for London, foundered four days after setting sail; *Lydia*, Captain Teague, foundered near Cape Henry; *Duke of Cumberland*, Captain Ball, sailing from the Canaries to Virginia, was lost nine leagues south of Cape Henry and 25 of her crew perished; at the same time a brig and a snow were lost in the area, all of the snow's crew perished.

Year 1760. Two English merchantmen were wrecked 25 miles south of Cape Henry: *Neptune*, Captain Burdon, and the *Thomas & Richard*, Captain Wilkinson, both arriving from London.

Year 1761. English merchantman *Russel*, Captain Calder, sailing for Barbados, lost when passing Cape Henry, crew and part of cargo saved.

Year 1762. English merchantman *Sally*, Captain Pritchard, sailing from Philadelphia to Lisbon, and two unidentified ships were lost off Cape Charles but both crews were saved.

Year 1764. Two merchantmen were lost: English ship *Brothers*, Captain Morrison, sailing for London, was wrecked near Cape Henry, but her crew was saved; American schooner *Friendship*, Captain Clark, sailing from Barbados to Philadelphia, was wrecked on November 25 a little south of Cape Henry, two of her crew perished.

Year 1766. English merchantman *Rogers*, Captain Wignell, arriving from Liverpool, wrecked on the Middle Ground, between capes Henry and Charles, but the crew was saved.

Year 1768. English merchantman *Charles*, Captain Waterman, arriving from London, was totally lost on Cobb Island; several of her crew perished.

Year 1769. During a hurricane on September 7 and 8, four large English merchantmen were wrecked on the York River and two on the James River. In November, the English merchantman *Randolph*, Captain Andrews, arriving from Bristol, wrecked off Cape Henry but all of her crew was saved.

Year 1770. English merchantman *Gorel*, Captain Rymey, arriving from Liverpool, lost three leagues north of Cape Charles, but most cargo was saved.

Year 1771. American merchantman *Kitty*, Captain Shaw, sailing for England, sank off Cape Charles during a gale.

Year 1772. Dutch merchantman *Jan Pierre*, Captain Veffer, sailing from the Caribbean to Amsterdam, foundered on December 24 near Cape Henry, her crew was saved.

Year 1775. Three English merchantmen were lost: *Hibernia*, Captain Morrison, arriving from Londonderry, wrecked during a violent storm on September 2 about 10 leagues south of Cape Henry; *Five Oak*, Captain Peaton, arriving from the Leeward Islands, totally wrecked on Hog Island; only two of the crew saved; and the *Minerva*, Captain Ewing, arriving from Londonderry, wrecked on September 4 at Cape Charles.

Year 1776. English merchantman *Molly*, Captain Collins, preparing to sail for Liverpool, was burned at Norfolk.

Year 1778. American warship *Lewis*, Captain Celey Saunders, was burned by the British in Carter's Creek on the Rappahannock River.

Year 1779. The worst maritime disaster suffered by the Americans during the Revolutionary War occurred in May of this year when naval forces under the British Admiral George Collier burned and destroyed 148 American naval and merchant vessels at Norfolk and surrounding areas.

Year 1781. During the British siege of Yorktown in October, at least six British warships and other smaller support vessels were sunk.

Year 1784. Ship of unknown registry, *Cox*, Captain Mason, sailing from Barbados to Philadelphia, wrecked on Assateague Island; crew was saved.

Year 1785. During September and October, many severe storms struck the vicinity of Virginia and several large ships were sunk or destroyed along the coasts and in the rivers. During one tremendous gale at Portsmouth, several large ships were carried a long way into the woods. Earlier in the year the English ship *Grange*, arriving from England, was wrecked at Cape Charles, but all of her cargo was saved.

198

Year 1786. American packet boat *Maryland*, Captain Brown, arriving from London, was wrecked on Cape Henry; her crew was saved.

Year 1787. English merchantman *Nonsuch*, Captain Wallace, arriving from London, was lost on the Middle Ground between capes Charles and Henry, her crew was saved.

Year 1788. During a bad gale at Norfolk on July 23, many unidentified ships were destroyed and sunk.

Year 1790. Six merchantmen were lost: Scottish ship *William*, Captain Church, sailing for Dublin, wrecked on Cape Charles; her cargo was saved; American ship *Jane & Dianna*, Captain Handwith, sailing from Norfolk to Spain, lost near Cape Henry; English ship *Kitty & Alice*, arriving from Jamaica, lost near Cape Henry; Scottish ship *Lovely Ann*, arriving from Glasgow, wrecked near Cape Charles; French ship *Fanny*, arriving from the Channel Islands, wrecked near Cape Charles; and the American ship *Flora*, Captain Finlay, sailing from London to Philadelphia, wrecked about 25 miles north of Cape Charles.

Year 1791. Three English merchantmen were lost: *Rainbow*, Captain Coward, sailing from Newfoundland to Philadelphia, near Cape Henry, her crew was saved; *Nanty*, Captain Foster, sailing to London, lost in Hampton Roads; and the *Swan*, Captain Dale, sailing for London, lost on Hog Island.

Year 1795. During a gale on August 2, a large unidentified ship sank off Cape Charles with a total loss of lives.

Year 1797. Two English ships were lost: merchantman *Martin*, sailing for London, lost at Hampton Roads; and the warship *H.M.S. Hunter*, 18 guns, Captain Tudor Tucker, wrecked December 27 on Hog Island, 75 of her crew of 80 perished.

Year 1798. Two merchantmen of unknown registries were lost: *Antony Mangin*, Captain Stafford, sailing from Hamburg to Baltimore, lost near Cape Charles; and the *Inclination*, Captain Coster, sailing from Bremen to Baltimore, wrecked on Hog Island.

Year 1800. English merchantman June, *Captain Rexburg*, sailing from Liverpool to Baltimore, was totally lost on Hog Island, only a few of the crew survived.

Year 1801. American merchantman *Suffolk*, Captain Doggett, sailing from New York to Norfolk, was totally lost on the Middle Ground between capes Henry and Charles, crew and passengers saved.

Year 1804. Ship of unknown registry, *Samuel Smith*, Captain Stiles, arriving from the Far East with a valuable cargo, wrecked south of Cape Henry; many of her crew perished.

Year 1805. American merchantman *Adventure*, Captain Smith, arriving from Jamaica, wrecked September 7 on Cape Henry, but her crew and some of her cargo were saved.

Year 1806. Two ships wrecked near Cape Henry: English merchantman *Sheperdess*, Captain Wells, arriving from London, crew and passengers saved; and the French warship *Impetueux*, 74 guns, forced ashore by two British frigates and destroyed.

Year 1807. American merchantman *Betsey*, Captain Tredwell, fully laden and ready to sail for Liverpool, was accidentally burned at anchor at Norfolk and sank.

Year 1808. English merchantman *William Murdock*, Captain Brooks, sailing in ballast from Rotterdam to the Potomac River, wrecked on Cape Charles in January but no lives were lost.

Year 1809. American merchantman *Robert*, Captain Stocking, sailing from Jamaica to Philadelphia, wrecked on August 31 at Cape Henry, but her crew was saved.

Year 1810. American merchantman *Lucy*, Captain Pickman, sailing from Madeira Island to Baltimore, wrecked on Cape Henry, but crew and some wine cargo were saved.

Year 1811. Two ships were lost: French privateer *Revanche du Cerf* was captured by an American naval vessel and taken into Norfolk, where it was stripped and burned on April 16; and an American ship, *Heroine*, Captain Maxwell, sailing from Lisbon to Norfolk, wrecked April 14 on Hog Island, but no lives were lost.

Year 1813. French ship *Tamerlane*, after being captured, was lost on Cape Henry; only a small part of the large amount of silver and gold specie saved.

Year 1818. American merchantman *Clotilda*, Captain Brotherdon, sailing from New Orleans to Philadelphia, wrecked on Cape Henry on March 5 and 11 men drowned.

Year 1821. During a hurricane that struck Norfolk on September 3, two American war frigates *Congress* and *Guerriere* plus a large number of brigs, schooners and smaller vessels were sunk or wrecked.

Year 1822. Four merchantmen were lost: one, unidentified, wrecked near the boundary line of Virginia and North Carolina, no lives were lost; Spanish ship *La Plata*, sailing from Havana to Baltimore, was totally lost on October 22 near Cape Charles, no lives were lost; Dutch ship *Janus*, Captain Windt, arriving from Bremen, totally wrecked on Cape Henry, no lives were lost; and a ship of unknown registry, *Seaflower*, Captain Bascombe, arriving in ballast from St. Vincent, lost near Cape Henry, crew and sails saved.

Year 1824. Two merchantmen were lost: English ship *Liverpool*, Captain Nash, arriving from Jamaica, lost March 10 south of Cape Henry, ship *Mary & Ann*, Captain Barlow, sailing from Havana to Philadelphia, wrecked November 19 on Hog Island Shoals.

North Carolina

Year 1526. A small unidentified Spanish brigantine, sent from Cuba on a voyage of exploration along the eastern coast of the U. S., was wrecked during the month of June at Cape Fear. The survivors made a smaller vessel from the wreckage and managed to reach Santo Domingo with great hardship.

Year 1585. English ship *Tiger*, on a voyage of exploration, wrecked on June 29 at Ocracoke Inlet but no lives were lost.

Year 1665. An unidentified English fly-boat was wrecked at Cape Fear but no lives were lost.

Year 1666. An unidentified English sloop wrecked at Cape Lookout but all cargo was salvaged by the survivors.

Year 1710. English warship *H.M.S. Garland* was wrecked November 29 on a small sandbar a little south of Currituck Inlet and 15 of her crew perished. The wreck sanded over before anything could be salvaged.

Year 1728. During a hurricane, an unidentified English ship was wrecked six miles seaward from Ocracoke Inlet and there were only a few survivors.

Year 1739. English merchantman *Adriatick*, Captain Hanney, sailing from London to Virginia, wrecked at Cape Hatteras with a large loss of lives.

Year 1741. Two English merchantmen were lost off Cape Hatteras: *Hoylin*, Captain Cunningham, arriving from Bristol, no lives were lost, and the *Woolford*, Captain Kenlock, sailing from Jamaica to London.

Year 1743. American coastal trader *George*, Captain Raitt, sailing from Boston to North Carolina, wrecked near Oregon Inlet but no lives were lost.

Year 1744. Two English merchantmen sailing for London were lost on Diamond Shoals: *Katherine & Elizabeth*, Captain Webster, and the *Neptune*, Captain Knowler.

Year 1749. During a hurricane on October 7 and 8, 11 English merchantmen were totally lost. At Ocracoke Inlet seven sank inside the bar and two were wrecked five miles north of the inlet; at Cape Fear the *Dolphin*, Captain Cleavers, sank; and the *John & Jane*, Captain Close, foundered nine leagues seaward of the Cape Fear bar.

Year 1750. During a hurricane on August 18, four ships of the New Spain Flota of Captain-General Juan Manuel de Bonilla were lost: the galleon *Nuestra Señora de la Soledad*, wrecked 10 leagues north of Ocracoke Inlet; the merchant nao *El Salvador* wrecked 15 leagues north of Ocracoke Inlet; an unidentified nao wrecked at Topsail Inlet and another at Drum Inlet. The Spaniards and the English recovered the majority of the treasure. During the hurricane an unidentified English merchantman was lost off Cape Hatteras with a total loss of lives.

Year 1751. English merchantman *Greyhound*, Captain Cook, sailing from Boston to North Carolina, wrecked during bad weather near Salmon Creek in the Chowan River, but no lives were lost.

Year 1752. Three merchantmen were lost: two unidentified schooners arriving from Virginia wrecked on the Ocracoke Bar; and an unidentified English brigantine, Captain Murray, sailing for London, wrecked near Cape Fear.

Year 1757. Three ships were lost at Cape Hatteras: American merchantman *Union*, Captain Hammond, from Rhode Island, in January; English packet boat *Virginia Packet*, Captain Ball, sailing from Bristol to Virginia; and an unidentified American schooner, Captain Hayman, sailing to the Leeward Islands.

Year 1758. Three English merchantmen were lost at Cape Hatteras: *Friendship*, Captain Briscal, arriving from England, no lives were lost; *Peggy*, Captain Abercrombie, sailing from Philadelphia to South Carolina; and the *Princess Amelia*, Captain Freizwell, sailing from Halifax to South Carolina.

Year 1759. English merchantman *Tyrrel*, wrecked July 3 off Bacon Island Roads, all of the crew were saved.

Year 1760. Six ships were lost: English merchantman *Nancy*, Captain M'Carroll, sailing from Philadelphia to Cape Fear, lost near the Ocracoke Inlet bar; and earlier in the year the English merchantman *Betsey*, Captain Leadbeater, was lost crossing this bar.

Year 1774. Two English merchantmen were lost: *Charming Betsey*, Captain Waugh, sailing from Baltimore to London, wrecked on Ocracoke Island, only a small part of her cargo was saved; and the *Sally*, Captain Keith, sailing from Maryland to Gibraltar, was lost on Cape Hatteras.

Year 1775. During a hurricane that struck the North Carolina coast on September 2, a large number of ships were lost, but only the English merchantman *Hector*, Captain Quince, arriving from London, lost on Frying Pan Shoals, was identified. Four other English merchantmen were lost during the year: *Royal Exchange*, Captain Daverson, bound for London, at Cape Lookout, all of her crew was saved; *Clementina*, Captain Weir, arriving from London, at Cape Hatteras; *Elizabeth & Mary*, arriving from England, lost entering Cape Fear Inlet; and the *Austin*, Captain Sarrat, sailing from Tobago to Liverpool, lost off Cape Hatteras.

Year 1776. Ship of unknown registry, *Aurora*, a brigantine, wrecked September 19 on Portsmouth Island.

Year 1777. English troop-transport *Aurora*, Captain Bishop, was lost on November 11 off Cape Hatteras, very few survivors.

Year 1783. American merchantman *Peggy*, Captain McNeil, sailing from the Virgin Islands to New York, was lost off Cape Hatteras, only a small part of her cargo was saved.

Year 1784. Ship of unknown registry, *Betsey*, Captain Flynn, sailing to Antigua, was totally lost near Cape Fear.

Year 1786. English ship *Britannia*, Captain Dunlop, arriving from England, wrecked south of the Cape Fear River, but no lives were lost.

Year 1788. During a hurricane on July 23 and 24, 17 ships were wrecked at Ocracoke Inlet but only a few lives were lost.

Year 1789. English merchantman *Molly*, Captain Baker, sailing from Dunkirk to Virginia, was wrecked at Cape Hatteras.

Year 1790. American ship *Pusey Hall*, Captain Simpson, sailing from Jamaica to Virginia, wrecked at Cape Lookout.

Year 1791. English merchantman *St. James Planter*, Captain Paxton, sailing from Jamaica to London, was lost near Cape Lookout but part of her cargo was saved.

Year 1792. Two merchantmen were lost: English ship *Pitt*, Captain Cook, arriving from Antigua, lost on the Ocracoke Inlet bar; and the American ship *Experiment*, Captain McDonald, sailing to New York, lost off Cape Hatteras.

Year 1793. Two American merchantmen were lost: the *Polly*, wrecked near Beaufort, no lives were lost; and the *Nancy*, Captain Beacon, sailing from Jamaica to Virginia, wrecked on a shoal off Currituck, no lives were lost.

Year 1795. During a bad gale on August 2, six unidentified ships were wrecked on the Ocracoke Inlet bar; during the same storm a fleet of 18 Spanish ships, sailing from Havana to Spain, was struck off Cape Hatteras; an undisclosed number of these ships were lost.

Year 1797. American sloop *Betsey*, lost on September 6 at Currituck Inlet.

Year 1798. American merchantman *Industry*, Captain Woodend, sailing from St. Vincent to Virginia, was lost on Cape Hatteras.

Year 1799. German immigrant ship *Christian*, Captain Deetjen, sailing from Bremen to Baltimore, was lost near Cape Lookout, no lives lost and part of cargo saved.

Year 1802. Two English merchantmen were lost on Cape Hatteras: *Expectation*, Captain Baker, sailing from Antigua to North Carolina, and the *Brunshill*, Captain Bacon, sailing from England to Virginia, her crew was saved.

Year 1804. Four ships were lost: American packet boat *Wilmington Packet*, wrecked on September 8 at Bald Point, after first striking on Frying Pan Shoals; English ship *Lydia*, Captain Hatton, sailing from Wilmington to England, lost on Cape Hatteras; American merchantman *Molly*, Captain Mill, arriving from Jamaica, wrecked near Cape Hatteras; and a Spanish merchantman, *Santa Rosa*, Captain Fernandez, sailing from Havana to Bilbao with a great amount of treasure aboard, was lost near Wilmington about the middle of November.

Year 1805. Portuguese merchantman *Fortuna*, Captain Rhode, sailing from Brazil to Baltimore, lost on Cape Hatteras; part of her cargo was saved.

Year 1810. Four merchantmen were lost: English ship *Rhine*, Captain Turnly, arriving from the Bahamas, lost crossing the Wilmington bar in September, no lives were lost; French ship *Marma*, sailing from Martinique to New York, lost on Cape Hatteras; English ship *Olympus*, arriving from England, was totally lost near Wilmington at the end of November; and the American ship *Lively Lass*, sailing from New Orleans to Liverpool, drifted onshore at Ocracoke Island at the end of September without any persons aboard.

Year 1811. English merchantman *Young Factor*, sailing for London, was lost crossing the Wilmington bar, but no lives were lost.

Year 1813. Two ships were lost: American pilot boat *Patriot*, lost during January at Nags Head, and the Spanish brig *San Antonio*, Captain Fabre, was totally lost on February 18 near Wilmington, but all of her crew were saved.

Year 1814. American gunboat #140 wrecked on September 23 on Ocracoke Island.

Year 1815. During a hurricane early in September, more than 20 ships were wrecked or sunk at Ocracoke Inlet and on Ocracoke Island. During the year, three other ships were lost: American brig *Atlanta* on November 8 on Diamond Shoals, but the crew was saved; English merchantman *Sero*, Captain Robinson, coming from Cuba, wrecked on September 25 off Cape Hatteras; and the American merchantman *Superior*, Captain Spence, sailing from Martinique to Philadelphia, lost October 3 near Cape Hatteras, crew and part of cargo saved.

Year 1816. Five merchantmen were lost: American ship *Eliza*, Captain Steele, sailing from Jamaica to Philadelphia, lost on Ocracoke Island, crew and part of cargo saved; American ship *Bolina*, Captain Lee, sailing from New York to Charleston, wrecked on Boddy Island on September 26, crew and part of cargo saved; American ship *Little Dick*, sailing from Jamaica to Wilmington, lost crossing the Wilmington bar; English ship *Nancy*, Captain Scott, sailing from the Virgin Islands to Edenton, wrecked on January 23 near Newburn but the crew was saved; and a ship of unknown registry, *Mary*, sailing from Norfolk to Trinidad, wrecked on April 15 on Currituck Beach, most of her cargo was saved.

Year 1817. Five merchantmen were lost. American ship *Voucher*, Captain Howland, sailing from New York to Charleston, wrecked November 19 at Chicamacomico, all of crew, passengers, and cargo saved; ship of unknown registry, *Emperor of Russia*, sailing from Amsterdam to Boston, lost March 18 near Currituck Inlet, crew and part of cargo saved; American ship *John Adams*, sailing from Charleston to Norfolk, lost May 19 on Cape Hatteras, crew and some cargo saved; ship of unknown registry, *Rosetta*, Captain Sissen, arriving from New York, lost March 4 crossing the Ocracoke Inlet bar, crew and all cargo saved; and the American ship *Mary & Francis*, Captain Marsh, sailing from Madeira to Baltimore, wrecked during March near Cape Hatteras but most of her cargo was saved.

Year 1818. Five merchantmen were lost. During a storm on October 3 two unidentified American ships were wrecked near Cape Hatteras and the English ship *Fly* sank on Frying Pan Shoals. The American ship *William Carlton* wrecked May 15 at Kill Devil Hills and the English brig *Georgia*, Captain Colesworth, coming from New York, was wrecked July 15 at Currituck Inlet, crew and most of wood cargo saved.

Year 1819. Two American ships were lost, the schooner *Phoenix*, Captain Coffin, sailing to Philadelphia, wrecked May 13 on Cape Hatteras, and the sloop *Revenge* during January at Currituck Inlet.

Year 1820. Three American ships were lost, the sloop *Henry* during January on Ocracoke Island; the merchantman *Islington*, Captain Wilson, on March 16 at Cape Hatteras, and the ship *Horatio*, Captain Martin, during April on Diamond Shoals.

Year 1821. Four merchantmen were lost. An unidentified English ship of about 125 tons with a cargo of rum wrecked at Cape Hatteras in September, with a total loss of lives; American ship *Charles K. Mallory*, Captain Driver, arriving from St. Thomas, wrecked September 10 on Cape Hatteras, with a total loss of lives; English ship *Martha*, sailing from Bermuda to New London, wrecked at Currituck Sands; and American schooner *Sophia*, Captain Massey, sailing from Philadelphia to Norfolk, wrecked 10 miles north of Currituck Inlet, only one survivor.

Year 1822. Three ships were lost, a ship of unknown registry, *Nereus*, Captain Bosse, sailing from Bremen to Virginia, totally lost January 1 on CapeHatteras; English merchantman *Statira*, sailing from Havana to London, lost on Frying Pan Shoals, no lives were lost; and the American schooner *Enterprize*, wrecked October 27 at New Inlet.

Year 1823. American ship *Peter Francisco*, Captain Reerson, sailing from New York to Mobile, wrecked October 7 on Bodies Island, crew, passengers, and all cargo saved.

Above

This pair of beautiful earrings, probably of Oriental origin, were found on one of the 1733 Spanish shipwrecks in the Florida keys.

Below

These colorful ceramic jars and jugs and glass spirit bottles came from the wreckage of an early American merchantman off Charleston, South Carolina.

Year 1824. Two ships were lost on the Ocracoke Inlet bar, the American schooner *Susan*, sailing from Demarara to Philadelphia, on June 1; and the French merchantman *Caroline du Nord*, Captain Grace, on January 19, no lives were lost.

Year 1825. During a hurricane on June 4, more than 25 unidentified ships were wrecked north of Ocracoke Inlet on the Outer Banks. During the year, seven other American ships were lost, *Washington*, coming from Jamaica, on January 24, at Ocracoke Island; *Nancy*, Captain Hatch, February 21, on the Ocracoke Inlet bar; merchantman *Horam*, Captain Eldridge, sailing from Boston to Jamaica, April 6, on the Ocracoke Inlet bar; schooner *Emulous*, January 22, at Kitty Hawk; schooner *Diomede*, January 23, at Kitty Hawk; schooner *Harvest*, Captain Murphy, November 18, at Bodie Island; and the schooner *Victory*, December, at Kitty Hawk.

South Carolina

Year 1520. Unidentified Spanish nao, Captain Lucas Vazquez de Ayllon, wrecked near Cape Romain, no lives were lost.

Year 1700. Scottish merchantman *Rising Sun*, lost during a hurricane on September 3 on the Charleston bar.

Year 1713. During a hurricane in September, a large number of ships were sunk and wrecked in Charleston harbor.

Year 1728. During a hurricane on September 14, a great part of the town of Charleston was destroyed and eight ships were sunk in the harbor and 15 badly damaged.

Year 1750. English merchantman *Caesar*, Captain Sparks, sailing from the Bay of Honduras for England, was forced to enter Charleston for repairs but was lost crossing the bar of this port.

Year 1751. Scottish merchantman *Martha*, Captain Shea, arriving from the Canary Islands, was wrecked on Cape Romain, all of her crew was saved.

Obverse and reverse of two Spanish eight-escudo coins dated 1708 that were recovered from the 1715 Spanish treasure fleet offshore Florida.

Year 1752. During a hurricane on September 15, more than 20 large English merchantmen and three warships were totally lost in Charleston harbor. On September 30, another hurricane struck and 12 more newly arrived English merchantmen were also sunk. In April the English merchantman *Bennet*, Captain Wadham, preparing to sail for London, was accidentally burned in Charleston harbor.

Year 1757. Slave ship of unknown registry, *Anamaboo*, Captain Ferguson, sailing from Africa to Rhode Island with a cargo of slaves, was totally lost near St. Helena Sound, only a few of the crew survived.

Year 1758. English merchantman *Marcella*, Captain Way, arriving from Lisbon, wrecked February 18 on a sandbank about three leagues from Charleston, totally salvaged and no lives were lost.

Year 1759. English merchantman *Judith*, Captain Martin, sailing from North Carolina to England, wrecked on Cape Romain.

Year 1761. Five ships were lost in Rebellion Road at Charleston during a hurricane on May 4: the English merchantman *Polly & Betsey*, Captain Muer; English merchantman *Success*, Captain Clark; English merchantman *Daniel*, Captain Lake; English ship *Britannia*, Captain Wilson; and an unidentified Bermudan schooner.

Year 1766. English merchantman *Speedwell*, Captain Redman, arriving from London, lost crossing the Charleston bar.

Year 1767. Two merchantmen were lost: Portuguese ship *St. Anthony*, Captain Arnold, sailing from Charleston to Oporto, foundered soon after leaving port, no lives were lost; and the English ship *Mary*, Captain Loveday, arriving from London, wrecked a bit south of Charleston but the crew, rigging, and sails were all saved.

Year 1768. English merchantman *York*, Captain Randell, sailing from Jamaica to London, forced into Charleston for repairs but lost in November while crossing the bar of this port, all cargo lost but crew saved.

Year 1770. English merchantman *Sergeant Glynn*, Captain Mogridge, arriving from London, totally lost near Port Royal Sound; no lives were lost.

Year 1775. English merchantman *Nancy*, Captain Cunningham, sailing from London to North Carolina, wrecked several leagues north of Charleston.

Year 1776. English warship *H.M.S. Acteon*, 28 guns, Captain Christopher Atkins, burned in Charleston harbor by her crew on June 29.

Year 1777. English warship *H.M.S. Cruiser*, 8 guns, Captain Francis Parry, was burned off Charleston by her crew to prevent its capture by the Americans.

Year 1780. During a battle off Charleston, a British fleet commanded by Vice-Admiral Arbuthnot, destroyed and sank three American naval vessels, *Bricole*, 44 guns; *General Moultrie*, 20 guns; and the *Notre Dame*, 16 guns. The British privateer *Vigilant*, 20 guns, Captain Thomas Goldesbrough, was burned at Beaufort.

Year 1781. Six ships were lost: English warships *Thetis* and *London* sank at the Charleston docks during a hurricane on August 9; English merchantman *Despatch*, arriving from Jamaica, was driven ashore near Charleston by several American privateers and totally lost; English troop-transport *Leeds Industry*, Captain Hobkirk, sank in Charleston harbor; ship of unknown registry, *Jamaica*, Captain McLeon, arriving from New York, capsized and sank in Charleston harbor; and the English merchantman *Port Morant*, sailing from Jamaica to London, wrecked October 10 on a sandbank called Martin's Industry, to the eastward of Port Royal, but no lives were lost.

Year 1784. Three English merchantmen were lost on the Charleston bar: *America*, Captain Jameson, arriving from Scotland; Swift, *Captain Craig*, arriving from St. Augustine; and the *Suffolk*, Captain Warton, sailing for London, part of her cargo was saved.

Year 1785. English merchantman *Dispatch*, Captain Shields, fully laden and ready to sail for London, totally lost at Georgetown harbor.

Year 1787. Two merchantmen were lost: English ship *Hope*, Captain Worsley, sailing to Hamburg, lost on the Charleston bar; and the Scottish ship *Three Friends*, Captain McElcheran, arriving from Tobago, wrecked near Charleston but some of her cargo was saved.

Year 1791. American ship *Governor Pinkney*, Captain Hall, sailing to Hispaniola, wrecked on the Charleston bar.

Year 1792. During a severe gale on October 30, several large unidentified merchantmen were lost in Charleston harbor.

Year 1796. Two English merchantmen were lost: *Powhaton*, Captain Shaw, sailing from Liverpool to Jamaica, on the Charleston bar, most of her cargo was saved; and the *Grampus*, arriving from Liverpool, wrecked southward from Charleston.

Year 1797. Two merchantmen were lost: English ship *Three Friends*, Captain Bradford, sailing to London, lost on the Charleston bar; and the American ship *Polly*, Captain Higgins, arriving from Havana, wrecked near Charleston.

Year 1799. Ship of unknown registry, *Seaflower*, Captain Williams, arriving from Jamaica, was lost on the Georgetown bar, some of her cargo was saved.

Year 1800. English merchantman *Argus*, Captain Johnson, sailing for Liverpool, was lost on the Charleston bar but most of her cargo was saved.

Year 1801. English ship *Patrick*, Captain Salmon, arriving from Honduras, was lost on the Charleston bar.

Year 1802. American ship *Monticello*, Captain Newell, coming from the Leeward Islands, wrecked on Morris Island but some of her cargo was saved.

Year 1804. During a hurricane on September 11, five ships were sunk and 11 severely damaged in Charleston harbor.

Year 1805. Two English merchantmen were lost in Charleston harbor: *Northumberland*, Captain Gibb, arriving from Jamaica, October 14, the crew was saved, and the *Jack Park*, sailing for Liverpool, while crossing the bar.

Year 1806. Two English slave ships were wrecked when attempting to enter Charleston harbor: *John*, Captain Cummings, and the *Swan*, Captain Smith, with no lives lost on either ship.

Year 1810. Two English merchantmen were lost near Charleston: *Sarah*, Captain Milner, sailing from Havana to Jamaica, on May 7 on Morris Island; and the *Cracklow*, arriving from London, several miles south of the harbor.

Year 1811. English ship *Benson*, Captain Wilmot, sailing from Honduras to London, wrecked on March 23 near Charleston.

Year 1813. During a hurricane at Charleston on August 27 and 28, a large number of ships were sunk in the river and harbor and others wrecked on the shore. On November 24 a sloop of unknown registry, *General Hodgkinson*, arriving from Curaçao, wrecked off Charleston.

Year 1814. English warship *H.M.S. Peacock*, 18 guns, Captain Richard Coote, during August, foundered off Charleston, total loss of lives.

Year 1815. Two merchantmen lost: English ship *Spring*, Captain Smith, sailing from Liverpool to Wilmington, was totally lost on Cape Romain Shoals during August but no lives were lost; and the American ship *Hercules*, Captain Duncan, arriving from Jamaica and the Bahamas, was totally lost off Charleston.

Year 1816. American ship *Harriet*, Captain Folson, sailing from Havana to Wilmington, wrecked on August 6 on Sullivan's Island.

Year 1818. English merchantman *Margaret*, sailing for Liverpool, wrecked August 9 on the Charleston bar, crew and cargo saved.

Year 1820. English ship *Dee*, Captain Dixon, arriving from Liverpool, was totally lost on December 24 to the southward of the Charleston Lighthouse, crew, four chests of specie, and mail saved.

Year 1821. Ship of unknown registry, *Minerva*, Captain Neilson, arriving from France, wrecked January 3 on Edisto Island, her crew was saved.

Year 1822. American ship *Calcutta*, Captain Winslow, arriving from Amsterdam, wrecked on April 10 about 4 miles north of the lighthouse on Folly Island.

Year 1824. English merchantman *Plantagenet*, Captain Key, from Liverpool, totally lost February 20 on the Charleston bar; her crew was saved.

Georgia

Year 1763. English merchantman *Friends Endeavour*, Captain Wake, sailing for London, was lost crossing over Sunbury bar, only her crew was saved.

Year 1769. English merchantman *Prudence*, Captain Smith, arriving from Cadíz, totally lost on Cumberland Island.

Year 1779. English warship *H.M.S. Rose*, 20 guns, Captain John Brown, was deliberately sunk in September to block the bar at the entrance of Savannah.

Year 1780. Two ships were lost: English warship *H.M.S. Defiance*, 64 guns, Captain Maximillian Jacobs, wrecked February 18 on the Savannah bar; and the English merchantman *Jamaica*, Captain Redman, arriving from Jamaica, was lost on the Savannah River.

Year 1781. English warship *H.M.S. Hope*, 16 guns, Captain William Thomas, wrecked off Savannah.

Year 1785. English merchantman *Polly*, Captain Newell, preparing to sail for London, accidentally burned in Savannah Harbor.

Year 1787. Scottish merchantman *Dutchess of Argyle*, Captain Miller, sailing from Jamaica to Philadelphia, wrecked on Cumberland Island but no lives were lost.

Year 1791. English merchantman *Eliza*, Captain Shelburn, arriving from Barbados, totally lost on the Savannah bar.

Year 1792. Ship of unknown registry, *Conception*, Captain Towers, arriving from Philadelphia, wrecked on St. Simon's Island.

Year 1794. English packet boat, *Grenada*, after being captured by a French privateer, was brought into Savannah Harbor and burned.

Year 1799. American brig *Minerva*, Captain Bunker, lost during April near St. Andrews Sound.

Year 1803. Scottish merchantman *Whidah*, Captain Balfour, arriving from Clyde, lost January 6 near Savannah, crew and part of cargo saved.

Year 1804. During a hurricane on September 11, a large number of unidentified ships were sunk in Savannah Harbor.

Year 1806. American merchantman *Mary*, Captain Firth, sailing to Barbados, was lost going down the Savannah River, crew and cargo saved.

Year 1808. Ship of unknown registry, *Triton*, Captain Cox, sailing from Amsterdam to Baltimore, was totally lost near Savannah.

Year 1810. Ship of unknown registry, *Pezzarro*, Captain Fosh, sailing for Liverpool. was wrecked at Savannah, crew and cargo saved.

Year 1811. Two American merchantmen were totally lost on the Savannah bar: *Active*, arriving from Lisbon, at the end of November, and the *Edward*, Captain Lewis, laden with timber for England.

Year 1815. Three English merchantmen were lost: *Mars*, Captain Taylor, arriving from London, on December 2, near Savannah, no lives were lost; *Achilles*, on the Martha's Industry Shoals; and the *Speculator*, Captain Hardy, on December 10, near Savannah, seven of her crew perished.

Year 1816. Two English merchantmen were lost near Savannah: *Velina*, Captain Wickham, arriving from England, on March 3, crew and part of cargo saved, and the *Braddock*, Captain Johnson, arriving from Liverpool, on November 21.

Year 1817. Three merchantmen were wrecked near Savannah: American ship *Goleah*, Captain Payne, arriving from France, in March; the American ship *Jupiter*, arriving from Havana; and the English ship *Rose in Bloom*, Captain Lake, sailing from New Orleans to Amsterdam, on May 6, crew and small part of cargo saved.

Year 1821. English ship *Jason*, Captain Thomson, arriving from England, wrecked on the South Breakers of the St. Simon's Island bar but no lives were lost.

Year 1824. English merchantman *Albion*, Captain Stephenson, sailing from Honduras to London, wrecked on St. Catherine's Island, only six survivors.

The Gulf Coast

Alabama

Year 1814. English warship *H.M.S. Hermes*, 20 guns, Captain William Henry Percy, was sunk while attacking the batteries in Mobile Bay on September 15.

Year 1821. American merchantman *Mississippi*, lost on June 20 at the entrance to Mobile Bay.

Year 1822. American merchantman *Margaret Ann*, Captain Bodfish, arriving from New York, wrecked on September 25 at Mobile Point, crew and some cargo saved.

Mississippi

Year 1643. Two unidentified Spanish caravels, sent on an exploration voyage from Veracruz, were wrecked on the south side of Ship Island, several lost from both crews. The island was named after these two shipwrecks.

Year 1818. American merchantman *Hibernia*, Captain Latham, sailing from Madeira to New Orleans, wrecked on Petit Bois Island; no lives lost.

211

Year 1819. American warship, the schooner *Firebrand*, 12 guns, 150 tons, crew of 75 men, Captain Cunningham, wrecked on a shoal off the west end of Cat Island during a hurricane in July.

Louisiana

Sometime before 1550. A Spanish fleet commanded by Captain Narvay, on a voyage of exploration, lost one of its ships at the entrance to the Mississippi River.

Year 1722. During a hurricane on September 12 and 13, a large number of unidentified ships were sunk at and near New Orleans.

Year 1772. Spanish merchant brigantine *Nuestra Señora del Amparo*, alias *El Principe de Orange*, Captain Pedro Días Baladonque, sailing from New Orleans for Veracruz, was struck by a hurricane on September 2 and wrecked at the entrance of the Mississippi River, where she quickly went to pieces, only six survivors.

Year 1779. A Spanish fleet of warships commanded by Governor Bernardo de Galvez, while preparing to attack the English fort at Baton Rouge, was struck by a hurricane on August 18, all ships, except one, were sunk. The number of ships lost was not stated, only the name of one of them: the *America La Reseda*.

Year 1780. During a hurricane that struck New Orleans on August 24, dozens of ships sunk in the Mississippi River and the lakes surrounding New Orleans, and the town was leveled.

Year 1782. French merchantman *Deux Freres*, sailing from New Orleans to London, was lost south of the port on the Mississippi River.

Year 1785. French merchantman *Savanne*, Captain Basques, arriving from Jamaica, was totally lost on a sandbar on the Mississippi River below New Orleans, some of her cargo was saved.

Year 1793. Four merchantmen were wrecked on the Mississippi River, south of New Orleans, during a storm in August. Two of them were American ships from Philadelphia, captains Towers and McClanahon.

Year 1812. During a hurricane on August 19 a large number of ships were lost at New Orleans and on Lake Ponchartrain.

Year 1817. American merchantman *Rolla*, arriving from Lisbon, wrecked on May 30 on the New Orleans bar.

Year 1821. During a severe gale on March 6, three ships were lost at New Orleans: an unidentified ship from Cuba; American merchantman *Blanch*, having arrived from Charleston, no lives were lost; and a French brig coming from France with a valuable cargo and $30,000 in specie aboard, many persons perished on this ship. Two other ships were lost the French merchantman *Navigatore, Captain Chaureaux, arriving from France, lost in March on Chandelier Island; and the English merchantman Hannah*, Captain Rose, arriving from Liverpool, on August 19, about 60 miles south of New Orleans on the Mississippi River.

Texas

Year 1553. About five days after the New Spain Flota sailed from Veracruz for Havana and Spain, it was struck by a hurricane and the 20 or more ships in this fleet were widely scattered over the Gulf of Mexico. Three of the ships managed to reach Spain and one, Veracruz; but none of the others were ever heard from. Three of these ships, all carrying substantial amounts of treasure, were wrecked on Padre Island, *San Estevan*, 220 tons, Captain Francisco del Mecerno; *Sancta Maria de Yciar*, 220 tons, Captain Alonso Ozosi; and an unidentified nao. On two of the ships, it is not known whether there were any survivors, but on the other, most of the crew and passengers reached shore only to be massacred by Indians. Only two persons survived and eventually reached civilization. In recent years, one of these wrecks has been located and a substantial amount of treasure and artifacts have been recovered.

Year 1766. During a hurricane on September 4, all five ships of a Spanish fleet carrying treasure from Veracruz to Spain were wrecked on Galveston Island: two were identified, *El Nuevo Constante*, and *La Caraqueña* (alias the *Guipuzcuana*). The majority of the treasure and persons on these ships were saved.

Year 1811. Spanish warship *San Pedro*, sailing from Veracruz to Spain, carrying more than 500,000 pesos in gold and silver specie, was wrecked on Padre Island. Salvors recovered most of the treasure shortly afterward.

Year 1818. During a hurricane on September 12, four ships of the pirate Jean Lafitte were wrecked on the northern tip of Galveston Island, but it is not known if they were carrying anything of value.

West Coast

California

Year 1540. In 1539, at the orders of the conquistador Hernán Cortez, three small caravels under the command of Captain Francisco de Ulloa explored the coast of California. Before reaching Californian waters, one of the ships was scuttled and another sent back to Mexico. The remaining ship, the 35-ton *Trinidad*, continued on alone and during the summer of 1540 was in the vicinity of San Diego. Due to sickness, all of the men were placed ashore, and during a storm the small vessel disappeared (apparently the anchor cable parted and the vessel drifted off to places unknown). In recent years men claim to have located this wreck and recovered substantial amounts of treasure. No proof has turned up, however, to substantiate the claim of its discovery, and there is little chance that it carried any treasure at all, except for the few personal effects of its crew.

Year 1579. During Sir Francis Drake's circumnavigation of the globe in the *Golden Hind*, he stopped at Drake's Bay — named after him — in what today is called the Point Reyes National Seashore to the west of San Francisco. After careening the ship, he decided to abandoned a small Spanish vessel he had captured along the west coast of Central American. We can assume that the scuttled vessel was first stripped of any valuables or usable items.

Year 1599. A large Manila galleon, the *San Agustín*, Captain Sebastian Cermeño, was sailing between Manila and Acapulco with a cargo of gold, silver, jewels, oriental porcelains, silks and other exotic Far Eastern products. While anchored at Drake's Bay she wrecked during a squall and was a total loss. Most of her crew was ashore at the time; all those aboard perished. I first located a part of the *San Agustín* in 1951 and again in 1989, but Federal authorities have refused permission to excavate the site.

Year 1600. The Capitana of a small squadron commanded by General Juan de Velasco, which was sent from Peru in search of Dutch warships reported cruising in the area of Panama, lost its rudder during a storm near Panama and drifted for weeks until it finally wrecked somewhere on the southern coast of California. But the only clue of her possible location is that it was somewhere north of San Diego.

Year 1823. A large French merchantman, *Nereide*, Captain Betaille, sailing from the Far East for South America, was lost somewhere on the coast of California and only 10 of the crew of more than 300 managed to reach civilization.

Oregon

Year 1707. Large Manila Galleon *San Francisco Xavier*, Captain Francisco Obregon y Avila, sailing between Manila and Acapulco was off course as she attempted to make landfall at Cape Mendocino off the California coast when she was wrecked on November 8 in a storm near the mouth of the Nehalem River. Nothing more is known of her fate or of the persons aboard her. Over the years large amounts of Chinese porcelain shards and of beeswax have been cast ashore during storms. One of the large pieces of beeswax now on display in a local museum bears the date 1679.

Year 1808. British trading ship Sea Otter, Captain Niles, of 120 tons, was wrecked on August 22 near the mouth of the Umpqua River and all but six men perished.

Washington

Year 1800. Russian trading vessel *St. Nicholas*, Captain Nikolai Bulagin, set sail from Sitka, Alaska on a trading voyage for otter skins when a gale caused her to wrecked on some rocks at the mouth of the Quillayute River, near Lapush, Washington.

The Great Lakes

Year 1679. Small French frigate *Griffon*, Captain Robert La Salle, sank during September carrying a small amount of gold specie aboard on Birch Island Reef, on Lake Huron.

Year 1721. French frigate *Le Jean Florin* sank on July 2 about 10 to 15 miles northeast of Erie, Pennsylvania, on Lake Erie and was reported to be carrying some treasure at the time.

Year 1764. French ship *Le Blanc Henri* wrecked on June 17 on Wolf Island Spit, near Kingston, Ontario, carrying some treasure aboard.

Year 1783. English sloop *Ontario* sank on November 23 about 3 miles off Oswego, on Lake Ontario, 190 persons perished and a great amount of treasure was lost.

214

Year 1803. American sloop *Lady Washington* vanished November 11 on Lake Ontario carrying a general cargo including a large amount of chinaware.

Chapter Three

Florida

Florida is the world center for underwater treasure hunting. More work has been done on shipwrecks in Florida waters than throughout the rest of the Western Hemisphere. There are several reasons for this activity. The Florida Keys and the east coast of Florida are lined with off-lying reefs and shoals which have claimed an extraordinary number of vessels. Because there are no safe refuges from bad weather, more ships have been lost in storms there than in many other areas. From the time of Columbus until the introduction of steamships almost all ships returning to Europe from the New World to the Old chose to sail up the dangerous Bahama Channel. Even in good weather, the prevailing winds and Gulf current pushed all shipping toward the coast of Florida. The abundance of shipwrecks attracted large numbers of "wrackers," who were established in the Bahamas from the early 18th century and working out of Key West from the second decade of the 19th century.

Moving forward to the 20th century...like California, Florida was one of the first places in the United States where skin diving and scuba diving caught on. Many divers, soon bored with spear fishing or underwater photography, switched their focus to old shipwrecks. Because it costs less to travel to Florida than to the Caribbean or other shipwreck-rich areas, divers from across the country who were interested in diving on shipwrecks began combing the reefs off Florida in quest of treasure and artifacts.

Even before skin diving caught on, there were a handful of professional treasure hunters: Art McKee, Bill Thompson, Ed Ciesinski and others, doing most of their exploring and salvaging in the Florida Keys. As early as 1950 they had located and worked on most of the ships of the fleet of 1733, including the *H.M.S. Winchester* and the *H.M.S. Loo*, and had recovered a wide variety of artifacts but very little treasure.

Their diving and salvage equipment was primitive by today's standards. Shallow-water helmets were used for diving, and most of excavation was done by hand or with small water-jets. With the introduction of scuba gear a new breed of treasure hunter followed in their wake, benefiting from better equipment, including air lifts for excavating and metal detectors for locating metallic deposits. They also enjoyed much greater freedom on the bottom with their advanced diving gear. For the most part they worked on the same wrecks as their predecessors, making even better discoveries. Most of these divers were part-time treasure hunters, working mostly during weekends or summer vacations.

For years controversy raged between the State of Florida and two groups of salvors. A young boy was spear fishing between Vero Beach and Fort Pierce and accidentally uncovered a large number of American gold coins on the site of an 1857 shipwreck which had been carrying a U.S. Army payroll. At the time of the discovery neither the boy nor his father, who helped him recover the coins, had a search or salvage permit. However, they reported their find to the state which took the customary 25 percent. The salvors reported recovering 582 gold coins. Sometime later the state, which employs a team of criminal investigators, brought the salvors to court, claiming that they had actually recovered 3,264 gold coins, valued at $271,000. After three years in the court the salvors lost everything.

Another group, led by Tom Gurr, discovered the Spanish merchant ship *San José* of the 1733 fleet outside the three-mile limit in 1968. During the summer of 1968 the divers recovered a large number of interesting artifacts valued at over $50,000. Then, after the new law was passed extending the state's control over coastal waters from three miles to 10 miles, Gurr was forced to stop his salvage operation. He threatened to sue the state, but the state finally gave him a lease on the *San José* wreck and, in gratitude, Gurr turned over half of what he had recovered during 1968, even though the wreck was not within the boundaries of the state at the time.

The Real Eight Company of Melbourne, Florida, was the first group in Florida to operate on a large scale, treating treasure hunting as a business. Real Eight was founded by the late Kip Wagner, who has been mentioned earlier in this book. Kip had been beach combing for years, using a World War II metal detector without any noteworthy finds, but in 1960 he located a large number of silver and gold coins along the beach between Sebastian Inlet and Fort Pierce. Since none of the coins were dated later than 1714, he assumed, correctly, that they were from a fleet of shipwrecks which had been lost in the area around 1714 or soon afterwards. Further research into historical documents convinced him that these coins were coming ashore from some of the 12 ships of the fleet of 1715 which were lost in a hurricane.

Not being a diver himself, Wagner assembled a group of divers, who were either in the military or worked at Cape Canaveral, and they began exploring the areas where the coins were washing ashore. They located several shipwrecks and began excavating with a hydrolift. Because they were all employed, they were limited to working on the wrecks during weekends and holidays; that is, if conditions permitted. All too often, the sea was too rough. In 1963 Real Eight decided the best course of action was to employ full-time divers. They signed a contract with Treasure Salvors, a group of divers from California led by Mel Fisher. Treasure Salvors had a modest amount of treasure hunting experience, but had never made a spectacular find. *Their luck was about to change!*

The Real Eight group had already recovered over 100,000 silver coins and a few gold ones as well. During the summer of 1964 Treasure Salvors hit it big, recovering over $1 million in gold specie and bullion as well as jewelry and other priceless artifacts. The two groups worked together until 1970, making substantial finds each year. Treasure Salvors then shifted operations to the Florida Keys in quest of the 1622 *Margarita* and *Atocha* shipwrecks. Real Fight continued working for several more years before going out of business.

About 10 years ago, after Fisher's discovery of the *Atocha* and the *Margarita*, he came back to the 1715 shipwrecks with a new company, Cobb Coin, Inc.. By invoking the Admiralty Arrest Act, Cobb Coin was able to assume ownership of the wrecks of the 1715 fleet and many others scattered between Fort Pierce and Sebastian Inlet. In addition to having several of their own vessels working these sites, Cobb Coin subleases the rights to many other treasure hunting groups to work these wrecks for a percentage of the finds.

The name of Mel Fisher is familiar to anyone who is fascinated by shipwrecks and sunken treasure, and I need say little more here about his numerous fabulous discoveries. In recent years he has extended his activities to the Bahamas and other areas of the Caribbean. A visit to his treasure museums in Key West and Sebastian is worthwhile for anyone interested in sunken treasure. In May 1993 I too opened the Port Royal Museum of Sunken Treasure on St. Petersburg Beach. It is a modern museum with hands-on activities and displays of countless treasures found in Florida waters, and from shipwrecks I have found and excavated in the Bahamas, the Caribbean, Mexico, South America, the Mediterranean and the Far East.

The State of Florida has very strict laws for locating and recovering objects from shipwrecks. In areas not covered by groups holding Admiralty Arrest Act permits you must deal with the Division of Historical Resources in Tallahassee, which controls all wrecks inside the three-mile zone. For the past three years they have been trying unsuccessfully to extend this area out to 200 miles. In the old days it was a simple process to get a search permit, which encompassed 18 square miles, or a pinpoint salvage permit which covered a one-mile radius. During the past few years, however, it appears that the state wants to put an end to all shipwreck work in Florida waters, and many in the business fear they may eventually succeed. Early in 1992 they shut down all shipwreck activities in the Florida Keys citing environmental concerns, and at the time of writing (Autumn 1993) this restriction is still enforced. There is now talk about prohibiting shipwreck work along the east coast as well.

Whereas, in the past salvors had only the Division of Historical Resources to deal with, today a salvor requesting even something as simple as a search permit must deal with four different state and federal agencies. One group of salvors, Historical Research and Development of Melbourne, has been trying in vain for three years to obtain a search permit for an area near Vero Beach. Recently, they believed they were finally going to get the permit. They had jumped through all the bureaucratic hoops and done everything they were told to do, including providing the Army Corps of Engineers with aerial photographs of the area they plan to explore. However, instead of receiving the permit they were informed that they must also provide underwater photographs of the complete sea floor in this area; not an easy task since underwater visibility is rarely more than a few feet. Severe restrictions such as these are driving salvors to other countries or to deep water areas where no permission is required — at least at this time.

Actually problems with the State of Florida go back quite a few years. In 1966 more than 100 groups and individuals applied for shipwreck permits from the state, but only 10 were issued. Since this naturally infuriated many people, a large number who had been refused leases joined forces and sued the state, but they lost the case. One state official, when notifying a diver that he was refused a permit, had four of his teeth knocked out by the frustrated diver.

Those fortunate enough to obtain a permit from the State of Florida must adhere to strict archaeological procedure. The state takes 25 percent of everything recovered, but has the right to buy part or all of the salvors' remaining share. After the division has been made between the state and the salvors, they are free to dispose of their share in any way they wish, but they must keep in mind that the IRS is lurking in the background for their eventual cut as well.

In addition to the wrecks I have listed in this chapter, there are several hundred others lost between 1540 and 1825 that are listed in original archival documents only as lost in the Bahama Channel, Straits of Florida or Gulf of Florida.

Shipwrecks in Florida's Waters

Year 1521. Spanish merchant nao *San Anton*, 100 tons, Captain Gonzalo Rodríguez, was lost in the Florida Keys after leaving Cuba en route to Spain.

Year 1525. A caravel that was part of the expedition of Don Lucas Vasqué de Ayllon, which sailed from Spain in 1524, was lost near Cape St. Helen and natives massacred 200 survivors.

Year 1528. During the expedition led by Panfilo de Narvaez, his four ships anchored in an area called Santa Cruz which is believed to be Sarasota Bay. Four ships under the command of Lieutenant Caraballo were sent to find a better harbor and one of them wrecked close to shore.

Year 1530. A book written in Spain in 1571 mentions a large number of ships lost at Key Largo and others near Cape Canaveral, but no supporting documents have been found in the Spanish archives.

Year 1535. Another 16th-century Spanish book mentions that a fleet of ships was lost in Espírito Santo Bay (believed to be Tampa Bay) and that a survivor named Juan Muñoz was rescued by a Spanish ship 14 years later.

Year 1545. A vessel was wrecked upon the coast of Florida and some of its crew of 200 were slain by natives and the remainder reduced to slavery.

Year 1549. Three unidentified Spanish vessels sailing between Mexico and Spain were lost near Key Largo and most of the people aboard the ships reached shore and lived with great hardships for several years until being rescued by a passing vessel.

Year 1550. Nao (type of vessel), *Visitación*, 200 tons, Captain Pedro de la Torre, sailing alone from Veracruz for Spain, was wrecked in the Florida Keys.

Year 1551. A Spanish ship returning to Spain was wrecked on December 2 during a storm somewhere in the Florida Keys and only 19 persons managed to reach shore and were later rescued. Apparently the ship was carrying treasure as several attempts were made in vain to locate the wreck and salvage her contents.

Year 1551. Nao *San Nícolas*, 200 tons, Captain Juan Christoval, was wrecked near Fort Pierce, and Indians recovered a great deal of what it carried. The ship was coming from Nombre de Diós and Cartagena on its way to Spain, and there was no mention of whether it stopped in Havana or of its cargo.

Year 1554. Nao *Santa Maria del Camino*, 350 tons, Captain Diego Díaz, owned by Sr. Bolaños, part of the Armada de Tierra Firme of Captain-General Bartolome Carreño, was lost on the coast of Florida; everything it carried was salvaged by the Spaniards.

Year 1554. The ship of *Farfan* (probably its owner) sank near Fort Pierce, richly laden with gold and silver, and Indians of the King of Ais recovered a great deal from the wreck.

Year 1555. Several ships of the Flota de Tierra Firme, commanded by Cosme Rodríguez Farfan, were separated from the convoy in the Bahama Channel after a storm hit and never heard of again.

Year 1556. Indians of the King of Ais were reported to have recovered, near Cape Canaveral, over a million pesos in bars of gold and silver and many precious pieces of jewelry made by the Indians of Mexico from ship or ships of the Nueva España Flota, of which it is said the son of Pedro de Menéndez was the general. The document containing this information is dated 1570, and although the Indians made this recovery in 1556, the ship or ships might have wrecked at an earlier date. The wording of the document makes it impossible to determine if only one ship, several or the whole fleet sank, but it was probably only one or several ships, otherwise there would have been a great deal more mention in other contemporary documents.

Year 1556. Three naos under the command of Captain Gonzalo de Carbajal, sailing from Puerto Rico to Spain, were lost on the coast of Florida. Only two were identified: *Sancta Salvador*, 120 tons, Captain Guillen de Lugo; and the other, with the identical name and weight, Captain Martín de Artalico.

Year 1559. A fleet of thirteen vessels sailed from Veracruz under the command of Don Tristan de Luna y Arellano, Governor of Florida, on June 11, where they planned to found a new colony. On August 14 the fleet anchored in the Bay of Santa Maria and on the night of September 19 it was struck by a tempest from the north, which lasted 24 hours and shattered five ships, a galleon and a bark to pieces with great loss of life. It swept a caravel with its cargo into a grove of trees more than the distance of a arquebus shot from the shore.

Year 1563. Two unidentified Spanish ships in the fleet of Pedro Menéndez de Aviles were lost on the west coast of Florida near Charlotte Harbor.

Above

Valued at about $10,000, this rare Spanish eight-real piece, dated 1733, was found on one of the 1733 wrecks in the Florida keys.

Below

Two gold Mexican-minted eight-escudo coins were recovered from the wreckage of the 1715 treasure fleet off the coast of Florida.

Year 1563. Spanish galleon *La Magdalena*, 250 tons, Captain Cristóbal Rodríguez, sailing between Havana and Spain was wrecked in a storm on a shoals off Cape Canaveral. Only 16 of the 300 people aboard reached shore. She was carrying over 50 tons of silver bullion and specie, 170 chests of worked silver (e.g. candle sticks, plates, etc.), 1,100 pounds of gold bullion, jewelry, plus other valuables belonging to the passengers. Six months after the disaster a salvage vessel from Havana failed to locate the wreck. In 1970 a bronze cannon was snagged in a shrimper's nets in the area where the ship was lost. It bore the date 1560, and more than likely belonged to the *La Magdalena*. Four years later another shrimper pulled up a bronze cannon in the same area. Its date is 1773 and is certainly from another wreck. Within five miles from where these cannon were found still another shrimper picked up a chest of some 3,000 four- and eight-real silver coins dating between 1748 and 1751.

Year 1564. A Spanish historian briefly mentions the loss of three ships of Don Juan Menéndez on the Florida coast near Fort Pierce.

Year 1565. Two ships of the French Huguenot explorer Jean Ribault were wrecked during a storm along the shore between Matanzas and Mosquito Inlets. Some of both crews drowned in attempting to reach shore, and Indians captured and killed most of the others.

Year 1567. On the coast of Florida, one of the naos of Pedro Menéndez de Aviles was lost.

Year 1567. While Spaniards were exploring the area of Tampa Bay in 1567 they discovered a trader from Portugal's Algarve region, the only survivor from a ship that had wrecked there, who had been living as a prisoner of the Indian chief Tocobaya. All others from the wreck had been killed by the Indians.

Sometime before 1570. The richly laden *Viscayo*, on which Don Anton Granado was a passenger, wrecked near Fort Pierce Inlet and the Indians of the King of Ais salvaged a great deal of her treasure.

Unidentified year sometime before 1570. A richly laden Spanish privateer, *El Mulato*, wrecked near Fort Pierce where the Indians recovered a great deal of her treasure.

Year 1571. Two galleons, *San Ignacio*, 300 tons, 22 iron cannon, Captain Juan de Canovas; and the *Santa Maria de la Limpia Concepción*, 340 tons, captain's name unknown, wrecked several leagues south of Cape Canaveral with almost a total loss of life on both ships. The few survivors managed to reach St. Augustine and report the disaster. Combined, these ships carried 2,500,000 pesos in treasures. Salvors only found fragments of the wrecks' wooden hulls on the beach.

Many coins and artifacts can be found buried in coral growth; here Bob Marx and an associate remove coral encrustation from an iron cannon.

Year 1571 or 1572. Two ships en route from Mexico to Santo Domingo to receive a cargo of sugar and hides were lost in a storm off Cape Canaveral, and as the surviving crew members were trekking the 30 leagues to the fort at St. Augustine, most of them were massacred by Indians.

Year 1572. Adelantado Pedro Menéndez de Aviles left St. Augustine for Havana with two small tenders and a bark. While sailing down the coast of Florida the vessels were separated by a storm. The bark reached Havana safely but the tender in which Aviles and some Jesuits were sailing was wrecked near Cape Canaveral. All 30 persons on board reached shore, however, and constructed a small fort from the wreckage. Sometime later they walked safely back to St. Augustine. The other tender wrecked onshore in the province of Ais, where the crew was killed and their vessel burned.

Year 1576. The Armada de Tierra Firme, commanded by Captain-General Cristóbal de Eraso, left Havana for Spain. A few days later the armada was struck by a tempest in the Bahama Channel and one of the naos was separated from the other ships. It arrived in a sinking condition at Puerto Escondido, which is near Puerto de las Palmas, on the coast of Florida, but soon after entering port the ship sank. Salvage operations were soon under way and all of its gold and silver was recovered.

Year 1577. Don Gutierres de Miranda wrote the King from Havana on February 13,1578, "While I was coming in a boat from St. Augustine to this town, off the Florida Keys three Indians came in a canoe out to me, from which I understood by signs that two vessels had been wrecked, which had been sent from this town in the month of August past. As I knew not their language, I brought one of them to this town, where they understand it, and he said that the loss of the ships was a fact and that the Indians had killed all the people except two, whom two caciques are holding captive."

Year 1579. Don Antonio Martínez Carvajal wrote to the King from Havana on November 3, 1579, stating that "we set out for St. Augustine and by reason of a tempest one of the two frigates we had was lost...the General and the rest of the people were saved from the wreck of said frigate, whence he went by land to the fort of St. Augustine." This wreck occurred somewhere on the east coast of Florida.

Year 1579. An unidentified Spanish nao returning to Spain with treasure aboard was totally lost on Key Largo reefs and a few survivors were rescued the following year by ambergris hunters from Cuba.

Year 1582. An unidentified Spanish nao was lost somewhere between Fort Pierce and Cape Canaveral and survivors managed to reach St. Augustine.

Year 1582. Another unidentified Spanish merchant nao was lost sailing between Mexico and Spain at Cape Canaveral and fragments of the wreck were found on the beach by soldiers from St. Augustine.

Year 1587. A hurricane hit the flota of General Francisco de Noboa and during the storm the nao of maestre Hernan García Marín sank off the coast of Florida with a great quantity of gold, silver and pearls, but almost all was saved and carried to the Capitana in a launch before the ship sank.

Year 1589. The Dutch historian Linschoten tells us that in 1589 all but one out of 100 large ships in the Tierra Firme Flota were wrecked in the Florida Channel, and that of 220 ships sailing that year for Spain and Portugal from various possessions of the Spanish Crown (Portugal was under Spanish rule at this time), only 14 or 15 arrived safely. No doubt Linschoten is grossly incorrect. The Spanish historian Duro states that 1589 was not a particularly bad year (but he goes on to say that 14 ships were lost at San Juan de Ulúa, in Veracruz, in 1590 due to a "norther"). From the abundance of documents for this year there is no doubt that Linschoten was wrong, because only four Spanish ships were lost and only one Portuguese ship, returning from Goa, in India, just one instance of false information on losses to Spanish shipping.

Year 1589. For protection against an English squadron that was known to be waiting for the return of Spanish ships from the West Indies, at the Kings orders the Armada and Flota de Tierra Firme and the Flota de Nueva España met in Havana, forming a convoy of about 100 ships, and sailed from Havana on September 9. Soon after entering the Bahama Channel the convoy was struck by a hurricane. The Almiranta of the Flota de Nueva España developed a bad leak and fired cannon for assistance, but before aid could reach her she sank at the mouth of the Bahama Channel in very deep water with a great treasure aboard. While running up the Bahama Channel before the hurricane, three merchant naos also sank in 30 fathoms of water in about 30 degrees of latitude. The names of only two were given in the documents: *Santa Catalina*, 350 tons, Captain Domingo Iañez Omi, owned by Fernando Omi, coming from Mexico, and the *Jesús María*, 400 tons, Captain Francisco Salvago, owned by Domingo Sauli, also coming from Mexico. There is no mention of what their cargoes consisted of, but it is certain that the Almiranta, at least, was carrying treasure.

Year 1591. A Spanish fleet of 75 ships left Havana after spending the winter there, leaving all of their treasure in Havana at the King's orders. The treasure reached Spain safely, bypassing an English blockade aboard small but fast zabras. After the convoy, consisting of ships from Mexico and South America, left Havana on July 27, it was beset by many storms and no less than 29 vessels were lost, many off the coast of Florida. This information was obtained from English sources, and as the Spanish sources for this year are vague on the matter, it cannot be disputed. Only one Spanish document, dated March 26, 1592, briefly states that "due to the fact that so many ships were lost returning from the Indies during the past year, there are very few ships available to be sent to the Indies for this year." Since the lost ships were not carrying treasure (at least not registered treasure or any belonging to the King) this is probably the reason there is so little mention of them in the Spanish documents.

Year 1592. A frigate coming from Havana to St. Augustine sank on the coast near Cape Canaveral, and all the men made it ashore where all but one were killed by the Indians before aid could reach them (and that one was being tortured when soldiers from St. Augustine arrived to save him).

Year 1600. Unnamed 200-ton nao (originally built in France), of Captain Diego Rodríguez, coming from Mexico in the Flota de Nueva España, sank on the coast of Florida.

Year 1611. Galleon *Santa Ana María del Juncal*, owned by Bernardo de Torres, in the New Spain Fleet of Captain General the Marquis de Cadereyta was wrecked on June 2 off Cape Apalachi and salvors were not able to recover any of the two million pesos in treasure the ship carried.

Year 1618. An unnamed patache, an advice boat from Veracruz, wrecked in March on its 28th day of sailing at "la Boca de Matasissos," on the coast of Florida. Some survivors reached St. Augustine safely but others were killed by Indians. Some mail and cargo washed ashore and was recovered by the Indians.

Year 1618. On October 10 the governor of St. Augustine received news from Indians that a very large ship had sunk near the Fort Pierce Inlet. He sent men to aid the 53 survivors who identified the ship as the *San Martín*, Almiranta of the Honduras fleet. The ship's cargo of indigo, cochineal and hides was washed all over the coast. Because a smaller unidentified nao sank nearby about the same time, the governor sent a frigate assigned to locate both wrecks. There was no other document telling the identity of the latter shipwreck, or if either ship was ever located by the Spaniards. In the summer of 1993 a rare bronze astrolabe was recovered from the *San Martín* by Kane Fisher.

Year 1619. On March 24 an unidentified ship coming from Campeche sank in the Florida Keys with a cargo of hides and indigo. All of the crew escaped to shore and reached St. Augustine.

Year 1621. An unidentified small patache, serving as an advice boat on a voyage from Veracruz to Spain, was capsized by a large wave about three leagues off the Dry Tortugas and sank. The number of persons aboard was not given, but 30 drowned and the rest reached one of the cays of the Dry Tortuga group. They were soon rescued, along with the mailbags they had saved from the ship, by a passing Spanish ship which they had signaled by lighting fires on the cay.

Year 1622. On the morning of September 4 a large convoy consisting of the Armada de Tierra Firme and the Tierra Firme Flota, commanded by the Marquis de Cadereita, sailed for Spain from Havana harbor against the better judgment of the main pilots of the convoy, who warned that there were imminent signs of a hurricane. On September 6 (some accounts give the date as the seventh) the convoy was struck by a fierce hurricane, which scattered the ships over a wide area. Nine were lost in the Florida Keys, and several others were probably lost on the high seas, as they were never accounted for.

The surviving ships got back to Havana in battered condition. All had lost their masts, and many had been forced to jettison cannon and parts of their cargoes. This disaster was considered the worst to have occurred to the flotas in over 50 years. Of the nine ships that were wrecked in the Florida Keys, three were treasure-laden galleons, five were merchant naos, and one a patache that served as a reconnaissance boat for the convoy. Only the locations of the three galleons and the patache are given in the documents, and only four of the nine are identified.

The galleon *Nuestra Señora de Atocha*, 600 tons, built two years earlier in Havana, Captain Jacome de Veider, owned by the Administrators of the Averia (a branch of the House of Trade in Seville that regulated and collected a special tax on all returning treasure and products from the New World for the maintenance of a fleet of warships that generally met all returning fleets off the Azores and escorted them on their final leg of the voyage to Spain), was lost in 10 fathoms off Matacumbe Key with a cargo valued at over one million pesos, consisting chiefly of silver bullion and specie with a small amount of tobacco for the king. The wreck was lost soon after the disaster, when a buoy placed over the wreck site was lost in bad weather; before it could be relocated, it was covered over by sand and never salvaged.

The galleon *La Margarita*, 600 tons, Captain Pedro Guerrero de Espinosa, carrying over half a million pesos in silver bullion and specie and a small amount of tobacco belonging to private merchants, sank near the Atocha, in five fathoms, off Matacumbe Key. The majority of the treasure on this shipwreck was recovered by salvage divers, but before they finished the wreck sanded over and the remainder of the treasure was lost. The Spanish salvors had reported locating the ballast pile of an older shipwreck nearby, from which they recovered several silver bars.

The galleon *N.S. del Rosario*, 600 tons, Captain Francisco Rodríguez Rico, owned by Admiral Gaspar de Vargas, was wrecked at the Dry Tortugas with about half a million pesos of silver bullion and specie aboard. Salvors recovered all of the treasure and 20 cannon from the wreck. The patache was wrecked near this galleon and everything of value aboard it was recovered.

Of the five merchant naos, only the identity of one is known: *Jesús y N.S. del Rosario*, 117 tons, originally built in Portugal, Captain Manuel Déaz, owned by Juan do la Torre. Neither her location nor that of the other four were precisely given, only that they were lost in the Florida Keys, in the vicinity of the other shipwrecks.

Treasure Salvors of Key West led by Mel Fisher located and salvaged both the galleons *Margarita* and *Atocha* with considerable publicity. Seahawk Deep Ocean Technology of Tampa located one of the smaller ships of this fleet in 1500 feet of water off the Dry Tortugas and partially salvaged it using an ROV.

Year 1622. Nao *Santa Ana María*, 180 tons, Captain Gongalo [sic] de la Rocha, sailing alone from Santo Domingo and Havana for Spain, was sunk in a storm on the high seas off the coast of Florida.

Year 1623. In early spring two galleons were sent to the Florida Keys to protect the salvors at work on *La Margarita* from attack by Dutch privateers who were reported cruising in that area. The Capitaña of this small squadron was wrecked on the Florida Keys, four leagues to windward of the shipwreck of the *N.S. de Atocha*, but none of the crew was lost. Ten days later these survivors reached Havana aboard rafts made from their shipwreck. The galleons carried 14 bronze cannon.

Year 1623. The Tierra Firme Flota, commanded by Captain-General Antonio de Oquendo, sailed from Havana on April 26. Upon reaching the mouth of the Bahama Channel it was struck by a storm that created waves so huge that the ships were tossed about like corks. The treasure-laden galleon *Espíritu Santa el Mayor*, 480 tons, Captain Antonio de Soto, opened up and sank so quickly that only 50 of the 300 persons aboard her could be saved by other ships, and all of her treasure, amounting to more than one million pesos, was totally lost. The Almiranta of the flota, the galleon *Santissima Trinidad*, 600 tons, Captain Ysidro de Cepida, also sank, but not as quickly, as there was time for several pataches to recover all of her treasure, which amounted to one million pesos, and all the people aboard her. Contemporary accounts differed as to the loss of both ships. Several state that they wrecked on the coast of Florida in the vicinity of Ais and others that they sank on the high seas.

Year 1624. An unidentified frigate sank on the coast of Florida sometime before July 30, and eight of the 12 iron cannon it carried, as well as several anchors, were recovered from it.

Year 1626. A small frigate en route to St. Augustine from Havana with the salaries of officials' and supplies ran aground on the bar at the entrance to St. Augustine and was a total loss. Only a few pipes of wine that washed ashore were recovered from this wreck.

Year 1627. When news of the above loss reached the viceroy of Mexico, he ordered a frigate sent from Veracruz with supplies and money to pay the garrison at St. Augustine, which was threatening to mutiny if not paid promptly. The governor of Florida, Don Luis de Rojas, wrote the King on February 15, stating that the frigate that had been sent from Veracruz had also wrecked on the same bar as the one in 1626 and was a total loss. The crew of the frigate, along with 12,000 pesos in eight-real silver coins were saved. Of the 200 barrels of flour it carried, only 11 were salvaged. The ship had also carried four bronze and four iron cannon, but only two of the iron cannon could be salvaged as mud covered the wreck over quickly.

Year 1630. Two galleons of the Armada de Tierra Firme were sent, under command of the Maestre de Campo Antonio de Oteyca, to carry supplies to St. Augustine from Havana but both were wrecked at the head of the Florida Keys. All of the men on both wrecks were saved and the 56 bronze and iron cannon on both wrecks were recovered and taken to Havana.

Year 1632. As a large convoy was making its way up the Bahama Channel, sailing from Havana to Spain, two ships were wrecked on the coast of Florida during the night of April 2 when they were separated from the convoy and currents forced them too close to shore. One was the *Almiranta de Honduras* and the other was an unidentified frigate coming from Maracaibo, Venezuela, with a cargo consisting mainly of cocoa. The location of the two wrecks was probably in the vicinity of present-day Miami, as an advice boat passing that area a few days later reported sighting two ships wrecked shortly after passing the head of the Florida Keys.

Year 1633. On November 15, the governor of Florida wrote to the King, "On the 10th of November, my soldiers captured three Englishmen from London. Their ship was carrying supplies and aid to the English settlement at Alxacan (probably somewhere in Virginia or New England), but it sank on our coast. Forty of them reached shore safely, but the Indians had killed all but the three my soldiers captured. I will send them back to Spain for questioning on the first available vessel." The location of their shipwreck was 70 leagues south of our town (St. Augustine).

Year 1634. On December 20 the governor of Florida wrote to Captain-General Antonio de Oquendo, wintering in Havana with his Armada de Tierra Firme: "I received news that a ship of the Flota de Nueva España, commanded by Captain-General Lope de Hoces, had wrecked on my coast. We found some Indians who told us that other Indians had salvaged some treasure off this wreck. We stationed some soldiers opposite the site of the wreck and sent others after the Indians who had recovered the treasure, but they were never located. I went with several canoes and some divers to the wreck and we recovered one million pesos in bullion and specie the ship had been carrying as registered cargo and took this treasure to my fort at St. Augustine."

Year 1638. British ship *Kinsdale*, Captain D. Dent, was wrecked on April 18 during a storm at Cape Florida and was a total loss.

Year 1641. A convoy consisting of the Nueva España Flota, commanded by Captain-General Juan de Campos, and the Armada de Barlovento (a squadron used for protecting returning flotas during time of war), was struck by a hurricane on September 27 in the latitude of 30 degrees north and five ships of the Flota were wrecked on the coast of Florida. Four of the five ships were merchant naos, and there were no survivors. Another was the patache of the Flota, which was located by another patache from Havana some days later. They found the wrecked patache about five leagues from the shore with some survivors still aboard. Others, including a priest, had tried to swim ashore but they were all eaten by sharks. Other ships in this same convoy were in such bad condition that they sank on the high seas. Another, the Almiranta of the Flota, lost all her masts and developed such a bad leak that she eventually drifted and was wrecked on a reef in the Bahamas called Abreojos, located north of Hispaniola. Today this reef is called Silver Shoals as a result of the more than two million pesos in silver that was lost on this shipwreck. The majority of the treasure was recovered about 40 years later by Sir William Phips.

Year 1660. An unidentified Spanish advice boat sailing from Panama for Spain was wrecked along the east coast at a place called Jega, which is believed to be around St. Lucie Inlet. A vessel was sent from St. Augustine which rescued the survivors but nothing else salvaged.

Year 1665. Spanish merchant nao *Santa Anna María* was wrecked on Key Largo on February 15 and there is no mention of what she carried or if she was salvaged.

Sometime before 1677. On May 4, 1677, the governor of Cuba sent Don Martín de Melgar with a frigate to salvage cannon from a Dutch ship that had wrecked at Key West.

Year 1683. Spanish galleon *Santissima Concepción*, alias *El Grande*, Admiral Manuel Ortíz Arosemena, after picking up treasures in Panama, Cartagena and Mexico totaling one million pesos in gold and silver specie and bullion, plus 77 chests of pearls, 49 chests of emeralds and 217 chests of "goods from the Orient" was wrecked on the east coast. One document states it was lost 12 hours sail north of Key Largo; another, "to the south of Cape Canaveral". Only four of the 500 persons aboard her managed to reach St. Augustine. Salvors only found ship's timbers on the beach and her treasures were never salvaged.

Sometime before 1685. The governor of Cuba sent two brigantines under the command of captains Martín de Riva and Pedro de Iriarte to St. Bernard's Bay, on the coast of Florida, to salvage what they could from several French ships that had been wrecked there. Divers recovered only four cannon and some other objects of little value.

Year 1688. Brief mention that an unidentified Spanish merchant nao was lost in the Florida Keys.

Year 1689. Frigate *N.S. de Concepción y San José* was lost at Key Largo.

Year 1695. British man-of-war *Winchester*, 50 guns, Captain John Soule, sailing from Jamaica to England, was wrecked near Cape Florida on some reefs.

Year 1696. British merchantman *Burroughs* (or *Smith*), from the port of Bristol, sailing from Port Royal, Jamaica, in a convoy of twelve or thirteen ships was wrecked on September 23 north of Jupiter Inlet.

Year 1696. British barkentine *Reformation*, Captain Joséph Kirle, sailing from Port Royal, Jamaica, in a convoy of twelve or thirteen merchant ships, sank on September 23 a bit north of Jupiter Inlet, close to shore. Her exact location was 27 degrees and 8 minutes of north latitude. She carried 25 passengers and crew, and her cargo consisted of sugar, rum, beef, molasses and some Spanish money.

Year 1696. British merchant bark *Nantwitch*, Captain John Smith, part of the same convoy as the above two ships, was wrecked south of Fort Pierce Inlet, about one-third of the distance between Fort Pierce and St. Lucie inlets.

Year 1698. Brief mention that two ships of unknown nationality were forced ashore on the coast of Florida about 40 leagues from the Island of New Providence in the Bahamas by a notorious pirate named Kelly.

Year 1700. British merchant-slave ship *Henrietta Marie* was sailing between Jamaica and England with a cargo of logwood, cotton, indigo, sugar and molasses when she wrecked just south of the Marquesas Keys to the west of Key West. This wreck was located by Treasure Salvors in 1972 and completely salvaged.

Year 1702. Eight unidentified British warships under the command of Commodore Moore were set on fire in St. Augustine Harbor to prevent their capture by two large Spanish warships in November.

Year 1705 or 1706. The governor of Florida wrote the King on January 31, 1706, stating that one of the two ships named *Santo Cristo de Maracaibo* sent by the viceroy of Mexico to bring supplies to St. Augustine sank eight leagues southwest of St. Augustine during a storm.

Year 1711. Merchant nao *N.S. del Rosario y San Cristóbal*, sailing alone from Havana to Spain, was lost on the coast of Florida in 30 degrees and 20 minutes of north latitude

Year 1715. At sunrise on July 24 a convoy consisting of 12 ships set sail from Havana Harbor for Spain. The convoy was composed of the five ships of the New Spain Flota, commanded by Captain-General Don Juan Esteban de Ubilla, six ships of the Squadron of Tierra Firme, commanded by Captain-General Don Antonio de Echeverz y Zubiza, and a French ship named *Grifon*, commanded by Captain Antonio Daire. The *Grifon* was not part of Ubilla's flota or Echeverz's squadron but just happened to be in Havana at the time and received permission to sail back to Europe in the convoy. Echeverz's Squadron had sailed from Spain and gone directly to Cartagena, Colombia, carrying assorted merchandise for sale at Cartagena, Portobelo and Havana.

Upon arriving in Cartagena, Echeverz sent word to the viceroy of Peru to send up the treasure of Peru and Chile to Panama City and generally transport it overland on mules to Portobelo, where the treasure was to be placed aboard the ships of the Squadron of Tierra Firme and carried back to Spain. Echeverz also notified the viceroy of New Granada in Bogota to send treasure and the governor of the Island of Margarita to send pearls.

Because the last Squadron of Tierra Firme had been destroyed near Cartagena in 1708 by an English fleet under the command of Admiral Wager, the viceroy of Peru did not send the treasure to Panama City as requested by Echeverz, but had it transported overland to Buenos Aires, then by ship to Spain. For some unknown reason, neither the viceroy of New Granada nor the governor of Margarita Island heeded the request. Instead of a large amount of treasure from South America, Echeverz received so little that it was hardly worth his effort. The only treasure he received was from the governor of Cartagena and his royal officials and some belonging to private individuals.

The royal treasure consisted of 46,095 pesos, six reales, and 10 maravedis in gold doubloons (escudos), 300 castellanos, seven tomines, six grains of gold dust, and 646 castellanos in two small gold bars. All of it was carried on Echeverz's Capitana. Also put aboard his Capitana were 19 gold bars valued at 26,063 pesos, 2,650 pesos in gold doubloons, 1,485 pesos in silver specie, three gold chains valued at 747 pesos, 47 serons of cocoa, and 1 1/2 tons of brazil wood (a valuable dyewood). Aboard his Almiranta he put eight gold bars valued at 8,978 pesos, 3,150 pesos in

232

gold doubloons, 175 pesos in silver specie, two chests of ceramic jugs, one chest of gifts, 232 tons of brazil wood, 28 serons of cocoa, one chest of vanilla, two chests of tortoise shells, and 650 cured half-hides.

Aboard the *N. S. de Concepción* he put 3,000 pesos in gold doubloons, four gold bars valued at 5,703 pesos, 15 serons of cocoa, one chest of vanilla, 15 3/4 tons of brazil wood, 1,440 cured half-hides and some tobacco. The ship *El Ciervo* carried only 96 tons of brazil wood. On his other two ships we know of no cargo or treasure being loaded aboard in Cartagena or Portobelo, but like all the ships in this squadron it is believed that they received a large cargo of tobacco in Havana. There is a possibility that there were actually seven ships in Echeverz's squadron, making a total of 13 sailing together from Havana, but the documents are confusing. Ubilla's flota consisted of eight ships when it sailed from Spain to Veracruz, but four were lost during a bad storm while in that port, and when he sailed from Veracruz for Havana he had only four ships. In Havana he added a small frigate to the flota.

Ubilla's Capitaña carried the following treasure and cargo: 611,409 pesos in silver specie for the King, 169,111 pesos in silver specie for the wages of the members of the Council of the Indies in Madrid, 2,559,917 pesos in silver specie belonging to private persons. All of this treasure was packed in 1,300 chests. The Capitaña also carried a modest amount of silver bars; 23 chests of silver-ware, one small chest containing an undisclosed number of gold doubloons, gold bars, and pearls; a small chest containing jewelry for the Queen; and another small chest of gold jewelry belonging to a nobleman. The cargo consisted of Chinese porcelain, indigo, cochineal, drugs, hides, brazil wood, gifts, copper disks and ceramic drinking vessels. In Havana it received 36,000 pesos worth of silver specie, gold disks, and several other bars that had been salvaged off a ship that sank in 1711.

The Almiranta also received a similar amount in Havana. It carried 990 chests of silver specie, of which 611,408 pesos belonged to the King and 2,076,004 pesos belonged to private persons. Other treasure consisted of 53 chests of silverware. Her general cargo was the same as that of the Capitana, but in addition she carried sarsaparilla, cocoa and three Chinese folding screens. Since documents indicated that she carried no gold treasure in any form, gold coins which Real Eight members found on this shipwreck must have been contraband.

The *Refuerzo* (also called the *Urca de Lima*) carried no royal treasure but did carry 81 chests and some loose sacks of silver specie valued at 252,171 pesos belonging to private persons. In addition it carried 13 chests of worked silver and, like the Capitaña and Almiranta, general cargo plus snuff and balsam.

The patache, which was a much smaller vessel than the above three of Ubilla's flota, carried no royal treasure but did carry 44,000 pesos of silver specie in 12 chests and some loose sacks of leather. Since Real Eight members have found a sufficient number of gold coins on this shipwreck in recent years, these coins were undoubtedly contraband. This ship also carried a general cargo which included incense.

Documents do not indicate whether the small frigate Ubilla bought in Havana carried any cargo or treasure, but it is unlikely that it carried treasure.

The total value of registered treasure carried on the four ships of Ubilla's flota, excluding the silverware, jewelry and a small number of gold coins, was

6,388,020 pesos. The total amount of treasure carried on three of the ships of Echeverz's squadron was 98,046 pesos in silver and gold specie, plus the 955 castellanos in gold dust and bars. The total carried in the overall convoy was 6,466,066 pesos and 955 castellanos. Records indicated virtually no gold coins on any of the ships, which means that those recovered by Real Eight divers were contraband. This is substantiated by the fact that most of the gold disks Real Eight found are not marked like registered gold bars.

After the convoy left Havana it made its way Up the Bahama Channel. During the night of July 30 it was struck by a fierce hurricane that wrecked all the ships upon the coast of Florida, with the exception of the *Grifon*, which miraculously escaped. Over a thousand persons lost their lives, including Ubilla and his principal officers. About 1,500 people reached shore by clinging to pieces of wreckage or swimming. Some of the survivors perished from exposure, thirst and hunger before aid reached them from Havana and St. Augustine.

Salvage efforts on the wrecks began immediately, and by the end of December the officials in charge of operations reported that they had already recovered all of the King's treasure and the major part of the treasure belonging to private persons, totaling 5,200,000 pesos. The following spring they recovered an additional small amount of treasure, so that by July, when the Spaniards ended all further salvage efforts, they had recovered a reported total of 5,241,166 pesos in silver specie and bars, excluding the gold specie and bars, silverware and general cargoes.

We know that after the Spaniards ended their salvage operations, English "wrackers" from Jamaica and the Bahamas also salvaged unknown amounts off these wrecks. When the Spaniards ended their salvage operations, there supposedly remained a total of 1,244,900 pesos of registered treasure, but the amount will never be known, as the survivors and salvors robbed unknown amounts.

Furthermore, we have no way of determining how much unregistered treasure remains. Gold in terms of weight was worth 16 times the value of silver and was the most common item smuggled back to Spain. Since there were no gold coins registered aboard the ships, it is possible that a substantial amount was being smuggled in this convoy.

Year 1731. Unidentified merchant nao was lost on the coast of Florida on a voyage between Havana and Spain, near the mouth of the St. John's River.

Year 1731. Unidentified Spanish frigate, Captain Joseph Piz, carrying the annual payroll for the garrison at Pensacola, wrecked near this port.

Year 1733. A merchant nao sailing alone back to Spain was lost at Rio Seco, on the coast of Florida.

Year 1733. On July 13 the Nueva España Flota, commanded by Don Rodrígo de Torres, set sail for Spain; documents give either 21 or 22 as the total number of ships in this fleet. The names of the ships are also confusing, since some ships had two: a religious name and an alias. However, the majority of the documents reveal that the following ships were in the fleet when it sailed from Havana.

1. The Capitaña *El Rubi*, 60 cannon, Captain Baltazar de la Torre y Alfaro, owned by the King (her tonnage not given in any document), carried 104 castellanos in worked gold, 3,200 pesos in gold specie, 5,080,285 pesos in silver specie and bullion, and 6,099 marcos in worked silver, all the property of private citizens.

2. The Almiranta *N.S. de Balvaneda* (alias *El Gallo*), 60 cannon, Captain Bernardo de Maturana, owned by the King (tonnage not given in any documents), carried 196 castellanos in worked gold, 3,200 pesos in gold specie, 4,895,216 pesos

in silver specie and bullion, 2,579 marcos in worked silver, and 285 marcos of "plata pasta," all the property of private citizens.

Note that the Capitaña and Almiranta also carried 1,519,527 pesos in silver specie and bullion, 4,110 "granos" in gold, an unspecified amount of worked gold and silver and copper ingots, all of which was the property of the King. The precise percentage of what each of the two ships carried of this amount is not given in the documents, only that it was equally divided aboard both ships. Documents also state that unspecified amounts of gold and silver specie and bullion were carried on both ships as the property of the Church of Spain.

3. Galleon *N.S. de Balvaneda* (alias *El Infante*), Captain Domingo de Sanz, owned by the King (neither the number of cannon nor tonnage given in the documents), carried 562,509 pesos in silver specie and bullion and 643 marcos in worked silver, plus large amounts of indigo, vanilla and ceramic jars, jugs and plates.

4. Pink *N.S. del Pópulo* (alias *El Pinque*), Captain Francisco Ibernon, owned by the King. Documents do not reveal the number of cannon, tonnage, or what cargo this small vessel carried.

5. Merchant nao *San José de las Animas* (sometimes listed as *San José y las Animas*), Captain Cristóbal Fernandez Franco, owned by José del Duque y Muñoz, English-built ship, 326 tons (number of cannon not given for any of the privately owned merchant ships), carried 30,435 pesos in silver specie and bullion, plus sugar, chocolate, indigo, cochineal, dyewoods, cocoa, hides, ceramic ware, tobacco, vanilla and various types of drugs.

6. Merchant nao *N.S. del Rosario (San Francisco Javier y San Antonio de Padua)*; the captain and owner was Don Luis Lozana, French-built of 205 1/3 tons, carried 12,000 pesos in silver specie and bullion and a cargo of products similar to that of the above ship.

7. Merchant nao *N.S de Belem y San Antonio de Padua*, her captain and owner was Don Luis de Herrira, English built, 242 1/4 tons, carried 12,000 pesos in silver specie and bullion, 359 marcos in worked silver, and a cargo similar to those of the above two ships.

8. Merchant nao *N.S. del Rosario, San Antonio y San Vicente Ferrer*, Captain Juan José de Arizón, owner Jacinto de Arizon carried 24,000 pesos in silver specie and bullion and a general cargo as the above ships; in addition, an item listed as tinta, which could either be coffee or some type of dye.

9. Merchant nao *N.S. del Carmen, San Antonio de Padua y las Animas*, captain and owner Don Antonio de Chaves, Genovese-built of 220 and 9/10 tons, carried no treasure, only a cargo similar to that of the above ships.

10. Merchant nao *N.S. de Belem y San Juan Bautista*, Captain Diego de la Corte y Andrade, owner Francisco Lebrum, foreign-built, 212 and 3/8 tons. This ship carried no treasure, only the usual cargo, and was probably better known by an alias, which is not revealed in the documents.

11. Merchant nao *N.S. de los Dolores y Santa Isabel* (alias *El Nuevo Londres*), Captain Antonio de Loaysa, owner Nicolas Fernandez del Castillo, English-built, 296 tons, carrying cargo plus an unspecified small amount of silver specie.

12. Merchant nao *N.S. del Rosario y Santo Domingo*, Captain Tomas de Astiguieta, owners were the captain and Doña María Teresa de Astiguieta (probably his wife), Spanish-built, 522 1/3 tons, carried 31,281 pesos in silver specie and bullion, 495 marcos in worked silver and the usual cargo.

13. Merchant nao *N.S. de los Reyes, San Fernando, y San Francisco de Paula,* Captain José Cabeza, owner Francisco de Soto y Posada, Genovese-built, 328 tons, carried 16,000 pesos in silver (not disclosed if in specie or bullion, or both), 226 marcos of worked silver, and the usual cargo.

14. Merchant nao *San Pedro,* Captain Gaspar López Gonzales, owner Gaspar de Larea Berdúgo, Dutch-built, 287 1/4 tons, carried 16,000 pesos in silver specie and bullion and the usual cargo plus several boxes of Chinese porcelain.

15. Merchant nao *San Felipe,* Captain José del Villar y Andrade, owner the Marquis de Canada, English-built of 485 tons, carried 34,000 pesos in silver specie and bullion, 326 marcos of worked silver, and the usual cargo.

16. Merchant nao *N.S. de las Angustias y San Rafael,* Captain Francisco Sanchez de Madrid, owner José Sanchez de Madrid, English-built, 328 1/2 tons, carried 27,000 pesos in silver specie and bullion, 605 marcos of worked silver, the usual cargo plus an unspecified amount of Chinese porcelain.

17. Merchant nao *El Gran Poder de Diós y Santa Ana* (alias the *Ana Agustina*) the captain and owner was Francisco Sanchez de Madrid (note: same name as that of above captain), built in Hamburg, Germany, of 181 3/4 tons, carried 14,000 pesos in silver specie and bullion, 139 marcos in worked silver and the usual general cargo.

18. Merchant nao *San Ignacio,* captain not identified, owner Francisco de Alzaibar, English-built, 292 4/5 tons, carried 12,000 pesos in silver specie and bullion, 696 marcos of worked silver in six boxes and the usual cargo plus some boxes containing gifts from China.

19. Merchant nao *San Francisco de Asis,* captain and owner was Cristóbal de Urquijo, English-built, 264 2/3 tons, no mention in any document of what its cargo was, but it can be assumed that it was the usual.

20. Merchant nao *San Fernando,* no data.

21. Frigate *Floridana,* no data.

22. A vessel only identified as a balandra (or schooner), which might be the reason for the different accounts stating that there were 21 or 22 ships in the fleet when it sailed from Havana. This type of vessel was quite small, and in some accounts it might not have been included as a ship of the fleet.

The following day after setting sail from Havana on July 13, the fleet sighted the Florida Keys. Around nine that evening the wind blew very strongly from the north. By sunup the following morning the wind had swung around to the south at hurricane force and prevented the ships from trying to reach the safety of Havana.

By nightfall of this same day, all or most of the ships had wrecked on the Florida Keys, scattered in different areas between Key Biscayne and Vaca Key. Many documents, as well as charts showing the locations of the wrecks, differ as to the names of the shipwrecks, their locations, and the total number of ships that were lost. Following are the probable locations of the lost ships:

1. Capitaña *El Rubi,* listed as wrecking at Cayo Tabamos in most documents and at Cayo Largo (Key Largo) in a few others.

2. Almiranta El Gallo, listed as being wrecked at Cayo de Vivoras in all the documents and charts.

3. Galleon *El Infante,* listed as wrecking at Cayo Tabamos in all documents and charts.

4. Pink *El Pinque,* listed as wrecking at the Cabeza de los Martires (head of the Florida Keys) and Key Biscayne in different documents and charts.

5. *San José de las Animas*, listed as wrecking at Cayo Tabamos. On one chart showing the locations of the shipwrecks of this fleet, a shipwreck denoted as *Africa* is shown in the same location that other charts show the *San José de las Animas*, which was probably her alias.

6. *N.S. del Rosario, San Francisco Javier y San Antonio de Padua*, listed in some documents as wrecking at Cayo de Vivoras and in others as having survived the hurricane and safely returned to Havana.

7. *N.S. de Belem y San Antonio de Padua*, listed in documents as wrecking at Cayo de Matacumbe el Viejo (Upper Matacumbe Key), but on the charts it is not shown by this name. However, the charts do list a shipwreck by the name of *Herrera*, which is probably the same ship, as the captain and owner of this ship was named Herrera.

8. *N.S. del Rosario, San Antonio y San Vicente Ferrer*, is not listed in any document or shown on the charts. However, on two charts a shipwreck named *Arizon*, the name of the captain and owner of this ship, is shown, and on another chart in the same location a shipwreck named *Terri* is shown as being lost at Cayo de Vivoras. Several documents also mention a ship named *Terri* (or Terry) as having been lost at Cayo de Vivoras; it is probably the same ship as above.

9. *N.S. del Carmen, San Antonio de Padua y las Animas*, is listed in both documents and charts as wrecking at Cayo de Matacumbe el Viejo, or Matacumbe Grande, both names used for Upper Matacumbe. In documents, this ship was sometimes called simply *Chaves*, the name of captain and owner, and on all the charts it was also denoted by the name *Chaves*.

10. *N.S. de Belim y San Juan Bautista* is mentioned in documents as being wrecked at Cayo de Matacumbe el Viejo (Upper Matacumbe) and not shown on any charts by this name. However, the charts do show a ship named *Tres Puentes* as being lost at Upper Matacumbe, and this was probably the ship's alias.

11. *N.S. de los Dolores y Santa Isabel* is not mentioned as being lost in the documents, nor shown on any of the charts, but she might have been mentioned by an alias.

12. *N.S. del Rosario y Santo Domingo* made it safely back to Havana.

13. *N.S. de los Reyes, San Fernando y San Francisco de Paula*, was wrecked at Cayo de Vivoras.

14. *San Pedro* is listed as wrecking at Cayo de Matacumbe el Mozo (Lower Matacumbe), and at Cayuelo de Matanzas.

15. *San Felipe* is not mentioned in any documents as being lost, nor returning to Havana, nor shown on any of the wreck charts.

16. *N.S. de las Angustias y San Rafael* wrecked at Cayo de Vivoras.

17. *El Gran Poder de Diós y Santa Ana* is listed by this name and by *Sanchez de Madrid*, the name of the cap tain and owner, as being wrecked at Cayo de Bocas del Leste (Vacas Key).

18. *San Ignacio*, listed as wrecking at Cayo de Bocas and Cayo de Vacas. One document calls this ship *San Ignacio de Urquijo*, which was the captain's name of the *San Francisco de Asis*. Since the documents do not reveal the name of the captain of the *San Ignacio*, it is possible that this was his name as well.

19. *San Francisco de Asis* was wrecked at Cayo de Vivoras.

20. *San Fernando* is not mentioned in the documents or shown on any charts as being lost, but it was probably mentioned by its alias, if it had one.

21. *Floridana* is listed in some documents as having escaped and in some others as being wrecked at Cayo de Vivoras.

22. The unidentified balandra is probably the Key Biscayne shipwreck mentioned in documents and shown on charts as *El Aviso* (an advice boat).

To add to the confusion, documents and charts mention the following ships as being wrecked at different places. They might be aliases for some of the ships that were wrecked or for those whose fate was not mentioned in documents. Or they might be ships that were not even part of the fleet but were sailing separately.

1. *El Sueco*, wrecked at Cayo de Bacas del Leste.

2. *Sanchez*, which is probably the *El Poder de Diós y Santa Ana*, wrecked at Cayo de Bacas del Leste.

3. *Murguia*, wrecked at Cayo de Matacumbe el Mozo.

4. *Ledieque*, wrecked at Cayo de Tavanos (probably the same place that is listed as Cayo Tabamos) .

5. *Valandrita*, wrecked at Matacumbe el Grande.

The Spaniards thoroughly salvaged on all these wrecks, and several, which were not identified by name, were refloated. Fifteen, which could not be refloated, were burned to the waterline after salvage operations were completed. Within three months of the disaster, the King was informed by royal officials in Havana that, not only had all of the registered treasure been recovered but a substantial amount of unregistered treasure as well. Much of the other cargo was also recovered but a great amount of it had been destroyed by the salt water, especially the sugar, indigo, and cochineal. What little the Spaniards failed to recover has been searched for in the past few decades, but very little of real value has been discovered other than various items of historical and archaeological value. Small numbers of silver coins have been found by modern-day salvors, but nothing of the magnitude such as has been recovered from the wrecks of the 1715 fleet.

Year 1734. Brief mention of a ship of Don Gerónimo Barroso (he could have been the captain or owner, or both) that was lost near Rio Seco on the coast of Florida.

Year 1741. Brief mention of an unidentified Spanish frigate being lost at Cayo de Lobos on the coast of Florida.

Year 1741. In March the *H.M.S. Wolf*, a 14-gun sloop, captain's name not given, was wrecked on the east coast of Florida. These British war-sloops generally carried eight regular iron cannon and 12 swivel guns, also called patereroes, which were counted as half a gun.

Year 1741. British merchantman *Naffaw* (*Nassau*), Captain Bradshaw, sailing from Jamaica for Bristol, England, lost on the Florida Keys; the crew was saved by a vessel bound for Virginia.

Year 1742. British man-of-war *H.M.S. Tyger* was lost in the Florida Keys, where the crew built a small fort from the wreck's timbers. The Spanish admiral Torres sent several small vessels to capture survivors, but the Englishmen beat them off.

Year 1742. Spanish galleon *Fuerte*, 60 cannon, lost near the *H.M.S. Tyger*. When Admiral Torres learned that his forces had been repelled by the crew of the *Tyger*, he sent this larger ship with a great number of Spanish soldiers aboard, but they wrecked themselves.

Year 1744. British man-of-war (called a frigate in some accounts) *H.M.S. Looe* (sometimes called *Loo*), 44 guns, Captain Uting, was lost in the Florida Keys along with a Spanish ship she had captured shortly before, but all the men on both ships

238

were saved. The site of the wreck was called la Pareda by the Spaniards, but shortly later the area was referred to as Looe Reef, the name it bears today. The date of the disaster was February 5.

Year 1748. British merchantman *Dolphin*, Captain Smith, sailing from Carolina to Antigua, and several other vessels were lost on the coast of Florida.

Year 1748. British ship *Dolphin*, Captain Bagat, bound for North Carolina, was captured by the Spaniards but soon afterward wrecked near Cape Florida.

Year 1748. American merchant vessel *Howlet*, on a trading voyage from Boston to the Gulf of Mexico, was driven ashore by strong winds near Cape Florida, where the crew was captured by Indians and put to death; except for a black slave who later escaped.

Year 1748. British warship *H.M.S. Fowey*, 20 guns, Captain Francis William Drake, was wrecked in the Florida Keys (area is known as Fowey Rocks), along with a Spanish merchantman named *Judith* (or *Judan*), which was carrying $57,000 (pesos) and a large cargo of cocoa. The crews of both ships and the cargo of the Spanish prize were all saved and transferred to a sloop and carried to Carolina.

Year 1748. British merchantman *Betsey*, Captain Slater, sailing from Jamaica to Bristol, was lost in the Gulf of Florida but the crew was taken up by a passing vessel.

Year 1752. The following ships were lost in the Gulf of Florida during a hurricane on October 22: British merchantman *Alexander*, Captain Mudis, sailing from Jamaica to London; British merchantman *Lancaster*, Captain Lowry, sailing from Jamaica to Lancaster; British merchantman *Dolphin*, Captain Pedrick, sailing from Jamaica to Liverpool; British merchantman *Queen Anne*, Captain Rymer, sailing from Jamaica to Bristol; British merchantman *May*, Captain Crawford, sailing from Jamaica to Glasgow; American merchantman *Rhode Island*, Captain Ball, sailing from Jamaica to New York; American merchantman *Statea*, Captain Jones, sailing from Honduras to Rhode Island; an unidentified Spanish man-of-war; an unidentified Spanish schooner; and three other ships of unknown identity.

Year 1763. British merchantman *Albinia*, sailing from Jamaica to London, was wrecked on the coast of Florida but the crew was saved.

Year 1763. Unidentified French sloop wrecked on the bar of St. Augustine. Another French sloop and a British schooner, *Charming Sally*, both wrecked a few miles south of St. Augustine in a storm.

Year 1763. British merchantman *Alexander*, Captain Johnson, sailing from Jamaica to London, was lost in the Florida Keys.

Year 1764. British ship *Industry*, Captain Lawrence, in the government service installed in Charleston, South Carolina, from New York bound for east and west Florida, having on board a number of craftsmen and other settlers and their families, was lost on the St. Augustine bar but the crew and all passengers were saved.

Year 1765. British ship *Grenville Packet*, Captain Curlett, with mail from Falmouth, in her route from Pensacola ran ashore on February 27 upon the Dry Tortugas and was lost but the crew was saved.

Year 1766. Unidentified Spanish ship from the Bay of Campeche, en route to Pensacola, wrecked off Isle of Rosey, within a few leagues of Pensacola. The ship was a total loss but her cargo was saved.

Year 1766. British or American ship *Nelly*, Captain Smith, sailing from Philadelphia to St. Augustine, was lost on the St. Augustine bar, crew and part of cargo saved.

Year 1766. British ship *General Conway*, Captain Bail, from Jamaica, was lost in the Florida Keys but the crew was saved.

Year 1766. Unidentified French ship, commanded by Monsieur Pierre Viaud, was wrecked on the coast of Florida between Pensacola and Mobile.

Year 1766. On October 22 and 23, a violent hurricane caused considerable damage to shipping in the harbor of Pensacola. This same hurricane also caused five large and richly laden Spanish galleons, sailing from Veracruz for Spain, to be wrecked in the Bay of St. Bernard, which is WSW from Pensacola.

Year 1767. Ship of unknown registry, the *Jason*, after being badly damaged in a storm, wrecked at Apalachion July 28.

Year 1768. Unidentified shipwreck shown on a chart as "A Wreck in 1768," located between Mount Tucker and Cape Kennedy.

Year 1768. Spanish ship *Jazo y Santa Ana* (alias *La Nimsa del Puerto*), captain's name unknown, sailing from Havana to Cadíz, was lost in the Florida Straits.

Year 1768. A vessel of Captain Codington, coming from Montego Bay, Jamaica, to Rhode Island with rum, in coming through the Florida Straits was set on fire by lightning and entirely consumed; all lives were lost.

Year 1768. Spanish ship *San Antonio*, Captain Font, from Havana, was lost on January 22 on a reef near Key West; the crew and passengers, after surviving for twenty-two days on this reef, were rescued by a turtling sloop and carried back to Havana.

Year 1768. British packet boat *Anna Theresa*, Captain Dyer, sailing from Pensacola to Falmouth, wrecked on the Florida Keys. On the morning of July 30 the British ship *Prince George*, Captain Collier, was sailing past the Florida Keys and saw the wreck aground on a reef and afire. Seeing three sloops anchored near the wreck, he sent a boat to investigate and was told that the crew of the ship had been carried to New Providence, the Bahamas. He was also told that a few days earlier a Spanish ship and a brig from Boston whose captain's name was Bostley had been lost in the same area.

Year 1769. British ship *Prince George*, sailing from London to St. Augustine, was lost going into St. Augustine

Diver investigates a bronze cannon from the shipwreck of the Spanish galleon *Maravillas*, from which numerous recoveries have been made.

Spanish Admiral's Rivulet thus called from his Encampent here after cast away in the Palmira Bay.

Hillsborough Stream

Palmira Bay, in which a Spanish Admiral was cast away: this Bay has its Name from the great Number of Palm (Cabbage) Trees growing here

Hillsborough Inlet

from the Shore

the Soundings

Huntingdon River

MAP
the General Survey of
T FLORIDA,

Leach
Shoal

Year 1769. British merchant snow *Ledbury*, Captain John Lorain, sailing from Jamaica to Bristol, was driven on shore about 15 leagues northward of Cape Florida, in a violent gale of wind on September 29, crew and part of cargo saved.

Year 1769. Unidentified shipwreck location shown on Bernard Romans' map of Florida as "Wreck 1769" at Mount Tucker, north of Cape Canaveral.

Year 1770. News reached London from Jamaica that a large Spanish ship, sailing from Caracas, Venezuela, for Cadíz, was wrecked in the Florida Keys during a violent gale of wind, ship and cargo totally lost.

Year 1771. British ship *Eagle*, arrived in Bristol from Jamaica, where it had left on July 26. The captain reported seeing five large ships and one brig wrecked in the Florida Keys and on the coast of Florida. One of the ships had lost her main and mizzen masts, and he noted that the current set very strong toward the Florida coast.

Year 1771. British ship *Hope*, Captain Clutsam, who, while passing through the Florida Straits, reported that he saw a Spanish man-of-war; sometime later it caught on fire and blew up.

Year 1771. Captain Bratt, who arrived in London in early October, reported seeing seven large ships wrecked on the shores of Florida.

Year 1771. Spanish merchant nao *El Nauva Victoriosa*, Captain Josif Varan, which had sailed from Cadíz on November 3, 1770, in a flota going to Veracruz, sank sometime in 1771 at the entrance of the Bahama Channel, on the head of the Florida Keys, in the vicinity of Key Largo, with only her crew being saved.

Year 1772. British merchantman *Maria Beckford*, Captain Boyd, was wrecked at Cape Florida and was a total loss.

Year 1772. British ship *Fortune*, Captain Richardson, sailing from Jamaica to London, was lost on November 18 near the coast of Florida, only two men drowned.

Above

Contemporary chart showing the exact location off the east coast of Florida where the Almiranta of the 1715 Spanish treasure fleet was lost.

Below

About 20 of these Spanish eight-escuda "Royals" have been recovered from the 1715 fleet; such a coin can net more than $100,000 on the open market.

Year 1773. A ship of unknown nationality, *Sally*, Captain Matthews, sailing from Lisbon to South Carolina, was lost on February 22 in a snowstorm near St. Augustine and all of the crew except the mate perished.

Year 1773. British merchantman *East Florida Merchant*, Captain Losthouse, sailing from London to St. Augustine, was lost on the St. Augustine bar and two-thirds of its cargo was saved.

Year 1773. British ship *Dove*, captain's name unknown, was lost on October 18 on the coast of Florida, en route from Africa to St. Augustine, 80 out of 100 slaves, plus the captain and two of the crew, were lost.

Year 1774. Captain Addis of the ship *Green River*, sailing from Jamaica to London, reported that on April 23 he saw a ship wrecked at Cape Florida without main or mizzen masts, and believed it was the *Mill*, Captain Hays, which was sailing in ballast from Jamaica to Boston.

Year 1774. British ship *Rhee Galley*, Captain Hunter, sailing from Honduras to Bristol, was lost in the Florida Keys.

Year 1774. Captain Magness of the ship *Ann & Elizabeth*, arrived in London from Jamaica and reported that on August 8 he saw a large brig onshore to the northward of Cape Florida being stripped by several wreckers.

Year 1774. British merchantman *Montague*, Captain Pickels, sailing from Jamaica to Liverpool, was lost at Cape Florida, but the crew and about 30 hogsheads of sugar were carried to New Providence Island in the Bahamas.

Year 1774. British ship *Diana*, Captain Buckley, sailing from Jamaica to Rhode Island, was lost on Cape Florida, the crew was saved, but the cargo and ship were a total loss.

Sometime before 1775. An historian wrote: "...a little cay lying before Matacumbe is a dreadful monument of this [Caloosa Indians' cannibalism] it is called Matanca [i.e., "slaughter"], from the number near 400 wretched Frenchmen, who being cast away, fell into the hands of these monsters."

Sometime before 1775. A British historian writing in 1775 stated that three Spanish galleons were wrecked near the Bay of San Bernard, which is somewhere along the west coast of Florida.

Year 1776. British ship *Belieze* [sic], Captain Gillis, sailing from Honduras to London, was lost on October 12 on the east coast of Florida.

Year 1777. A ship of unknown nationality, *Minerva*, Captain Callahan, was lost on the east coast of Florida.

Year 1777. On May 16 the Spanish ship *Begoña* entered Cadíz. Coming from Veracruz it had sighted an English vessel of Captain Williams just ready to sink off the coast of Florida. The Spaniards rescued the crew from this ship and took them to Cadíz.

Year 1777. British ship *Claudina*, Captain Valliant, sailing from London to Pensacola, was totally lost on the coast of Florida.

Year 1778. British warship *H.M.S. Otter*, 10 guns, Captain John Wright, was wrecked off the east coast of Florida.

Year 1778. During a hurricane on October 9, 14 large and many small ships were sunk at Pensacola, among which were the *Sarah & Elizabeth*, Captain Tovet, laden with lumber for Jamaica, and the *Mary*, Captain Blackwell, both of British registry.

Year 1778. British ship *Mary*, Captain Hoincastle, sailing from Jamaica to London, was lost in December off Cape Florida in attempting to escape from two American privateers.

Year 1778. Spanish merchantman *N.S. del Carmen*, sailing between New Orleans and the Canary Islands was wrecked on Anastasia Island.

Year 1779. Privateeering vessel of unknown nationality was wrecked just north of New Smyrna and 50 of her crew were captured and taken to St. Augustine.

Year 1781. Spanish frigate *Francesa*, Captain Andromaca, carrying a large cargo of war materials, ran aground on April 19 on a shoal in Pensacola Bay. The exact location of this shipwreck is shown on a chart in the Naval Museum of Madrid.

Year 1781. British warship *H.M.S. Mentor*, 20 guns, Captain Robert Deans, was burned at Pensacola.

Year 1782. Brief mention that an English ship sank on the Florida Keys sometime during the year.

Year 1782. British ship *Fanny*, Captain Farquar, sailing from Jamaica to Liverpool, on March 7 ran aground to the northward of Cape Florida and broke up quickly, people and 'some cargo rescued by a privateer from Nassau.

Year 1783. British ship *Mary*, Captain Stafford, sailing from St. Augustine to London, was lost on the St. Augustine bar on April 19.

Year 1783. British merchantman *Tony*, Captain Welsh, sailing from Charlestown to St. Augustine and London, was lost on the St. Augustine bar.

Year 1785. Captain Earl of the ship *Joséph*, sailing from Honduras to England, on August 31 reported seeing a large ship wrecked on the Florida Keys. Two small vessels were near her on the inside of the reef.

Year 1786. Spanish brigantine *La Esclavitúd* carrying 40,000 pesos in silver specie from Havana to the garrison at St. Augustine was unable to enter this port due to bad weather and soon after disappeared without a trace. Two other supply vessels sailing with it were lost on shoals off Cape Canaveral. Later this same year two other Spanish supply ships heading for St. Augustine were also lost off Cape Canaveral.

Year 1787. A vessel sailing from Jamaica to London picked up the crew of a British ship wrecked on the east coast of Florida.

Year 1787. British ship *Noble Bounty*, Captain Herbert, sailing from Jamaica to London, was wrecked on the Cape Florida Reef but her crew was saved by the *Friendship*, Captain Black.

Year 1788. British ship *Betsey*, Captain Grant, sailing from Nassau to Florida, was lost on the Mosquito bar on the coast of Florida.

Year 1788. British merchantman *Evenly*, Captain Hebden, sailing from Honduras to London, was wrecked on the Florida Keys.

Year 1788. British merchantman *Mary & Jane*, Captain Pennymont, sailing from Jamaica for Liverpool, was lost on the Florida shore but the crew was saved.

Year 1789. British merchantman *Hazard*, Captain New, sailing from Honduras to London, was totally lost near Cape Florida but the crew was saved.

Year 1789. British ship *Fly*, Captain Walker, sailing from Jamaica to Africa, was lost on the Florida Keys.

Year 1790. A ship of unknown nationality, *Santa Marie*, Captain Wicks, sailing from St. Augustine to Havana, was lost on the St. Augustine bar.

Year 1790. British merchantman *Elizabeth*, Captain Sims, came from Jamaica to Bristol after having run aground on the coast of Florida, where it was refloated by throwing part of its cargo overboard. On August 12, Captain Sims, then in 25 degrees and 4 minutes of latitude, saw four ships on the Florida reef. On the August 19 he saw two other ships at Cape Florida wrecked on the reef: the *Apollo*, Captain Cragg, and the *Edmund & George*, Captain Rainy; both had been bound for London. Two other ships had been on shore in Florida but got off by throwing some cargo overboard.

Year 1790. British merchantman *Hope*, Captain Chappel, sailing from Jamaica to Charlestown, was lost on the coast of Florida.

Year 1791. British merchant brig *Lively*, Captain Morse, sailing from Jamaica for Bristol, was lost in the Florida Keys but most of her cargo was saved.

Year 1792. Captain Graham of the ship *Mary*, on June 5 reported seeing a large ship wrecking on the Florida Keys. It was a total loss, and although he was within a mile of her he could not establish her identity.

Year 1792. Captain M'Donald of the ship *Trelaumey Planter* on August 14 reported sighting a ship ashore on Carysford Reef with several wreckers about her.

Year 1792. American merchantman *Lovely Ann*, Captain Green, sailing from Jamaica to New York, was lost in the Florida Keys.

Year 1793. British warship *H.M.S. Carysford*, a frigate of 28 guns, Captain Francis Laforey, was lost on Carysford Reef in the Florida Keys.

Year 1793. British merchantman *General Clark*, Captain Lilburn, sailing from Jamaica to Savannah, was totally lost on a reef of the Florida Keys but the crew was saved.

Year 1794. British merchantman *Catherine Green*, Captain Rose, sailing from Jamaica for London, was wrecked on August 8 on a reef in the Florida Keys but most of her cargo was saved.

Year 1795. American merchantman *Noah's Ark*, captain's name unknown, sailing from New Orleans to Philadelphia, was lost in the Florida Keys.

Year 1796. A brig of unknown nationality, *Hope*, Captain West, sailing from Havana to a port in America, was lost near Cape Florida.

Year 1796. British naval transport *Maria*, Captain Giltchrist, sailing from Jamaica, was lost on Ludberry Reef in the Florida Keys.

Year 1796. British merchantman *Speedwell*, Captain Brownlow, sailing from Honduras to Charlestown, was lost on August 28 on Carysford Reef, crew and ship's materials saved.

Year 1796. A ship of unknown nationality, *Jolly Tar*, captain's name unknown, sailing from Jamaica to Norfolk, was wrecked on the coast of Florida, crew and cargo saved.

Year 1797. A number of American vessels were cast away on the east coast of Florida during a hurricane on October 15 or 16. Some were also lost in the Bahamas.

Year 1798. British ship *Flora*, Captain Scott, sailing from Charlestown to Havana, was lost on the Florida Keys.

Year 1799. British sloop-of-war *Amaranthe*, Captain John Blake, 14 guns, was wrecked on the coast of Florida on October 25 and twenty-two of the crew of eighty-six were lost.

Year 1799. An unidentified Spanish sloop, after being captured by a New Providence privateer was wrecked on Nov. 12 just south of Key Largo and only her crew were saved.

Year 1800. A ship of unknown nationality, *Hector*, captain's name unknown, sailing from Havana to Nassau, was lost on a reef in the Florida Keys.

Year 1801. American ship *Eagle*, Captain Dennet, sailing from Havana to Philadelphia, was wrecked on December 15 on the Florida side of the Maranzie Reef in the Florida Keys, crew and cargo saved.

Year 1802. British ship *Neptune*, Captain Cushley, sailing from New Orleans to Nassau, was lost on the coast of Florida, crew and most of cargo saved.

Year 1802. A ship of unknown nationality, *Neptune*, Captain Cosbury, sailing from New Orleans to Greencock, out 14 days from New Orleans, was lost on the coast of Florida, crew and small part of cargo saved.

Year 1802. American schooner *Phoebus*, Captain Dominique, sailing from Norfolk, was lost on the St. Augustine bar.

Year 1803. A Spanish ship and a Spanish snow, both from Cadíz, were wrecked and totally lost in January on the Mocus Reef on the Florida Shore.

Year 1803. British merchantman *Maria*, captain's name unknown, sailing from Honduras to Charlestown, wrecked on the Florida coast; crew, materials and cargo saved.

Year 1803. British merchantman *Britannia*, Captain Wright, sailing from Jamaica to London, was lost on the Florida Keys but part of her cargo was saved by wreckers and carried to Nassau.

Year 1804. American merchantman *Calliope*, Captain Nash, sailing from Jamaica to Virginia, was lost on the reefs of the Florida Keys.

Year 1804. During a fierce northeast gale on September 6 or 7, eight ships were sunk in St. Augustine Harbor.

Year 1805. British warship *H.M.S. Fly*, Captain Powell Bast Pellew, was wrecked in May on the Carysford Reef and all 121 men of the crew were saved. Gilly states that the wreck occurred on March 3.

Year 1805. British merchantman *Rattler*, Captain Balmond, sailing from Honduras to London, was totally lost on Carysford Reef and only a small part of her cargo was saved.

Year 1805. A ship of unknown nationality, *Providence*, Captain Gibson, sailing from New Orleans to Bordeaux, wrecked on September 17 in the Florida Keys.

Year 1805. A ship of unknown nationality, *Andromache*, Captain Hickles, sailing from Jamaica to New York, was wrecked on December 6 in the Florida Keys. The principal part of her cargo Was salvaged and carried to Nassau.

Year 1806. British schooner *H.M.S. Zenobia*, 10 guns, captain's name unknown, wrecked on the coast of Florida and the crew was lost.

Year 1806. A ship of unknown nationality, *Maria*, Captain Rundle, sailing from Jamaica to Halifax, was wrecked on the Dry Tortugas.

Year 1807. A ship of unknown nationality, *Sea Flower*, Captain Pitch, sailing from Jamaica and Havana to New York, lost on Florida's east coast.

Year 1807. British merchantman *Flora*, Captain Adams, sailing from New Orleans to Liverpool, was wrecked on the coast of Florida.

Year 1808. American merchantman *Ohio*, Captain Hall, sailing from Jamaica to New York, was wrecked on January 15 near Cape Florida but the crew and a great part of the cargo were saved.

Year 1810. During a hurricane at the end of October, five American ships were wrecked on the Florida shore and went to pieces, but the greatest part of their cargoes were recovered.

Year 1810. British merchantman *Susan*, Captain Beard, sailing from Amelia Island to Clyde, was lost at Amelia Island, crew and cargo saved.

Year 1810. American merchantman *Fame*, Captain Bennett, sailing from New Orleans to Liverpool, was lost on the coast of Florida but the crew was saved.

Year 1810. Two British merchantmen, *Hanover*, Captain Baxter, and *George*, Captain Decone, sailing from Liverpool to Amelia Island, were lost about October 20 on Amelia Island.

Year 1810. Four merchantmen of unknown nationality were lost about October 25 on the Florida shore: *Caroline*, Captain Curtis, sailing from New Orleans to Liverpool; *Union*, captain's name unknown, sailing from Havana to London; *African*, Captain García, sailing from Havana to New York; and the *Triton*, Captain Hand, sailing from Havana to Richmond.

Year 1810. American schooner, name of ship unknown, Captain Fowler, sailing from St. Mary's to Savannah, laden with salt and cotton, was wrecked at St. Augustine.

Year 1811. British merchantman *Cabinet*, Captain Montgomery, sailing from New Orleans to Liverpool, was lost October 26 on a reef of the Florida Keys, crew and most of cargo saved.

Year 1811. British merchantman *Minerva*, Captain M'Nelly, sailing from Londonderry to Amelia Island, was lost on March 2 on Amelia Island but crew was saved.

Year 1811. Ship identified only by its name, *North Star*, was wrecked at Amelia Island.

Year 1811. A ship of unknown nationality, *Horatio*, Captain Turner, was totally wrecked at Amelia Island.

Year 1811. British merchantman *Lady Provost*, Captain Clary, struck on a bar at Amelia Island and was lost on May 9.

Year 1811. Two British merchantmen were lost at Amelia Island: *Windsor*, Captain Low, sailing from Liverpool to Savannah and Amelia Island, wrecked on Amelia Bar; and the *Maria*, Captain Forster, sailing from London to Amelia Island, was blown up at Amelia Island.

Year 1811. On October 17 the Spanish ship *Araucana*, Captain Benmto de la Rigada (with an official rank of Teniente de fragata), sailed from Havana with mail for Spain, but was totally wrecked on Elliot Key in a hurricane on October 26. The crew came ashore on this key and was picked up by a vessel and carried to Nassau and then Havana.

Year 1811. In October the *Eagle*, sailing from Liverpool, and the *Maria*, of and to London, with five of six other vessels, names unknown, were lost on Amelia Island bar.

Year 1811. A ship of unknown nationality, *Fair Weather*, captain's name unknown, sailing from Amelia Island to England, was lost on Amelia Island bar.

Year 1811. British merchantman *Mary*, Captain Forbes, was totally lost at Amelia Island in October.

Year 1811. British ship Earl Bathurst, Captain Heron, sailing from Liverpool, was wrecked at Pensacola.

Year 1811. Pirate schooner *La Franchise*, after fighting a battle with U.S. Gunboat #162 on August 7, was set on fire by her crew near Pensacola and totally lost with a considerable amount of treasure aboard.

Year 1812. American merchantman *Orion*, Captain Brown, sailing from Aux Cayes to Philadelphia, was lost on February 20 on a reef in the Florida Keys.

Year 1812. British ship *Betsey*, Captain Telley, sailing from St. Vincent, was totally lost at Amelia Island.

Year 1812. British merchantman *Highlander*, Captain Cuthbert, sailing from Jamaica to London, was lost on July 15 on Carysford Reef, the crew was picked up by the ship Hopewell.

Year 1812. American ship *Juno*, Captain Pratt, sailing from New Orleans to Boston, was lost on June 16 on the Carysford Reef.

Year 1813. Spanish merchantman *Flor de Guadiana*, captain's name unknown, with between 800 and 900 bags of cotton aboard, was driven on shore at Amelia Island and broke up during a violent storm on September 17.

Year 1814. Spanish merchantman *Americano*, Captain Abreu, sailing from Havana to Lisbon, was wrecked on July 26 on a reef in the Florida Keys.

Year 1814. Ship identified only by its name, *Santa Rosa*, coming from Liverpool, was lost on Amelia Island bar.

Year 1814. Ship identified only by its name, *Oscar*, bound for Liverpool, was burned at Amelia Island.

Year 1814. Spanish ship *Intripido*, commanded by Alferez de Navío Marquis del Moral, was wrecked on a beach at Pensacola during a storm.

Year 1814. A ship of unknown nationality, *Nicholas-Adolph*, Captain Hoas, was lost on November 10 on the Amelia Island bar, part of her cargo was saved.

Year 1815. Spanish ship *Empecinada*, six guns, commanded by Captain Juan Villacencio, left Havana on December 19, 1814, with four other Spanish ships. On January 8, 1815, due to bad weather, it wrecked at Amelia Island bar while trying to enter the port, where it immediately went to pieces; crew and cargo saved.

Year 1815. Spanish ship *Volador*, 10 cannon, commanded by Captain Joaquín Veal, entered the port of Pensacola on March 25 carrying a large cargo of goods and rifles. That night a strong wind arose which caused the ship to run aground, and it soon went to pieces. Two of the crew and all of the ship's cargo were lost.

Year 1815. Ship identified only by its name, *Santa Anna*, coming from Bermuda, was lost on March 7 off Amelia Island.

Year 1815. A ship of unknown nationality, *Watt*, Captain M'Gee, sailing from Jamaica to New York, was lost on a reef in the Florida Keys.

Year 1815. Spanish ship *Jerusalem*, captain's name unknown, sailing from Havana to Africa, was lost on November 13 on a reef of the Florida Keys, crew and cargo saved.

Year 1815. An unidentified ship was reported to be wrecked on Carysford Reef on December 6.

Year 1816. The following vessels were wrecked in the Gulf of Florida during violent gales between June 5 and 8 *Atlas*, Captain Thompson, of and heading for Glasgow, coming from Jamaica, on a reef in the Florida Keys; *Martha Brae*, Captain Farish, from Jamaica to Whitehaven, near Cape Florida, with loss (total) of cargo and two men; *Cossack* from Havana to Hamburg in the Florida Keys, crew and part of cargo saved; *General Pike*, Captain Emery, from Charlestown to Matanzas, Cuba, at Sound Point, part of its cargo saved; and the *Zanga*, Captain Russell, of Nassau, at Sound Point, all of its cargo saved.

Year 1816. The following ships of unknown nationality were wrecked near St. Augustine in early June: *Huron*, Captain Snow, sailing from Charlestown to St. Mary's; the schooners *Due Bill* and *Water Witch*, of Savannah; and several unidentified vessels.

Year 1816. British ship *Three Sisters*, captain's name unknown, of and heading for Nassau, from New York, was lost on the Carysford Reef.

Year 1816. American ship *Three Sisters*, Captain Arnington, of New York, bound for New Orleans, was wrecked on August 30 on Carysford Reef; the crew was saved.

Year 1816. Two ships of unknown nationality were wrecked "at Florida": *Rebecca*, captain's name unknown, sailing from Cadíz and Havana to Savannah; and *Catherine Osmond*, Captain Vicaiz, sailing from Havana to Salem. Parts of their cargoes were saved and carried to Nassau.

Year 1816. American merchantman *Frolic*, Captain Kennedy, sailing from Havana to Charleston, was wrecked on Anastasia Island, crew and cargo saved.

Year 1816. A ship of unknown nationality, *Sir John Sherbroke*, Captain Cowan, sailing from Jamaica to New York with a general cargo and $60,000 in specie, struck a reef off the Dry Tortugas and the ship went to pieces. The crew was saved and made off with the specie.

Year 1816. British merchantman *Magdalen*, Captain Sawyer, sailing from New Orleans to Liverpool, was wrecked on a reef in the Florida Keys, its cargo was saved.

Year 1816. British merchantman *Neptune*, Captain Conolly [sic], sailing from Amelia Island to Jamaica, wrecked on the Amelia Island bar and went to pieces.

Year 1816. Ship identified only by its name, *Amiable Antoinetta*, sailing from Charlestown, wrecked on December 26 near St. Augustine, crew and cargo saved.

Year 1817. The ship *Hambro*, Captain Patterson, sailing from St. Ubes to Savannah was wrecked about March 12 at a distance of 12 miles to the south of St. Augustine, the crew was saved but the cargo was a total loss.

Year 1817. Ship identified only by its name, *Anna Maria*, sailing from New Orleans to Philadelphia, wrecked on Bason Bank off east Florida on March 23, the crew was saved, also the few dry goods she had on board.

Year 1817. Ship identified only by its name, *Julian*, sailing from St. Ubes to Savannah, was lost on March 15 at Anastasia Island, crew, passengers, and part of cargo saved.

Year 1817. The ship *Brandt*, coming from New Orleans arrived in New York on June 3 and reported seeing a ship and a brig aground on Carysford Reef with eight wreckers around them.

Year 1817. A ship of unknown nationality, *Europa*, Captain Rich, sailing from St. Jago de Cuba for America, wrecked in May on a Florida Keys reef.

Year 1817. American merchantman *Despatch*, Captain Field, sailing from Havana for Charlestown, wrecked on June 15 on Carysford Reef, crew and cargo saved.

Year 1817. Portuguese ship *Marquis de Pombal*, captain's name unknown, sailing from Pernambuco to Oporto, was captured by the Patriola, an insurgent privateer, but was run aground on May 5 on a reef in the Florida Keys; her cargo was saved and carried to Nassau.

Year 1817. British merchantman *Sisters*, Captain Swiney, sailing from Jamaica to London, was lost on August 3 on Grand Cayman Island but her crew was picked up by the ship *Unity*, Captain Lambourn, sailing from Jamaica to London. The *Unity* was then lost on August 13 on Carysford Reef and the crews of both ships were saved by another passing ship.

Year 1817. American brig *Merrimack*, captain's name unknown, sailing from Havana to New York, was wrecked in the Florida Keys and her cargo was completely los,t but her crew was saved and taken to Nassau by the wreckers.

Year 1817. A ship of unknown nationality, *Venus*, Captain Pinder, sailing from Jamaica to New York, was lost on the east Florida coast, crew and part of cargo saved.

Year 1818. American merchantman, *Betsey*, Captain Grafton, sailing from Havana to Rhode Island, was lost on a reef in the Florida Keys, part of her cargo was saved and carried to Nassau.

Year 1818. A large plain ship with yellow sides and black-painted parts was seen wrecked on the Carysford Reef about August 15.

Year 1818. British merchantman *Solway*, Captain Bennett, sailing from Jamaica to Withsharon, wrecked August 10 on a reef of the Florida Keys. Eighteen different wrecking vessels were reported to have recovered the greatest part of her cargo.

Year 1818. British merchantman *Quebec*, Captain Fiott, sailing from Jamaica to London, was totally lost on a reef in the Florida Keys on August 7; only her crew was saved.

Year 1818. A ship of unknown nationality, *Eliza*, Captain Murphey, sailing from Jamaica to Philadelphia, was lost on Carysford Reef, crew and six boxes of dollars saved.

Year 1818. British merchantman *Acasta*, Captain Parkin, sailing from Jamaica to Liverpool, was wrecked sometime before December 5 on the Dry Tortugas, crew and most of cargo saved.

Year 1819. Ship identified only by its name, *Bonee Adelle*, coming from Havana, was wrecked on the coast of east Florida on February 5, only the crew was saved.

Year 1819. A brig with a white bottom and a white streak was seen wrecked on a reef along the Florida Keys on February 24.

Year 1819. French ship *Modeste*, Captain D'Barron, was wrecked at Key Largo on May 21.

Year 1819. American ship *General Jackson*, Captain Taylor, sailing from New Orleans for Rotterdam, was wrecked on Cape Florida but most of her cargo was saved.

Year 1819. British merchantman *Sandwich*, Captain Fraser, sailing from Havana to Guernsey, was wrecked in the Florida Keys and only a small part of her cargo was saved.

Year 1819. A ship of unknown nationality, *Anie of Scarbro* [sic], Captain Stanley, en route to England, was lost June 29 on a reef in the Florida Keys, only five of the crew were saved.

Year 1819. On August 12 a large vessel was seen aground on Carysford Reef with three small vessels presumably anchored nearby.

Year 1819. Two American ships were driven over a reef in the Florida Keys and lost: the brig *Barilla*, Captain Jones, sailing from New Orleans to Philadelphia, and the schooner *Lively*, Captain Avery, sailing from New Orleans to Baltimore. The cargoes of both vessels were saved.

Year 1821. American ship *Hope for Peace*, Captain Baker, sailing from New Orleans for Charlestown, was dismasted and overset in the Gulf Stream on January 25. The ship then drifted and wrecked on the coast of Florida on January 30 but the crew was saved.

Year 1821. A ship of unknown nationality, *Supply*, Captain Fisher, sailing from Jamaica to Havana, heading for the Cape Verde Islands, was totally lost on the coast of Florida at a latitude of 26 degrees and 20 minutes during a heavy gale on January 26 but the crew was saved.

Year 1821. At the end of February a ship was seen wrecked and totally dis-masted on Carysford Reef.

Year 1821. British merchantman *Pearl*, Captain Johnson, sailing from Havana to Gibraltar, was lost near Cape Florida on March 8, only the captain and four of the crew survived.

Year 1821. French ship *Royal Desire*, Captain Feuardant, sailing from Havana to Le Havre, was lost early in June near the Florida Coast but the crew was rescued.

Year 1821. During a hurricane September 15 several ships were lost in Pensacola Bay.

Year 1821. A ship of unknown nationality, *Cosmopolite*, Captain Selliman, sailing from Charlestown to New Orleans, was wrecked during a gale on September 14 in the Florida Keys.

Year 1821. American sloop *General Jackson*, captain's name unknown, was wrecked on the coast of Florida but the crew was saved and carried to Havana, arriving there on October 5.

Year 1822. American naval schooner *USS Alligator*, 198 tons, 12 guns, Captain Dale , was wrecked on November 19 on a reef which now bears it name in the Florida Keys, only about 100 yards from the lighthouse on Alligator Reef

Year 1822. English brig *Nelson*, captain's name unknown, was wrecked on the Florida shore on January 31; the crew was saved and taken to Jamaica.

Year 1822. British merchantman *Frances & Lucy* Captain Barnaby, sailing from Jamaica to Halifax, was lost on a reef in the Florida Keys on January 14.

Year 1822. On April 25, a full-rigged brig was reported wrecked on Carysford Reef. Two other brigs were also aground on Ledbury Reef, one appeared to be over the reef, and there were six or seven wreckers around the two wrecks.

Year 1822. British merchantman *Ann of London*, Captain Campbell, sailing from Havana to Buenos Aires, was lost around the end of April on the east Florida Keys, only part of her cargo was saved.

Year 1822. A French brig laden with indigo, logwood, and mahogany, coming from Honduras, was wrecked on the east Florida Keys around the end of April.

Year 1822. On May 19 a ship with plain yellow sides was reported wrecked on Carysford Reef.

Year 1822. During a hurricane on July 7 the sloop *Lady Washington* ran aground on Ship Island near Pensacola.

Year 1822. British merchantman *Neptune*, Captain Duncan, sailing from Jamaica to Dublin, was wrecked on the east Florida shore and broke up quickly.

Year 1822. On June 27 a large vessel was seen wrecked on a reef in the Florida Keys with six large wrecking vessels around her.

Year 1822. British ship *Waterloo*, Captain Kelcher, sailing from Jamaica to Cork, was wrecked during October on the east Florida shore but all of its cargo was saved and carried to Nassau.

Year 1823. American sloop *Leopard*, captain's name unknown, sailing from St. Augustine to Havana, was lost in the Florida Keys but the crew was saved and taken to Havana.

Year 1823. American merchantman *Franklin*, Captain Taper, sailing from Philadelphia for Pensacola, was wrecked in the Florida Keys, crew and principal part of cargo saved and taken to Nassau.

Year 1823. Ship identified only by its name, *Andromache*, sailing from Jamaica to New York, was wrecked November 18 on a reef in the Florida Keys.

Year 1823. Spanish ship *Intripido*, commanded by Captain José Usel de Guimbarda, was lost in the Bay of Pensacola.

Year 1824. British merchantman *George III*, Captain Danning, sailing from Honduras to Dublin, was lost February 24 on Carysford Reef, only her crew was saved.

Year 1824. On March 14 a brig, painted black with a white streak, was seen wrecked on a reef in the Florida Keys.

Year 1824. The sloop *Theodore*, reported that a British brig, sailing from Honduras to England, was wrecked on a reef in the Florida Keys. The *Theodore*, was driven away from the wreck by American wreckers.

Year 1824. On March 26, in latitude of 25 degrees, near Caesar Creek, a long black vessel with painted ports was seen wrecked on a reef with her masts cut down.

Year 1824. A ship of unknown nationality, *Swift*, Captain Miller, coming from Havana, was wrecked at night on Long Island: 900 boxes of sugar and all the indigo and cochineal she had on board were saved by wreckers and landed at Key West.

Year 1824. On August 5 a large bright-sided American brig, deeply laden, was seen wrecked on the southwestern end of Carysford Reef with several wreckers alongside.

Year 1824. On August 29 a large brig was seen wrecked on the Florida coast near Palmerstone Inlet with several small vessels around her.

Year 1824. British brig *Sarah*, Captain Rowe, laden with logwood and mahogany, was wrecked eight miles from St. Johnson's bar.

Year 1824. Ship identified only by its name, *Ceres*, coming from New Orleans, was wrecked on the Dry Tortugas but the crew was saved and carried to Havana.

Year 1825. French merchantman *Pointe-a-Pitre*, captain's name unknown, sailing from New Orleans to Bordeaux, was lost on a reef in the Florida Keys on February 7, crew and part of cargo saved.

Year 1825. Ship identified only by its name, *Johan Carl* (or *Carl John*), sailing from Havana to the Mediterranean, was lost in the Florida Keys, and out of a thousand boxes of sugar aboard only 74 were saved.

Chapter Four

Mexico

I am frequently asked which area of the Western Hemisphere I prefer for old shipwrecks. My answer has always been Mexico because of the vast number of virgin shipwrecks lying in its waters. Unlike the Bahamas or Florida, where salvors have been picking shipwrecks clean for centuries, most colonial shipwrecks in Mexico (except for ships lost close to Veracruz) were not salvaged, or only partially so. This is because many ships were lost off desolate areas of the Yucatan Peninsula, or on small cays or reefs in the Gulf of Mexico. Even if survivors managed to reach civilization, they couldn't report a wreck's location with any accuracy. Most of the coastline of the Yucatan Peninsula even today is barren, and outstanding landmarks are few and far between.

In addition to shipwreck locations I have listed in this chapter, there are no doubt many others on which no documentation has survived; if indeed, anything was ever written about them. This would include small trading vessels that plied between Mexico, Cuba and other Caribbean ports as well as privateering and pirate vessels of various nationalities.

The reason there is little mention of ships lost on the Pacific side of Mexico is that in the old days there was virtually no shipping in those waters. There were the annual departures and arrivals of the Manila Galleons, but none were known to have been lost in Mexican waters. Trade between Mexico, Panama and Peru was prohibited, except on rare occasions, in an effort to prevent the carrying of contraband.

It must be remembered that prior to 1600 the town of Veracruz was located 15 miles west of the present port city, so any ships listed as being lost at or near Veracruz before that date were located at the site of the old town. Ships mentioned as being lost at San Juan de Ulza are today located in the present harbor of Veracruz, as the former name is no longer in use. In the past 50 years a great deal of

255

dredging has been done in Veracruz harbor and vast amounts of treasure and artifacts have been brought up by accident, but a great deal remains. Many of the shipwrecks listed as having been lost at Veracruz may no longer exist because of this extensive dredging and land reclamation.

When a ship was reported as "lost on the Coast of Campeche," this did not necessarily mean near the present port of Campeche, as the whole Yucatan Peninsula was known as the Coast of Campeche as late as 1800. Some of the place names I have used in this chapter are no longer used on modern charts or maps but can be found on old nautical charts.

From my own experience I know that most of the eastern section of the Yucatan Peninsula can be worked the year around, but in the Gulf of Mexico the best season is summer, when the strong north winds don't blow. Except around the mouths of rivers or in large commercial ports the underwater visibility is generally as good as in the Bahamas.

The Mexican Government is very strict about foreigners working on shipwreck sites in their territorial waters, and in recent years several treasure-hunting parties have been arrested for diving illegally in Mexican waters. Permission can be obtained only through CEDAM or CEDAM International.

CEDAM (Club of Explorations and Aquatic Sports of Mexico) was founded in 1959 by Pablo Bush Romero, a noted sportsman and businessman. The first marine archaeological society created in the Western Hemisphere, its function was not just to undertake serious salvage work but to protect all ancient shipwrecks from being plundered. Members of CEDAM have participated annually in large-scale expeditions in Mexican waters and have recovered a great deal of interesting artifacts from various sites.

From its inception CEDAM admitted U.S. citizens as members and CEDAM International was formed in the U.S. in 1966 by those interested in salvaging shipwrecks around the world as well as in Mexican waters. Combined, the two groups, which work jointly on Mexican shipwreck sites each summer have over a thousand members.

Permission to work on shipwrecks in Mexican waters is rarely given. Occasionally permission may be granted by the Instituto Nacional de Arqueologia y Historia in Mexico City.

Shipwrecks in Mexican Waters

Year 1511. When Hernán Cortez stopped at Cozumel Island in 1519 he found a Spaniard there named Jeronimo de Aguilar, a native of Ecija, Spain. In 1511 they and 15 other men and two women left Darien for the Island of Santo Domingo, but their ship was blown off course and wrecked on the Alacrán Reef in the Gulf of Mexico. In the ship's boat they reached Yucatan, where most of their companions were sacrificed by the Indians.

Year 1519. After Cortez began the conquest of Mexico, he had nine of the ten vessels the Spaniards had arrived at San Juan de Ulza in either burned or sunk. Various accounts differ as to how the ships were destroyed; however, all accounts agree that all the ships were stripped of everything of value, such as rigging, cordage, etc., before they were destroyed. None of the accounts indicate what type of ships they were, except that some were large and others small. During the summer of 1958 a group of divers led by Pablo Bush Romero attempted to locate these shipwrecks but didn't because the land has built out farther into the sea and the area in which these ships were lost is believed to be under land.

Year 1519. A nao of Captain Diego Camargo sank in the Tampico River and all of the men aboard her were lost.

Year 1524. The lawyer Alonso Zuazo, who was then the governor of Santiago de Cuba, sailed from there in January of 1524 to visit Cortez in Mexico. On January 20 his ship wrecked on Los Triangulos and quickly went to pieces. Only 43 people were saved, and Zuazo lost his books and a great deal of gold, silver and jewels. The wreck occurred near a small cay, 10 paces wide and 100-150 paces long. There was another small cay located about three leagues away, from which they obtained water. From the wreckage of the ship they built a small boat and eventually reached Veracruz. Other accounts of this event place the wreck on Los Alacránes, but from the description of the area it was most likely on Los Triangulos.

Year 1526. *La Nicolasa* sank at Isla Cancun near Isla Mujeres. This was a ship sailing from Cuba to Veracruz with supplies for the conquistadors. A CEDAM expedition recovered several lombard cannon from this wreck in 1959, and a few years earlier several fishermen from Isla Mujeres recovered a bronze cannon in excellent condition.

Year 1527. When conquistador Francisco de Montejo began the conquest of Yucatan in 1527, he ordered two of his ships, a brigantine and a caravel, burned at Punta Soliman on the coast of Quintana Roo, between the ruins of Tulúm and Xehla. I located the site of these wrecks in 1957 and recovered a small anchor, iron cooking caldron, miscellaneous iron fittings, various ceramic shards and some ballast stones.

Year 1527. Two naos of the armada of General Alvaro de Saavedra, which were sent by Cortez from the west coast of Mexico to search for the ships of Loaysa, were believed to have been lost on the Straits of Gaspar, near the coast of Mexico, but the exact location of this strait is not known. The names of the ships were the *Santiago* and *Espíritu Santo*.

Year 1532. An unidentified brigantine, built in Mexico at the orders of the Marquis del Valle to make new discoveries in the South Seas (Pacific Ocean), was lost on the coast of Mexico near Aldeanueva.

Year 1539. Loss of the ship carrying the explorer Francisco de Ulloa, who after exploring the Gulf of California headed north and was never again heard from.

Year 1545. An unidentified merchant nao coming from Spain was lost "on the reefs of Veracruz" and all of its cargo worth over 100,000 pesos, was totally lost, but the people were saved.

Year 1545. An unidentified ship of the Flota de Nueva España was wrecked because of a norther on Isla de Terminos and the survivors reached Campeche in a canoe.

Year 1552. After the New Spain Treasure Fleet had taken aboard its treasures and was preparing to set sail from Veracruz for Havana and Spain, a terrible hurricane struck on Sept. 2, and 12 ships were wrecked. Most of their cargoes were recovered soon afterwards.

Year 1553. Merchant nao *La Magdalena*, 150 tons, Captain Juan Rodríguez, sailing from Veracruz to Spain, was lost on the coast of Mexico but all the gold she carried was recovered and taken to Spain in another ship.

Year 1555. Nao *Espíritu Santo*, 220 tons, Captain Damyan Martín, preparing to sail for Spain, was sunk in the port of San Juan de Ulza but all the gold and silver she carried was salvaged.

Year 1555. On January 21 the nao *Santa María la Blanca*, 220 tons, Captain Francisco de Santana, owned by Diego Felípe, was lost. One document states she sank in the port of San Juan de Ulza and another that she was lost on some reefs as she was leaving port. All of her cargo, which consisted of 850,000 pesos de oro, 28,000 marcos of silver (recovered from three naos that had been wrecked on the coast of Florida in 1554) and a large amount of cochineal, were salvaged but 85 people were drowned.

Sometime before 1557. In 1557 the bishop of Yucatan, Diego de Landa, wrote that about 15 years earlier a bark was lost with many people and a great amount of dry goods near the Bay of Ascensión, on the coast of Quintana Roo. The ship foundered and everyone, except a man named Majuelas and four others, was lost. The five men clung to a fragment of the ship's mast and floated for three or four days trying to reach one of the small islands in this bay. Only Majuelas survived. He built a small raft and reached the mainland.

Above

Just part of the vast number of gold coins and jewelry that have beem recovered from the wreck of the Spanish galleon *Maravillas*.

Below

Artifacts that were recovered from the wreck of the Spanish merchantman *Matanceros*, lost in 1741 off the coast of Yucatan.

258

Year 1558. On February 6 19 merchant naos under the command of General Pedro de Ruelas sailed from Sanlúcar de Barrameda for the Indies. After making a Caribbean landfall, Ruelas took 11 of the ships and sailed for Cartagena. The other eight, under the command of Admiral Antonio de Aguayo, sailed for Mexico. When they were in sight of Roca Partida, which was about 50 leagues from Veracruz,they were struck by a storm that lasted three days. The urca of Maestre Pedro de Mata was lost near Rio Alvarado and 60 persons aboard her were drowned. Another nao, *La Inglesa*, was lost nearby and only the people aboard her were saved. The remaining six ships entered San Juan de Ulúa on May 23.

Year 1565. An unidentified nao coming from Cabo Verde (probably with a cargo of African slaves) wrecked on the coast of Coatzacoalcos during a norther and her captain, Juan Gallego, and some of the crew were saved. Some of the general merchandise she carried was later salvaged.

Year 1566. The nao *El Santo Crucifijo de Burgos*, 400 tons, Captain Sebastian de Porras, one of the merchant ships in the Flota de Nueva España of Captain-General Juan Velasco de Barrio, was wrecked on the coast of Coatzacoalcos while enroute to Veracruz.

Year 1566. After the aforementioned Flota had anchored and was in the process of discharging its cargo in the port of San Juan de Ulza, a norther struck the port on October 4 and caused a great deal of damage to the ships, sinking an unidentified ship of Captain Armijo.

Year 1567. The Flota de Nueva España, commanded by Captain- General Cristóbal de Eraso and numbering over 20 merchant naos, sailed from Sanlúcar on July 7 and entered the port of San Juan de Ulza during the first week of October. On the night of October 16 a strong norther struck the port and three of his naos were sunk but the people and most of their cargoes were saved.

Year 1568. The Flota de Nueva España, commanded by Captain- General Francísco de Luxan and Admiral Juan de Ubillo, sailed from Sanlúcar near the end of July and reached San Juan de Ulza on September 21, where they found eight ships under the command of the English sea dog John Hawkins already anchored in port. Most sources vary as to the number of ships Hawkins had (five to eight). Although a truce was effected by the opposing forces, a battle broke out and the Almiranta of the Flota, the *Santa Clara*, 500 tons, Captain Alonso Arfran, was blown up and sank carrying 184 quintales (100 pounds) of mercury. During the battle five or six of the English ships were also burned or sunk (Spanish sources say six; English sources say five). The names of five are known: *Jesús, Swallow, Grace of God, William & John* and *Angel*. Although Hawkins's flagship the *Jesús* was lost, he escaped aboard the *Minion*; another ship, the *Judith*, under command of Francis Drake, also escaped and reached England.

Author and other members of his team with thousands of objects recovered from from the Spanish merchantman *Matanceros* off the coast of Yucatan.

Year 1571. Four merchant naos of the Flota de Nueva España, commanded by Captain-General Cristóbal de Eraso, sailing from Sanlúcar to Veracruz, were wrecked on the coast of Tabasco in October or November. The ships were: the urca *San Juan*, 300 tons, Captain Luis Guttiirez; nao *La María*, 550 tons, Captain Alonso Rodríguez de Norruega; nao *Santa Catalina*, 400 tons, Captain Andres de Paz; and the nao *La Magdalena*, 886 tons (a very large ship for this period), Captain Gonzalo Monte. Extensive salvage operations were carried out on all these wrecks and most of the mercury, wine and other types of merchandise were recovered.

Year 1574. The Flota de Nueva España, commanded by Captain-General Antonio Manríquez, sailed from Spain with 27 ships on June 29 and, after reaching the Gulf of Mexico, was struck by a storm that scattered the ships widely. The nao *Sanct'Ana*, 300 tons, Captain Pedro de Paredes, and two unidentified naos owned by Antonio Sanch de Armas and a man identified only by the surname of Carrejas, were sunk. An unidentified urca was also wrecked on the coast of Coatzacoalcos and five men were drowned but all of its cargo was saved.

Year 1582. The Flota de Nueva España, commanded by Captain-General Alonso de Quiñones and consisting of 39 ships, sailed from Sanlúcar on June 20 and reached Veracruz on September 18 or 19. The Almiranta *Nuestra Señora de la Rosa*, 650 tons, Captain Alonso Conquero, and an unidentified small nao were sunk inside the port. The Almiranta was carrying 450 quintales of mercury, all of which was recovered.

Year 1584. The Flota de Nueva España, commanded by Captain-General Diego de Alcega and consisting of 47 ships, sailed from Sanlúcar on July 11. On September 10 four naos of this flota wrecked on Las Cabezas, which is located 10 leagues from Veracruz. One of these naos was carrying mercury, but there is no mention if the mercury, or any of the cargoes of the other ships, was salvaged.

Year 1585. After the New Spain Treasure Fleet arrived in Veracruz this year and their cargoes were unloaded, nine of the ships were wrecked in a storm.

Year 1586. The Flota de Nueva España, commanded by Captain-General Francisco de Nova Feijo and consisting of 55 ships, sailed from Sanlúcar on July 18. While passing in sight of Cabo Catoche, two naos were wrecked: *Santa María de Begonia*, 140 tons, Captain Cristóbal Sanch Melgareza, and the *Santiago El Mayor*, 200 tons, Captain Vasco Martin. The nao *La Trinidad*, 125 tons, Captain Gaspar de Cubas, was also lost on the coast of Tabasco.

Year 1588. The Flota de Nueva España, commanded by Captain- General Martín P de Olozabal and consisting of 52 ships, sailed from Sanlúcar on July 5 and had an uneventful voyage until reaching the Gulf of Mexico, where on September 23 it was struck by a storm that separated many of the ships from the main convoy. Although the storm lasted for several days, none of the ships were lost. All were then reunited with the main convoy and entered Veracruz in September. The Almiranta *Ascension*, 500 tons, Captain Juan de Lambarri (the last ship in the convoy to enter the port) was struck by a freak wind and sank on a reef at the port entrance. Most of her mercury was quickly salvaged.

Year 1590. The Flota de Nueva España, commanded by Captain- General Antonio Navarro de Prado and consisting of 63 ships, sailed from Sanlúcar on August 1. Early in November the flota was struck by a fierce norther while in the Gulf of Mexico and 16 ships were lost along the Mexican coast. The surviving ships entered Veracruz on November 8. Only four of the lost ships were identified: nao *La Trinidad*, 280 tons, Captain Bernardo de Paz, lost trying to enter Veracruz during the storm; a Portuguese nao, *La Piedad*, 180 tons, Captain Cristóbal Sanchéz Melgarejo, lost on the bar of Veracruz with only 18 persons saved but most of its cargo; nao *N.S. del Socorro*, 220 tons, Captain Pedro Díaz Franco, lost in the Canal Gallega in Veracruz; and the Portuguese nao *N.S. de la Concepción*, 130 tons, Captain Miguél Rodríguez, which was lost near Veracruz. More than a thousand men and over two million pesos in cargo were lost on the 16 ships.

Year 1597. The Flota de Nueva España, commanded by Captain-General Pedro Menindez Márquez and consisting of 68 ships, sailed from Cadíz on June 22 and entered San Juan de Ulúa on August 30. Two ships were wrecked at the entrance of this port: nao *San Buenaventura*, 700 tons, Captain Pedro de Venaotoqui, and nao *Lu Pandora*, 600 tons, Captain Julio L de Cubeleus. The accident occurred when the fluke of an anchor on the bow of *La Pandora* caught the rigging of the *San Buenaventura*, which was sailing too close to it, causing them to collide and sink.

Year 1597. A hurricane struck the port of San Juan de Ulúa on September 22 and two ships were sunk: nao *San Buenaventura*, 250 tons, Captain Pedro de Bestiqui, and nao *La María*, 140 tons, Captain Manuel de Gaya. (Note the similarity between the námes of the two captains of two ships named "San Buenaventura" of the same flota)

Year 1600. The Flota de Nueva España, commanded by Captain- General Pedro D'Escobar Melgarejo, sailed from Cadíz on May 15 with 60 ships in the convoy. A hurricane struck the flota on September 12, when it was about 20 leagues from the coast of Villa Rica, and six ships were lost. Three of them sank soon after the storm began: nao *San Antonio de Padua*, 300 tons, Captain Juan de Morales; nao *Santa Catalina de Siena*, 280 tons, Captain Andrés Ximinez, and an unidentified nao, 700 tons, Captain Mathea Letieta, which was carrying a great deal of mercury.

Two other ships, unidentified, disappeared and were presumed to have sunk. One was 350 tons and its captain was Rafael Ferrifino. During the same storm a small patache of 50 tons, Captain Ganucho, was also wrecked on the coast of Tabasco and 60 men were drowned. After the hurricane abated, the ships that survived rejoined the main convoy and continued on to Veracruz, which they sighted on September 26, but when a norther began blowing, the ships were forced to anchor offshore for the night.

Some of them anchored in the lee of Isla de Sacrificios and many were forced to cast their cannon, anchors and part of their cargoes overboard to prevent them from capsizing. The nao of Captain Juan Minquez cast 500 ceramic jugs of wine and 160 jugs of olive oil overboard off this island.

Before the norther died out, eight more ships were lost: frigate *La Caridad*, 300 tons, Captain Francisco Morales, owned by Augustino de Paz, was wrecked near Isla Verde and 30 men were drowned; nao *Santa María del Juncal*, 100 tons, captain's identity unknown, was wrecked near Isla de Gavias and later divers recovered part of her cargo; nao *San Pedro*, 300 tons, Captain Diego de Bodes, was wrecked on the coast near the Medellin River and some of her cargo washed ashore; nao *La Catalina*, 100 tons, Captain Duarte de Quiros, was wrecked on the coast about five leagues from Coatzacoalcos and only her men and 40 or 50 new muskets were recovered; a Scottish-built felibote, *N.S. del Rosario*, 170 tons, Captain Hernan García, was wrecked on the coast at Las Aguas Locas and many pipes of wine from her were washed ashore and recovered; English-built frigate *San Benito*, 135 tons, Captain Lazaro de Arpide, struck the coast near the Alvarado River and some pipes of wine were salvaged. French-built ship *Santa Buenaventura*, 125 tons, Captain Juan Francísco Grimaldi, sank near the Tuscla River, off the Sierras de San Miguél, and 60 persons were drowned. Some pipes of wine from her washed ashore and were recovered; nao *La Esperanza*, 400 tons, Captain Tomas Gallardo, struck on the coast near Mimcapa and 13 men were drowned. All 110 boxes of mercury she carried were lost.

Some brief contemporary accounts state that all 14 ships were lost when trying to enter Veracruz, but other accounts written in greater detail tell what actually happened. The total loss of life was reported to be about one thousand persons, and the value of the ships and their lost or jettisoned cargoes was valued at more than 10 million pesos. French and English contemporary accounts date this occurrence as 1601, perhaps because news of it reached these two countries at a late date.

Year 1604. Shortly after the Flota de Nueva España, commanded by Captain-General Juan Gutiérrez de Garibay, reached Veracruz on September 5, the nao *Santa María de Begonia*, 700 tons, Captain Sanctor de Bengochea, carrying 239 quintales of mercury as well as a general cargo of merchandise, was lost inside the harbor.

Year 1605. The Armada de Barlovento, consisting of five ships commanded by Admiral Fajardo, surprised 17 Dutch ships near Manzanillo (engaged in trading contraband merchandise with unscrupulous Spanish colonists of Mexico) and gave battle. Two of the Dutch ships were sunk during the battle and the others escaped.

Year 1610. Soon after the Flota de Nueva España, commanded by Captain-General Pedro de Armendariz, reached Veracruz, on September 10 a hurricane struck and many frigates were lost on the coast near the port.

Year 1610. An unidentified ship, carrying over a million pesos in gold and silver and coming from Peru to Mexico, was wrecked by strong winds about a league from shore on the coast of Zacatula, 53 persons were drowned and 32 saved. Many pieces of the wreck, as well as some boxes, drifted ashore the same day. Divers recovered some of the treasure.

Year 1610. The galleon *N.S. de la Piedad*, Captain Martín Ruíz, 250 tons and 27 iron cannon, was sailing between Callao, Peru, and Acapulco with over a million pesos in gold and silver specie and bullion to be carried on next year's Manila Galleon sailing to the Philippines. When the ship was about a league off the port of Zacatula a sudden squall caused it to capsize and sink with all of the treasure. Fifty-three of the crew were lost, and since the ship went down in deep water none of the treasure was salvaged.

Year 1611. Shortly before the New Spain Treasure Fleet was ready to sail for Havana and Spain in March, four large galleons were wrecked in Veracruz: the *San Lorenzo*, Captain Diego García of 280 tons; the *La Concepción*, Captain Bernardo de Paz of 450 tons; the *N.S. de la Antigua*, Captain Antonio de Lobrano of 450 tons; and the *N.S. del Rosario y Santo Tomas*, Captain Juan de Medína of 550 tons. No mention if any of their treasures were ever recovered.

Year 1611. After the Flota de Nueva España, commanded by Captain-General Antonio de Oquendo, was anchored in San Juan de Ulúa and all of the cargoes had been taken ashore, on December 4 the Almiranta *San Pablo*, 600 tons, commanded by an unidentified admiral, sank during a storm.

Year 1614. A special armada of 21 warships of various sizes, was dispatched to the Indies under the command of Admiral Juan Bermúdez de Castro to search for pirates and contraband traders. Several ships were lost on the coast of Campeche.

Year 1614. The Flota de Nueva España, commanded by Captain-General Juan de la Cueva y Mendoza and consisting of 41 ships, sailed from Cadíz on July 7. Seven unidentified merchant naos of this flota, which carried over a million and a half pesos in merchandise and 876 quintales of mercury, were wrecked during the night on the coast of Yucatan between Cabo Catoche and Isla Mujeres. Salvage boats were sent from Havana, but very little was recovered, because the ships broke up quickly and their cargoes were buried deep under sand.

Year 1615. The Flota de Nueva España, commanded by Captain-General Martín de Vallecilla and consisting of 41 ships, sailed from Cadíz on July 6. On August 30, when the flota was 20 leagues from Islas Tranquilo and Arena in 22 fathoms of water, it was struck by a storm from the southeast and the nao *San Miguél*, 500 tons, Captain Gaspar Conquero, with a cargo of 700 pipes of wine, 3,000 ceramic jugs of wine, 150 boxes of mercury and 75 bales of general merchandise, split in two and quickly sank. Nothing was saved, not even the crew or passengers.

On September 4 the flota reached Veracruz and the nao *Espíritu Santo*, 100 tons, Captain Juan Ortuño de Olano, ran aground. Attempts to pull her off the shoals were successful, but then she sank in deeper water. While she was sinking, over a thousand men were put aboard her and, working quickly, threw most of the cargo into boats alongside.

Year 1616. The Flota de Nueva España, commanded by Captain-General Juan de la Cueva y Mendoza and consisting of 39 ships, sailed from Cadíz on July 7. It was struck by a storm while only six leagues from the entrance of the port of Veracruz and the nao *N.S. de la Candelaria*, 200 tons, Captain Antonio de Obregón, sank; crew and part of cargo saved.

Year 1617. The Flota de Nueva España, commanded by Captain-General Juan de Salas y Valdes and consisting of 31 ships, sailed from Cadíz on July 16 and reached Veracruz on September 17. While entering port the nao of Captain Domingo de la Guardia sank, but was totally salvaged.

Year 1618. The Flota de Nueva España, commanded by Captain-General Carlos de Ibarra and consisting of 23 ships, sailed from Cadíz on July 6 and reached Veracruz on September 16. While in the Gulf of Mexico the flota was struck by a storm and one unidentified nao sank but her cargo was saved.

Year 1621. As the Flota de Nueva España, commanded by Captain Juan de Benavídes y Bazan, was leaving the port of Veracruz, the nao *N.S. del Rosario*, 370 tons, caught fire and sank but her silver was saved and transferred to the Capitana and Almiranta.

Year 1623. The navío, *N.S. de la Piedad*, Captain Pascual Farina (probably Portuguese), coming from Angola with a cargo of 282 African slaves, was wrecked at Isla Mujeres. Two frigates were sent from Veracruz for the survivors, the crew and 170 of the slaves.

Year 1623. A Captain Sancho de Urdanivia was sent with war materials from Spain to Punta de Araya, Venezuela, but on his return to Spain his ship was wrecked on Cozumel Island.

Year 1623. Navío *La Candelaria*, 250 tons, Captain Juan de Paternina, sailing from Santo Domingo to Spain, was wrecked on Cozumel Island.

Year 1623. The Armada de Tierra Firme, commanded by Captain-General Antonio de Oquendo, was forced to spend the winter in Havana when many of its ships were damaged in a storm while sailing up the Bahama Channel. Because of a shortage of victuals in Havana, a patache was sent to Mexico for supplies, but was lost at Cabo de Contón. Its men and artillery were saved.

Possibly before 1628. On December 3, 1628, the governor of Cuba wrote to the King from Havana, "Because of bad weather they have not been able to search for the Almiranta [which was lost at Matacumbe Cay in the Florida Keys], but at my own expense I sent a frigate, two longboats and two canoes to salvage a galleon that I received notice had been lost in the Bahía de la Ascensión and los Bajos de San Martín on the coast of Mexico." This was probably one of the Honduras galleons, which disappeared in 1627.

Year 1628. As the Flota de Nueva España, commanded by Captain-General Juan de Benavídes y Bazan, was leaving Veracruz for Havana and Spain near the end of July, the frigate *Larga* was wrecked at the entrance of the port. The flota returned while the cargo of this ship was salvaged, then set sail again on August 8.

Year 1628. The Flota de Nueva España, commanded by Captain-General Hierónimo Gómez de Sandoval and consisting of 21 ships, sailed from Cadíz on July 15 and reached Veracruz on September 15. In October an advice boat was sent from Veracruz to carry the news of the flota's safe arrival back to Spain but sank on the coast of Campeche, crew and mail saved.

Year 1628. A hurricane struck the coast of Yucatan on September 8 and many ships and frigates were sunk. This was the same day that the Dutch privateer Peit Heyn with a fleet of warships belonging to the Dutch West Indian Company captured the entire Flota de Nueva España, commanded by Captain-General Juan de Benavídes y Bazan, in Matanzas, Cuba.

Year 1628 or 1629. A registered nao, sailing alone from the Canaries to Veracruz, was wrecked on the coast near Coatzacoalcos, between Veracruz and Campeche. All of her cargo was salvaged and, when brought to Veracruz, the royal officials discovered that over half of her cargo was contraband. Shortly afterward, another nao from the Canaries arrived in Veracruz, and when the officials learned that she too was carrying a great deal of contraband, they tried to seize the ship. However, the ship escaped and later wrecked on the coast of Campeche. Slaves, pepper, wine and clothes were salvaged from the wreck.

Year 1629. The governor of Yucatan wrote the King stating that during the month of April they had suffered a great deal of terrible weather and many coastal frigates were lost. A great number of items washed ashore from the wrecks, most of which was contraband. One Indian found three small bars of gold worth over 5,000 pesos.

Year 1631. The Flota de Nueva España, commanded by Admiral Manuel Serrano and consisting of 19 ships, sailed from Veracruz for Havana and Spain on October 14. The flota was carrying 3,644,198 pesos in silver and gold, 5,408 arrobas (25 pounds each) of cochineal, 3,879 arrobas of an inferior grade of cochineal, 15,413 arrobas of indigo, 10,018 pounds of silk from China, 71,788 hides, 6,858 quintales of brazilwood, 7,972 quintales of palo de Campeche (wood), 119 boxes of chocolate and 91 quintales of molasses.

All of the treasure was carried aboard the Capitaña, Almiranta, and the naos of the captains Baltasar de Espinosa, Baltasar de Amesqueta, and Francisco Niculas. About a week out of port the flota was struck by a hurricane and all ships were lost.

The Capitaña, *N.S. del Juncal,* sank eight leagues north of the Bajo de las Arcas and only 35 of the 335 people on board were saved by escaping in a small boat. The location of the wreck was never rediscovered and nothing was ever salvaged. The nao *San Antonio,* Captain Antonio Lajust, was wrecked one league to windward of the port of Tabasco but most of the cochineal aboard was salvaged. The nao of Captain Baltasar de Espinosa (some documents give his name as España) was wrecked very close to the port of Tabasco and 164,954 pesos in specie, 23 silver bars, 50 marcos in silver objects and nine marcos in golden objects were recovered from her by divers. Two other merchant naos were wrecked on the coast of Campeche but nothing was salvaged. The identities and fate of the other ships of this flota were never discovered.

Year 1635. The *San Juan el Feo,* a nao of the Flota de Nueva España, commanded by Captain-General Martin de Vallecilla, was burned and totally lost in the port of Veracruz.

Year 1647. A galleon identified only by the name "*Santiago*" sank in the "Sonda de Campeche," either near the Bahía de la Ascensión or Bahía del Espíritu Santo. Its people, 276 souls, reached a small island and then made boats and rafts from the wrecked galleon and reached the mainland. Salvage vessels were sent out but the wreck site was never located.

Year 1647. The Flota de Nueva España, commanded by Captain-General Pablo de Paradas and consisting of only 13 ships, sailed from Cadíz on July 13 and reached Veracruz on September 10. During the winter two ships of this flota, a merchant nao and a patache, and a merchant nao that had arrived from Venezuela were sunk in port because of a norther.

Year 1649. A French pirate ship was sunk on the coast of Tabasco and 26 pirates were captured and sent back to Spain in the Flota de Nueva España, commanded by Captain-General Juan de Pujadas.

Year 1650. Unidentified ship carrying Fray Antonio Jesús María left Havana on July 6 and was wrecked on Alacrán Reef on July 15 due to an error by the navigator. Survivors, eight persons drowned, lived on the keys for 55 days until they made a raft from pieces of the wreck and headed toward the mainland, but in passing a nearby key they found survivors from another ship that had wrecked there three years earlier.

Year 1651. Unidentified merchant nao was lost on the "playa de Jalkun" on the coast of Yucatan.

Year 1657. Unidentified nao of an inward-bound Flota de Nueva España was lost on the coast of Campeche, only the men were saved.

Year 1659. Sometime before June four merchant naos of the Armada de Tierra Firme, under the command of the Marquis de Villarubia en route from Cartagena to Havana, were lost on the coast of Yucatan. Only one was identified, the *Santiago,* which had wrecked on the east side of Cozumel during a bad storm. Three hundred survivors were rescued two months later weak from thirst, hunger and exposure. The other three naos were mentioned only as being wrecked "on the coast of Yucatan" during the same storm.

Year 1668. Manila Galleon *Santa María de los Valles*, Admiral Nicolas Curi de Leyba, 1,500 tons, and 68 bronze and 22 iron cannon, with 778 persons and over three million pesos in treasure aboard, was anchored off Acapulco awaiting the arrival of the customs and other royal officials, when just two days before Christmas a fire broke out and she quickly sank in 60 fathoms, taking 330 persons and all of her treasure to the bottom.

Year 1672. Brief mention in an English document that earlier in the year four Spanish ships were wrecked on the coast of Campeche during a hurricane.

Year 1675. Two unidentified New England ketches that were en route to Trist ran aground on the backside of Alacrán Reef and were lost.

Year 1675 or 1676. Brief mention that a great quantity of silver pieces of eight were discovered from an unidentified shipwreck located in several fathoms of water on the coast of Tampico.

Year 1683. Navío *El Santo Cristóbal, San Agustín y La Magdalena*, Captain Ignacio Antonio de Zarantes, owned by Santiago de la Hava Llaquano, built in Holland, 70 tons, en route from Spain to Tabasco, stopped in Veracruz to be careened, as she was leaking badly. While being careened she caught fire and was totally lost.

Sometime before 1689. Brief mention that some years earlier the navío *Santiago* was lost on the coast of Yucatan and that the location of the wreck was about midway between Chinchorro Reef and Bahía del Espíritu Santo, in 18 degrees of latitude. A Captain Arreynaza was reported to have located the wreck a few years after it was lost, but there was no mention if he carried out any salvage operations on the wreck.

Year 1700. Unidentified British ship was wrecked on Alacrán Reef; Richard Falconer was either its captain or was a passenger aboard.

Year 1702. While the Flota de Nueva España, commanded by Captain-General Fernando Chacón was preparing for its departure for Spain, the Almiranta of this flota, *Santa María de Teasanos*, Captain Martín Gonzalez de Vergara, sank at San Juan de Ulza on January 14.

Year 1706. The main patache of the Flota de Nueva España, the navío *N.S. de Europa y San Jos y San Francisco de Padua*, captain and owner Don Manuel Alphonso de Nariega, built in England, 193 tons, sank within sight of Veracruz as the flota was entering port.

Year 1706. An advice boat, navío *N.S. de la Concepción y San Joséph y Las Animas*, Captain Francisco Barcaeztequi, built in England, 68 tons, enroute from Spain to Veracruz, was chased by an English privateer and ran aground at Conil on the coast of Yucatan. The captain and all his men got ashore, along with the mail they were carrying. The English salvaged the entire cargo, rigging, sails and ship's fittings before setting it on fire.

Year 1715. While the Flota de Nueva España, commanded by Captain-General Juan Estevan de Ubilla, was in Veracruz, along with many merchantmen and warships, a norther struck on the night of March 28, causing a great deal of damage both to shipping and the town. Twelve ships were lost, of which four belonged to Ubilla's flota. The ships lost were the following: *Gobierno*, Captain Miguél de Lima; a nao belonging to Pedro de Córdova; a nao belonging to Francisco de Chaves; a newly built frigate from Campeche, Captain Ledesma; nao *Santiago*, Captain Aguirre; small patache owned by the King; small merchant schooner, Captain Alvarado; privateer vessel *El Talla Piedra*; frigate owned by Captain

Barriga; brigantine owned by the King; merchant nao owned by a Greek merchant from Havana; and the frigate *Miseria de Maracaibo.*

Year 1719. A squadron of three large galleons carrying mercury to Veracruz from Spain, commanded by Admiral Francisco de Cornejo, identified as the Capitaña, Almiranta, and *Santo Cristo de Maracaibo,* were totally lost on the coast of Campeche.

Year 1725. The Capitaña of the Flota de Nueva España, commanded by Admiral Antonio Serrano, caught fire and was totally lost in Campeche Sound, in the Gulf of Mexico, and over four hundred lives were lost.

Year 1726. The navío *N.S. de la Concepción* was burned in the Gulf of Campeche on April 9.

Year 1732. A small squadron carrying mercury to Veracruz, under the command of Jefe de Escuadra Gabriel Pérez de Alderete, sailed from Cadíz on August 18, 1731, but had a very difficult voyage and did not reach Veracruz until early in January 1732. The large galleon *N.S. de la Concepción,* Captain Quiroga, sank soon after the squadron entered Veracruz and 500 lives were lost.

Year 1733. The warship *N.S. de la Concepción,* one of two ships sent to escort the Flota de Nueva España back to Spain and commanded by Captain-General Rodrigo de Torres, was lost in Veracruz sometime during spring before the flota departed. This flota was later lost during a hurricane in the Florida Keys.

Year 1735. The Flota de Nueva España, commanded by Lt. General Manuel Lopez Pintado, entered Veracruz on February 24 and a navío, Santa Rosa, owned by the King and carrying mercury, was lost trying to enter with the flota during a norther. The crew was saved but not the mercury or any other cargo.

Year 1737. The navío *N.S. de Belem y San Antonio y San Francisco de Asis* was lost in Veracruz between the "Bajo de los Cochinos y el Baluarte del Bonete."

Year 1737. An unidentified nao or frigate sank nine leagues south of the Alvarado River, near Veracruz.

Year 1738. Brief mention of the navíos *Incendio* and *Lanfranco* being lost in Veracruz.

Year 1741. News reached England early in 1742 that the large galleon *Europa,* commanded by Admiral Spinola, was lost in the Gulf of Mexico when sailing from Havana to Veracruz.

Year 1741. The merchant nao *N.S. de los Milagros* (alias *El Matanzero*), 270 tons, built in Matanzas, Cuba, Captain Cristóbal de Montano, owned by the Marquis de Casa Madrid, was wrecked "on the coast of Campeche," near Acúmal, Quintana Roo, on February 22. The ship was partially salvaged soon after the disaster and again salvaged in recent years by myself and CEDAM. More information about the history of this wreck and our recent salvage work can be obtained from my book, *Always Another Adventure,* World Publishing Company, 1967.

Year 1743. In January the British warship *H.M.S. Oxford,* 70 guns, Captain Perry Mayne, was wrecked in the Gulf of Mexico.

Year 1749. A navío that left Cadíz on October 16, 1748, sailing suelto to Veracruz, the *San Antoñio de Podera y N.S. del Rosario* (alias *La Bella Sara*), captain and owner Don Joseph Beatura de Rapaldizan, sank in Veracruz soon after it arrived in January 1749.

Year 1751. Navío *San Geronimo* (alias *El Retiro*), Captain Manuel Delfín, owned by Alberto Nicholas Diaz Faxardo and Manuel Silvestre de Ziancaro, sailed from Cadíz on August 6 carrying 10,000 quintales of mercury and other cargo. It struck on a reef 12 leagues to the south of Cabo Catoche, between Isla Contoy and Isla Mujeres.

Year 1752. Five ships of the Flota de Nueva España, commanded by Captain-General Cristóbal de Eraso, sank on the coast of Tabasco.

Year 1755. Navío *San Raymundo Thae*, Captain Juan Franco de Vilnava, sailed from Cadíz on August 8 and was lost on the coast of Campeche. All of the crew was saved and most of the cargo (of general merchandise) was salvaged.

Year 1758. Brief mention that a merchant nao, *El Retiro*, was lost on the coast of Campeche.

Year 1760. Merchant nao, *La Fetis*, Captain José Antonio Rivero, sank on its return voyage to Spain after leaving Cartagena, on the east side of Cozumel Island.

Year 1761. British merchant ship *Tates*, sailing from Cartagena to England, was lost in March on Cozumel Island, but its people and money were saved and boats were sent from Campeche to recover her cargo.

Year 1763. A Spanish frigate, *Mercurio*, which sailed from Cadíz in August with a convoy carrying mercury to Veracruz, was lost near Cabo Catoche.

Year 1765. The merchant nao *N.S. de la Luz y San Maura*, Captain Lorenzo de Villas, sailed from Cadíz on March 9 and five days after entering Veracruz caught fire and sank losing most of her cargo.

Year 1772. A navío of many guns, *Castilla*, captain the Marquis de Casina, was lost during a violent norther in Veracruz on "el bajo de los Hornos." All those aboard were saved, but the cargo, 700 large chests of fine cochineal, was lost.

Year 1772. Spanish frigate *N.S. de Guadalupe* (alias *La Tetis*), Captain Juan Gil del Barrios, sailed from Cadíz for Honduras on April 15. She then sailed from Omoa, Honduras, for Spain with a cargo of silver and land products. On December 5 it wrecked on Chinchorro Reef. Of the 29 chests of silver aboard her, all but three were salvaged. In Lloyd's List it mentions that the ship was carrying 1,580 serons of indigo, which was totally lost.

Year 1780. Frigate *Santa Maria* (or *Santa Marta*), 38 cannon, Captain Andres Valderrama, part of the squadron commanded by Don Juan Bautista Bonet, was lost near the coast of Yucatan on "Bajo de las Mesas de Contreras," which is two miles from land, and sank in three fathoms of water on a sandy bottom. Her entire cargo consisted of war materials.

Year 1781. A large ship named *Santa Ana*, coming from Callao, Peru, to Mexico was lost on a shoal in Acapulco Harbor. This same shoal, which is only 40 meters wide, was named Santa Ana after the ship.

Year 1783. A large Spanish warship, *Dragon*, 60 cannon, captain the brigadier Miguél de Sousa, was lost on "Bajo Nuevo," in the Gulf of Campeche, and 60 of the crew were drowned.

Year 1786. Spanish ship *San Rafael* was lost in the Gulf of Mexico.

Year 1794. Spanish ship *N.S. del Carmen* (alias *Las Animas*) was lost on Cayo Culebra, one of the Cayos de la Cadena, located five leagues from the port of Az... (rest of word faded on the document) on the coast of Yucatan.

Year 1797. Spanish advice boat *San Carlos*, sent from San Blas by the Marquis de Banceforte and commanded by Teniente de Fragata Ramón de Saavedra, sailed to San Francisco, California, with news of war with Great Britain. On March 23 it sank near the port of Yerba Buena and only its people were saved.

Year 1799. On September 28 the British warship *H.M.S. Fox*, 32 guns, commanded by Lt. William Wooldridge, was wrecked in the Gulf of Mexico but the crew was saved.

Year 1801. British warship *H.M.S. Meleager*, 32 guns, Captain Honorable T. Bladen Capel, 215 men on board, was lost on June 9 on the westernmost triangle key in the Gulf of Mexico but all its men were saved.

Year 1803. Spanish merchant ship *Maria*, Captain Uxaboxa, sailing from Bilbao to Veracruz, was lost in the Gulf of Mexico.

Year 1803. Spanish merchant ship *N.S. del Carmen* (alias *La Princesa*), Captain Remachn, sailing from Cadíz to Veracruz with a valuable cargo, was totally lost in the Gulf of Mexico.

Year 1804. British merchantman *Catherine*, Captain Hayward, sailing from New Orleans to Liverpool, was lost in the Gulf of Mexico.

Year 1805. Spanish frigate *N.S. de la O* [slc], 64 guns, Captain Miguél de Palacios, was lost in Veracruz during a norther but was completely salvaged.

Year 1808. Spanish frigate *Muros* was lost in the Gulf of Mexico but all her crew was saved.

Year 1808. Spanish schooner *Felicidad*, Captain José del Castillo, was struck by lightning and blew up while anchored in Veracruz.

Year 1809. Spanish brigantine *Volador*, 18 cannon, commanded by Teniente de Navío Pedro María de Piedrola, was lost on August 17 in the port of Veracruz "sobre la zapata del Castillo de San Juan," and everyone aboard, 143,000 pesos in specie, and most of the ship's equipment were saved.

Year 1811. American ship *Sally*, Captain Perkins, coming from New York, was lost in January near Campeche.

Year 1816. British ship *Rhine*, Captain Gordon, sailing from New Orleans to Campeche, was lost off the coast of Campeche.

Year 1816. Spanish schooner *Cantabria*, commanded by Teniente de Fragata Antonio Valera, was lost on the Alvarado River on June 9 and eight men were drowned.

Year 1816. British sloop-of-war *H.M.S.Tay*, 20 guns, Captain Samuel Roberts, was sailing from Campeche to Jamaica with about two million pesos in treasure when it was lost on Alacrán Reef on November 11. None of the 135 men in her crew were lost. This wreck was located by CEDAM and partially salvaged.

Year 1816. British sloop-of-war, *H.M.S. Bermuda*, 10 guns, Captain John Pakenham, was wrecked on November 25 near the bar of Tampico and, of 76 men in her crew, only one was lost.

Year 1818. Spanish frigate *Ifigen*, 38 cannon, commanded by Capitan de Fragata Alejo Gutiirrez de Ribalcava, sank in the harbor of Campeche.

Year 1819. British ship *Frances Ann*, Captain Mossup, coming from St. Thomas, Virgin Islands, to Campeche, was lost on October 28 off Cabo Catoche.

Year 1819. Spanish brigantine *Consulado*, 14 cannon, commanded by Teniente de Navío Cipriano Mauleon, and the schooner *Guma* were sunk during a storm at Veracruz on December 30, over 120 men were lost.

Year 1822. British merchantman *Holiday*, Captain Stewart, sailing from Liverpool to Campeche, was wrecked on May 6 on the Alacrán Reef but the crew was saved.

Year 1822. American merchantman *Dido*, Captain Dario, coming from Philadelphia, was lost near Alvarado on December 21.

Year 1822. American merchantman *Catherine Jane*, Captain Storer, sailing from New York to Veracruz, was lost eastward of Veracruz.

Year 1823. British merchantman *Nancy*, Captain Butterfield, sailing from Cuba to Montego Bay, Jamaica, was leaking badly and intentionally wrecked on Cabo Catoche to prevent it from sinking; but most of its cargo was saved.

Year 1824. American ship *Harriet*, Captain Davidson, sailing from New Orleans to Tampico with a valuable cargo aboard, was lost between Soto la Marina and Tampico.

Year 1824. French ship *Cacique*, Captain Roy, sailing from Bordeaux to Veracruz, was totally lost in the Gulf of Mexico on May 9, but her crew was saved and arrived at the port of Sisal, Yucatan.

Year 1824. A ship of unknown nationality, *Sancho Panza*, Captain Harris, sailing from New York to Tampico, was lost on Alacráan Reef; crew and passengers saved.

Year 1824. American ship *Alabama*, Captain Kirk, sailing from Philadelphia to Alvarado ran aground after crossing the bar at the entrance to this port, but all of her cargo was recovered.

Chapter Five

Lesser Antilles

Year-around working conditions in the Lesser Antilles are better than those of the other, larger islands of the Caribbean, which are subject to more hurricanes and storms. Because of the prevailing northeasterly winds, however, the windward, or eastern, side of the Lesser Antilles is continually battered by large ocean swells rolling in off the Atlantic, which makes diving generally difficult and hazardous. Off the eastern side of Barbados, for example, the average size of the swells is over 20 feet. Furthermore, since there are very few safe harbors or anchorages on the eastern side of most of these islands, a large vessel is needed for serious work on shipwreck sites. There are occasional days, generally during the hurricane season, when diving conditions are more favorable. Strong ocean swells still roll in and caution must be exercised. With the exception of a few harbors, such as Trinidad's Port of Spain, and Bridgetown in Barbados, the underwater visibility is excellent around all of these islands.

The Dutch government prohibits shipwreck search and salvage around their islands, except by accredited archaeologists and the government takes 100 percent. The French government has a law requiring that an archaeologist must supervise any work undertaken on shipwrecks in their waters. The salvor keeps 40 percent of what he recovers and the French government has the right to purchase all or any part of the 40 percent belonging to the salvor at a price determined by the government.

The British government requires a potential salvor to obtain a permit from the Admiralty Office in London before working on a site, but no ruling has been passed yet as to what percentage of the recovery a salvor will receive. In a letter to me the Admiralty Office stated that although it has received numerous requests for permission to salvage various wrecks around the British West Indian Islands, it has not granted any permits, as the law governing the salvaging of

273

ancient shipwrecks is not too clear and will have to be modified and rewritten. Since some of the islands require permits, make certain to check before going ahead with plans.

Shipwrecks in Anguillan Waters

Year 1628. Two unidentified Spanish merchant naos sailed from Puerto Rico for Spain and one of them wrecked on December 12 on the north side of this island. Frenchmen from St. Kitts salvaged some of its cargo.

Year 1733. English merchantman *Castle Shallop*, owned by Sir William Stapleton, sailing from St. Kitts to England with a cargo of sugar, was wrecked on the south side and only the rigging was salvaged.

Year 1755. Two ships were lost on the north side: English merchantman *Brown Gally*, Captain Belson, sailing from Rhode Island to the Leeward Islands, and an unidentified large French merchantman sailing from Martinique to France.

Year 1763. English merchantman *Temple*, Captain Campbell, sailing from Liverpool to Jamaica, struck on a reef and quickly went to pieces but most of the crew were saved.

Year 1772. Two large Spanish warships, escorting 18 merchant naos of the Flota de Nueva España, were wrecked off the east end of the island: galleon *El Buen Consejo*, 70 guns, Captain Julio de Urcullo, and the galleon *Jesús, María y Joséph* (alias *El Prusiano*), 40 guns, Captain Juan Baptista de Echeverria. Most of their cargoes were salvaged by the English from surrounding islands.

Year 1773. English merchantman *William*, Captain Stoodley, sailing from London to the West Indies, was wrecked.

Year 1811. During a hurricane on October 8, several unidentified American merchantmen were wrecked on the north side of the island.

Shipwrecks in St. Martin's Waters

Year 1631. An unidentified Dutch merchantman was wrecked off the south side of this island when it was chased by several ships of the Windward Armada, commanded by Admiral Azevelo. While the Spanish admiral's ship was cruising to pick up survivors from the Dutch wreck, a sudden storm caused it to sink. There were only eight survivors from both wrecks.

Year 1780. Dutch merchantman *Wynhandelet*, Captain Froon, sailing from this island to Ireland, was totally lost while at anchor during a hurricane on the south side of the island.

Year 1781. A richly laden Portuguese merchantman, *Santissimo Trinidade*, Captain Dos Santos, sailing from Brazil to Amsterdam, was wrecked and only a small part of its valuable cargo was salvaged.

Year 1792. During a hurricane on August 1 two unidentified ships foundered in the oyster pond.

Year 1801. English warship *H.M.S. Proselyte*, 32 guns, Captain George Fowke (some accounts have a Henry Whitly as captain), wrecked on a reef on the south side of the island (which is now named Proselyte Reef). None of the crew of 215 were lost. In 1960 I spent several days exploring this wreck, which lies in depths of from 15 to 50 feet. I located six anchors, at least 20 cannon, and there were several hundred tons of pig iron ingots, which were used for ballast during the period this ship was lost. A great section of the wreck was covered over by thick coral growth but some parts were off the reef on a sandy bottom.

Year 1811. During a hurricane on October 7, several unidentified ships were wrecked.

Shipwrecks in St. Barthelemy's Waters

Year 1707. During a hurricane on August 29 a large unidentified ship was sunk in the harbor.

Year 1791. During a severe gale in September, three unidentified ships were wrecked on the island.

Year 1792. American merchantman *Nelly*, Captain Shelly, sailing from Antigua to America, was wrecked.

Year 1792. During a hurricane on August 1, ten unidentified ships were totally destroyed in the main harbor and there was a great loss of life.

Year 1811. French ship *Guernsey*, Captain Collinette, was totally lost in June and most of her crew perished.

Year 1811. During a hurricane on October 7 a total of 40 ships, most of them American vessels that had come into the harbor for shelter from the hurricane, were wrecked or sunk.

Year 1813. English warship *H.M.S. Subtle*, 10 guns, Captain Charles Brown, foundered near the island and the crew of 50 perished.

Year 1815. During a hurricane on September 18, 60 ships, most of them American vessels that had entered the harbor for shelter from the hurricane, were wrecked or sunk. A Swedish sloop-of-war was also lost here.

Year 1819. During a hurricane in September, half the town was totally destroyed and washed into the sea and all of the shipping was rendered a mass of ruins at the head of the bay.

Year 1821. During a hurricane on September 10, many unidentified sloops and schooners were totally lost in the port.

Shipwrecks in Saba's Waters

Year 1567. Spanish advice boat *La Regla*, four guns, Captain Julio Rodriquez Espinosa, was wrecked on the east side of the island while sailing from Spain to Puerto Rico with mail and passengers.

Year 1733. English slave ship *Bristol*, Captain Payne, sailing from Africa to Jamaica with a cargo of slaves, was wrecked on this island during a hurricane in June.

Shipwrecks in St. Eustatius' Waters

Year 1690. During an earthquake on April 6, more than half of the main town, which was located on the west side of the island, was cast into the sea and several hundred lives were lost. At this time the town was used mainly as a base for privateers and contraband traders of various nationalities, so that many of the buildings that fell into the sea were warehouses full of plunder and contraband, the overall value of which exceeded a million pounds sterling. The ruins of these sunken buildings are still visible and are located off the bluff of Orange Town, the island's only settlement. I visited this site in 1960 and with only fins and mask recovered a large number of bottles, intact pieces of ceramicware, clay smoking pipes, bricks and two muskets. For some years the College of William and Mary has been working on this site with meager results.

Year 1733. During a hurricane in June, two unidentified English merchantmen were wrecked.

Year 1737. During a hurricane in October a large fleet of homeward-bound English merchantmen sought shelter off Orange Town but twenty of them were sunk.

Year 1758. Italian merchantman *Duke Compagni*, Captain Lambaldi, sailing from this island for Amsterdam after loading a valuable cargo of merchandise for which it received many chests of silver specie, was wrecked as it attempted to round the north side but all of the crew and most of the specie were saved.

Year 1766. During a violent hurricane on September 21, several unidentified merchant ships were totally lost off Orange Town.

Year 1772. During a hurricane in August, all 400 houses in Orange Town were blown down and the Dutch church was thrown into the sea.

Year 1780. During a hurricane on October 9, seven Dutch ships were totally lost on the coast at North Point and not a soul survived. Orange Town was leveled to the ground and between 4,000 and 5,000 persons perished.

Year 1786. During a hurricane in August a large number of ships of different nationalities were lost around the island.

Year 1791. During a hurricane around the end of October, two large Dutch merchantmen were lost off Orange Town.

Year 1792. During a hurricane on August 1, one large Dutch ship and several of other nationalities were totally lost off the west side. A Spanish brig, sailing between St. Kitts and the island, sank and there were only two survivors.

Underwater archeologist carefully tags the timbers of a 17th-century Dutch shipwreck found off the island of St. Martin.

Shipwrecks in St. Kitts' Waters

Year 1629. During a Spanish attack led by Captain-General Fadrique de Toledo to dislodge the French and English who had recently settled on this island, four small ships were sunk by Spanish cannon fire in the port of Basseterre, off the west side of the island.

Year 1630. Unidentified merchant rulo of the New Spain Flota, Captain-General Miguel de Echazarreta, was wrecked on the east side of the island and among the many drowned was the new governor of Santiago, Cuba.

Year 1642. During a hurricane, 23 English ships of various oizoo woro wrecked at Basseterre, but there was little loss of life, as most of the crews were ashore.

Year 1650. During two different hurricanes a total of 28 merchantmen of different nationalities, a great number of lives, and over a half-million pounds sterling in cargoes were lost in and near Basseterre.

Year 1651. During a hurricane, nine English and 12 Dutch ships were wrecked in Basseterre.

Year 1652. During a hurricane, four or five fully loaded English merchantmen were totally lost off Sandy Point, on the west side of the island.

Year 1667. While an English squadron of warships was attempting to recapture the island from the French, it burned one French and one Dutch ship, both of which were anchored at Basseterre.

Year 1680. During a hurricane on August 3, two shallops were wrecked at Basseterre.

Year 1690. English merchantman *Thornhills Hill* was wrecked on June 1 against rocks off the west side of the island.

Year 1707. During a hurricane on August 30, two English warships were wrecked: *H.M.S. Child's Play*, 24 guns, Captain George Doyley, at Palmetto Point, and the *H.M.S. Winchester*, off Sandy Point. The cannon from both wrecks were salvaged.

Year 1733. During a hurricane in June, 12 ships were sunk at Basseterre, three of them identified as English ships: the *Nassau*, *Stapleton* and *Ancient Britain*. A ship that had just arrived at Sandy Point from Philadelphia suffered a total loss of lives and cargo.

Diver removes coral encrustation from a small breech-loading swivel gun recovered from a late-17th-century pirate ship near the island of St. Eustatius.

Year 1737. During an October hurricane an English merchantman, *Captain Sutton*, main cargo rum and sugar, was sunk at Basseterre and only one of the crew survived.

Year 1741. Irish merchantman *Rebecca & Martha*, Captain Copythorn, coming from Cork, was wrecked on the east side of the island.

Year 1747. During hurricanes on September 21 and October 24 a total of 24 ships were totally lost at Basseterre, most of them fully loaded with cargoes of sugar for England. All were English merchantmen: *Owen Gally*, Captain Wood; *Rising Sun*, Captain Parker; *Pretty Patsey*, Captain Hays; *Duke of Marlborough*, Captain Denn; *Cornwally*, Captain Swoard; *Rowlandson*, Captain Watson; *Emma*, Captain Faulker; *Mary*, Captain Watson; *Swallow,* Captain Watts; *Plante*, Captain Cains; *Parkham Pink*, Captain Aberdam; *Nisbitt*, Captain Hall; the others were not identified.

Year 1751. During a violent gale on July 24, several ships were wrecked at Basseterre, but only one was identified: the Irish merchantman *Friendship*, Captain Bodkin, sailing to Cork, none of the crew was saved.

Year 1754. During a hurricane on September 13, five unidentified ships were wrecked at Basseterre.

Year 1758. During a hurricane an English privateer vessel with 200 persons aboard sank at Sandy Point with a total loss of life.

Year 1765. During a hurricane in August, nine unidentified English merchantmen and one French mail boat were lost around the island.

Year 1766. During a gale on September 18 the English merchantman *Betsey*, Captain Mathews, ready to sail for England, was wrecked at Sandy Point and only some rigging was salvaged from it.

Year 1766. During a hurricane in October, 13 English merchantmen and two Dutch sloops were wrecked off the west side of the island and at Basseterre.

Year 1772. During a hurricane two ships were totally lost: the English merchantman *Apollo*, Captain Manning, and Scottish merchantman *Thistle*, Captain Hunter.

Year 1773. English merchantman *Charlotte*, Captain Williamson, arriving from London, was wrecked off the east side of the island.

Year 1775. During a hurricane in October a large number of unidentified ships were lost.

Year 1776. During a hurricane on September 6, two unidentified ships were wrecked and three others sank at Basseterre.

Year 1779. English storeship *H.M.S. Supply*, 20 guns, Captain John Lockhart Nasmyth, was accidentally burned at Basseterre.

Year 1780. During a hurricane on October 11 and 12, described as the worst in over a century, more than 100 ships of different nationalities and sizes were totally lost all around the island and the loss of lives was in the thousands.

Year 1781. American privateer *Earl of Cornwallis*, 18 guns and 100 men, sank at Basseterre and a large number of the crew perished.

Year 1782. During an attack by several French warships, the English merchantman *Douglas*, Captain Webster, recently arrived from London, was burned near Basseterre.

Year 1785. During an August 26 hurricane five English merchantmen were wrecked in Deep Bay, only three of them identified: *Thomas*, Captain Furber; *Spooner*, Captain Lorban; and the *Betsey*, Captain Basdon.

Year 1791. During a severe gale several ships were wrecked in and near Basseterre but only one was identified: the English merchantman *Yucatan*, Captain Barton, sailing from Cork to Jamaica.

Year 1792. Before August 1, three English merchantmen were lost on the island: *George & Margaret*, Captain Ashington, sailing to London; *Isabella*, Captain Carnage, sailing to Glasgow; and the *Britannia*, Captain Woodyear, sailing to London.

Year 1792. During a hurricane on August 1 and 2, more than 20 ships of different nationalities were lost around the island.

Year 1793. During a hurricane on August 12, 30 merchantmen (English and American) were lost, and only a few of the English ships were identified by name: *Hoppitt, Letitia, Flying Delight, Indian Castle, Polly* and *Nancy*.

Year 1807. During a gale on July 26, two schooners, two sloops, and the English merchantman *Maria*, Captain Williams, bound for London, were wrecked on the island.

Year 1811. Three English merchantmen were lost around the island: *Sussex*, only partially loaded; *Venus*, Captain Moore, sailing to Quebec; and the *Dart*, just arrived from England. All three crews were saved.

Year 1813. During a hurricane that occurred on July 23, 17 ships were wrecked: 10 were American ships seized as war prizes, three were American coastal schooners and four were English merchantmen: *John & William*, just arrived from France; *Britannia*, Captain Paulson, sailing to England; *Colonest*, Captain Oliver; and the *Bottle*, Captain Ford.

Shipwrecks in Nevis' Waters

Year 1629. During an attack by the Spanish, one unidentified small English merchantman was wrecked on the west side of the island.

Year 1667. During a battle between 30 French and 10 English warships on April 10 in Nevis Roads, one of the English ships was accidentally blown up by her own crew and most of the men aboard her perished.

Year 1669. During a hurricane on August 16 a large British privateer was totally lost off Charlestown, the island's main port and town.

Year 1690. An earthquake struck the whole island at 7 a.m. on April 6 and most of the town of Charlestown, including the main fort, was cast into the sea. Records concerning this disaster are very brief and vague, and there is no mention of the number of buildings lost, value of property lost, nor of the total loss of lives. During an exploratory dive on the site in 1961, I located at least 50 different brick buildings that were protruding above the sandy sea floor. No doubt many more are buried. Most of the site is in depths of 20 to 30 feet of water, but the walls of the main fort are near shore in only 8 to 10 feet of water, where I sighted over 20 huge iron cannon.

Year 1728. English merchantman *Campbell*, Captain Goodwin, coming from Bristol, was captured by a French pirate, but on September 10 she was wrecked in a gale at Nevis Point.

Year 1747. During a hurricane on September 21, eight vessels were wrecked around the island: five sloops, one schooner, a large prize snow and an English merchantman *Mary*, Captain Herbert, preparing to sail for London.

Year 1761. English merchantman *Princess Ann*, Captain Tampert, sailing from Barbados to Ireland, was wrecked at Green Point but her cargo of rum was saved.

Year 1772. During a hurricane a large unidentified English merchantman carrying 500 hogsheads of sugar was totally lost.

Year 1779. During a hurricane on September 4, several large French warships of the fleet of the Count d'Estaing, then anchored off Charlestown, were totally lost.

Year 1782. On January 25, the English warship *H.M.S. Solebay*, 28 guns, Captain Charles Holmes Everritt, while trying to elude three French ships that were chasing it, was wrecked at Nevis Point and burned by its crew before they escaped ashore.

Year 1790. During a hurricane in August, 20 unidentified English merchantmen were wrecked in the vicinity of Charlestown and Nevis Point.

Year 1792. During a hurricane on August 1 the English merchantman *Sarah & Ann*, sailing to London, was totally lost and nothing of her cargo was salvaged.

Year 1804. Two English ships wrecked on the island: merchantman *Friends*, Captain Donald, coming from London, and the warship *H.M.S. Drake*, 14 guns, Captain William Ferriss, on a reef near the island but none of the crew of 86 were lost.

Year 1808. English merchantman *Grace*, Captain Taylor, coming from London, was totally lost January 30 on a reef at the northeast end of the island, crew and part of cargo saved.

Year 1811. During a hurricane on October 7 a ship of unknown registry, *Rachael*, was totally lost.

Year 1819. During a hurricane on September 21 and 22, the Venezuelan cruiser *Brutus* was wrecked.

Year 1823. A mailboat of unknown registry, *Mackey*, was totally lost on January 16, only the mail was saved.

Shipwrecks in Montserrat's Waters

Year 1666. During a hurricane in September a large number of unidentified French warships were wrecked on the island.

Year 1681. During a hurricane on October 14 an unidentified merchantman coming from New England was wrecked.

Year 1744. Irish merchantman *Two Brothers*, Captain Brown, coming from Cork, was wrecked but her cargo was saved.

Year 1747. During a hurricane on September 21 a sloop, several shallops, and two English merchantmen were lost: *Imperial Anne*, Captain Buder, and *Friends Goodwill*, Captain Lesley. And during a hurricane that struck on October 24 the English ship *London Packet*, Captain Tirnam, was totally lost.

Year 1754. During a September 13 hurricane, eight unidentified English merchantmen were wrecked in Plymouth Harbor, island's main port and town.

Year 1766. During a hurricane in October a large number of homeward-bound English merchantmen were totally lost on the west side of the island.

Year 1775. English merchantman *Gill*, Captain Craig, sailing from St. Eustatius to St. Vincent Island, sank during a hurricane on July 31.

Year 1807. Two English merchantmen were wrecked during a gale on July 26: *Lady Parker*, bound for London, and *Eliza*, Captain Summers, bound for Bristol.

Shipwrecks in Barbudan Waters

Year 1695. Unidentified Spanish merchant nao, Captain Francisco Morales, carrying 13,000 pesos to pay the garrisons at Maracaibo, was wrecked off the east side of the island. All of the specie and a great deal of merchandise were recovered by divers.

Year 1749. English slave ship *Pearl*, Captain Dighton, coming from Africa with a cargo of slaves, was wrecked here and 70 slaves and 11 of the crew were drowned.

Year 1749. English merchantman *Nancy*, Captain Dlam, sailing from Bristol to Jamaica, wrecked November 2; only a small part of her cargo saved.

Year 1752. Scottish merchantman *Prince Charles*, Captain Walsh, sailing from Dublin to Jamaica, was wrecked on the south end of the island.

Year 1755. French slave ship *Hazard*, sailing from Africa to Hispaniola, was wrecked and more than 80 slaves were drowned.

Year 1760. English warship *H.M.S. Griffin*, 20 guns, Captain Thomas Taylor, was wrecked during October.

Year 1761. A ship of unknown registry, *Boscawen*, Captain Hawkins, sailing from Virginia to Barbados, wrecked and none of her cargo was saved.

Year 1763. Two English merchantmen were wrecked: *Royal Duke*, Captain Tory, sailing from Guadeloupe to London; and the *John*, Captain Simpson, sailing from England for the West Indies.

Year 1780. Two English ships wrecked: merchantman *Ceres*, Captain Howes, sailing from London to Antigua, part of her cargo was saved; and privateer *Fortune Teller*, Captain Kay, the crew was saved.

Year 1782. English merchantman *Telemacko*, sailing from London to Nevis, wrecked on November 9, crew and small part of cargo saved.

Year 1785. American ship *Betsey*, Captain Woodman, coming from South Carolina, was totally lost near the island.

Year 1790. American merchantman *Nelly & Nancy*, Captain Dennison, sailing from North Carolina to Guadeloupe, was lost on July 2 but the crew was saved.

Year 1792. Spanish warship *Lanzerota*, 24 guns, Captain Ignacio Perez, was wrecked on July 23 and very little was saved except for the crew.

Year 1793. American ship *Grand Sachem*, Captain Cairnes, sailing from St. Helena to Massachusetts, was wrecked on a reef.

Year 1795. American merchantman *Jeanette*, Captain Anderson, sailing from New England to St. Thomas, was wrecked on the north side of the island, crew and some cargo saved.

Year 1797. Scottish ship *Castle Semple*, sailing from Glasgow to the West Indies, was totally lost near the island.

Year 1799. American merchantman *Seaforth*, Captain Phelan, sailing from New York to Barbados, was captured by a French privateer and shortly after wrecked on a reef, most of her cargo was lost.

Year 1801. Three ships of unknown registry were wrecked near the island: *Argo*, Captain Pindar, sailing from Nassau to Surinam; unidentified sloop sailing from Nassau to Surinam; and an unidentified brig sailing from New England to Antigua.

Year 1807. English merchantman *Triton*, Captain Newhall, sailing to Antigua, wrecked on April 29, the crew was saved.

Year 1809. Three English merchantmen were wrecked: *Julia*, Captain Snow, coming from Cadíz, most of her cargo was saved; *Farrrier*, Captain Young, sailing from Newcastle to Honduras, only the crew was saved; and the *Kingston*, Captain Bruton, sailing from Liverpool to St. Croix.

Year 1810. English ship *Adventure*, Captain MacMillon, sailing from Lancaster to St. Thomas, was wrecked during August but her crew was saved.

Year 1813. English warship *H.M.S. Woolwich*, 40 guns, Captain Thomas Ball Sullivan, wrecked on November 6.

Year 1817. French ship *Jeune Adolphe*, sailing from Guadeloupe to France, wrecked on August 2 but her crew was saved.

Year 1819. A ship of unknown registry, *Speculation*, Captain Colburn, coming from Bermuda, was totally lost off the north part of the island on August 25.

Year 1821. Three ships were lost near the island: French merchantman *Martiniquin*, Captain Garcin, sailing from Martinique to France, lost off the west end on July 24; English merchantman *Hound*, Captain Stronnack, sailing from St. Vincent to London, was totally lost off the southwest end, her crew was saved; and the Spanish brig San Josif, 150 tons, coming from Spain with a cargo of olive oil, brandy, paper, and almonds, wrecked on April 7.

Year 1822. American merchantman *Monitor*, Captain Whitter, sailing from Philadelphia to St. Eustatius.

Shipwrecks in Antigua's Waters

Year 1666. During a hurricane two unidentified English warships were lost in English Harbor with a great loss of life.

Year 1681. During a hurricane on September 6, an unidentified English ship, Captain Gadbury, was totally lost in the main harbor.

Year 1740. English merchantman *Eagle*, Captain Long, sailing from London to South Carolina, was wrecked on a reef.

Year 1744. Two ships were lost: English merchantman *Cape Fear Merchant*, Captain Allen, coming from Bristol, wrecked on the bar while entering the main harbor but most of her cargo was saved; and an unidentified Spanish privateer was destroyed by an English warship after it was forced ashore near the south shore.

Year 1745. English warship *H.M.S. Weymouth*, Captain Calmady, wrecked on February 16 on a reef near Sandy Island off St. John's Road.

Year 1747. Two English ships were lost: the *Shirley*, Captain Sherbourn, coming from Boston, driven onshore by some French privateers; and an unidentified sloop lost during a hurricane on September 21

Year 1748. Two unidentified English vessels, a brig and a schooner, wrecked off Pope's Head and were totally lost.

Year 1754. During a hurricane on September 13, more than 10 unidentified ships were wrecked off St. John's Harbor.

Year 1762. English slave ship *Nancy*, Captain Bare, coming from Africa, was lost near Sandy Island but the slaves and crew were saved.

Year 1768. English slave ship *Dorsetshire*, Captain Traud, coming from Africa, was wrecked on a reef but the slaves and crew were saved.

Year 1770. An unidentified Spanish ship was wrecked on the island, only her crew was saved.

Year 1772. During a hurricane on August 30, several English merchantmen sank in St. John's Harbor and four or five English warships were lost in English Harbor.

Year 1773. American ship *Nester*, Captain Rowland, sailing from New England to Trinidad, was wrecked on the island.

Year 1774. An unidentified French ship, sailing from Guadeloupe to France, was wrecked on a shoal located three miles from the island; only a small part of her cargo of sugar was saved.

Year 1779. Dutch merchantman *Sarah & Rachel*, Captain Almers, sailing from Amsterdam to St. Eustatius, was lost near the island, only her crew was saved.

Year 1782. Unidentified merchantman, bound for Belfast, sank shortly after leaving St. John's Harbor.

Year 1786. English merchantman *Friendship*, Captain Bowen, sailing from Bristol to Honduras, wrecked on a reef but her crew was saved.

Year 1791. French merchantman *Aviance*, Captain Gamare, sailing from France to Hispaniola, was wrecked on Long Island, off Antigua.

Year 1797. English slave ship *Lively*, Captain Bell, coming from Africa, was wrecked on the east end of the island.

Year 1802. Four English merchantmen were wrecked: *Britannia*, Captain Brown, coming from Demarara; *Phaeton*, Captain Billings, coming from Baltimore with a cargo of salt, off Boon Point; *Echo*, Captain Johnson, sailing from London to Jamaica, on Diamond Rock, most of her cargo was saved; and the *Parras*, Captain Sleigh, coming from Bristol, on Guana Island.

Year 1803. American ship *Alice Bridger*, coming from New York, wrecked on a reef near St. John's Harbor.

Year 1804. During a hurricane on September 4 the English warship *H.M.S. De Ruyter*, 32 guns, Captain Josiph Becket, was sunk in Deep Bay and none of her crew of 250 men were lost.

Year 1805. English merchantman *Successful Noney*, sailing to Liverpool, was wrecked on August 16 near Sandy Island.

Year 1809. English ship *Friends*, Captain Gourley, sailing from Clyde to St. Thomas, wrecked on a reef, most of her cargo was saved.

Year 1811. During a hurricane on July 7 the English warship *H.M.S. Guachapin*, 10 guns, Captain Michael Jenkins, was wrecked on Rat Island; during the same storm the *H.M.S. Gloire* was forced to cast all her guns overboard in English Harbor.

Year 1816. English merchantman *Europe*, Captain Huddlestone, arriving from Liverpool, burned on August 7 off St. John's Harbor, one man lost.

Year 1817. Canadian ship *New Providence*, Captain Butler, arriving from Halifax, wrecked on the south side of the island on October 17.

Year 1821. German merchantman, *Philip & Emelie*, Captain Rentz, sailing from Hamburg to St. Thomas, was wrecked on Belfast Reef on the north side of the island on June 27 and only a small part of her cargo was saved.

Year 1823. Two ships were lost: American schooner, *Hope*, arriving from Norfolk, wrecked on Little Bird Island on the north side of Antigua; and English merchantman, *Sisters*, Captain Douthwarte, sailing from Demarara to London, wrecked on a reef on the south side of the island.

Shipwrecks in Aves' (or Bird Island) Waters
Located 130 miles southwest of Guadeloupe

Year 1689. Spanish merchant nao *Santa Ana Maria*, sailing from Cad to Veracruz, was wrecked while carrying a valuable cargo of mercury and general merchandise.

Year 1705. Unidentified English merchantman, 24 guns, with a main cargo of iron bars and barrels of nails, was wrecked. Eleven days later a French ship rescued the survivors and recovered most of her cargo.

Year 1774. American slave ship *Rising Sun*, Captain Allanson, sailing from Africa to America with a cargo of slaves, was wrecked on the island.

Shipwrecks in Guadeloupe's Waters

Year 1595. During an English privateering voyage to the West Indies led by Francis Drake and John Hawkins, the ship *Richard* was stripped and then scuttled on the west side of the island because she sailed too slowly.

Year 1603. The New Spain Flota, commanded by Captain-General Fulgencio de Meneses, made the customary stop to water on the southwest side of the island. An onshore breeze caused three of the ships to be wrecked; Capitana *San Juan Bautista*, 700 tons, 45 bronze guns, Captain Domingo de Licona; nao *La Rosa*, Captain Juan Diaz Canpillo; the third was not identified. The value of the cargoes lost on these ships was over a million pesos, and 250 men were left behind to salvage the wrecks. Soon after the flota sailed, however, they were attacked by Carib Indians and fled the island before they could recover anything. A few months later the Spaniards captured a French pirate vessel near Puerto Rico that had on board ten of the bronze cannon lost on the Capitaña.

Year 1609. Spanish merchant nao *San Juan Bautista*, Captain José de Ybarra, sailing from Cadíz to Veracruz, sank after anchoring in the same area in which the above three ships had wrecked. Carib Indians prevented the Spaniards from salvaging her valuable cargo.

Year 1618. An unidentified French privateer was wrecked on the east side of the island. Two years later six of the survivors were rescued by an English merchantman bound for Virginia.

Year 1630. Shortly after the New Spain Flota, commanded by Captain General Roque Centeno, anchored for water off the south end of the island, the galleon *Nuestra Señora del Pilar*, 1,100 tons, Captain Alonso García del Castillo, sank for no apparent reason quite close to shore but was completely salvaged.

Year 1656. During a hurricane a large number of French ships were totally lost at the port of Basseterre and around Maria Galante Island.

Year 1666. On August 12 there was a major sea battle between a French fleet and an English fleet commanded by Lord Willoughby. The French lost over 12 major warships and the English lost two near the Isle de Saints. Two days later a hurricane struck and over 50 ships were lost, including all 15 of Lord Willoughby's fleet. The walls of the fort at Basseterre were washed into the sea, carrying many 14-pound cannon with them.

Year 1691. Several English warships forced a French frigate of Admiral De Casse's fleet ashore on the Isle de Saints.

Year 1713. During a hurricane in September, over 40 ships of different nationalities were lost at Basseterre and other nearby anchorages.

Year 1759. English bomb vessel *H.M.S. Falcon*, eight guns, Captain Mark Robinson, was wrecked on the Isle de Saints.

Year 1760. Four English merchantmen were wrecked: *Prosperity*, Captain Wilson, arriving from Cork, chased onshore by a French privateer; *Armstrong*, Captain Muntford, arriving from Belfast, chased ashore by the French near Chatron Point and totally lost; *Deliverance*, Captain Whyte, sailing from London to Virginia, wrecked on the Isle de Saints; crew was saved; an unidentified ship of 200 tons arriving from Virginia wrecked on the Isle de Saints; some of her crew perished.

Year 1762. During a hurricane in July, six unidentified English merchantmen were sunk at Basseterre and several others near Maria Galante Island.

Year 1765. During a hurricane on July 31, 17 English merchantmen were lost at Basseterre but only one was identified: the *Friendship*, Captain Rivoira.

Year 1766. During a hurricane on October 6, more than 50 large English ships were lost at different ports around the island; and near the Isle de Saints 12 inbound slave ships from Africa were also totally lost.

Year 1774. A small English trading vessel, *Rose*, Captain Carline, arriving from Dominica, was wrecked at Grand Terre.

Year 1776. During a hurricane on September 6, more than 40 ships of various nationalities were wrecked around the island.

Year 1786. During a hurricane on September 10, three unidentified English ships were sunk at Basseterre.

Year 1792. French warship *Didon*, 44 guns, was wrecked and totally lost at Pointe-a-Pitre.

Year 1794. English troop-transport *H.M.S. Britannia* was accidentally burned at Basse Terre.

Year 1797. English merchantman *Cornwallis*, sailing from Antigua to Liverpool, was captured by the French and then wrecked off Pointe-a-Pitre.

Year 1800. English ship *Catherine & Francis*, Captain Smith, sailing from Bermuda to Martinique, was wrecked on Maria Galante Island.

Year 1801. French merchantman *Syren*, Captain Rohde, sailing from France to St. Thomas, was wrecked on the east side of the island.

Year 1809. Four warships were lost: the British destroyed two French warships of 40 guns each, *Loire* and *Seine*, on December 18 at Anse la Barque; English sloop *H.M.S. Carieux*, 18 guns, Captain Henry George Moysey, wrecked on September 25 at Petit Terre on Maria Galante Island; and the English warship *H.M.S. Unique*, 12 guns, Captain Thomas Fellowes, burned at Basseterre on May 31.

Year 1810. English merchantman Point-a-Petre, sailing for London, was lost during a gale on July 29 off Pointe-a-Pitre.

Year 1811. English warship *H.M.S. Grouper*, four guns, Captain James Atkins, wrecked on October 21 on the main island.

Year 1814. English warship *H.M.S. Rapide*, six guns, wrecked on the Isle de Saints.

Year 1821. A ship of unknown registry, *Kate*, Captain Purdy, sailing to Halifax with a large amount of specie aboard, was captured by pirates and scuttled near Deseada Island.

Year 1822. English ship *Virginia*, Captain Burt, sailing from Dominica to Antigua with a large number of soldiers, wrecked on July 20 on the Isle de Saints, but crew and passengers were saved.

Year 1823. American ship *Superior*, Captain Shaw, was wrecked on December 20 on Maria Galante Island, crew and cargo saved.

Year 1824. Two French merchantmen were wrecked on the main island: *Petit Louis*, Captain Videau, arriving from France, and the *France*, Captain Gerard, leaving for France.

Shipwrecks in Dominican Waters

Year 1565. Unidentified Spanish ship wrecked on the island and the Carib Indians captured and ate most of the survivors. When John Hawkins stopped there for water a few months later he rescued the few remaining survivors.

Year 1567. Before the New Spain Flota of Captain-General Juan Velasco de Barrio sailed from Veracruz for Spain word came that there were two English fleets waiting to intercept the flota, one near Havana and the other near the mouth of the Bahama Channel. To protect the treasure they decided to sail back to Spain by a very unusual route. Hugging the coast of Yucatan the flota turned south, passing south of Jamaica. They planned to sail toward the Virgin Islands, then head directly for Spain. However, when nearing Puerto Rico they were forced to run before a bad storm and six of the major ships of the flota, carrying over three million pesos in treasure, wrecked near the northwest tip of Dominica. The lost ships were: the Capitaña, *San Juan*, 150 tons, Captain Benito de Santana; the Almiranta, *Santa Barbola*, 150 tons, Captain Vicencio Garullo; galleon *San Felipe*, 120 tons, Captain Juan Lopez de Sosa; nao El Espíritu Santo, 120 tons, Captain Juan de Rosales; and two unidentified naos of 120 tons each. The storm prevented any of the other ships in the flota from stopping to pick up the treasure or the survivors, most of whom reached shore, where they were all massacred by the Carib Indians.

According to several Indians, captured the following year by salvors who came to the island, the Indians hid all the treasure in caves. But even under torture they would not reveal the location of the treasure, and there is no record of it being recovered.

Year 1605. As the New Spain Flota approached Guadeloupe to stop for water, an unidentified nao became separated during the night and anchored at Dominica. A large Dutch warship appeared and, after a brief battle, sank the nao. There were only a few survivors, whom the Dutch rescued and placed ashore on Puerto Rico.

Year 1766. During a hurricane in the month of October, five English merchantmen were totally lost at Roseau: *Phoenix*, Captain Knight, just arriving from Bristol; *Three Friends*, Captain Reef, recently arrived from Newfoundland; and three unidentified vessels.

Year 1769. During a hurricane on July 26, 13 ships were totally destroyed at Roseau but only one was identified: the English merchantman *Edward & Ann*, Captain Adnet. Two unidentified sloops were also sunk at Prince Ruperts Bay.

Year 1772. During a hurricane on August 30, 18 unidentified English merchantmen were sunk or wrecked at Roseau; several cannon from the fort were also washed into the sea.

Year 1776. During a hurricane on September 6, two ships were wrecked on the west side of the island: English merchantman *Mary & Jane*, Captain Gerdner, arrived from Lancaster; and the Scottish merchantman *Hunter*, Captain Robinson, some of her cargo was recovered.

Year 1780. During a hurricane on October 9 the newly built French frigate *Juno*, 40 guns, was wrecked on the east side of the island and over three hundred men perished.

Year 1787. The island suffered from three different hurricanes this year. On August 3 an English slave ship and several schooners were lost. Another on August 23 sank an English slave ship, three brigs and many smaller ships. The third hurricane, on August 29, caused another English slave ship and two brigs loaded with rum to be sink at Roseau.

Year 1792. During a hurricane on August 1, 14 English ships were lost in various ports on the west side of the island. Only one was identified: merchantman *Olive*, which was ready to sail for England.

Year 1796. English warship *H.M.S. Berbice*, 20 guns, Captain John Tresakar, was wrecked during November on a reef near the island.

Year 1804. English merchantman *Nufus*, Captain Sandland, coming from London, was wrecked with a valuable cargo.

Year 1808. English merchant schooner *Stag*, Captain Derbyshire, was wrecked at Roseau during a gale on July 14, crew and most of cargo saved.

Year 1809. During a gale on August 1 or 3, three ships were wrecked: an unidentified American schooner at Roseau; an unidentified British ship on the northern tip of the island; and the English warship *H.M.S. Lark*, 18 guns, Captain Robert Nicholas, off Point Palenqua, with three of her crew of 121 perishing.

Year 1813. During a hurricane in August, 16 ships were totally lost near and in the port of Roseau.

Shipwrecks in Martinique's Waters

Year 1636. Spanish warship *San Salvador*, Captain Sancho de Urdanibia, carrying a cargo of war materials to Venezuela for an attack against the Dutch on Curagao, was wrecked in two fathoms on the south side of the island. Because the island was under French control, the Spaniards threw its 26 bronze cannon overboard and set the ship afire before escaping. The French tried to reach the wreck, but it blew up before they could get any of its cargo.

Year 1666. When the governor of Barbados heard that there were six richly laden French ships in the Bay of All Saints on the island, he sent the *H.M.S. Coventry* and four other large English ships to capture them. When the French saw the English approaching the bay they set fire to all six of their ships, but the English managed to save all but one, which sank. Then, on the following day, while the English were transferring the plunder to their own ships, a storm struck and all five English ships sank. The French recovered over 80 large cannon from these wrecks as well as other items.

Year 1667. Accounts differ as to what happened on the island this year. One states that a large English fleet commanded by Admiral Sir John Harman entered the main port, Fort of France, and burned 20 French warships and merchantmen at anchor. The other account places the event at Governor's Bay and states that 19 French warships, three fireships, and some Dutch merchantmen were burned and sunk.

Year 1680. During a violent hurricane on August 3, over 20 large French ships and two English ships were totally lost in Cul-de- Sac Bay and the loss of lives was great.

Year 1687. French merchantman *Our Lady of Hope*, Captain Serres, coming from Marseilles, was wrecked on a reef six miles off the east side of the island.

Year 1691. An English warship commanded by Captain Arther forced an unidentified French warship to run aground near Fort of France.

Year 1695. During a hurricane in October, six or seven large French ships and several smaller ones were totally lost on the west side of the island and more than 600 men perished aboard them.

Year 1740. During a hurricane in October, two large French warships and many merchantmen were sunk or wrecked in different ports of the island.

Year 1744. A large unidentified Spanish merchantman, sailing from Cadíz to Cartagena, was forced ashore and destroyed on the south side of the island by several ships of the English fleet commanded by Commodore Knowles.

Year 1745. A fleet of 40 large French merchantmen escorted by two warships was sailing around the south side of the island, when it was attacked by the English fleet of Admiral Townsend and 30 of the merchantmen and the two warships were forced ashore and destroyed by the English. The cargoes on the merchantmen were valued at over 15 million livres.

Year 1761. During an attack on the island by an English fleet commanded by Sir James Douglas, one of the ships wrecked near a battery several miles north of Fort of France. She was the *H.M.S. Raisonable*, 64 guns, Captain Molyneux Shuldham, crew and most of stores saved. The French later recovered her cannon.

Year 1762. English merchantman *Brilliant*, Captain Boyd, sailing from London to the West Indies, foundered off the south part of the island but all of her crew was saved.

Year 1763. American ship *New Hampshire*, Captain Knight, coming from New England, was lost while entering the port of Fort of France, crew and cargo saved.

Year 1765. During a hurricane in July 33 large French merchantmen and many small vessels were lost in different ports on the west side of the island.

Year 1766. During a hurricane in October, 28 French and eight English ships were lost at Fort of France; nine other English ships were lost at Flemish Bay; and at La Trinite Bay, 18 unidentified ships were totally lost.

Year 1774. French slave ship *Geraundeau*, Captain Duckerson, arriving from Africa with 450 slaves, was wrecked on the south side of the island, slaves and crew saved.

Year 1776. During a hurricane on September 6, more than 100 French and Dutch merchantmen, all in a convoy preparing to sail for Europe, were totally lost at Point Pitre Bay and more than 6,000 persons were drowned.

Year 1779. Barely had the island recovered from a previous hurricane when an even worse one struck on August 28. This time more than 70 ships were lost all over the west side of the island, and among the many lives lost were some of the survivors from the last hurricane.

Year 1780. The English merchantman *Diligence*, Captain Orr, coming from England, was captured by a French privateer near the island and taken into Fort Royal Bay, where she was burned along with the ship that had captured her, as 10 English warships were coming to her rescue.

Year 1780. A hurricane that struck on October 12 was the worst ever to hit the island. No two accounts agree as to the number of ships lost. A French convoy of 40 large troop transports that had just reached the island was totally destroyed in some port on the west side. Four large French warships were sunk with a total loss of men in Fort Royal Bay. Three English warships of the fleet of Admiral Rodney were wrecked on the west side of the island: *H.M.S. Andromeda*, 28 guns; *H.M.S. Laurel*, 28 guns; and the *H.M.S. Deal Castle*, 24 guns. An English ship, probably a supply ship of Rodney's fleet, the *Endymion*, was lost on the island. Some accounts place the total number of ships of different nationalities lost on the island at more than 150.

Year 1788. During a hurricane in September more than 50 large French ships were totally destroyed in various ports of the island. Most of the town of Caravel, along with the majority of its inhabitants, was swept into the sea.

Year 1794. Two ships were wrecked on the island: American sloop *John*, Captain Richardson, coming from Virginia, and the English troop-transport *Generous Friends*, Captain Harrison, arriving from London.

Year 1796. A ship of unknown nationality, *Diana*, Captain Deare, sailing from India to America, was forced to enter a port on the west side of the island and burned to prevent it from falling into the hands of some English warships.

Year 1801. Four English merchantmen were wrecked on the east side of the island: *Edward*, Captain Nash, sailing from London to Honduras; *Hope*, Captain Thompson, sailing from London to Tortola; *Madona*, Captain Vollum, arriving from London; and the *Pacific*, Captain Wilson, also arriving from London.

Year 1802. Three English ships were wrecked on the island: merchantman *Dispatch*, Captain McIntire, sailing for Quebec, part of her cargo was saved; merchantman *Susannah*, Captain Stanton, sailing for Dublin; and the slave ship *Kennion*, Captain Robinson, sailing from Africa to Jamaica.

Year 1807. English warship, *H.M.S. Thames*, Captain Willoughby, was captured by the French off Barbados but later wrecked near Diamond Rock on the south side of the island.

Year 1809. On January 9 the English warship *H.M.S. Morne Fortunee*, 12 guns, Captain John Brown, was wrecked on the island, and 41 of her crew of 65 perished. During an English attack against the French, the English sank the French warship *Amphitrite*, 40 guns, on February 4, at Fort of France. On February 24 the French burned two of their other warships in the same port to prevent their capture: *Rossollis* and *Carnation*, both of 18 guns.

Year 1811. Early in the year the American merchantman *Spring Bird*, Captain Lambert, coming from New England, was wrecked on the island. During a hurricane on July 8, four or five unidentified ships were lost at Cul-de-Sac Bay.

Year 1814. Two Canadian ships were wrecked on the island: sloop *Margaret*, coming from New Brunswick, was lost at Grand Passage Bay but her crew was saved; and the brig *General Hunter*, Captain Perkins, arriving from Halifax, was lost at Fort of France.

Year 1813. During a hurricane in August a total of 42 ships of different nationalities were lost in various ports of the island and more than 3,000 persons perished.

Year 1815. French merchantman *Madame Royale*, arriving from France, was totally lost on the east side of the island on June 7, no survivors.

Year 1816. Two French merchantmen wrecked on the island: *Caroline*, Captain Monnier, sailing from France to Louisiana, in May, crew was saved; and the *Stanislaus*, Captain Berthelet, arriving from France, on September 15.

Year 1823. French ship *Alfred*, Captain Mony, arriving from France, wrecked on Diamond Rock.

Shipwrecks in St. Lucia's Waters

Year 1780. During a hurricane on October 10 the following ships were sunk: American merchantman *Champion*, Captain Hall, arriving from New York; English merchantman *Dolphin*, Captain Morrison; and three English warships: *H.M.S. Cornwall*, 74 guns, Captain Timothy Edwards; *H.M.S. Vengeance*, 32 guns; and the *Beaver's Prize*, 18 guns.

Year 1781. English warship *H.M.S. Thetis*, 32 guns, Captain Robert Linzee, was wrecked on the west side of the island.

Year 1783. English merchantman *Barbara*, Captain Perry, arriving from Liverpool, wrecked on the northern part of the island, crew and part of cargo saved.

Year 1800. English slave ship *Prince John*, Captain Hestor, arriving from Africa, lost on the east side of the island, crew and slaves saved.

Year 1805. English schooner *Dolphin*, coming from Barbados with rum, was wrecked on the east side of the island.

Year 1809. English merchantman *Lancashire Witch*, sailing from Liverpool to Barbados, was totally lost on the east side of the island; her crew was saved.

Year 1817. During a hurricane on October 21, seven large English merchantmen were sunk on the west side of the island, more than 200 men perished.

Year 1823. American merchantman *Suffolk*, sailing from Demarara to New York, was wrecked on the east side of the island on September 15 but her crew was saved.

Shipwrecks in St. Vincent's Waters

Year 1635. Two unidentified Spanish merchant naos were wrecked on the east side of the island while sailing from Spain to Cartagena. Survivors were found on this island in 1667 by the first English settlers.

Year 1780. During the famous October 10 hurricane the English warship *H.M.S. Experiment*, 50 guns, and the French warship *Juno*, 40 guns, were destroyed on the east coast of this island with almost a total loss of lives.

Year 1784. English slave ship *Africa*, Captain Brown, arriving from Africa with a cargo of slaves, wrecked while entering the port of Kingstown, crew and slaves saved.

Year 1792. English packet boat *Willoughby Bay*, was wrecked on the east side of the island on September 21, mail and crew saved.

Year 1793. A large unidentified ship, apparently English-built, drifted ashore on the east side of the island and quickly went to pieces. No one was on board at the time it wrecked.

Year 1817. Dring a hurricane on October 21, ten large unidentified English umerchantmen wrecked or sank at Kingstown.

Year 1818. English merchantman *William*, Captain Landells, sailing from Tobago to London, wrecked on the east side of the island on May 27, crew and some cargo of rum saved.

Shipwrecks in Barbados' Waters

Year 1666. During a hurricane in July a large unidentified English warship was wrecked on the east side of the island.

Year 1669. During a hurricane on November 1, many ships were wrecked on the island and over 1,500 coffins from the island's main cemetery were swept into the sea.

Year 1675. During a hurricane on September 1, 12 large unidentified English merchantmen, some of them loaded with sugar and rum, were sunk at Bridgetown.

Year 1693. During a hurricane in October, 17 unidentified English merchantmen were sunk in the vicinity of Bridgetown.

Year 1694. During a hurricane on September 27, 26 English merchantmen were sunk in Carlisle Bay and more than a thousand men perished.

Year 1700. During a hurricane two large and two small unidentified ships were lost.

Year 1716. A pirate ship of Captain Martel sank a sloop that was guarding the entrance to Carlisle Bay. The following day an English warship chased the pirate ship of 24 guns around the island and sank it by cannon fire on the east side of the island.

Year 1748. An unidentified richly laden French merchantman, sailing from France to Martinique, was wrecked on the east side of the island. An English sloop-of-war, *Serpent*, wrecked on the island and seven crewmen perished.

Year 1749. During a hurricane in October, six ships were sunk near Bridgetown but only the English merchantman *Nancy*, sailing from Bristol to Jamaica, was identified.

Year 1751. English merchantman *Argo*, Captain Alleyne, sailing for London, wrecked shortly after leaving Carlisle Bay but her crew was saved.

Year 1757. During a hurricane in July, eight unidentified ships were lost at Carlisle Bay and Bridgetown. In November an American ship, *George*, Captain Hardy, coming from Philadelphia, wrecked on the island.

Year 1758. During a hurricane on August 23 the following ships were wrecked or sunk in Carlisle Bay: an English privateer brigantine, Captain Franklin; American merchantman *Aurora*, Captain Campbell, coming from North Carolina; American ship *Jenny & Sally*, Captain Boulton, arriving from South Carolina; English merchantman *Rose*, Captain Elmore, arriving from Bristol; and two ships of unknown registry: *Good Intent*, Captain Tucker, and *David & Susanna*, Captain Bartlett. At Bridgetown, six unidentified ships were also lost.

Year 1761. Scottish merchantman *Blakeney*, Captain Murford, coming from Belfast, was forced ashore on the east side of the island by a French privateer and quickly went to pieces, crew and some cargo saved.

Year 1762. Two merchantmen wrecked on the island: English ship *Greyhound*, Captain Walsh, driven ashore by a French privateer on January 8, her cargo was saved; and Irish ship *Cato*, Captain Houseman, sailing from Cork to Guadeloupe, near the entrance to Carlisle Bay, only her crew was saved.

Year 1765. During a gale or hurricane in August, seven large English merchantmen were lost in Carlisle Bay; at Bridgetown the Scottish ship *Josiph*, Captain McNabb, ready to sail for Dublin, was sunk but her cargo was recovered.

Year 1767. English slave ship *Rebecca*, Captain Brodie, arriving from Africa, wrecked on a reef near Long Bay on November 17, crew, slaves and cargo of ivory and wax saved.

Year 1772. Two English ships were wrecked on the east side of the island: packet boat *Barbadoes*, Captain Twine, arriving from Bristol, burned after running up on a reef; and the merchantman *Cunriff*, Captain Clapp, arriving from London and Cork, only a small part of her cargo was saved.

Year 1773. A ship of unknown registry, *Hill*, Captain Coffin, was struck by lightning and blew up off Bridgetown, most of her crew perished.

Year 1775. During a gale on August 25 the Scottish packet boat *Duncannon*, Captain Goddard, arriving from England, wrecked near Carlisle Bay, crew and mail saved. During a hurricane on September 2 the English ship *Ostall*, Captain Temple, coming from Newfoundland, was wrecked on the island.

Conservation expert inspects large gold chain recovered from a 1622 Spanish shipwreck by the ROV *Merlin* in 1,500 feet of water off the Dry Tortugas.

Year 1776. Two ships were wrecked on the east side of the island: English slave ship *Patty*, Captain Johnson, arriving from Africa, crew and slaves saved; and the French ship *Industry*, Captain Carcaud, sailing from Marseilles to Barbados, her crew was saved.

Year 1779. Privateer ship *Pickering*, 20 guns, forced on shore by the *H.M.S. Aurora* and then burned.

Year 1780. During the famous hurricane of October 10, over 20 ships were wrecked around the island. A large number of other ships were blown out to sea, most of them never again heard from. Two English ships, *Happy Return* and the *Edward*, Captain Peoples, which had been blown away during the hurricane, made it back to the island but sank upon returning. One of the main buildings of the Naval Hospital at Bridgetown was carried into the sea by large waves.

Year 1782. English slave ship *Lark*, Captain Blackhouse, arriving from Africa, wrecked on the east side of the island, crew and all of its 320 slaves saved.

Year 1784. English merchantman *Euphrates*, Captain Smith, coming from London, was totally lost on a reef on the eastern side of the island but the crew was saved.

Year 1785. American ship *Rose*, Captain Savage, coming from Philadelphia, was wrecked at Round Rock but part of her cargo was saved.

Year 1786. During a hurricane on September 2, various accounts state "that every ship in Carlisle Bay was lost." Only two were identified: Scottish ship *Hibernia*, Captain McConnel, and the English merchantman *Generous Planter*, Captain Sands.

Year 1790. American ship *Betsey*, Captain Brown, sailing from Georgia to Grenada, was totally lost on the east side of the island but her crew was saved.

Year 1791. English slave ship *King George*, Captain Howard, arriving from Africa, wrecked on the east side of the island and only 80 of its 360 slaves were saved.

Year 1792. English slave ship *Garland*, Captain Sherwood, arriving from Africa, wrecked on Cobler's Rock, crew and slaves saved.

Year 1794. Scottish merchantman *Kingston*, coming from Glasgow, wrecked on Cabbin Rock Reef, on the east side of the island.

Year 1798. English schooner *Star*, shortly after sailing for Trinidad on June 30, was wrecked in a gale on the southern part of the island.

The large gold bar at the top of these ingots and jewelry from a 17th-century Spanish shipwreck weighed 36 pounds and was unmarked, indicating it was contraband.

Year 1799. Two English merchantmen were wrecked on Cobler's Rock: *Edwards*, Captain Wilson, arriving from England, and the Mary, *Captain Leigh*, arriving from Liverpool.

Year 1801. Two English ships wrecked on the east side of the island: packet boat *Grantham*, Captain Ball, sailing from England to Jamaica, crew and passengers saved; and the merchantman *Chance*, Captain Peters, the crew was saved.

Year 1804. Large richly laden Portuguese merchantman *Francizhena*, Captain Carros, sailing from Brazil to Lisbon, wrecked on the east side of the island and many men perished.

Year 1806. English merchantman *Maryann*, Captain Mack, sailing from Newcastle to Grenada, wrecked on the island.

Year 1807. Four ships were wrecked on the island: English ship *Nelly*, Captain Adamson, arriving from Trinidad, near Bridgetown; American brig *Lark*, Captain Worrel, arriving from Surinam, on the south part of the island; English ship *Cicero*, Captain Turner, sailing from London to Jamaica, on Cobler's Rock; and the English merchantman *Bridgetown*, sailing from London to Jamaica, also on Cobler's Rock.

Year 1808. English troop transport *Majestic*, burned and sank in Carlisle Bay, no lives were lost.

Year 1809. English sloop-of-war *H.M.S. Glommen*, 18 guns, Captain Charles Pickford, wrecked in Carlisle Bay in November, no lives were lost.

Year 1810. Canadian schooner *Laura*, wrecked during a gale on August 12 at Pier Head, the crew was saved.

Year 1812. Canadian merchantman *Cruden*, sailing from Newfoundland to Grenada, wrecked on Cobler's Rock on March 7.

Year 1813. Two English mail packet boats *Sprightly* and *Lady Spencer*, were wrecked on the east side of the island on July 23.

Year 1814. Two English merchantmen were lost on the island: *Jane*, Captain Ranof, sailing from London and Madeira to Dominica, on the east side of the island, crew and cargo saved; and the schooner *Jonathan*, forced on Marida Reef by an American ship and then destroyed by cannon fire, most of her cargo of dry goods and rum was lost.

Year 1815. Three merchantmen were lost on the island: Scottish ship *Elizabeth*, Captain Duncan, sailing from England to St. Vincent, on the east side of the island; English ship *Sylph*, Captain Davidson, sailing from Gibraltar to the West Indies, totally lost on August 10 on a reef near the northern end of the island; and a ship of unknown registry, *M'Dowall*, coming from Dominica, on Kettlebottom Rock.

Year 1816. During a hurricane on September 15, two English ships were totally lost on the island: brig *Commerce*, arriving from England, and the sloop *Economy*, arriving from St. Lucia.

Year 1821. English packet boat *Lady Georgiana*, Captain Spencer, totally lost in Carlisle Bay on September 1.

Shipwrecks in Grenadine Waters

Year 1611. An unidentified French slave ship carrying over 400 slaves was wrecked on one of the islands of the Grenadines. Spaniards later rescued most of the slaves and killed all of the Frenchmen.

Year 1653. During the month of July a large unidentified French ship was totally lost near one of the smaller cays in this chain of islands.

Year 1675. During a hurricane in August an unidentified Portuguese slave ship was wrecked on Bequia Island and a large amount of ivory went down.

Year 1768. English merchantman *Nancy*, Captain Hamilton, sailing from Bristol to Nevis, was lost on one of the islands but her crew was saved.

Year 1769. English merchantman *Rose*, Captain Farr, sailing from London and Madeira to Jamaica, was wrecked on the east side of Carriacou Island.

Year 1782. English merchantman *Rebecca*, Captain Sim, sailing from Demarara to Barbados, was totally lost on the east side of Bequia Island.

Year 1794. A ship of unknown registry, *Adventure Baptista*, Captain Blanckley, was wrecked on a reef near Carriacou Island.

Year 1818. American schooner *Lily* was wrecked on one of the Grenadines and only the captain was saved.

Year 1821. English merchantman *March*, sailing from London to Grenada, was wrecked at Carriacou Island in April and was totally lost.

Shipwrecks in Grenadan Waters

Year 1768. During a hurricane on August 9 the following ships were sunk at St. George's Harbor: English ship *Industry*, Captain Wilkinson, arriving from Barbados; Dutch ship, Captain Simpson, arriving from St. Eustatius; and three unidentified brigs. At Grand Once, the English slave ship *Molly*, Captain Woodburn, coming from Africa, was wrecked.

Year 1769. English slave ship *Sally*, Captain Tonkey, arriving from Africa, wrecked in Grand Roy Bay on June 19, crew and slaves saved.

Year 1772. English merchantman *Champion*, Captain Glover, arriving from Bristol, was lost at St. George's Harbor.

Year 1773. English sloop *Ann*, Captain Knotsford, wrecked on a reef near Bacolet, three men were lost.

Year 1774. Two merchantmen were lost: Scottish ship *Morris & MoUy*, Captain Weatherhead, while sailing out of Mergain for Dublin; and the English ship *Rochard*, Captain Bartlet, while leaving Grenville Bay on August 3 for London; some of their cargo was saved.

Year 1780. During the famous hurricane of October 10 the following ships were lost: 19 unidentified Dutch merchantmen sank in Grenville Bay; Swedish merchantman *Prince Frederick Adolph*, Captain Lonstroom, in St. George's Harbor; French ship *Two Sisters*, Captain Townseau, on the east side of the island; French privateer *Comte de Durant*, Captain Lamster, on the south side of the island; and three other French and seven English merchantmen were lost in other ports of the island.

Year 1787. English merchantman *Lady Hughes*, Captain Dommet, was totally lost on the island but her crew was saved.

Year 1788. American ship *Mary Ann*, Captain Dale, arriving from Virginia, wrecked on the north side of the island on December 2.

Year 1790. Two English merchantmen wrecked on the island: *Hope*, Captain Blackman, and the *Arnelia*, Captain Burgess, the latter on the north end of the island.

Year 1791. American merchantman *Ann & Bridget*, Captain Shaftoe, arriving from Boston, wrecked on the island.

Year 1793. Two ships were lost on the east side of the island: English slave ship *Fanny*, Captain Moore, arriving from Africa; only two of the crew were saved; and a ship of unknown registry, *Charlotte*, Captain Cummings.

Year 1794. English merchantman *Mary*, Captain Johnson, was totally lost leaving Grenville Bay while sailing for London.

Year 1798. American ship *Elizabeth*, arriving from New York, wrecked on a reef near St. George's Harbor but most of her cargo was saved.

Year 1800. English merchantman *Charlotte*, Captain Buttery, arriving from London, was wrecked on the south side of the island but most of her cargo was saved.

Year 1801. English ship *Love*, Captain Death, arriving from England, wrecked while entering St. George's Harbor but all of her cargo was saved.

Year 1804. English brig *Surprise*, while leaving for Trinidad, was wrecked at the entrance to Grenville Bay, but all of her cargo of rum was saved.

Year 1805. Large Portuguese merchantman *Armida*, Captain Silva, sailing from Brazil to Venezuela, was wrecked at Point Saline on December 20, most of her cargo was lost.

Year 1807. English sloop *Neptune*, Captain Hunt, arriving from London, wrecked on the island.

Year 1813. English merchantman *Four Brothers*, sailing for London, was wrecked on the east side of the island.

Year 1816. Richly laden Spanish merchant nao *Virgen del Rosario*, Captain Gale, coming from Spain, wrecked on January 22 at Point Saline, only a small part of her cargo was saved.

Year 1822. Two English merchantmen, *Sophia* and the *Columbine*, Captain Bannatyne, sailing from Tobago, were wrecked on the east side of the island, both crews and cargoes were saved.

Year 1824. English sloop *Arrow*, Captain Williams, wrecked on La Bays Rock but her crew was saved. The ship was in ballast at the time.

Shipwrecks in Tobago's Waters

Year 1572. Five unidentified Spanish merchant naos, sailing from Spain to Veracruz, were wrecked on the island but most of their cargoes were later salvaged by divers from Margarita Island.

Year 1677. A big battle took place between a French fleet under Admiral Estres and a Dutch fleet under Vice-Admiral Herr Binkes in Palmit Bay. The French fleet was burned and sunk; the number of ships or their identities are not known. The Dutch also lost several ships.

Year 1787. English sloop *Tabago* was totally lost on August 16 on a reef east of Englishman's Bay, on the north side of the island.

Year 1792. Unidentified French ship of Captain Steur, sailing from Demarara to Amsterdam, was wrecked on the island.

Year 1800. Two English merchantmen were wrecked on the island: *Recovery*, Captain Abercromby, sailing to London, and the *Mary Ann*, Captain Craig, arriving from London. Some cargo from both ships was saved.

Year 1801. English ship *Rebecca*, Captain Reed, arriving from London, wrecked on the east end of the island but the crew was saved.

Year 1803. English merchantman *Catherine*, Captain Bodkin, arriving from London, wrecked on the north side of the island.

Year 1805. English merchantman *Rosalia*, Captain Ferguson, arriving from London, wrecked on a reef while attempting to enter Tyrrel Bay.

Year 1807. English merchantman *Eclipse*, Captain Vaughan, was totally lost in Courland Bay but her crew was saved.

Year 1812. English ship *Fame*, Captain Mumford, sailing from Madeira to Tobago, wrecked on August 21 on the island.

Year 1813. English merchantman *Trafalgar*, Captain Pines, sailing for Bristol, was wrecked off the island's east end in June; some cargo was saved.

Shipwrecks in Trinidad's Waters

Year 1731. Spanish merchant nao *N. S. de la Concepción*, Captain Gotibo, wrecked on Maracas Bar, only her crew was saved.

Year 1780. English merchantman *Friends*, Captain Wood, arriving from Africa, wrecked on the east side of the island; few of the crew were saved.

Year 1782. English warship *H.M.S. Rattlesnake* was wrecked on the island, one of the crew perished.

Year 1797. As an English fleet of warships commanded by Sir Henry Harvey approached to capture the island from the Spaniards on February 17, the Spaniards burned five large warships off Chaguaramas to prevent them from falling into the hands of the English: Capitana *San Vicente*, 80 guns, Brigadier Jeronimo Mendoza; Almiranta *Arrogante*, 74 guns, Captain Rafael Bennazar; galleon *Gallardo*, 74 guns, Captain Gabriel Sorondo; galleon *San Damasco*, 74 guns, Captain José Jordan; and the frigate *Concha*, 34 guns, Captain Manuel Urtizabel. Amateur divers located these wrecks and recovered a few artifacts from them.

Year 1800. Two English ships were wrecked on the island: merchantman *Charlotte*, Captain Crow, arriving from Africa, the crew was saved; and the warship *H.M.S. Dromedary*, 20 guns, Captain Bridges W. Taylor, on August 10, at Parasol Rock, but the crew was saved.

Year 1802. Scottish merchantman *Swan*, arriving from Glasgow, wrecked in the Bocas on September 20.

Year 1803. English slave ship *Kate*, Captain Good, arriving from Africa, wrecked on the east side of the island, ten people were lost.

Year 1806. Scottish ship *Governor Picton*, arriving from Clyde, wrecked on the south side of the island on April 19, only her crew was saved.

Year 1810. Canadian ship Polly, Captain Bell, arriving from Newfoundland, sank at Port of Spain but her crew was saved.

Year 1816. English merchantman *Lion*, Captain Grove, sailing to Demarara, wrecked on the east side of the island but her crew was saved.

Year 1821. Spanish ship *Tamar*, arriving from Puerto Rico, was wrecked in the Bocas, crew and some cargo saved.

Chapter Six

Bermuda

Bermuda, in relation to its size, has more shipwrecks than any other area in the Western Hemisphere, with the possible exceptions of the Florida Keys and Cape Hatteras, North Carolina. Although on charts it is nothing more than a dot located 800 miles from the United States, Bermuda played an important role in early navigation. All the Spanish ships, as well as those of other European nations sailing in the waters of the New World, attempted to pass within sight of Bermuda on their homeward-bound voyages, using it as a checkpoint in their haphazard navigation.

Most of the ships bringing colonists to North America either made stops there or passed within sight of the island. Because these islands are very low in elevation and generally concealed by mist or haze, sighting them was not an easy task and many ships ran up on reefs, some of which are as far as 10 miles out.

From the earliest days many Bermudans were engaged in salvaging wrecks throughout the West Indies. When William Phips first reached the treasure galleon on Silver Shoals, he discovered that Bermudan wreckers had already beat him to it. During World War II a great deal of salvaging for scrap iron went on around the island and many cannon and anchors were raised.

The first major treasure recovery in the 20th century was made in 1955 by Teddy Tucker, a Bermudan and descendant of the first governor of Bermuda (who, ironically, got into trouble over salvaging a Spanish galleon, the *San Antonio*, wrecked in Bermuda in 1621, when he was accused of pocketing a large amount of the recovered cargo). Teddy himself located this same wreck about 10 years ago and recovered a large number of artifacts from it. In 1950, while combing the reefs with a glass-bottom bucket to locate several of his fish traps after a storm, he discovered six coral-encrusted cannon in a small sand pocket on a shallow reef.

He didn't return to the site until the summer of 1955, when, after recovering the cannon for a local museum, he began excavating by hand (using a table-tennis paddle to fan the sand away). His first find was a beautiful gold bar weighing 32 ounces. In less than a week he discovered two small cakes of gold, two smaller gold bars, several gold-studded pearl buttons, and a gold, emerald-studded cross that sold for $100,000. This wreck is believed to date from the late 16th century.

For many years Tucker has been working at salvaging a wide assortment of wrecks, sometimes under the sponsorship of the Smithsonian Institution. The waters are so clear around Bermuda that he located over 100 wrecks using a light plane, a helium balloon or by just standing on the bow of a boat to look through the near-transparent water. Tucker is one of the hardest workers of all the divers I know, thinking nothing of spending eight or ten hours below each day. His many discoveries are due to hard work, not luck.

The most notable wrecks Tucker has worked on are an unidentified Spanish merchant nao dating to 1560; the *San Antonio*; Virginia Company merchantmen *Eagle* and *Virginia Merchant*, 1659 and 1660, respectively; an unidentified Spanish nao dating around 1700; the *Sir George Arthur*, an English merchantman, 1778; an unidentified French merchantman, around 1780; the *Caesar*, an English merchantman, 1818; and the French warship *L'Herminie*, 1839.

In June 1958 amateur skin-diver Robert Downing discovered the wreck of the *Sea Venture*, the ship that brought the first colonists to Bermuda in 1609. With Teddy Tucker's assistance, he salvaged the wreck, which is of great importance to Bermudan history.

Another native Bermudan, Harry Cox, a wealthy businessman, has been prowling the reefs for as long as Tucker and has located a large number of shipwrecks. His most spectacular discovery occurred in the summer of 1968, when he excavated the remains of a Portuguese ship sunk ca. 1580. Among the many items Cox recovered are several gold bars, gold circlets, an assortment of rare mint-condition gold Portuguese cruzado coins, a solid gold, double-linked chain 15 feet long, a gold manicure set backed by two golden caryatids, an assortment of Spanish silver coins, a pearl cross mounted on a gold frame, several gold rings, and a brass astrolabe, one of the few ever found on shipwrecks anywhere.

There are others who spend their spare time working old wrecks. Brian Malpus, who earns his living as a policeman, worked with Tucker for many years; then, on his own focusing on 16th- and 17th-century Spanish shipwrecks. Although he hasn't discovered much treasure, his wrecks have yielded a fascinating array of "things;" e.g., a silver bosun's whistle, many types of intact ceramicware, pewterware and a few Spanish silver coins.

Although Bermudans generally work wrecks during the summer, work on many sites can be carried on most of the year, except when passing hurricanes cause huge swells to break on the reefs. Certain areas are now restricted and are under control of the Bermuda Maritime Museum. In many areas no permits are necessary to explore wreck sites, but application for salvage leases must be made to the Receiver of Wrecks. The salvor may keep all that he recovers, but the Bermudan government has the right to purchase any or all of what is recovered from a wreck at a fair price.

Shipwrecks in Bermudan Waters

Year 1500-10. According to noted 19th century British historian Defroy, Bermuda is named after a Spanish ship, *La Bermuda*, that wrecked there not long after Columbus's discovery of the New World. Other historians claim that the island is named after its discoverer, a Spaniard named Juan Bermúdez.

Year 1533. An unidentified Spanish merchant nao owned by Johan de Leon carrying an undisclosed amount of gold and pearls, was lost on the reefs. Three years later, two ships sailing from Santo Domingo for Spain passed close to Bermuda and sighted fires on the island but wind and current prevented them from investigating. They recommended to the King that a small ship be sent to pick up the survivors and treasure, but no documents reveal if this was done.

Year 1543. A Portuguese slave ship, sailing from Santo Domingo with seven Spanish merchantmen, wrecked on a reef four leagues from the nearest land, at the north end of Bermuda. The 30 survivors got ashore in the ship's boat and made many return trips to the wreck, bringing ashore supplies and part of its cargo. After 60 days on the island they sailed for Santo Domingo in a vessel constructed from timbers of the shipwreck. They reported sighting the remains of several other shipwrecks on the reefs.

Year 1550. Unidentified merchant nao, owned by Rodrigo Vago and sailing in the Nueva España Flota, was badly damaged in a storm about 70 leagues west of Bermuda and drifted until it struck a reef at Bermuda. It carried a large amount of gold and silver, none of which was reported recovered.

Year 1551. A hurricane that lasted for ten days struck the Tierra Firme Armada of Captain-General Sancho de Viedma after it cleared the Bahama Channel. His Capitiña sprang a bad leak and was deliberately run up on a reef, where her cannon and 150,000 ducats in treasure were saved. Another ship of this fleet, the *Santa Barbola*, 400 tons, Captain Alvarez de los Rios, owned by Cosme Rodríguez Farfan, was also wrecked on a reef but all her treasure was saved.

Year 1560. When the Tierra Firme Flota of Captain-General Pedro de la Roelas was in sight of Bermuda a storm struck and the Capitaña disappeared without a trace, either sinking in deep water or on the reefs of Bermuda.

Year 1563. When the Nueva España Flota of Captain-General Juan Menéndez was in the vicinity of Bermuda, his Capitaña and several merchant naos disappeared without a trace. One of these is believed to be the unidentified Spanish wreck (dated 1560) that Tucker located.

Year 1584. When the New Spain Treasure Fleet consisting of 51 ships was in the vicinity of Bermuda it was struck by a hurricane and six unidentified ships went down in deep water. A small vessel on 120 tons coming from Honduras was also wrecked on the reefs of Bermuda.

Year 1588. Unidentified merchant nao of Pedro Menéndez, carrying a cargo of indigo, cochineal, logwood, and a small amount of silver specie, wrecked on a reef.

Year 1593. A French ship owned by Monsieur Charles de la Barbotiere sailed from Laguna, Hispaniola, and was wrecked on December 17 against a reef in the northwestern part of Bermuda that the captain reported was seven leagues from the nearest shore. In a makeshift raft, 26 of the 50 persons on board reached shore. They later made a small vessel from the wreck and reached France.

Year 1596. Merchant nao San Pedro, 350 tons, Captain Hieronimo de Porras, of the Nueva España Flota of Captain-General Pedro Menéndez Marquez, was wrecked near the island. It could be this wreck on which Tucker made his big find in 1955.

Year 1603. Unidentified galleon in the Tierra Firme Armada, Captain-General Luis Fernandez de Cordova, separated from the convoy during a storm and was wrecked at Bermuda. Most of the treasure aboard was recovered and, together with the survivors, was rescued 22 days later. Crew reported seeing many earlier shipwrecks on the island.

Year 1605. Merchant nao *Santa Ana*, 200 tons, sailing from Honduras to Spain with a general cargo, sank near Bermuda, only the people on her were saved.

Year 1609. A squadron of nine English vessels sailed from Plymouth, England, with colonists and supplies for Jamestown, Virginia. The flagship *Sea Venture*, Admiral Sir George Somers, was wrecked at Bermuda and the survivors founded the first settlement on the island.

Year 1619. An unidentified pinnace, manned mostly by Dutchmen but with a few Englishmen aboard, wrecked on the northwest shoals of Bermuda and went quickly to pieces before anything could be saved. It was returning from a privateering voyage in the West Indies.

Year 1619. English merchantman *Warwick*, owned by the Virginia Company, was wrecked in Castle Harbor during a storm in November after it had discharged its cargo and passengers from England. In 1967 this wreck was discovered with the help of a magnetometer by Tucker and several Smithsonian people.

Year 1621. Merchant nao *San Antonio*, 12 cannon, owned by Simón de Vidacar, was wrecked in Bermuda while the rest of the convoy it was sailing with rode out a storm within sight of the island. Its cargo consisted of 5,000 hides, 1,200 quintals of brazilwood, 6,000 pounds of indigo, 30,000 pounds of tobacco, 5,000 pounds of sarsaparilla, and gold and silver worth 5,000 pounds sterling in English currency. Bermudans under the direction of the governor recovered most of its cargo, and the survivors were shipped to England several months later.

Year 1622. During a storm that struck the Nueva España Flota of Captain-General Fernando de Sousa, two ships were lost off Bermuda: nao *San Ignacio*, 150 tons, Captain Domingo Hernandez, and the nao *Nuestra Señora de la Limpia Concepción*, 116 tons, Captain Juan Calzado.

Year 1639. Two small vessels, sailing in the convoy of the Tierra Firme Armada, Captain-General Gerónimo Gomez de Sandoval; urca *La Viga*, Captain Mathew Lorenzo, and the pattachuelo *El Galgo*, a prize vessel captured by the Spaniards, were wrecked on October 22 at Bermuda. The wreck site of *La Viga* was given as three leagues from the main village in Bermuda, and survivors from both wrecks reached shore carrying some silver with them.

Year 1644. An English chart of Bermuda dated 1740 had the following information marked on it:

"Among these rocks which extend above three leagues to the northeast of the island are a great number of wrecks and amongst others that of a rich Spanish ship lost about the year 1644. It was once discovered, but it is now fished for in vain. Off the southwest and west northwest section of the island are great numbers of rocks at three to four leagues distance from land, whereby an abundance of ships have been lost.

Year 1659. English merchantman *Eagle*, Captain Whitby, owned by the Virginia Company, sailing from Plymouth, England, to Jamestown, Virginia, with trade goods and passengers was wrecked on January 12 on a reef. This wreck was discovered and partially salvaged by Tucker.

Year 1660. English merchantman *Virginia Merchant*, Captain Robert Burk, owned by the Virginia Company, sailing from Plymouth to Jamestown, was wrecked on March 26. Of the 189 persons aboard only 10 were saved. This wreck has also been discovered and partially salvaged by Tucker.

Year 1669. During a hurricane a large unidentified ship was sunk at Castle Harbor in Bermuda.

Year 1684. Spanish navío *San Salvador*, Captain Pedro de Arvide, 567 tons, owned by Admiral Manuel Casadeite, sprung a bad leak and wrecked at Bermuda. After the survivors reached shore in small boats the Spaniards set the ship afire to prevent the Bermudans from salvaging her cargo.

Year 1744. English merchantman *Friendship*, Captain Hooper, sailing from St. Kitts for Barbados, was driven off course by a storm and lost near Bermuda.

Year 1744. English ship *Mary & Hannah*, Captain Savage, sailing from Genoa, Italy, for Carolina (both North and South Carolina were called just Carolina at this time) was lost at Bermuda.

Year 1747. English merchantman *Tryton*, Captain Gibbons, sailing from Carolina to London, was lost near Bermuda.

Year 1747. A ship of either American or British registry, *Dorothy and Elizabeth*, Captain Simpson, sailing from Boston for the Leeward Islands, was lost on the reefs of Bermuda.

Year 1749. English ship *Leoftoffe*, Captain Fielding, coming from Jamaica, was lost off Bermuda.

Year 1750. English ship *Margaret*, Captain Gallagar, sailing from London to Antigua, was lost near Bermuda.

Year 1753. A large unidentified Danish ship, carrying 700 hogsheads of sugar, was lost on the reefs of Bermuda.

Year 1757. English ship *Mary*, Captain Daniel, sailing from Philadelphia to Antigua, was lost near Bermuda.

Year 1757. American sloop *Hunters Galley*, Captain Clement Conyers, sailing from St. Eustatius Island to South Carolina with a general cargo, lost at Bermuda on January 11.

Year 1758. English ship *Britannia*, Captain Sorogham, sailing for London, struck on a bar leaving Bermuda and sank in eight fathoms of water.

Year 1760. English ship *Mancheoneal*, Captain Morgan, sailing from London to Bermuda, was wrecked on the west side of the island but part of its cargo was saved.

Year 1761. English man-of-war *Griffin*, 20 guns, was lost off Bermuda on October 25; 50 of her crew were drowned.

Year 1762. English merchantman *Judith Maria*, Captain Ball, sailing from Jamaica to Bristol, England, was wrecked at Bermuda in August, crew, some cargo, and ship's stores saved.

Year 1763. English brigantine *Katherine*, Captain Simondson, sailing from Philadelphia to Jamaica, was wrecked on a reef on April 4, four of the crew drowned.

Year 1764. English ship *Peggy*, Captain M'Carthy, sailing from South Carolina to Lisbon, wrecked on a reef on March 18 and her hull slid off into seven fathoms of water but all the people on board were saved.

Year 1765. A snow of unknown registry, *Duke*, Captain French, sailing from South Carolina to Oporto, Portugal, was wrecked on a reef.

Year 1766. English merchantman *Fairfax*, Captain Copithorn, sailing from Virginia to Bristol, was wrecked at Bermuda but part of her cargo was saved.

Year 1766. English ship *Elizabeth*, Captain Trattle, sailing from New England to Antigua, was wrecked at Bermuda.

Year 1768. American ship *Penn*, sailing from North Carolina to Bristol, was wrecked on the reefs.

Year 1769. Two ships, sailing from Jamaica to London, were wrecked in December on a reef five or six miles northwest of the island: the *Martin*, Captain Mitchell, and an unidentified vessel. A few days later the English ship *Allitude*, Captain Rains, sailing from Carolina to Tortuga, wrecked near the two other ships.

Year 1775. English merchantman *Industry*, Captain Lowes, sailing from Limerick to Virginia, was wrecked at Bermuda on April 13, part of her cargo was saved.

Year 1777. English warship *H.M.S. Repulse*, 32 guns, Captain Henry Davies, foundered off Bermuda.

Year 1777. Spanish privateering vessel *Mark Antonio*, Captain Jean-Bautiste Hugonne, sailing from St. Eustatius to Cape Henlopen, was wrecked on the island on July 18.

Year 1779. English ship *Nancy*, Captain Manley, sailing from Jamaica to Bristol, was lost entering a port in Bermuda.

Year 1780. During a terrible hurricane on October 18, over 50 ships were wrecked or driven aground on the island.

Year 1781. English merchantman *Lord Frederick*, sailing from Clyde, Scotland, to Charleston, South Carolina, was wrecked at Bermuda.

Year 1783. Three English warships were lost on the island: *H.M.S. Cerberus*, a 32-gun frigate, Captain Sir Jacob Wheate, was wrecked shortly after leaving Castle Harbor; *H.M.S. Pallas*, 36 guns, Captain Christopher Parker, ran ashore on St. George's Isle; and the *H.M.S. Mentor*, 16 guns, Captain R. Tullidge, was wrecked on a reef.

Year 1783. A Dutch merchantman, *Stadt Cortrycht*, Captain Harmong, sailing from Dominica Island to Ostend, Holland, carrying a cargo of sugar, was wrecked on a reef while attempting to enter a harbor on June 24.

308

Year 1784. Two merchantmen were wrecked on the reefs of Bermuda: Scottish brig *Betsey*, Captain Camarn, sailing from St. Kitts to Cork, Ireland, lost in March, crew and most of cargo saved; and an Irish ship, *Lord Donegal*, Captain Campbell, sailing from Belfast to Virginia, lost on February 9, crew and small part of cargo saved.

Year 1786. American ship *Kingston*, Captain Farrer, sailing from North Carolina to Grenada Island, was lost off Bermuda but her people were saved.

Year 1787. A ship of unknown registry, *Swift*, Captain M'Donald, sailing from Grenada Island to Newfoundland, was lost off Bermuda but her crew was saved.

Year 1788. During a hurricane on July 26 a large number of ships were wrecked on the southwestern side of Bermuda.

Year 1700. French ship *Marie Therese*, Captain Guathier, sailing from Santo Domingo to Bordeaux, France, was lost near Bermuda, only a few bales of cotton were saved.

Year 1792. French ship *Grand Annibal*, Captain Caisergues, sailing from Santo Domingo to Marseilles, was lost off Bermuda.

Year 1792. French brig *Le Grand Aanictl*, 350 tons, sailing from Hispaniola to Marseilles with a rich cargo, struck a reef on July 4 off the west side of Bermuda. at a great distance from shore, then slid off into deep water. The captain and several passengers drowned but other survivors reached the island in a boat with only the clothes on their backs. (Note that this may be the same ship listed above as *Le Grand Aanictl*.)

Year 1794. English warship, the brig *Actif*, 10 guns, Captain John Harvey, foundered off Bermuda on November 26.

Year 1794. Two merchantmen of unknown registry were lost about the same time near the island: *George Douglas*, sailing from Havana to Newfoundland, was wrecked on a reef on the north side of the island, then slid off into deeper water; and the brig *Harriet*, Captain Monteath, was wrecked on the south side of the island.

Year 1795. Three merchantmen of unknown registry were lost around the island prior to June: *Minerva*, Captain Arnet, sailing from Norfolk, Virginia, to Tobago Island, was wrecked on a reef, crew and part of cargo saved; an unnamed brig of Captain Clark, sailing from Newhaven, England, to St. Vincent's Island, was wrecked on the north side of the island; and an unidentified ship sailing from Madeira Island to Baltimore.

Year 1796. Two American vessels were lost: the schooner *Polly*, coming from Norfolk, and the ship *Nancy*, Captain Mitchell, sailing from Philadelphia to Jamaica. The latter's crew was saved.

Year 1800. American brig *Humber*, Captain Clough, sailing from New York to Havana, was wrecked on a reef prior to April.

Year 1801. Three merchantmen were lost: American ship *Dispatch*, Captain Ramsey, sailing from Nevis Island to New England, wrecked on a reef, crew and part of cargo saved; a ship of unknown registry, *Ebenezer*, Captain Sharman, sailing to Santo Domingo; and another ship of unknown registry, the *Mary Ann*, Captain Greave, sailing from New York to Montserrat Island, only the crew was saved.

Year 1802. Two American merchantmen were lost on January 1 because of fog: brig *Commerce*, Captain English, sailing from New England to St. Croix Island; and the schooner *Roebuck*, Captain Forester, sailing from Boston to the West Indies, both wrecked on reefs, crews and part of cargoes saved.

Year 1803. American merchantman *Margaret*, Captain Muir, sailing from Virginia to Barbados, was lost near the island on January 19.

Year 1804. Two merchantmen were lost: English ship *Providence*, Captain Burnet (or Barnick), sailing from Havana to Spain, on October 20, only the crew was saved; and a ship of unknown registry, *Surprise*, Captain Renshaw, sailing from the Cape of Good Hope to Philadelphia, prior to July.

Year 1805. American ship *Hunter*, Captain Slout, sailing from New York to Martinique Island, was wrecked on November 30, crew and part of cargo saved.

Year 1806. French ship *Pamela*, Captain Demeul, sailing from Quebec to Jamaica, was lost prior to March. Two merchantmen of English registry were wrecked in December: *Loyal Sam*, coming from London with a valuable cargo, and the *Three Friends*, Captain Pullinge, coming from Philadelphia. Both were lost in gales.

Year 1807. Three ships were wrecked on the reefs: the English warship *H.M.S. Subtle*, eight guns, Captain William Dowers, lost on October 26 near Somerset Island; American ship *Rosannah*, Captain Mull, sailing from Baltimore to Venezuela, lost on February 23; and a ship of unknown registry, the *Merchant*, Captain Day, coming from New London, Connecticut, on March 21.

Year 1808. A ship of unknown registry, *Batavia*, Captain Houghton, sailing from Trinidad to Liverpool, was lost on the Bermuda bar, only the crew was saved.

Year 1809. English ship *William Grey*, Captain King, sailing to Jamaica, was wrecked on a reef on August 29 on the west side of the island, crew and most of cargo saved.

Year 1810. English merchantman *William & Mary*, Captain Clifton, with a cargo of sherry wine, was wrecked in February, crew and part of wine saved.

Year 1811. Three merchantmen of unknown registry were wrecked on reefs: small vessel *Montgomery*, Captain Bignell, coming from Bristol, four of the crew were saved and three drowned; ship *Frederick*, Captain White, sailing from New York to the West Indies, on February 1; and the ship *Eliza*, Captain Lord, sailing from New York to Guadeloupe, on April 30, but her cargo was saved.

Year 1812. Three ships were wrecked on the reefs: English warship *H.M.S. Barbados*, 28 guns, Captain Thomas Huskisson, lost on September 29 at Sable Island, only one of the crew of 195 was lost; Spanish ship *Pensacola del Sol*, sailing from Pensacola, Florida, to London, struck a reef on the west side of the island on March 29 but her cargo was saved; and another Spanish ship, *Antonia*, sailing from Havana to Tenerife in the Canary Islands, was wrecked on a reef north of the island on October 24; crew and small part of cargo saved.

Year 1813. During a hurricane that struck the island on August 1, a large number of ships were driven ashore or sunk in the harbor. Two English ships were wrecked on reefs: *Lady Emily*, a packet boat, was lost in June but the crew and passengers were saved; the merchantman *Pacific*, sailing from Halifax to Barbados, was lost on December 27, only the crew was saved.

Year 1815. During a hurricane on August 7, many vessels were driven ashore or sunk. On August 15 the English warship *H.M.S. Dominica*, 14 guns, Captain Richard Crawford, was wrecked on a reef.

310

Year 1816. English ship *Duke of Wellington*, Captain Williams, sailing from London for Bermuda and Jamaica, was wrecked on a reef in March off the west side of the island; only a small part of her stores was saved.

Year 1817. Three ships of unknown registry were lost: *Peter*, Captain Chadwick, coming from East Florida, wrecked on a reef in February; *Elizabeth*, Captain Largie, sailing from Barbados to America, on February 19; and the *Emma*, Captain Morgan, sailing from New York to St. Vincent's Island, wrecked on a reef on October 5, crew and part of cargo saved.

Year 1818. Six merchantmen were lost: English ship *Caesar*, Captain James Richardson, sailing from Newcastle, England, to Baltimore with a cargo of bricks, bottles, and grindstones, wrecked on a reef on May 17 but part of her cargo and rigging were saved (this site has been partially salvaged by Tucker); American ship *Hope*, coming from New York, was wrecked at the island on August 30 during a gale; English ship *Alfred the Great*, sailing from Jamaica to London, was wrecked on a reef on the west side of the island on September 8, part of her cargo was saved; English ship *Admiral Durham*, sailing from Demerara to Bermuda, wrecked during a gale on a reef off the west side of the island on December 23, one of the crew drowned and some of her cargo of rum was saved; the American ship *Mary*, sailing from New York to St. Thomas, and an unidentified English brig, coming from Barbados to Bermuda, wrecked on reefs off the southwestern point of the island on December 25.

Year 1819. Three merchant ships were lost: French ship *Lydia*, sailing from Bordeaux to New York, was lost near the island, crew, passengers, and part of cargo saved; a ship of unknown registry, *St. Helena*, sailing from Jamaica to Quebec, wrecked on a reef on May 18, only a small part of her cargo was saved; and English ship *Hamilton*, Captain Adams, coming from Antigua, was wrecked on the east side of the island.

Year 1821. American ship *Pallas*, coming from Savannah, was lost on June 17.

Year 1822. American brig *Indian Chief*, Captain M'Vicar, sailing from Jamaica to New Brunswick, was wrecked on a reef on the north end of the island on January 12.

Year 1823. Three merchantmen wrecked on the reefs: Dutch ship *Vriendscaap*, Captain de Jong, sailing from Surinam to Amsterdam, off the west end of the island on May 2; American schooner *Collector*, Captain Hall, sailing from St. John's, New Brunswick, to Bermuda and South America with a general cargo, on May 26; and the American ship *Mary*, Captain Campbell, sailing from Philadelphia to St. Thomas, off the northern part of the island on August 15, crew and part of cargo saved.

Year 1824. American ship *Cyno*, Captain Dessey, sailing from New York to St. Croix, was totally lost on a reef off the northwestern part of the island on August 5.

Famed Bermuda salvor Teddy Tucker poses with a 17th-century clay pipe that he recovered from a shipwreck and actually uses today.

Chapter Seven

The Bahamas

The Bahama Archipelago is unquestionably one of the best areas for working on shipwrecks in the Western Hemisphere. It has a marvelous combination of gin-clear water, close to ideal year-around weather conditions and a vast number of ancient shipwrecks. Its proximity to the United States is a big advantage for American divers, because there is less expense involved in working a wreck site close to home. For this reason, the Bahamas runs a close second to Florida for shipwreck search and salvage.

The biggest discovery of sunken treasure in the Bahamas is an on-going story about a wreck called the *Maravillas*. I discovered this fabulous galleon wreck in 1972 after years of searching, and the site is still yielding treasures today. For me the story began in 1960 while I was doing research in the General Archives of the Indies in Seville. Delving into primary documents, I found more than 15,000 pages of documents dealing with the *Maravillas*, as well as three contemporary charts showing her location. Despite all of these archival aids, it took me five years of determined searching before I finally found her.

This gold and emerald cross was found by Teddy Tucker in the wreck of the Spanish galleon *San Pedro*, lost in 1595 off the coast of Bermuda.

After bringing up what we then decided was several million dollars worth of treasure (at today's prices it would be more like $20 million), I had a falling out with the Bahama Government and was prevented from continuing my excavation of the wreck site. Several other firms followed behind me with significant finds. For about 10 years after this, the wreck was abandoned and forgotten.

In 1987 Marex International, Inc. of Memphis, Tennessee, decided to try their luck. In the past seven years, led by Herbo Humphries, they have recovered over $10 million more in treasure and expect to find at least another $100 million before the wreck is completely worked. Last summer while following a scattered trail of *Maravillas* treasures they chanced upon two 16th-century wrecks that have also yielded significant treasure.

As early as a century before Nassau was first settled by the English in the early 1700s, Bermudan wreckers established bases in different areas of the Bahamas and carried out salvage work. After Nassau was settled, wreck salvage work, or "wracking" as they called it, was the inhabitants' principal occupation until as late as the end of the American Civil War. Many of today's wealthy Bahamian families got their start through the "wracking" business. Even now Bahamian fishermen use their glass-bottom buckets not only to locate conch and turtles but in the hope of stumbling across a good treasure wreck. Tales of these fishermen's discoveries are as numerous as the Bahamas' islands and cays, but rarely can any of them be verified.

There are several exceptions, however, that I know about personally. About 10 years ago a fisherman from Grand Cay showed me some gold and silver bars and several hundred gold coins he had discovered somewhere nearby, but I never learned where he had found them. Fishermen in 1933 recovered a metal safe containing approximately $100,000 in American gold coins, dating from the American Civil War on a reef off the north side of Green Turtle Key. Several years later, another fisherman recovered "a boatload" of silver and gold bars off a reef in the Exuma Chain. Incredibly, all of this treasure was sold for its metal value alone.

After a storm in 1947 three Bahamian fishermen discovered five large silver bars and a substantial number of silver coins on a beach on the south side of Gorda Cay. News of their discovery spread quickly, and Art McKee, an American diver from Florida, appeared on the scene the following year. One of the fishermen showed McKee the location of two small ballast piles offshore from the area where they had discovered the treasure. They were the site of the two Spanish salvage boats that

316

had wrecked in 1657 while trying to carry some of the treasure salvaged off the galleon *Nuestra Señora de las Maravillas*, sunk north of Memory Rock in 1656.

McKee, equipped with helmet diving equipment, spent several days laboriously moving all the ballast rock. It was well worth the effort, for he discovered three silver bars, a number of iron cannon bars and some ceramic shards. Next, in 1950 two Nassau businessmen, Roscoe Thompson and Howard Lightbourn, claimed to have discovered another silver bar from one of the same ballast piles. However, rumor has it that their silver bar was actually one of the five the fishermen had found on the beach and that they bought it from them for only $50. During the past 20 years there have been at least two dozen expeditions around Gorda Key, but no one has reported making any other important discoveries.

Four American divers, Gary Simmons, Dick Tindale, Jack Slack and Bissel Shaefer, announced in January 1965 that they had accidentally stumbled on a treasure wreck near Lucaya Beach and recovered an immense treasure. At first their find was reported to be worth over $20 million, but this amount gradually dwindled. Several numismatists hired by the Bahamian government placed the find's total value at only $40,000, a far cry from $20 million. Actually, the find might someday reach $20 million if this group or another group eventually discovers the main section of the wreck from which their silver coins came or the other Spanish galleon that sank nearby at the time. Both galleons, carrying a great deal of treasure, were captured in 1628 by a Dutch fleet in Matanzas Bay, Cuba, and then lost while returning to Holland with the Dutch fleet.

In 1968 Dr. Manson Valentine and Dimitri Rebikoff discovered several submerged buildings off the northern tip of Andros Island and what initially appeared to be an ancient seaport off the west end of Bimini. The press trumpeted that they had found the sunken continent of Atlantis. They made no such claim, although they were convinced the remains were of pre-Columbian origin.

No permission is required for divers to explore for shipwrecks in the Bahamas. To salvage a wreck, however, a permit must be obtained from the Ministry of Transportation. Permits are granted on each wreck site for periods of five years. Salvors keep 75 percent of what is recovered, and the Bahamian government receives 25 percent. Several years ago an American diver who salvaged a shipwreck without a permit was arrested and sentenced to a year in prison.

In my files I have over 3,000 Bahamian shipwrecks, but I have selected for the following list only those of which I have a fairly accurate location or those of special importance.

Shipwrecks in Bahamian Waters

Year 1500. In July or August, two unidentified caravels of the four sailing in the squadron of Vicente Yañez Pinzón, from Brazil to Spain, were wrecked near Crooked Island.

Year 1528. Spanish nao *Santa María de la Concepción*, 110 tons, 14 iron cannon, Captain Blas de Navarra Oleo, sailing directly from Mexico for Spain was lost somewhere near a small cay to the south of Bimini in a storm. It carried what was described as a "vast amount of Aztec treasures" which Cortez and his conquistadors had plundered from Montezuma and his people, It must have been a very large amount as the crew had to jettison most of the ship's ballast in Veracruz because of the treasure's weight.

Year 1551. Unidentified galleon, owned by the viceroy of Mexico, Don Luis de Velasco, sailing in the Nueva España Flota, commanded by Captain-General Sancho de Viedma, separated from the convoy during a storm, was wrecked on Silver Shoals, then sank in deeper water. Divers were able to recover only 150,000 pesos of the treasure it carried.

Year 1552. Portuguese slave ship *San Anton Do Brasil*, also known as *El Dorado*, 120 tons, number of cannon unknown, sailed from the west coast of Africa to Nombre de Diós, Panama, with a cargo of slaves. While in port it was seized by the port captain and placed in the service of the Spanish Crown. An immense Inca treasure had been discovered in a cave near Cuzco, Peru, and rather than wait for the annual treasure fleet to arrive to carry it to Spain, it was decided to use this Portuguese ship. Most of the treasure consisted of gold statues, ingots and jewelry valued at over 780,000 castellanos. The ship made a brief stop at Cartagena, Colombia, where it picked up quantities of pearls from Margarita Island and an undisclosed amount of gold and emeralds from Bogota. The ship wrecked eight miles north of Bimini in a storm. A shoal in this area is named El Dorado Shoal after this famous disaster. In 1981 I located three of the anchors from the *El Dorado* wreck using a magnetometer. Then I was attacked by a mako shark which ripped open my upper arm and shoulder. By the time I returned to the wreck several weeks later the anchors had disappeared and the location was lost. Months of magnetometer work failed to find her because all the cannon are bronze and the only ferrous materials on the wreck were the anchors which had been removed. Since my original discovery a number of groups have unsuccessfully sought the wreck.

Year 1554. Two unidentified ships carrying a great amount of silver suffered from a storm in the Bahama Channel and soon after were wrecked on one of the Bahama islands near Hispaniola, but all the persons and treasure were taken ashore. A small frigate was made from the remains of both wrecks and sent to Cuba, but it sank on the way and only two were saved from it. Salvors were sent from Cuba but they were unable to locate the island where the survivors and silver were marooned.

Year 1559 Spanish galleon, *Santa María De Los Remedios*, 300 tons, captain's identity and number of persons aboard not known, was carrying 32 iron cannon and sailing between Veracruz and Spain without making the customary stop at Havana because pirates were reported in that area. She was carrying 768,440 pesos in gold and silver, plus an unspecified amount of exotic goods from the Orient such as porcelain, jewelry, jade, silks and spices. She was working her way up the Bahama Channel in a convoy when she became separated from the convoy's other 87 vessels in a bad storm which destroyed the rudder and one of her masts. Wind and currents drove the *Remedios* on a reef three to four leagues east of Great Issacs cay near the northwestern edge of the Great Bahama Bank. A few survivors managed to reach Cuba in a ship's longboat but repeated attempts failed to locate the wreck.

Year 1564. Spanish galleon *Santa Clara*, 300 tons, Captain Juan Díaz Bozino was carrying 1,217,000 pesos in treasure from South America and sailing in the fleet commanded by Captain General Estéban de las Alas. Driven off course during a storm she wrecked and was lost several miles north of Memory Rock on the Little Bahama Bank — most likely on the reef called the Dry Bar. Salvors sent to recover her treasure initially reported they had located her and were recovering all her treasure but when it was taken to Havana, royal officials found the salvaged treasure was from another Spanish wreck which had disappeared without trace four years earlier. Salvors returned to the area the following season but failed to find any traces of the Santa Clara.

Year 1567. Unidentified urca of Captain Gonzalo de Peñalosa was wrecked on Cayo Romano in the Little Bahama Channel.

Year 1599. A Spanish merchant ship owned by Hernando del Castillo was sailing to Havana when it was captured by some pirates. The Spaniards and their cargo were taken aboard the pirate vessel, which soon after anchored on Great Inagua Island. The Spaniards escaped in a small boat and headed for Cuba, but en route they stopped at a large cay for water and accidentally discovered an enormous treasure of gold and silver bars and pieces of artillery from ships that must have wrecked there. They took some of the treasure with them, then other vessels were sent from Cuba and picked up the remainder.

Year 1628. Dutch privateers commanded by Admiral Piet Heyn captured the entire Spanish treasure fleet in Matanzas Bay, Cuba, where the Spaniards had run the ships aground. Five of the largest were refloated by the Dutch who couldn't cram all the plunder on their own ships. A storm struck the victorious fleet when it was about to pass Grand Bahama Island and two of the richly laden Spanish galleons, the *Santa Gertrudes* and the *Santa Ana*, both of 600 tons, were separated from the convoy and driven eastward. One first struck on a shallow reef off present-day Lucaya (Freeport) and then wrecked about three miles to the east. The other was reported to have wrecked "within a cannon shot distance" to the east of the first one. They would be in the vicinity of Pinder Point Village — where there is a place still named Golden Rock because, according to local lore, fishermen about 150 years ago found a large amount of gold and silver on the sea floor.

Year 1641. Galleon *N.S. de la Concepción*, 680 tons, Captain Hernando Rodríguez, sailing in the Nueva España Flota of Captain-General Juan de Campos, was separated from the convoy during a storm in the Bahama Channel and drifted without masts or rudder until wrecking on the north side of Silver

Shoals. Most of the 600 persons aboard managed to swim to a nearby sandbar. Makeshift rafts and boats were constructed from the wreck, and they carried about 200 of the survivors toward Santo Domingo, but only a few ever reached safety. By the time a rescue vessel reached the area, everyone on the sandbar had perished. Weather prevented salvage operations for several months, and when the weather finally moderated, the sandbar had been washed away and the rescuers couldn't locate the site. The story of Sir William Phips' recovery of the treasure from this galleon in 1687 is well-known, but for some reason a myth has persisted that he did not recover it all. The fact is that he recovered almost twice the amount declared in the ship's registers and other salvors, before and after Phips, recovered considerable amounts of treasure and there is reason to believe more remains.

Year 1644. Three unidentified English privateers in the squadron of General Jacob Jackson were wrecked on Arcas Reef in the Old Bahama Channel.

Year 1656. Galleon *N.S. de la Maravillas*, 650 tons, Admiral Mathias de Orellanas, was the Almiranta in the Tierra Firme Armada of Captain-General Marquis de Montenegro, and sank in five or six fathoms of water on the Little Bahama Bank, about 20 miles north of Memory Rock, after first colliding with another galleon during the night when the whole convoy found itself in shallow water and veered seaward. Of the more than 700 persons on this ship, only 56 were saved. Spaniards began salvage operations soon afterward and, during the next three years, recovered over one million of the five million pesos of treasure on this wreck.

When shifting sands covered the wreck over completely, they had to abandon future salvage operations. Phips stopped at the site of this wreck in 1681, but was able to recover only a small amount of silver specie because of the sand over it. In modern times, many treasure hunters have searched for this wreck, but most of them looked in the Florida Keys where other authors placed the site of the wreck until I discovered documents in Spain that told of its true location. I passed this information on to a group from Miami in 1960 and they spent several years searching for the wreck, but to no avail. They in turn gave it to others. I located it in 1972.

In 1657 two small salvage vessels, carrying some of the treasure from this wreck to Puerto Rico, were wrecked on the south side of Gorda Cay. The survivors buried some of the treasure on the cay and most of it, as well as most of what was still on the wrecks, was recovered the following year. The three silver bars discovered by Art McKee, and the one by Roscoe Thompson and Howard Lightbourn, came from these two wrecks.

Year about 1660. An unidentified English ship, Captain Sayle, was wrecked on Eleuthera Island. Sayle went to Virginia in a small boat, returning later in a larger vessel to rescue the survivors.

Year 1669. Spanish galleon *N.S. de Buena Esperanza*, 650 tons, 32 cannon, Captain Domingo Ypenarreita, carrying 3,250,000 pesos in treasure was wrecked on the Little Bahama Bank near the edge of the Gulf Stream in less than five fathoms of water. The location is 10 to 12 miles north of Memory Rock. Of the 478 souls aboard only 63 were rescued by another ship in the same convoy. When salvors from Havana found the wreck site in 1670 it was almost totally covered over by sand and they only recovered two anchors. The following year another salvage attempt was made but no trace of the wreck was found.

Year 1669. English ship *Port Royal*, Captain John Russel, was wrecked in latitude 26 degrees and 14 minutes at Munsake Island, near Abaco, on January 12. Modern charts do not show an island by this name.

Year before 1687. On a chart drawn in 1687 by a Captain Solman of the Little Bahama Bank, three shipwreck locations are shown: Copper Wreck, bearing 10 degrees from Memory Rock, in latitude 27002'11" North, about 1 1/2 miles from the edge of the bank; Genovese Wreck, bearing northwest by about 3 1/2 English leagues from the Copper Wreck, in latitude 27010'11" North, about half a mile from the edge of the bank; Plate Wreck, bearing 15 degrees and 10 nautical miles from the Genovese Wreck, in about 6 fathoms of water, in latitude 27020'11" North, and about three nautical miles from the edge of the bank.

Year 1694. Dutch merchantman *Jufron Gertrud*, Captain Derrick Loffrey, carrying 74,000 pieces of eight and a great quantity of merchandise, was wrecked near Great Isaac Cay. Survivors reached Nassau in a small boat and salvors returned to the wreck, recovering all of the treasure and most of her cargo. They sighted another wreck nearby and again recovered things of value.

Year 1702. Unidentified American brigantine was chased by pirates and forced to run aground on Eleuthera Island, where they plundered her. They also forced another unidentified ship to wreck at Mayaguana Island, where they burned her to the waterline after plundering her.

Year 1704. A Bermudan privateer commanded by Captain Peniston captured an unidentified French merchantman sailing from Martinique to France with a cargo of sugar, indigo, cocoa and drugs. After some of the cargo was transferred to the privateer's vessel, the French ship was wrecked on Great Abaco Island.

Year 1705. English packet boat *Barbadoes* was wrecked December 28 on Great Inagua Island, mail and money saved.

Year 1713. Large French merchantman, *Count de Paix*, Captain Lewis Doyer, sailing from Hispaniola to France with a cargo of gold dust, ambergris, sugar, indigo and other products, was wrecked on Great Inagua and only the gold dust and ambergris was saved.

Year 1714. Galleon *San Juan Evangelista*, part of the Armada de Barlovento, sailing from Veracruz to Puerto Rico and Santo Domingo with 300,000 pesos in treasure to pay the royal officials and military at both islands, was struck by a storm in the Bahama Channel and wrecked in 27 degrees of latitude in four fathoms of water near Grand Bahama Island. Salvors recovered all of the treasure and the ship's cannon.

Year 1715. An unidentified Spanish warship with 200 men aboard, sailing from Havana to St. Augustine, Florida, with chests of silver specie to pay the garrison there, was wrecked on the Little Bahama Bank. Salvors from Havana recovered all of the treasure and then burned the wreck.

Year 1723. Ship identified only by the name *Petatch*, which may be the English spelling for a "patache" was wrecked near Bimini.

Year 1724. Unidentified French frigate was wrecked at Caye de Argent (or Silver Cay), on the Caicos Bank.

Year 1731. English merchantman *Bridget & Kitty*, Captain Minshall, sailing from Jamaica to Liverpool, was wrecked on Little Inagua Island but her crew were saved.

Year 1741. Unidentified Spanish nao was wrecked on Lobos Cay, near the Old Bahama Channel.

Year 1744. An unidentified Spanish merchantman of 300 tons and 200 men, sailing from Cadíz for Mexico with a cargo valued at over 300,000 pounds sterling, was forced ashore on Sugar Cay by the famous American privateer Captain Lamprier, whose ship was also wrecked nearby.

Year 1750. English merchantman *Duke of Cumberland*, Captain Prenton, sailing from Jamaica to London, was lost March 27 on the Acklin Keys, crew and part of cargo saved.

Year 1751. English merchantman *Katherine*, Captain Richards, sailing from Jamaica to Bristol, was lost on Great Inagua Island; the crew was saved.

Year 1751. English merchantman *Duncanon*, Captain Elphinston, sailing from Jamaica to London, was lost on the Hogsties in the Windward Passage but the crew were saved.

Year 1751. English merchantman *Jane*, Captain Caton, sailing from Jamaica to London, was wrecked off Acklin's Key but the crew was saved by a French vessel.

Year 1751. English ship *Warwick*, Captain Manepenny, sailing from Philadelphia to Hispaniola, was lost August 8 at Atwood Key but the crew was saved.

Year 1752. English merchantman *Lord Duplin*, Captain Thompson, sailing from Jamaica to Liverpool, was wrecked on the Hogsties but the crew were saved.

Year 1753. American merchantman *Polly*, Captain Walker, sailing from Rhode Island to Jamaica, was lost on Silver Shoals near the Spanish galleon that wrecked there in 1641.

Year 1754. French merchantman *Anna Maria*, sailing from Hispaniola to France with a cargo of indigo and sugar, was wrecked at Crooked Island.

Year 1755. A ship of unknown registry, *John and Rebecca*, Captain Rice, sailing from Jamaica to Philadelphia, was lost June 8 on Great Inagua Island.

Year 1758. Spanish ship *Caesar*, sailing from Havana to Spain, was lost on Annagabes Island but her crew was saved. This island has a different name today, as no island by this name is shown on any charts of the Bahamas.

Year 1758. A ship of unknown registry, *St. Francis*, sailing from Philadelphia to Antigua was forced ashore on Sandy Cay by a French privateer.

Year 1760. A ship of unknown registry, *Prince Ferdinand*, Captain Caznean, sailing from Boston to Jamaica, lost January 17 on Great Inagua Island but the crew was saved.

Year 1761. English merchantman *Eagle Gally*, Captain Nash, sailing from Jamaica to Bristol, was wrecked on the Hogsties but her crew was saved.

Year 1762. English merchantman *Gambia*, Captain Whiting, sailing from Jamaica to Bristol, was lost on West Caicos Island but the crew was saved.

Year 1763. English ship *Peter Beckford*, Captain Lovelace, sailing from Jamaica to London, was lost on a reef at San Salvador Island.

Year 1763. English merchantman *Patty*, Captain Clark, sailing from Bristol, was lost near Nassau.

Year 1764. Large French ship *Le Bernard*, sailing from Hispaniola to France, was totally lost July 4 on Turks Island.

Year 1765. English merchantman *Medway Planter*, Captain Leslie, sailing from Jamaica to London, was lost April 25 on a reef near Cat Island but her crew was saved.

Year 1765. A very large Spanish galleon named *El Santiago El Grande* was sailing between Havana and Spain with over two million pesos in treasure aboard when she wrecked and went down in 17 feet of water on the Great Bahama Bank 35 to 40 miles southeast of Bimini and seven miles southeast of Beak Cay in the Riding Rock Chain. Huge seas drove the ship far onto the shallow bank where it broke up and was covered by shifting sands. Within a few years of the disaster the exact location of this wreck appeared on printed navigation charts and then on countless subsequent charts. Despite this pinpoint location, recurring attempts by contemporary and modern salvors have failed to locate this rich wreck.

Year 1768. English merchantman *Defiance*, Captain Carook, sailing from Honduras to London, was lost March 21 on the Little Bahama Bank, but her crew was saved.

Year 1768. Two American ships were lost on the Caicos Bank: *Beggars Benizon*, Captain Rogers, lost May 31 while sailing from Charleston, South Carolina, to Jamaica; and *The Charm*, Captain Peggy Stinton, sailing from North Carolina to Jamaica.

Year 1769. English merchantman *Meylor*, Captain Tyler, sailing from Bristol and Boston to Jamaica, was lost at Caicos but her crew was saved.

Year 1769. American ship *Nancy Gaer*, sailing from Hispaniola to Georgia, lost May 17 on Great Inagua Island but her crew was saved.

Year 1770. A large unidentified merchant sloop was wrecked on a reef at Long Key and salvors recovered several chests of Spanish silver species from it.

Year 1772. English merchantman *Merredith*, Captain Peacock, sailing from Jamaica to London, was lost on San Salvador Island and her cargo totally lost, but crew saved.

Year 1772. An unidentified three-decked merchantman was lost on the southwest cay of the Caicos Bank.

Year 1773. English merchantman *John*, Captain Madge, sailing from Jamaica to Bristol, was lost off Gun Cay, to the south of Bimini, but her crew was saved.

Year 1774. A ship of unknown registry, *Palliser*, was lost on New Providence Island.

Year 1774. Three unidentified ships were wrecked on the Little Bahama Bank, north of Memory Rock, but the current was too strong for several passing ships to send rescue boats.

Year 1774. Two English ships were lost on Great Inagua Island: *Hanover Planter*, Captain M'Cullock, sailing from Jamaica to Philadelphia, crew and cargo saved; and the *Martha*, Captain M'Intosh, sailing from Jamaica to London, most of her cargo of rum and sugar saved.

Year 1775. During a hurricane on November 2, at least 11 merchantmen and several English warships were lost in the Windward Passage near the Caicos Islands.

Year 1775. A ship of unknown registry, *Expectation*, Captain Wake, was lost August 10 on the windward side of Long Island, crew and part of cargo saved.

Year 1775. Two ships were lost on the Hogsties: unidentified French ship coming from Port au Prince, and English merchantman *Port Morant*, Captain Raffles, from Jamaica to London, carrying a cargo of rum and sugar, crew clung to rocks for 10 days until rescued.

Year 1780. English warship *H.M.S. Sterling Castle*, lost October 6 on Silver Shoals and went to pieces in a few minutes, only a small number were saved after floating on wreckage for days.

Year 1781. American ship *Pink*, Captain Hasrwen, sailing from New York to Jamaica, was lost in January on Silver Shoals but her crew was saved.

Year 1784. A ship of unknown registry, *David*, Captain Boyd, was lost April 30 at New Providence Island.

Year 1785. French ship *Marquis de Castries*, sailing from Cape Fran, Hispaniola, to France, was totally lost on the Caicos.

Year 1785. Three ships were lost at New Providence Island: English transport *Hope Sherrer*, during a hurricane in September, totally lost; a ship of unknown registry, *Sally*, Captain Croskill, wrecked at Nassau on October 24; and American ship *Rodney*, Captain Jenkins, sailing from Florida to Jamaica, sprung a leak and sank on the Samphire reefs near Nassau.

Year 1786. Bahamian ship *Bahama*, sailing from Honduras to Nassau, was totally lost during a gale at Bimini on March 4.

Year 1786. American merchantmen were lost at Turks Island: *Sally*, Captain Alexander, sailing from Jamaica to Maryland; and the *Porgey*, Captain Dickson, sailing from New York to Jamaica.

Year 1787. English merchantman *Charlotte*, Captain Potter, sailing to London, and several unidentified ships were lost at Nassau.

Year 1787. Large three-decked English merchantman was wrecked on the south end of Acklins Key, but her crew was saved.

Year 1787. Three ships were lost on Great Inagua Island: American ship *Mercury*, Captain Hemsley, sailing from Charleston, South Carolina, to Jamaica; English ship *Jane*, coming from Jamaica; and an unidentified French brig, most of crew and part of cargo saved.

Year 1788. English merchantman *Lord North*, Captain Maver, sailing from Liverpool for Nassau, was lost on San Salvador Island but part of her cargo was salvaged.

Year 1788. Spanish brigantine of war, *Infanta*, 18 cannon, Captain Casmiro de Madrid, was wrecked on the reefs of Little Inagua Island, only the crew was saved.

Year 1789. French ship *Bonne Mere*, 350 tons, Captain David, sailing from Hispaniola to France, was totally lost on San Salvador.

Year 1790. English merchantman *Triton*, sailing from Jamaica to England, lost June 19 on the Hogsties, crew and part of cargo saved.

Year 1790. French ship *Le Belisaire*, Captain Kelly, sailing from Hispaniola to Philadelphia, was lost on Salt Pond Reef, crew and part of cargo saved.

Year 1790. English warship *H.M.S. Endymion*, Captain Woodriff, wrecked on a shoal 4 miles southwest of Sand Key, near Turks Island, in nine feet of water, but her crew was saved.

Year 1791. Four ships were wrecked on Great Inagua Island: American ship *St. George*, Captain Vincent, sailing from Jamaica to North Carolina, part of her cargo was saved; English merchantman *Simon Taylor*, carrying cargo of rum and cotton, on May 25, passengers and crew were saved; an unidentified French frigate, sailing from Hispaniola to France, on May 10, troops and crew all saved; and the French warship *La Fouvette*, 20 guns, sailing from Hispaniola to France, on November 26. After jettisoning all of her guns, provisions, water casks and part of her ballast, she got off the reef and went to Jamaica for repairs.

Year 1791. Irish merchantman *Two Sisters*, Captain Sedley, sailing from Cork to Nassau, lost at Royal Island, near New Providence Island.

Year 1791. Two ships were lost near the northeastern end of Turks Island: American brig *Mary*, Captain Telfair, sailing from New York to Jamaica, on October 25; and the English brig *Dartmouth*, Captain Kimm, on October 26.

Year 1791. Two ships were lost near Great Abaco Island: American ship *Robert & Mary*, Captain Cameron, sailing from Wilmington to Barbados, on the North Cay near the island; and the English merchantman *Concord*, Captain Forresdale, sailing from London to Nassau, close to the island, part of her cargo was saved.

Year 1792. French slave ship *L'Armitie*, Captain Jabalet, sailing from Africa to Havana with a cargo of slaves and ivory, lost near Cay Santo Domingo in the Old Bahama Channel.

Year 1792. American ship *Three Sisters*, Captain Spears, sailing from South Carolina to Nassau, lost on Guana Cay but her crew was saved.

Year 1792. English merchantman *Cohen*, Captain Davis, sailing from Jamaica to Liverpool, lost near Fish Key.

Year 1792. Canadian ship *Felicity*, Captain Doty, coming from New Brunswick, Canada, lost near Turks Island.

Year 1792. French ship *Neckar*, Captain Voltearo, sailing from Santo Domingo to France, was wrecked on the Hogsties.

Year 1792. Two ships wrecked on Great Inagua Island: French merchantman *Patrice*, Captain Largement, from Hispaniola to France; and the American ship *Lark*, Captain Barry, from Santo Domingo to New England.

Year 1792. Two ships were lost on the Caicos Bank: English ship *Friendship*, Captain Riche, sailing from Philadelphia to Jamaica, on the Great Caicos Reef; and an unidentified merchantman on the southwestern part of the bank.

Year 1793. American ship *Hannah*, Captain Bright, from Hispaniola to Wilmington, lost on Long Island. Her crew was lost.

Year 1794. English merchantman *Active*, Captain Howard, sailing from Jamaica to London, wrecked at Cat Cay, south of Bimini, part of her cargo was saved.

Year 1794. American ship *Calcutta*, Captain Orange, sailing from New York to Havana, was lost on the Atwood Keys.

Year 1794. A ship of unknown registry, *Eliza*, Captain Huggins, sailing from Nassau to Santo Domingo, lost on the Crooked Island Reef.

Year 1796. English warship *H.M.S. Narcissus*, 24 guns, Captain Percy Fraser, wrecked on Sandy Key, near Nassau, her crew was saved.

Year 1796. Two ships were lost on the Great Inagua Island reef: English merchantman *Hestor*, Captain Pearson, sailing from Santo Domingo to London, in July, crew was saved; and the American ship *Eagle*, Captain Byrnes, sailing from Santo Domingo to Baltimore; only a small part of her cargo was saved.

Year 1797. Two ships lost on Great Inagua Island: Jamaican privateer *Nelly*, sailing from Jamaica to Nassau, and the American schooner *William*, sailing from Baltimore, most of her cargo was saved.

Year 1798. American ship *Jenny*, Captain Knox, sailing from Havana to Philadelphia, wrecked on Mantanilla Reef, on the Little Bahama Bank, but her crew was saved.

Year 1798. A ship of unknown registry, *Eliza*, Captain Grant, sailing from the Azores to Santo Domingo, lost September on Grand Caicos Island but her crew was saved.

Year 1799. English merchantman *Cecilia*, Captain Roach, sailing from Jamaica to Liverpool, lost on the Hogsties, her crew was saved.

Year 1799. American ship *Hamilton*, Captain Noval, sailing from Savannah to Jamaica, lost on the Caicos Bank.

Year 1800. English merchantman *Doudswell*, Captain M'Lean, coming from London, was lost at New Providence Island but her crew was saved.

Year 1800. During August the English warship *H.M.S. Lowestoffe* and eight merchantmen carrying cargoes of colonial produce valued at over 600,000 pounds sterling were totally wrecked on Great Inagua Island.

Year 1801. During a hurricane in July over 120 ships of various descriptions and sizes were wrecked, sunk or thrown on the beach near and at Nassau. Only a slave ship named *George* was identified.

Year 1801. English merchantman *Supply*, Captain Wallace, sailing from Honduras to London, was wrecked at Mohairs Key, near New Providence Island.

Year 1801. In December a large English merchantman coming from Jamaica was wrecked on the Hogsties but slipped off the reef and sank in deeper water before she could be identified.

Year 1801. American ship *Endeavour*, Captain Russel, sailing from North Carolina to the Bahamas, was lost on Long Island.

Year 1801. Three American ships were lost near Little Caicos Island: *Acress*, Captain Lynch, sailing from New York to Jamaica, on July 25; *Hope*, Captain Edmoundson, and the *Hannah*, Captain Larson, both sailing from Philadelphia to Jamaica.

Year 1801. Six English merchantmen were wrecked at the same time, August 10, on the reefs of Great Inagua Island: *Auspicious*, Captain Procton; *Milton*, Captain Robley; *Jason*, Captain Watt; *Bushy Park*, Captain Brown; *Fanny*, Captain Warden, and an unidentified ship.

Year 1802. Spanish merchantman *Argonauta*, carrying a very rich cargo, totally lost at Mantanilla Reef, on the Little Bahama Bank.

Year 1802. English merchantman *Mars*, Captain Patterson, sailing from Jamaica to London, wrecked on the Hogsties, part of her cargo was saved.

Year 1802. Three ships were lost near New Providence Island: American ship *Fancy*, Captain Wilson, coming from Philadelphia; English slave ship *Agnes*, Captain Kitts, coming from Africa, slaves and crew saved; and the English merchantman Ranger, *Captain Lea*, arriving from London.

Year 1802. Two ships lost at Turks Island: Canadian ship *Minerva*, Captain Potter, coming from New Brunswick, in January; and the American ship *Nancy*, Captain Nevesin, sailing from Virginia to Jamaica, on October 28.

Year 1802. American ship *General Oglethorp*, sailing from Charleston, South Carolina, to Havana, wrecked on a reef six miles north of Whale Key and quickly went to pieces, 10 crewmen and 13 slaves drowned. In the same area, five or six other ships were also lost, one of which was an African slave ship.

Year 1803. Two American merchantmen were wrecked on Great Abaco Island: *Lilly*, Captain M'Camen, sailing from Georgia to Nassau, on December 5; and the *Adventure*, Captain Bashford, sailing from Charleston to Havana.

Year 1804. English ship *Morne Fortunee*, Captain Dale, lost December 3 at Crooked Island.

Year 1804. Two American ships were wrecked on Great Inagua Island: *Lark*, Captain Swan, on February 16, and the *Thomas*, Captain Cobb, on February 5, both sailing from Virginia to Jamaica.

Year 1805. Two Jamaican ships were lost at Fortune Island: *Ruby*, Captain M'Intosh, and the *John*, Captain Williamsboth bound for the United States.

Year 1805. American ship *Zephyr*, Captain Pace, sailing from Virginia to Jamaica, was lost on Grand Caicos Island.

Year 1806. American merchantman, *Pyomingo*, Captain Latimer, sailing from London to New Orleans, was wrecked in the Berry Islands.

Year 1806. American ship *Jefferson*, sailing from New York to Jamaica, was totally lost February 14 on the Mayaguana Reef.

Year 1806. Three ships wrecked on Turks Island: American ship *Heron*, Captain Cullum, sailing from Wilmington to Jamaica; English merchantman *Harnet*, Captain Curry, sailing from Jamaica to Halifax; and the Canadian ship *Ann*, Captain Mackie, sailing from Quebec to Jamaica, but part of her cargo was saved.

Year 1806. Seven ships lost on the Caicos Bank: American merchantman *Eagle*, Captain Toby, sailing from Boston to Jamaica, on July 27; Canadian ship *Jane*, Captain Boyd, sailing from Halifax to Jamaica, on February 19, crew saved; English ship *Martha*, Captain Yates, coming from Liverpool; and four unidentified ships.

Year 1806. American merchantman *Polly*, Captain Bigby, sailing from Jamaica to Wilmington, on September 13; English ship *Speedwell*, Captain Fairbotham, sailing from Jamaica to Liverpool, during a hurricane on September 13; and the English ship *Mentor*, Captain Bellowly, carrying the cotton and stores salvaged from the wreck of the *Speedwell*.

Year 1806. Four ships were wrecked on Great Inagua Island: American merchantman *Isaac*, Captain Pearson, sailing from Philadelphia to Jamaica, on September 15; American ship *Rattlesnake*, Captain Bessel, sailing from Jamaica to North Carolina, in September; American ship *Brandy Wine*, Captain Miller, sailing from New York to Jamaica; and the English warship *H.M.S. Wolfe*, a sloop of 18 guns, Captain G. C. Mackenzie, 121 in the crew, none of which was lost, on September 4.

Year 1807. American ship *Franklin*, sailing from New York to Jamaica, lost February 26 on Great Inagua Island, the crew was saved.

Year 1807. English merchantman *Harmony*, sailing from Bristol to the West Indies, was totally lost in the Berry Islands, the crew was saved.

Year 1807. Four ships lost on the Caicos Bank: American packet *John*, Captain Sabe, sailing from Washington to Jamaica, lost April 14; a ship of unknown registry, *Martha*, Captain Jackson, coming from St. Vincent Island, the crew was saved; American ship *Four Friends*, Captain Jouffet, sailing from South Carolina to Jamaica, crew and cargo saved; and the English merchantman *Lady Warren*, Captain Kingsbury, sailing from Santo Domingo to London, on November 28, crew and passengers saved.

Year 1807. English merchantman *Sir Charles Hamilton*, sailing from Liverpool to Santo Domingo, was totally lost on Turks Island.

Year 1808. English warship *H.M.S. Bermuda*, 18-gun schooner, Captain William Henry Byam, wrecked April 22 at Memory Rock, on the Little Bahama Bank, the crew was saved. (Note: Within a 300-yard radius of Memory Rock there are seven old shipwrecks; all appear to have been thoroughly salvaged.)

Year 1808. American ship *Hiram*, Captain Anner, sailing from New York to Havana, lost July 21 on Great Abaco Island, crew and part of cargo saved.

Year 1808. English ship *Elizabeth and Mary*, Captain Graff, sailing from Haiti and Jamaica to London, wrecked April 23 on Grand Caicos Island.

Year 1809. English merchantman *Victorina*, sailing from Liverpool to New Providence Island, wrecked on the west end of this island, December 9.

Year 1809. American merchantman *Mary*, Captain Smith, sailing from Cape François, Hispaniola, to Philadelphia, lost on the Caicos Bank; crew was saved.

Year 1809. Two ships wrecked on Turks Island: English merchantman *John*, Captain Yates, sailing from Liverpool to Nassau, on August 13; crew and part of cargo saved; and the American ship *Ann*, Captain Nixon, sailing from Amelia Island, Florida, to Jamaica, on May 15, crew and cargo saved.

Year 1810. A ship of unknown registry, *Orion*, Captain Brown, sailing from Philadelphia to Havana, was wrecked October 28 on Pelican Key, four of the crew drowned.

Year 1810. English merchantman *Ann*, Captain Robins, sailing from Santo Domingo to Bristol, wrecked October 27 in the Berry Islands, crew and part of cargo saved.

Year 1810. Two ships wrecked at New Providence Island: a ship of unknown registry, *Olympus*, sailing from New Orleans to England, wrecked in November; and the English ship *Three Brothers*.

Year 1810. English ship *Good Hope*, Captain Folger, sailing from London to Baltimore, lost near San Salvador Island, October 30, the crew was saved.

Year 1810. French ship *Transit*, Captain Vaux, coming from Haiti, totally lost on a reef off the southwestern end of Great Inagua Island.

Year 1810. English merchantman *Clarendon*, sailing from Jamaica to London, lost December 11 at Atwood Key, the crew was saved.

Year 1810. Two ships lost at Turks Island: American ship *Orient*, Captain Hunter, sailing from New York to Jamaica, the crew was saved; and the English ship *Schomer*, Captain Howe, sailing from Haiti to London, September 20, the crew was saved.

Year 1810. Two American merchantmen wrecked near Great Abaco Island: schooner *Elizabeth Ann*, Captain Blake, coming from Haiti, November 1; and the *Convention*, Captain Allen, sailing from New York to Havana, October 24.

Year 1811. American merchantman *Union*, Captain M'Known, sailing from Virginia to Jamaica, wrecked January 21 on Great Caicos Reef, the crew was saved.

Year 1811. English packet boat *Prince of Wales*, Captain Paquet, coming from Jamaica, wrecked on the Great Inagua Island Reef on July 19, crew, passengers, mail, and specie saved.

Year 1811. Two ships lost near Turks Island: American ship *Fox*, Captain Lippcatt, sailing from New York to Jamaica, December 23, the crew was saved; and the Canadian ship *Harmony*, Captain Penniston, sailing from Newfoundland to Jamaica.

Year 1812. English warship *H.M.S. Southampton*, 32 cannon and commanded by Captain Sir James Lucas Leo, was sailing between Jamaica and England carrying "68 chests of Spanish specie" when she wrecked on a reef which still bears her name, about nine miles north of Conception Island. The exact position given by the ship's navigator for the wreck was 24 degrees and three minutes north latitude and 69 degrees and 57 minutes west longitude. Admiralty documents written six years after the disaster indicate that "only about half of the specie was ever recovered." Several years ago well-known underwater photographers Ron and Valerie Taylor briefly visited this reef and located a large number of cannon while leading sports divers from a cruise ship. From photographs they sent me it appears that they chanced upon the Southampton.

Year 1812. American ship *Neutrality*, Captain Kimball, sailing from Jamaica to Georgia was totally lost January 13 at Cats Key, south of Bimini, the crew was saved.

Year 1812. English merchantman *Brown*, Captain Brough, sailing from Santo Domingo to London, wrecked October 5 on the Little Caicos Bank, the crew was saved.

Year 1812. Four ships were lost near Great Abaco Island: American ship *Twin Sisters*, Captain Owen, sailing from Baltimore to Havana, February 18, crew and most of cargo saved; American ship *Carlton*, Captain Davis, sailing from Virginia to Havana, April 16, crew and part of cargo saved; and the Scottish ship *Irmelinda*, Captain Graham, sailing from Clyde to Nassau, November 9.

Year 1813. English packet boat *Hinchinbrook*, sailing from Jamaica to England, wrecked at San Salvador Island July 19, only one person drowned.

Year 1813. English warship *H.M.S. Algerine*, a cutter, Captain Carpenter, wrecked May 20 near Great Abaco Island, the crew was saved.

Year 1813. English merchantman *Hotspur*, Captain Marshall, sailing from Santo Domingo to London, wrecked July 25 on Atwood Key, the crew was saved.

Year 1813. Bahamian ship *Fair Bahamian*, Captain Graham, sailing from Nassau to Havana, totally lost August 26 at Cat Cay, south of Bimini.

Year 1813. English ship *Forester*, Captain Jackson, sailing from Bermuda to Jamaica, lost September 26 on Turks Island, the crew was saved.

Year 1813. Two English warships wrecked on Silver Shoals: *H.M.S. Laurestinus*, 22 guns, Captain Alexander Gordon, October 22, the crew was saved; and the *H.M.S. Persian*, 18-gun sloop, Captain Charles Bertram, in seven fathoms of water, none of her crew of 121 men was lost.

Year 1813. During a violent gale at Nassau on July 26, over 40 ships were wrecked, sunk, or cast ashore. Only one was identified: English ship *Dart*, Captain Sweeting, sailing from Jamaica to Nassau, most of her cargo was saved.

Year 1813. During the same gale the English ship *Conck*, sailing from Nassau to Jamaica, was wrecked on Eleuthera Island.

Year 1814. Portuguese mail boat *Corriero Lisbonere*, sailing from Liverpool to Havana, was totally lost January 27 on the Little Bahama Bank.

Year 1814. A ship of unknown registry, *Moreau*, Captain Crosby, sailing from Amelia Island, Florida, to Nassau, was lost on the Nassau Bar.

Year 1814. Spanish merchantman *María Antonia*, sailing from Florida to Havana, was lost in February on a reef near Great Abaco Island, the crew was saved.

Year 1814. English ship *Sir James Yeo*, Captain Humble, sailing from Jamaica to Halifax, wrecked on Bird Rock near Crooked Island but most of her cargo was salvaged.

Year 1814. A ship of unknown registry, *Rose*, Captain Morris, sailing from Haiti to Hamburg, Germany, totally lost in August at Atwood Key.

Year 1815. American ship *Warrior*, Captain Dickenson, sailing from New York to Havana, lost June 30 on the Great Bahama Bank to the west of Andros Island, the crew was saved.

Year 1815. American merchantman *William & Mary*, Captain Ross, sailing from Haiti to Baltimore, wrecked August 23 on the Hogsties, the crew was saved.

Year 1815. Two Spanish merchantmen were lost, one at the beginning of the year and one at the end, while sailing between Havana and Spain. On January 6 the *Barcelones*, captain's name unknown, had part of her cargo salvaged but over 100,000 pesos in gold and silver coins were never found. *The Juncta* of Captain Capillo was lost on December 26 and the crew was rescued by a passing ship. A fraction of the more than 175,000 pesos in coinage that went down with her was reportedly recovered by Bahamian salvors. Strangely, both ships were reported to have been lost two to three miles north of West End, Grand Bahama island close to the edge of the Little Bahama Bank.

Year 1815. A ship of unknown registry, *Cameleon*, sailing from Norfolk to Havana, was lost on Great Abaco Island.

Year 1815. American ship *Sceptre*, Captain Simpson, sailing from Philadelphia to New Orleans, was lost on New Providence Island

Bob Marx is shown with some of the tens of thousands of coins recovered from the wreck of the 1656 galleon *Maravillas*, which he found in the Bahamas in 1972.

Year 1815. Three ships were lost near Great Inagua Island: a ship of unknown registry, *Port Royal*, sailing from New York to Jamaica; American ship *Intrepid*, Captain Martin, sailing from Jamaica to Baltimore, crew and part of cargo saved; and the American frigate *Statira*, on February 27, the crew was saved.

Year 1815. American merchantman *Farmer*, Captain Thompson, sailing from Nassau to South Carolina, was lost during a severe gale on June 19 on Wood Key, the crew was saved.

Year 1815. A ship of unknown registry, *Urbana*, Captain Brittain, sailing from New York to Jamaica, lost on Turks Island, the crew was saved.

Year 1815. English merchantman *Eliza Ann*, Captain Little, sailing from Honduras to London, wrecked at Memory Rock.

Year 1815. English ship *Incle*, Captain Thatcher, sailing from Bermuda to Jamaica, wrecked on the Caicos Bank.

Year 1815. Irish ship *Forest*, Captain Lascell, coming from Norfolk, totally lost December 2 on Great Exuma Island, the crew was saved.

Year 1816. American ship *Savannah*, Captain Bowers, sailing from Liverpool to New Orleans, was totally lost on the Macories Reef in the Old Bahama Channel, the crew was saved.

Year 1816. American merchantman *Cooler*, sailing from Philadelphia to Jamaica, wrecked on Mouchoir Bank, near Turks Island, the crew was saved.

Year 1816. A ship of unknown registry, *Swallow*, Captain Mossop, sailing from Savannah, Georgia, to Jamaica, wrecked December 10 on a reef at the north end of Eleuthera Island, the crew was saved.

Year 1816. Bahamian ship *Antelope*, Captain Teder, sailing from Nassau to St. Vincent Island, wrecked in October at Atwood Key.

Year 1816. A ship of unknown registry, *Mary*, Captain Jerault, coming from the Virgin Islands, was wrecked on the Berry Island, crew and part of cargo saved.

Year 1816. English ship *Phoenix*, sailing from Havana to Nassau, wrecked in March on the Mantanilla Reef, the crew was saved.

Year 1816. English merchantman *Aldbro*, Captain Suthoff, sailing from Honduras to London, totally lost September 28 near Memory Rock, the crew was saved.

These two handsome bronze cannon are among the valuable items that have been recovered from the wreck of the Spanish galleon *Maravillas* in the Bahamas.

Year 1816. American ship *Benjamin*, Captain Cushman, sailing from Boston to Havana, wrecked September 21 near Grand Bahama Island, crew and part of cargo saved.

Year 1816. English ship *Robert*, Captain Wilkes, sailing from Nassau to Liverpool, wrecked on a reef off Egg Island.

Year 1816. English ship *Britannia*, Captain Middlemas, sailing from Jamaica to New York, wrecked December 24 on Ackland Key, part of her cargo was saved.

Year 1816. Three American merchantmen were lost near Bimini: Expedition, *Captain Clare*, and the *Charter*, both sailing from Baltimore to Havana, wrecked near Great Isaac Key, the crews were saved; and the *Lardegable*, Captain Leon, sailing from Charleston, South Carolina, to Havana, was totally lost on the Little Isaac Key but the crew was saved.

Year 1816. Five ships were lost near Great Abaco Island: Spanish ship *Rosa*, sailing from Africa to Havana with 300 slaves, all people were saved; American ship *Minerva*, Captain Robinson, sailing from New York to Havana, totally lost March 8; American ship *William & Mary*, Captain Cooper, sailing from Philadelphia to Havana, October 17; American ship *New Orleans*, Captain Booth, crew and cargo saved; and the American ship *Alompre*, Captain Prior, sailing from New York to New Orleans, the crew was saved.

Year 1816. Three ships wrecked on the Caicos Bank: English ship *Amwell*, Captain Hawkins, sailing from London to Jamaica, December 19, at Great Caicos, crew and part of cargo saved; a ship of unknown registry, *Fair Trader*, Captain Haze, sailing from Philadelphia to Cuba, September 23, on the North Caicos Reef; and the American ship *Ann*, Captain Grant, sailing from South Carolina to Jamaica, December 25, the crew was saved.

Year 1816. Six ships were lost near Great Inagua Island: American ship *Nile*, Captain Tumley, sailing from New York to Jamaica, March 26, crew and cargo saved; American merchantman *Milford*, Captain Dukehard, coming from Baltimore, December 23, crew and part of cargo saved; a ship of unknown registry, *Mary*, sailing from Haiti to Baltimore, August 30; and three unidentified ships during June, one of which was carrying a considerable amount of money.

Year 1817. German merchantman *Christiansand*, Captain Berge, sailing from Hamburg to Havana, wrecked near Guinches Key, in the Old Bahama Channel, June 28, crew and some of specie saved.

Year 1817. American merchantman *Fame*, Captain Salisbury, sailing from Boston to Havana, lost January 12 near Harbour Island; crew was saved.

Year 1817. American ship *Mohawk*, Captain Harding, sailing from New York to Haiti, wrecked in August on Crooked Island, crew and part of cargo saved.

Year 1817. Spanish merchantman *Rosa*, wrecked near Little Isaac Island (called Las Profetas by the Spanish) in October, on a reef 13 nautical miles and bearing 73 degrees from above island.

Year 1817. American ship *Miriam*, sailing from Baltimore to Jamaica, wrecked March 27 on Great Inagua Island, her cargo was saved.

Year 1817. American merchantman *Workenston*, Captain Wilkens, sailing from New England to Veracruz, wrecked on North Caicos Key, crew and part of cargo saved.

Year 1817. Two ships wrecked on the Great Bahama Bank: American ship *Morning Star*, Captain Bishop, sailing from South Carolina to Havana, January 20; and an unidentified Dutch ship, sailing from Amsterdam to Havana, on the south edge of the bank in July.

Year 1817. Seven ships were lost near Great Abaco Island: American merchantman *Louisa*, Captain Hayes, sailing from Philadelphia to Havana, in April, part of her cargo was saved; Bahamian ship Do, *Captain Miller*, sailing from Philadelphia to Nassau, November 7, crew and part of cargo saved; a ship of unknown registry, *Adeline*, Captain Marre, sailing from Savannah to Havana, crew and part of cargo saved; American ship *Industry*, Captain Sweet, coming from Boston, March 22; American merchantman *Robert Potter*, sailing from Norfolk to Havana, April 17; American ship *Natchez Belle*, sailing from New York to New Orleans, March 23, crew and cargo saved; and the American merchantman *Frances Mary*, Captain Jennings, sailing from New York to New Orleans, February 12.

Year 1818. During a bad gale at Nassau on December 14, many ships were wrecked and sank.

Year 1818. American ship *Margaret*, Captain Hughes, sailing from Haiti to New York, wrecked March 1 near Little Inagua Island, crew and cargo saved.

Year 1818. English merchantman *Keddington*, Captain Bacon, sailing from Jamaica to London, lost April 1 at Atwood Key, crew and part of cargo saved.

Year 1818. English ship *Neptune*, Captain Foller, coming from Antigua, lost September 29 at Turks Island.

Year 1818. English ship *King George*, Captain Cook, sailing from Jamaica to London, lost on a cay near Bimini, most of her cargo was saved.

Year 1818. Ship of unknown registry, *Neptune*, Captain Hallowell, sailing from France to New Orleans, was totally wrecked February 5 near James Point on Eleuthera Island, the crew was saved.

Year 1818. French merchantman *Alexander*, sailing from France to Havana, wrecked in March near New Providence Island, crew and part of cargo saved.

Year 1818. Two ships of unknown registry wrecked on Silver Shoals: schooner *Alexander*, Captain Stewart, totally lost August 7, from Jamaica; and the *John*, bound for Jamaica, on October 10 or 1;, crew was saved.

Year 1818. American ship *Jane*, Captain Woodward, sailing from Savannah to Jamaica, wrecked on August 16 near Crooked Island, some of her cargo was saved.

Year 1818. Four ships were wrecked near Memory Rock: Spanish merchantman *Echo*, Captain Rodríguez, sailing from Veracruz to Venezuela, crew and over $100,000 in specie saved; English ship *Elizabeth*, sailing from Jamaica to Liverpool, on March 22; English merchantman *Two Brothers*, Captain Holmes, sailing from New Orleans to Liverpool, the crew was saved; English brig *British Trader*, Captain Gemmell, coming from Jamaica, March 22, but got afloat again after throwing part of her cargo overboard.

Year 1818. American ship *Horizon*, Captain Johnson, sailing from Philadelphia to New Orleans, wrecked on Fish Key, near Great Abaco Island.

Year 1818. Five ships were wrecked on Great Abaco Island: a ship of unknown registry, *Shakespeare*, sailing from Le Havre to America, in March; American ship *Caroline*, Captain Seymour, sailing from Norfolk to New Orleans, March 4; English merchantman *Sir John Doyle*, Captain Watts, sailing from Havana to Santiago de Cuba, on September 13, part of her cargo was saved; American packet boat *Savannah*, Captain Fowler, sailing from New York to Mobile, October 14, crew, passengers, and cargo saved; and the American ship *Rival*, sailing from Boston to Mobile, November 18, crew, passengers, and cargo saved.

Year 1818. American schooner *Lily*, sailing from Port au Prince, Haiti, to Great Exuma Island, wrecked on Andros Island, the crew was saved.

Year 1818. Scottish merchantman *Pomona*, Captain M'Naught, sailing from Jamaica to Glasgow, lost April 10 on the Caicos Bank, crew, rum, and sails saved.

Year 1819. A ship of unknown registry, *Sero*, Captain Murdock, sailing from Philadelphia to Cuba, totally lost July 27 at Turks Island .

Year 1819. English ship *Golden Fleece*, sailing from Jamaica to Liverpool, wrecked in January on Long Key, crew and cargo saved.

Year 1819. A ship of unknown registry, *Constantia*, Captain Johnson, sailing from Haiti to France, wrecked April 22 on Ginger Key, cargo was saved.

Year 1819. American schooner *Walton Grey*, sailing from Baltimore to Havana, wrecked in the Berry Islands, most of her cargo was saved.

Year 1819. American ship *Hazard*, Captain Crocker, sailing from Boston to Mobile, wrecked January 3 near Nassau, crew and part of cargo saved.

Year 1819. A large unidentified brig was wrecked on the Crooked Island Reef before April 25.

Year 1819. English packet boat *Princess Charlotte*, sailing from Jamaica to England, wrecked in early April on the Hogstie Reef, crew, passengers, mail, and specie (with the exception of about $30,000) saved.

Year 1819. Portuguese ship *Bom Successo*, coming from Brazil with a cargo of sugar, cotton, rice, and hides, was wrecked at Little Island, near Rum Key, most of her cargo was salvaged.

Year 1819. English merchantman *Fairfield*, Captain Elias, sailing from Haiti to Liverpool, wrecked on a reef at Atwood Key on March 28, crew and some of cargo saved.

Year 1819. American brig *George Washington*, Captain Baker, sailing from New York to New Orleans, was totally wrecked at Green Turtle Cay, near Great Abaco Island.

Year 1819. Two American ships wrecked on Great Abaco Island: merchantman *George Washington*, Captain Brethoff, sailing from New York to Havana, January 1, crew and small part of cargo saved; and the sloop *Altezara*, Captain Glover, totally lost at Hole in the Wall.

Year 1819. Five ships wrecked on the Caicos Bank: an unidentified Dutch brig, sailing from Hamburg to Havana, with a valuable cargo of silks, April 13; American ship *Jonus*, sailing from New York to Haiti, crew and part of cargo saved; Belgian merchantman *Elizabeth Elenor*, Captain Rose, sailing from Antwerp to Havana, April 2, crew and part of cargo saved; Canadian ship *Herman*, Captain Milne, sailing from New Brunswick to Jamaica, part of her cargo was saved; and an unidentified American schooner.

Year 1820. American ship *Atlantic*, Captain Homer, sailing from Boston to Hispaniola, totally lost December 30 in the Crooked Island Passage, the crew was saved.

Year 1821. Two ships lost near Cat Cay, south of Bimini: Canadian ship *Prince Regent*, Captain Wickes, sailing from Jamaica to Halifax, on September 5, the crew was saved; and the German ship *Rapid*, Captain Hinman, sailing from Havana to Hamburg.

Year 1821. English merchantman *Cuba*, Captain M'Gowan, sailing from Liverpool to Havana, totally lost October 15 on Mayaguana Island; all members of the crew were saved.

Year 1821. American brig *Leopard* was wrecked during a gale on September 14 near Great Exuma Island.

Year 1821. Two ships were lost on Great Abaco Island: American brig *Perseverance*, sailing from Charleston, South Carolina, to Havana, June 9, the crew was saved; and a ship of unknown registry, *Hero*, Captain Riebeiro, sailing from New York to Havana, in June; the ship's crew and most of cargo saved.

Year 1821. Spanish ship *Santa Rosa*, Captain Torres, sailing from Philadelphia to Havana, lost in March on Egg Island, the crew was saved.

Year 1821. English ship *Sovereign*, Captain Pierson, sailing from Jamaica to London, was totally wrecked November 17 on the Hogsties, crew and cargo saved.

Year 1821. English merchantman *Posthumous*, Captain Fisher, lost at Saynee Island, the crew was saved. (Note: Today there is no Bahamian island by this name.)

Year 1821. Irish ship *James Munroe*, Captain Harwood, carrying a cargo of salt, wrecked on St. Nicolas Key, the crew was saved.

Year 1821. English brig *Harriet*, sailing from Savannah, wrecked on Ginger Cay, the crew was saved.

Year 1821. Two ships wrecked near Great Inagua Island: Canadian merchantman *Hope*, Captain Tucker, sailing from Jamaica to New Brunswick, September 13; and the English ship *Anne*, Captain Hodnett, sailing from Bermuda to Jamaica, May 6, near the northeastern end of the island.

Year 1822. English merchantman *Loyalty*, Captain Atkinson, sailing from Jamaica to London, wrecked January 27 on the Hogsties, crew and part of cargo saved.

Year 1822. Two ships were lost on Castle Island: American schooner *Jane*, Captain Miller, sailing from Boston to Havana, part of her cargo was saved; and the English brig *Jemima*, coming from Maracaibo, Venezuela, the crew was saved.

Year 1822. Four American merchant ships wrecked on the Great Bahama Bank: *Maryland*, *Savannah Packet*, *Nancy* and *Speedy Peace*, the latter sailing from Mobile to New York; the crews of all ships were saved.

Year 1822. American merchantman *Falmouth*, carrying a cargo of soap, lumber, and candles, wrecked near the Exuma Keys.

Year 1822. Two ships were lost on the Caicos Bank: a ship of unknown registry, *Westmoreland*, Captain Majoribanks, sailing from Quebec to Jamaica, totally lost December 5, her crew was saved; and the English ship *Draper*, Captain Brown, sailing from Bermuda to Jamaica, on November 28, crew and passengers saved.

Year 1822. Four ships wrecked on Great Abaco Island: Spanish ship *Jupiter*, Captain de Minchaca, sailing from Malaya to Havana, crew and part of cargo saved; Canadian ship *Ann*, sailing from Jamaica to New Brunswick, prior to February 21; American ship *Ranger*, Captain Eldridge, sailing from South Carolina to Havana, totally lost January 26; and the American ship *Washington*, Captain Taylor, sailing from New York to New Orleans in ballast.

Year 1822. English merchantman *Britannia*, Captain Preble, sailing from Haiti to Wilmington, totally lost November 19 on Sugar Key; crew was saved.

Year 1822. Scottish ship *Jemima*, Captain Doyle, wrecked April 2 on a reef near Crooked Island, part of her cargo was saved.

Year 1822. Canadian ship *Harriet*, Captain Hitchins, sailing from Jamaica to Halifax, wrecked April 26 on the Mira Por Vos Keys, her crew was saved.

Year 1822. Scottish merchantman *Favorite*, Captain Davis, sailing from Glasgow to Canada, wrecked May 7 on Ragged Island.

Year 1822. Unidentified merchant brig wrecked at Ackland Key, the crew was saved.

Year 1822. Two ships of unknown registry wrecked near Great Inagua Island: brig *Hope*, Captain Tooker, coming from Jamaica, her crew was saved; and an unidentified vessel.

Year 1822. Three ships were totally wrecked at Turks Island: American ship *Washington*, Captain Berry, sailing from New York to Haiti, October 17, her crew was saved; a ship of unknown registry, *Merrimack*, Captain Miltimore, sailing to Haiti, crew and part of cargo saved; and the Canadian ship *Harriet Newell*, Captain Corfield, sailing from New Brunswick to Jamaica, December 1, crew and part of cargo saved.

Year 1823. Cuban ship *Rio*, sailing from Philadelphia to Havana, wrecked in the Berry Islands.

Year 1823. Three ships wrecked on Sugar Key: French ship *Ville de St. Pierre*, Captain Scolan, sailing from France to Havana, the crew was saved; a ship of unknown registry, *Warren*, sailing from France to Havana with 400 tons of wine; and an unidentified Dutch ship, sailing from Hamburg to Havana, with a very valuable cargomost of their cargoes were saved.

Year 1823. A ship of unknown registry, *Victoria*, Captain M'Killop, sailing from Jamaica to Halifax, wrecked on the Mayaguana Reef, got off, but then was wrecked off the western end of Crooked Island, November 10, where she went to pieces.

Year 1823. American ship *Orion*, Captain Smith, sailing from Haiti to Wilmington, wrecked December 8 on the Mayaguana Reef, crew and cargo saved.

Year 1823. English ship *Wanderer*, totally wrecked on Double Headed Shot Key, June 3, crew and passengers saved.

Year 1823. A ship of unknown registry, *Delight*, sailing from Jamaica to Philadelphia, wrecked near Nassau, part of her cargo saved.

Year 1823. American schooner *Richard*, Captain Harvey, sailing from New York to Jamaica, lost September 11 on Turks Island, crew and most of cargo saved.

Year 1823. Two unidentified Jamaican vessels, a brig and a schooner, were wrecked on the Hogsties.

Year 1823. Spanish brig *Estrella*, sailing from Puerto Rico to Havana, was lost near Great Isaac Key.

Year 1823. Bahamian schooner *Sarah Ann*, Captain Bannatyne, coming from Cuba, wrecked March 5 on Green Key.

Year 1823. A ship of unknown registry, *Friendship*, Captain Wells, sailing from Jeremie to Portsmouth, New Hampshire, wrecked at Castle Island, crew and most of cargo saved.

Year 1823. Two ships lost on the Caicos Bank: Spanish ship *Bella Dolores*, captured by a Colombian privateer and then wrecked June 9; and the American ship *Fabius*, Captain Higgins, sailing from Wilmington to Haiti, totally lost, her crew was saved.

Year 1823. Five ships wrecked on Great Abaco Island: American schooner *Jane*, Captain M'Williams, sailing from South Carolina to Havana, crew and cargo saved; American merchantman *Essex*, Captain Ladiew, sailing from Rhode Island to Havana; American ship *Franklin*, Captain Taper, sailing from Philadelphia to Venezuela; a ship of unknown registry, Remittance, Captain Heter, sailing from New York to Havana; and the American ship Catherine Rogers, Captain Griffiths, sailing from New York to Mobile.

Year 1824. During a hurricane on September 11, several unidentified ships were wrecked at Rum Key.

Year 1824. American ship *Joseph*, Captain Holdrige, sailing from Mobile to New York, totally lost June 3 on the Little Bahama Bank, near Memory Rock.

Year 1824. French ship *Eolus*, Captain Dickinson, sailing from Morlaix, France, to Mobile, wrecked on Eleuthera Island.

Year 1824. English brig *Providence*, Captain Dunn, sailing from Gibraltar to Havana, wrecked August 8 near Great Exuma Island.

Year 1824. English ship *Cleo*, Captain Heath, sailing from Bath to Havana, lost February 23 on Grand Bahama Island, part of her cargo was saved.

Year 1824. American schooner *Three Sisters*, Captain Allen, coming from Jamaica, wrecked on the Hogsties.

Year 1824. Three ships wrecked on the Caicos Bank: American schooner *Franklin*, Captain Stevenson, sailing from Boston to South America; a ship of unknown registry, *Europa*, Captain Allen, sailing from Liverpool to Havana, June 14, crew and cargo saved; and the Bahamian sloop *Maria*, Captain Bartlett.

Year 1824. Three ships wrecked on Great Abaco Island: American schooner *George Washington*, Captain Smith, sailing from Philadelphia to Havana, her cargo was saved; a ship of unknown registry, *Chace*, Captain Anderson, sailing from Charleston, South Carolina, to Havana, her crew was saved; and the English ship *Albert*, Captain Philip, sailing from Gibraltar to Mexico, part of her cargo was saved.

Year 1824. American ship *Live Oak*, Captain Brill, sailing from Gibraltar to Havana, wrecked December 1 near Harbour Island, crew and cargo saved.

Year 1824. Two American ships wrecked at Turks Island: *Panopea*, Captain Bogle, sailing from South Carolina to Jamaica, December 25, most of her cargo was saved; and the *Jerome Maximilian*, sailing from New York to Haiti, wrecked December 30 with no one aboard.

Year 1825. English mail boat *Havana Packet*, Captain Jenkins, sailing from England to Jamaica, wrecked March 13 on the Caicos Bank.

Year 1825. American ship *North America*, sailing from Nassau to Key West, wrecked near Bimini.

Year 1825. Three ships wrecked on reefs near Mayaguana Island: American ship *Strong*, Captain McGill, sailing from Haiti to Baltimore, part of her cargo was saved; English merchantman *Woodstock*, Captain Paton, sailing from Jamaica to London, small part of her cargo was saved; and the Spanish ship *San Francisco de Paula* (alias *Orionon*), Captain Pugol, sailing from Barcelona to Havana, the crew was saved.

Year 1825. English ship *Doris*, Captain White, sailing from Santo Domingo to England, was totally lost near Great Inagua Island, her crew was saved.

Year 1825. American merchantman *Betsy*, Captain Hilton, sailing from New England to Cuba, was totally lost on Double Headed Key, all of crew except one were murdered by pirates.

Chapter Eight

Cuba

Cuba was considered the most strategically located island in the Caribbean for more than three centuries. Virtually all shipping en route to Mexico, Central America or the southern sections of the present United States from Europe or Africa — and all shipping to Europe or ports in North America coming from the Caribbean, Mexico and Central and South America — had to sail close by the island.

When Old World countries were at war with one another, their privateering vessels generally cruised in search of enemy ships off the western tip of Cuba, which all Europe-bound ships using the Bahama Channel had to pass. The Windward Passage between the eastern tip of Cuba and Haiti was used by shipping at times to avoid capture, but because of the difficult navigation through the Bahamian Archipelago, this route was a last resort. Storms, faulty navigation and sea battles caused the loss of more than 700 ships in Cuban waters between the beginning of the 16th century and 1825. I have listed only those for which accurate locations are given or ships of major importance, e.g. a vessel carrying important cargo.

Under the Castro government, no foreigners are permitted to salvage shipwrecks or even sail in Cuban territorial waters. Since Castro came to power, three American treasure-hunting expeditions had the misfortune to accidentally shipwreck in Cuban waters. In two of these cases the divers were held captive for several months even though their original destinations were not in Cuban waters. Cuban patrol vessels extend their cruising grounds well out of their own territorial waters, ostensibly to try to intercept Cuban-exile raiders working out of Florida and the Bahamas. Recently a shrimp-boat captain reported sighting a large number of bronze cannon on a reef in Cay Sal Bank, which is in Bahamian waters, but when a group of Miami divers went there to recover these cannon, they were chased away by a Cuban gunboat.

There are several unconfirmed stories of American divers recovering treasure in the vicinity of the Isle of Pines prior to Castro's takeover, but I have been unable to verify these reports. In 1957 an amateur diver from Havana sent me photographs of several silver bars he had recovered from Matanzas Bay. He asked me to help him in salvaging more treasure, but I wasn't able to get to Cuba before the revolution. I identified the bars (from markings on them) as belonging to one of the Spanish ships wrecked in this bay in 1628 during the attack of the great Dutch privateer Piet Heyn. No doubt there is a great deal more treasure from this disaster in Matanzas Bay. Since Castro himself is an avid diver, I'm surprised he hasn't attempted to locate this treasure to augment Cuba's depleted treasury.

Shipwrecks in Cuban Waters

Early 16th century. The famous Spanish historian Oviedo mentions, without giving the year, that a ship sailing from Santo Domingo to Cuba was wrecked on the coast of Cuba and that a Juan de Rojas and his wife, María de Lobera, were aboard.

Prior to 1515. An unidentified small Spanish caravel, carrying a valuable cargo, was lost in the port of Cumanacan, at the mouth of the Bani River.

Prior to 1518. Merchant nao *Jesús Nazareno y Nuestra Señora de Guadalupe*, 112 tons, Captain Bartolomé Antònio Garrote, owned by Tomas José Caro, carrying a cargo of tobacco, developed a bad leak after leaving Havana for Spain and was sunk in the port of Guarico, after most of its cargo was removed.

Year 1519. An unidentified caravel, sailing from the port of Santa María del Antigua, Colombia, for Santo Domingo, was forced (because of bad weather) to pass on the northern coast of Cuba, where it wrecked. Huge waves later tossed the ship over 100 yards ashore.

Year 1521. Merchant nao *San Anton*, 100 tons, Captain Gonzalo Rodríguez, sailing from Havana to Spain, lost on a reef on the northwestern coast of the island.

Year 1525. An unidentified ship commanded by Juan de Avalos, a relative of Cortez, was wrecked during a hurricane west of Havana, en route to Veracruz with supplies for the conquistadors. Of the 80 persons aboard, only eight survived. This occurred toward the end of October.

Year 1527. During a hurricane on October 14, two large ships of the fleet of Admiral Panfilo Narvaez were lost in the port of Trinidad after arriving from Santo Domingo.

Year 1537. During a hurricane, two ships were lost: the nao *San Juan*, arriving from Spain with a valuable cargo of merchandise, was lost five leagues east of Havana; and the nao *Santa Catalina*, 200 tons, Captain Francisco López, carrying gold and silver from Mexico, sank in Havana Harbor.

Year 1544. Nao *Santa Marta de la Isla*, 180 tons, Captain Vicente Martín, sailing with treasure from Nombre de Diós to Havana, was wrecked on the coast near Havana.

Year 1552. After the regular Tierra Firme Treasure Fleet set sail from Nombre de Diós with the South American treasures, a galleon sailing between Peru and Panama, which had been presumed lost earlier, arrived at Panama with over two million pesos in treasure. This treasure was quickly transferred overland to Nombre de Diós to be stored until the next year's fleet arrived. However, when pirate vessels were sighted in the area, the governor decided to safeguard the treasure by placing it aboard the *Santa María de Finisterra*, Captain Juan Rodríguez Zarco, 210 tons, and sending it to Havana. Shortly after arriving in Havana the ship capsized for no apparent reason and went down with the treasure in 120 feet of water. Repeated salvage attempts failed to recover the treasure.

Year 1552. Merchant vessel, *Sant' Andres*, Captain Vicente Hernandez, owned by Sebastian Gonzalez, arriving from Honduras with a small amount of treasure and other cargo, was wrecked and partially salvaged.

Year 1555. Nao *Santa María de Villacelan*, 220 tons, Captain Mateo de Vides, carrying treasure from Panama and Cartagena to Spain, was wrecked on the coast near Matanzas Bay.

Year 1556. Four ships of the Tierra Firme Armada, Captain-General Alvaro Sanchez de Aviles, were wrecked on the coast between Cape San Anton and Havana on May 24 during a storm: nao *La Magdalena*, 220 tons, Captain Cristóbal Garcia, and the nao *La Concepción*, 220 tons, Captain Juan Diaz Bozino, both carrying treasure; and two unidentified caravels of 80 tons each.

Year 1563. A large convoy of ships sailed from Spain for the New World and, after stopping for water at Guadeloupe, those going to South America and those to Mexico split up in two groups. The Nueva España Flota was commanded by Captain-General Pedro de las Roelas. On July 18, six ships of this flota were wrecked on the Jardines Reefs on the southern coast of Cuba, in 21 degrees of north latitude at a distance of 12 leagues from the Isle of Pines: the Capitana, *San Juan Bautista*, 150 tons, Captain Juan de Arenas; nao *San Juan*, 250 tons, Captain Gaspar Luys; galeza (ship propelled by oars or sail) *San Salvador*, 350 tons, Captain Pedro Menéndez Marquez; nao *N.S. de la Consolación*, 300 tons, Captain Juan de Barrios; nao *Santa Margarita*, 300 tons, Captain Gonzalo Monte; and the nao *N.S. de la Concepción*, 250 tons, Captain Pedro del Corro. All six ships were carrying large amounts of mercury as well as cargoes of general merchandise. The Capitaña was also carrying Archbishop Salcedo, who was reported carrying a great amount of church and personal treasure. The wrecks were reportedly in 1 1/2 to 4 fathoms of water. Ships were sent from Havana to rescue the survivors and undertake salvage operations, but only a small part of the mercury and merchandise were recovered and none of the treasure of Archbishop Salcedo was located.

Year 1563. Nao *San Andres*, 300 tons, Captain Marco de Napoles, sailing from Cartagena and Panama with treasure, was wrecked in Havana Harbor.

Year 1565. Three unidentified Spanish warships under the command of Admiral Estéban de las Alas, sent to the Caribbean to destroy enemy privateers, were wrecked on the island; only the crews were saved.

Year 1567. An unidentified urca, 300 tons, Captain Gonzales de Peñalosa, sailing from Veracruz to Santo Domingo, carrying several chests of silver to pay the officials and soldiers garrisoned in Santo Domingo, was lost near Cayo Romano.

Year 1576. Nao *Jesús María*, Captain Diego de Alvendin, wrecked at Puerto Escondido, after being chased by pirates.

Year 1577. An unidentified nao in the Tierra Firme Armada of Captain-General Cristóbal de Eraso was separated from the convoy in a storm and forced to enter Puerto Escondido, where it sank. The gold and silver it carried was recovered.

Year 1586. Unidentified nao, sailing from Spain to Veracruz in the Nueva España Flota of Captain-General Francisco de Novoa, was lost at Cape San Anton around the end of September.

Year 1593. Two treasure-laden naos, sailing from Veracruz to Spain in the Nueva España Flota of Captain-General Martín Perez Olozabal, were lost near Havana: *Santa María de San Vicente*, 180 tons, Captain Miguel de Alcata; and the *N.S. del Rosario*, 220 tons, Captain Cristóbal Castellanos. The treasure from both ships was taken off before they sank.

Year 1595. Merchant navío *San Gabriel*, 140 tons, Captain Pedro de Morillo, part of the Nueva España Flota, commanded by Captain-General Marcos de Aramburu, was wrecked in Havana Harbor, but its silver was recovered by divers.

Year 1599. Merchantman *San Julian*, 230 tons, arriving from Panama with an a small amount of treasure was wrecked near Morro Castle during a storm and went down in deep water.

Year 1605. Merchant nao *Trinidad* was wrecked near Havana, only a few persons aboard this ship were saved.

Year 1605. A small mail boat, *Captain Diego Ruiz*, sank in Havana Harbor after striking on the mast of another shipwreck.

Year 1606. Navío *San Francisco*, Captain Antonio Cardosa, 100 tons, arriving from Santo Domingo sank in deep water in Havana Harbor.

Year 1606. Unidentified warship in the Armada de Barlovento, commanded by Admiral Juan Alvarez, sent to the Caribbean to capture foreign shipping, was wrecked on the Los Jardines Reefs, near the Isle of Pines.

Year 1610. Unidentified English privateering vessel, sailing from Plymouth, England, with 150 men on board, sank near the Isle of Pines; there were only eight survivors. This ship was carrying a large amount of treasure captured from Spanish shipping.

Year 1612. Small unidentified advice boat, sailing from Cartagena to Spain, was wrecked on the Isle of Pines.

Year 1613. Treasure-laden galleon *Los Peligros*, while preparing to sail for Spain, caught fire and sank in Havana Harbor.

Year 1616. During a hurricane near the end of September, more than 30 unidentified ships were sunk in several ports of Oriente Province, many by being dashed to pieces against other ships.

Year 1618. Frigate *San Francisco*, 80 tons, Captain Juan d'Esquibel, sailing as an advice boat between Veracruz and Spain, was lost during a storm while attempting to enter Matanzas Bay, no lives were lost and divers recovered the mail and cargo.

Year 1618. An unidentified Portuguese merchantman, sailing in the Nueva España Flota of Captain-General Vallecillas, for some unknown reason set fire to his ship as the convoy was entering the port of Havana.

Year 1621. Advice boat *La Concepción*, 50 tons, Captain Francisco Rodríguez, sailing from Veracruz to Spain, was wrecked on Cayo del Visal, near the entrance to Rio de Puercos, most of the crew drowned but the mail was recovered.

Year 1628. A small squadron of privateers owned by the Dutch West India Company attacked two Honduras galleons near Cabo San Anton, forcing one ashore and capturing the other. The cargo of the wrecked ship consisted mainly of indigo and a small amount of silver specie, but only a small part of the indigo was recovered by divers from Havana.

Year 1628. Another Dutch West India Fleet, commanded by Admiral Piet Heyn, cornered the Nueva España Flota, commanded by Captain-General Juan de Benevides y Bazan, near Havana and forced it into Matanzas Bay on September 8, where all 24 Spanish ships were wrecked on the shoals. Some of the treasure on the flota ships was thrown overboard before the Dutch fleet entered the bay and the Spaniards fled ashore without firing a shot to protect the treasure or their ships. The Dutch estimate the value of the treasure they took from the ships at 15 million Dutch guilders; an amount greater than the total captured from Spanish shipping by privateers and pirates since the discovery of the New World. The treasure was so great that it could not be carried aboard the 28 ships of Piet Heyn, so he refloated four of the largest Spanish ships and used them to carry some of the treasure back to Holland. Two of these Spanish ships became separated from the Dutch fleet in bad weather and wrecked near present day Freeport, Grand Bahama Island. A small part of the treasure that one of these ships was carrying was discovered several years ago.

Year 1629. A Dutch privateer forced the 400-ton nao *Santiago*, Captain Andrés de la Calde, coming from Honduras, to be run aground near Havana, where it was totally lost.

Year 1629. An unidentified advice boat, sailing between Spain and Veracruz, was forced ashore near Cabo de Cruz by a Dutch privateer but the crew escaped with the mail.

Year 1633. A large unidentified Portuguese galleon, sailing in the Tierra Firme Armada of Captain-General Antonio de Oquendo, hit a reef and sank at the entrance to Havana Harbor, the crew was all saved and her artillery was later recovered by divers.

Year 1634. Unidentified merchant nao carrying the Mastre de Campo Francisco Riano y Gamboa to Spain, was sunk in the port of Muriel on October 5.

Year 1634. The galleon *San Juan Agustín*, Captain Bartolomé de Larríba, part of a four-galleon squadron commanded by Captain Sancho de Urdaniba to help escort the Nueva España Flota to Spain, was wrecked during the night in a storm about 15 leagues from Havana, between Rio de Puercos and Bahía Honda, and 40 of the crew were drowned.

Year 1635. Merchant urca owned by Captain Diego de Larrasa, was attacked by a Dutch warship off Cape Corrientes and wrecked on the shore but the crew escaped.

Year 1636. During a hurricane that struck Havana, many houses and warehouses were carried into the sea by torrential floods, a large number of cannon and some of the ramparts of Morro Castle were also flung into the sea.

Year 1636. When the Nueva España Flota, Captain-General Juan de Vega Bazan, arrived from Veracruz and entered Havana, its Capitana, *N.S. de la Limpia Concepción*, 600 tons, Captain Alonso Hidalgo, carrying a large amount of treasure, hit a rock near Morro Castle and sank, but rapid action of many nearby ships saved all of the treasure and artillery before she went down.

Year 1636. On January 20, two Dutch privateers forced an urca of Captain Juan de Urrutia, which was coming from Maracaibo to Havana with a cargo of cocoa, to run aground at Cape San Anton. After her crew reached shore the Dutch stripped everything of value off the ship.

Year 1638. A Dutch privateering fleet commanded by the famous Dutch admiral known by the nickname "Wooden Leg" attacked the Tierra Firme Armada of Captain-General Carlos de Ibarra. The battle ensued for two days while the Armada attempted to reach Havana. One of the Spanish galleons, the *N.S. de Arancacu*, 600 tons, Captain Sancho de Urdaniva, was so badly damaged by cannon fire that, after all of its treasure was transferred to other galleons, it was taken into the port of Bahía Honda and set afire. Later, divers retrieved 15 of the 20 large cannon from the burned hulk, but the other five were buried under sand and could not be raised. All of the other Spanish ships made port safely.

Year 1638. A fleet of Dutch privateers were cruising off Cabo de San Antonio waiting for Spanish ships when a hurricane caused seven of them to be totally lost near this cape.

Year 1639. Merchant urca *Hercules* sank during a storm near Cayo de Libizas, located 22 leagues west of Havana, because she was overloaded. Four frigates with divers sent from Havana recovered all 20 of her cannon, eight of which were bronze.

Year 1640. Admiral "Wooden Leg" returned again to the Caribbean in an attempt to duplicate Piet Heyn's feat of capturing a treasure fleet; but while cruising near Havana waiting for the Nueva España Flota, a hurricane wrecked seven of his warships on the coast near Xaimanita, Baru, Mosquitos, and La Herradura, located three, seven, nine and 11 leagues, respectively, from Havana. The Spaniards captured many of his men and recovered some cannon from a few of the wrecks.

Year 1641. After the Nueva España Flota, commanded by Admiral Juan de Campos, set sail from Havana for Spain, it was struck by a hurricane in the Bahama Channel and many ships were lost. Four ships of this flota were driven back to Cuba, where two were wrecked near Havana; another wrecked six leagues from Santiago de Cuba, and the other entered this port.

Year 1642. The nao *N.S. de Atocha y San Joséf*, 400 tons, Captain Gerónimo Beleno, reached Santiago de Cuba, and after making repairs, left this port for Havana in January. Within sight of Havana a storm struck and the nao was wrecked only a musket-shot distance from the Fort of La Puntal. During this same storm a galleon, *Peña de Francia*, of the Armada de Barlovento, sank six leagues from Havana with a total loss of lives. Eight months later salvors found this wreck completely buried in sand and they were unable to recover anything.

Year 1647. When the Tierra Firme Armada of Captain-General Pedro de Ursua entered Havana, arriving from Cartagena with large amounts of treasure, its Capitaña, *San Joséf y San Francisco de Paula*, 400 tons, Captain Jacobo de Oyanguren, and an unidentified patache were sunk at the entrance to the harbor.

Year 1648. When a pirate ship was sighted cruising off Havana, the governor armed two large merchantmen and sent them to capture or destroy it, but both ran aground at a small port near Havana and were totally lost. The pirate ship entered the port and cut the throats of many of the survivors.

Year 1660. The frigate *La Gallardino*, Captain Juan Gomez Brito, coming from Puerto Rico, was wrecked on a small reef described as about half the size of the main plaza of Havana, where waves are always breaking, located 12 to 14 leagues north of Rio de Puercos.

Year 1672. Merchant navío *N.S. de la Concepción y San Francisco*, Captain Juan Ignacio de Cuellar, was accidentally burned in Havana Harbor.

Year 1672. A Jamaican privateer commanded by Captain Robert Hewytt, captured a Spanish bark, which was later wrecked at Boga Pavillion, one of the small cays on the south coast of Cuba.

Year 1681. Merchant navío *N.S. de la Concepción y San Ignacio*, one of the ships in the Nueva España Flota of Captain-General Fernando Ponce, was wrecked on the shoals of Los Organos, located 14 leagues from Havana.

Year 1687. Galleon *N.S. del Rosario y San Joséph*, built in Havana, 424 tons and owned by Governor Francisco Blanco, sank while entering Havana after her sea trials.

Year 1689. Galleon *San lose y N.S. del Rosario*, Captain Francisco Blanco, 230 tons, sank at the entrance of Havana harbor; divers recovered her 42 iron cannon and cargo of tobacco.

Year 1693. English warship *H.M.S. Mordaunt*, 46 guns, Captain Francis Maynard, was wrecked on the Los Colorado Reefs on November 21 with a total loss of life.

Year 1695. Two treasure-laden galleons were wrecked near Havana: *N.S. de la Soledad y San Ignacio de Loyola*, near the entrance of the port, all of her treasure was recovered; and the Almiranta *N.S. de las Mercedes*, Captain Juan Velez de Larres, at Simarina, near Havana, most of her treasure was recovered.

Year 1696. An unidentified navío wrecked at Playa de Sabarimar, seven leagues east of Havana, in 35 feet of water, during a storm, she was completely salvaged soon afterward.

Year 1699. Merchant navío *Santiago*, 228 tons, Captain Salvador Vanegas, returning to Spain with a cargo of no great value, was wrecked on the Los Jardines Reefs, near the Isle of Pines.

Year 1702. A French fleet of warships commanded by Chateaurenault was sent to Havana to escort some Spanish treasure galleons back to Spain, but the vice-admiral's ship was burnt in Havana Harbor.

Year 1703. Another French fleet, commanded by Admiral Ducasse, was sent to Havana to escort Spanish ships back to Spain, and the French man-of-war *El Bueno* was wrecked at Castle de la Punta in Havana.

Year 1705. American privateer ship *New York*, Captain Tongerlou, chased a Spanish ship of 24 guns and 600 tons coming from the Canary Islands and forced it to run aground about one league from Baracoa; its cargo of wine and brandy was saved.

Year 1705. During a hurricane, four large Spanish warships and most of their crews were lost in Havana Harbor.

Year 1707. Two French frigates, *Diamante* and the *El Conde Torigin*, were wrecked on the Bajos de Santa Isabel, about three leagues from Bahía Honda and half a league from shore. One was carrying a cargo of logwood and the other 30 tons of iron bars as ballast.

Year 1711. Five ships of the Nueva España Flota were wrecked during a norther on December 16 about 5 leagues west of Havana: one was its Almiranta, *Santisima Trinidad*, which carried a large treasure, Captain Diego de Alarcón y Ocaño of the Armada de Barlovento; the other four were flota naos, of which only one was identified, the *N.S. del Rosario, San Jos y Las Animas*. Divers were quickly employed and by January 4 they had recovered over 1,700,000 pesos in treasure from the wrecks. The total amount of treasure carried on these ships was not stated in the documents.

Year 1715. An unidentified ship bringing 85 chests of silver and 50 silver bars, salvaged in 1970, was wrecked during a storm at Jaimanita, located five leagues from Havana, but divers recovered all of its treasure.

Year 1715. Brief mention that a Spanish ship named *Santisima Trinidad* was lost on Los Pasajes Shoals near Havana.

Year 1721. Treasure-laden galleon *San Juan*, Captain Francisco Maldonado, was lost entering Havana Harbor.

Year 1726. An unidentified French merchant brigantine, sailing to the Mississippi River, ran aground at Cabo Frances but the majority of her cargo was salvaged.

Year 1727. Two unidentified French warships commanded by Admiral du Rochet were wrecked on the reefs of Jardines de la Reina, on the southern coast of the island, a bit to the east of Jaqua, and when salvors were sent there they reported sighting several other wrecks in the same area.

Year 1731. Merchant navío *San Antonio de Padua* (alias *Hercules*), 174 tons, Captain Pedro Sanz y Sagardia, carrying a cargo of mercury, was wrecked in Bahía Mangle, located between Puerto de Principe and Bayano.

Year 1740. Large galleon *Invencible*, of the squadron of Admiral Rodrigo de Torres, was struck by lightning after anchoring in Havana Harbor and blew up, causing great damage to the city as well. This ship carried four million pesos in treasure, none of which was recovered.

Year 1741. Small unidentified Spanish frigate was wrecked on Cayo Lobos.

Year 1744. Two unidentified Spanish privateering vessels were run ashore near Santiago de Cuba by two New England privateering ships.

Year 1745. Two American privateering ships from Philadelphia drove a Spanish sloop ashore at Matanzas Bay and carried her cargo away.

Above

This elaborate drawing carefully depicts workmen involved with the construction of an 18th-century galleon in Havana, Cuba.

Below

For everyday use the Spaniards utilized copper coins such as these, called maravedis or vellon, which can be found on many New World shipwrecks.

Part of the Ind. of CUBA.

Year 1748. An English squadron of warships commanded by Admiral Knowles attempted to capture the Nueva España Flota, Captain-General Spinola. During the battle near Havana, the Almiranta of the flota lost her masts and was forced to run aground on the coast, where the Spaniards set her afire. Within an hour she blew up, scattering the beach with many of the more than 10 million pesos in treasure she carried. A merchant nao of this flota was lost in Ensenada de Vixiras, 95 leagues east of Havana attempting to escape from the English warships.

Year 1749. A large unidentified ship was wrecked on the Jardines Reefs, near Cape San Anton.

Year 1751. Galleon *San Antonio y San Felix*, Captain Ocana, sailing from Cartagena for Spain, was lost during a storm on the coast between capes San Anton and Corrientes, crew and 400,000 pesos saved.

Year 1752. During a hurricane on September 26, 16 unidentified ships were lost near Havana.

Year 1753. English merchantman *Griffin*, Captain Brown, sailing from Jamaica to London, was lost off Cape San Anton.

Year 1755. Two American merchantmen, *Salisbury*, Captain Ash, and the *Delight*, Captain Fry, both sailing from Honduras to New York, were wrecked on the Los Colorados Reefs. The *Delight*, after throwing overboard part of her cargo, was able to get off the reef; the *Salisbury* lost all of its crew, except for a cabin boy.

Year 1757. English merchantman *Hawke*, Captain Caine, sailing from Jamaica to London, wrecked on November 3 on the Los Colorados Reef.

Year 1758. Two unidentified English merchantmen were lost on the Los Colorados Reef, sailing from Jamaica to England.

Year 1758. English ship *Lion*, Captain Brown, sailing from Jamaica to Bristol, was wrecked on Isla Blanca, on the northern coast of Cuba, crew and part of cargo saved.

Above

Contemporary chart showing the exact location where five British warships were lost off the northwest coast of Cuba in the 18th century.

Below

Spanish olive jars and other artifacts found on an unidentified late-16th-century merchantman off the coast of Bermuda.

351

Year 1760. English warship *H.M.S. Harwich*, 50 guns, Captain William March, wrecked October 4 on the Isle of Pines.

Year 1761. English merchantman *Scorpion*, Captain Quay, sailing from Jamaica to Liverpool, wrecked on the Jardines Reef, near the Isle of Pines.

Year 1762. Shortly before the Spaniards surrendered Havana to the English on June 3, they sank their three largest warships at the entrance to the harbor: galleon *Neptuno*, 70 guns, Captain Pedro Bermudas; galleon *Asia*, 64 guns, Captain Francisco Garganta; and the galleon *Europa*, 60 guns, Captain Jos Vicente. During the English attack on the city, the frigate *La Victoria*, Captain Carlos Joseph de Sarria, sank in the port on "la Colonia del Sacramento."

Year 1762. One English warship, *H.M.S. Chesterfield*, and four transports bringing reinforcements to hold the city of Havana in English hands, wrecked on Cayo Confite, north of Havana, but no lives were lost.

Year 1762. After the English captured the city of Havana, three English warships sank at the entrance of the port while leaving for England with plunder: *Providence*, Captain Strenham, *General Wolfe*, 440 tons, and the *Lion*, 293 tons.

Year 1763. A small advice boat sent from Spain, *N.S. de las Mercedes*, Captain Ram Ortís Delgado, was wrecked at Cape San Anton on January 26.

Year 1763. A ship of unknown registry, Havana, Captain Hale, sailing from New England to Jamaica, was lost off Cape Maize.

Year 1765. English merchantman *Hare*, Captain Colly, sailing from Jamaica to Liverpool, was wrecked on the Colorado Reef, but the crew was saved.

Year 1766. Unidentified Spanish nao, carrying the cargo of the nao *El Nuevo Constante* (which had sunk 75 leagues from the mouth of the Mississippi River), sank between El Morro and La Punta in Havana Harbor.

Year 1768. During a hurricane that struck Havana on October 15, 69 nine ships were sunk, of which 17 belonged to the King. Of these, only five were identified: navío *Tridente*; three frigates, *Nancy*, *Perle* and the *Dorado*; and the packet boat *San Francisco de Paula*. Over 5,000 buildings were also destroyed in the city and the surrounding countryside.

Year 1768. English merchantman *Black River*, Captain M'Taggart, sailing from Jamaica to London, was wrecked on the Isle of Pines but the crew was saved.

Year 1768. A ship of unknown registry, *Neptune*, Captain Hodgson, sailing from Honduras to Leghorn, Italy, was lost in Bahía Honda but the crew was saved.

Year 1770. English hydrographic ship, commanded by Lieutenant John Payne, was wrecked on the Colorado Reef in 22 degrees and 22 minutes of latitude, about four leagues from Cape Buena Vista. Spaniards rescued them and took them to Havana where they were embarked on a ship for Jamaica, which was also wrecked at Cape San Antonio on February 19.

Year 1770. Three other ships were lost on the Colorado Reef this year: English warship *H.M.S. Jamaica*, Captain Talbot, all of the crew was saved; English merchantman *Britannia*, Captain Lawrie, coming from the Bay of Honduras; and the American ship *Nonsuch*, Captain Hall, sailing from Jamaica to South Carolina, the crew was rescued from a raft they constructed from the wreck.

About 1771. English schooner *Rebecca*, Captain Pedro Anson, was wrecked on the Shoals of Santa Isabel. The crew was rescued by a boat from Havana and carried to its port.

Year 1772. During a hurricane on July 20, more than 150 ships of various sizes and nationalities were destroyed in the ports and on the coast.

Year 1773. English merchantman *George*, Captain Stenton, sailing from Jamaica to London, was wrecked on the Colorado Reef.

Year 1773. English ship *Mary*, Captain Aspinal, sailing from Jamaica to London, was wrecked on the Isle of Pines; eight of the crew reached Grand Cayman Island in the ship's longboat.

Year 1776. English merchantman *Rebecca*, Captain Stott, sailing from Jamaica to Bristol, was wrecked on the Colorado Reef but the crew was saved.

Year 1777. American merchantman *Sally*, Captain Thompson, sailing from Jamaica to New York, was totally lost on the Jardines Reef, some of the crew were saved.

Year 1778. During a hurricane (date not stated), many ships were lost in and around Havana Harbor.

Year 1780. During a hurricane on October 3, 13 English warships were lost on the Jardines Reefs on the south coast of the island. They were in the squadron commanded by Sir Hyde Park, sailing from Jamaica to Pensacola, Florida: *Thunderer*, 74 guns; *Stirling Castle*, 64 guns; *Phoenix*, 44 guns; *La Blanche*, 42 guns; *Laurel*, 28 guns; *Andromeda*, 28 guns; *Deal Castle*, 24 guns; *Scarborough*, 20 guns; *Beaver's Prize*, 16 guns; *Barbadoes*, 14 guns; *Camelon*, 14 guns; *Endeavour*, 14 guns; and the *Victor*, 10 guns. Most of the crews on these ships were lost.

Year 1783. Scottish merchantman *Blandford*, Captain Troup, sailing from Jamaica to Scotland, was totally lost on the Isle of Pines.

Year 1784. Spanish brigantine *Carlota*, arriving from Spain, sank at the entrance of Matanzas Bay on December 23.

Year 1784. English ship *Mercury*, Captain Taylor, sailing from Africa and Jamaica to Bristol, was wrecked on the Jardines Reef on March 13.

Year 1785. English merchantman *Port María*, Captain Potter, sailing from Jamaica to London, was totally lost on the Jardines Reefs on the south side of the island but the crew was saved.

Year 1785. Scottish merchantman *Friendship*, Captain Curry, sailing from Jamaica to Dublin, was lost in Havana Harbor.

Year 1786. Spanish frigate of war *Santa Tecla*, Captain Carlos Chacon, burnt completely in Havana Harbor.

Year 1787. Two merchantmen lost in the Colorado Reef: English ship *Ranger*, Captain Patterson, sailing from Jamaica to Bermuda, five men were drowned; and the Irish ship *Hannah*, Captain Williamson, sailing from Jamaica to Cork, struck on a sunken rock a few leagues northeast of the reef on August 2 but the crew reached Havana in 13 days in the ship's boat.

Year 1788. Spanish schooner *Carmen*, wrecked at Punta Sabanilla, near Havana.

Year 1790. English merchantman *Flora*, Captain Fatheringham, sailing from Jamaica to Leith, was lost on the Jardines Reef, near the Isle of Pines.

Year 1791. Ship of unknown registry Ally, Captain Sparling, sailing from Africa and Dominica to Havana, wrecked on Cayo Romano, crew and cargo saved.

Year 1791. A hurricane on June 21 caused the house of a count named Barretos, at Puestes Grandes, to be swept into the sea. He had died the same day, so his coffin went into the sea.

Year 1792. During a hurricane on October 29 an unidentified brig was carried 100 yards ashore at Alares Castle in Havana; two ships were wrecked near Batabano and four others wrecked along the coast.

Year 1792. Two unidentified English merchantmen were wrecked near the Isle of Pines.

Year 1792. Four merchantmen were lost on the Jardines Reef: English ship *Good Intent*, Captain Kennedy, sailing from Jamaica to London; English ship *Sarah*, sailing from Jamaica to Liverpool, her cargo of sugar was lost but some rum and lumber were saved; Scottish ship *Eliza Partridge*, Captain Trenham, sailing from Jamaica to Dublin, crew and part of cargo saved; and the Scottish ship *Charming Mary*, Captain English, sailing from Jamaica to Dublin; part of her cargo of sugar, rum, coffee, ginger and castor oil was saved.

Year 1793. English merchantman *Albion*, Captain Mentor, sailing from Jamaica to Bristol, sank off Cape San Antonio after colliding with another ship but her crew was saved.

Year 1794. During a hurricane at Havana on August 27 and 28, 76 ships were totally lost and others damaged. Of those lost, 12 were Spanish warships and the others were merchantmen of different countries. Only two ships were identified: Spanish warship *Flor*, and the English merchantman *Sandown*, Captain Apsey, sailing from Jamaica to Havana. Most of the cargoes were later salvaged.

Year 1796. During a hurricane on October 2 and 3, five unidentified ships were totally lost in Havana Harbor.

Year 1797. Spanish frigate of war *Palas*, 34 guns, Captain Pedro Saenz de la Guardia, part of a Spanish squadron going after an English squadron, wrecked in two fathoms of water on "el placer de Cayo Blanco," near the Colorado Reef but the ship was later completely salvaged.

Year 1797. Spanish warship *Ventura*, Captain Luis Cabaleri, was wrecked at Punta del Palo while chasing a pirate ship; several men were drowned.

Year 1798. American ship *Mable*, Captain Reynolds, sailing from Jamaica to New York, was lost on the Colorado Reef but the crew was saved.

Year 1799. Spanish frigate *Guadalupe*, Captain Joseph de la Encina, was wrecked on Cape San Antonio on March 15 and 147 persons perished.

Year 1800. English warship *H.M.S. Diligence*, 18 guns, Captain Charles Baynton Hodgson, was wrecked in September on a shoal near Havana; crew was saved.

Year 1801. English warship *H.M.S. Bonetta*, 18 guns, Captain Thomas New, was wrecked on the Jardines Reef on October 25 but the crew was saved.

Year 1802. Two English merchantmen, sailing from Jamaica to London, were wrecked on the Isle of Pines: *Diana*, Captain Williams, on July 19; and the *Westmoreland*, Captain Smellie, but her crew was saved.

Year 1803. An unidentified French ship of Captain Gilbert was wrecked on the Shoals of Los Jardines del Rey.

Year 1805. English merchantman *Paget*, Captain Straycock, sailing from Jamaica to London, was wrecked at Cape San Antonio.

Year 1805. English warship *H.M.S. Barracouta*, 10 guns, Captain Joel Orchard, was wrecked on Jordan Key on October 2 but the crew was saved.

Year 1806. American merchantman *Albert*, Captain Hall, sailing from Boston to Jamaica, was wrecked at Cape Maize; part of her cargo was saved.

Year 1807. Spanish schooner *Piedad*, Captain José Fernandez de la Peña, sailing from Cartagena to Havana with mail, ran aground on January 19 in Baní but people, mail, and cannon were saved.

Year 1807. Two American ships were wrecked on the Colorado Reef: *Merry Quaker*, Captain Brown, sailing from Jamaica to New York, on January 9; and the *Lewis Williams*, Captain O'Brien, sailing from New Orleans to New York, March 23, but the crew was saved.

Year 1808. English warship *H.M.S. Muros*, 24 guns, Captain Archibald Duff, lost at the entrance to Balia Honda but the crew was saved.

Year 1809. Canadian ship *Cyrus*, Captain Lovitt, sailing from Jamaica to Halifax, was lost on Cape Comentes.

Year 1809. A ship of unknown registry, *Spanish Junta*, Captain Murray, sailing from London to Havana, was lost on Stoney Point Reef, located about three miles from Guazava Key on the north side of Cuba, but the crew was saved.

Year 1809. Two merchantmen were wrecked near the Isle of Pines: Scottish ship *Ann Phillippa*, sailing from Jamaica to Glasgow, on January 22; and a ship of unknown registry, *Tartaruga*, Captain Smith, sailing from Bahía, Brazil, to Havana, on a reef 12 leagues east-southeast of the Isle of Pines.

Year 1810. A ship of unknown registry, *May*, Captain Laughton, was burnt at Havana on July 25 but the crew was saved.

Year 1810. During a hurricane at Havana from October 23 to 26, 32 ships were sunk or wrecked, and the pier, church and 60 buildings were carried into the sea.

Year 1811. Two English merchantmen were wrecked at the Isle of Pines: *Louisa*, Captain Folger; and the *Hannah*, Captain Ellis, on January 29, both sailing from Jamaica to London.

Year 1811. American ship *Alexander*, Captain Hall, sailing from Jamaica to the United States, was totally lost on Cape Cruz at the end of May.

Year 1811. American schooner *Phoebe*, Captain Murray, was burnt off Santiago de Cuba but the crew was saved.

Year 1811. English ship *Edward Foote*, Captain Smart, sailing from Jamaica to London, was lost off Havana in February but her crew was saved.

Year 1812. During a hurricane on October 14 at Trinidad de Cuba a number of unidentified ships were sunk.

Year 1813. A ship of unknown registry, *Catalena*, Captain Ferrer, sailing from San Andres Island to Jamaica, was wrecked on White Key, near Trinidad de Cuba, July 24, crew and part of cargo saved.

Year 1813. Canadian ship *Olive*, Captain Vandirey, sailing from Jamaica to Halifax, was lost on September 17 near the Isle of Pines but the crew was saved.

Year 1813. Two English ships were wrecked at Havana: *Nancy*, Captain Bowden, sailing from Jamaica to London, October 8, very little of her cargo was saved; and the *Lancaster*, Captain Andrews, bound to Liverpool, July 21.

Year 1814. Two English ships sailing from London to Havana were totally lost near Havana on February 2: *Navigator*, Captain Preda, and the *Esther*, Captain Newman.

Year 1815. American ship *Pacific*, Captain Clark, sailing from Santo Domingo to Boston, was lost on July 13 on the Jardines Reef, crew and small part of cargo saved.

Year 1815. A ship of unknown registry, *Sarah*, Captain Kelly, sailing from Jamaica to Halifax, was lost entering Havana Harbor on January 14.

Year 1816. English sloop-of-war *H.M.S. Briseis*, 10 guns, Captain George Domett, wrecked on a reef November 5 near Punta Pedras; crew was saved.

Year 1816. Spanish frigate-of-war *Atocha*, 40 guns, Captain Lorenzo Noriega, caught on fire and sank in Havana Harbor on July 4.

Year 1816. During a violent gale on June 14, 12 or 14 unidentified ships were wrecked in Trinidad de Cuba Harbor.

Year 1816. A ship of unknown registry, *Clara*, sailing from Rio de la Hacha, Colombia, to Jamaica, put into Santiago de Cuba in distress and sank soon after.

Year 1816. Bahamian ship *Minerva*, Captain Whitehead, sailing from Jamaica to the Bahamas, was lost on Cape Maize.

Year 1817. A ship of unknown registry, *Lark*, Captain Knight, sailing to Havana, was wrecked on September 17 on the Nuevitas Reef, crew and part of cargo saved.

Year 1817. English ship *Jane*, Captain M'Bride, sailing from Jamaica to Greenock, England, wrecked near Cape Corrientes on June 9, crew and passengers saved.

Year 1817. Three ships wrecked near Havana: a ship of unknown registry, *Hercules*, during February; English brig *Prince Regent*, arriving from the Bahamas with a cargo of salt, during a gale on March 3; and the English brig *Liberty*, December 20, but her cargo was completely salvaged.

Year 1818. French ship *Clementine*, after arriving from St. Malo, France, during a storm on December 15, wrecked in Havana Harbor, crew and part of cargo saved.

Year 1818. Scottish merchantman *Amelia*, Captain Williams, sailing from Jamaica to Clyde, Scotland, wrecked on the Jardines Reef, near the Isle of Pines, on May 2.

Year 1818. Three merchant ships were wrecked on the Colorado Reef: English ship *Mariner*, Captain Whillis, sailing from London to Havana, crew, silver and gold specie and small part of cargo saved; American ship *Berkeley*, Captain Dent, sailing from Jamaica to Virginia, during a gale on November 17 (after being plundered by Spaniards she was set afire but her crew was saved); and the American ship *Joan*, sailing from Jamaica to Norfolk, July 4, crew and part of cargo saved.

Year 1819. Scottish ship *Sir Thomas Graham*, Captain Thomson, sailing from Jamaica to Havana, was lost in March on the Jardines Reef.

Year 1819. English merchantman *Syren*, Captain Clark, sailing from Jamaica to London, was totally wrecked on a rocky point near Cape San Antonio on June 9, only her crew was saved.

Year 1821. Two English merchantmen wrecked near Cape San Antonio: *Aristides*, sailing from Liverpool to New Orleans, was captured by pirates and then wrecked; and the *Duke of Bedford*, Captain Holliday, sailing from Jamaica to London, quickly went to pieces.

Year 1821. During a gale on September 13, four unidentified Spanish vessels and the American schooner *Olive Branch*, Captain Smith, were lost in the port of Gibara.

Year 1821. A ship of unknown registry, *Devon*, Captain Carlisle, sailing from Jamaica to Cork, wrecked on a reef off Cape Corrientes on September 16, only some of her crew were saved.

Year 1821. A ship of unknown registry, *Villorius*, Captain M'Kernly, sailing from the Plata River, Argentina, to Havana, was wrecked at Baracoa at the end of September, most of her cargo was saved.

Year 1821. French ship *Amie*, Captain Falvey, sailing from Haiti to Havana, lost on September 13 off the Isle of Pines, only the crew was saved.

Year 1821. English ship *Hall*, sailing from Jamaica to Liverpool, was wrecked at Havana on April 30 during a gale, small part of her cargo was saved.

Year 1821. American ship *Two Brothers*, Captain Blackman, sailing from Charleston, South Carolina, to Matanzas Bay, was wrecked on Cayo Blanco, located about 30 miles east of Matanzas.

Year 1821. American merchantman *Hannah*, Captain Lewis, sailing from Santiago de Cuba to Philadelphia, wrecked during September on the Colorado Reef.

Year 1822. French ship *Actif*, Captain Belliard, sailing from Havana to Le Havre, was lost near Nuevitas.

Year 1822. A ship of unknown registry, *Union*, Captain Munro, sailing from Jamaica to Nova Scotia, was lost on a reef 16 leagues from Matanzas Bay.

Year 1822. Bermudan ship *Carso*, Captain Peabody, sailing from Jamaica to Bermuda, was wrecked two leagues east of Havana on January 5.

Year 1822. Spanish frigate of war *Ligera*, 40 guns, sank in the port of Santiago de Cuba.

Year 1823. Large Spanish ship *Churrieca*, Captain Aspurua, sailing from Cadíz, Spain, to Veracruz, was totally destroyed by fire near Morro Castle, in Havana Harbor, in April, with a cargo worth over $100,000.

Year 1823. A ship of unknown registry, *Eliza & Polly*, Captain Forsyth, after leaving Havana, wrecked a few miles west of it.

Year 1823. A ship of unknown registry, *Freetown*, arriving from Jamaica in ballast, was lost on June 10 entering Santiago de Cuba.

Year 1823. A ship of unknown registry, *Caesar*, Captain Jars, sailing from Hamburg, Germany, to Havana, was wrecked on Cayo Romano but her cargo was saved by wreckers and carried to Nassau.

Year 1824. Two ships were wrecked at Cape Corrientes: a ship of unknown registry, *Fleetwood*, Captain Herring, sailing from Jamaica to London, on June 2; and the French ship *Reparateur*, Captain Freore, sailing from Cuba to Bordeaux, France, on June 1.

Year 1824. Spanish ship *General Palafox*, Captain Abente, sailing from Cadíz to Havana, was totally lost near the Isle of Pines.

Year 1824. A ship of unknown registry, *Azores*, Captain Bedford, sailing from Jamaica to Trinidad de Cuba, was lost while entering this port on March 2 but her crew was saved.

Year 1825. Two ships were lost on the coast near Matanzas Bay: American ship *Arinthea Bell*, Captain Pearson, sailing from Baltimore to Havana, crew and part of cargo saved; and a large Dutch ship found with no crew aboard but the decks running with blood (believed to have been plundered and set adrift by pirates).

Year 1825. A ship of unknown registry, *Telegraph*, Captain Dixon, coming from Alvarado, Mexico, was wrecked near Havana.

Chapter Nine

Hispaniola

Although there are a great number of interesting shipwrecks around this huge island very little salvage work has been undertaken. Both the governments of Haiti and the Dominican Republic have laws regarding the salvaging of shipwrecks by foreigners. About a dozen shipwreck projects have been undertaken in the past 10 years or so.

In 1955 millionaire Edwin Link and Mendel Peterson of the Smithsonian Institution attempted to locate Columbus's *Santa María*, which was wrecked at Cape Haitian in 1492, and although they didn't locate the shipwreck they claimed to have discovered an iron anchor from it. Similar anchors, also claimed to be from this shipwreck, have been found in the same area by Haitian fishermen. In 1967 a group from New Jersey undertook an expedition after this same shipwreck and claimed to have discovered it, but I have been unable to confirm their claim.

Over the years dredging operations in the port of Santo Domingo have exposed large numbers of artifacts and gold and silver coins. On a recent trip to Santo Domingo I was told by naval officers that some of their divers had recovered several thousand gold coins off a shipwreck a few miles east of the port of Santo Domingo.

In many articles and books concerning sunken treasure, authors claim that the port of Puerto Plata (Silver Port) on the north coast of the island was a staging and departure port for homeward-bound Spanish treasure ships. This is untrue. The port was named for another reason. When Columbus first sighted it, the large mountain behind the port was covered with a silver-colored cloud. For this reason he named it Silver Port.

Another erroneous tale which appears in sunken treasure literature concerns a large table made of solid gold: It was supposedly lost in 1502 near Mona Island. The truth is that a very large gold nugget was found on the island, and when the governor wrote to Spain telling of the loss of the ship carrying the nugget, he said "that it was big enough to eat off of," meaning that it was as large as a plate and not a table.

Weather and working conditions on shipwreck sites are about the same as they are throughout the rest of the Caribbean, and the calmest months are during the hurricane season, (obviously when no hurricane is imminent). Of the more than 430 ships that have been lost around Hispaniola, I have listed only those whose locations are fairly accurately given and those that are of major interest. In many cases documents stated simply that ships were lost on or at Hispaniola.

Shipwrecks in Hispaniolan Waters

Year 1492. Columbus's flagship, the caravel *Santa María*, was wrecked on a reef in Caracol Bay, near Cape Haitian. Columbus and the survivors from this wreck stripped the ship of all its wood, fittings, and supplies, which they used to build a fort with the intention of waiting until Columbus could return to rescue them on his second voyage. If anything of this wreck remains on the reef, it would probably be only ballast stones (if the ship carried any). A few years ago archaeologist Dr. Catherine Deagan of the University of Florida discovered fragments of the ship's hull and metal fittings on the land site of La Navidad where the shipwrecks survivors built a fort and small settlement. ·

Year 1494. On Columbus's second voyage he founded a settlement on the north coast and named it Isabela. Two of his caravels, *Mariagalante* and *Gallega*, are believed to have been lost there during a hurricane.

Year 1495. During the month of October a hurricane struck the port of Isabela and six or seven caravels were reported lost here. One account states that two of Columbus's ships, *San Juan* and *Cordera*, and four ships of the explorer Juan Aquardo were lost. Another account states that these six plus another of Columbus's ships, the *Gallega*, were lost. This second account may be confusing the loss of the *Gallega* during the hurricane in 1494 with the 1495 hurricane.

Year 1500. Two unidentified caravels of the explorer Vicente Yaqez Pinzón were wrecked during a storm on the Shoals of Babura.

Year 1501. Two unidentified naos of the captains Rodrigo de Bastidas and Juan de la Cosa, with cargoes of gold nuggets and dust as well as brazilwood and other products, were lost in Puerto Principe.

Year 1502. Columbus was in the port of Santo Domingo while a large fleet of 30 caravels and naos was preparing to sail for Spain. He attempted to prevent their departure, claiming there were signs of a hurricane. But Governor Bobadilla, who was his enemy, would not heed his advice, and the fleet sailed, carrying a large amount of gold (including the plate-size nugget) and other valuables. The fleet, commanded by Admiral Antonio de Torres, left port around the beginning of July, and 30 or 40 hours later the hurricane struck and all but four ships were lost. Most of them wrecked on the coasts eight to 10 leagues east of the port; others sank on the high seas near Mona Island. More than 500 persons perished.

About 1505. After the fleet of the lawyer Lucas Vazquez de Ayllon reached Santo Domingo from Spain, one ship, *El Breton,* was sent to carry colonists to new lands, but bad weather forced into Puerto Plata, where it sank at anchor.

Year 1508. During a hurricane on August 3 in which most of the town of Santo Domingo was leveled, more than 20 unidentified caravels and naos were sunk or wrecked in the port or along the nearby coast. When the hurricane first struck, many ships threw their cannon overboard in the port to lighten the ships.

Year 1509. Another hurricane struck this same port on August 8 and 18 or 20 ships of various sizes, including several that Columbus's son Diego had just brought from Spain, were sunk. During this same storm a small vessel owned by a religious named Mariscal was wrecked on the small key of Alto Volo, located 50 leagues west of the port of Santo Domingo, with six of the eight persons aboard drowning.

Year 1524. Four merchant ships left the port of Santo Domingo on their way to Spain carrying a considerable amount of gold which had been found on Hispaniola. A storm forced them into the port of Puerto de Plata on the north coast where they all wrecked.

Year 1526. Nao *SantaMaría,* 110 tons, Captain Pedro Nuñez, sank in Puerto Plata after loading aboard a cargo of sugar. Other accounts place the sinking in 1524 and 1525.

Year 1528. Unidentified ship of Captain Alonso Duran was wrecked in the port of Puerto Real sometime before April.

Year 1541. A small French pirate vessel with a crew of only 35 men captured and plundered a large Spanish merchantman, then wrecked it on Mona Island.

Year 1542. Nao *San Miguel,* a ship in the fleet of Admiral Francisco de Montejo, sailing from Santo Domingo to Spain, was lost near Cape Cabrón, about 15 leagues from Puerto Plata, carrying a large amount of gold and silver.

Year 1545. Two hurricanes struck the town and port of Santo Domingo. The first occurred on August 20 and many ships in port were lost. The second, which was even worse, occurred on September 18 and destroyed all the ships not lost in the first hurricane. Roughly 10 ships were lost in the Ozama River in the port, five near the fort, several others by the house of Columbus, more on the coast near the port and one ship of Captain Cruzado on Saona Island. The total number of ships lost during this second hurricane was 18 to 20.

Year 1547. During a hurricane the nao *San Juan,* 200 tons, Captain Martín de Zavalo, sailing from Spain to Nombre de Díos, Panama, was wrecked in Puerto Hermoso. Another account gives the date as 1549.

Year 1551. A French pirate ship with a crew of 150 men was wrecked on the coast of Iaguana and only a few escaped.

Year 1551. The flotas of Nueva España and Tierra Firme joined in Havana with the Armada de Tierra Firme, commanded by Captain-General Sancho de Veidma, and entered the Bahama Channel for the return to Spain. During a storm in the channel, the galleon *San Miguel,* 200 tons, Captain Salvador Garrido, owned by the viceroy of Mexico, Don Luis de Velasco, carrying a very valuable cargo of gold and silver specie and bullion, lost her mainmast and rudder and drifted until wrecking on a reef between Cape Frances and Cape Cabrón. about 30 leagues from Puerto de Plata. All of her people were saved and divers recovered all of her treasure.

Year 1552. A terrible hurricane struck the port of Santo Domingo on August 29 and three navíos and a patache were lost with 130 men.

Year 1553. Treasure-laden nao *La Salvadora*, Captain Juan Rodríguez, sailing from Mexico to Spain, was caught in a storm in the Bahama Channel, losing all her masts, and drifted until wrecking on the coast near Monte Cristi. All of her gold and silver was recovered by divers.

Year 1553. During a hurricane that struck the port of Santo Domingo, 16 merchantmen, loaded and ready to set sail for Seville, were totally lost. At the same time, three naos and one patache, commanded by Cristsbal Colón (the nephew of the famous discoverer), were also lost on the coast.

Year 1554. A small armada was sent out from Santo Domingo in pursuit of a pirate vessel that had captured a number of local vessels. While anchored at La Yaguana a hurricane sank six of these ships.

Year 1556. Nao *San Bartolome*, 120 tons, Captain Blas Alonso, sailing from Santo Domingo to Spain, was wrecked on the coast near the port of Santo Domingo shortly after sailing but divers recovered her cargo of gold, silver, and hides.

Year 1564. Nao *SantaMarta de Guadalupe*, 250 tons, Captain Salvador Gomez, after receiving the cargo of gold and silver from a ship that had sunk in the Bahama Channel during a storm, lost her masts and drifted until it wrecked near Monte Cristi, where divers later recovered all of the treasure she carried.

Year 1584. An oared galley, *Santiago*, sent from Santo Domingo to search for pirates, was wrecked on the reefs in front of Puerto de Plata, all of the galley slaves perished.

Year 1595. Nao *Nuestra Señora del Rosario*, Captain Melchor de los Reyes, 150 tons, sailing between Santo Domingo and Havana was totally lost at Cabo de Tiburón.

Year 1603. An unidentified merchant nao in the Nueva España Flota of Captain-General Fulgencio de Meneses, sailing from Spain to Veracruz, was wrecked on the southern coast of the island.

Year 1605. An unidentified Spanish advice boat was lost on Mona Island enroute from Spain to Santo Domingo.

Year 1609. Small navío *San Vicente Ferrer*, 84 tons, Captain Gaspar Alvarez, sailing from Puerto Rico to Havana and Spain, was wrecked near Samana Bay, only her crew was saved.

Year 1611. Navío *Santa María de la Gracia*, Captain Juan Baptista de Leon, 150 tons, was sunk while at anchor in the Port of Santo Domingo but her cargo was removed before the disaster.

Year 1623. Navío *N.S. de la Concepción*, Captain Thomas de Santa Ana, 150 tons, had just arrived from Angola with ivory tusks, gold dust and slaves when she sank near the entrance to the port of Santo Domingo.

Year 1626. Nao *La Candelaria*, 300 tons, Captain Juan de Patermina, sailed from Santo Domingo for Spain with three other naos, all carrying only island productsand no treasure. But near La Saona Island, three enemy ships gave chase and forced it to run aground on this small island, where it broke into pieces and sank.

Year 1629. Nao *N.S. de la Concepción y San Francisco*, Captain Hernando Mateos de Vera, 500 tons, was sailing in that year's New Spain Fleet. She was leaking so badly that she was forced into port at Santo Domingo. While at anchor she went down with a cargo of mercury and other merchandise.

Year 1631. An unidentified Dutch warship was wrecked during a storm near the port of Santo Domingo.

Year 1635. The Spaniards launched an attack on the Island of Tortuga, where pirates had been living for about six years. During the attack the Spaniards burned two ships and one pinnace after murdering all of the pirates and their families.

Year 1652. During a hurricane in September the English ship *Honest Seaman* was cast ashore at Porto Piña.

Year 1658. Portuguese slave ship of Captain Juan Bautista Pluma sank in Santo Domingo Harbor, and the divers who recovered twelve iron cannon of six- to eight-pound shot from the wreck, were paid 158 reals in silver.

Year 1669. English privateering frigate *Oxford*, 240 tons, caught fire on January 12 while anchored at the Isle of Ash and blew up with a loss of over two hundred lives. The ship had just returned from a successful attack on Portobelo, Panama, and was carrying a great deal of plunder.

Year 1670. During a storm in October, when the privateer Henry Morgan was waiting for other ships to join his fleet, 10 of his 11 ships were run ashore on the Isle de Vache, all except three were refloated.

Year 1673. An English privateering ship that operated out of Port Royal, Jamaica, the *Jamaica Merchant*, Captain Knapman (with Henry Morgan aboard) wrecked on February 25 on the east side of the Isle de Vache (also called Vaca and Vacour), because of the pilot's faulty navigation. Five or six days later they were rescued by another Jamaican privateering vessel and carried back to Jamaica. The governor of Jamaica sent salvage sloops to the wreck site and 20 large cannon and 212 cannonballs were recovered.

Year 1677. A Dutch fleet attacked all the French ships in the port of Petit-Goave and, after sacking them, burned them.

Year 1680. During a hurricane at the port of Santo Domingo on August 15, 25 French warships commanded by the Comte de Estre and several Spanish merchantmen carrying a very valuable cargoes of treasures from South America, were all lost; there were only a few survivors.

Year 1702. An English fleet forced ashore a large French man-of- war at Petit-Goave. Rather than let it fall into English hands, the French blew it up. Nearby, the English captured and burned two French merchantmen.

Year 1706. English warship *H.M.S. Dunkirk Prize*, 24 guns, Captain George Purvis, while in pursuit of a French ship on October 18, ran on a rock off Cape Frances and broke into pieces.

Year 1721. An unidentified nao, sailing from Spain to Veracruz, was wrecked in Sancana Bay.

Year 1724. The Nueva España Flota, commanded by Captain- General Baltasar de Guevara, sailed from Veracruz on August 25, but after leaving the Bahama Channel and heading toward Bermuda, a hurricane forced it to head south and an undisclosed number of ships, heavily laden with treasure, were lost in the area of Samana Bay. Its Capitana, *N.S. de Guadalupe y San Antonio*, sank on September 12 in deep water near this bay; the Almiranta *La Tolosa* wrecked at Cape Samana, and other merchant naos wrecked on the reefs of the bay. Over 120 lives were lost, but all the ships, with the exception of the Capitana, were completely salvaged.

Year 1737. During a hurricane on October 5 at the port of Santo Domingo, the whole town was leveled and a large number of ships were wrecked or sank at anchor in the harbor.

Year 1742. English warship *H.M.S. Tiger*, 50 guns, Captain Edward Herbert, wrecked on January 12 on a small key near Tortuga Island.

Year 1747. An English privateer forced a large French privateer to run ashore near Monte Cristi but her crew was saved.

Year 1749. French merchantman *Atlas*, Captain Tegail, was lost leaving the port of Cape Frances while sailing for Bordeaux but the crew was saved.

Year 1754. During a September hurricane at the port of Santo Domingo, 12 merchantmen were wrecked and more than 1,700 hogsheads of sugar were lost with them.

Year 1757. English warship *H.M.S. Assistance* chased two French privateering vessels, along with an English vessel they had captured, into Tiberón Bay, where the French had a fort. The French burned all three vessels near the shore under the guns of the fort.

Year 1762. French warship *Dragon*, 64 guns, was wrecked at Cape François.

Year 1770. French merchantman *Mecca*, Captain Merle, sailing from Hispaniola to Bordeaux, was wrecked near Cape François.

Year 1772. During a violent gale at the end of August, 28 French ships were lost near the northwestern tip of the island, and 280 bodies were washed ashore the following morning.

Year 1772. English merchantman *Intelligence*, Captain Hubbert, was lost on January 2 entering Cape François; 21 slaves drowned and most of her cargo was lost.

Year 1774. English slave ship *Ellis*, Captain Rylands, sailing from Africa and Barbados to Jamaica, was lost on the Isle of Ash but her crew and all 450 slaves were saved.

Year 1779. French warship of the fleet of the Count D'Estaing, *Tounant*, was badly damaged in a storm and sank a few days afterward at Cape François around the beginning of December.

Year 1782. Two large English warships drove the French warship *Scipion*, 74 guns, ashore near Cape François on October 18.

Year 1783. A ship of unknown registry, *Delight*, Captain Anderson, sailing from Grenada Island to Havana, was wrecked on June 3 at Tortuga Island, part of her cargo was saved.

Year 1784. A ship of unknown registry, *Friendship*, Captain Reily, sailing from Dublin to Philadelphia, was wrecked at Cape François.

Year 1785. English ship *Cornwallis*, Captain M'Gowan, sailing from Antigua to Port Royal, Jamaica, was wrecked during a hurricane on August 25 at Neve Bay and totally lost but the crew was saved.

Year 1788. During a hurricane at Port-au-Prince on August 16, more than 25 ships were lost. Another 25 were wrecked on the coasts nearby.

Year 1790. Large Scottish merchantman *Active*, Captain Douglas, sailing from Glasgow to Jamaica, was lost on the Isle de Vache on March 7, crew and part of cargo saved.

Year 1792. French merchantman *Clement*, Captain Omalin, sailing for Bordeaux, was lost leaving the port of Santo Domingo.

Year 1792. French merchantman *Jume Eiema*, Captain Camden, after arriving from Bordeaux, was lost in the Harbor of Cape François.

Year 1796. English warship *H.M.S. Salisbury*, 50 guns, Captain William Mitchell, wrecked on May 13 on Isle de Avanche but none of her crew of 343 men was lost.

Year 1796. English sloop-of-war *H.M.S. Cormorant*, 18 guns, Captain Thomas Gott, accidentally blew up at Port-au-Prince and 95 of her crew of 121 men were lost.

Year 1797. English warship *H.M.S. Tartar*, 28 guns, Captain Charles Elphinstone, was wrecked on July 1 when leaving the port of Puerto de Plata but none of her crew of 195 men was lost.

Year 1798. A ship of unknown registry, *Cornelia*, Captain Gilbert, sailing to Charleston, South Carolina, was lost in the port of Jeremie, on the northwest Tiburón Peninsula of Haiti.

Year 1802. English merchantman *Arethusa*, Captain Dods, sailing from London to Jamaica, was wrecked on the Isle of Ash, crew and part of cargo saved.

Year 1803. English warship *H.M.S. Garland*, 22 guns, Captain Frederick Cottrell, was wrecked at Cape François in November.

Year 1806. Two French warships, *Imperial*, 120 guns, and the *Diomede*, 74 guns, were sunk during action with an English fleet commanded by Vice-Admiral Sir J. T. Duckworth off the port of Santo Domingo.

Year 1808. English schooner-of-war *H.M.S. Flying Fish*, 12 guns, Captain J. Glassford Gooding, was wrecked on December 15 on a reef eastward of Point Salines, but her crew was saved.

Year 1808. Ship of unknown registry, *Catherine*, Captain Dohlin, sailing from St. Thomas, Virgin Islands, to Jacmel, Haiti, was lost on December 19 on the reef at Saona Island.

Year 1809. English merchantman *Queen*, Captain Sherwood, sailing to London, was wrecked near the Aux Cayes.

Year 1810. English merchantman *Caerwent*, Captain Browner, sailing to London, was lost on May 31 when leaving Jacmel Harbor, Haiti.

Year 1810. During a gale on September 27, about 10 Haitian vessels were driven ashore at Jeremie, and the English ship *Ellen* was wrecked near Aux Cayes.

Year 1812. American merchantman *Frederick William*, Captain Henchman, sailing from Lisbon to Boston, was wrecked on Isle de Vache on May 17; four of the crew perished.

Year 1816. During a hurricane on September 19, all of the shipping at Port-au-Prince was wrecked or sunk.

Year 1816. English ship *Shark*, arriving from London, was accidentally burned at Port-au-Prince about February 4.

Year 1817. American schooner *Roxana*, coming from Nantucket, was lost on Isle de Ash; crew and part of cargo saved.

Year 1817. French ship *Jean Marie*, Captain Bowie, sailing from Marseilles to Hispaniola, wrecked on the coast near Samana Bay around the end of May, crew and part of cargo saved.

Year 1818. American ship *Latona*, Captain Low, sailing from London to New Orleans, was lost in Samana Bay, but her crew was saved.

Year 1819. A ship of unknown registry, *Sally*, Captain Brockesby, sailing from Amsterdam to Havana, was totally lost near Puerto Principe.

Year 1819. An unidentified brig, sailing to England, was lost on July 30 at Port-au-Prince; and a Scottish merchantman, *Lord Belhaven*, sailing from Glasgow to Port-au-Prince, was lost about 20 miles from this latter port.

Year 1821. English ship *Favorite*, Captain Hayward, coming from Jamaica, was wrecked on April 19 at St. Jago port but her crew was saved.

Year 1821. American merchantman *Intrepid*, Captain Crofts, arriving from Charleston, South Carolina, was wrecked in Jacmel Harbor, Haiti, during a gale on January 30.

Year 1821. A ship of unknown registry, *Felix*, Captain Condon, was lost on Cape Engano on July 2.

Year 1821. During heavy gales from September 2 to 4, four merchantmen were wrecked at the Aux Cayes: a ship of unknown registry, *Peace*, Captain Clarkson, and three American ships: *Rover*, Captain Johnson, *Ann*, Captain Berchier, and an unidentified vessel.

Year 1822. American ship *Commerce*, Captain M'Knight, sailing from St. Thomas, Virgin Islands, to Hispaniola, was totally lost on Cape St. Nicolas Mole on June 10 but her crew was saved.

Year 1823. American ship *Jefferson*, Captain Marlore, sailing from Philadelphia to Dominica Island, was totally lost on January 10 on the Isle de Vache but her crew was saved.

Year 1824. A Jamaican cutter, *Swallow*, Captain Robertson, sailing from Jamaica to Barbados, was wrecked due to strong currents on Isle de Vache on November 12, crew and part of cargo saved.

Above

This ornate bowl of a clay smoking pipe, c. 1690, was one of the many relics recovered by Bob Marx from the sunken city of Port Royal, Jamaica.

Below

Examples of uncleaned and cleaned "Pilar Dollars," Spanish eight real coins; the cleaned coin was preserved in an electrolytic reduction bath.

GENERAL PLAN

OF THE TOWN OF

PORT ROYAL

Surveyed in June 1827
BY
PHILLIP A. MORRIS
C.S

Coast before the Great

Great Street

Kings Wharf

Thame

Mr...Wharf

Street

Street

Fort James

Sea Coast before the Great Earthquake

Fishery

High

Chapel

Wash House

Water Tank

Store

Dory

Kitchen

Receiving Room

Bathing Room

Hospital St

St

Street

Lime

McQuinns Wharf

McEowans Wharf

The Garrison Wharf

Land belonging to the Government

Chapter Ten

Jamaica
and the Cayman Islands

Between 1504 and 1825, over 900 ships of many nationalities and descriptions were lost in Jamaican waters, but in this chapter I have again listed only shipwrecks for which a fairly exact location is given or those of special interest.

There are very few Spanish shipwrecks around Jamaica because the island was one of the least important colonies in Spanish America and very few ships visited it. The inhabitants were very poor and unable to purchase goods from Spain; nor did they have precious metals or other products to ship back to Spain. There were periods in the 16th and 17th centuries when no large ship put in at Jamaica for as long as 10 years. It wasn't until the English captured Jamaica in 1655 that the island prospered and large numbers of ships visited. In the past two decades, there have been at least 10 large-scale treasure expeditions to Pedro Shoals; and although many interesting artifacts have been recovered from several wreck sites, very little treasure has been found. The Jamaican government has enforced strict laws concerning old shipwrecks, and in 1967 and 1968 three American diving groups were arrested there for illegally diving. The

These Spanish silver coins were among the treasures, relics and artifacts recovered by the author from the sunken city of Port Royal.

government now requires a salvage group to apply for a permit and then post a bond of $10,000 as a guarantee that the shipwreck will be excavated properly and the salvors won't disappear with their recovery before splitting with the government which offers one of the most unattractive agreements of any country in the Western Hemisphere. It receives 100 percent of all artifacts recovered, as well as 50 percent of any treasure, and it has the right to purchase any or all of the 50 percent of the treasure belonging to the salvor at bullion value. Unless the Jamaican government makes a more attractive division arrangement with potential salvors, I doubt if any serious work will be undertaken on the numerous shipwrecks in these waters.

Fortunately, I worked on the other side of the fence when I lived in Jamaica. Employed as the government marine archaeologist from 1965 to 1968, I had no problems about obtaining a fair shake with what I recovered; the government received every single item my team recovered. Most of my time was spent excavating the sunken city of Port Royal, but I also found time to explore several dozen shipwreck sites around the island. Our excavation of Port Royal remains the largest underwater excavation undertaken anywhere in the world. Although limited by insufficient funds, we managed to recover an incredible number of artifacts.

The sunken city of Port Royal is considered the most important marine archaeological site in the Western Hemisphere. The sudden cataclysm that caused Port Royal to sink into the sea is quite similar to the volcanic eruption that destroyed the Roman city of Pompeii in A.D. 79. When archaeologists began excavating Pompeii they uncovered a fantastic time capsule of history. The site was covered very quickly by volcanic ash and remained virtually untouched for almost 2,000 years. After a long, arduous excavation and close study of the findings, archaeologists were able to determine what life was like in Pompeii at the time of the disaster. Because of the similarity in the way the two cities met their end, a thorough excavation of Port Royal should reap similarly dramatic results.

Port Royal was founded very shortly after the British captured Jamaica from the Spaniards in 1655. It first served as a base for the English invasion fleet and soon afterward became the principal army garrison on the island. During the next decade (1660-70), Port Royal was the most important buccaneering base in the West Indies. Henry Morgan is only one of hundreds of successful privateers who brought immense riches in plunder into the boozy, bawdy town from raids on Spanish settlements and shipping. When in 1670 Spain and England

370

signed a peace treaty, the heyday of the privateers ceased but Port Royal continued to prosper.

By the time of the earthquake in 1692 Port Royal had been transformed from a deserted cay to the most important trading center in the New World. The spacious harbor was always crowded with shipping, and the amount and variety of goods that passed over its wharves was astonishing. Contraband trade with the Spanish colonies brought in even greater riches than the plunder obtained by the privateers. From historical documents we know that the town consisted of 2,000 buildings, the majority of which were brick, and many were two stories high. The population was about 8,000 and, although most contemporary accounts claim that the vast majority of the inhabitants were "Godless men," there were several Protestant churches (including a Quaker meeting house), a Roman Catholic chapel and a synagogue.

The wharves, warehouses and houses of the wealthy merchants were located on the harbor, or north side of the town, where the water was deep enough for ships of large tonnage to tie up right against the shore. Three large forts, Charles, James and Carlisle (the latter two sank during the earthquake), as well as several smaller batteries protected the town. The most outstanding buildings were the King's house, where the island's council met; the governor's house; St. Paul's Church (Anglican); the Exchange, the center for the town's main business transaction; the Marshallsea, a prison for men; and Bridewell, a prison for women.

At 20 minutes before noon on June 7, 1692, disaster struck: an earthquake quickly followed by a tidal wave. Within a matter of minutes, nine-tenths of the town had either sunk or slid into the sea and no more than 10 acres of land remained out of the water by the end of the day; and over 20 ships were sunk by the tidal waves. More than 2,000 lives were lost that day, and within a month an additional 3,000 persons died from epidemics that followed the disaster. Most of the survivors moved across the harbor and founded the town of Kingston. Salvage operations began on the very day of the disaster and continued for many years, but the bulk of what was lost during the disaster was missed by the salvors because of deep water or collapsed buildings.

The first six months of our project we mapped the overall site, locating the walls of the buildings buried under sediment with long metal rods, locating large metallic deposits with metal detectors, and removing tons of modern debris that covers the overall site.

The actual excavation began on May 1, 1966, and was carried on six days a week, with each diver averaging nine hours under water a day until June 1968, when the excavation was brought to a halt because of a vast backlog of artifacts awaiting proper preservation. Using a four-inch-diameter airlift, we systematically excavated a rectangular hole 400 feet by 150 feet to an average depth of 15 feet below the sea floor. We estimated that this area originally contained about 30 to 40 buildings at the time of the disaster, and by comparing the owners' initials on pewter and silverware with the old property records we were able to identify the owners of many of these buildings and how they were used.

Although the majority of the buildings had been private homes, we also located two taverns, a carpenter's shop, a silversmith's shop, the fish and meat markets and two turtle crawls. In this same area we also located two shipwrecks dating from the 1692 disaster and a French warship that sank during a hurricane in 1722.

Working conditions were terrible. Underwater visibility was never more than a few inches and constant landslides of sediment into a hole where the divers were working resulted in 24 accidents requiring medical attention. On several occasions divers were trapped under brick walls that collapsed on them. In coral-encrusted iron objects alone, we recovered over 50,000 items such as tools, weapons, apothecary items, household articles, ship's fittings and thousands of other artifacts still awaiting preservation. Other artifacts included 2,000 glass bottles, 12,000 clay smoking pipes, over 500 pewter and silver items and 2,500 copper and brass items, as well as two large hoards of silver coins and numerous pieces of valuable jewelry.

Yet we barely scratched the surface of this unique site. Because this section was slated to be dredged for use as a deep-water port, we excavated what was the least important section of the sunken city. Since the total area we uncovered is less than five percent of the overall site, there are still many years worth of work left. A preservation laboratory was built to cope with the vast amount of material we recovered. Still, before all the artifacts were preserved the government ran out of funding and, to my great frustration, threw many artifacts back into the sea. The Institute of Nautical Archaeology of Texas A&M University taught students underwater archaeological techniques.here for several summers. They concentrated on mapping the site and ound few artifacts..

The Cayman Islands

Crystalline waters, abundant marine life and friendly people who welcome visitors have made the Cayman Islands a mecca for divers.

They go there primarily for underwater photography and spear fishing, but ballast piles and many iron cannon have been located around all three of the Caymans. All wrecks are Crown property. A search permit must be obtained to look for a wreck; and if a salvage permit is granted, anything recovered from a wreck must be turned over to the British government, which will give a share to the salvor.

More than 325 documented ships sank around the Cayman Islands, which lay in the path of sailing vessels plying between Cuba, the last stop before setting out on the open ocean for Europe, and the Spanish Main. Over the years, amateur and professional divers have discovered a substantial amount of sunken treasure in the Caymans. One of the most valuable and historically important finds was also the most serendipitous. In 1970, a young couple from Dalton, Georgia, was snorkeling off the beach in front of the Holiday Inn on Grand Cayman Island when they spotted a metallic glint on the sandy bottom in water no more than waist-deep. To their great astonishment it turned out to be a gold cross covered with diamonds. They began fanning the fine white sand and within minutes had uncovered a few links of what proved to be a thirteen-foot (4-m) gold chain. In spite of their excitement, they managed to keep mum and rented scuba equipment to search the area more thoroughly.

What they pulled out of the gin-clear water that day ranks as one of history's most phenomenal treasure finds. Under a thin layer of sand they found a large bar of platinum dated 1521, seven bars of silver, many pieces of silver jewelry and a cache of more than 300 pounds (135 kg) of gold objects, still smooth and gleaming after centuries underwater. There were heavy gold discs, a gold bracelet in the form of a serpent covered with emeralds, more than 50 gold Aztec figurines and an impressive gold signet ring of European origin.

The dazed young couple not only struck it rich; but also solved a 450-year-old mystery. The signet ring held the answer to the question of what had become of the *Santiago*, a conquistadors' ship laden with Aztec plunder that disappeared in 1522 en route from Mexico to Spain. The coat of arms on the massive ring was that of the de León family of Spain, whose most illustrious member was Juan Ponce de Leon, the discoverer of Florida. The captain of the Santiago was his brother, Rodrigo, who accompanied Cortez to Mexico, and evidently lost his ship off Grand Cayman Island.

Shipwrecks in Jamaican Waters

Year 1504. On Columbus's fourth and last voyage of discovery, he lost two of his ships, the *Capitaña* and *Santiago*, in St. Anne's Bay, on the northern coast of Jamaica. After spending some months exploring along Panama and Central America, where he was forced to abandon two of his caravels, he started for Santo Domingo but ran out of food and water. The two ships mentioned above were leaking very badly because of sea worms. When he was off the northern coast of Jamaica, contrary winds prevented him from heading toward his destination, and since both ships were barely afloat, he was forced to enter St. Anne's Bay, where he ran both ships aground to prevent them from sinking. For a year he and his men lived in the fore-and-aft castles of the two vessels, which were the only parts above the water, before they were finally rescued.

Using historical data and assisted by Dr. Harold Edgerton of M.I.T. with his sediment-penetrating sonar equipment we located both of these shipwrecks in February of 1968 and carried out a small excavation on one of the wrecks to obtain samples of artifacts to positively identify our discovery.

Year 1512. A small caravel under the command of Valdivia, the regidor of Darien, was sailing from Panama to Hispaniola for supplies and reinforcements and carrying a great deal of treasure it had obtained from the Indians when it struck upon Pedro Shoals, about 130 miles south of the island of Jamaica. The caravel broke up quickly and the crew was unable to escape with anything more than a small boat, in which it drifted for thirteen days until reaching the Yucatan peninsula.

Year 1579. The Capitaña *La Trinidad*, 350 tons, Captain Manuel de Rodas, on which Captain-General Alvaro Manrique was traveling, was lost on the south side of Jamaica. No details on whether it was carrying any treasure at the time.

Year 1602. A large unidentified merchant nao, sailing in the Nueva España Flota of Captain-General Alonso de Chaves Galindo, carrying a great deal of merchandise and missionaries from Spain to Yucatan, wrecked in bad weather on Pedro Shoals when it was accidentally separated from the convoy. After the ship broke up on the reef, survivors made rafts and reached the southern section of Jamaica in a few days. A salvage boat dispatched by the governor of Jamaica failed to locate the shipwreck. The owner of the ship was Tomi Cano, one of Spain's leading ship designers.

Year 1636. An unidentified zabra, sailing between Maracaibo, Venezuela, and Jamaica, was wrecked on Pedro Shoals, but most of the ship's cargo was salvaged.

Year 1662. A Spanish merchant ship, sailing from Caracas, Venezuela, to Veracruz, was wrecked on Bajo Nuevo Shoals, striking on a reef and quickly breaking up. Forty persons drowned and only a few reached Jamaica. This shoal is located about 150 nautical miles south of the western tip of Jamaica. Since Colombia claims jurisdiction over it, permission must be obtained from the Colombian government before salvaging a wreck there.

Year 1670. During a hurricane on October 7, about 20 English warships and a large number of privateering vessels were wrecked in Kingston Harbor.

Year 1691. Four galleons, part of the Tierra Firme Flota, the Marquis de Vado, sailing between Cartagena, Colombia, and Havana, were wrecked on Pedro Shoals, 776 persons were saved from these wrecks by fishing boats from Port Royal. The lost ships were: the Almiranta, Admiral Leonardo de Lara; *Nuestra Señora del*

Carmen, Captain Salvador Velez de Guevara; *N. S. de la Concepción*, Captain Pedro Azpil Cueta; and the *Santa Cruz*, Captain Vicente López. As soon as the wrecks were abandoned by the Spaniards, salvage sloops from Port Royal descended upon them. Because England and Spain were then at peace, and the Spaniards were able to demand all the treasurethat was recovered. The British agreed that the treasure should be seized and turned over to the Spaniards; however, because many chests of treasure were concealed by the salvors, there is no way to know just how much was salvaged. The Spaniards also carried on their own salvage operations, and as late as 1698 salvage boats from Havana were recovering cannon from these wrecks.

Year 1692. During the earthquake which caused Port Royal to sink into the sea on June 7 the British warship *H.M.S. Swan* of 305 tons and 32 cannon also sank amongst the ruins of the city. Nearby an unidentified French prize ship was also lost. Both wrecks were salvaged by the author during his excavation of the sunken city in 1965-68.

Year 1699. Small Spanish advice boat *Jesús, María y José*, 80 tons, sent from Veracruz to Santo Domingo, was wrecked on the north coast of Jamaica.

Year 1714. During a hurricane that struck Kingston Harbor on August 9, several large English men-of-war were sunk as well as several small trading sloops and schooners.

Year 1726. During a hurricane that struck the island on October 22, over 50 ships of different descriptions were wrecked or sunk at Port Morant, St. Anne's Bay, Port Royal, and Kingston Harbor. At Port Royal, several dozens of wooden houses were also blown into the harbor.

Year 1730. Spanish galleon *Genovesa*, 54 guns, Captain Francisco Guiral, sailing from Cartagena to Havana, struck on a reef on Pedro Shoals and was lost. She was sailing alone and not in a convoy at the time, carrying over three million pesos in gold and silver plus many important passengers, several of whom drowned with the crew. Soon after the ship wrecked, an English frigate, the *H.M.S. Experiment*, arrived and took off the survivors and a large amount of the treasure. Other salvage vessels arrived from Port Royal and recovered undisclosed amounts of treasure and many of the ship's cannon. The ship broke up within a few weeks, however, and a great deal of the treasure was scattered and buried under sand. Over the years, various treasure hunters have claimed to have found this wreck. I've examined artifacts that they recovered and have been able to determine conclusively that what was locatedwas a Spanish shipwreck at least 50 years younger than the *Genovesa* that happened to lie in the same area.

Year 1741. English merchantman the *London*, Captain Hayes, was almost fully loaded for her voyage to London when she was accidentally destroyed by fire in Old Harbour.

Year 1741. An English troop transport, *Vease Pink*, Captain Horn, was lost in July on the Morant Keys, off the south coast of Jamaica, where she hit a reef and broke up quickly, with most of the persons aboard drowning.

Year 1744. A Spanish privateering vessel was sunk by the *H.M.S. Solebay* under the watch tower at Pedro Point. The present lighthouse is located near the ruins of the watch tower, and there are four different old wrecks in 30 feet of water, one of which might be this one.

Year 1744. During a hurricane that struck the island in October, 105 ships (nine warships and 96 merchantmen) were wrecked or sunk in Kingston Harbor and Port Royal. Many of the wharves and warehouses in Kingston which were full of merchandise were also swept into the harbor. Only five of the warships that were lost were identified: *H.M.S. Albans*, 50 guns, Captain William Knight; *H.M.S. Greenwich*, 50 guns, Captain Edward Allen; *H.M.S. Bonetta*, 14 guns, Captain William Lea; bomb ship *H.M.S. Thunder*, eight guns, Captain Thomas Gregory; and the store ship *H.M.S. Lark*, no guns, captain's name unknown. Many of these ships were refloated and a great amount of their cargoes recovered. In shallow water on the western side of Kingston Harbor I have dived on over 30 different wreck sites from this disaster, and although not using any excavation equipment, I recovered a wide variety of ceramicware, bottles, clay pipes, cannonballs and other artifacts.

Year 1747. Two English merchantmen were lost entering Port Morant, on the eastern end of the island: *Culloden*, Captain Harris, coming from London, and the *Pembeston*, Captain Nunns, coming from Liverpool.

Year 1748. English merchantman *Dragon*, Captain Lawson, with a cargo of sugar and rum, wrecked leaving St. Anne's Bay, on her way to London.

Year 1748. English merchantman *Greyhound*, Captain Palliser, with a cargo of sugar, molasses, rum, and some silver specie, was chased ashore near Cape Morant by two Spanish privateers.

Year 1748. English merchantman *Industry*, Captain Graham, sailing from Boston to Kingston, was lost off Port Morant.

Year 1748. English merchantman *Happy Success*, Captain Paterson, was lost leaving Port Antonio, heading for London, but part of her cargo was recovered.

Year 1749. English merchantman *Dragon*, Captain Wall, was lost on May 14 at Port Morant, only the crew was saved.

Year 1751. During a hurricane on September 25, 24 merchant ships and one man-of-war were lost in Kingston Harbor and at Port Royal. The warship was the *H.M.S. Fox*, 20 guns. Four of the merchantmen were American, one was Dutch and the others English.

Year 1752. English merchantman *Phebe*, Captain Lawson, coming from Liverpool, was wrecked on September 17 on the Morant Keys with a rich cargo of trade goods and some pieces of artillery for the island's forts.

Year 1755. English ship *Montfort*, Captain Clutson, sailing from Kingston to Bristol, carrying several chests of specie, was wrecked on the Morant Keys but the treasure was recovered.

Year 1755. Large Spanish galleon *La Andalucia*, sailing alone from Cartagena to Spain, was wrecked on Pedro Shoals on June 9, treasure and crew saved.

Year 1757. English merchantman *Craven*, Captain Stewart, sailing to London with a cargo of sugar products, was lost leaving St. Mary's harbor.

Year 1760. English merchantman *Sally*, Captain Bland, sailing for London, was lost on the reefs near St. Anne's Bay, but her crew and most of the cargo saved.

Year 1762. A large unidentified Spanish merchantman, laden with indigo, cocoa and specie, sailing from Venezuela to Veracruz, was wrecked on the coast near Port Morant, most of her cargo was salvaged.

Year 1762. English merchantman *Prince George*, Captain Clapperton, coming from London, was lost in a gale while entering the harbor of Martha Brae, only the crew was saved.

Year 1764. English ship *Marquis of Grandby*, Captain Calvert, coming from London, struck a rock near Portland Bight and went to pieces quickly, only the crew was saved.

Year 1765. English merchantman *Fanny*, Captain Boyd, coming from London, was sunk at Pidgeon Island, in Old Harbour, on March 8.

Year 1766. English merchantman *Portland*, Captain Kendal, after arriving from London, was lost in Manchioneal Bay.

Year 1766. English ship, a snow, *Friendship*, Captain Johnson, coming from Tortola, Virgin Islands, was wrecked onshore February 16, three miles west of Annotto Bay, crew and part of cargo saved.

Year 1766. During a hurricane on August 18, 17 ships were wrecked in Kingston Harbor, and others were lost at Black River, Savanna la Mar and Port Morant.

Year 1768. English merchantman *Minerva*, Captain Smith, loading for a voyage to London, was accidentally burned on April 19, having on board 300 hogsheads of sugar and 17 puncheons of rum, very little of which was saved.

Year 1769. English merchantman *Lyon*, Captain Irwin, sailing for London, was lost leaving the harbor of Oracabeza.

Year 1770. English slave ship *Cecelia*, Captain Dunn, coming from Africa with a cargo of slaves, was wrecked in the Morant Keys.

Year 1770. English merchantman *King David*, Captain Broad, was sunk in Port Royal Harbor, when it struck upon a large anchor sticking up from the sea floor.

Year 1770. English ship *Industry*, Captain Haste, arriving from Liverpool, was wrecked on the Palisadoes, several miles east of Port Royal, and was a total loss.

Year 1770. English merchantman *Caesar*, Captain Raffes, sailing to London, was lost on a reef west of Port Morant on July 23.

Year 1774. Unidentified Dutch slave ship, coming from Africa with over 500 slaves on board, was wrecked in the Morant Keys.

Year 1774. American ship *Jamaica Planter*, Captain M'Fadden, coming from Boston with a cargo of trade goods, and another vessel identified only by the captain's name "Todd" were both lost on Plumb Point, near Port Royal.

Year 1776. A ship of unknown registry, *Caton*, Captain Glyn, coming from Africa with a cargo of slaves, ivory and beeswax, was lost due to fire at Kingston.

Year 1779. Jamaican schooner *Speedwell*, on a sponging and wrecking voyage to the Bahamas, was lost leaving Manchioneal Bay.

Year 1779. English warship *H.M.S. Glasgow*, 24 guns, Captain Thomas Lloyd, was accidentally lost by fire on June 19 at Kingston.

Year 1780. A hurricane on February 23 caused six large ships to sink at Montego Bay: *Echo*, Captain Cragie, from London; *Petersfield*, Captain Thomas, from Bristol; *Nancy*, Captain Marshall, from Bristol; *Hero*, Captain Logget, from New York; *Cornelia*, Captain Smith, from New York; *Orangefield*, Captain Farris, from New York; and the *Charles and Martha*, Captain Elston, from Liverpool.

Year 1780. American ship *Pallas*, arriving from Charleston, South Carolina, with trade goods, was lost entering Port Morant on March 24.

Year 1780. During a hurricane in October, many ships were lost at various ports. At Lucea Harbor the *H.M.S. Badger* was sunk. At Port Morant, three large ships were thrown over a quarter of a mile onshore and were totally lost.

Year 1781. A ship of unknown registry, *Duke of Cumberland*, Captain Le Geyt, arriving from St. Eustatius Island, was lost entering Montego Bay.

Year 1781. During a hurricane that struck Jamaica on August 1 and 2, many ships were destroyed. In Kingston Harbor, 90 ships of various descriptions were wrecked or sunk; another 30 were lost at Port Royal; and 73 were lost in other ports of the island. The *H.M.S. Pelican*, 24 guns, Captain Cuthbert Collingwood, was wrecked on the Morant Keys. This wreck was discovered by a group of treasure-hunters from Florida who recovered a small bronze cannon, one gold coin and other artifacts. But they worked on it for only one day before being driven away by a Jamaican naval launch.

Year 1782. English warship *H.M.S. Hinchinbrooke*, 20 guns, Captain Nelson, wrecked on a reef off St. Anne's Bay. This wreck was reportedly located by a Jamaican diver in 1965.

Year 1782. English merchantman *Blagrove*, Captain M'Neil, with a cargo of sugar products, was sunk in Buckness Bay due to a leak.

Year 1783. English merchantman *Ann & Mary*, Captain Graham, sailing to London, was wrecked on rocks while leaving Kingston.

Year 1783. Spanish merchant nao *N.S. de la Concepción*, Captain Joaquin Fernandez, sailing from Cartagena to Cadíz, Spain, was wrecked on the Morant Keys on November 15; only a small part of her cargo was salvaged.

Year 1784. Hurricane struck the island on July 30 and more than 80 ships were destroyed or sunk in various ports around the island. At Port Royal, many houses were blown into the harbor.

Year 1785. A hurricane struck the island prior to October and more than 50 ships were wrecked or sunk in Kingston Harbor and Port Royal. Several others were lost at Savanna la Mar, Bull's Bay and Bush Cay in Old Harbour.

Year 1785. English merchantman *John*, Captain Churnside, sailing to Bristol, was wrecked at John's Point, near the west end of the island; part of her cargo was saved.

Year 1786. A hurricane struck the island on October 20 and about 20 ships were lost at Kingston Harbor and several others at Montego Bay.

Year 1787. Two English ships were wrecked on the reefs near Port Royal: slave ship *Enterprize*, Captain Wilson, arriving from Africa with a cargo of slaves; and merchantman *Marianne*, arriving from Santo Domingo.

Year 1790. English ship *Columbus*, Captain Mason, laden with sugar products for Leith, England, burned at Bluefields.

Year 1790. English merchantman *Two Friends*, Captain Brookbank, sailing to England, was wrecked in Old Harbour, most of the cargo was saved.

Year 1791. Jamaican sloop *Fly*, Captain Saise, driven onshore by wind on November 18 in St. Anne's Bay.

Year 1791. Scottish merchantman, a brig, *Exuma*, Captain Aylward, loaded with sugar and rum, bound for Dublin, wrecked onshore at Oracabeza by strong winds and quickly went to pieces.

Year 1792. American merchantman *Scipio*, Captain Carr, after arriving from Virginia, was wrecked during a storm on April 11 at Annotto Bay, most of her cargo of timber was washed ashore.

Year 1792. Irish merchantman *Ritson*, Captain Fairclough, was lost due to fire on June 20 at Old Harbour.

Year 1792. English merchantman *Rosemary*, Captain Woodham, loaded with sugar, struck a reef and sank at Jack's Bay.

Year 1792. American ship *Griffin*, Captain Vassey, sailing to Savannah, was wrecked on the Port Royal Bank on December 19.

Year 1793. English merchantman *Emerald*, Captain Kilgour, struck on her own anchor and sank with 400 hogsheads of sugar in Martha Bay.

Year 1793. Seven ships were wrecked or sunk in a gale at Montego Bay: *Langrest*, Captain Fitzhenry; *Active*, Captain Williams; *Young Eagle*, Captain Jones; *Palliseer*, Captain James, all arriving from London; the other three were not identified.

Year 1794. English warship *H.M.S. Rose*, 28 guns, Captain Mathew Henry Scott, was wrecked on June 28 at Rocky Point.

Year 1794. Scottish ship *Sampson*, Captain Bowie, sailing to Santo Domingo and London, was lost in Cow Bay.

Year 1795. English ship *Hankey*, Captain Kirky, sailing to London, sank in Port Antonio, crew and cargo saved.

Year 1796. English warship *H.M.S. Undaunted*, 38 guns, Captain Robert Winthrop, was wrecked on August 27 in the Morant Keys. She was originally the French warship *Arethuse* captured by the English.

Year 1796. English warship *H.M.S. St. Pierre*, Captain Christopher Paule, was wrecked on February 12 on some rocks off Point Negril.

Year 1796. English slave ship *Old Dick*, Captain Birdy, arriving from Africa with a cargo of slaves, gold dust and ivory, wrecked near Morant Bay, slaves and part of cargo saved.

Year 1796. English merchantman *Maria*, sailing to Exeter, England, was lost on a reef near Port Royal.

Year 1797. Scottish ship *Hope*, arriving from Glasgow, was lost on the Palisadoes, near Port Royal.

Year 1798. English ship *Carletch*, Captain Hamilton, arriving from New Brunswick, Canada, was lost near Jack's Bay, part of her cargo was saved.

Year 1798. English troop ship *Aurora*, Captain Milner, was wrecked at Old Harbour.

Year 1800. Two English merchantmen were wrecked in a gale at Oracabeza: *St. Andrew*, Captain Howard, from London; and the *Mary Ann*, Captain Bannerman.

Year 1800. English merchantman *Britannia*, Captain Compton, sailing to London, was lost at Buckner's Bay, none of her cargo was saved.

Year 1800. English merchantman *King George*, Captain Eilbeek, sailing from Kingston to London, was lost on Pedro Point but the crew was saved.

Year 1801. English ship *Lady Milford*, Captain Higgs, sailing to London, was lost on a reef near Savanna la Mar, all memb ers of the crew and part of the cargo was saved.

Year 1802. A violent gale struck the island on February 23 and many ships were driven ashore at Montego Bay, Annotto Bay, and Rio Bueno.

Year 1802. Three merchantmen were lost at Oracabeza during a gale: English ship *Generous Planter*, Captain Beattie; English ship *Fortune*, Captain Saunders; and the American brig *William*, Captain Clark.

Year 1802. Two English merchantmen were lost at Rio Bueno: *Jupiter*, Captain Plank, was burned; and the *Grace*, Captain Cook, wrecked; both were total losses.

Year 1802. During a violent gale on March 16 four unidentified ships were totally lost at Port Antonio and two in Buckner's Bay: English merchantman *Hannah*, Captain Lenox, from Greenock, England; and an unidentified American schooner.

Year 1803. American schooner *Mary*, Captain White, was totally lost in St. Anne's Bay on December 25.

Year 1804. American merchantman *Sisters*, Captain Richards, arriving from the Canary Islands with a cargo of wine and brandy, was lost on the reefs at the entrance to Port Royal.

Year 1804. English merchantman *Triumph*, Captain Johnson, arriving from New Brunswick, Canada, was burned in January at Kingston and was a total loss.

Year 1804. English ship *Henry Addington*, Captain Lacey, arriving from London, was wrecked on Barebush Cay in Old Harbour on April 14.

Year 1804. English merchantman *Margaret*, Captain Goodwin, sailing for London, was lost in Manchioneal Harbour on July 12.

Year 1805. Two English warships foundered near Jamaica: schooner, *H.M.S. Redbridge*, 10 guns, Captain Francis Blower Gibbs, in May; and *H.M.S. Orquijo*, 18 guns, Captain Charles Balderson, in October.

Year 1805. English merchantman *Scarbro*, Captain Scott, bound for London, sprung a leak and sank at Port Royal.

Year 1805. Two merchantmen were lost at Plaintain Garden: American ship *Minerva*, Captain Harding, sailing to Boston; and the English ship *William*, Captain M'Iver.

Year 1805. English merchantman *Jamaica*, Captain Clarke, bound for London, was totally lost during a gale on John's Point on June 30, but some of her cargo of rum was saved.

Year 1806. English merchantman *Vulcan*, Captain Gardner, bound for Bristol, was totally lost on Bare Bush Keys on July 26.

Year 1806. A ship of unknown registry, *Hercules*, Captain Cushing, arriving from Boston and sailing to the Spanish Main, was wrecked at Pedro Point on March 3.

Year 1806. American ship *Venus*, Captain Dony, arriving from New York, was totally lost at Rio Bueno in December.

Year 1807. American ship *Jane*, Captain Rust, arriving from Boston, was wrecked in Montego Bay on February 14.

Year 1808. Two English ships were wrecked at Bare Bush Key in Old Harbour: the frigate *Daedalus*, July 30, where three men were drowned; warship *H.M.S. Meleager*, 36 guns, Captain Frederick Warren, July 30. This wreck was located about 10 years ago and a large anchor raised, which is now on exhibit in Port Royal.

Year 1808. Two merchantmen were lost on the reefs at the entrance to Manchioneal Harbour: Jamaican schooner *Robert*, Captain Clarke, fully loaded, June 16; and the English ship *Dryade*, Captain Hoisbro, sailing to London, April 15, crew and small part of cargo saved.

Year 1810. Large Spanish warship *N.S. del Amparo*, carrying a valuable cargo of mercury and wine from Spain to Veracruz, was wrecked in the Morant Keys.

Year 1810. English troop-transport *Hannah*, Captain Harrison, was lost in Montego Bay on September 1 but the crew was saved.

Year 1810. English ship *Humphreys*, Captain Hastings, sailing to Honduras, was wrecked on Half Moon Key near Old Harbour on February 28.

Year 1810. English merchantman *Mary*, Captain Stafford, bound for London, was wrecked at Port Maria, December 18, during a gale; 167 hogsheads of sugar were lost.

Year 1811. American merchantman *Active*, after arriving from Boston, was wrecked near Port Royal on May 14, but part of her cargo was saved.

Year 1811. American ship *Ohio*, Captain Sinclair, arriving from Portsmouth, England, wrecked in Plaintain Garden River on November 14.

Year 1812. During a hurricane from October 12 to 14 a great number of ships were destroyed in Kingston Harbor.

Year 1812. English merchantman *Leander*, Captain Keen, arriving from Liverpool, was totally lost at Alligator Pond.

Year 1812. English merchantman *Mariner*, Captain Allurd, sailing to London, was wrecked at Oracabeza in December.

Year 1813. Five ships were lost around Port Royal prior to July: English warship *H.M.S. Colibri*, 18 guns, Captain John Thompson wrecked in Port Royal Harbor; English brig-of-war *H.M.S. Rhodion*, arriving from Portobelo, Panama, wrecked on shore two miles from Port Royal on February 20; Jamaican sloop *Chance*, arriving from Cuba with a cargo of cotton, sank in Port Royal Harbor during a gale on July 18; Scottish merchantman *Mercater*, sailing to Glasgow, wrecked on the Port Royal Keys; and an unidentified American ship sank in Port Royal Harbor.

Year 1813. On July 13, both a hurricane and an earthquake struck, causing 12 large ships to be lost at Kingston; 40 to 50 small vessels were lost at Port Royal; and eight ships at Morant Bay.

Year 1814. English ship *Hibernia*, Captain Vaas, arriving from Halifax, was lost on the Morant Keys on November 17.

Year 1814. English merchantman *Metcalf*, bound for London, was lost in April, sailing out of Port Maria.

Year 1814. English warship *H.M.S. Halcyon*, was wrecked off Annotto Bay in May but the crew was saved.

Year 1815. American merchantman *Planet* (or *Patent*), arriving from New York, was wrecked near Frankfork Bay during a gale on October 18-19.

Year 1815. Jamaican schooner *Mary*, Captain Brackenbridge, sailing from Kingston, was wrecked in Orange Bay.

Year 1815. American ship *Watson*, arriving from New York, was driven ashore at Blue Hole and went to pieces on October 18, all of the cargo was lost and 13 men drowned.

Year 1815. Two ships were lost on the reefs at Port Antonio: Spanish brig *Solo*, Captain Dick, arriving from Cuba, eight men drowned; and the Jamaican schooner *Two Friends*.

Year 1815. During a bad gale in October, two ships were lost at Port Maria, one in Orange Bay, one in Annotto Bay, and another at Goat Island.

Year 1816. A warship of unknown nationality, *Briseis*, sailing to Nassau, was lost on November 5 at Pedro Point, crew and greater part of stores saved.

Year 1816. A ship of unknown registry, *Anaconda*, Captain Pinel, sailing to Philadelphia, wrecked near Montego Bay but part of its cargo was saved.

Year 1816. English ship *Eliza*, Captain Johnston, arriving from Canada, was wrecked on the Grand Reef at Negril on March 8.

Year 1816. American ship *Agnes*, Captain Livingston, arriving from Charleston, South Carolina, wrecked entering Annotto Bay on December 23.

Year 1817. American ship *Isabella*, Captain Roach, sailing to Philadelphia, was wrecked in February on the Morant Keys.

Year 1817. Jamaican sloop *Happy Return*, with a cargo of sugar, was lost on June 11 coming out of Port Maria Harbor but the crew was saved.

Year 1817. Two ships wrecked in Morant Bay: English brig *Johanna*, Captain Caldwell, and the American schooner *Mary*, Captain Eswell.

Year 1817. Canadian ship *Five Sisters*, arriving from Nova Scotia, wrecked in St. Anne's Bay on December 20 but, some of her cargo was saved.

Year 1818. Bahamian ship *Duke of Wellington*, Captain Chancellor, arriving from Norfolk, Virginia, wrecked in Montego Bay on November 11.

Year 1818. Two ships were lost near Kingston Harbor: English ship *Triton*, Captain Carzia, arriving from Liverpool, totally lost on December 5 off Plumb Point, passengers, crew, and part of cargo saved; and the Jamaican sloop *Young March*, Captain Brown, wrecked at Healthshire Point on February 11 but part of her cargo was saved.

Year 1819. Bermudan ship *Julian*, Captain Brown, sailing to Bermuda, wrecked at Orange Bay, crew and cargo saved.

Year 1819. English merchantman *Ann*, Captain Fortune, sailing to Cuba, capsized on August 1 and sank near Oracabeza but the crew was saved.

Year 1819. Jamaican cutter *John Shand*, Captain Tucker, was totally lost in Port Morant on January 1.

Year 1820. English ship *Martins*, Captain Ramsey, sailing from Coro, Venezuela, to Kingston was wrecked on the Morant Keys on December 14; crew and most of cargo of mules saved.

Year 1821. Bahamian ship *Three Brothers*, Captain Hanson, was lost off Port Antonio on February 14.

Year 1821. English ship *Mackerel*, Captain Thompson, sailing to the Spanish Main, wrecked on September 20 near Port Morant.

Year 1821. American sloop *Brutus*, Captain Brakenbridge, was lost at Downers Bluff on September 19.

Year 1821. Scottish ship *Countess of Bute*, sailing between Kingston and Montego Bay, was lost on Sandy Reef Key on February 8; the crew was saved.

Year 1821. Canadian ship *Lowland Lass*, Captain Kyle, arriving from New Brunswick, was totally lost in St. Mary's Bay but the crew was saved.

Year 1822. Two ships of unknown registry were lost at Montego Bay: *Mary Charlotte*, Captain Richards, but the crew was saved; and an unidentified ship.

Year 1822. Dutch ship *Johanna*, Captain Benoist, sailing to Cura, wrecked off Rocky Point on a reef, crew and cargo saved.

Year 1823. Spanish ship *Graciosa*, sailing from Cadíz to Honduras, wrecked on Bajo Nuevo Shoals in April but the crew was rescued by a Dutch schooner.

Year 1824. English cutter *H.M.S. Dwarf*, 10 guns, Captain Nicholas Gould, wrecked on a pier at Kingston on March 3, one man was lost.

Year 1824. American merchantman *Thomas & Edward*, Captain Chevenick, arriving from Wilmington, North Carolina, sank near Kingston.

Shipwrecks in Cayman Island Waters

Year 1631. Unidentified Dutch ship, carrying 30 iron cannon, owned by the Dutch West India Company, was wrecked on Grand Cayman Island.

Year 1715. English sloop *H.M.S. Jamaica* lost her mast in a storm and drifted on the rocks on Grand Cayman Island, where it was lost but the crew was saved.

Year 1722. During a hurricane about the beginning of September, the pirate ship *Morning Star*, Captain George Bradley, was totally lost on the reefs of Grand Cayman Island but the crew was saved.

Year 1730. Spanish patache *Señor San Miguel*, Captain Juan Bautista de la Hondel y Zevallos, was wrecked on Little Cayman Island. She was sailing in the Nueva España Flota, Admiral Rodrigo de Torres, en route to Veracruz from Spain, and none of her cargo of mercury was salvaged.

Year 1764. English merchantman *Augustus Caesar*, Captain Duffell, sailing from Jamaica to London, was lost on Grand Cayman Island but her crew was saved.

Year 1766. English merchantman *Mary*, Captain Sullivan, sailing from Jamaica to London, was wrecked on Grand Cayman Island.

Year 1774. Spanish merchantman *Infante*, Captain Aspillage, sailing from Bilbao, Spain, to Havana, was lost at Little Cayman Island but her crew was saved.

Year 1783. English merchantman *Catherine*, Captain Miller, sailing from Jamaica to Bristol, was lost in the Cayman Islands, a small part of her cargo was salvaged and sold in Jamaica.

Year 1783. Two English merchantmen were lost on Grand Cayman Island: *Fidelity*, Captain Hewson, sailing from Jamaica to London, with crew and part of the cargo saved; and the snow *Rodney*, which was sailing from Jamaica to London.

Year 1794. English warship *Convert*, 32 guns, Captain John Lawford, was wrecked on Grand Cayman Island on February 8, but her crew was saved. Originally she was the French warship *Inconstant* until captured by the English.

Year 1794. English merchantman *Fortune*, Captain Merryman, sailing from Jamaica to Bristol, was lost on Grand Cayman Island; crew was saved.

Year 1795. English merchantman *Maria*, Captain Allison, sailing from Jamaica to Liverpool, was lost in the Cayman Islands but part of her cargo was saved.

Year 1806. A ship of unknown registry, *Allegator*, Captain Rust, sailing from France to New Orleans, was lost on Grand Cayman Island but the crew was saved.

Year 1807. American merchantman *Three Brothers*, Captain Jeffries, sailing from Jamaica to New York, was totally lost on December 17 off the Cayman Islands.

Year 1808. English merchantman *Cygnet*, Captain Bale, sailing from Jamaica to London, was lost in the Cayman Islands.

Year 1810. Scottish merchantman *Duncan*, sailing from Jamaica to Dublin, was lost in the Cayman Islands.

Year 1810. English merchantman *Cambria*, Captain Robertson, sailing from Jamaica to London, was lost on Grand Cayman Island.

Year 1812. English merchantman *Lion*, Captain Wilmot, sailing from London to Honduras, was lost on Grand Cayman Island on June 4 but the crew was saved.

Year 1817. English merchantman *Sisters*, Captain Swiney, sailing from Jamaica to London, was lost on August 3 on Grand Cayman Island but the crew was saved.

Year 1819. English merchantman *Constantine*, Captain Allen, sailing from Jamaica to London, wrecked on Grand Cayman Island at the end of July but most of her cargo of coffee was saved.

Year 1822. Canadian schooner *Dorchester*, coming from St. John's, New Brunswick, was wrecked on Grand Cayman Island.

Year 1823. A ship of unknown registry, *Grove*, Captain Reid, sailing from Cadíz to Veracruz, was lost on June 1 at Grand Cayman Island, but her crew was saved.

Year 1823. Large American schooner, sailing from the Mediterranean to New Orleans, was wrecked on Grand Cayman Island in September but part of her cargo of wine and silks was saved.

Year 1824. Spanish merchantman *Zamore*, sailing from France to Mexico, was wrecked on Grand Cayman Island but her crew was saved.

Gold ring with the De Leon coat-of-arms found off Grand Cayman, which helped identify the wreck of a ship sunk in 1522 while carrying Aztec plunder back to Spain.

Chapter Eleven

Puerto Rico
and the Virgin Islands

Puerto Rico

Compared with the majority of the other Caribbean islands, Puerto Rico has relatively few shipwrecks predating 1825 in her waters. Jamaica, for example, although only slightly larger than Puerto Rico, has over 900 recorded ship disasters that predate 1825, and even the small island of Anegada in the British Virgin Islands has at least four times the number of shipwrecks that Puerto Rico has.

There are various explanations for the scarcity of wrecks around Puerto Rico. The island is high in elevation and can be sighted at quite a distance from sea, which decreases the possibility of a ship running upon its shores. Unlike many of the other islands, e.g. Barbuda or most of the Bahamas, there are very few dangerous offshore reefs, thus eliminating the danger of ships running aground.

The waters surrounding virtually the whole coastline of Puerto Rico are quite deep and there are very few, if any, shoals or sandbanks. The question of how much maritime traffic there was around Puerto Rico must also be considered. Since the island lacked pre-

These two gold rings that came from the wreckage of an unidentified Portugese slave ship of the mid-16th century were found off Puerto Rico.

cious metals and other important export commodities and was never considered an important settlement by the Spaniards, there was very little shipping directed there during the 16th, 17th, and 18th centuries. In fact, there were occasional periods of as long as five years when no ships from Spain reached the island or left the island sailing for Spain. Most of the maritime commerce during this period was with small coastal sailing vessels that plied between Hispaniola and Puerto Rico.

The Nueva España Flota made its Caribbean landfall each year at either Martinique, Guadeloupe or Dominica islands, where it usually stopped to obtain fresh water and fruits. Then it would pass within sight of the southern coast of Puerto Rico on its way to Veracruz, generally in early summer, before the hurricane season. Around the middle of the 17th century, when the above three islands were settled by foreigners, the flota changed its pattern and began making the Caribbean landfall near the islands of St. Barthelemy or Anguilla, then passing within sight of Puerto Rico's northern coast while heading west to Veracruz. Throughout the three centuries of the flota system, only a few of these ships were lost off Puerto Rico.

Permits are required here for all shipwreck-related work. Puerto Rico enjoys relatively good weather the year around, except during the hurricane season. The United States National Park Service has several archaeologists and historians working in San Juan and they, along with several historians at the University of Puerto Rico, can be helpful in identifying and dating artifacts recovered from shipwrecks in this area.

Shipwrecks in Puerto Rican Waters

Year 1515. Caravel, *San Nicolas*, 80 tons, Captain Domingo de Guedin Bermeo, owned by Antonio de Norcia of Seville, sailing from Spain for Puerto Rico and Santo Domingo, sank in the harbor of San Juan "en una isleta llamada Berberia" sometime before October 25.

Year 1524. Nao *Santa María*, Captain Juan Pérez de Arecabal, owned by Juan L, of 110 tons, sailing between Spain and Yucatan with supplies for the conquistadors in Mexico, was lost off the North Coast of Puerto Rico.

Prior to 1550. Unidentified caravel lost "on the coasts of Puerto Rico" and only the people saved off it.

Year 1550. Merchant nao *Santa María de Jesús*, Captain Diego Bernal, en route from Spain to Mexico, was lost one league from the port of San Juan. The governor of the island wrote stating that this ship was one of the richest galleons ever to come to the Indies. Some salvage work was undertaken on the wreck but the majority of the cargo was not recovered. The accident occurred shortly before August 27.

Year 1554. Three naos, *San Salvador*, *Doña Juana* and *Regina Caelis* of the Nueva España Flota of Don C. Rodríquez Farfan, were lost in the port of San Juan but the majority of their cargoes were salvaged.

Year 1562. Nao *San Estivan*, 120 tons, Captain Lazaro Morel, was lost "at San Juan de Puerto Rico."

Year 1606. Two ships entered Sanlúcar de Barrameda in Spain on January 10 and reported that on October 26, 1605, while sailing from Santo Domingo to Spain, the Capitana of their fleet sank because of a leak when they were north and south of Punta de la Aguada and only the men were saved.

Year 1623. Sometime before September 22, eight merchant ships left Santo Domingo for Spain but one of them was run aground by bad navigation and was lost on the northern coast of Puerto Rico.

Year 1623. Galleon *N.S. de Begoña*, of a squadron of the Armada de Mar Oceano, commanded by Captain-General Thomas de Larraspuru, was lost on a shallows inside the port of San Juan. As the squadron was entering the port, a rain squall struck and caused this ship to run aground and then sink in deeper water. It was carrying only war munitions as its cargo, part of which was later salvaged along with some of the ship's cannon. No lives were lost in the disaster.

Year 1625. During the Dutch attack on San Juan, the Dutch totally destroyed by fire a merchant nao of 300 tons.

Year 1625. After the attack upon San Juan by the Dutch, one of the Dutch urcas sank in the harbor as the enemy fleet was sailing from that port. The Spaniards later salvaged six iron cannon from this wreck.

Year 1649. A Swedish ship of 200 tons was wrecked on a small island near Puerto Rico named Isla Palominos. This ship carried 16 cannon, two of which were brass, and the Spaniards recovered all of them from the wreck and imprisoned the Swedes.

Year 1659 or 1660. An advice boat, or aviso, owned by Captain Francisco de Liende, on its way from Spain to Veracruz, was forced to enter San Juan because of a bad leak, and sank soon after. Only a part of the mail, papal bulls and a little money was recovered.

Year 1673. Unidentified French ship reported to have hit a reef and sunk off Puerto Rico during February. Its location was not given in this letter, but in another one in the same legajo there was a brief mention that a ship was wrecked this same year at El Arecibo, and it was probably the same ship.

Year 1673. The French governor of the Island of Tortuga, located off the northern coast of Haiti, had a large warship built, which he named *Ogeron*. It was manned by 500 pirates of various nationalities and sent by this governor to aid in the capture of Curaçao. But when it was off the west side of Puerto Rico, a violent storm wrecked the ship on the rocks near some islands called Guadanillas, where it quickly broke up. Most of the pirates made it ashore to Puerto Rico but were massacred the next day by the Spaniards.

Prior to 1720. The pirate Captain George Lowther captured two ships near Puerto Rico: a small ship from Bristol of Captain Smith and a Spanish privateer that had just captured the ship of Captain Smith. After stripping both prizes he burned them near the island.

Year 1720. Warship *Carlos V*, 50 cannon, was lost during a hurricane at Puerto Rico and over 500 men drowned.

Year 1720. Spanish ship *La Victoria* lost in Bahía Anegada, at Puerto Rico.

Year 1739. Spanish galleon *N.S. del Pilar y San Antonio*, Captain Domingo Casares Goicochea, bound from Maracaibo for Cadíz, was lost near Puerto Rico but the people and goods were saved.

Year 1742. A Spanish sloop privateer was chased onshore and dashed to pieces and another of 24 cannon and full of men was sunk off Puerto Rico in an engagement with the *H.M.S. Scarsborough*, Captain Liste.

Year 1743. The *H.M.S. Litchfield* arrived at Kingston, Jamaica, on November 8, reporting that she had sunk a Spanish privateer on the west end of Puerto Rico and burned a Spanish sloop in Bahía La Aguada.

Year 1745. Unidentified French ship of 36 guns was accidentally lost while entering the port of San Juan.

Year 1764. British merchantman *Elizabeth*, Captain Alexander, going from Antigua to London, foundered off Puerto Rico but crew and captain saved.

Year 1780. British merchantman *Revenge*, Captain Kerr, sailing from Newfoundland to Jamaica, was lost at Puerto Rico.

Year 1787. A slave ship of British registry, *Sisters*, Captain Alworthy, going from Africa to Havana, was overset by a strong gust of wind while in the Mona Passage on May 17 with 500 slaves on board. All except two crew members and three slaves perished.

Year 1804. A large number of ships were sunk off the western end of Puerto Rico during a severe hurricane on September 3.

Year 1818. German ship *Nautilus*, Captain either Korff or Miltenburg, was lost off the northern coast of Puerto Rico.

Year 1818. Spanish schooner *Eugenia*, two cannons, Captain Francisco Gómez, was lost at Puerto Rico on August 13.

Year 1821. Spanish brigantine schooner *Proserpina*, 10 cannon, lost on the coast of Aguadilla.

Year 1822. British ship *Fountain*. Captain Howard, of St. John's, New Brunswick, going from Trinidad to Boston, was lost on December 23 on the island of Puerto Rico but the crew was saved.

The Virgin Islands

The waters of both the American and British Virgin Islands offer a good cross-section of shipwrecks of various types and nationalities. The wrecks span the centuries; although there is only one documented 16th-century shipwreck and but a few wrecks from the 17th century. Virtually no shipping of any kind passed through or even near the Virgin Islands until late in the 17th century, when sailing patterns of the Nueva España Flota were changed. In the early days this flota, after making its Caribbean landfall at Guadeloupe or a nearby island, would then head for Mexico, passing within sight of the southern coast of St. Croix. In later years, the flota made landfall at Anguilla or St. Barthelemy and passed around the northern edge of the Virgin Islands, generally sighting Anegada.

Several historians claim that, prior to 1850, over 100 ships were wrecked off low-lying Anegada, including some of the Nueva España Flota. The other islands in this group are considerably higher and could be spotted even in the night. Consequently, they were less of a hazard to navigation and have fewer wrecks. Most of the wrecks occurred in bad weather when the ships were driven by stress of wind and seas upon the reefs and islands.

No permits are required to work on shipwrecks in the American Virgin Islands; however, to work a shipwreck in the British Virgin Islands a permit must be obtained from the Keeper of Wrecks in Roadtown on the Island of Tortola. The weather pattern is about the same as for Puerto Rico.

The Virgin Islands have long been a major center for diving, and although many wrecks were accidentally discovered by amateurs, no serious attempts have been made to salvage any wrecks. The only major wreck discovery in these waters occurred in February 1969, when the harbor was being dredged at Roadtown. The dredge buckets brought up over four hundred artifacts, which included silver and pewter plates, cutlery, a silver sword handle, a cutlass, carpenter's tools, various types of shot, clasp knives, a flintlock rifle, ship fittings, caulking tools, clay pipes and different types of rigging.

Dr. Edward Towle, former director of the Caribbean Research Institute, which is affiliated with the College of the Virgin Islands, created a department of Marine Archaeology during the spring of 1968.

Shipwrecks in Virgin Island Waters

Year 1523. Two merchant naos, sailing from Spain for Santo Domingo, one under command of Captain Francisco Vara and the other under Captain Diego Sanchez Colchero, were lost in the Virgin Islands. The location of Vara's ship was given only as on some "shallows," but Colchero's was reported wrecked on the Island of Anegada. After several days, Colchero was able to refloat his ship by having most of its cargo and anchors thrown overboard. Then, going two leagues away, they located Vara's wrecked ship but could save only the men.

Year 1625. The governor of Puerto Rico wrote the King of Spain stating that an English-built ship of 70 tons with 18 men on it sank at Anegada Island. They had sailed from Virginia for Bermuda to salvage a shipwreck, but the ship was damaged in bad weather and driven onto the reefs of Anegada.

Year 1647. The *Bark*, commanded by Jean Pinart, carried French settlers from St. Christopher's and was burned by Spaniards, most likely in one of St. John's harbors.

Year 1652. Prince Maurice in the British ship *Defiance*, while privateering in the Caribbean with a convoy commanded by his brother, Prince Rupert, admiral of Charles I of England, wrecked off Anegada.

Year 1678. Unidentified French frigate, part of the war fleet of the Comte D'Estrees, was wrecked on Crab Island.

Year 1683. British naval officer Captain Carlile of the *H.M.S. Francis* wrote, "31 July 1683, attacked a pirate ship at anchor in the harbour of Charlotte Amalie, of 32 guns and six patararoes, by the name of *La Trompeuse*, commanded by the Frenchman John Hamlin ... setting her afire and she blew up...."

Sometime between 1692 and 1705. In a description of Anegada, Pere Labat, a French missionary wrote, "It is said that a year ago a great Spanish galleon laden with treasure was wrecked on Anegada, and that the treasure was buried on the island. There it still remains, or so they say, because most of the men who buried it were lost at sea, and the few survivors did not know where the treasure was hidden and were never able to find it. This treasure has caused many men including several filibusters to waste their time. I knew a man who stayed four or five months on the island, digging and sounding. He said he had found something, but no one has yet found the real treasure...[Speaking of another shipwreck he wrote]...one of our priests was wrecked on L'Isle Noyee or Anegada and was captured with the rest of his crew by the people of Panestown, also known as Virgin Gorda. He told me that he had remained a prisoner for two months with these Englishmen on Panestown..."

Year 1713. Captain Lewis Doyer, of French ship *Le Count de Poix*, sailing from Santo Domingo to Havre de Grace, France, wrecked on Anegada.

Year 1730. An English-built ship converted to a Spanish treasure galleon, *N.S. de Lorento y San Francisco Xavier*, 212 tons, commanded by Captain Juan de Arizon, coming from Spain and sailing in convoy with a fleet of treasure galleons commanded by General Manuel López Pintado for Cartagena and Portobelo, sank on Anegada Island.

Year 1731. Unidentified Spanish galleon, carrying a very valuable cargo of quicksilver (mercury) destined for the silver and gold mines of Mexico (where it was used in the refining process), wrecked on the reefs of Anegada.

Year 1734. "While I was in England, they [the inhabitants of Anguilla, Spanish Town (Virgin Gorda) and Tortola] pyrated upon a Spanish ship wrecked on the Anegadas...."

Year 1738. Spanish warship *Victory*, commanded by Captain Don Carlos Casamara, was cast away on the Anegada Shoals.

Year 1742. Spanish merchant ship *San Ignacio*, belonging to the newly formed Caracas Company, was lost on Anegada Island.

Year 1742. Spanish warship *St. Auguasies* (English spelling of its name, possibly the same ship as Ignacio mentioned above), from 30 to 60 guns, was wrecked on Anegada on March 20, 1742, and 400 of its 600 persons were drowned. It was sailing with two other warships from San Sebastian, Spain, for Havana, carrying 2,000 troops and supplies.

Year 1749. British merchantman *Purcell*, Captain Fuller, from Bristol for Tortola, was lost on the rocks near Tortola.

Year 1750. Sloop returning from the wreck of the *N. S. de Soledad* (lost on Cape Hatteras, North Carolina), and supposedly carrying the valuables from that ship, wrecked off Anegada.

Year 1751. *Katherine*, commanded by Captain Richards, sailing from Jamaica to Bristol, was lost on Anegada but the crew was saved.

Year 1757. Spanish merchantman *El Cesar*, Captain Josef Bernabe Madero, owned by the Marquis de Casa Madrid, was lost on Anegada Island.

Year 1758. Spanish merchantman *Santa Rosa* wrecked on the reefs of Anegada.

Year 1760. *Prince Ferdinand*, Captain Caynoon, sailing from Boston to Jamaica, was lost on Anegada Reef but her crew was saved.

Year 1769. British merchantman *Graham*, Captain M'Intosh, was cast away off the back reef of St. Croix, both ship and cargo were a total loss but the crew was saved. The *Graham* had been sailing from Grenada to London.

Year 1769. British ship *Brothers*, Captain Briggs, from Virginia for Lisbon, sprung a leak at sea and, bearing away for the West Indies, ran ashore upon a reef off St. Croix; both ship and cargo were lost but the crew was saved.

Year 1769. *Nancy Gaer* was lost off Anegada but her crew was saved.

Year 1773. British ship *Lord Mount Cathell*, Captain Fisher, previously commanded by the late Captain Taylor, was lost on the island of St. Croix in July; only part of the cargo was saved.

Year 1775. *Martha*, Captain McIntosh, sailing from Jamaica to London, was lost May 25 on Anegada.

Before 1775. Written on a chart of the Virgin Islands was the following note, "On Anegada is Ye Treasure Point, so called by ye freebooters from the gold and silver supposed to have been buried there abouts after the wreck of a Spanish galleon".

Year 1775. A Spanish snow called *Spirito Santo* (or *Espíritu Santo*), bound from La Coruña, Spain, to Havana, wrecked March 19 on the rocks of Anegada (at the point called the Horseshoe); the people and a great part of the cargo were saved but the vessel was lost.

Year 1776. British slave ship *Fox*, Captain Jones, from Africa for America, was lost at St. Thomas.

Year 1778. Dutch ship *Neptune*, Captain Spranges, lost at Tortola.

Year 1781. British merchantman *Swallow*, Captain Heblethwaith, of Liverpool, was lost coming out of Tortola but the crew was saved.

Year 1782. Originally a Spanish ship taken by the British on September 14, 1779, the *Santa Monica*, Captain John Linzee, was lost near Tortola. All of her crew but one were saved, as well as many of her guns, stores, and cargo.

Year 1783. *Ortello*, Captain Johnson, sailing from Africa to Tortola, was cast away in Tortola; 213 slaves were saved.

Year 1784. British ship *Ranger*, Captain Stewart, from Tortola to London, was lost on a reef of rocks near Tortola.

Year 1785. *Constantine*, Captain Langdon, sailing from Dominica to Bristol, lost in a hurricane August 26 on Thatch Island near St. Thomas; crew saved.

Year 1786. American ship *Cruger*, Captain Williams, from Philadelphia to St. Croix, was wrecked on September 3 on the Horseshoe Reef of Anegada.

Year 1789. British ship *Neptune*, Captain Casey, of London, was lost at the Island of St. John, Virgin Islands.

Year 1790. Spanish ship *El Rayo*, sailing from Bilbao to Puerto Rico, ran ashore on Anegada but the crew abandoned her safely.

Year 1792. Spanish ship *Nevarro* (probably correctly spelled "*Navarro*"), Captain Belandia, from St. Andero (Santander), Spain, to Havana, was lost at Anegada Island.

Year 1792. During a hurricane on August 1 two vessels were wrecked on the Island of St. Thomas, and a packet boat was run aground at Tortola Island.

Year 1793. British slave ship *Recovery*, Captain Walker, from Africa, was blown out of Nevis Roads (on Nevis Island) and driven by winds and wrecked on Tortola Island.

Year 1793. A ship of unknown nationality, but probably French, named *Christopher*, Captain Mollyneaux, from Africa, struck on a submerged anchor in the harbor of St. Croix and sank.

Year 1795. British ship *Hebe*, Captain Gray, from Cork to Jamaica, was lost on the rocks near Tortola.

Year 1795. British ship *Perseverance*, Captain Oriel, from Dublin to Jamaica, was totally lost on the north side of Anegada near Tortola.

Year 1796. British merchant ship *Jamaica*, Captain Alexander, from Tobago and Grenada to London, was captured by the French and run ashore at St. Croix.

Year 1797. British ship *Mary*, Captain Hunter, from Africa, was lost near St. Croix but her cargo was saved.

Year 1801. British ship *Albion*, Captain Robertson, from Montserrat to London, was lost at Tortola.

Year 1801. Ship, nationality unknown, named *Lavinia*, Captain Elles, from Tortola to Quebec, was lost near Tortola but a great part of her cargo was saved.

Year 1803. British ship *General Abercrombie*, Captain Booth, from Africa to West Indies, was lost at St. Croix but most of her cargo was saved.

Year 1805. British merchant ship *Ocean*, Captain Brown, from St. Vincent's Island to Bristol, was lost near the Island of Tortola.

Year 1806. British ship *Partridge*, Captain Miller, from Bristol and the Island of Madeira to St. Thomas, was lost near Tortola but part of her cargo was saved.

Year 1807. British merchant ship *Henry*, Captain Retson, of Liverpool, was lost off Water Island, St. Thomas, on April 26.

Year 1808. British frigate *Astrea*, 32 guns, Captain Edward Heywood, was lost on May 23 on a reef at the Island of Anegada, only four men were lost.

Year 1808. Spanish felucca was lost off Anegada; three men were lost.

Year 1809. British ship *Good Hope*, Captain Watson, from London to the Spanish Main, was lost near Anegada but most of the cargo was saved.

Year 1809. British war brig *Dominica*, Captain Charles Welsh, 10 guns, foundered near Tortola, 62 of her crew of 65 perished, including the captain.

Year 1810. Spanish merchant ship *Aftrivedo*, Captain Laporta, coming from Tarragona, was lost on July 22 on Anegada Island but part of the cargo was saved and carried to Tortola.

Year 1810. British ship *London*, Captain Cromie (might be Cramie), from London to Haiti, was lost on Anegada Island.

Year 1810. Unidentified ship lost off Anegada.

Year 1811. American brig *Lioness* wrecked on Anegada Reef.

Year 1812. British ship *Ocean*, Captain Stewart, from London to Honduras, totally lost in February on Anegada Reef but the crew was saved.

Year 1812. Spanish ship *N.S. de la Victoria*, coming from Malaga, was lost on December 5 on Anegada Reef.

Year 1813. A brig, name unknown, struck a rock between Buck Island and St. Thomas and stuck there. Incident took place the same day the *Thomas* of Bristol, coming from St. Vincent, struck the same rock and was run ashore to keep from sinking.

Year 1813. Spanish ship *Anrora* (correct spelling is probably "Aurora") Captain Aldayturriaga, from Cadiz to Veracruz, was totally lost on Anegada on November 29 but the crew was saved.

Year 1814. A ship of unknown nationality, *Caroline*, Captain DaSilva, from Madeira to Jamaica, was lost off Tortola on November 15 but the crew was saved and carried to Puerto Rico.

Year 1815. British ship *Marina*, Captain Littlewood, from Barbados to St. John and New Brunswick, was wrecked on a small island to the westward of St. Thomas but part of her cargo was saved.

Year 1816. British cutter *Jane* was lost on the north side of Tortola, her port of origin, at the end of February.

Year 1816. British ship *Dash*, Captain Falls, of London, from Puerto Rico to Barbados, with 120 head of oxen, was totally lost on May 23 on Anegada Reef, the crew, 20 head of oxen, and some rigging were saved.

Year 1816. British ship *Warwick*, Captain Simpson, from Liverpool to St. Thomas, struck a rock between Buck Island and St. Thomas and was lost with her cargo but the crew was saved.

Year 1817. A ship of unknown nationality, *Arabella*, Captain Spiller, from Para, Brazil, to New York, was totally lost near St. Thomas.

Year 1817. A ship of unknown nationality *Mary*, Captain Autman, from Jamaica to Veracruz, was lost on Anegada.

Year 1817. American ship *Falcon*, Captain Brothoff, wrecked at Anegada on May 26.

Year 1817. A large unidentified Spanish ship with over 300 African slaves aboard ran aground on the Horseshoe part of Anegada. After throwing many heavy objects overboard she was light enough to be pulled off and proceeded on her voyage.

Year 1818. *Paterson* sank at Anegada.

Year 1818. British ship *Bulwark*, from New Brunswick to Jamaica, wrecked on Anegada on December 13.

Year 1819. Portuguese ship *Dona Paulo*, Captain Viana, of Para, totally wrecked on the Anegada Shoals the night of September 2, 35 African slaves and the crew were saved.

Year 1819. British ship *Agno*, Captain Park, from London to (St.) Petersburg, lost on the south end of Hogland (Hog Island?) in the Virgin Islands.

Year 1819. During a hurricane in September an unidentified vessel was driven onshore at Tortola.

Year 1819. English ship *Ajax* wrecked, captain and three men drowned, off Anegada, September 1819.

Year 1819. American schooner *Maxwell* sank at Anegada.

Year 1819. American schooner *James Edwards* sank at Anegada.

Year 1819. Danish brig *Volvent* sank at Anegada.

Year 1819. British brig *Argus* sank at Anegada.

Year 1819. A dreadful hurricane struck St. Thomas as well as throughout the Leeward Islands on September 20-22. At St. Thomas alone, 104 vessels were totally lost.

Year 1821. A ship of unknown nationality, *Mary*, Captain Hellyer, from New York to St. Thomas, was lost on February 22 on Anegada Shoals but the crew and cargo were saved.

Year 1821. American ship *General Brown*, Captain Godfrey, from New York to the west end of Puerto Rico, was totally wrecked on the Anegada Shoals but most of its cargo was saved and sold at Tortola.

Year 1821. British ship *Bryon* (or *Byron*), Captain Anderson, of and for Cork from Trinidad, was totally lost on Anegada Shoals on November 23 but the crew and passengers were saved.

Year 1822. British ship *Sophia Sarah*, Captain Stairs, of and from Halifax to Jamaica, was totally lost in July on the Anegada Shoals but the crew and part of her cargo were saved.

Year 1822. American brig *Caroline*, from Boston to Puerto Rico, was totally lost on Anegada Shoals about November 25.

Year 1822. Spanish felucca on Anegada.

Year 1823. British schooner *Sophia*, of Antigua, bound to Curaçao with cargo of mahogany wood, ran on the Anegada Reef and was totally lost, crew, rigging, and part of cargo saved.

Year 1823. British ship *Eliza*, Captain Filliul, from Liverpool to St. Thomas, wrecked on Horseshoe Reef near Anegada, cargo and crew saved.

Year 1823. British ship *Acadia*, Captain Venham, of and for Trinidad from Puerto Rico, lost on the Anegada Shoals on March 4, only about fifty head of cattle were saved.

Year 1823. British ship *Union*, Captain Purrington, from Barbados to Bath, was lost on December 12 on Anegada.

Year 1824. American ship *James Barron*, Captain Fisher, from Charleston, South Carolina to Barbados, was totally lost on January 7 on the Anegada Reef.

Year 1824. French ship *Aimable Eulalie*, Captain Alleaume, from Guadeloupe to Le Havre, wrecked on Anegada Shoals in May, only a small part of the cargo was saved.

Year 1824. British ship *Sector*, from Trinidad to St. Thomas, wrecked on Anegada Shoals on May 6, crew and some of cargo of dry goods saved.

Year 1824. A ship of unknown nationality, *Angelica*, Captain Treby, from New York, was totally wrecked on Buck Island, off St. Croix, crew and small part of cargo saved.

Chapter Twelve

Central America
and Off-Lying Areas

When compared with most areas of the Western Hemisphere, Central America and the areas adjacent to it do not have a large number of shipwrecks. The main reason for this is because of the relatively small amount of shipping in these waters during the period covered in this book. There were only a few, relatively insignificant and small, Spanish settlements along the coastline of Central America on both the Caribbean side (the Spanish Main) and the Pacific side. Only the ports in Panama, which served as transshipment points between Spain and Peru, were considered of major importance.

Throughout most of the 16th, 17th and 18th centuries, shipping in the Pacific Ocean between ports of Mexico, Panama and all South American ports was forbidden. During the same period the only important shipping on the Caribbean side of Central America was carried on by the Honduras galleons, two of which were permitted to sail annually between Spain and Honduras. There were many years when none sailed, however, sometimes for periods as long as 10 years, especially in wartime. In the 18th century, when the English started settling British Honduras and some of the Bay Islands, shipping increased, and so did the number of ship losses. Most of these ships carried insignificant cargoes, such as mahogany and dyewoods.

In this chapter I have excluded over 100 shipwrecks, most of them English and dating after 1650, because documentary references to their locations are vague, e.g. the "in the Bay of Honduras" or "on the Coast of Honduras." Until the early 19th century the whole of the Caribbean coastline of Central America from Panama up to Yucatan was simply called "Honduras." And all of the western

Caribbean, from the Cayman Islands west, was called the "Bay of Honduras" — not merely the body of water near the coast.

All areas covered in this chapter require permits from the appropriate governments. Except for a few small-scale expeditions off Panama, and my work at Providencia and Serana and Seranilla Banks, there has been almost no work on old wrecks in these areas.

Shipwrecks in Central American Waters

Year 1526. A small unidentified Spanish merchant nao, sailing between Santo Domingo and Venezuela, encountered a severe storm and lost its masts and rudder. After drifting for six days it was wrecked on a reef in front of Southwest Key (now Serrana Bank). Only one man, identified as Master Pedro Serrano, reached the key safely. The others drifted away on pieces of the wreckage and were lost. He lived on the key for eight years before a passing ship sighted his smoke signals and picked him up. The bank was named after him. I located this shipwreck several years ago and recovered a number of interesting artifacts from it.

Year 1531. While Pedro Serrano was living on Southwest Key, an unidentified Spanish ship was wrecked on a reef about six miles to the east of Southwest Key. The only survivor from this wreck managed to reach Southwest Key and he lived with Pedro Serrano until both were rescued in 1534.

Year 1534. Several months after Pedro Serrano and his companion were rescued, another unidentified Spanish ship, carrying a large amount of treasure on board, was wrecked on the reefs at the eastern end of Serrana Bank. A few survivors from this wreck reached Jamaica in a small boat, but there are no records indicating if the treasure from it was ever recovered.

Year 1552. Nao *Santa Catalina*, Captain Alonzo Galdamez, 200 tons, carrying 330,000 pesos in treasure while sailing between Cartagena and Havana was wrecked and totally lost on Serranilla Bank.

Year 1571. Small Spanish merchant nao *Nuestra Señora de la Limpia Concepción*, sailing from Spain to Panama, was wrecked on a reef off Old Providence Island. Using documentation from the Archives of the Indies, I located this shipwreck in 1964 and partially salvaged it the following year.

Year 1605. Seven treasure-laden galleons of the Armada de Tierra Firme, commanded by Captain-General Luis de Córdova, were struck by a hurricane between Serrana and Serranilla banks. One of the ships managed to return to Cartagena and two others reached Jamaica. The other four, carrying over eight million pesos in treasure, were wrecked on Serranilla Bank. They were the Capitaña *San Roque*, 600 tons, Captain Ruy Lopez; Almiranta *Santo Domingo*, 747 tons, Captain Diego Ramírez; *Nuestra Señora de Begonia*, 500 tons, Captain Pedro Muñoz de Salto; and the *San Ambrosio*, 450 tons, Captain Martín de Ormachea. Although there were no survivors from these four wrecks, the Spaniards sent out salvage teams all over the western Caribbean trying unsuccessfully to locate them. They were accidentally located in 1667 by Spanish fishermen from Cuba who recovered an undisclosed amount of silver coins from two of the wrecks. During the following six years Spanish authorities sent many expeditions to salvage these wrecks but all failed because of bad weather. Several modern-day expeditions, including one of my own in 1963, have attempted to salvage these rich wrecks but constant bad weather and incessant large seas that break over the reef where the wrecks lie have foiled us all. From the air I sighted six large ballast piles in the target area. Artifacts I found on the inside of the reef date from the period of the disaster, and I'm sure that at least one of the six ballast piles is one of these 1605 wrecks.

Year 1633. While the Armada de Tierra Firme, commanded by Captain-General Antonio de Oquendo, was sailing between Cartagena and Havana, it encountered a bad storm near Serrana Bank. The galleons *Almiranta* and *San Juan*, both carrying a great amount of treasure, were wrecked on Serrana Bank; there are no records indicating if they were ever salvaged.

Year 1641. The Spaniards sent an expedition commanded by Admiral Pimienta from Cartagena to dislodge the English from their newly founded settlement on Old Providence Island. The Spanish attack was successful, but one of the ships of the attacking squadron, a Portuguese nao, *Santa María de la Ayuda*, of 230 tons, struck on a reef off the western end of the island and sank in 10 fathoms of water.

Year 1643. A small Spanish frigate of six bronze cannon was sent from Portobelo with supplies for the Spanish garrison on Old Providence Island but was wrecked en route on a reef at San Andrés Island, located 55 miles south of Old Providence Island.

Year 1666. A small Spanish warship was sent from Cartagena to dislodge a band of pirates living in Old Providence Island. Faulty navigation caused it to wreck on the reefs of Quita Sueño Bank, located north of the island.

Year 1675. An unidentified large Dutch warship was wrecked on Roncador Reef, located to the east of Old Providence Island. Some survivors managed to reach the southern coast of Cuba in a raft, where they were captured by the Spaniards.

Year 1688. Several Spaniards petitioned the King of Spain for permission to salvage several very rich galleon wrecks located near Swan's Island, but they neither identified the ships nor when they were lost. Records do not indicate if they were granted permission.

Year 1788. English merchantman *Richard*, Captain Watson, sailing from Jamaica to Honduras, was wrecked at San Andrés Island but the crew was saved.

Year 1794. English merchantman *June*, Captain Gardner, sailing from Honduras to London, was wrecked at Old Providence Island on August 17.

Year 1796. Spanish frigate *Palas*, 34 cannon, Captain Pedro Saenz de la Guardia, was wrecked at Old Providence Island on December 29.

Year 1801. Spanish merchantman *El Paysano*, Captain Chicey, sailing to Jamaica, was wrecked near San Andrés Island, her crew was lost.

Year 1816. American schooner *Charming Sally*, Captain Vincent, sailing from South Carolina to Cartagena, was wrecked on Serrana Bank.

Year 1817. American merchantman *Rolla*, Captain Lewis, coming from Philadelphia, was wrecked in April on Serranilla Reef but all of the crew was saved.

Year 1819. Three English merchantmen were wrecked on some reefs located south of San Andrés Island: *St. Lawrence*, Captain Williamson; *Friends*, Captain Howard; and the *Beckles*, Captain Hall.

Belize

Year 1749. During a hurricane on September 18, more than 20 English merchantmen were totally lost on the coast and off-lying keys and reefs.

Year 1751. English merchantman *Monmouth*, Captain Wadham, sailing to London, was wrecked on Glover's Key but the crew was saved.

Year 1751. Two sloops from Rhode Island and a snow from Jamaica were lost on the "North Keys."

Year 1764. English merchantman *Mary Oxford*, coming from Jamaica, was wrecked on Turneffe Island.

Year 1769. English merchantman *Liberty*, Captain Beard, coming from Jamaica, was wrecked on the southern end of Chinchorro Reef but her crew was saved.

Year 1771. American ship *Andrew*, Captain Passgrove, sailing from Honduras to Philadelphia, was wrecked October 22 on Chinchorro Reef.

Year 1773. American merchantman *Industry*, Captain Glen, sailing from Honduras to New York, carrying a cargo of indigo and mahogany, was wrecked on Chinchorro Reef.

Year 1774. Two ships wrecked on Glover's Reef: English merchantman *Argyle*, Captain Fisher, about five leagues from the southwestern end of the reef; and the American ship *Polly*, Captain Waid, sailing to New York, on the northeastern end of the reef; crews and part of cargoes saved.

Year 1776. Irish merchantman *Hercules*, Captain Norwood, sailing from Honduras to Dublin, was wrecked on Chinchorro Reef.

Year 1780. English ship *Live Oak*, sailing to Jamaica with a cargo of mahogany, was wrecked on the coast at Black River; the crew was saved.

Year 1786. English merchantman *Assistance*, Captain Galt, coming from Jamaica, was lost crossing the bar at Black River.

Year 1786. Unidentified Scottish ship, Captain Carr, was wrecked on Glovers Reef, but the crew was saved.

Year 1787. During a hurricane on September 2, more than 30 English merchantmen were wrecked on the coast and off-lying areas. Of these, 15 were lost in the port of Belize. The only ship identified by name was H.M.S. Triumvirate, lost at St. Georges Key, which was carrying a large amount of silver specie.

Before 1792. An English chart dated 1792 states that some years earlier a Spanish galleon named *Sant' Yaga* was lost off the Three Brothers, which are several small keys near the northeastern tip of Ambergris Key.

Year 1793. English gunship *H.M.S. Advice*, four cannon, Captain Edward Tyrell, was lost to the leeward of Key Bokell but her crew was saved.

Year 1793. English merchantman *Chance*, Captain Reed, coming from Jamaica, was wrecked on Glovers Reef.

Year 1803. English merchantman *Fishburn*, Captain Leake, sailing to London, was lost on a reef near Belize on February 19.

Year 1804. A ship of unknown registry, *Mentor*, Captain Simpson, coming from Jamaica, was lost on "the Main Reef" near Belize, but part of her cargo was saved.

Year 1807. English ship *General Don*, Captain Messeroy, coming from France, was lost on Glovers Reef.

Year 1808. English merchantman *Perseverance*, Captain M'Nutt, coming from Jamaica, lost near Belize on December 20 but the crew was saved.

Year 1814. A ship of unknown registry, *Pompey*, Captain Cowan, was wrecked on "the Main Reef" on March 31, but her cargo of wine was saved.

Year 1815. Scottish merchantman *Lord Blandtyre*, Captain M'Lea, coming from Jamaica, was wrecked in August on the "Southern Four Keys."

Year 1818. American ship *Enterprize*, Captain Wayne, sailing from the Bahamas to New Orleans, was lost on March 9 near Belize; crew was saved.

Year 1818. English merchantman *John Winslow*, Captain Hodges, coming from Liverpool, was lost on July 26 on the "Main Reef," cargo and crew saved.

Year 1819. English merchantman *Vestol*, Captain Hutchinson, sailing to London, was wrecked on Corker Key in August, crew and part of cargo saved.

Year 1821. English merchantman *Barrosa*, Captain Anderson, coming from London, was totally lost on November 8 on the "Southern Fourth Reef," crew and most of cargo saved.

Year 1821. French ship *Ceres*, Captain Mourant, coming from France, was wrecked on July 18 on Chinchorro Reef; only the crew was saved.

Year 1822. American ship *Phoebe Ann*, sailing to New York, was wrecked near Belize about April 11.

Year 1822. English ship *Comet*, Captain Merrill, sailing to England, was wrecked on Ambergris Key on August 16.

Honduras

Year 1524. After learning of the revolt of Captain Olid, Cortez sent two ships of soldiers commanded by Captain Francisco de las Casas to quell the mutiny. After entering the port of Trizano de la Cruz, a battle ensued between the mutineers and de las Casas's ships in which one of Olid's vessels was sunk by cannonfire. Soon after, a violent gale hit the port and both of de las Casas's ships were sunk.

Year 1530. Two large ships from Spain arrived in the port of Trujillo, with supplies and the new governor of that province, Don Diego de Albitez. Only minutes after anchoring, both ships were wrecked by a violent gust of wind and only a small part of their cargoes was salvaged.

Year 1545. A big unidentified galleon commanded by Captain Nicolas Castellon sailed from Puerto Caballos for Spain with a large number of passengers and a great amount of gold. She was wrecked at Cabo de Honduras and the majority of her passengers and gold was lost.

Year 1605. Two large galleons were sent from Spain to the port of Trujillo and met with misfortune. As the Almiranta was entering port it was struck by lightning and sank quickly, with only eleven of the 101 persons aboard being saved. After the Capitaña had taken on a valuable cargo in that port, including a substantial amount of gold and silver, it sailed for Spain. But the following day a storm drove it ashore on the coast, where it quickly went to pieces. Several months later, pieces of the wreck, including some bodies and a few bars of gold and silver, were found on a beach, but the wreck was never located.

Year 1607. A squadron of twelve Dutch ships entered the port of Puerto Caballos and attempted to capture two Spanish galleons that were then loading for the voyage to Spain. During the battle that ensued and lasted for a period of nine days, one Dutch ship was sunk in the port and the other left without capturing the two Spanish galleons.

Year 1617. Two galleons sent from Spain to Honduras were lost. The Capitaña *La Limpia Concepción de Nuestra Señora* sank on September 28 while entering Trujillo, and several days before the Almiranta *Santiago* had wrecked on Guanaja Island.

Year 1618. The following year, Spain sent only one galleon to Honduras, and it too met with disaster. She was the 450-ton galleon *San Francisco*, Captain Sebastian Rodriguez de Caranca, and when attempting to enter the port of Santo Tomas de Castilla she wrecked and totally lost on a reef. Of her 30 bronze cannon only two were salvaged, and of her cargo only a few casks of wine.

Year 1644. Six English warships were sighted off the port of Santo Tomas de Castilla on May 12, and to prevent the capture of a frigate that had just arrived from Veracruz, the Spaniards quickly took off her cannon and then sank the ship at the mouth of the port.

Year 1647. Shortly after two large galleons from Spain had arrived at Trujillo, they were quickly unloaded and then sunk by the Spaniards, as they believed that an English fleet was coming to attack that port.

Year 1660. The Spanish nao *Santiago*, part of the Tierra Firme Flota of Captain-General Juan de Echeverri, sailing from Cartagena to Havana, was wrecked near a deserted island off the coast of Honduras. Most of the persons aboard the ship managed to reach the island and spent 53 days there building a small vessel from the timbers of their wreck.

Year 1690. Because of a shortage of mercury in Mexico, the viceroy sent a small ship with over a million pesos in silver specie aboard to buy mercury in Peru. Several days after sailing from Acapulco, it was struck by a storm and soon afterward wrecked near a point of land on the southwest side of the Gulf of Fonseca. Salvors were able to recover only a small part of the treasure, as most had been buried under shifting sands.

Year 1751. English merchantman *Lamport*, Captain M'Namara, carrying a cargo of 300 tons of logwood to England, was wrecked on Roatan Island.

Year 1768. English merchantman *Ward*, Captain Kelly, sailing from Honduras to the Windward Islands, was wrecked on Utila Island.

Year 1769. English merchantman *Windsor*, Captain Burden, sailing to England, was wrecked on Roatan Island but most of its cargo was saved.

These three Portugese ingots — one bears the date 1537 — minted in Olinda, Brazil, were recovered from a wreck off Salvador, Brazil.

Year 1773. A ship of unknown registry, *St. Paul*, Captain Maes, sailing from Montserrat Island to Honduras, was lost on Roatan Island but the crew was saved.

Year 1774. Scottish merchantman *Willingmaid*, Captain Bray, was accidentally burned while at anchor at Guanaja Island.

Year 1785. English merchantman *Quebec*, Captain Rattle, sailing from Honduras to Bristol, was wrecked at Guanaja Island.

Year 1803. English merchantman *Oliver*, Captain Hood, sailing for England with a cargo of logwood, was wrecked on Uffla Island.

Nicaragua

Year 1577. Unidentified Spanish nao, carrying a large number of religious from Cartagena to Trujillo, Honduras, was wrecked about 20 leagues south of Cabo Gracias a Dios.

Year 1680. An unidentified English privateer, coming from Jamaica, was wrecked several leagues north of Cabo Gracias a Dios.

Year 1766. English sloop *Fanny*, Captain Henderson, coming from Jamaica, was lost October 31 off Cabo Gracias a Dios; the warship *Fox*, sailing from Puerto Caballo to Havana, was wrecked at Cabo Gracias a Dios.

Costa Rica

Year 1567. Small Spanish advice boat *La Rapidez*, Captain Hernando Martín López, was wrecked near the mouth of the San Juan River, on the Caribbean side of the country.

Year 1675. Two unidentified merchant naos, sailing from Callao, Peru, to Acapulco, each carrying several chests of silver specie as well as several tons of mercury, were wrecked near Cabo Blanco on the Nicoya Peninsula, which is in the Pacific.

On an 18th-century shipwreck off the coast of Honduras, co-author Jenifer Marx, above, holds a gold scabbard tip next to a cannon, while she and another diver pick up gold and silver coins below.

Panama

Year 1503. While Columbus was on his fourth voyage of discovery, two of his caravels were so worm-eaten that he was forced to scuttle them. The *Gallega* was scuttled near Santa María de Belem and the *Vizcaina* off Portobelo. Both vessels were first stripped of all items of value.

Year 1514. Two or three small Spanish ships, under the command of Governor Pedrarias Davila, were lost during a storm near Cabo Tiburón, on the Caribbean side of the isthmus.

Year 1544. At the orders of the conquistador Francisco de Pizarro, an undisclosed number of ships were scuttled in the port of Nombre de Diós after being stripped of their cannon and rigging.

Year 1551. An unidentified Spanish nao of the Tierra Firme Flota of Captain-General Sancho de Viedma, was wrecked on the coast about 25 leagues from the port of Nombre de Diós.

Year 1563. While the Tierra Firme Flota of Captain-General Antonio de Aquayo was anchored in Nombre de Diós, seven ships were sunk during a storm. None had their cargoes aboard at the time, the cannon from five of them were recovered.

Year 1567. An unidentified merchant nao of the Tierra Firme Flota of Captain-General Diego Flores de Valdes struck upon an anchor in a shallow area while entering Nombre de Diós and sank with all of her cargo still aboard.

Year 1584. Shortly after the Tierra Firme Flota of Captain-General Francisco de Novoa Feijo entered the port of Nombre de Diós, two merchant naos sank with their cargoes from Spain still aboard: *Espíritu Santo*, 500 tons, Captain Cristóbal García de la Vega, and an unidentified nao of 300 tons, Captain Nufio Rodriquez.

Year 1609. An unidentified Portuguese caravel, coming from Angola, Africa, with a cargo of slaves, ivory and gold dust, sank a bit north of the Bay of Acla but all of her cargo and slaves were saved.

Year 1619. Several flat-bottomed boats that were transporting treasure from Panama to the galleons anchored in Portobelo overturned on the Chagres River and a large amount of treasure was lost.

Year 1631. The Almiranta of the South Seas Armada, the galleon *San José* while carrying a great amount of treasure from Callao, Peru, to Panama, was wrecked on a reef about 40 leagues from Panama City, between the islands of Garachine and La Galera. Divers were quickly sent to the wreck site and recovered 25 of the ship's 28 cannon and over a million pesos in treasure. A year later the president of Panama reported that more than 400,000 pesos in silver specie and 44 silver bars remained on the wreck, but diving operations had to be suspended because of rough seas and fast currents; also because the remainder of the treasure was buried under sand.

Year 1632. The patache *Margarita*, owned by Miguél de Garnica, was wrecked at Isla del Rey, located 15 leagues from Panama City, but her complete cargo of silver bullion and specie was recovered.

Year 1634. Two unidentified Spanish merchant naos were sunk during a storm in the port of Portobelo but the cargoes and cannon from both wrecks were salvaged.

Year 1635. While the Tierra Firme Armada, commanded by Captain-General Carlos de Ibarra, was in Portobelo loading on the treasure for Spain, one galleon the *Santa Ana María* was in such bad condition from multiple leaks that she was stripped and then sunk.

Year 1670. While approaching the coast of Panama before his attack on Panama City, the flagship of the pirate Henry Morgan and four other ships in his fleet were wrecked on a reef at the mouth of the Chagres River. After the five were stripped of all valuable items they were burned to the waterline by the pirates.

Year 1681. After the Tierra Firme Armada, commanded by the Marquis de Bienes, had taken on treasure and set sail from Portobelo it was struck by a storm that scattered many of the ships to various places near the coast of Panama. An unidentified rich treasure galleon of Captain Antonio de Lima struck on a reef off Punta de Brujas and quickly broke up with more than 280 persons drowning and her treasure totally lost. The merchant nao *Chaperon* sank at the mouth of the Chagres River with only 11 eleven men lost; and another nao, *La Boticaria*, was wrecked on a reef near Isla de Naranjos, but only two men were lost and some of her cargo was eventually recovered.

Year 1740. During the English attack led by Admiral Vernon against Portobelo, a small Spanish sloop was sunk at Portobelo and two large Spanish vessels were sunk at the mouth of the Chagres River.

Year 1746. A Spanish privateer, *Golgoa*, was driven ashore near Portobelo by two English warships after a short battle and quickly went to pieces.

Year 1818. Two schooners were wrecked near Portobelo during a storm: the *Lion*, coming from Jamaica, and an unidentified vessel from Havana.

Year 1819. A large French brig, *Jeune Robert*, was totally lost on Sapelo Island, on the Caribbean side of the isthmus.

Chapter Thirteen

South America

The majority of shipping off the East Coast of South America was Portuguese during the 16th, 17th, and 18th centuries. Hundreds of wrecks must have occurred, but relatively few locations are known today because of the almost total destruction of old Portuguese documents. All South American countries have laws regarding the salvaging of shipwrecks. Brazil has the law most favorable to salvors. The government takes only 20 percent of a find. Colombia's law is similar to Florida's. The salvor gets 75 percent and the country 25 percent of all treasure and artifacts recovered. In addition, a foreigner must post a bond of about $25,000. Although the salvor retains 75 percent of everything he recovers, no gold in any form can leave Colombia; and if a Colombian museum wishes to obtain anything belonging to a salvor, they can buy it at a price they deem reasonable.

I have excluded over 400 shipwrecks from this chapter for the reasons cited in previous chapters.

Shipwrecks in South American Waters

Colombia

Year 1504. During an exploration voyage along the coast of Colombia the flagship of Captain Cristobal García was wrecked on a reef near Punta de Canoas, between Cartagena and Barranquilla. The crew was rescued by the two other vessels in the flotilla, but an undisclosed amount of gold nuggets and emeralds that the explorers had traded from the natives sank with the ship.

Year 1504. Another flotilla of four larger vessels commanded by Captain Juan de la Cosa was sent later this same year to continue exploring and mapping the Colombian coast, but all four were wrecked during a storm in the Bahía de Uraba and 175 of the 200 men on board the naos were drowned.

Year 1513. A large nao was sent from Santo Domingo to the new Spanish settlement named Darien, located close to the present boundary of Panama and

409

Colombia. The nao was carrying a large number of colonists and supplies, but the pilot erred in his navigation and the ship wrecked a bit west of Darien; there were only a few survivors.

Year 1542. Three unidentified ships carrying over a half-million pesos in gold and silver were sunk near Boca Chica, in Cartagena Harbor, while entering the port. At the admiral's orders the convoy's chief pilot was hanged. Divers recovered only a small part of the treasure, reported to be in a depth too great for them to work in.

Year 1544. A large unidentified Spanish nao, carrying a bishop to Cartagena from Spain along with a rich cargo of merchandise, was wrecked on the coast near Santa Marta.

Year 1545. An unidentified Portuguese slave ship arriving from Angola was wrecked during a storm in December on Salmedina Reef just outside the entrance to Cartagena.

Year 1546. An unidentified Spanish merchant nao was wrecked on a reef near Cartagena and 13 thirteen of the 104 persons aboard perished.

Year 1553. After the Tierra Firme Armada, commanded by Captain-General Bartolome Carreño, sailed from Nombre de Diós with a great amount of treasure, the navío *Santa María de Villacelan*, 120 tons, Captain Martin García, was wrecked on the coast about 10 leagues south of Cartagena, but all of her treasure was salvaged by Indian divers brought from the pearl fisheries of Margarita Island.

Year 1553. Nao *San Marcos*, Captain Pedro Lerida, 120 tons, sailing in the armada of General Carreño between Nombre de Diós and Cartagena was lost near the entrance to this port but all treasures she carried were salvaged.

Year 1556. Unidentified merchant nao of Captain Juan Estevan sank while at anchor in Cartagena harbor; but all treasure was recovered by Indian divers.

Year 1559. A richly laden unidentified galleon sailing from Nombre de Diós with over 900,000 pesos in gold and silver aboard parted from its convoy and attempted to enter Cartagena Harbor at night, but the pilot missed the entrance and the ship ran aground a bit south of the port and quickly broke up. Only a small amount of the treasure was recovered.

Year 1562. Treasure-laden nao *Santa María de Begonia*, 250 tons, Captain Cosmo Andrés, ran aground when entering Cartagena Harbor and was lost but all of her treasure was saved.

Year 1564. An unidentified treasure-laden galleon in the Tierra Firme Armada, commanded by Captain-General Estiban de las Alas, was wrecked on a reef near Cartagena and 13 persons drowned. The wreck fell off the reef into deeper water before her treasure could be saved, and divers were unable to recover anything because of the depth of the wreck.

Year 1572. Treasure-laden galleon *San Felipe*, 550 tons, Captain Galdómez, caught fire while sailing between Nombre de Diós and Cartagena and was run aground near Isla Tesoro, where it blew up before the majority of the treasure she carried could be taken off.

Year 1575. Shortly before the Tierra Firme Armada was to sail for Havana, two unidentified galleons collided while at anchor in Cartagena and one of them, carrying an immense treasure in silver bullion and specie, sank. The water's depth permitted divers to recover only some of the ship's rigging and a few bronze cannon.

Year 1578. After the armada of General Miguel de Eraso reached the port of Cartagena, two of the galleons, the *San Tadio* and *Sant' Andrés*, were found to be unfit for further use. They were stripped and sunk in the deepest part of the bay.

410

Year 1594. A late 17th-century atlas of the Pacific coast of South America of the area of the River St. Jago and the Bay of St. Matheo (sic.) states, "The little river between St. Jago and St. Matheo cannot be seen till you come near it from which comes out into the sea a shoal of rocks one and a half leagues on which was cast away John Philipo Castro, a great pilot of this sea with the ship *Clarius* in the year 1594, in said ship was a vast treasure and many other rich ships have also been cast away on the same shoals." This wrecks lies on the Pacific coast of Colombia.

Year 1599. In June of this year a fleet of Dutch privateers sank seven Spanish ships along the coast of Colombia, but only one, the *Cuervo Volante* was identified and she was driven ashore at the entrance to the port of Cartagena.

Year 1600. Unidentified merchant nao of Captain Bodes, coming from Margarita Island with a large amount of pearls, was wrecked near the mouth of the Medellín River.

Year 1615. Soon after arriving from Spain the nao *Nuestra Señora del Rosario*, 250 tons, Captain Baltazar Rodriquez Carreno, sank at anchor in Cartagena Harbor.

Year 1616, A small unidentified ship, coming from Venezuela with a cargo consisting mainly of tobacco, ran aground while entering the port of Santa Marta.

Year 1626. Treasure-laden galleon of the Tierra Firme Armada, Captain-General Tomas de Larraspuru, the *Nuestra Señora de la Candelaria*, 600 tons, Captain Juan de Campos, was wrecked on the Salmedina Reef when the Armada was leaving Cartagena en route to Havana but most of her treasure was recovered by divers.

Year 1629. Due to bad leaks the galleon *Nuestra Señora de la Concepción y San Francisco*, 550 tons, sank while at anchor in Cartagena Harbor, but she had no treasure or other cargo aboard.

Year 1631. While the Tierra Firme Armada, Captain-General Tomas de Larraspuru, was sailing between Portobelo and Cartagena, an unidentified patache was wrecked on a reef off Isla Baru.

Year 1632. An unidentified patache, sailing from Margarita Island to Cartagena with a valuable cargo of pearls, was wrecked on Isla Tesoro but most of the pearls were recovered by divers.

Year 1634. When the Tierra Firme Armada, under Captain-General Antonio de Oquendo, was arriving at Cartagena, coming from Portobelo with a vast amount of treasure, four ships were lost: galleon *San Juan Bautista*, 600 tons, Captain Hernan Martínez de Velasco, was wrecked on Salmedina Reef but her treasure and cannon were recovered; patache *Nuestra Señora del Carmen*, 80 tons, was wrecked at the entrance of Boca Chica but was totally salvaged later; two merchant naos, *Nuestra Señora del Rosario*, 450 tons, and the *Los Tres Reyes*, 600 tons, sank because of leaks shortly after entering the inner harbor. A week later an unidentified merchant nao from Santo Domingo sank after accidentally striking some part of the sunken patache at Boca Chica.

Year 1637. The patache of the Tierra Firme Armada, Captain- General Carlos de Ibarra, was sailing between Venezuela and Cartagena with a cargo consisting of 60 tons of copper ingots when it wrecked on a reef near Cartagena. Salvors recovered most of the cargo.

Year 1640. With the outbreak of war between Spain and Portugal this year, the Tierra Firme Armada intercepted the richly laden Portuguese Armada when it was sailing between Brazil and Portugal and forced it to sail with the Spanish Armada to Cartagena.Even though the leader of the Portuguese Armada, Admiral Rodrigo Lobad da Silva, had no idea that there was a war between the two countries, he suspected foul play. When the armadas were entering Cartagena harbor, he deliberately wrecked his three richest galleons on a reef near the entrance of Boca Grande. The treasure on these three galleons consisting of gold, diamonds and other precious stones was estimated at over five million pesos, and records do not state if any of it was ever recovered.

Year 1652. An unidentified Spanish advice boat was wrecked off Cabo de la Vela. Her crew reached shore but was captured and eaten by the Carib Indians. These same Indians recovered the mail from the wreck and sold it to the Spaniards.

Year 1660. An unidentified Portuguese slave ship struck on a rock in one and one-half fathoms of water near Punta de la Canoa, then sank in deeper water.

Year 1680. An unidentified advice boat arriving from Spain was totally lost on the Salmedina Reef.

Year 1681. After the Tierra Firme Armada, Captain-General Marquis de Brenes, sailed from Cartagena for Portobelo, four ships were lost: galleon *Santa Teresa*; galleon *Nuestra Señora de la Soledad*; merchant nao *Nuestra Señora de la Asunción*; and the patache *Nuestra Señora de la Encarnación*. Where and why these four ships were lost is not found in the documents. After receiving the treasure at Portobelo, the armada returned to Cartagena, then sailed for Havana. But shortly after leaving Boca Chica, four more ships were wrecked on nearby reefs: galleons *Santa Teresa* (another by the same name as the one above) and *Santiago*; an unidentified small nao; and the armada's patache. The loss of treasure and lives was great, and only four persons were rescued from all four ships.

Year 1682. The galleon *Catheresa* sank in sight of Cartagena Harbor, but records do not indicate whether she was in a convoy or carried any treasure. The records do indicate that in 1963 several bronze cannon were recovered from this wreck.

Year 1697. A French fleet under the command of Admiral Pointé attacked Cartagena, and to prevent the French from entering the inner harbor the Spaniards sank two large galleons near Castillo Santa Cruz and then burned two other large ships, two galleys and many small vessels in the inner harbor to prevent their capture by the French. The French bomb galliot *Eclatant* was so badly damaged by Spanish cannonfire that the French burned it in the harbor before leaving.

Year 1705. The French merchantman *La Armona*, which had permission to trade with the Spaniards, was wrecked on Salmedina Reef while carrying a valuable cargo of merchandise.

Year 1707. While giving chase to a small French sloop, the English warship *H.M.S. Margaret* was lost at Punta de la Canoa.

Year 1708. The richest single Spanish galleon ever lost in the Western Hemisphere was the *San José*, carrying over 11 million pesos in treasure. Because of the War of Spanish Succession, no treasure had been sent from South America to Spain in six years, and a fleet of 17 ships arrived at Portobelo to receive the treasure. Since only four of the ships were heavily armed, all of the 22 million pesos in treasure received at Portobelo was placed on these four ships: the Capitaña *San José*, 64 guns; the Almiranta *San Martín*, 64 guns; the galleon *Gobierno*, 44 guns; and an unidentified urca commanded by Captain Francisco Nieto. As the fleet was approaching Cartagena, an English squadron commanded by Commodore Wager appeared on the horizon between the Spanish fleet and Cartagena and closed in on the Spaniards. Soon afterward a battle ensued between the four Spanish ships and the English warships which continued into the night. The *San José* exploded and quickly sank, with only five of her crew of 600 surviving. The *Gobierno* was captured by the English, the urca was run aground and set afire by the Spaniards on the tip of the Baru Peninsula and the *San Martín* managed to reach the safety of Cartagena, along with the other Spanish merchantmen that carried no treasure. The exact location of the *San José* is not given in the records, only that it sank off Baru Island. Most of the treasure on the urca was later recovered by the Spaniards.

Year 1740. An unidentified Spanish merchant nao was lost near Isla de los Sombreros.

Year 1741. Spanish warship *Guipuzcoa*, 70 guns, was sent from Cartagena to search for some English privateers operating near Santa Marta, but during a storm she was wrecked near the entrance to Santa Marta.

Year 1741. During the English attack on Cartagena led by Admiral Vernon, the Spaniards sank six galleons, six large warships and several merchant naos in the harbor. Only the warships and a French merchantman were identified: *Galicia*, 70 guns; *San Carlos*, 70 guns; *Africa*, 60 guns; *San Felipe*, 80 guns; the French ship *Le Leon de Nantes*, Captain José Lesvin. All the other Spanish ships were scuttled across the mouth of the outer harbor near Castillo Grande to prevent the English ships from entering the port. The following day the two remaining Spanish warships *Conquistador*, 60 guns, and the *Dragon*, 60 guns, were also sunk in the inner channel of the port. Most of the superstructures of the Spanish ships remained above the water, and were burned to prevent the English from obtaining anything of value from them. The English captured, stripped and burned a large Spanish ship, the *Galicia*, which unsuspectingly entered the harbor.

Year 1751. Spanish merchant nao *Nuestra Señora del Carmen* (alias *Bristol*), Captain Joséph de Artecona, coming from Cadíz, was wrecked on Sunzen Shoals, near San Bernardo Island.

Year 1761. A terrible storm struck Cartagena on December 12 and two large unidentified Spanish warships were wrecked in the harbor. During the same storm, many cannon from the two forts at Santa Marta were thrown into the sea.

Year 1765. English merchantman *Friendship*, Captain Morgan, coming from Jamaica, was wrecked off Punta Gallinas.

Year 1773. Spanish nao *San Joséph*, Captain Arestiqui, arriving from Cadíz, was lost while entering Cartagena Harbor.

Yerr 1790. Spanish warship *San Miguel*, Captain Juan Elizalde, struck a submerged rock between Punta de la Canoa and El Palmarita and then sank in 14 fathoms of water on January 3 with only one of her crew drowning.

Year 1793. Spanish merchant nao *Nuestra Señora de Cortijo* (alias *La Serrana*) wrecked on the north side of the point of Isla de Galera Zamba.

Year 1795. Spanish warship *Victoria*, 10 guns, Captain Francisco de Raula Escudero, was wrecked on March 28 on the shallows of Bajo de Negrillo, located near Cartagena. She was originally a French ship captured by the Spaniards.

Year 1801. English warship *H.M.S. Legere*, 18 guns, Captain Cornelius Quinton, was wrecked in Jamba Bay, east of Cartagena, on February 2; one of her crew of 121 men was lost.

Year 1808. A ship of unknown registry, *Chalmers*, Captain Tyack, bringing slaves from Africa to the West Indies, was wrecked on February 24 near Cabo de la Vela, its crew and slaves were all saved.

Year 1808. Two English warships were wrecked within sight of Cartagena: the brig *H.M.S. Bassora*, 12 guns, Captain James Violett, on February 13; none of her crew of 50 was lost; and the frigate *H.M.S. Raposa*, 10 guns, on February 15; the crew was saved.

Year 1813. English merchantman *Confeance*, Captain Molloy, coming from Jamaica, was lost at the end of March near Cartagena.

Year 1814. English merchantman *Clara*, Captain Roberts, coming from Jamaica, sank on September 23 off St. Blas, in the Gulf of Darien, the crew was saved.

Year 1817. A ship of unknown registry, *Martin*, Captain Bull, sailing from Barcelona to Santa Marta was lost on December 10 near Rio de la Hacha, crew and part of cargo saved.

Year 1818. Spanish schooner *Amistad*, Captain Manuel de Zaragosa, wrecked on the bar of the Magdalena River; the captain and several of the crew perished.

Year 1822. English merchant brig *Martins*, Captain Ramsey, coming from Jamaica, was wrecked off Cartagena.

Venezuela

Year 1531. Three Spanish merchant naos commanded by Captain Diego de Ondas were lost in the Gulf of Venezuela, near the entrance of Lake Maracaibo.

Year 1561. An unidentified caravel carrying the Count of Nieva, the new viceroy of Peru, and other important persons was lost on the coast of the Paraguana Peninsula and there were no survivors.

Year 1586. Two Spanish galleys were sent after a French pirate vessel anchored at Puerto Santo on Margarita Island, and during the battle the French ship exploded and 46 of the 50 Frenchmen aboard her were lost.

Year 1590. Small bark *Santiago*, Captain Pedro Vasco, 25 tons, after being loaded with the year's accumulation of pearls from Margarita Island was ready to set sail for Cartagena when she was seized by local inhabitants who claimed they hadn't been paid for their labor for many years. One of the crew still aboard chopped a hole in the side of the vessel and she quickly sank with all the pearls aboard.

Year 1605. The Dutch had established a thriving salt industry at Punta de Araya several years earlier, and this year a large armada of Spanish warships was sent after the Dutch. They surprised 22 Dutch ships there, burned and sank all of them, then massacred all the Dutchmen.

Year 1610. As the Tierra Firme Armada, Captain-General Hierónimo, was sailing between Spain and Cartagena, its Capitaña, *San Felipe*, 850 tons, 42 bronze cannon, Captain Gaspar de Vargas, and the patache of the armada were wrecked off the east side on Bonaire Island. Over a period of five years divers recovered all the cannon from both wrecks as well as a great amount of the cargo of the Capitana.

Year 1613. An unidentified patache carrying a large amount of pearls was wrecked on Aves Island. Two years later the owner of the vessel stated that it had not yet been salvaged.

414

Year 1622. Unidentified patache was wrecked on Islà Beata in Lake Maracaibo.

Year 1622. An unidentified frigate owned by the King of Spain, carrying 30,000 pesos' worth of tobacco, sank near the port of Coro.

Year 1630. Merchant nao *Nuestra Señora de L'Antigua*, Captain Benito Sanchez, sank on June 1 on the north side of Tortuga Island (not to be confused with the island of the same name located off Hispañiola) and was later salvaged by the Dutch.

Year 1648. Frigate *Nuestra Señora de la Concepción*, Captain Pedro Soberanis, 100 tons, was sunk near the town of Gibraltar on Lake Maracaibo but her cargo was salvaged.

Year 1660. Three large unidentified Spanish naos commanded by Captain Antonio Campos were lost in Lake Maracaibo.

Year 1669. While the pirate Henry Morgan was attacking and sacking various settlements on Lake Maracaibo, three large frigates of the Windward Armada, commanded by Admiral Alonso de Espinosa, were sent to fight the pirates. The three Spanish ships were anchored under the guns of the fort at the entrance to Lake Maracaibo, and the pirates had to pass there when leaving the lake. The pirates sank one with the use of a fire ship, the Spaniards burned another to prevent its capture and the third was captured by the pirates.

Year 1678. A French fleet consisting of 18 warships and two privateers, commanded by Count D'Estre, was sent to capture Curaçao from the Dutch. During the night of May 3 all but one of the warships and one of the privateers were totally lost on a reef on Aves Island. Over 1,200 men perished and 250 brass and 300 iron cannon were lost. The Dutch salvaged most of the cannon, and later the French recovered most of those not recovered by the Dutch.

Year 1733. Spanish navío *San Miguél* wrecked near the port of Cumana and was later salvaged by the English.

Year 1734. Unidentified Spanish schooner was wrecked on the reefs in front of Puerto de la Guayra on the mouth of the Orinoco River.

Year 1763. English merchantman *Edward*, Captain Darby, sailing from Hispañiola to Curaçao, was wrecked on Aruba Island.

Year 1766. Irish merchantman *John & Stephen*, Captain Kent, sailing from Cork to Curaçao, was wrecked on August 10 during a storm on Bonaire Island but most of her cargo was saved.

Year 1779. Spanish advice boat *San Antonio*, sailing from Caracas to Spain, was wrecked on June 4 on Bonaire Island.

Year 1780. A ship of unknown registry, *Good Hope*, Captain Dirks, coming from France, was totally lost near Curaçao Island.

Year 1784. During a hurricane that struck Curaçao, several large ships were wrecked in the main harbor and others forced to sea, where they were lost without a trace.

Year 1791. Spanish ship *San Francisco de Paula* was totally lost on the bar at the entrance to Lake Maracaibo.

Year 1802. A ship of unknown registry, *Escape*, coming from Martinique Island was lost near Curaçao.

Year 1803. Spanish schooner of war *San Carlos*, Captain Juan Casteñeda, lost in May on Aves Island during a voyage from Puerto Rico, crew and some cannon saved.

Year 1807. English warship *H.M.S. Pert*, 14 guns, Captain Donald Campbell, wrecked on October 16 on Margarita Island.

Year 1807. English warship *H.M.S. Fiery*, 12 guns, Captain Thomas Price, foundered on November 11 near Curaçao Island; most of the crew perished.

Year 1808. English slave ship *Chalmers*, coming from Africa, was wrecked on Margarita Island.

Year 1808. English warship *H.M.S. Volador*, 16 guns, Captain Francis George Dickins, wrecked on October 24 in the Gulf of Coro.

Year 1808. During a hurricane on October 16 that struck the Island of Curaçao, many of the buildings in the main town were carried into the sea, as well as many graves in the churchyard and cannon from the forts.

Year 1809. Scottish merchantman *Jason*, Captain Stewart, sailing to Curaçao Island, was wrecked on August 17 on Orchella Island, the crew and a small part of her cargo was saved.

Year 1809. English merchantman *Penelope*, Captain Boon, sailing from London to Curaçao, was lost near Curaçao, crew and part of cargo saved.

Year 1813. Spanish brigantine-of-war *Manuel*, Captain Martín María Espino, sank in Puerto Cabello on April 27, crew and some equipment saved.

Year 1815. A large fleet of Spanish warships and troop transports was sent from Spain to suppress the revolution in Venezuela, and after reaching the Caribbean the fleet anchored off Coche Island, located near Margarita Island. One of the largest warships in the fleet was the *San Pedro*, Almirantra, 64 guns, Captain Javier de Salazar. During the afternoon of April 24 the ship caught fire and blew up, killing more than 50 men. More than 800,000 pesos in silver specie were aboard, as well as tons of weapons and munitions, which the explosion scattered over a wide area. Salvage operations began the following day, and as late as 1871 salvors were still recovering treasure. Incomplete records, however, make it impossible to know just how much was recovered or if anything remains. In recent years, amateur divers from Caracas have recovered a few cannon and artifacts from this wreck.

Year 1817. Dutch merchantman *Ceres*, Captain Jucometti, sailing from Rotterdam to Curaçao, was wrecked on December 27 on Bonaire Island, only a small part of her cargo was saved.

Year 1819. Spanish merchantman *Mariposa*, sailing to Spain, was totally lost on Aves Island but her crew was saved.

Year 1822. English merchantman *Mary*, Captain Richardson, coming from London, was wrecked on September 17 on the bar in front of the port of Maracaibo but the crew was all saved.

Year 1822. English merchantman *Robert*, Captain Neilson, coming from Liverpool, was wrecked on a reef near the port of Maracaibo on May 20 but most of her cargo was saved.

Year 1822. Scottish ship *Thetis*, coming from Clyde, was lost near the port of La Guaira, part of her cargo was saved.

Year 1822. American ship *Eliza*, Captain Bicker, sailing from New York to Curaçao, was lost on November 30 off Bonaire Island.

Year 1822. American schooner *Cecila*, Captain Hampton, sailed from Curaçao with a valuable cargo of dry goods, cocoa, indigo, etc., then sank off the west end of Curaçao.

Year 1822. During a bad gale that struck the port of La Guaira on December 22, over 20 large ships of different nationalities were lost.

Year 1824. A ship of unknown registry, *Caledonia*, sailing from Philadelphia to La Guaira, wrecked on Los Roques Reefs, part of her cargo of soap and flour was saved.

Year 1824. American merchantman *Morning Star*, Captain Waring, sailing from New York to Curaçao, was totally lost on November 14 on Aves Island, only the crew was saved.

West Coast

Year 1584. Nao *Trinidad*, Captain Domingo de Celaya, owned by Martín de Cubierta, 400 tons, in an armada sailing between Spain and the Philippines under command of Admiral Gamboa, was wrecked and totally lost in February in the Straits of Magellan.

Year 1586. During a violent earthquake in Peru, two or three large unidentified merchant naos that had just arrived from Mexico were sunk in the port of Callao.

Year 1600. During a storm the Spanish merchant nao *San Juan Bautista* sank in the port of Valparaiso, Chile, but her cargo was salvaged.

Year 1600. Spanish caravel *Buen Jesús*, 60 tons, Captain Francisco de Ibarra, was approaching the port of Valparaiso when it sighted Dutch warships commanded by Admiral Oliver von Noort. Because the caravel carried no cannon and the Dutch were certain to capture it, the captain ordered her cargo (which consisted of over 125,000 pesos in gold and silver bullion and specie) thrown overboard.

Year 1610. A large Spanish nao, carrying over one million pesos in gold and silver, was wrecked on its voyage to Panama, several leagues south of the port of Chiclayo, and divers were able to recover only about 150,000 pesos from it.

Year 1612. An English chart of the 17th century had the following inscription on it: "On a shoal off the River Fama on the coast of Ecuador was cast away Domingo Anotto in the ship of *Gonzalo Beltram* in the year 1612 and in her was abundance of plate and other treasure."

Year 1623. A large fleet of Dutch warships attacked the port of Callao and burned eleven large Spanish ships anchored there at the time.

Year 1632. A large merchant nao owned by Martin López Caballón was sailing from Panama to Callao with 125 slaves and a merchandise valued at one million pesos. On February 27 it was lost on some rocks at Las Hormigas, located seven leagues from Callao, and everyone aboard perished except two men, one of them the pilot who was hanged for losing the ship.

Year 1644. Five Dutch privateering ships entered the port of Valdiva, Chile, and sank a Spanish ship containing over 100,000 pesos in gold and silver bullion, believing it was just a local trading vessel.

Year 1647. During an earthquake that struck Peru and Chile on May 13, large numbers of ships were lost in ports and on the coasts of both countries. At the port of Arica, Chile, the navío *San Nicholas*, with more than a million pesos of treasure, was lost. Divers recovered only a small part of this treasure.

Year 1647. A 17th century English chart of the coast of Chile bears the inscription, "Meyo Gallego was cast away here" south of Chiloe Island near the San Estevan River."

Year 1650. Spanish warship *San José* sailed from Concepción, Chile, with soldiers, supplies, and over 125,000 pesos in silver specie for several garrisons located to the south. On March 26 it wrecked at Punta Dotolauquen, near the port of Valdivia, and although most of the crew and soldiers made it ashore they were massacred by hostile Indians.

Year 1654. In May, four large galleons sailed from Callao, for Panama with several years' accumulation of treasure from the mines of South America. On a dark rainy night, the Capitana, commanded by Admiral Francisco de Sosa, was wrecked on Chanduy Reef, near the mouth of the Guayaquil River, in Ecuador. It quickly broke up and almost everyone aboard perished. Salvors recovered only a small amount of the more than three million pesos in treasure aboard before the wreck was buried under shifting sands within days of the disaster.

Year 1665. An unidentified ship carrying gold and silver ore was wrecked near the small port of Itata near Concepción, Chile. She was totally lost and all aboard perished.

Year 1680. An unidentified Spanish merchantman sailing from Callao to Guayaquil, Ecuador, carrying over 1,000,000 pesos in specie, was wrecked in August near Santa Clara, Ecuador.

Year 1684. Spanish nao *San Juan de Diós*, sailing from Callao to Concepción, Chile, and carrying the new bishop of Concepción and other important persons, was totally lost on Playa de Panque, Chile.

Year 1685. An unidentified Spanish merchant nao caught fire and sank at Callao. A diving bell was used to recover her cannon and cargo.

Year 1688. An unidentified merchant nao owned by Nicolas de Zarza, not carrying any cargo at the time, wrecked near Esmeraldas, close to the port of Amapola.

Year 1721. English pirate ship *Speedwell*, Captain George Shevelocke, carrying a large amount of plunder it had obtained by attacking Spanish settlements and shipping, was wrecked on rocks while entering a cove on one of the Juan Fernandez islands. Survivors managed to recover the greater part of their treasure, then built a schooner from the wreckage and escaped.

Year 1721. Treasure-laden galleon *Jesús María y Limpia Concepción* was wrecked on Chanduy Reef, Ecuador. Records do not indicate if she was ever salvaged.

Year 1746. On October 28, Peru suffered the worst earthquake since it was colonized by the Spaniards. Both Lima and the port of Callao were leveled and thousands of persons perished. At Callao, 23 ships were wrecked or sunk, of which only two were identified: galleon *San Fermín*, 30 guns, and the merchant nao *Santo Cristo de Leon*. In the port of Guacacho, another merchant nao *San Cristóbal*, was sunk.

Year 1760. A large galleon, *San Martín*, Captain Caconba, sank during a voyage between Valparaiso and Callao but her crew was saved.

Year 1762. Three Spanish trading frigates, *Encarnación, San Juan Evangelista* and *San Judas Tadio*, were wrecked among the islands of the Chiloe archipelago, Chile.

Year 1765. After arriving from Spain at Valparaiso, and with most of her cargo taken off, the galleon *San Lorenzo del Arco*, Captain Juan Lacomba, sank in port.

Year 1770. The largest ship to sail directly from Spain to Chile was the 1,200-ton galleon *L'Orriflamme*, which originally was a French warship. Her cargo was valued at over four million pesos and she carried a crew and passengers numbering over 700. During a storm she was totally lost on the coast near Valparaiso, and there were only a few survivors. Salvage attempts were made, but very little was recovered.

Year 1788. Spanish galleon *Nuestra Señora de la Balvanera*, 470 tons, Captain Antonio Ordoñez, was wrecked on the Guapacho Reefs near the port of San Carlos, Chile. All of her crew perished and several chests of gold and silver specie were never recovered from her.

Year 1800. Spanish frigate-of-war *Leocadia*, 34 guns, Captain Antonio Barreda, was wrecked on November 7 near Punta Santa Ilena, Ecuador, carrying over two million pesos in treasure. Of her crew, passengers and English prisoners, 140 perished and 48 were badly injured. Within three weeks salvors had recovered the greatest part of her treasure.

Year 1822. English merchantman *Mar*, Captain Quincey, sailing from Rio de Janeiro to Valparaiso, was totally lost off Conceicas, located near Valparaiso.

Year 1823. Italian merchantman *Diana*, sailing from Italy to Lima, entering the port of Pisco, Peru, and passing between the islands of Gallon and Maise, struck a rock in nine feet of water and immediately sank but her crew was saved.

East Coast

Year 1573. Portuguese East Indiaman, *Santa Clara*, commanded by Don Francisco de Sousa sailed from the Far East with over eight million cruzadoes in treasure and cargo aboard. Off the Cape of Good Hope two ships of the same fleet were leaking so badly that their treasures valued at six million cruzadoes were also transfer to the Santa Clara — making her the richest ship to ever sail from the Far East. En route to Lisbon the fleet stopped for water and provisions at Salvador, Brazil. Six hours after leaving port on January 6 when the fleet was four to six leagues north of Salvador, a fierce storm struck and the *Santa Clara* was totally lost on some reefs on the coast. Of the 667 souls aboard only six survived. None of her cargo was ever recovered.

Year 1582. Three Spanish merchant naos, *Capitaña*, *Almiranta* and *Santiago*, commanded by Captain Juan Ortíz de Zarate, were sunk in the Plata River, close to Buenos Aires.

Year 1582. Spanish warship *Santa María de San Vicente*, Captain Juan de Villaviciosa, owned by Juan de Arieta, sailing between Spain and the Philippines, was wrecked and totally lost at Rio de Janeiro, Brazil.

Year 1584. Spanish nao *Santa María*, Captain Pedro de Scarco, owned by Juan Aguilar Osoria, sailing between Spain and Buenos Aires, wrecked on Santa Catalina Island, Brazil.

Year 1625. The Spanish urca *Puerto Cristiana* was sent to search the seas for Dutch ships and while doing so wrecked on a reef at Pernambuco (today called Recife), Brazil; the men and cannon were saved.

Year 1625. An unidentified Dutch urca which escaped the Spanish attack on Salvador, Brazil, to dislodge the Dutch who had captured the port, was lost near Cape San Augustine, Brazil, with a great amount of treasure it had captured from two Portuguese ships.

Year 1625. In 1624 a large Dutch fleet captured Salvador (Bahía de Todo los Santos), the most important town in Brazil. During the attack several small Portuguese merchantmen were sunk. The following year a massive armada of Portuguese and Spanish warships commanded by Captain-General Fadrique de Toledo was sent to recapture the town from the Dutch. During the attack three unidentified Dutch warships were sunk by cannonfire and a Portuguese warship was wrecked on the reefs near the entrance to this port.

Year 1648. Dutch privateering fleet commanded by Admiral Witte de Witt set up a blockade off the port of Salvador, Brazil. Two large Portuguese warships went out to give battle and during the ensuing action the Dutch flagship Utrecht grappled with the Portuguese ship *Rosario*. Seeing he was losing, the Portuguese admiral set fire to his powder magazine and both ships blew up and went to the bottom with more than 550 men. The *Utrecht* was carrying a considerable amount of treasure at the time. Both wrecks were located in 1979 and some treasure has been recovered.

Year 1668. The *Sacramento*, flagship of the Portuguese navy, commanded by Admiral Francisco Correa da Silva, carrying a very valuable cargo and over 1,000 people, was just about to enter the port of Salvador, Brazil, when she overset in a squall and went to the bottom in 130 feet of water. This 900-ton ship carried 82 bronze cannon, most of which have been removed since fishermen accidentally discovered the site in 1976, but very little treasure has been found to date.

Year 1673. Spanish merchant nao *San Joséph*, Captain Sebastian de la Menarala, sank shortly after sailing for Spain from Buenos Aires.

Year 1679. Spanish galleon *Jesús, María y Joséph*, 350 tons, Captain José L de Villavicencio, sank while anchored at the mouth of the Plata River during a violent storm; all of its crew of 74 men perished.

Year 1681. Spanish nao *Nuestra Señora del Milagro*, 129 tons, Captain Cristóval de Aquenné, sank on October 19 while at anchor off Buenos Aires with nothing of value.

Year 1687. A fleet of 19 Dutch merchantmen was wrecked during a storm off Cayenne, French Guiana, and over 700 men died.

Year 1688. Two unidentified French warships were wrecked on a reef near Paramaribo, Surinam, due to faulty navigation.

Year 1698. A large richly laden Portuguese carrack was wrecked on the coast near present-day Georgetown, British Guiana; over 400 persons died and only three survived. Nothing of the one and one-half million cruzados in treasure the ship carried was ever recovered.

This valuable brass and silver sword handle was recovered from a mid-17th-century Dutch shipwreck off the coast of Colombia.

Year 1722. A small unidentified French merchantman was wrecked on Devil's Island, located off French Guiana.

Year 1726. The largest amount of gold ever lost in this hemisphere was aboard the Portuguese flagship *Santa Rosa*, sunk off the coast of Brazil. Powerfully armed with 66 bronze cannon and a crew of more than 700, she carried over 26 tons of registered gold bullion and specie, plus an unknown amount of contraband gold. Sailing from Salvador, she was to make a stop at Recife before heading for Portugal. A fire broke out aboard the ship when she was only a few hours south of Recife, in the vicinity of Cape San Augustine, and she blew up and sank in a matter of minutes. Only six persons survived the disaster. She now lies somewhere at a depth of between 300 and 600 feet

Year 1750. Spanish merchant frigate *La Purísima Concepción y San Francisco de Asis*, owned by the Marquis de Casa Madrid, sank during a bad storm at the mouth of the Plata River, which is the boundary between the present-day countries of Uruguay and Argentina.

Year 1752. Large French East Indiaman, *Prince*, Captain Morén, with a cargo valued at over 5 million livres aboard, caught fire off the coast of Brazil and was run aground near Natal, where she was totally lost. Of her crew of over 400, only nine survived.

Year 1752. Spanish merchant frigate *Esperanza*, coming from Cadíz, was wrecked near Rio de Janeiro and all except the captain perished. She was carrying 624,232 pesos in treasure from Peru.

Year 1752. Spanish galleon *Nuestra Señora de Luz*, sailing for Cadíz with two million pesos of treasure, sank near Buenos Aires; all but 62,000 pesos was recovered by divers.

Year 1753. Spanish galleon *Nuestra Señora del Rosario*, 460 tons, Captain Poloni, carrying 819,752 pesos in treasure from Peru, sank at the mouth of the Plata River but her crew was saved.

Above

Chinese porcelain figurines of royal officials recovered from a Portugese East Indiaman of the early 18th century off the coast of Recife, Brazil.

Below

This display of Chinese porcelain was recovered from another Portugese East Indiaman lost off Salvador, Brazil, in 1737.

Year 1762. An unidentified English ship was lost on the Plata River. , Because of a strange phenomenon caused by a freak wind parts of the river went dry in 1793, and many wrecks, including this one, were left high and dry; many things were salvaged.

Year 1776. Spanish frigate-of-war *Clara*, 30 guns, was wrecked on Banco Inglés, located off Montevideo, and 120 persons of her crew were lost.

Year 1776. A ship of unknown registry, *M of Marbourn*, coming from Africa with a cargo of slaves, was wrecked near Cayenne, French Guiana.

Year 1779. English merchantman *Prince Edward*, Captain Clerk, sailing from Australia to London, was lost near Cape Frio, Brazil.

Year 1801. Two English slave ships, *Enterprize* and *Earl*, of Liverpool, Captain Hume, both coming from Africa, were lost on the coast of Surinam.

Year 1805. English merchantman *Duke of Clarence*, Captain Killiner, arriving from Liverpool, was sunk at the mouth of the Plata River.

Year 1805. Spanish warship *Asunción*, 36 guns, Captain Juan Domingo Deslobbes, was wrecked on the Plata River during May.

Year 1807. English merchantman *Mary*, Captain Athol, sailing from Montevideo to Virginia, was lost near Aracaju, Brazil; two of her crew were drowned.

Year 1807. Three ships were lost on the Plata River: French privateer *Dart*, Captain Le Pelley, all hands perished; a privateer of unknown nationality, *Venus*, the crew was saved; and the English troop-transport *Royal Charlotte* during a gale on March 10.

Year 1809. Two English ships were lost on the Plata River: merchantman *Fanny*, Captain Bonsfield, shortly after sailing for London; the crew was saved; and the warship *H.M.S. Agamemnon*, 64 guns, Captain Jonas Rose.

Year 1809. Spanish merchantman *Galzo*, Captain Echeverriara, sailing from Cadíz to the Plata River, was wrecked near Montevideo but part of her cargo was saved.

Year 1809. Portuguese merchantman *Fama de Lisboa*, Captain Ramos, coming from London, was lost on August 18 while entering Recife, Brazil, but the crew was saved.

Year 1809. Portuguese ship *San Juan Rey de Mar*, sailing from Maraham to Cayenne, was wrecked at Para, Brazil.

Year 1810. Two English merchantmen were lost on the Plata River: brig *Adventure*, after arriving from Rio de Janeiro; and the ship *Little Venus*, Captain Bamber, heading for Liverpool.

Year 1813. Spanish ship *Fernando Septimo*, was burned at anchor in La Ensenada, near Buenos Aires, by the revolutionaries from Montevideo.

Year 1815. English warship *H.M.S. Cygnet*, 16 guns, Captain Robert Russell, was wrecked off the Courantyne River, which is the boundary between Surinam and British Guiana.

Suggestions for Further Reading

Bibliography

Shipwreck Locations

Anonymous, *Shipwrecks and Disasters at Sea*, 1851, London.

Bachard, Robert G., Scuba Northeast, *Shipwrecks: Rhode Island to New Jersey*.

Barrington, George, *Remarkable Voyages and Shipwrecks*, 1883, London.

Barry, James P., *Wrecks and Rescues of the Great Lakes*, 1981, San Diego.

Berg, Daniel, *Wreck Valley*, 1986, New York.

Tropical Shipwrecks, 1989, East Rockaway, NY.

Berman, Bruce D., *Encyclopedia of American Shipwrecks*, 1972, Boston.

Bowen, Dana Thomas, *Shipwrecks of the Lakes*, 1952, Daytona Beach.

Boyer, Dwight, *True Tales of the Great Lakes*, 1971, New York.

Burgess, Robert, *Sinkings, Salvages and Shipwrecks*, 1970, New York.

Florida's Golden Galleons, 1982, New York.

Cardone, Bonnie J. & Smith, Patrick, *Shipwrecks of Southern California*, 1989, Los Angeles.

Deperthes, Jean L., *Histoire des Naufrages*, 3 vols., 1828, Paris.

Douglas, Darren, *Guide to Shipwreck Diving: Southern California*, 1990, Houston.

Duffy, James, *Shipwrecks and Empire*, 1955, Cambridge, Mass.

Duro, Fernandez Cesareo de, *Armada Española*, 9 vols., 1878, Madrid.

Farb, Richard M., *Guide to Shipwreck Diving: North Carolina*, 1990, Houston.

Farb, Roderick, *Shipwrecks: Diving the Graveyard of the Atlantic*, 1989, Houston.

Frederick, James, *Diver's Guide to River Wrecks*, 1982, New York.

Fleming, Robert M., *Primer of Shipwreck Research and Records for Skin Divers*, 1971, Milwaukee.

Gentile, Gary, *Shipwrecks of New Jersey*, 1987, New York.

Advanced Wreck Diving Guide, 1988, New York.

Gibbs, James Atwood, *Shipwrecks of the Pacific Coast*, 1957, Portland.

Disaster Log of Ships, 1971, Seattle.

Hocking, Charles, *Dictionary of Disasters at Sea During the Age of Steam: 1824-1962*, 2 vols., 1969, London.

Hoehling, Adolph A., *Great Ship Disasters*, 1971, New York.

Lost at Sea, 1984, Harrisburg, PA.

425

Horner, Dave, *Shipwrecks, Skin Divers and Sunken Gold*, 1965, New York.
   The Treasure Galleons, 1971, New York.
Hudson, Kenneth, *The Book of Shipwrecks*, 1979, London.
Huntress, Keith, *Narratives of Shipwrecks and Disasters*, 1974, Ames, Iowa.
Jenney, Jim, *In Search of Shipwrecks*, 1980, New York.
Keatts, Henry, *Dive into History: U-Boats*, 1986, New York.
   Field Reference to Sunken U-Boats, 1987, New York.
   New England's Legacy of Shipwrecks, 1988, New York.
LaFrance, Jean, *Les Epaves du Saint-Laurent 1650-1760*, 1972, Montreal.
Layton, J.F., *Memorable Shipwrecks and Seafaring Adventures*, N.D.,
   Glasgow.
Lonsdale, Adrian L. and Kaplan, H.R., *Guide to Sunken Treasure in American
   Waters*, 1964, Arlington, VA.
Marshall, Don B., *California Shipwrecks*, 1978, Seattle. *Oregon Shipwrecks*,
   1984, Portland.
Marx, Robert F., *Shipwrecks of the Virgin Islands 1523- 1825*, St.Thomas,
   Shipwrecks in the Waters of Puerto Rico, 1969, San Juan,
   Shipwrecks in Florida Waters, 1971, Melbourne FL.
   Shipwrecks in Mexican Waters, 1971, Mexico City.
   Shipwrecks of the Western Hemisphere 1492-1825, 1971, New York.
   Spanish Treasures in Florida Waters, 1978, Boston
McDonald, Kendall, *The Wreck Detectives*, 1972, London.
   The Treasure Divers, 1977, London.
Morris, Paul C. and Quinn, William, *Shipwrecks in New York Waters*, 1989,
   Orleans, MA.
Meylach, Martin, *Diving to a Flash of Gold*, 1986, Port Salerno, FL.
Neider, Charles, *Great Shipwrecks and Castaways*, 1952, New York.
Nesmith, Robert I. and Potter, John S., Jr., *Treasure: How and Where to Find
   It, 1968, New York.*
Paine, Ralph D., *Lost Ships and Lonely Seas*, 1942, Garden City, NY.
Potter, John S., Jr., *The Treasure Diver's Guide, Revised Edition*, 1988, New
   York.
Quinn, William, *Shipwrecks Around Cape Cod*, 1973, Orleans, MA.
   Shipwrecks Around New England, 1978, Orleans, MA.
   Shipwrecks Around Maine, 1983, Orleans, MA.
   Shipwrecks Along the Atlantic Coast, 1988, Orleans, MA.
Ratigan, William, *Great Lakes Shipwrecks and Survivals*, 1989, New York.
Rattray, Jeannette, *Perils of the Port of New York*, 1973, New York.
   Shipwrecks, Life-Saving and Salvage on Long Island, 1978, New York.
Rieseberg, Harry E. and Mikalow, A.A., *Sunken Treasure Ships of the World*,
   1965, New York.
Sands, John O., *Yorktown's Captive Fleet*, 1983, Newport News, VA.
Scoville, Dorothy R, *Shipwrecks of Martha's Vineyard*, 1972, Gayhead, MA.
Shepard, Birse, *Lore of the Wreckers*, 1961, Boston.
Shomette, Donald G., *Shipwrecks of the Civil War*, 1973, Washington, D. C.
   Shipwrecks on the Chesapeake and its Tributaries 1608- 1978, 1982,
   Centerville, MD.

Snow, Edward R., *Great Storms and Famous Shipwrecks of the New England Coast*, 1943, Boston.
Pirates, Shipwrecks and Historical Chronicles, 1981, New York.
Spyglass Publications, *Snorklers' and Divers' Guide to Shipwrecks of Florida's Southeast Coast*, 1989, Miami.
Stick, David, *Graveyard of the Atlantic*, 1952, Chapel Hill, NC.
Stirling, Nord B., *Treasure Under the Sea*, 1957, Garden City, NY.
Stonehouse, Frederick, *Isle Royale Shipwrecks*, 1974, Marquette, MI.
Trupp, Philip Z., *Tracking Treasure*, 1986, Washington, D.C..
Villiers, Alan J., *Wild Ocean: The Story of the North Atlantic and the Men Who Sailed It*, 1957, New York.
Voynick, Stephen M., *The Mid-Atlantic Treasure Coast: Coins, Beaches and Treasure Shipwrecks from Long Island to Maryland's Eastern Shore*, 1984, Wallingsford. PA.
Watson, Milton H., *Disasters at Sea*, 1987, London.
Wilkins, Harold T., *Hunting Hidden Treasures*, 1929, New York.
Williams, Mark, *Sunken Treasure*, 1980, London.
Wood, Walter, *Survivors' Tales of Famous Shipwrecks*, 1932, London.
Wrigley, Ronald, *Shipwrecks: Vessels That Met Tragedy on Northern Lake Superior*, 1985, Cobalt, Ontario.
Zinck, Jack, *Shipwrecks of Nova Scotia*, 1975, Windsor, Nova Scotia.

The Ships and their History

Artiñano y de Galdacano, Gervasio de, *La Arquitectura Naval Española*, 1920, Madrid.
Historia del Comercio de Las Indias, 1917, Barcelona.
Baker, William A., *Colonial Vessels*, 1962, Barre, MA.
Sloops & Shallops, 1966, Barre, Mass.
Boxer, Charles R., *The Dutch Seaborne Empire: 1600-1800*, 1965, New York.
The Portuguese Seaborne Empire: 1415-1825, 1969, New York.
Chaunu, Huguette and Pierre, *Seville et L'Atlantique (1504- 1650)*, 9 vols., 1955, Paris.
Clowes, William L., *The Royal Navy*, 3 vols., 1898, Boston.
Cowburn, Philip., *The Warship in History*, 1965, New York.
Duhamel Du Monceau, Henri L., *Elements de l'Architecture Navale*, 1758, Paris.
Duro, Fernandez Cesareo de, *La Armada Española*, 9 vols., 1895-1903, Madrid.
Disquisiciones Nauticas, 6 vols., 1876-81, Madrid.
Fincham, John, *A History of Naval Architecture*, 1851, London.
Hamilton, Earl J., *American Treasure and the Price Revolution in Spain, 1501-1650*, 1934, Cambridge, MA.
Haring, Clarence H., *Trade and Navigation Between Spain and the Indies in the Time of the Hapsburgs*, 1918, Cambridge, MA.
The Buccaneers in the West Indies, 1910, Cambridge, MA.
Landstrom, Bjorn, *The Ship*, 1961, New York.
Martinez-Hidalgo, Jose Maria, *Columbus' Ships*, 1966, Barre, Mass.

Marx, Robert F., *The Treasure Fleets of the Spanish Main*, 1968, Cleveland.
  The Battle of the Spanish Armada: 1588, 1965, Cleveland.
Morison, Samuel Eliot, *Admiral of the Ocean Sea*, 1942, Boston.
Pares, Richard, *War and Trade in the West Indies*, 1936, New York.
Parry, J. H. *The Age of Reconnaissance*, 1963, London.
  The Spanish Seaborne Empire, 1966, New York.
Schurz, William L., *The Manila Galleon*, 1939, New York.
Veitia Linage, Joseph de, *Norte de la Contratación de las Indias Occidentales*, 1672, Seville.

Early Salvage and Underwater Archaeology

Arnold, J. Barto, *The Nautical Archaeology of Padre Island*, 1978, New York.
Bass, George F., *Underwater Archaeology*, 1966, New York.
Blair, Clay, Jr., *Diving for Pleasure and Treasure*, 1960, Cleveland.
Bush Romero, Pablo, *Under the Waters of Mexico*, 1964, Mexico City.
Cleator, Philip Ellaby, *Underwater Archaeology*, 1973, London.
Davis, John, *Treasure, People, Ships and Dreams*, 1977, San Antonio, TX.
Davis, Robert H., *Deep Diving and Submarine Operations*, 1951, London.
Diole, Philippe, *4,000 Years Under the Sea*, 1954, New York.
Dugan, James, *Man Under the Sea*, 1956, New York.
  Men Under Water, 1965, New York.
Dumas, Frederic, *Deep-Water Archaeology*, 1962, London.
Franzen, Anders, *The Warship Vasa*, 1960, New York.
Frost, Honor, *Under the Mediterranean*, 1963, London.
Johnstone, Paul, *The Archaeology of Ships*, 1974, London.
Karraker, Cyrus H., *The Hispaniola Treasure*, 1934, Philadelphia.
Latil, Pierre de and Rivoire, Jean, *Man and the Underwater World*, 1954, London.
Marx, Robert F., *They Dared the Deep*, 1967, New York and Cleveland.
  Pirate Port: The Story of the Sunken City of Port Royal, 1967, New York and Cleveland.
  The Underwater Dig, 1990, Houston.
Martin, Colin, *Full Fathom Five: Wrecks of the Spanish Armada*, 1975, London.

Diving and Modern Salvage

Allen, Geoffrey, *The Guns of the Sacramento*, 1978, London.
Ballard, Robert D., *The Discovery of the Titanic*, 1987, New York.
Borhegyi, Suzanne de, *Ships, Shoals and Amphoras*, 1961, New York.
Carrier, Rick and Barbara, *Dive: The Complete Book of Skin Diving*, 1955, New York.
Ciampi, Elgin, *Skin Dive*, 1960, New York.
Cousteau, Capt. Jacques Yves, *The Silent World*, 1953, New York.
  The Living Sea, 1963, New York.
Earle, Peter, *The Wreck of the Almiranta*, 1979, London.

Ellsberg, Edward, *On the Bottom*, 1929, New York.
  Men Under the Sea, 1939, New York.
Falcon-Barker, Capt. Ted, *Roman Galley Beneath the Sea*, 1964, New York.
Garrett, Charles, *Treasure Recovery from Sand and Sea*, 1990, Dallas.
Giquere, Jon-Paul, *Salvage Laws for Weekend Divers*, 1981.
Gores, Joseph N., *Marine Salvage*, 1971, New York
Grissim, John, *The Lost Treasure of the Concepción*, 1980, New York.
Library of Congress, A descriptive list of treasure maps and charts in the
  Library of Congress, 1973, Washington, D.C.
Link, Marion C., *Sea Diver, A Quest for History From the Sea*, 1959, New
  York.
Lyon, Eugene., *The Search for the Atocha*, 1979, N. Y.
Marx, Robert F. and Jenifer, *The Search for Sunken Treasure*, 1993 Toronto
Marx, Robert F., *Always Another Adventure*, 1967, Cleveland.
  Still More Adventures, 1976, New York.
  The Lure of Sunken Treasure, 1973, New York.
  Sea Fever, 1972, New York.
  Quest for Treasure, 1982, Dallas.
  Diving for Adventure, 1979, New York.
  Sunken Treasure: How to Find It, 1990, Dallas.
Masters, David, *The Wonders of Salvage*, 1924, New York.
  Epics of Salvage, 1952, Boston.
Mathewson, Duncan, *Treasure of the Atocha*, 1987, New York.
McKee, Alexander, *History Under the Sea*, 1968. London.
  How We Found the Mary Rose, 1982, London.
Morris, Roland, *Island Treasure*, 1969, London.
Nesmith, Robert I., *Dig for Pirate Treasure*, 1958, New York.
Northeast Marine Advisory Council, *Sportsdivers Handbook for Historical
  Shipwrecks*, 1982, Durham, NC.
Owen, David M., *A Manual for Free Divers*, 1955, New York.
Peterson, Mendel, *History Under the Sea*, 1969 Washington.
Rackl, Hanns-Wolf, *Diving Into the Past: Archaeology Underwater*, 1968,
  New York.
Rebikoff, Dimitri, *Free Diving*, 1956, New York.
Slack, Jack, *Finders Losers*, 1967, New York.
Stenuit, Robert, *The Deepest Days*, 1966, New York.
Taylor, Joan du Plat, editor, *Marine Archaeology*, 1965, London.
Throckmorton, Peter, *The Lost Ships*, 1964, Boston.
  Shipwrecks and Archaeology, 1969, Boston.
Tucker, Teddy, *Treasure Diving with Teddy Tucker*, 1966, Bermuda.
Wagner, Kip (as told to Taylor, L. B., Jr.), *Pieces of Eight*, 1967, New York.
Wilkes, Bill St. John, *Nautical Archaeology-A Handbook for Skin Divers*,
  1971, New York.

Preservation

Albright, Alan, "The preservation of small water-logged wood specimens with polyethylene glycol," *Curator*, 1966, Vol.IX, No.3, pp. 22-34.

Barkman, Lars, *The Preservation of the Vasa*, no date, Stockholm.

Caley, Earle R., "Coatings and encrustations on lead objects from the Agora and the method used for their removal," *Studies in Conservation*, 1955, Vol. 2, No. 2, pp.49-54.

Erickson, Egon, and Tregel, Svend, *Conservation of Iron Recovered from the Sea*, 1966, Copenhagen.

Graham, John Meredith, *American Pewter*, 1949, Brooklyn.

Katsev, Michael, and Doornick, Fredrick van, "Replicas of iron tools from a Byzantine shipwreck," *Studies in Conservation*, August 1966, Vol.11, No. 3, pp. 133-42.

Organ, R. M., "The conservation of fragile metallic objects," *Studies in Conservation*, November 1961, Vol. 6, No.4, pp.135-36.

Pittsburgh Plate Glass Company, "Embedding Objects in Selectron 5000 Resins," 1946, Pittsburgh.

Plenderleith, H. J., *The Conservation of Antiquities and Works of Art*, 1956, London.(The most comprehensive work on the subject.)

Smith, James B., Jr., and Ellis, John P., "The preservation of underwater archaeological specimens in plastic," *Curator*, 1963, Vol. VI, No. 1, pp. 32-36.

Thomas M. W., and Dunton, John V. N., *Treatment for Cleaning and Preserving Excavated Iron Objects*, 1954, Williamsburg, Va.

Townsend, Samuel P., "Heat methods of preserving cast iron artifacts recovered from salt water," Report presented at the Third Conference on Underwater Archaeology, Miami, FL, March 23- 25, 1967.

Identification of Artifacts

Artillery

Foulkes, Charles, *The Gun Founders of England*, 1937, Cambridge, England.

Gibbon, John, *The Artillerist's Manual*, 1863, New York.

Grant, Michael, Armada Guns, 1961, London.

Hime, Henry W. L., *The Origin of Artillery*, 1915, London.

Hogg, Oliver F. G., *English Artillery 1325-1716*, 1963, London.

Manucy, Albert, *Artillery Through the Ages*, 1949, Washington, D.C.

Mountaine, William, *The Practical Sea-gunners' Companion or an Introduction to the Art of Gunnery*, 1747, 3rd edition, London.

Muller, John, *A Treatise of Artillery*, 1780, 3rd edition, London.

Museo del Ejercito, Catalogo del Museo del Ejercito, 4 vols., 1956, Madrid.

Robins, Benjamin, *New Principles of Gunnery*, 1742, London.

Saint-Remy, Pierre Surirey de, *Memoires d'artillerie*, 2 vols., 1741, The Hague, Holland.

Smith, George, *An Universal Military Dictionary*, 1779, London.

430

Streete, Thomas, *The Use and Effects of the Gunne* (sic), 1674, London.
Thomas, Capt., *A Treatise on Gunpowder*, 1789, London.
Vigon, Jorge, *Historia de la Artilleria Española*, 3 vols., 1947, Madrid.

Weapons

Greener, W. W., *The Gun and its Development*, 9th edition, 1967, New York.
Jackson, H. J., *European Hand Firearms of the 16th, 17th & 18th Centuries*.
Peterson, Harold L., *The Treasury of the Gun*, 1962, New York.
  Arms and Armor in Colonial America, 1526-1783.
  Daggers and Fighting Knives of the Western World.
Stone, George Cameron, *A Glossary of the Construction, Decoration and Use of Arms and Armor in all Countries and in all Times*, 1934, New York. (The most comprehensive work on the subject.)
Tunis, Edwin, *Weapons: A Pictorial History*, 1954, Cleveland and New York.
Wilkinson, Frederick, *Swords and Daggers*, 1968, New York.

Navigation Instruments

Brewington, M. V., *Navigating Instruments*, 1963, Salem, Mass.
Garcia France, Salvador, *Instrumentos Nauticos en el Museo Naval*, 1959, Madrid.
Mountaine, William, and Wakely, Andrew, *The Mariner's Compass Rectified*, 1754, London.
Waters, David W., *The Art of Navigation in England in Elizabethan and Early Stuart Times*, 1958, London.
Zinner, Ernst, *Astronomische Instrumente*, 1967, Munich.

Clay Smoking Pipes

Brongars, G. A., *Nicotiana Tabacum*, 1964, Amsterdam.
Dunhill, Alfred, *The Pipe Book*, 1924, New York.
Harrington, J. C., "Dating stem fragments of 17th and 18th century tobacco pipes," Bull. Arch. Soc., 1954, Vol. 4.
Marx, Robert F., "Clay smoking pipes recovered from the sunken city of Port Royal: May 1, 1966-September 3, 1967," March 1968.
  "Clay smoking pipes recovered from the sunken city Of Port Royal: October 1,1967-March 31, 1968," August 1968. (Both reports published by the Jamaica National Trust Commission, Kingston, Jamaica.)
Oswald, Adrian, *English Clay Tobacco Pipes*, 1967, London.

Glassware and Bottles

Buckley, Francis, *The Glass Trade in England in the 17th Century*, 1914, London.
Corning Glass Museum, *Glass from the Corning Glass Museum*, 1965, Corning, N.Y.
Frothingham, Alice Wilson, *Hispanic Glass*, 1941, New York.
Harrington, J. C., *Glassmaking at Jamestown*, 1953, Richmond, Va.
Hayes, E. Barrington, *Glass Through the Ages*, 1966, Baltimore.

Honey, W. B., *Glass*, 1946, London.

Hume, Ivor Noel, "Dating English glass wine bottles," *Wine and Spirit Trade Record*, February 1955.

Here Lies Virginia, 1963, New York.

Lee, Ruth Webb, *Victorian Glass*, 1939, Framington, Mass.

Marx, Robert F., "Wine glasses recovered from the sunken city of Port Royal: May 1, 1966-March 31, 1968," Jamaica National Trust Commission, Kingston, Jamaica, May, 1968.

"Glass bottles recovered from the sunken city of Port Royal, Jamaica: May 1, 1966-March 31, 1968," Caribbean Research Institute, St. Thomas, VI, January, 1969.

McKearin, Helen and George, *Two Hundred Years of American Blown Glass*, 1956, New York.

Rider, Dennis, *A History of Glass Bottles*, 1956, London.

Ruggles-Brise, Sheelah, *Sealed Bottles*, 1949, London.

Gold Plate

Castro, J. P. de, *The Law and Practice of Marking Gold and Silver Ware*, 1935, London.

Heal, A., *The London Goldsmiths, 1200-1800*, 1935, Cambridge, England.

Hill, H. D., *Antique Gold Boxes, Their Lore and Their Lure*, 1953. New York.

Jackson, C. J., *English Goldsmiths and Their Marks*, 1949, London.

Jones, E. A., *Old English Gold Plate*, 1907, London.

Prideaux, W. S., *Memorials of the Goldsmiths' Company, 1335-1815*, 2 vols., 1896-97, London.

Silverware

Cripps, W. J., *Old English Plate, Ecclesiastical, Decorative and Domestic: Its Makers and Marks*, 1926, London.

Jackson, C. J., *An Illustrated History of English Plate, Ecclesiastical and Secular*, 2 vols., 1926, London.

Jones, E. A., *Old Silver of Europe and America*, 1928, London and New York.

Wyler, S. B., *The Book of Old Silver: English, American, and Foreign*, 1947, New York.

Pewterware

Bell, Malcolm, *Old Pewter*, 1905, New York.

Cotterell, Howard H., *Old Pewter: Its Makers and Marks*, 1929, London. (The most comprehensive work on the subject.)

Markham, C. A., *Pewter Marks and Old Pewterware*, 1909, London.

Welch, C., *History of the Worshipful Company of Pewterers of London*, 1902, London.

432

Pottery and Porcelain

Chaffers, William, *The New Collector's Handbook of Marks and Monograms on Pottery and Porcelain*, 1914, London.

Cushion, J. P., and Honey, W. B., *Handbook of Pottery and Porcelain Marks*, 1956, London.

Frothingham, Alice Wilson, *Talavera Pottery*, 1944, New York.
Lustreware of Spain, 1951, New York.

Garner, Frederic H., *English Delftware*, 1948, New York.

Godden, Geoffrey A., *British Pottery and Porcelain*, 1966, New York.

Goggin, John M., "The Spanish olive jar, an introductory study," Yale University publications in Anthropology, No. 62, 1960, New Haven.
"Spanish Majolica in the New World: Types of the 16th to 18th Centuries," 1968, New Haven.

Savage, George, *Porcelain Through the Ages*, 1963, Baltimore.

Shepard, Anna O., *Ceramics for the Archaeologist*, 1965, Washington, D.C.

Thorn, C. Jordan, *Handbook of Old Pottery and Porcelain Marks*, 1965, New York.

Towner, Donald C., *English Cream-Colored Earthenware*, 1957, London.

Watkins, Lura W., *Early New England Potters and their Wares*, 1950, Cambridge, Mass.

Wills, Geoffrey, *The Book of English China*, 1964, New York.

Spanish Coinage

Beals, Gary, *Numismatic Terms of Spain and Spanish America*, 1966, San Diego.

Dasi, Tomas, *Estudio de los Reales de a Ocho*, 5 vols., 1950, Valencia, Spain.

Harris, Robert P., *Pillars and Portraits*, 1968, San Jose, California.

Lopez-Chaves y Sanchez, Leopoldo, *Catalogo de la Onza Española*, 1961, Madrid.
Catalogo de la Media Onza o Doblon de a Cuatro, 1961, Madrid.
Catalogo de las Onzas de la America Independiente, 1961, Madrid.

Nesmith, Robert I., *The Coinage of the First Mint of the Americas at Mexico City*, 1955, New York.

Pradeau, Alberto F., *Numismatic History of Mexico from the Pre-Columbian Epoch to 1823*, 1938, Los Angeles.

Yriarte, Jose de., *Catalogo de los Reales de a Ocho Españoles*, 1955, Madrid.

Coinage of Other Nations

Brooke, George C., *English Coins From the 7th Century to the Present Day*, 1932, London.

Ciani, Louis, *Catalogue de Monnaies Francaises*, 3 vols. 1926-31, Paris.

Dieudonne, A., *Monnaies Royales Francaises*, 1916, Paris.

Lindheim, Leon, *Facts and Fiction About Coins*, 1967, Cleveland; New York.t

Peck, C. Wilson, *English Copper, Tin and Bronze Coins: 1558-1958*, 1960, London.

Santos, Leitao & Cie., *Catalogo de Moedas Brasileiras de 1643 a 1944*, No date, Rio de Janeiro.

Wood, Howland, *The Coinage of the West Indies, and the Sou Marque*, 1915, New York.

Yeoman, R. S. *A Catalog of Modern World Coins*, 1965, Chicago.
A Guide Book of United States Coins, 1965, Chicago.

Brass and Copper Objects

Marx, Robert F., "Brass and copper items recovered from the sunken city of Port Royal: May 1, 1966-March 31, 1968," Jamaica National Trust Commission, Kingston, Jamaica, May 1968.

Wills, G., *Collecting Copper and Brass*, 1954, Glasgow. Privately published.

Miscellaneous Reference Books

Bradford, Ernle, *Four Centuries of European Jewelry*, 1953, Feltham, England.

Bruton, E., *Clocks and Watches*, 1965, London.

Hume, Ivor Noel, *A Guide to Artifacts of Colonial America*, 1970, New York. (This comprehensive book is useful in the identification of hundreds of types of artifacts, such as bells, buckles, buttons, cooking vessels, cutlery, locks and padlocks and tools.)

Marx, Jenifer, *The Magic of Gold*, 1978, New York.

Marx, Jenifer, *Pirates and Privateers of the Caribbean*, 1993, Malabar, Fl.

Mercer, Henry C., *Ancient Carpenters' Tools*, 1960, Doylestown. PA.

Form for Ordering...

Ram Books

Please send these Treasure Hunting Texts:

___ Let's Talk Treasure Hunting $14.95
___ Modern Metal Detectors $14.95
___ Treasure Recovery from Sand & Sea. . $14.95
___ Sunken Treasure: How to Find It. $14.95
___ Treasure from British Waters. . . . . $ 7.95
___ The New Successful Coin Hunting . . . $12.95
___ Buried Treasures You Can Find. $14.95
___ Modern Electronic Prospecting . . . . . . $ 9.95
___ Weekend Prospecting. . . . . $ 3.95
___ Gold Panning is Easy . . . . $ 9.95
___ An Introduction to Metal Detectors . . . $ 1.00
     (No shipping/handling charge)

True Treasure Tales

___ Secret of John Murrell's Vault. . . . . . . $ 4.95
___ Missing Nez Perce Gold . . . . $ 4.95

Ram Publishing Company
P.O. Drawer 38649
Dallas, TX 75238
FAX: 214-494-1881
(Credit Card Orders Only)

Please add $1 for
each book
(maximum of $3
  handling charges.)

Total for items $_____

8.25% Tax (Texas residents) $_____

Handling Charge $_____

                  TOTAL $_____

    Enclosed check or money order

    I prefer to order through
☐ MasterCard
☐ Visa
By telephone:
1-800-527-4011   _____
                      Credit Card Number

_____

Expiration Date   **Phone Number (8 a.m. to 4 p.m.)**

_____

Signature (Credit Card orders must be signed.)

_____

NAME

_____

ADDRESS (For Shipping)

_____

CITY, STATE, ZIP